Handbook of Research in International Marketing

A UCONN CIBER SUPPORTED RESEARCH INITIATIVE

CIBER is a program of the US Department of Education. The CIBER program's mandate is to enhance US competitiveness in the global business arena through activities involving US businesses, educators, and students.

Handbook of Research in International Marketing

Edited by

Subhash C. Jain

University of Connecticut, USA

Edward Elgar
Cheltenham, UK • Northampton, MA, USA

© Subhash C. Jain 2003

Published by
Edward Elgar Publishing Limited
Glensanda House
Montpellier Parade
Cheltenham
Glos GL50 1UA
UK

Edward Elgar Publishing, Inc.
136 West Street
Suite 202
Northampton
Massachusetts 01060
USA

A catalogue record for this book
is available from the British Library

Library of Congress Cataloguing in Publication Data
State of the Art of Research in International Marketing Conference (2001 :
    University of Connecticut)
    Handbook of research in international marketing / edited by Subhash C. Jain.
        p. cm.
    'This book grew out the State of the Art of Research in International Marketing
    Conference held at the University of Connecticut in October 2001'—Pref.
        Includes index.
        1. Export marketing—Research—Congresses. 2. Foreign trade promotion—
    Research—Congresses. 3. Export marketing—Research—United States—
    Congresses. 4. Foreign trade promotion—Research—United States—
    Congresses. I. Jain, Subhash C., 1942– II. Title.

    HF1416.S698 2001
    658.8'48'072—dc21

                                                                    2003049105
    ISBN 1 84064 946 1 (cased)

Printed and bound in Great Britain by MPG Books Ltd, Bodmin, Cornwall

Contents

Contributors

Preet S. Aulakh holds the Pierre Lassonde Chair in International Business at the Schulich School of Business, York University.

Nancy R. Buchan is an Assistant Professor of Marketing in the School of Business at the University of Wisconsin, Madison.

S. Tamer Cavusgil is University Distinguished Faculty and the John W. Byington Endowed Chair in Global Marketing at Michigan State University. He also serves as the Executive Director of MSU-CIBER.

C. Samuel Craig is the Catherine and Peter Kellner Professor and Director of the Entertainment, Media and Technology Program at New York University's Stern School of Business.

Susan P. Douglas is the Paganelli-Bull Professor of Marketing and International Business at New York University's Stern School of Business.

Robert L. Engle is currently Associate Professor of International Business at the Lender School of Business at Quinnipiac University in Hamden, Connecticut.

M. Krishna Erramilli is Associate Professor and Head of the Marketing and International Business Division at the Nanyang Business School, Nanyang Technological University in Singapore.

F. Esra Gençtürk is an Assistant Professor of Marketing at Koç University. Previously, she was an Assistant Professor of Marketing and International Business at the University of Texas at Austin.

David A. Griffith is Associate Professor of Marketing at the University of Hawaii.

Hillary Haley is a PhD student in the Department of Psychology at UCLA. She received her BA in Psychology from Columbia University in 1996.

Louise A. Heslop (MSc Guelph, PhD Western Ontario) is Professor of Marketing at the Eric Sprott School of Business, Carleton University, Ottawa, Canada, and has worked as a Senior Research Officer in the Social and Economics Studies Division at Statistics Canada.

G. Tomas M. Hult, a native of Sweden, is Associate Professor of Marketing and Supply Chain Management and Director of the Center for International Business Education and Research (MSU-CIBER) in the Eli Broad Graduate School of Management at Michigan State University, and a Founding Research Member of the FedEx Center for Supply Chain Research, Memphis, Tennessee.

Subhash C. Jain is Professor of Marketing, Director of the Center for International Business Education and Research (CIBER) funded by the US Department of Education, and Director of the GE Global Learning Center endowed by GE Capital Corporation, in the School of Business, University of Connecticut.

Johny K. Johansson was named the McCrane/Shaker Professor in International Business and Marketing at Georgetown University in 1989.

Destan Kandemir, a native of Turkey, is a PhD Candidate in the Eli Broad Graduate School of Management at Michigan State University.

Masaaki Kotabe holds the Washburn Chair of International Business and Marketing, and is Director of Research at the Institute of Global Management Studies at the Fox School of Business and Management at Temple University.

V. Kumar (VK) is the ING Chair Professor of Marketing, and Executive Director, ING Center for Financial Services in the School of Business, University of Connecticut.

Paul Matthyssens is Professor of Industrial and International Marketing at Limburgs Universitair Centrum and the University of Antwerp in Belgium and at Erasmus University in the Netherlands.

David B. Montgomery is the S.S. Kresge Professor of Marketing Strategy – Emeritus at the Stanford Graduate School of Business and Business Dean at Singapore Management University. He was Executive Director at the Marketing Science Institute (1995–1997), Academic Trustee

(1994–2001), and is currently a member of the Executive Directors Council (1997–present)

Cheryl C. Nakata is Assistant Professor of Marketing and International Business at the University of Illinois at Chicago.

Nicolas Papadopoulos (MBA Washington State, DBA Athens) is Professor of Marketing and International Business and Director, International Business Study Group, at the Eric Sprott School of Business, Carleton University, Ottawa, Canada.

Pieter Pauwels is Assistant Professor of Marketing at Maastricht University (The Netherlands).

Ilkka A. Ronkainen serves on the faculty of marketing and international business at Georgetown University's McDonough School of Business as well as docent of international marketing at the Helsinki School of Economics.

John K. Ryans, Jr holds the Bridgestone Professorship in International Marketing at the Graduate School of Management at Kent State University.

Saeed Samiee is the Collins Professor of Marketing and International Business at the University of Tulsa. He is also a TU Director for the Institute of International Business Education in Moscow, Russia, a joint project with the Moscow Institute of Electronics Engineering.

Ravi Sarathy is Professor of Management and International Business, in the College of Business Administration at Northeastern University.

Bernd H. Schmitt is Professor at Columbia Business School and Director of the Center on Global Brand Leadership.

Camille P. Schuster is a Professor of Marketing at Xavier University. She received her PhD from Ohio State University and MA from Arizona State University.

Narasimhan Srinivasan is an Associate Professor of Marketing at the School of Business, University of Connecticut.

Charles R. Taylor is Professor of Marketing at Villanova University.

P. Rajan Varadarajan is Distinguished Professor of Marketing and holder of the Ford Chair in Marketing and E-Commerce, Mays Business School, Texas A&M University at College Station.

Allen M. Weiss is Associate Professor and a Tappan Fellow of Marketing in the Marshall School of Business at the University of Southern California.

Manjit S. Yadav is an Associate Professor of Marketing and Mays Faculty Fellow, Department of Marketing, Mays Business School, Texas A&M University.

Attila Yaprak is Professor of Marketing and International Business and Director of the Center for International Business Studies at Wayne State University.

Shi Zhang is Assistant Professor at the Anderson Graduate School of Management, UCLA.

Shaoming Zou is Assistant Professor of Marketing and International Business at the University of Missouri, Columbia.

Foreword

The tragic events of September 11th have dramatically heightened our nation's concern for homeland security. While this will remain an important national focus in the future, we must not lose sight of the fact that our nation's place in the twenty-first century will also be determined by the extent to which our business firms can compete internationally. As trade barriers continue to fall, customers' needs and preferences converge across markets, and pressure on American firms to generate greater economies of scale and scope intensifies, business must explore and exploit growing international markets.

In order to supply US firms with business leaders capable of looking beyond national borders and leading the global activities of their firms, US universities must enhance the international orientation and expertise of their faculty and students. The Centers for International Business Education and Research (CIBER) program of the US Department of Education was launched over a decade ago to help achieve this goal. A Reagan administration initiative, the program was authorized under the Omnibus Trade and Competitiveness Act of 1988 and is now administered in the US Department of Education under Title VI, part B of the Higher Education Act as amended.

The CIBER program awards grants to leading business schools throughout the country to establish and operate Centers for International Business Education and Research. These CIBERs serve as national resources for teaching and outreach in business, foreign languages, and cultures and for conducting cutting-edge research on key international business topics of managerial relevance and significance.

This book, *Handbook of Research in International Marketing*, represents one CIBER-sponsored research activity in the field of international marketing. Recognizing the potential benefit of assembling the world's top international marketing scholars in a single venue, the University of Connecticut CIBER organized a conference: 'State-of-the-Art Research in International Marketing'. The fact that four other CIBERs (Michigan State University and the universities of Memphis, Wisconsin and California, Los Angeles) co-sponsored the program is an example of the cooperative relationships among CIBERs encouraged by the US Department of Education – relationships that significantly enhance the scope of the CIBER program and maximize its impact on issues affecting the competitiveness of US managers.

The interaction of 24 top international marketing scholars from colleges and universities around the world during this conference represented a major opportunity for examining the state-of-the-art research in this important field. Scholars presented and debated their views on a broad spectrum of current and emerging international marketing issues and took advantage of this unique opportunity to seek feedback from respected colleagues around the world on the direction of their own research. The papers included in this book encompass virtually all areas of international marketing and should be of great value in shaping the future research of emerging international marketing scholars. I believe these research efforts will directly and indirectly guide US managers and enhance their ability to compete in world markets. As such, I consider the completion of this book to be a success in fulfilling CIBER statutory program objectives.

Given the high quality of the chapters in this book and the overwhelmingly positive response of participating scholars, I know all CIBERs will share my opinion that this was a highly successful endeavor. This co-operative effort is but one of many examples of resource sharing among CIBER universities. As the CIBERs begin a new 4-year funding cycle in fall 2002, we can expect increased linkages and outreach to US institutions of higher education beyond the funded CIBER group.

I thank Dr Subhash Jain, the editor of this book for asking me to write this foreword and wish the contributing authors success in their future research endeavors.

Susanna Easton
Program Specialist
International Education and Graduate
Programs Service
US Department of Education
Washington, DC, USA

Preface

This book grew out of the State of the Art of Research in International Marketing Conference held at the University of Connecticut in October 2001. The conference involved international marketing scholars located all over the world, thereby setting an example of global coordination in productive research. The conference, supported by the Centers for International Business Education and Research at the University of Connecticut, University of Memphis, Michigan State University, University of California at Los Angeles, and the University of Wisconsin, provided a unique opportunity for stimulating thinking and for generating new ideas through formal presentations and discussions.

The chapters contained in this book address research issues about the way international marketing actually does function, as well as theoretical explorations of how it perhaps should function. The book gives PhD students and faculty a vital perspective on international marketing research. It fulfills an important objective of the conference to involve faculty in thinking seriously about the challenges and opportunities ahead in international marketing research and teaching. In some respects, the book creates a distinctive model of international marketing research. Some chapters have broken through the bounds of traditional disciplines and methodologies to borrow whatever tools and concepts are needed for a particular inquiry. Others have been less concerned with testing existing theory than with generating new insights. Still others strive for results that are operationally significant for managers. Many chapters are drawn to problems that are broad in scope, and yet offer insights that are of considerable value for advancing the state of the art.

Beyond exploring research findings, the conference sustained and enlivened the dialogue among the participants with different cross-cultural backgrounds and interests. From that melding of perspectives many insights emerged that can revitalize research of upcoming scholars and refine current professional outlook relative to international marketing. In that spirit of cooperative endeavor, I feel honored to introduce this collection.

This book would not be possible without the willingness of the scholars from around the world to travel to the University of Connecticut to participate in the conference within a few weeks of the September 11th tragedy. I owe them a great deal of gratitude to let the conference go on despite worldwide uncertainty in the wake of terrorist attacks. I sincerely thank Sarah Beaton and Susanna Easton at the US Department of Education for their encouragement in this endeavor. I am obliged to Susanna Easton for writing a foreword to this book. 1 appreciate the support of CIBER directors at the University of Memphis, Michigan State University, UCLA and the University of Wisconsin for cosponsoring this program.

A major endeavor such as this would never have been complete without the help and guidance of many people. I would like to thank Dean Thomas Gutteridge and many others at the School of Business, University of Connecticut for their administrative help, financial support and hospitality. A special mention of appreciation must go to the Associate Director of our CIBER, Kelly Dunn, for planning, coordinating, and implementing numerous tasks to make the program successful. She did a marvelous job of bringing off a complex event. I would like to thank the staff of our International Programs office, especially PhD student Piotr Chelminski, graduate assistants Paula Ehlers and Mami Nishimune, and student workers Amy Hotsko, Dom DaFonte and Jennifer Graham for their administrative support. 1 would also like to make special mention of Kelli Francis, our student employee who compiled and edited this text. My thanks go to her for all of her hard work. My grateful appreciation goes also to Alan Sturmer of Edward Edgar Publishing who has been instrumental in publishing this book. I am indebted to Senior Desk Editor Karen McCarthy in the UK office of Edward Elgar for the super job of seeing the book to completion. Finally, my wife Sadhna not only made it possible for me to live through the experience, but gave me intellectual and moral support in countless ways.

Subhash C. Jain
June 2003
Storrs, Connecticut, USA

PART I

Introduction

1. State-of-the-art review of research in international marketing management

Masaaki Kotabe*

INTRODUCTION

International marketing underwent fundamental changes in the last two decades. Global political and economic liberalization trends created tremendous business opportunities and challenges for international marketers. For instance, the emergence of regional trading blocs in the form of the EU (European Union), NAFTA (North American Free Trade Agreement), and MERCOSUR (Mercado Común del Sur) have necessitated reorganization in the production and marketing strategies of firms. The changes in strategy include serving different markets from one production source or the shifting of production facilities for greater efficiency.

The Asian financial crisis in the latter half of the 1990s provided a significant reality check on the wisdom of globally integrated strategy development. Wildly fluctuating exchange rates make it difficult for multinational companies to manage globally integrated but geographically scattered activities. Indeed, many companies are scurrying to speed steps toward making their procurement, manufacturing, and marketing operations in Asian countries more local. Since the yen's sharp appreciation in the mid-1980s, Japanese manufacturers have moved to build an international production system less vulnerable to currency fluctuations by investing in local procurement and local marketing (*Nikkei Weekly* 1998).

Two fundamental counteracting forces have always shaped the nature of marketing in the international arena over the years. The same counteracting forces have been revisited by many authors in such terms as 'standardization vs. adaptation' (1970s), 'globalization vs. localization' (1980s), and 'global integration vs. local responsiveness' (1990s). Terms have changed, but the quintessence of the strategic dilemma that multinational firms face today has not changed and will probably remain unchanged for years to come.

* The author acknowledges Shruti Gupta for providing research assistance during this project.

The importance of these changes is reflected in the development of new research streams in international marketing (Cavusgil and Li 1992; Douglas and Craig 1992; Aulakh and Kotabe 1993; Pieters et al. 1999), those of market globalization (Levitt 1983; Douglas and Wind 1987; Jain 1989; Firat 1997), and collaborative business arrangements (including strategic alliances) (Thorelli 1986; Contractor 1990; Beamish and Killing 1997).

These trends have imparted added importance to research in international marketing, but it is not clear how research in the field has coped with this broadened responsibility in a fast-changing environment. Past reviews of research in international marketing (Boddewyn 1981; Albaum and Peterson 1984; Bradley 1987; Douglas and Craig 1992; Aulakh and Kotabe 1993) highlighted deficiencies of the discipline in two aspects: that international marketing research was fragmentary and exploratory without a strong theoretical framework, and that it lacked the methodological rigor compared with the generic (or domestic) research in international marketing. While the first deficiency in international marketing research was attributed to the opportunistic nature (Albaum and Peterson 1984) and lack of synthesis (Bradley 1987) of international marketing research, the latter was attributed to the inherent difficulties encountered in research involving more than one country (Aulakh and Kotabe 1993). Difficulties stemmed from financial constraints in data collection, problems of data comparability in cross-cultural research and the implementation of methodological techniques in foreign markets. There have been various attempts to address the problems encountered in international marketing research (e.g. Craig and Douglas 2000).

We examine the state of the art in research in international marketing in the last decade (1990–99), with particular emphasis on the conceptual framework and theory development in the field. While earlier review articles (e.g. Cavusgil and Li 1992; Douglas and Craig 1992; Aulakh and Kotabe 1993) classified the research streams fairly broadly encompassing macro-environment issues to marketing management to buyer behavior, macro-environment issues did not receive much research attention in the 1990s. Therefore, this chapter focuses on micro issues including buyer behavior and managerial issues

RESEARCH IN INTERNATIONAL MARKETING MANAGEMENT

This chapter reviews micro/managerial topics in international marketing. Research for this review spanned more than 200 articles in the journals from marketing and other related business areas that are listed on the ProQuest database. A list of journals represented in this survey is provided in the Appendix. Although the list is not comprehensive, it covers sufficiently the domain of research in international marketing management. Indeed, a large majority of articles published in the 1990s deal specifically with issues related to marketing management rather than macro-environments that affect marketing management practices.

First, we examine research in both organizational and personal consumer behavior as it represents the initial interfaces between firms and customers. In particular, the effect of country of origin in consumer behavior received a significant amount of research attention. Second, research in various modes of entry and their performance implications is examined. Third, the literature on the marketing mix strategy is highlighted, as it constitutes the crux of marketing. Fourth, research in global strategy and strategic alliances is covered. Both marketing and strategy researchers generally share common research interests in these strategy-related issues. Researchers in marketing tend to be more interested in market performance implications of global strategy and strategic alliances, while strategy researchers seem to place more emphasis on theoretical reasoning for those strategies. The topics covered in this review are summarized in Table 1.1.

ORGANIZATIONAL AND CONSUMER BEHAVIOR

1. Organizational Buying Behavior

Only one article was cited in this area. A study of organizational buyer behavior of the Gulf States was carried out by Baker and Abu-Ismail (1993). In examining the organizational environment and its impact on buying decisions, five specific issues were considered – buying tasks, the composition of the buying group and its behavior, the impact of bureaucracy on buying decisions, the concept of time and the influence of country of origin effects.

2. Consumer Behavior

International consumer behavior studies provide an alternative to international marketing research by focusing on consumers, instead of relying on countries as a basis for analysis (Wang 1999). Research in this area includes:

- Impact of culture on consumer behavior.
- Universality of American consumer behavior models to the international context.

Table 1.1 Topics covered in the review

Organizational and Consumer Behavior
  1. Organizational Buying Behavior
  2. Consumer Behavior
  3. Country of Origin
Market Entry Decisions
  1. Initial Mode of Entry
  2. Specific Modes of Entry
    a. Exporting
    b. Joint Ventures
Local Market Expansion: Marketing Mix Decisions
  1. Global Standardization vs. Local Responsiveness
  2. Marketing Mix
    a. Product Policy
    b. Advertising
    c. Pricing
    d. Distribution
Global Strategy
  1. Competitive Strategy
    a. Conceptual Development
    b. Competitive Advantage versus Competitive Positioning
    c. Sources of Competitive Advantage and Performance Implications
  2. Strategic Alliances
    a. Learning and Trust
    b. Recipes for Alliance Success
    c. Performance for Different Types of Alliances
  3. Global Sourcing
    a. Global Sourcing in a Service Context
    b. Benefits of Global Sourcing
    c. Country of Origin Issues in Global Sourcing
  4. Market Performance
    a. Determinants of Performance
    b. Different Interpretation of Performance

- Debate over global consumer homogeneity versus heterogeneity.
- Descriptions of international consumer behavior.

Culture and consumer behavior
The impact of culture on salient consumer behavior constructs of perception, information processing, value systems and self-concept is reviewed (McCort and Malhotra 1993). The impact of religion (a key determinant of culture) on consumer behavior is studied with a sample of Japanese and

American Protestant consumers (Sood and Nasu 1995). The impact of culture in moderating consumer's opinion exchange behavior is explored by Dawar, Parker and Price (1996). Results indicate that the cultural characteristics of power distance and uncertainty avoidance influence the focus of consumers' product information search activities, but not their tendencies to share product-related opinions with others.

Universality of American consumer behavior models
Samli, Wills and Jacobs (1993) alert the reader that the assumption that existing American consumer behavior knowledge is applicable to all cultures is deterrent to international consumer behavior theory development. Effectiveness of international marketing strategies depends a lot on the understanding of international markets at the macro level and consumer behaviors. It is in this context that Wills, Samli and Jacobs (1991) suggest that separately developed consumer behavior models versus a global one would prove to be more effective in international marketing strategy. Such a consumer behavior model would incorporate the following dimensions – learning, involvement, diffusion-adoption and culture context. Samli (1994) offers an international consumer behavior model that focuses on environmental and cultural factors and dwells on the theory that culture forms personality, which in turn modifies consumer behavior. Chao (1993) questions how international consumers evaluate products that are produced by strategic alliances involving multiple firms and multiple countries. In this research, a more complex form of the country of origin effect of product evaluation is examined. Despite the above, Lee and Green (1991) found support for the applicability of the Fishbein Behavioral Intentions Model in a South Korean consumer sample.

Descriptive consumer behavior
Research was conducted on the attitudes of Japanese consumers towards foreign countries and products (Nishina 1990). The results showed that in comparison to domestic products, foreign products were thought to be appealing in terms of design and individuality, but not necessarily in terms of function and quality. From the impact that global philanthropy has on consumer behavior, Collins (1993) makes the observation that in the 1990s, on a global scale, a more 'caring' global consumer seems to be evolving. Difference between the consumer behavior of oil-producing and non-oil-producing nations in their decisions to purchase imported goods is observed by Metwally (1993). In a sample drawn from Japanese consumers, the study revealed differences on issues of ethics among the consumers that provides theoretical support for expanded research in the domain of cross-national consumer ethics and highlights the needs for managers to consider

possible differences in the ethical behavior of consumers when entering a new international market (Erffmeyer, Keillor and LeClair 1999).

Consumer heterogeneity versus homogeneity
In a consumer behavior survey of comparable samples from the United States, Mexico, the Netherlands, Turkey, Thailand, and Saudi Arabia, the results suggest the existence of both global consumer segments that transcend national boundaries and a local consumer segment (Yavas, Verhage and Green 1992). In a sample representing 38 nationalities, it is found that there are few differences in the use of quality signals across cultures for a high priority segment of consumers globally (Dawar and Parker 1994).

3. Country of Origin

Although the country of origin (COO) research falls under the domain of consumer behavior research, it will be treated separately as it has carved out its own niche in international marketing research. This line of research has continued to be a breeding ground for extensive academic research. The pattern of research in this domain can be traced to the following themes:

- Conceptual refinement.
- COO and information processing.
- Establishing further proof for robustness of COO measure.
- Proof against robustness of COO measure.
- Measurement issues.

Conceptual refinement
The COO construct is decomposed into the following components – country of product design, country of parts manufacture and country of product assembly – by Insch and McBride (1998). Their results indicate that these three COO components do affect consumer perceptions of design quality, manufacturing quality and overall quality for each product in distinctly different ways. Another study reveals that COO effects can only be understood with respect to consumer ethnocentrism, where low ethnocentric consumers are more likely to use country cues as objective information about product quality (Brodowsky 1998). Further, Klein, Ettenson and Morris (1998) add that consumer animosity toward a country has a significant negative impact on buying decisions above and beyond the effect of consumer ethnocentrism.

Country of origin and consumer information processing

A schema-based knowledge representation framework is developed to examine the effects of COO on product evaluations (Kochunny et al. 1993). Results indicate that consumers possess a COO schema and that COO schema affect consumers' retention of information about products as well as their judgments. The cognitive structures that influence a person's use of the COO factor in product evaluation are discussed by Janda and Rao (1997). It is suggested that the COO may be an outcome of a combination of two processes – cultural stereotypes and personal beliefs.

Establishing further proof for robustness of country of origin measure

Research was conducted to identify consumer expertise and the type of attribute information as moderating the effects of COO on product evaluations (Maheswaran 1994). Another study found that in buying foreign products, US consumers base their decision not simply on COO cue, but on tradeoffs with price, warranty and other product attributes (Lee and Kim 1992). Research shows that perception of quality was most strongly affected by COO followed by product evaluations other than quality. COO had its smallest effect on purchase intention (Lim, Darley and Summer 1994). The extent to which the risk attitudes, political convictions and COO associations of individuals affect the buying decision of a product from a controversial source country is explored with special reference to Eastern Europe (Johansson, Ronkainen and Czinkota 1994). In a meta analysis, it is indicated that COO has a larger effect on perceived quality than on attitude towards the product or purchase intention (Verlegh and Steenkamp 1999). COO with brand name is found to be a robust determinant in consumer decision making in a cross-cultural context (Hulland 1999). An initial test of the animosity model of foreign product purchase in PRC revealed that animosity towards a foreign nation will negatively affect the purchase of products produced by that country independent of judgment of product quality (Klein, Ettenson and Morris 1998). In an experimental setting, the salience of COO was tested along with global brand name on product evaluation (Tse and Gorn 1993). In contrast to the general notion that a well-known global brand will override the COO effect, it was found that the COO was an equally salient and more enduring factor in consumer product evaluation. Research by Thakor and Katsanis (1997) indicates that while foreign branding affects product evaluations more than COO, the uni-cultural or multi-cultural nature of the research context is influential in determining which brands are seen as 'foreign'.

Proof against robustness of country of origin measure
In a large scale, cross-national consumer survey conducted in US, Canada, UK, Netherlands, France, West Germany, Greece and Hungary, the study provided some tentative evidence that product images may influence, or may be influenced by country images (Papadopoulos and Heslop 1990). Using conjoint analysis, the study found that the influence of COO on product evaluation is relatively weak when examined in the context of multiattribute modeling (Akaah and Yaprak 1993). In two separate studies, Ahmed and d'Astous (1996) found that favorableness of a brand or country of origin cue is considerably modified when a consumer is provided with additional product-related information. In a study of Dutch consumers, they were found to place little importance on country of origin as a choice cue and trusted more on their ability to evaluate the product themselves (Liefeld et al. 1996).

Measurement issues
Tests of internal reliability and validity were conducted across different countries and samples to assess the strength of a final 14 item semantic differential scale with success (Martin and Eroglu 1993).

MARKET ENTRY DECISIONS

1. Initial Mode of Entry

Research in this area has focused its attention in three areas:

- To lay a conceptual foundation for understanding the choice of entry mode.
- Entry mode choice in service firms and how they differ from manufacturing firms.
- Managerial how-to's – in other words, how managers make their decisions on the choice of entry mode.
- Tools for market entry.

Conceptual foundation
The literature continues to draw from the transaction cost/internalization and organizational capability perspectives, and even on concepts from the economics of industrial organization (Otto 1997). Bjorkman and Eklund (1996) address the question why some companies follow the sequence of operational modes used by foreign investors as explained by the Uppsala internationalization model, while others deviate from the 'traditional' establishment chain as proposed in the above model.

Buckley and Casson (1998) present a fully integrated analysis of foreign market entry decisions encompassing a choice between exporting, licensing, joint venturing and wholly owned foreign investment. A special feature of the model is the distinction between investment in production facilities and investment in distribution facilities – a distinction that according to the authors has been overlooked in international business literature.

An evolutionary perspective in analyzing multinational enterprise (MNE) entry and expansion in the global market proposes four stages of development – preparation, entry, expansion and experience (Geng 1998). The model explores the evolving objectives of the MNE at each stage and discusses the strategic transitions with respect to mode and scale, operations management, marketing strategies and human resources.

Camino and Cazorla (1998) examine the foreign market entry decisions by small and medium-sized enterprises and indicate that meaningful differences in the internationalization of firms do exist, although most SMEs follow the sequential or evolutionary process predicted by internationalization theory. Using the case of the Upjohn Company, the test for reliability and validity of the internalization and internationalization theories in the context of market entry is performed by Fina and Rugman (1996).

A multi-dimensional measure of managers' perception of international market entry risk is developed by Tan (1996). Lampert and Jaffe (1996) examine the country of origin effects on international market entry that determines the consumer protection of imported products and their value. Another study examines the contraction of foreign market operations and exit from foreign markets when MNEs face market turbulence and decline (Hadjikhani and Johansson 1996).

A comparison and contrast of the mode of foreign market entry decision is presented with the recommendation that the organizational capacity framework is better adept with today's business context (Madhok 1997). Using the theories of transaction cost, internalization and resource based view of the firm, a new framework of entry mode choice is developed where six different types of entry modes are distinguished based on location factors and complementarity (Moon 1997). A conceptual framework examines how host-country, home-country and industry-specific factors along with operation-related factors such as location and the level of local government affect the mode of entry decision and formation of alliances (Tse and Yigang 1997).

Entry mode choice in service firms
A mail survey of 175 US service firms exhibits a wide diversity in the choice of entry mode patterns (Erramilli 1990). Findings from the survey reveal that customized services are more likely to be marketed via highly

integrated entry modes that give the firm a great degree of control over its international marketing operations.

Following debate over how service firms choose their modes of entry, one study advances a classification scheme that allows some services to be grouped with manufactured goods in terms of entry mode choice (Ikechi and Sivakumar 1998). A conceptual model of factors affecting the entry mode choice of service firms is also proposed.

Managerial how-to's

Based on a series of interviews with managers at two international companies, a study by Maignan and Lukas (1997) reveals that managers' mental models or representations developed for domestic markets guide the choice of entry mode for international markets. In a study examining the experience of entering the Chinese market by six UK companies, it is suggested that equity joint ventures are a major route into the Chinese market (Wilson 1997). A list of strategies for US firms entering the restructured markets of Poland, Hungary and Czechoslovakia is offered by Dedee and Pearce (1995). Further, in another study, baseline information about how US companies entered the opening markets of the former Soviet bloc countries that are fraught with risk of different types and of different levels is provided by Shama (1995).

Tools for market entry

The approach of brand alliances is suggested as a more effective market entry tool given the large expenditures that firms face in order to build brand awareness and brand image in a foreign market (Voss and Tansuhaj 1999). A systematic understanding of the new product learning that takes place between consumers in two countries – a pair of lead and lag countries – can provide insights for a firm's international market entry decisions (Ganesh, Kumar and Subramaniam 1997). Market entry strategy is also identified by Li (1995) as one of the determinants of survival of foreign subsidiaries in international markets. Another study by Mitchell, Shaver, and Yeung (1994) reveals that successful foreign market entry is related to the extent of foreign presence in an industry at the time of entry.

2. Specific Modes of Entry

Exporting

Exporting has been one of the most frequently studied areas in the literature. Most of the academic work revolved around the following issues:

- Conceptual foundation.
- Exporting and the marketing mix.
- Determinants of exporting.
- Export performance.
- Exporting and small business.
- Factors for export success.
- Barriers to exporting.
- Exporting and strategic alliances.

Conceptual foundation   Leonidou and Katsikeas (1996) provide a comprehensive review of the main models on the export development process, identify their structural characteristics, evaluate the methodologies used for their validation, and analyze the key conceptual issues emerging from their assessment. Stump, Athaide and Axinn (1998) offer an integrative approach that combines the behavioral and attitudinal dimensions to define export commitment. The concept of relational exchange between exporters and importers is explored through a model that hypothesizes that cultural distance influences relational exchange which is in turn mediated by exporting performance and opportunism (Lee 1998a).

Exporting and the marketing mix   One study defines export pricing strategies and processes currently being used by exporting firms, what influences the adoption of these strategies, and how these strategies differ across cultures (Myers 1997). The transformation of the export product portfolios is examined from a sample in Greece (Chryssochoidis 1996). According to the main findings, the foreign versus domestic market dependence of the focus exporters had a major effect in the transformation of the export product portfolios from initiation to development of exports. Export market characteristics such as local government regulation, infrastructure differences, export market lag, cultural differences, end-user differences in tastes and preferences, and competitive intensity affect ideal and actual product adaptation is investigated by Johnson and Arunthanes (1995).

Determinants of exporting   The impact of organizational culture in a firm's export intention is explored by Dosoglu-Guner (1999). The four dimensions of organizational culture are market, adhocracy, hierarchy and clan cultures. The results indicate that clan culture decreases and adhocracy culture increases the firm's probability of exporting.

Export performance   A longitudinal study of exporting firms examines the relationships among the managers' beliefs about exporting, their export intentions, subsequent exporting behavior and future exporting intentions

(Axinn et al. 1995). Using a sample of New Zealand exporting firms, a study by Brendan (1997) indicates that segmenting the managers based on their awareness levels of export schemes can lead to better export performance. Patterson, Cicic and Shoham (1997) suggest that the satisfaction with the export relationship contributes to export performance and future export intentions. Morgan and Katsikeas (1998) discovered that the strength of perceived exporting problem is inversely related to the export intensity of the firm. The role of managerial characteristics as influences on the export behavior of the firm are reviewed by Leonidou, Katsikeas and Piercy (1998). A generalized export performance measure, the EXPERF scale, which can be applied to multiple countries is developed by Zou, Taylor and Osland (1998).

Exporting and small business In the context of small and medium-sized firms, the factors that make a small firm a successful exporter are discussed (Gray 1997; Nakos, Brouthers and Brouthers 1998; Zafarullah, Ali and Young 1998). Earlier, Calof (1994) examined the direct and indirect effects of firm size by studying three dimensions of export behavior – propensity to export, countries exporting to and export attitudes of manufacturers. A survey of characteristics of the internationalization processes pursued by small Italian exporting companies confirms the validity of some premises of the stages theory, but it is noted that companies are free to follow other routes and or pursue individualized processes of development abroad (Dalli 1994).

Factors for export success The adequacy of government export incentive programs as well as managers' awareness of these incentives are identified as the two key determinants of the success of export development strategies (Kotabe and Czinkota 1992; Kumcu, Harcar and Kumcu 1995). The findings show that level of export interest, export exploration and company size have a higher explanatory power on awareness than other company characteristics. When exporting to developing countries, the findings of the study by Sriram and Manu (1995) highlight the importance of taking the country of destination into account when planning export marketing strategies. Two marketing factors identified to be most important to successful exporting were gathering marketing information and communicating with markets (Howard 1995). Finally, Leonidou, Katsikeas and Piercy (1998) investigate managerial characteristics as influences on the export behavior of firms.

Barriers to exporting An attempt is made to review, assess and synthesize existing empirical research on factors impeding the initiation, development, or sustainment of export activities (Leonidou 1995). The role of cultural distance and managerial decision-making style are explored variables in why some firms perceive barriers to export as being more important than other firms or why some firms perceive a given barrier as more important than it is for another company (Shoham and Albaum 1995).

Exporting and strategic alliances   A model is advanced that suggests the determinants of exporters' intentions to form strategic alliances with their foreign exchange partners (Lee 1998b). Relational exchange, exporting performance and the duration of the business relationship are identified as factors affecting exporters' intentions to form strategic alliances.

Joint ventures
Research in this area examined the following issues:

- Joint venture performance.
- Selection international joint ventures.
- The element of learning in joint ventures.

JV performance   One study examined the performance of international joint ventures in the context of a global aerospace industry (Dussauge and Garrette 1995). Strategic value analysis as an indicator of performance is applied in the evaluation of a Chinese joint venture (Mills and Chen 1996). In the context of international strategic technology partnerships, joint ventures are disproportionately represented in relatively mature industries (Hagedoorn and Narula 1996). Factors that explain joint ventures performance in China are identified as level of partner commitment, the number of joint venture partners, sociocultural distance among partners, product/industry characteristics, foreign control, and joint venture location in China (Hu and Chen 1996). Kim (1996) studies international joint ventures in the context of developing countries to reveal four types of IJVs and four patterns of IJV development.

Selection of international joint ventures   Buckley and Casson (1996) provide a conceptual model that offers a range of predictions about the formation of joint ventures within industries, across industries, across locations, and over time. In a study that examines whether wholly owned subsidiaries are better than joint ventures, Chao and Yu (1996) indicate that for a small open economy under tariff protection, the desirable policy is 100 percent foreign ownership of subsidiaries, coupled with export-share requirement.

Learning in joint ventures   Organizational characteristics, structural mechanisms and contextual factors that influence knowledge acquisition from the foreign parent in international joint ventures are examined by Lyles and Salk (1996).

Country-choice strategies

In order for product introduction to be successful, corporations must identify countries and test market cities that offer a good fit with firm's overall marketing strategy (Hoffman 1997). A two-stage model is presented by the author that combines the concepts of marketing strategy, the management science technique of goal programming and microcomputer technology for an efficient and effective evaluation of international markets.

International market choice of small entrepreneurial high-tech firms is largely shaped by the interests of various network players (Coviello and Munro 1995). Early relationships with large firms are recognized as being particularly influential in the entrepreneurial high-tech firm's internationalization process.

MARKETING MIX DECISIONS: LOCAL MARKET EXPANSION

This section examines the studies relating to the global standardization debate, followed by a discussion on the international marketing mix variables of product policy, advertising, pricing, and distribution.

1. Global Standardization vs. Local Responsiveness

Four isolated studies were identified in the international marketing literature reviewed for this chapter. The findings of each study are summarized below:

- Kotabe and Duhan (1991, 1993) examine Japanese executives' perceptions of the veracity of various PIMS strategy principles developed from analysis of the pooled experience of businesses in the United States. While some differences exist, their findings generally suggest that most of the PIMS principles and strategic orientations found to exist in the United States are perceived by Japanese executives to apply in Japan.
- A new perspective on the marketing mix standardization debate suggests that clusters should be a function of the marketing mix elements instead of the more popular country clustering approach (Ayal and Nachum 1994).
- Sullivan (1992) points to the conflict or tension between global standardization and local responsiveness in multinationals.

- An empirical investigation of MNEs that implement a global standardization program versus those that do not revealed that there were no identifiable performance differences between the two samples (Samiee and Roth 1992).

The common theme in all of the above four studies is that the focus among the academicians seems to be on evaluating the effectiveness of a global standardization program in the context of multinationals.

2. Marketing Mix

Product policy
A bulk of the studies in this domain examined the following two key concepts:

- Determinants of new product development and management in international markets.
- Success of new products.

Determinants of new product development   As new technologies are becoming more complicated, R&D consortia become a popular tool for new product development (Hongcharu 1999). The marketing–R&D interface exerts a positive impact on new product performance in foreign markets (Li 1999). In a study of 13 Japanese, American and European multinational companies, observations reveal that global new product development processes vary in terms of the involvement of overseas subsidiaries in project teams and the generation of new product concepts (Mohan, Rosenthal and Hatten 1998). It was found that when the knowledge about different product design requirements among overseas markets or plants is tacit, firms employ cross-national product development teams and use overseas subsidiaries as sources of new product concepts. Literature suggests that product innovation introduced later in a country results in faster diffusion as the consumers in the lag market have an opportunity to learn about the new product from the consumers in the lead market. This finding is used to provide some preliminary guidelines for manufacturers regarding selection of foreign markets and the timing and order of entry decisions for new products (Ganesh, Kumar and Subramaniam 1997). Investigating the relationship between marketing and new product development, a study in East Asia revealed that marketing skills derived from marketing resources and the proficiency in conducted marketing activities are important in new product development (Song, Montoya-Weiss and Schmidt 1997). The role of the Internet overseas in new product development is also examined (Quelch and Klein 1996).

Success of new product   Speed in new product introduction in the market is a critical dimension of competition faced by many firms in the global marketplace. A model explains that new product success is largely determined by the speed to market, which in turn is an outcome of technological familiarity, product differentiation, competitive intensity and internal R&D skills (Yeoh 1994). A study conducted in PRC indicated that relative product advantage and the acquisition of marketing information were highly correlated with new product success (Parry and Song 1994). Unlike the findings from Canadian firms, the level of competitive activity, the timing of the product launch and the level of proficiency in executing activities in the early stages of the product development process were identified as other indicators of new product success in China. A country's innovativeness contributes to the successful introduction of new products in the global markets (Lee 1990). In a more applied setting, with the emergence of the European Union, diffusion rates of new products introduced during the first and second halves of the unification process were found to vary (Ganesh 1998).

In addition to the above two discussed core areas, isolated studies examined the ability of a firm to develop new products as being crucial for an industrial firm to start exporting (Rynning and Anderson 1994); and how in a multicountry environment, variations in media availability has predictable effects on the speed and pattern of new product sales (Tellefsen and Takada 1999).

Advertising
Some work has also been conducted in the area of international advertising strategy and its impact on other marketing related decisions. The two key areas that have received most of the research attention are:

- Advertising standardization versus customization.
- International advertising strategy.

Other studies have also examined advertising effectiveness in an international context. Here, the use of culturally relevant stimuli in international advertising is investigated to determine how these culturally relevant aspects are interpreted by the intended audience (Leach and Liu 1998). Visual ads have been found to be more effective than verbal ads in a global campaign (Kernan and Domzal 1993). Attitudes toward the ad and advertised product in a collectivist cultural setting are found to be more positive when the advertisements depict consistencies in cultural norms and roles than when there are inconsistencies (Gregory and Munch 1997).

Advertising standardization   In a review of a 40-year debate over standardization versus adaptation advertising issues, Agarwal (1995) indicates that academicians have mostly advocated the adaptation approach, while the practitioners have alternated between the two approaches with a trend towards standardization. This degree of advertising standardization adopted by firms and 'what is' standardized varies across a standardization spectrum (Harris 1994). However, the opportunities for advertising standardization are most likely to occur in less affluent, developing markets (James and Hill 1991). Additionally, advertising standardization is more likely to be effective in country clusters which are segregated based on their economic and cultural similarities and their media availability and usage (Sriram and Gopalakrishna 1991).

In the context of Asian markets such as Hong Kong, Taiwan, Singapore and PRC, a regionalization approach is found to be more effective than a global standardization perspective for advertising (Tai 1997). Contrasting this finding, Zandpour and Harich (1997) provide evidence that countries that are not necessarily a part of a geographic region may exhibit similar advertising preferences in spite of cultural differences and lack of regional proximity. Counteracting the benefits of a regionalization approach, Nevett (1992) indicated that British and American consumers had very different preferences in terms of their advertising needs. However, in terms of standardization, Alexander and King (1995) highlight the universality of leisure themes in international advertising across a sample of 500 billboard and print advertisements from 33 nationalities.

The scope of multi-country campaigns have attracted much attention but have often been overshadowed by the standardization–adaptation debate (Hill and Shao 1994). Additionally, the role of the advertising agency has been found to be negligible in the decision to standardize. One study has found evidence that suggests that standardization of advertising is on the decline (Kanso 1992).

International advertising strategy   One study showed unique characteristics at each stage of internationalization for a firm from a newly industrialized country (Chao, Choi and Yi 1994). International advertising in addition to several other factors was identified as one of the major factors affecting the decision of Middle Eastern consumers to purchase imported goods (Metwally 1993). The impact of international advertising of processed foods and beverages, pharmaceuticals, tobacco and alcoholic beverages has also been examined (Baudot 1991).

Pricing
Many authors note that research in international pricing issues is a neglected area in international marketing management when compared

with the other marketing mix variables (Aulakh and Kotabe 1993; Samli and Jacobs 1994; Myers and Cavusgil 1996). Therefore our literature search revealed that research in this domain tends to be scattered with no observable pattern or trend.

In a conceptual framework, Myers and Cavusgil (1996) identify the factors that influence the export pricing process and the reasons why firms adopt the export pricing strategies that they do. The relationship between firms' strategies in international pricing and performance is explored. Research has tried to build a set of rules and processes for international price setting (Cavusgil 1996). An empirical study investigated the relationship between international pricing and Western European economic integration (Gaul and Lutz 1994). The results suggest that price differences that can be observed in the Western European market decrease when influence on final prices exerted by exporting firms increases. Research on how to set international pricing suggests a technique called strategic choice that can help a manager understand tradeoffs made by different customer segments to set price discrimination and product differentiation policies (Sinclair 1993). More recently, Clark, Kotabe and Rajaratnam (1999) have developed a conceptual framework to link international marketers' pricing strategy to the impact of exchange rate pass-through on international pricing and offered testable propositions.

Distribution

The only article that reflected on the conceptual underpinnings of international channels of distribution was the research by Kale and McIntyre (1991). The study suggested that international channel relationships should reflect the underlying cultural tenets of the society.

Research in this area focused on the following broad issues:

- Channel cooperation and conflict.
- Channel performance.
- Channels and MNE performance.
- Standardization versus adaptation debate.
- Applied issues.

Channel cooperation and conflict   This is a popular area of research in this field. Shoham, Rose and Kropp (1997) examine this construct within the context of international channels. Two determinants of international channel conflict are identified – distribution system quality and cultural distance between exporters' home and international target countries. In a study of 135 British international trade intermediaries, discussion centered around the factors that enhance cooperation and reduce conflict between an intermediary and its suppliers, and the impact of conflict and cooperation on the maintenance of long-term relationships (Balabanis 1998).

Channel performance   Channel performance can be enhanced by relying on certain nonmarket forms of governance – control and flexibility (Gilliland and Bello 1997). Of the two forms of control, output control along with flexibility is identified as enhancing export channel performance, with process control having no performance effect. Gillespie and McBride (1996) indicate that with smuggling as a popular form of illegal channel in emerging markets competing with more legitimate channels of distribution, US multinationals will face new challenges relating to strategic planning, etc. With respect to Canadian operations, a mail survey revealed that the lower the financial performance in the foreign market relative to Canadian operations, the lower the satisfaction with the international marketing channel (Klein and Roth 1993). Within the context of the Saudi car market, it is indicated that the level of economic development and culture impacts the channel structure, operations and its performance (Ahmed and Al-Motawa 1997).

Channels and MNE performance   Appropriate distribution channels along with high commitment of top management are identified as important determinants of international marketing success in large multinational corporations (Cavusgil and Kirpalani 1993). Access to distribution channel is identified as a market entry barrier (among several others) in international consumer markets (Karakaya 1993).

Standardization vs. adaptation debate   It is noted that in the existing literature on this issue, both academicians and practitioners concur that market channels cannot be standardized. However, given this challenge, a conceptual framework for the possible standardization of global marketing channels is presented (Rosenbloom, Larsen and Mehta 1997).

Applied issues   Fahy and Taguchi (1995) point to the changing landscape of the Japanese distribution system that is less intimidating and relatively more easily accessible by US multinationals. On a last note, how to pick the right foreign distributors by small and medium sized firms (who lack sophisticated market research/decision analysis tools to assist them) is answered by the Analytical Hierarchy Process, which serves as a highly flexible and versatile substitute (Yeoh and Calantone 1995).

GLOBAL STRATEGY

The literature review was performed to advance the knowledge in the four sub-areas as identified by Douglas and Craig (1992): competitive strategy, strategic alliances, sourcing and multinational company performance.

1. Competitive Strategy

Three broad issues seem to be dominant in mainstream research:

- Theoretical and conceptual development to help in understanding the role of competitive strategy.
- Difference between competitive advantage and competitive positioning.
- Sources of competitive advantage in international marketing strategy and performance implications.

Conceptual development

A resource-based strategic management model of MNE market entry demonstrates the value of this new conceptual framework to the understanding of competitive strategy of MNEs (Tallman 1991). The integration-responsiveness framework in the choice of the models of international strategy is less helpful for devising competitive strategy (Taggart 1998). A contingency framework illustrates how national and political institutions of a country impact the effectiveness of an MNE's international strategies (Murtha and Lenway 1994). Application of the Porter–Dunning Diamond model of international competitiveness is used to explain the current situation and the further development of the international competitive strategy of mainland China's manufacturing sector (Liu and Song 1997).

Competitive advantage versus competitive positioning

Strategy literature in the 1990s tried to differentiate between two sources of competitive strategy – competitive advantage and competitive positioning. A firm experiences competitive advantage in terms of its core competencies. A firm's competitive positioning, on the other hand, raises the need for important strategy choices beyond the core competencies of a single corporation. Competitive positioning strategy interacts with internationalization strategy in the formulation of an overall strategy (Morrison and Roth 1992).

Sources of competitive advantage and performance implications

A firm's competitive strategy along with other key variables such as market orientation, experience and product characteristics plays an important role in the development of International Manufacturing Configuration (IMC) strategies (Dubois, Toyne and Oliff 1993). Competitive advantage is a key determinant of international marketing strategy (Lim, Sharkey and Kim 1993). In a study of 56 large US-based multinational firms in Latin America, competitive advantages were found to be significant in firm performance. The only advantages that were consistently significant were proprietary technology, a firm's goodwill based on brand or company name and economies of scale in production (Grosse 1992). This study identifies the sources of competitive advantage that significantly impact firm performance. Manufacturing policies are identified as a primary source of sustainable competitive advantage (Carr 1993). The three additional Ps of service firms (physical evidence, participants and process) are also identified as sources of competitive advantage (Collier 1991).

Samli and Jacobs (1995) suggest that in order to achieve the strongest international competitive advantage, there must be cooperation between the public and business sectors. Competitive advantage along with location-specific advantages should be integrated in the design of a firm's overall international strategy. In other words, the basic task of strategy is to identify the geographical location of a firm's functional activities and to integrate these activities across the various locations. Roth (1992) suggests that selective globalization (when a firm defines its global strategy around a narrow subset of the value chain) may lead to the most effective outcomes.

2. Strategic Alliances

The value of cooperation realized in the 1980s in the strategy literature is still recognized as an important contributor to firm success in a global economy. The only article identified on the conceptual foundation of strategic alliances defines it as a manifestation of inter-organizational cooperative strategies, entailing the pooling of specific resources and skills by the cooperating organizations in order to achieve common goals (Varadarajan and Cunningham 1995). The motives for firms to enter into strategic alliances as identified by the above authors are: gaining access to new markets, accelerating the pace of entry into new markets, sharing of research and development, manufacturing, and/or marketing costs, broadening the product line/filling product, and learning new skills.

With the exception of the above research piece, literature in this area has focused its interest in three broad areas:

- Issues of learning and trust in alliances.
- Recipes for alliance success.
- Performance issues for different types of alliances.

Learning and trust

Work by Varadarajan and Cunningham (1995) provides a conceptual foundation for understanding strategic alliances and the role of marketing in the nature of such alliances. Inkpen (1998) investigates the potential of international strategic alliances for learning and knowledge acquisition. A study by Hamel (1991) suggests that not all alliance partners are equally adept at learning and that asymmetries in learning might alter the relative bargaining power of partners. A difference between convenience and strategic alliances is examined. It is maintained that although all international corporate alliances provide learning, this learning does not necessarily always lead to strategic learning (Samli, Kaynak and Sharif 1996). The notion of trust in a special form of strategic alliance–non-equity-based international cooperative alliance was examined. Results showed that partner cultural sensitivity was an important contributor to trust building in such alliances (Johnson, Cullen and Sakano 1996).

Recipes for alliance success

Interfirm relationship networks are strategic resources that can be shaped by managerial action and industry events (Ravindranath, Balaji and Prescott 1998). Managing relationships with strategic alliance partners as well as with their customers, employees, channel partners etc. is key to a firm's long-term success in a global economy (Beckett-Camarata, Camarata and Barker 1998). There are different types of alliances each with their own respective type of performance implication (Dussauge and Garrette 1995). One study suggests a framework to analyze the likely success factors of international strategic alliances and to assist companies in their efforts to avoid picking the wrong alliance partners (Brouthers, Brouthers and Wilkinson 1995). Strategic alliances defined as interfirm partnering – should be examined to analyze the stability of alliance networks in a global context and also if market leaders tend to dominate the alliance partnership. To achieve a mature and coherent global order in a rapidly changing world, it is suggested that government and business must reconcile economic interests by fostering collaborative international alliances (Halal 1993).

Performance for different types of alliances

Patterns of similarities and differences in the forms of strategic alliances among the Triad Powers are examined. Equity participation plays a somewhat larger role in the United States and Europe. Japan, on the other hand, was characterized by a dominance of contractual agreements over joint ventures and equity participation forms (Terpstra and Simonin 1993). An analysis of 473 strategic alliances revealed that equity joint ventures are preferred to contracts when cultural differences between partner firms are greater and when alliances involve upstream rather than downstream value chain activities (Sengupta and Perry 1997). Real application of the performance of international strategic alliances (ISAs) is examined in the case of China, where, results show that ISAs outperform joint ventures and wholly owned subsidiaries. However, ISAs also bear more financial risks in terms of liquidity and solvency (Luo 1996).

3. Global Sourcing

Isolated studies examined the role of global sourcing as a critical factor in a variety of competitive strategies, differentiated between opportunistic and strategic sourcing (Samli, Browning and Busbia 1998) and offered suggestion on how to reduce uncertainty associated with supplier selection in global markets (Min, Latour and Williams 1994). However, the three broad areas most popularly studied in this domain are the following:

- Global sourcing in a service context.
- Benefits of global sourcing.
- Country of origin issues in global sourcing.

Global sourcing in a service context
A growing area of interest has been to investigate the comparability of product versus services sourcing strategies. The market performance of global sourcing strategies of service firms is investigated by Kotabe, Murray and Javalgi (1998). Using the TCA paradigm, Murray and Kotabe (1999) investigate the locational (domestic vs. global sourcing) and the ownership (internal vs. external sourcing) aspects of service sourcing strategies. Performance implications are also discussed.

Benefits of global sourcing
Despite eroding market share, US firms have consolidated their global profitability levels by skillfully exploiting their technological prowess through technology transfer and offshore sourcing (Kotabe and Swan 1994). The sourcing strategies used by European and Japanese firms have implications for the transferability of the firm's product and manufacturing process technology (Kotabe 1993). Lower costs are not the only benefit of global sourcing. Some of the other more strategic benefits include

potential for a lasting advantage in technical supremacy, penetration of growth markets and high speed (Fagan 1991). Global sourcing is identified as one of the reasons that allows for relationship building between firms and their suppliers (Sharma and Sheth 1997). A contingency framework studies the moderating influence of product innovation, process innovation and asset specificity on the relationship between the sourcing strategy and the product's strategic and financial performance (Murray, Kotabe and Wildt 1995). The results show that the moderators are significant for only financial performance and not strategic. A study of US-based subsidiaries of foreign MNEs, shows that internal component sourcing and internal sourcing of non-standardized components from abroad is related to the highest sales growth (Murray, Kotabe and Wildt 1995; Murray, Wildt and Kotabe 1995).

Country of origin issues in global sourcing
Global sourcing is addressed as a type of commodity bundling of components with implications for the country of origin effect (Choi 1993). In this case, the 'made in a developing country' might pose a problem for the company (Choi 1993; Witt and Rao 1992).

4. Market Performance

The literature here has focused on two sets of issues:

- Determinants of performance – what factors determine High MNE performance.
- An environmental interpretation of performance.

Determinants of performance
The chosen mode of ownership (joint ventures or wholly-owned subsidiaries) is associated with the behavior and performance of overseas subsidiaries (Chowdhury 1992). Financial performance was found to be higher when management practices in the multinational work unit were congruent with the national culture (Newman and Nollen 1996). Performance was found to be enhanced by budget communication between subunits of multinationals when reliance on budget control and environmental dynamism is high (Hassel and Cunningham 1996). Sources of competitive advantage such as proprietary technology, goodwill based on the firm's brand and company name and economies of scale in production are significant predictors of multinational performance (Grosse 1992). The need to develop better international products and to improve the multinational performance in international marketing efforts is mentioned by Wills, Samli and

Jacobs (1991); simply stated, this means that managers should know when to globalize or localize marketing practices. Kotabe (1990) notes that the interaction between product and process innovation is a crucial determinant of market performance of European and Japanese multinationals.

Different interpretations of performance
Corporate environmental performance is different from the traditional interpretation of performance in financial terms (Epstein and Roy 1998). In this perspective, a multinational's performance depends on whether it adopts global or local standards to meet the environmental requirements. Yet another determinant of performance is stakeholder satisfaction (Greeno and Robinson 1992). This study revealed that companies that aggressively consider the environmental implications of all parts of their organization, processes and products, as they set strategies for the future to satisfy stakeholder needs, will be high performers in the future.

DIRECTIONS FOR FUTURE RESEARCH

Having surveyed the international marketing management literature published in the 1990s, we have to ask if the research deficiencies addressed in the last two decades have been addressed. In the early 1990s, Douglas and Craig (1992) lamented that strategy issues were a sadly neglected area in international marketing and that marketing's role in global strategy was largely ignored.

Based on the 1990–99 international marketing management literature, we have to express the same concern despite a large number of articles in this area. Researchers in international marketing continue to borrow concepts and theories from the management and strategy literature, and tend to relate them to market performance. Management and strategy researchers tend to focus on the supply side of the dyadic relationships between firms and customers, while marketing researchers tend to focus on the demand side of the relationships. In a positive light, international marketing researchers complement management and strategy researchers in subjecting supply-side theories to demand-side considerations. However, studies in international marketing do not appear to have affected the direction of management and strategy research in any significant way.

Market segmentation and target marketing are two major concepts uniquely developed in the marketing literature with focus on the demand (customer) side. Yet, studies in these areas are scarce in both domestic and international marketing literature. This area of research would have some profound impact on supply-side strategy research if sufficiently developed.

In particular, benefit and intermarket segmentation concepts appear promising for further development in the international marketing literature.

In the generic (domestic) context, marketing as a discipline has gradually moved from economic issues to behavioral issues. For example, marketing was developed as a study of distribution channels and logistics at
the dawn of the twentieth century. Today, logistics is not generally considered as part of the marketing discipline. Even economics of new
product development is increasingly considered outside the mainstream
marketing field. On the other hand, behavioral research, as well as quantitative applications, in consumer behavior, promotion, and channel management has become mainstream. In the international area, the same
forces have been at work. Consequently, there have been a disproportionately large number of studies in consumer behavior (particularly country
of origin effects), modes of entry (particularly exporting), and channel
performance.

The focal area of marketing is the marketing mix strategy, encompassing
product, price, promotion, and distribution management. Studies that
address various aspects of the marketing mix were limited to the standardization vs. adaptation issue. Part of the limited attention to each aspect of
the marketing mix is due to the difficulty of conducting empirical research.
Product development has become so technically and technologically
complex that this area is increasingly better examined by researchers in the
engineering fields, or jointly by those in engineering and marketing fields.
Pricing has always been one of the most difficult areas of research in marketing as firms are not willing to share pricing and cost information.
Promotion – in particular, advertising-related research, such as advertising
effectiveness and global advertising – and consumer behavior have
attracted many marketing researchers, due mainly to the relative ease of
collecting data for theory testing. Research in distribution management is
more or less limited to such behavioral issues as dyadic trust and power
(control) relationships. Although global sourcing issues (including procurement and supply chain management) are considered part of the broadly
defined domain of marketing (Douglas and Craig 1992), studies in these
areas appear to be gradually migrating to the strategy literature and away
from the contemporary domain of marketing.

One area where marketing has genuine strengths is research methodology. As the marketing discipline has evolved into a strongly psychology-
based behavioral discipline, researchers have paid serious attention to the
reliability and validity of measurement issues. However, it should be noted
that international marketing research is faced with many more operational
difficulties and pitfalls in conducting empirical research than is generic,
domestic-bound research. Consequently, international marketing research-

ers may not be able to address those measurement and other methodological issues as effectively as would be possible in domestic research.

Another issue that shaped the nature of international business in the 1990s is that of regionalization as evidenced by the formation of various trading blocs including the European Union, NAFTA, and MERCOSUR, among others and by regional crises in Southeast Asia and Latin America. As a result, the fundamental strategic dilemma between integration (supply-side consideration) and local responsiveness (demand-side consideration) has intensified rather than weakened. Until mid-1990s the frame of mind of most business researchers and practitioners was that management of the configuration and coordination of globally scattered value-chain activities was possible. I call it a global 'scatter' strategy. Then since the second half of the 1990s we have begun to doubt the wisdom of such simplicity. We posit that a more self-contained localized 'delivery' systems perspective will gain prominence as the unexpected and wild fluctuations of the exchange rates will prevent multinational firms from effectively managing the set of globally scattered value-chain activities. Regional trade blocs will form currency areas in which exchange rates are stable relative to each other, which will reinforce localization of production and marketing. Regionalization of global strategy may be an apt characterization. If so, then how to manage global marketing in fragmented production and delivery systems will become an important managerial issue that begs for further investigation.

The emergence of e-commerce in recent years will also have a pervasive impact on the way marketing is practiced around the world. Due to some time lag in conducting research and the publication process, we expect a flurry of research publications on e-commerce to start appearing in the first decade of the twenty-first century. Thanks to the Internet revolution, information lag as well as geographical distance between countries has shrunk enormously. One fundamental assumption about the physical and mental distance behind the international product cycle thesis has become irrelevant for strategy development. It does not necessarily mean, however, that market needs are converging. Indeed, people around the world are expressing their ethnic and cultural differences more openly than ever before. Therefore, despite some regional integrations, other regions are Balkanizing across cultural and religious lines even within the same country (e.g. the Basque region in Spain and Scotland in the UK). Thus, the fundamental strategic dilemma between integration and local responsiveness remains. With the advancement of the Internet and e-commerce in international business, an online scale vs. offline market sensitivity dilemma may well characterize the first decade of the twenty-first century.

In general, international marketing researchers have always been interested in the ever-changing market environments and/or methodological rigor as cherished by their domestic counterparts for research publication purposes. As a result, international marketing researchers have tended to focus their research attention either on topics *de jour* or on research areas in which a large database can be developed. The first group of international marketing researchers tend to focus on interesting but unstructured topics that are difficult to theorize on or apply existing theory to, and thus engage in exploratory research. Although exploratory research is interesting, it tends to lack in transferability of its research framework and findings in explaining other related topics. The second group of international marketing researchers tend to focus on such behavioral research areas as country of origin, modes of entry, and trust/power relationships in the marketing channel, in which rigorous research methodology is applied for scholarly publication. Both groups of international marketing researchers face different criticisms. The first group is criticized for conducting atheoretical research, while the second group is criticized for overdoing research in mature areas in which additional contribution to the literature is increasingly very limited.

In conclusion, there remain many important research areas that have eluded serious academic inquiry. The increased technical complexity of marketing issues, particularly the marketing mix strategy, calls for more interdisciplinary work across traditional functional confines than in the past. Collaborative work by a group of researchers across national boundaries also facilitates data collection and promotes cultural sensitivity in conducting marketing research.

APPENDIX

List of Journals Reviewed

Marketing Journals	General Business Journals
• *European Journal of Marketing*	• *Academy of Management Journal*
• *Industrial Marketing Management*	• *Business Horizons*
• *International Journal of Advertising*	• *International Journal of Management*
• *International Journal of Research in Marketing*	• *Journal of Business Research*
	• *Journal of Business Strategy*
• *International Marketing Review*	• *Journal of Economic Psychology*
• *Journal of Consumer Marketing*	• *Journal of International Business Studies*
• *Journal of Advertising Research*	
• *Journal of Consumer Research*	• *Journal of Management Studies*
• *Journal of Euro-Marketing*	• *Journal of Product Innovation Management*
• *Journal of Global Marketing*	
• *Journal of International Consumer Marketing*	• *Journal of World Business*
	• *Long Range Planning*
• *Journal of International Marketing*	• *Management International Review*
• *Journal of International Marketing and Marketing Research*	• *Organization Science*
	• *Review of Business*
• *Journal of Macromarketing*	• *Sloan Management Review*
• *Journal of Marketing*	• *Strategic Management Journal*
• *Journal of Marketing Research*	
• *Journal of Marketing Theory and Practice*	
• *Journal of the Academy of Marketing Science*	
• *Psychology and Marketing*	

REFERENCES

Agarwal, M. (1995), 'Review of a 40-year Debate in International Advertising', *International Marketing Review*, **12** (1), 26–49.
Ahmed, A. and A. Al-Motawa (1997), 'Communication and Related Channel Phenomena in International Markets: The Saudi Car Market', *Journal of Global Marketing*, **10** (3), 67–82.
Ahmed, S. and A. d'Astous (1996), 'Country of Origin and Brand Effects', *Journal of International Consumer Marketing*, **9** (2), 93–115.
Akaah, I. and A. Yaprak (1993), 'Assessing the Influence of Country of Origin on Product Evaluations', *Journal of International Consumer Marketing*, **5** (2), 39–53.
Albaum, G. and R.A. Peterson (1984), 'Empirical Research in International Marketing', *Journal of International Business Studies*, **15** (Spring/Summer), 161–73.

Alexander, J. and N.D. King (1995), 'Leisure Themes in International Advertising: A Content Analysis', *Journal of International Consumer Marketing*, **8** (1), 113–14.

Aulakh, Preet S. and Masaaki Kotabe (1993), 'An Assessment of Theoretical and Methodological Development in International Marketing: 1980–1990', *Journal of International Marketing*, **1** (2), 5–28.

Axinn, C.N., R. Savitt, J.M. Sinkula and S.V. Thach (1995), 'Export Intentions, Beliefs and Behaviors in Smaller Industrial Firms', *Journal of Business Research*, **32** (1), 49–56.

Ayal, I. and L. Nachum (1994), 'A Fresh Look at the Standardization Problem: Classifying LDCs in the Marketing Mix Content', *Journal of International Marketing and Marketing Research*, **19** (1), 17–36.

Baker, M. and F. Abu-Ismail (1993), 'Organizational Buying Behavior in the Gulf', *International Marketing Review*, **10** (6), 42–61.

Balabanis, G. (1998), 'Antecedents of Cooperation, Conflict and Relationship Longevity in an International Trade Intermediary's Supply Chain', *Journal of Global Marketing*, **12** (2), 25–46.

Baudot, B. (1991), 'International Issues in the Advertising of Health-related Products', *European Journal of Marketing*, **25** (6), 24–37.

Beamish, P.W. and J.P. Killing (1997), *Cooperative Strategies*, San Francisco: New Lexington Press.

Beckett-Camarata, J.E., M. Camarata and R.T. Barker (1998), 'Integrating Internal and External Customer Relationships through Relationship Management: A Strategic Response to a Changing Global Environment', *Journal of Business Research*, **41** (1), 71–81.

Bjorkman, I. and M. Eklund (1996), 'The Sequence of Operational Modes Used by Finnish Investors in Germany', *Journal of International Marketing*, **4** (1), 33–55.

Boddewyn, J.J. (1981), 'Comparative Marketing: The First Twenty-five Years', *Journal of International Business Studies*, **12** (Spring/Summer), 61–79.

Bradley, M.F. (1987), 'Nature and Significance of International Marketing: A Review', *Journal of Business Research*, **15**, 205–19.

Brendan, J.G. (1997), 'Profiling Managers to Improve Export Promotion Targeting', *Journal of International Business Studies*, **28** (2), 387–420.

Brodowsky, G.H. (1998), 'The Effects of Country of Design and Country of Assembly on Evaluative Beliefs about Automobiles and Attitudes Toward Buying Them: A Comparison Between Low and High Ethnocentric Consumers', *Journal of International Consumer Marketing*, **10** (3), 85–113.

Brouthers, K., L. Brouthers and T. Wilkinson (1995), 'Strategic Alliances: Choose Your Partners', *Long Range Planning*, **28** (3), 18–36.

Buckley, P.J. and M. Casson (1996), 'An Economic Model of International Joint Venture Strategy', *Journal of International Business Studies*, **27** (5), 849–76.

Buckley, P.J. and M. Casson (1998), 'Analyzing Foreign Market Entry Strategies: Extending the Internalization Approach,' *Journal of International Business Studies*, **29** (3), 539–61.

Calof, J. (1994) 'The Relationship Between Firm Size and Export Behavior Revisited', *Journal of International Business Studies*, **25** (2), 367–87.

Camino, D. and L. Cazorla (1998), 'Foreign Market Entry Decisions by Small and Medium-sized Enterprises: An Evolutionary Approach', *International Journal of Management*, **15** (1), 123–9.

Carr, C. (1993), 'Global, National and Resource Based Strategies: An Examination', *Strategic Management Journal*, **14** (7), 551–68.

Cavusgil, S.T. and V.H. Kirpalani (1993), 'Introducing Products Into Export Markets: Success Factors', *Journal of Business Research*, **27** (1), 1–15.

Cavusgil, S.T. and T. Li (1992), *International Marketing: An Annotated Bibliography*, Chicago: American Marketing Association.

Cavusgil, S.T. (1996), 'Pricing for Global Markets', *Journal of World Business*, **31** (4), 66–78.

Chao, C. and E. Yu (1996), 'Are Wholly Foreign Owned Enterprises Better Than Joint Ventures?', *Journal of International Economics*, **40** (1), 225–47.

Chao, D.S., J. Choi and Y. Yi (1994), 'International Advertising Strategies by NIC Multinationals: The Case of a Korean Firm', *International Journal of Advertising*, **13** (1), 77–93.

Chao, P. (1993), 'Partitioning Country of Origin Effects: Consumer Evaluations', *Journal of International Business Studies*, **24** (2), 291–306.

Choi, C.J. (1993), 'A Note on Commodity Bundling and Global Sourcing', *Journal of Global Marketing*, **7** (2), 117–23.

Chowdhury J. (1992), 'Performance of International Joint Ventures and Wholly Owned Subsidiaries', *Management International Review*, **32** (2), 115–34.

Chryssochoidis, G.M. (1996), 'Successful Exporting: Exploring the Transformation of the Export Product Portfolios', *Journal of Global Marketing*, **10** (1), 7–31.

Clark, T., M. Kotabe and D. Rajaratnam (1999), 'Exchange Rate Pass-through and International Pricing Strategy: A Conceptual Framework and Research Propositions', *Journal of International Business Studies*, **30** (2), 249–69.

Collier, D.A. (1991), 'New Marketing Mix Stresses Service', *Journal of Business Strategy*, **12** (2), 42–6.

Collins, M. (1993), 'Global Corporate Philanthropy', *European Journal of Marketing*, **27** (2), 46–59.

Contractor, F.J. (1990), 'Contractual and Cooperative Forms of International Business: Towards a United Theory of Model Choice', *Management International Review*, **30**, 31–54.

Coviello, N. and H.J. Munro (1995), 'Growing the Entrepreneurial Firm: Networking for International Market Development', *European Journal of Marketing*, **29** (7), 49–62.

Craig, C.S. and S.P. Douglas (2000), *International Marketing Research*, 2nd edn, New York: Wiley.

Dalli, D. (1994), 'The Exporting Process: The Evolution of Small and Medium Sized Firms Towards Internationalization', *Advances in International Marketing*, **6**, 85–110.

Dawar, N. and P. Parker (1994), 'Marketing Universals: Consumers Use of Brand Name, Price', *Journal of Marketing*, **58** (2), 81–96.

Dawar, N., P. Parker and L. Price (1996), 'A Cross-Cultural Study of Interpersonal Information Exchange', *Journal of International Business Studies*, **27** (3), 497–516.

Dedee, J.K. and J.A. Pearce (1995), 'Eastern Euro-Markets: Strategies for United States Firms', *International Journal of Management*, **12** (3), 315–25.

Dosoglu-Guner, B. (1999) 'An Exploratory Study of the Export Intention of Firms: The Relevance of Organizational Culture', *Journal of Global Marketing*, **12**, 45–63.

Douglas, S.P. and C.S. Craig (1992), 'Advances in International Marketing', *International Journal of Research in Marketing*, **9** (4), 291–318.

Douglas, S.P. and Y. Wind (1987), 'The Myth of Globalization', *Columbia Journal of World Business*, **22** (Winter), 19–30.

Dubois, F.L., B. Toyne and M.D. Oliff (1993), 'International Manufacturing Strategies of U.S. Multinationals', *Journal of International Business Studies*, **24** (2), 307–33.

Dussauge, P. and B. Garrette (1995), 'Determinants of Success in International Alliances', *Journal of International Business Studies*, **26** (3), 505–31.

Epstein, M. and M.J. Roy (1998), 'Managing Corporate Environmental Performance: A Multinational Perspective', *Academy of Management Journal*, **16** (3), 284–96.

Erffmeyer, R.C., B.D. Keillor and D.T. LeClair (1999), 'An Empirical Investigation of Japanese Consumer Ethics', *Journal of Business Ethics*, **18** (1), 35–50.

Erramilli, M.K. (1990) 'Entry Mode Choice in Service Industries', *International Marketing Review*, **7** (5/6), 50–63.

Fagan, M. (1991), 'A Guide to Global Sourcing', *Journal of Business Strategy*, **12** (2), 21–6.

Fahy, J. and F. Taguchi (1995), 'Reassessing the Japanese Distribution System', *Sloan Management Review*, **36** (2), 49–62.

Fina, E. and A. Rugman (1996), 'A Test of Internalization Theory and Internationalization Theory: The Upjohn Company' *Management International Review*, **36** (3), 199–213.

Firat, A.F. (1997), 'Educator Insights: Globalization of Fragmentation – A Framework for Understanding Contemporary Global Markets', *Journal of International Marketing*, **5** (2), 77–86.

Ganesh, J. (1998), 'Converging Trends Within the European Union: Insights from an Analysis of Diffusion Patterns', *Journal of International Marketing*, **6** (4), 32–48.

Ganesh, J., V. Kumar and V. Subramaniam (1997), 'Learning Effects in Multinational Diffusion of Consumer Durables: An Exploratory Investigation', *Journal of the Academy of Marketing Science*, **25** (3), 214–28.

Gaul, W. and U. Lutz (1994), 'Pricing in International Marketing and Western European Economies', *Management International Review*, **34** (2), 101–25.

Geng, C. (1998), 'The Evolutionary Process of Global Market Expansion: Experiences of MNCs in China', *Journal of World Business*, **33** (1), 87–110.

Gillespie, K. and B. McBride (1996), 'Smuggling in Emerging Markets: Global Implications', *Journal of World Business*, **31** (4), 40–54.

Gilliland, D. and D.C. Bello (1997), 'The Effect of Output Controls, Process Controls and Flexibility on Export Channel Performance', *Journal of Marketing*, **61** (1), 22–38.

Gray, B.J. (1997), 'Profiling Managers to Improve Export Promotion Targeting', *Journal of International Business Studies*, **28** (2), 387–420.

Greeno, L. and S. Robinson (1992), 'Rethinking Corporate Environmental Management', *Columbia Journal of World Business*, **27** (3), 222–32.

Gregory, G.D. and J.M. Munch (1997), 'Cultural Values in International Advertising: An Examination of Familial Norms and Roles in Mexico', *Psychology and Marketing*, **14** (2), 99–119.

Grosse, R. (1992), 'Competitive Advantages and Multinational Enterprises in Latin America', *Journal of Business Research*, **25** (1), 27–43.

Hadjikhani, A. and J. Johansson (1996), 'Facing Foreign Market Turbulence: Three Swedish Multinationals in Iran', *Journal of International Marketing*, **4** (4), 53–74.

Hagedoorn, J. and R. Narula (1996), 'Choosing Organizational Modes of Strategic Technology Partnering: International and Sectoral Differences', *Journal of International Business Studies*, **27** (2), 265–85.

Halal, W.E. (1993), 'Global Strategic Management in a New World Order', *Business Horizons*, **36** (3), 5–11.

Hamel, G. (1991), 'Competition for Competence and Inter-Partner Learning Within International Strategic Alliances', *Strategic Management Journal*, **12**, 83–104.

Harris, G. (1994), 'International Advertising Standardization: What do the Multinationals Actually Standardize?', *Journal of International Marketing*, **2** (4), 13–31.

Hassel, L.G. and G.M. Cunningham (1996), 'Budget Effectiveness in Multinational Corporations: An Empirical Test of the Use of Budget Controls Moderated by Two Dimensions of Budgetary Participation Under High and Low Environmental Dynamism', *Management International Review*, **36** (3), 245–66.

Hill, J.S. and A.T. Shao (1994), 'Agency Participants in Multicountry Advertising: A Preliminary Examination of Affiliate Characteristics and Environments', *Journal of International Marketing*, **2** (2), 29–49.

Hoffman, J. (1997), 'A Two Stage Model for the Introduction of Product into International Markets', *Journal of Global Marketing*, **11** (1), 65–86.

Hongcharu, B. (1999), 'An Analysis of Different Opinions on Consortia for Research and Development and Consortia for Manufacturing in New Product Development', *Journal of International Marketing and Marketing Research*, **24** (1), 35–44.

Howard, D. (1995), 'The Role of Export Management Companies in Global Marketing', *Journal of Global Marketing*, **8** (1), 95–110.

Hu, M. and H. Chen (1996), 'An Empirical Analysis of Factors Explaining Foreign Joint Ventures Performance in China', *Journal of Business Research*, **35** (2), 165–73.

Hulland, J.S. (1999), 'The Effects of Country-of-Brand and Brand Name on Product Evaluation and Consideration: A Cross-Country Comparison', *Journal of International Consumer Marketing*, **11** (1), 23–40.

Ikechi, E. and K. Sivakumar (1998), 'Foreign Market Entry Mode Choice of Service Firms', *Journal of the Academy of Marketing Science*, **26** (4), 274–92.

Inkpen, A.C. (1998), 'Learning and Knowledge Acquisition through International Strategic Alliance', *Academy of Management Executive*, **12**, 69–80.

Insch, G. and B. McBride (1998), 'Decomposing the Country of Origin Construct: An Empirical Test of Country of Design, Country of Parts and Country of Assembly', *Journal of International Consumer Marketing*, **10** (4), 69–91.

Jain, Subhash C. (1989), 'Standardization of International Marketing Strategy: Some Research Hypotheses', *Journal of Marketing*, **53** (1), 70–79.

James, W.L. and J.S. Hill (1991), 'International Advertising Messages: To Adapt or Not To Adapt', *Journal of Advertising Research*, **31** (3), 65–72.

Janda, S. and C.P. Rao (1997), 'The Effect of Country of Origin Related Stereotypes and Personal Beliefs on Product Evaluations', *Psychology and Marketing*, **14** (7), 689–702.

Johansson, J., I. Ronkainen and M. Czinkota (1994), 'Negative Country of Origin Effects: The Case of New Russia', *Journal of International Business Studies*, **25** (1), 157–76.

Johnson, J.L. and W. Arunthanes (1995), 'Ideal and Actual Product Adaptation in US Exporting Firms: Market Related Determinants and Impact on Performance', *International Marketing Review*, **12** (3), 31–47.

Johnson J.L., J.B. Cullen and T. Sakano (1996), 'Setting the Stage for Thrust and

Strategic Integration in Japanese–U.S. Cooperative Alliances', *Journal of International Business Studies*, **27** (5), 981–1004.

Kale, S. and R.P. McIntyre (1991), 'Distributional Channel Relationships in Diverse Cultures', *International Marketing Review*, **8** (3), 31–46.

Kanso, A. (1992), 'International Advertising Strategies: Global Commitment to Local Visions', *Journal of Advertising Research*, **32** (1), 10–15.

Karakaya, F. (1993), 'Barriers to Entry in International Markets', *Journal of Global Marketing*, **7** (1), 7–25.

Kernan, J.B. and T.J. Domzal (1993), 'International Advertising: To Globalize, Visualize', *Journal of International Consumer Marketing*, **5** (4), 51–72.

Kim, S.C. (1996), 'Analysis of Strategic Issues for International Joint Ventures: Case Studies of Hong Kong–China Joint Venture Manufacturing Firms', *Journal of Euro Marketing*, **4** (3), 55–70.

Klein, J.G., R. Ettenson and M.D. Morris (1998), 'The Animosity Model of Foreign Product Purchase: An Empirical Test in the People's Republic of China', *Journal of Marketing*, **62** (January), 89–100.

Klein, S. and V.J. Roth (1993), 'Satisfaction with International Marketing Channels', *Journal of the Academy of Marketing Science*, **21** (1), 39–45.

Kochunny, C., E. Babakus, R. Berl and W. Marks (1993), 'Schematic Representation of Country Image: Its Effects on Product Evaluations', *Journal of International Consumer Marketing*, **5** (1), 5–26.

Kotabe, M. (1990), 'Corporate Product Policy and Innovative Behavior of European and Japanese Multinationals', *Journal of Marketing*, **54** (2), 19–34.

Kotabe, M. (1993), 'Patterns and Technological Implications of Global Sourcing Strategies: A Study of European and Japanese Multinational Firms', *Journal of International Marketing*, **1** (1), 26–43.

Kotabe, M. and M.R. Czinkota (1992), 'State Government Promotion of Manufacturing Exports: A Gap Analysis', *Journal of International Business Studies*, **23** (4), 637–58.

Kotabe, M. and D.F. Duhan (1991), 'The Perceived Veracity of PIMS Strategy Principles in Japan: An Empirical Inquiry', *Journal of Marketing*, **55** (January), 26–41.

Kotabe, M. and D.F. Duhan (1993), 'Strategy Clusters in Japanese Markets: Firm Performance Implications', *Journal of the Academy of Marketing Science*, **21** (Winter), 21–31.

Kotabe, M., J.Y. Murray and R.G. Javalgi (1998), 'Global Sourcing of Services and Market Performance: An Empirical Investigation', *Journal of International Marketing*, **6** (4), 10–31.

Kotabe, M. and S.K. Swan (1994), 'Offshore Sourcing: Reaction, Maturation and Consolidation', *Journal of International Business Studies*, **25** (1), 115–40.

Kumcu, E., T. Harcar and M.E. Kumcu (1995), 'Managerial Perceptions of the Adequacy of Export Incentive Programs: Implications for Export Lead Economic Development Policy', *Journal Of Business Research*, **32** (2), 163–75.

Lampert, S. and E.D. Jaffe (1996), 'Country of Origin Effects on International Market Entry', *Journal of Global Marketing*, **10** (2), 27–52.

Leach, M.P. and A.H. Liu (1998), 'The Use of Culturally Relevant Stimuli in International Advertising', *Psychology and Marketing*, **15** (6), 523–46.

Lee, C. (1990), 'Determinants Of National Innovativeness and International Market Segmentation', *International Marketing Review*, **7** (5), 39–60.

Lee, C. and R. Green (1991), 'Cross-Cultural Examination of the Fishbein Behavioral Intent', *Journal of International Business Studies*, **22** (2), 289–96.

Lee, D. (1998a), 'The Effect of Cultural Distance on the Relational Exchange Between Exporters and Importers: The Case of Australian Exporters', *Journal of Global Marketing*, **11**, 7–22.

Lee, D. (1998b), 'Developing International Strategic Alliances Between Exporters and Importers: The Case of Australian Exporters', *International Journal of Research in Marketing*, **15**, 335–48.

Lee, H. and C. Kim (1992), 'The Relative Effects of Price, Warranty and Country of Origin on Consumer Products Evaluations', *Journal of Global Marketing*, **6** (2), 55–80.

Leonidou, L. (1995), 'Empirical Research on Export Barriers: Review, Assessment and Synthesis', *Journal of International Marketing*, **3** (1), 29–43.

Leonidou, L.C. and C.S. Katsikeas (1996), 'The Export Development Process: An Integrative Review of Empirical Models', *Journal of International Business Studies*, **27** (3), 517–51.

Leonidou, L.C., C.S. Katsikeas and N.F. Piercy (1998), 'Identifying Managerial Influences on Exporting: Past Research and Future Directions', *Journal of International Marketing*, **6**, 74–102.

Levitt, T. (1983), 'The Globalization of Markets', *Harvard Business Review*, **61** (May–June), 92–102.

Li, J. (1995), 'Foreign Entry and Survival: Effects of Strategic Choices on Performances in International Markets', *Strategic Management Journal*, **16** (5), 333–51.

Li, T. (1999), 'The Impact of the Marketing – R&D Interface on New Product Export Performance: A Contingency Analysis', *Journal of International Marketing*, **7** (1), 10–33.

Liefeld, J.P., L.A. Heslop, N. Papadopoulos and M. Wall (1996), 'Dutch Consumer Use of Intrinsic, Country-of-Origin, and Price Cues in Product Evaluation and Choice', *Journal of International Consumer Marketing*, **9** (1), 57–81.

Lim, J., W. Darley and J. Summer (1994), 'An Assessment of Country of Origin Effects Under Alternative Presentation Formats', *Journal of the Academy Of Marketing Science*, **22** (3), 274–82.

Lim, J., T. Sharkey and K.I. Kim (1993), 'Determinants of International Marketing Strategy', *Management International Review*, **33** (2), 103–31.

Liu, X. and H. Song (1997), 'China and the Multinationals: A Winning Combination', *Long Range Planning*, **30** (1), 74–83.

Luo, Y. (1996), 'Evaluating the Performance of Strategic Alliances in China', *Long Range Planning*, **29** (4), 534–42.

Lyles, M. and J. Salk (1996), 'Knowledge Acquisition from Foreign Partners in International Joint Ventures', *Journal of International Business Studies*, **27** (5), 877–903.

Madhok, A. (1997), 'Cost, Value and Foreign Market Entry Mode: The Transaction and the Firm', *Strategic Management Journal*, **18** (1), 39–61.

Maheswaran, D. (1994), 'Country of Origin as Stereotype: Effects of Consumer Expertise and Attribute Strength on Product Evaluations', *Journal of Consumer Research*, **21** (2), 354–66.

Maignan, I. and B.A. Lukas (1997), 'Entry Mode Decisions: The Role of Managers, Mental Models', *Journal of Global Marketing*, **10** (4), 7–22.

Martin, I. and S. Eroglu (1993), 'Measuring a Multi-Dimensional Construct: Country Image', *Journal of Business Research*, **28** (3), 191–210.

McCort, D.J. and N. Malhotra (1993), 'Culture and Consumer Behavior: Toward an Understanding of Cross-Cultural Consumer Behavior in International Marketing', *Journal of International Consumer Marketing*, **6** (2), 91–128.

Metwally, M.M. (1993), 'Attitudes of Middle Eastern Consumers Towards Imported Products', *Journal of International Marketing and Marketing Research*, **18** (2), 81–93.

Mills, R.W. and G. Chen (1996), 'Evaluating International Joint Ventures Using Strategic Value Analysis', *Long Range Planning*, **29** (4), 552–62.

Min, H., M. Latour and A. Williams (1994), 'Positioning Against Foreign Supply Sources in an International Purchasing Environment', *Industrial Marketing Management*, **23** (5), 371–83.

Mitchell, W., J.M. Shaver and B. Yeung (1994), 'Foreign Entrant Survival and Foreign Market Share: Canadian Companies' Experience in United States Medical Sector Markets', *Strategic Management Journal*, **15** (7), 555–67.

Mohan, S., S.R. Rosenthal and K.J. Hatten (1998), 'Global New Product Development Processes: Preliminary Findings and Research Propositions', *Journal of Management Studies*, **35** (6), 773–96.

Moon, H.C. (1997), 'The Choice of Entry Modes and Theories of Foreign Direct Investment', *Journal of Global Marketing*, **11** (2), 43–64.

Morgan, R. and C. Katsikeas (1998), 'Exporting Problems of Industrial Manufacturers', *Industrial Marketing Management*, **27**, 161–76.

Morrison, A. and K. Roth (1992), 'A Taxonomy of Business-Level Strategies in Global Industries', *Strategic Management Journal*, **13** (6), 399–418.

Murray, J.Y. and M. Kotabe (1999), 'Sourcing Strategies of U.S. Service Companies: A Modified Transaction Cost Analysis', *Strategic Management Journal*, **20** (9), 791–809.

Murray, J.Y., M. Kotabe and A.R. Wildt (1995), 'Strategic and Financial Performance Implications of Global Sourcing', *Journal of International Business Studies*, **26** (1), 181–205.

Murray, J.Y., A.R. Wildt and M. Kotabe (1995), 'Global Sourcing Strategies of U.S. Subsidiaries of Foreign Multinationals', *Management International Review*, **35** (4), 307–24.

Murtha, T.P. and S.A. Lenway (1994), 'Country Capabilities and the Strategic State: How National Political Institutions Affect Multinational Corporations' Strategies', *Strategic Management Journal*, **15**, Special Issue, 113–30.

Myers, M.B. (1997), 'The Pricing Processes of Exporters: A Comparative Study of the Challenges Facing US and Mexican Firms', *Journal of Global Marketing*, **10** (4), 95–115.

Myers, M.B. and S.T. Cavusgil (1996), 'Export Pricing Strategy–Performance Relationships: A Conceptual Framework', *Advances in International Marketing*, **8**, 159–78.

Nakos, G., K. Brouthers and L.E. Brouthers (1998), 'The Impact of Firm and Managerial Characteristics on Small and Medium-Sized Greek Firms' Export Performance', *Journal of Global Marketing*, **11** (4), 23–47.

Nevett, T. (1992), 'Differences Between American and British Television Advertising: Explanations and Implications', *Journal of Advertising*, **21** (4), 61–72.

Newman, K.L. and S.D. Nollen (1996), 'Culture and Congruence: The Fit Between Management Practices and National Culture', *Journal of International Business Studies*, **27** (4), 753–79.

Nikkei Weekly (1998), 'Manufacturers Reshape Asian Strategies', January 12, pp. 1 and 5.

Nishina, S. (1990), 'Japanese Consumers: Introducing Foreign Products/Brands into the Japanese Markets', *Journal of Advertising Research*, **30** (2), 35–46.

Otto, A. (1997), 'Internationalization and Market Entry Mode: A Review of Theories and Conceptual Frameworks', *Management International Review*, **37** (2), 27–42.

Papadopoulos, N. and L. Heslop (1990), 'National Stereotypes and Product Evaluations in a Socialist Country', *International Marketing Review*, **7** (1), 32–48.

Parry, M.E. and X.M. Song (1994), 'Identifying New Product Successes in China', *Journal of Product Innovation Management*, **11** (1), 15–41.

Patterson, P., M. Cicic and A. Shoham (1997), 'A Temporal Sequence Model of Satisfaction and Export Intentions of Service Firms', *Journal of Global Marketing*, **10** (4), 23–43.

Pieters, R., H. Baumgartner, J. Vermunt and T. Bijmolt (1999), 'Importance and Similarity in the Evolving Citation Network of the International Journal of Research in Marketing', *International Journal of Research in Marketing*, **16** (June), 113–27.

Quelch, J. and L. Klein (1996), 'The Internet and International Marketing', *Sloan Management Review*, **37** (3), 60–76.

Ravindranath, M., R.K. Balaji and J. Prescott (1998), 'Networks in Transition: How Industry Events Reshape Interfirm Relationships', *Strategic Management Journal*, **19** (5), 439–59.

Rosenbloom, B., T. Larsen and R. Mehta (1997), 'Global Marketing Channels and the Standardization Controversy', *Journal of Global Marketing*, **11** (1), 49–64.

Roth, K. (1992), 'International Configuration and Coordination Archetypes', *Journal of International Business Studies*, **23** (3), 533–50.

Rynning, M.R. and O. Anderson (1994), 'Structural and Behavioral Predictors of Export Adoptions', *Journal of International Marketing*, **2** (1), 73–90.

Samiee, S. and K. Roth (1992), 'The Influence of Global Marketing Standardization on Performance', *Journal of Marketing*, **56** (2), 1–18.

Samli, A.C. (1994), 'Towards a Model of International Consumer Behavior: Key Considerations and Research Avenues', *Journal of International Consumer Marketing*, **7** (1), 63–85.

Samli, A.C., J.M. Browning and C. Busbia (1998), 'The Status of Global Sourcing as a Critical Tool of Strategic Planning: Opportunistic Versus Strategic Dichotomy', *Journal of Business Research*, **43** (3), 177–87.

Samli, A.C. and L. Jacobs (1994), 'Pricing Practices of American Multinational Firms: Standardization vs. Localization Dichotomy', *Journal of Global Marketing*, **8** (2), 51–73.

Samli, A.C. and L. Jacobs (1995), 'Achieving Congruence Between Macro and Micro Generic Strategies: A Framework to Create International Competitive Advantage', *Journal of Macromarketing*, **15** (2), 23–33.

Samli, A.C., E. Kaynak and H. Sharif (1996), 'Developing Strong International Corporate Alliances: Strategic Implications', *Journal of Euro-Marketing*, **4** (3), 23–36.

Samli, A.C., J.R. Wills and L. Jacobs (1993), 'Developing Global Products and Marketing Strategies: A Rejoinder', *Journal of the Academy of Marketing Science*, **21** (1), 79–84.

Sengupta, S. and M. Perry (1997), 'Some Antecedents of Global Strategic Alliances Formation', *Journal of International Marketing*, **5** (1), 31–50.

Sharma, A. (1995), 'From Exploiting to Investing: An Empirical Study of Entry Strategies of U.S. Firms to the Former Soviet Bloc', *Academy of Management Journal, Best Paper Proceedings*, 197–200.

Sharma, A. and J.N. Sheth (1997), 'Supplier Relationships: Emerging Issues and Challenges', *Industrial Marketing Management*, **26** (2), 91–100.

Shoham, A. and G. Albaum (1995), 'Reducing the Impact of Barriers to Exporting: A Managerial Perspective', *Journal of International Marketing*, **3** (4), 85–106.

Shoham, A., G.M. Rose, and F. Kropp (1997), 'Conflict in International Channels of Distribution', *Journal of Global Marketing*, **11** (2), 5–22.

Sinclair, S. (1993), 'A Guide to Global Pricing,' *Journal of Business Strategy*, **14** (3), 16–20.

Song, M., M.M. Montoya-Weiss and J.B. Schmidt (1997), 'The Role of Marketing in Developing Successful New Products in South Korea and Taiwan', *Journal of International Marketing*, **5** (3), 47–69.

Sood, J. and Y. Nasu (1995), 'Religiosity and Nationality: An Explanatory Study of Their Effect on Consumer Behavior in Japan and the United States', *Journal of Business Research*, **34** (1), 1–10.

Sriram, V. and P. Gopalakrishna (1991), 'Can Advertising be Standardized Among Similar Countries? A Cluster Based Analysis', *International Journal of Advertising*, **10** (2), 137–50.

Sriram, V. and F.A. Manu (1995), 'Country of Destination and Export Marketing Strategy: A Study of U.S. Exporters', *Journal of Global Marketing*, **8** (3), 171–91.

Stump, R., G.A. Athaide and C.N. Axinn (1998), 'The Contingent Effect of the Dimensions of Export Commitment on Exporting Financial Performance: An Empirical Examination', *Journal of Global Marketing*, **12** (1), 7–25.

Sullivan, D. (1992), 'Organization in American MNCs: The Perspective in Europe', *Management International Review*, **32** (3), 237–51.

Taggart, J.H. (1998), 'Strategy and Control in the Multinational Corporation: Too Many Recipes', *Long Range Planning*, **31** (4), 571–85.

Tai, S.H.C. (1997), 'Advertising in Asia: Localize or Regionalize?', *International Journal of Advertising*, **16** (1), 48–61.

Tallman, S.B. (1991), 'Strategic Management Models and Resource-Based Strategies Among MNEs in a Host Market', *Strategic Management Journal*, **12** (Summer), 69–82.

Tan, S.J. (1996), 'Risks Assessment in International Market Entry: A Multi Dimensional Approach', *International Journal of Management*, **13** (3), 370–80.

Tellefsen, T. and H. Takada (1999), 'The Relationship Between Mass Media Availability and the Multicountry Diffusion of Consumer Products', *Journal of International Marketing*, **7** (1), 77–96.

Terpstra, V. and B.L. Simonin (1993), 'Strategic Alliances in the Triad: An Exploratory Study', *Journal of International Marketing*, **1** (1), 4–26.

Thakor, M.V. and L.P. Katsanis (1997), 'A Model of Brand and Country Effects on Quality Dimensions: Issues and Implications', *Journal of International Consumer Marketing*, **9** (3), 79–100.

Thorelli, H.B. (1986), 'Networks: Between Markets and Hierarchies', *Strategic Management Journal*, **7** (1), 37–51.

Tse, D. and G. Gorn (1993), 'An Experiment on the Salience of Country of Origin in the Era of Global Brands', *Journal of International Marketing*, **1** (1), 57–77.

Tse, D. and P. Yigang (1997), 'How MNCs Choose Entry Modes and Form Alliances: The China Experience', *Journal of International Business Studies*, **28** (4), 779–805.

Varadarajan, P.R. and M.H. Cunningham (1995), 'Strategic Alliances: A Synthesis of Conceptual Foundations', *Journal of the Academy of Marketing Science*, **23** (4), 282–96.

Verlegh, P. and J.-B.E.M. Steenkamp (1999), 'A Review and Meta Analysis of Country of Origin Research', *Journal of Economic Psychology*, **20** (October), 521–46.

Voss, K.E. and P. Tansuhaj (1999), 'A Consumer Perspective on Foreign Market Entry: Building Brands through Brand Alliances', *Journal of International Consumer Marketing*, **11** (2), 39–58.

Wang, C.C.L. (1999), 'Issues and Advances in International Consumer Research: A Review and Assessment', *Journal of International Marketing and Marketing Research*, **24** (1), 3–21.

Wills, J., A.C. Samli and L. Jacobs (1991), 'Developing Global Products and Marketing Strategies: A Construct and a Research Agenda', *Journal of the Academy of Marketing Science*, **19** (1), 1–11.

Wilson, I. (1997), 'Entering the Chinese Market', *Journal of International Marketing and Marketing Research*, **22** (3), 139–46.

Witt, J. and C.P. Rao (1992), 'The Impact of Global Sourcing on Consumers: Country of Origin Effects on Perceived Risk', *Journal of Global Marketing*, **6** (3), 105–29.

Yavas, U., B.J. Verhage and R.T. Green (1992), 'Global Consumer Segmentation Versus Local Market Orientation', *Management International Review*, **32** (3), 265–72.

Yeoh, P.L. (1994), 'Speed to Global Markets: An Empirical Prediction of New Products', *European Journal of Marketing*, **28** (11), 29–53.

Yeoh, P.L. and R.J. Calantone (1995), 'An Application of the Analytical Hierarchy Process to International Marketing – Selection of a Foreign Distributor', *Journal of Global Marketing*, **8** (3), 39–65.

Zafarullah, M., M. Ali and S. Young (1998). 'The Internationalization of the Small Firm in Developing Countries: Exploratory Research from Pakistan', *Journal of Global Marketing*, **11** (3), 21–40.

Zandpour, F. and K.R. Harich (1997), 'Think and Feel Country Clusters: A New Approach to International Advertising Standardization', *International Journal of Advertising*, **15** (4), 325–44.

Zou, S., C.R. Taylor and G.E. Osland (1998), 'The EXPERF Scale: A Cross-National Generalized Export Performance Measure', *Journal of International Marketing*, **6** (3), 37–58.

2. Market orientation, learning orientation, and innovativeness in the global marketplace: moderating roles of organizational memory and market turbulence

G. Tomas M. Hult and Destan Kandemir

INTRODUCTION

Recent research by Baker and Sinkula (1999a), Han, Kim and Srivastava (1998), and Hurley and Hult (1998) have centered on various aspects of the effects of market orientation, learning, and innovativeness on performance. For example, Hurley and Hult (1998) conceptually integrated thoughts on these constructs, but only tested the learning → innovativeness link in their study of 9648 people in 56 groups of a large research and development agency of the US federal government. Han, Kim and Srivastava (1998) studied the market orientation → innovativeness link, but omitted learning both conceptually and empirically from their study of 134 banks. Baker and Sinkula (1999a) specifically set out to integrate the thoughts by Hurley and Hult (1998) and Han, Kim and Srivastava (1998). As such, they tested a model involving market orientation, learning, innovativeness, and performance using a sample of 411 firms drawn from the D&B database.

While the Baker and Sinkula (1999a) study helps to clarify some of the integrative relationships involving market orientation, learning, and innovativeness discussed in the two studies by Hurley and Hult (1998) and Han, Kim and Srivastava (1998), their conceptual development is rather simplistic when, in all likelihood, the relationships are bound to be more complex. For example, Baker and Sinkula (1999a) make the assumption that all modeled relationships are linear without any diminishing return or 'turning point' (i.e. a point where, for example, more global market orientation may in fact result in no additional performance improvement or where it may even be detrimental to performance). This begs the question: can a focus on achieving too much market orientation, learning, and/or innovativeness be detrimental to performance? Our study is designed to address this research issue with a focus on global operations and within the confines of the established theoretical linkages provided by Baker and Sinkula (1999a), Han, Kim and Srivastava (1998), and Hurley and Hult (1998).

Additionally, we integrate thoughts on global market turbulence (Jaworski and Kohli 1993) and global organizational memory (Moorman 1995; Moorman and Miner 1997) into the framework. Specifically, we propose that it is theoretically plausible that any relationship involving global market orientation be affected, on a contingency basis, by global market turbulence. Similarly, any relationship involving global learning orientation seems likely to be affected by global organizational memory. To achieve its objective, we will briefly review the relevant literature and present testable hypotheses, followed by a presentation of the methods (sample, measurement, and model testing approaches), results, and a discussion of implications.

HYPOTHESIS DEVELOPMENT

The hypothesized model is depicted in Figure 2.1. The basic model of the relationships involving global market orientation, learning orientation, innovativeness, and performance is founded in the work by Baker and

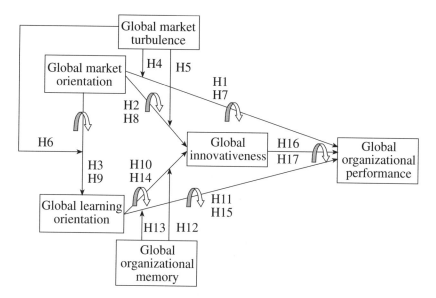

Figure 2.1   The conceptual model

Sinkula (1999a) who based their model conceptualization on works by Han, Kim and Srivastava (1998) and Hurley and Hult (1998). The inclusion of global organizational memory is motivated primarily by the work of Moorman and colleagues (e.g. Moorman 1995; Moorman and Miner 1997). The modeling of market turbulence in this context fits with current conceptualizations in strategic marketing research (e.g. Glazer and Weiss 1993; Han, Kim and Srivastava 1998; Jaworski and Kohli 1993; Moorman and Miner 1997; Slater and Narver 1994). Each hypothesized relationship is briefly justified in the next paragraphs.

Market orientation has been found to affect performance positively in a number of studies (e.g. Jaworski and Kohli 1993; Narver and Slater 1990). Recently, market orientation has also been linked positively to both innovativeness (Han, Kim and Srivastava 1998; Hurley and Hult 1998) and learning orientation (Baker and Sinkula 1999a; Hurley and Hult 1998). Thus, we test the following relationships in our study on global operations:

H1: Global market orientation is positively associated with global organizational performance.

H2: Global market orientation is positively associated with global innovativeness.

H3: Global market orientation is positively associated with global learning orientation.

However, a number of scholars have argued that market turbulence influences relationships involving market orientation (e.g. Jaworski and Kohli 1993; Narver and Slater 1994). As such:

H4: Global market turbulence moderates the relationship between global market orientation and global organizational performance.

H5: Global market turbulence moderates the relationship between global market orientation and global innovativeness.

H6: Global market turbulence moderates the relationship between global market orientation and global learning orientation.

At the same time, it is plausible to argue that a focus on developing more market orientation at some point will result in no additional global benefits and may very well even be detrimental to performance (cf. Johanson and Vahlne 1977). Thus:

H7: There is a positive U-shaped relationship between global market orientation and global organizational performance.

H8:   There is a positive U-shaped relationship between global market orientation and global innovativeness.

H9:   There is a positive U-shaped relationship between global market orientation and global learning orientation.

Similar to market orientation, learning orientation has been found to affect innovativeness (Hurley and Hult 1998) and performance positively (e.g. Baker and Sinkula 1999a, 1999b; Hult 1998; Hult and Ketchen 2001; Hult, Ketchen and Nichols 2002; Hult et al. 2000). Thus:

H10:   Global learning orientation is positively associated with global innovativeness.

H11:   Global learning orientation is positively associated with global organizational performance.

However, an argument can be made that learning as a general phenomenon is affected by what the organization already knows (e.g. Sinkula 1994). Using this logic, an argument can be made that organizational memory affects the relationships involving learning as an antecedent. Thus:

H12:   Global organizational memory moderates the relationship between global learning orientation and global innovativeness.

H13:   Global organizational memory moderates the relationship between global learning orientation and global organizational performance.

Again, however, learning orientation is unlikely to result in an indefinite positive effect on innovativeness and performance. At some point, an expectation of diminishing return or potentially even a negative return is bound to materialize. To test this contention, the following hypotheses are set forth:

H14:   There is a positive U-shaped relationship between global learning orientation and global innovativeness.

H15:   There is a positive U-shaped relationship between global learning orientation and global organizational performance.

Finally, a number of studies have found significant relationships between innovativeness and performance (e.g. Han, Kim and Srivastava 1998; Hurley and Hult 1998). Thus:

H16:   Global innovativeness is positively associated with global organizational performance.

That said, one would assume that such a positive relationship between innovativeness and performance is not indefinite. Perhaps previous studies have simply involved organizations that are in the upward sloping phase of the relationship, resulting in a linear positive relationship between innovativeness and performance. Thus, conceptually one would assume that a turning point exists in the curve. We test this contention via the following hypothesis:

> H17: There is a positive U-shaped relationship between global innovativeness and global organizational performance.

METHOD

Sample

The sample used to test the developed model in Figure 2.1 was drawn from the database of Dun & Bradstreet commercial information services. Strategic business units (SBUs) with a significant global market focus and an identifiable marketing executive were included in the study. These individuals had titles such as 'marketing manager', 'sales and marketing manager', 'vice president of marketing', 'vice president of sales', and 'marketing director'. One SBU per firm was targeted to obtain data that are reasonably generalizable.

One thousand surveys were mailed to the marketing executives along with a cover letter explaining the purpose of the study and its confidentiality in terms of responses. The surveys were returned via preaddressed and postage-paid envelopes. In total, we received responses from 249 SBUs, for an overall response rate of 26.3 per cent (after incorporating the 54 non-deliverable surveys). These SBUs had an average number of employees of 6357 (range: 620 to 17 843), had existed 44 years (range: 4 to 160 years), were primarily product (57.8 per cent) versus service oriented (42.2 per cent), with an average of 25.0 per cent of their total in foreign sales (range: 5.9 per cent to 88.0 per cent).

The extrapolation procedure suggested by Armstrong and Overton (1977) was used to assess non-response bias based on the study data. No significant differences were found between early and late respondents on the subjective scales in the study and a select set of demographics.

Measurement

The results of the measurement analysis are presented in Table 2.1a, including means, standard deviations, average variances extracted, construct reliabilities, loadings, and fit indices. Table 2.1b reports the correlations and shared variances for the study constructs.

All measures were drawn from extant research. As such, the following scales/sources were used: market orientation (competitor orientation, customer orientation, and interfunctional coordination; Narver and Slater 1990), learning orientation (team, systems, learning, and memory orientations; Hult 1998; Hult et al. 2000), innovativeness (Hurley and Hult 1998), competitor-based performance (Deshpandé, Farley and Webster 1993), overall performance (Jaworski and Kohli 1993), market turbulence (Jaworski and Kohli 1993), and organizational memory (Moorman 1995; Moorman and Miner 1997). To study global business phenomena, each scale item was modified to emphasize 'global' aspects (the modified survey items are available from the authors).

After the data were collected, the measurement scales were subjected to a rigorous testing process involving a series of dimensionality, reliability, and validity assessments. The psychometric properties were evaluated via confirmatory factor analysis (CFA) using LISREL (Jöreskog et al. 2000). The model fits were evaluated using the DELTA2 index (Bollen 1989), the relative noncentrality index (RNI) (McDonald and Marsh 1990), and the comparative fit index (CFI) (Bentler 1990), which have been shown to be the most stable fit indices by Anderson and Gerbing (1988) (cf. Hu and Bentler 1999). Utilizing these criteria, the CFA model resulted in a reasonably good fit to the data with DELTA2, RNI, and CFI all being 0.89 ($\chi^2 = 2537.2$, df = 1208, RMSR = 0.06) after deleting six items from the analysis. In addition, the remaining items were found to be reliable and valid when evaluated based on each item's error variance, modification index, and residual covariation.

Within the confirmatory factor analysis setting, composite reliability was calculated using the procedures outlined by Fornell and Larcker (1981) based on the work of Werts, Lin and Jöreskog (1974). We also examined the parameter estimates and their associated *t*-values, and assessed the average variance extracted for each construct (Anderson and Gerbing 1988; Bagozzi and Yi 1988). The composite reliabilities for the 12 scales ranged from 0.71 to 0.93 (Table 2.1a). The factor loadings ranged from 0.42 to 0.97 ($p < 0.01$), and the average variances extracted ranged from 38.5 per cent to 78.3 per cent (Table 2.1a). Overall, after scale purification, the six latent constructs, involving 12 dimensional scales, were found reliable and valid in the context of this study.

Table 2.1a Summary statistics of the measurement analysis

Variable	Mean	Std Dev	Variance (%)	Reliability	Loadings
Competitor Orientation (CO)	5.13	1.18	55.8	0.83	0.69–0.77
Customer Orientation (CU)	5.20	1.18	67.8	0.91	0.71–0.89
Interfunctional Coordination (INT)	4.45	1.12	59.4	0.88	0.65–0.85
Team Orientation (TO)	4.94	1.17	67.0	0.89	0.75–0.88
Systems Orientation (SO)	4.68	1.17	69.5	0.90	0.75–0.89
Learning Orientation (LO)	5.67	0.99	72.0	0.88	0.76–0.94
Memory Orientation (MO)	4.22	1.17	58.5	0.85	0.71–0.81
Innovativeness (IN)	5.08	1.27	73.0	0.92	0.80–0.91
Competitor Performance (CP)	5.00	1.27	38.5	0.71	0.50–0.79
Overall Performance (OP)	5.44	1.27	78.0	0.88	0.85–0.91
Organizational Memory (OM)	4.93	1.34	78.3	0.93	0.78–0.97
Market Turbulence (MT)	4.66	1.31	50.0	0.73	0.42–0.91

Notes:
$n = 249$.
$\chi^2 = 1885.3$, df $= 923$.
$\Delta 2 = 0.89$, RNI $= 0.89$, CFI $= 0.89$, RMSR $= 0.06$.

Table 2.1b *Intercorrelations and shared variances of the study variables*

	CO	CU	INT	TO	SO	LO	MO	IN	CP	OP	OM	MT
CO	—	0.42	0.49	0.31	0.29	0.20	0.23	0.32	0.08	0.06	0.21	0.03
CU	0.65	—	0.52	0.45	0.41	0.36	0.35	0.30	0.09	0.12	0.18	0.04
INT	0.70	0.72	—	0.45	0.46	0.25	0.42	0.35	0.20	0.15	0.25	0.07
TO	0.56	0.67	0.67	—	0.62	0.32	0.37	0.28	0.08	0.12	0.11	0.02
SO	0.54	0.64	0.68	0.79	—	0.29	0.41	0.26	0.04	0.12	0.18	0.04
LO	0.45	0.60	0.50	0.57	0.54	—	0.31	0.21	0.04	0.06	0.06	0.04
MO	0.48	0.59	0.65	0.61	0.64	0.56	—	0.24	0.04	0.08	0.16	0.06
IN	0.57	0.55	0.59	0.53	0.51	0.46	0.49	—	0.08	0.12	0.26	0.04
CP	0.29	0.31	0.45	0.29	0.21	0.20	0.19	0.29	—	0.29	0.12	0.01
OP	0.25	0.35	0.39	0.34	0.34	0.25	0.29	0.34	0.54	—	0.08	0.03
OM	0.46	0.43	0.50	0.33	0.42	0.25	0.40	0.51	0.34	0.29	—	0.04
MT	0.18	0.21	0.27	0.15	0.19	0.19	0.25	0.19	0.09	0.18	0.21	—

Note: The correlations are included in the lower triangle of the matrix. All correlations are significant at the 0.05 level except the relationship between CP and MT, which is insignificant. Shared variances are included in the upper triangle of the matrix.

Model Testing

Testing of the hypotheses was accomplished via the analyses of three polynomial OLS regression models with all predictor variables entered at the
same time. Summated indices were used for market orientation (composed
of equal weights scores of competitor orientation, customer orientation,
and interfunctional coordination), learning orientation (composed of
equal weights scores of team, systems, learning, and memory orientations),
innovativeness, performance (composed of equal weights of overall and
competitor-based performance), market turbulence, and organizational
memory. The summated variables were mean-centered to reduce the potential effects of collinearity associated with variables in polynomial regression
modeling.

To incorporate the U-shaped relationships, a second-order polynomial
regression model was used (Neter, Wasserman and Kutner 1983). Regression
was chosen for the hypothesis testing due to sample size limitations and the
complexity of modeling both multiple interaction and multiple quadratic
relationships (cf. Ping 1995). Three regression models were used to test the
hypothesized relationships. The following regression model was analyzed
with learning orientation as the criterion variable:

$$LO = \alpha + \beta_1(MO) + \beta_2(MO^*MT) + \beta_3(MO)^2 + e,$$

where LO = global learning orientation, MO = global market orientation,
and MT = global market turbulence. The following regression model was
analyzed with innovativeness as the criterion variable:

$$IN = \alpha + \beta_1(MO) + \beta_2(LC) + \beta_3(MO^*MT) + \beta_4(LC^*OM) +$$
$$\beta_5(MO)^2 + \beta_3(LC)^2 + e,$$

where the additional variables of IN = innovativeness and LO = learning
orientation were included in the analysis. Finally, the following regression
model was analyzed with performance as the criterion variable:

$$P = \alpha + \beta_1(MO) + \beta_2(LC) + \beta_3(IN) + \beta_4(MO^*MT) +$$
$$\beta_5(LC^*OM) + \beta_6(MO)^2 + \beta_7(LC)^2 + \beta_6(IN)^2 + e,$$

where the additional criterion variable of P = performance was included in
the model.

In these models, the key to whether the relationships are U-shaped
depends on the second derivative that contains only the β for the squared

term. Thus, $LC = \alpha + \beta_1(MO) + \beta_2(MO*MT) + \beta_3(MO)^2 + e$, the first derivative is $\beta_1 + 2 * \beta_3$ (meaning a maximum or minimum at $[(MO) = \beta_1/(2 * \beta_3)]$ and the second derivative is $2 * \beta_3$. If the second derivative is positive ($\beta_3 > 0$), it is a U-shaped curve. If $\beta_{15} < 0$, it is an inverted U. Corresponding logic applies to $(LC)^2$ and $(IN)^2$.

As a part of the model testing analyses, we examined the skewness (range: -0.19 to -0.81) and kurtosis (range: -0.60 to 0.82) assumptions; both analyses resulted in acceptable values for all variables. Additionally, we confirmed that the data did not violate the assumptions of independence in the regression models ($VIF < 3.59$) and had normally distributed error terms (Kolmogorov–Smirnov < 1.28).

RESULTS

Figure 2.2 summarizes the significant relationships found in the three polynomial regression models used to test the 17 hypotheses. These results are now discussed.

Learning Model

Using learning orientation as the criterion variable, both market orientation ($\beta = 0.78$, *t*-value $= 17.28$, $p < 0.01$) and the moderator MO*MT ($\beta =$

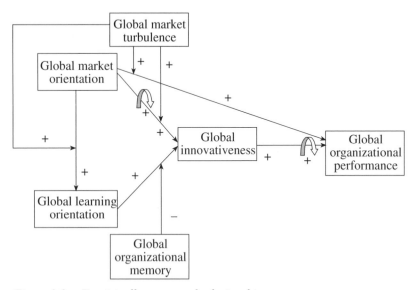

Figure 2.2   Empirically supported relationships

0.09, t-value$= 2.06$, $p < 0.05$) were significant predictor variables, but not the quadratic variable $(MO)^2$. The adjusted R^2 for the model was 0.60. As such, H3 and H6 were significant.

Innovativeness Model

Using innovativeness as the criterion variable, a number of significant relationships as well as relationships approaching significance were found. Market orientation ($\beta = 0.62$, t-value$= 7.66$, $p < 0.01$), the moderator variable of MO*MT ($\beta = 0.08$, t-value$= 1.53$, $p = 0.13$), and the quadratic variable of $(MO)^2$ ($\beta = 0.17$, t-value$= 2.29$, $p < 0.05$) were significant predictors. Since both the moderator and quadratic variables were significant, we conducted one additional test to examine the effects of the MO*MT moderator before and after the break in the U-shaped curve. Both the positive and negative relationships involving MO and IN were influenced by a positive MO*MT moderator. Additionally, learning orientation ($\beta = 0.12$, t-value$= 1.51$, $p = 0.13$) and the moderator of LO*OM ($\beta = -0.14$, t-value$= 2.28$, $p < 0.05$) approached accepted levels for significance and are therefore noteworthy. The adjusted R^2 for the model was 0.44. As such, H2, H5, H8, H10, and H12 were significant.

Performance Model

Using performance as the criterion variable, three significant relationships and one additional relationship approaching significance were found. Market orientation ($\beta = 0.35$, t-value$= 3.19$, $p < 0.01$), innovativeness ($\beta = 0.21$, t-value$= 2.38$, $p < 0.05$), and the quadratic term of $(IN)^2$ ($\beta = 0.12$, t-value$= 1.65$, $p < 0.10$) were found to be significant predictors. Additionally, the moderator of MO*MT ($\beta = 0.09$, t-value$= 1.50$, $p = 0.14$) approached accepted levels for significance. The adjusted R^2 for the model was 0.18. As such, H1, H4, H16, and H17 were significant.

CONCLUSION

In this study, we extend recent research by Baker and Sinkula (1999a), Han, Kim and Srivastava (1998), and Hurley and Hult (1998) regarding the effect of market orientation, learning orientation, and innovativeness on performance. Our contribution is twofold. First, we offer a more comprehensive depiction of the relationships among the constructs. Second, we integrate the moderating roles of organizational memory (e.g. Moorman 1995; Moorman and Miner 1997) and market turbulence (e.g. Jaworski and Kohli

1993) into the framework. In this conclusion, we elaborate briefly on each of the two areas of contribution.

Comprehensive Model Depiction

Excluding the moderators, the general thrust of the linkages in our model follows the framework proposed by Baker and Sinkula (1999a) with two exceptions. First, we included a direct effect of market orientation on learning orientation based on work by Slater and Narver (1994). Second, we modeled all relationships as both direct and quadratic to incorporate the notion that the positive effects of marketing orientation, learning orientation, and innovativeness are not indefinite on either intermediate or bottom-line outcomes.

In terms of market orientation (MO), the findings indicate that MO works at multiple levels to affect performance. MO has an effect on performance directly as well as indirectly through innovativeness and learning orientation (again via innovativeness). Thus, MO functions as a foundation for the market-based organization. In this capacity, MO serves as an important building block for learning and innovation activities but also that of bottom-line performance. Additionally, the relationship between MO and innovativeness was found to be U-shaped. Thus, the MNC should expect a diminishing and, as we found, perhaps detrimental effect of market orientation on innovativeness when investing too many resources into being market oriented.

In terms of learning orientation (LO), the findings indicate that LO has a positive effect on innovativeness. However, we found no direct effect of LO on performance nor did we find a quadratic effect of LO on either innovativeness or performance. These results suggest that LO is valuable to the MNC in the context of mediating the link between market orientation and innovativeness, subsequently affecting performance. However, at least for MNCs, it is clear that LO by itself does not lead to a competitive advantage. Instead, what the MNC learns needs to result in either an innovative product or process as an intermediate outcome before realizing the effect on organizational performance.

In terms of innovativeness (IN), the findings indicate that IN has a positive effect on performance but that this positive effect is only effective to a certain point. Our findings show a positive U-shaped relationship between IN and performance, meaning that too much innovativeness can be detrimental to organizational performance. Thus, MNCs need to balance its innovativeness relative to its focus on more stable operations to achieve success.

Moderating Roles of Organizational Memory and Market Turbulence

In this study, we hypothesized market turbulence to be a moderator on all relationships involving market orientation. Our rationale is that market turbulence has an influence on the effect of market orientation on various intermediate and bottom-line outcomes. Likewise, our logic is that relationships involving learning orientation and its effect on intermediate and bottom-line outcomes be affected by organizational memory.

In terms of market turbulence (MT), the findings indicate that MT is positively moderating all three hypothesized relationships involving MO. First, MT moderates the relationship between MO and LO. Second, MO moderates the relationship between MO and IN. Third, MO moderates the relationship between MO and performance. This indicates that the positive effect of MO in terms of achieving a high degree of learning, innovativeness, and performance will be affected by the nature of the environment. Presumably, in low turbulent environments there is not the same need to be as market oriented to achieve learning, innovativeness, and performance at a high level as it is in more turbulent environments.

In terms of organizational memory (OM), the findings indicate that OM is negatively moderating the relationship between LO and IN. This finding supports theoretical arguments by Sinkula (1994). Sinkula (1994, p. 41) suggests that LO is 'a function of information need, which is in turn a function of the organization's environment, age and experience'. Organizations that achieve the most benefit from LO are the ones that can unlearn established routines and are able to replace them with routines that ultimately result in a competitive edge (Nystrom and Starbuck 1984). Thus, while OM can serve as a foundation for learning (and could theoretically be modeled as a direct effect on LO), OM can also be detrimental to the effect of LO on IN.

REFERENCES

Anderson, James C. and David W. Gerbing (1988), 'Some Methods for Respecifying Measurement Models to Obtain Unidimensional Construct Measurement', *Journal of Marketing Research*, **19** (November), 453–60.

Armstrong, J. Scott and Terry S. Overton (1977), 'Estimating Nonresponse Bias in Mail Surveys', *Journal of Marketing Research*, **14** (August), 396–402.

Bagozzi, Richard P. and Youjae Yi (1988), 'On the Evaluation of Structural Equation Models', *Journal of the Academy of Marketing Science*, **16** (2), 74–94.

Baker, William E. and James M. Sinkula (1999a), 'Learning Orientation, Market Orientation, and Innovation: Integrating and Extending Models of Organizational Performance', *Journal of Market-Focused Management*, **4** (4), 295–308.

Baker, William E. and James M. Sinkula (1999b), 'The Synergistic Effect of Market Orientation and Learning Orientation on Organizational Performance', *Journal of the Academy of Marketing Science*, **27** (4), 411–27.

Bentler, Peter M. (1990), 'Comparative fit indexes in structural equation modeling', *Psychological Bulletin*, **107**, 238–46.

Bollen, Kenneth A. (1989), *Structural Equations with Latent Variables*, New York: Wiley & Sons.

Deshpandé, Rohit, John U. Farley and Frederick E. Webster, Jr (1993), 'Corporate Culture, Customer Orientation, and Innovativeness in Japanese Firms: A Quadrad Analysis', *Journal of Marketing*, **57** (January), 23–37.

Fornell, Claes and David F. Larcker (1981), 'Evaluating Structural Equation Models with Unobservable Variables and Measurement Error', *Journal of Marketing Research*, **18** (February), 39–50.

Glazer, Rashi and Allen M. Weiss (1993), 'Marketing in Turbulent Environments: Decision Processes and the Time-Sensitivity of Information', *Journal of Marketing Research*, **30** (November), 509–21.

Han, Jin K., Namwoon Kim and Rajendra K. Srivastava (1998), 'Market Orientation and Organizational Performance: Is Innovation a Missing Link?', *Journal of Marketing*, **62** (October), 30–45.

Hu, Li-tze and Peter M. Bentler (1999), 'Cutoff Criteria for Fit Indexes in Covariance Structure Analysis: Conventional Criteria Versus New Alternatives', *Structural Equation Modeling*, **6** (1), 1–55.

Hult, G. Tomas M. (1998), 'Managing the International Strategic Sourcing Function as a Market-Driven Organizational Learning System', *Decision Sciences*, **29** (1), 193–216.

Hult, G. Tomas M., Robert F. Hurley, Larry C. Giunipero and Ernest L. Nichols, Jr (2000), 'Organizational Learning in Global Purchasing: A Model and Test of Internal Users and Corporate Buyers', *Decision Sciences*, **31** (2), 293–325.

Hult, G. Tomas M. and David J. Ketchen, Jr (2001), 'Does Market Orientation Matter? A Test of the Relationship Between Positional Advantage and Performance', *Strategic Management Journal*, **22** (9), 899–906.

Hult, G. Tomas M., David J. Ketchen, Jr and Ernest L. Nichols, Jr (2002), 'An Examination of Cultural Competitiveness and Order Fulfillment Cycle Time within Supply Chains', *Academy of Management Journal*, **45** (3), 577–86.

Hurley, Robert F. and G. Tomas M. Hult (1998), 'Innovation, Market Orientation, and Organizational Learning: An Integration and Empirical Examination', *Journal of Marketing*, **62** (July), 42–54.

Jaworski, Bernard J. and Ajay K. Kohli (1993), 'Market Orientation: Antecedents and Consequences', *Journal of Marketing*, **52** (July), 53–70.

Johanson, Jan and Jan-Erik Vahlne (1977), 'The Internationalization Process of the Firm – A Model of Knowledge Development and Increasing Foreign Market Commitments', *Journal of International Business Studies*, **8** (Spring/Summer), 23–32.

Jöreskog, Karl G., Dag Sörbom, Stephen Du Toit and Mathilda Du Toit (2000), LISREL 8: *New Statistical Features* 2nd edn, Chicago, IL: Scientific Software International, Inc.

McDonald, Roderick P. and Herbert W. Marsh (1990), 'Choosing a Multivariate Model: Noncentrality and Goodness of Fit', *Psychological Bulletin*, **107** (2), 247–55.

Moorman, Christine (1995), 'Organizational Market Information Processes:

Cultural Antecedents and New Product Outcomes', *Journal of Marketing Research*, **32** (August), 318–35.

Moorman, Christine and Anne S. Miner (1997), 'The Impact of Organizational Memory on New Product Performance and Creativity', *Journal of Marketing Research*, **34** (February), 91–106.

Narver, John and Stanley Slater (1990), 'The Effect of a Market Orientation on Business Profitability', *Journal of Marketing*, **54** (October), 20–35.

Neter, J., W. Wasserman and M. Kutner (1983), *Applied Linear Regression Models*, Homewood, IL: Irwin.

Nystrom, P.C. and W. Starbuck (1984), 'To Avoid Organizational Crises, Unlearn', *Organizational Dynamics*, **13** (Spring), 53–65.

Ping, Robert A., Jr (1995), 'A Parsimonious Estimating Technique for Interaction and Quadratic Latent Variables', *Journal of Marketing Research*, **32** (August), 336–47.

Sinkula, James M. (1994), 'Market Information Processing and Organizational Learning', *Journal of Marketing*, **58** (January), 35–45.

Slater, Stanley F. and John Narver (1994), 'Does Competitive Environment Moderate the Market Orientation–Performance Relationship?', *Journal of Marketing*, **58** (January), 46–55.

Werts, Charles E., Robert L. Lin and Karl G. Jöreskog (1974), 'Interclass Reliability Estimates: Testing Structural Assumptions', *Educational and Psychological Measurement*, **34**, 25–33.

3. The dynamics of international market withdrawal

Pieter Pauwels and Paul Matthyssens

This study focuses on the decision-making process of international market withdrawal within the scope of international market portfolio management. A comparative study of eight withdrawal cases in four multinational firms results in a six-phased decision-making model that is driven by threat-rigidity behavior, failure-induced learning and political dynamics. Two types of international market withdrawal are identified. On the one hand, a tactical withdrawal is the outcome of threat-rigidity and exploitative learning at the level of executive management. A strategic withdrawal, on the other hand, is characterized by a process of failure-induced exploratory learning initiated by middle-level challengers. In contrast to a tactical withdrawal, which remains an isolated decision and does not interfere with other international ventures of the business unit, a strategic withdrawal turns out to be a germ of strategic (re)orientation of the business unit's entire international market portfolio. Whether a market withdrawal turns out to be tactical or strategic ultimately depends on the autonomy, the amount and the relevance of challengers' market and business knowledge.

INTRODUCTION

A multinational firm regularly optimizes its international market portfolio through expansions, extensions and retractions. Given limited resources, changing market opportunities may require resetting priorities in the current portfolio, including the withdrawal of less promising ventures. However, market interconnectedness and other exit barriers may turn this exercise into a complex decision (Douglas and Craig 1995, 1996). This study focuses on international market withdrawal as a strategic instrument within the logic of international market portfolio management. International market withdrawal is defined as a firm's or business unit's decision to reduce its engagement in market-related activities in a foreign product/market combination.

The obvious practical relevance of international market withdrawal (see for instance: Birkinshaw and Ritchie 1993; Calof and Beamish 1995; Benito 1997) stands in sharp contrast to the relative neglect in the literature. Most classic handbooks on international business and global marketing do not or hardly mention this phenomenon. Compared to an extensive industrial organization track on causes of exit and exit barriers (e.g. Harrigan 1985) and work on divestment in organizational behavior (e.g. Duhaime and Schwenk 1985), exit and divestment studies in international business are scarce. In the 1980s Jean Boddewyn studied foreign direct divestment, which was put forward as the reverse of FDI (e.g. Boddewyn 1983). Later, Welch and Luostarinen (1988) conceptually developed the broader phenomenon of 'de-internationalization'. Only recently, Fletcher (2001) and Lamb and Liesch (2002), among others, presented promising endeavors to include and explain withdrawal in a (more dynamic) internationalization process theory. Except for Crick (2002) who focuses on the perceptions of why exporting is discontinued, empirical studies of causes, processes and outcomes of international market withdrawal have not been published yet.

The objective of this chapter is to explore international market withdrawal within the decision-making unit and to understand the 'how' and 'why' of this phenomenon in the context of a particular internationalization process of a business unit. As such, we aim at unraveling the process of international market withdrawal and at understanding how this phenomenon fits in the overall internationalization of the firm. In the next section, the methodology of this study is presented. In the third section, the analytic outcome is discussed and summarized in a six-phased process model, comprising specific propositions for future validation. The final section summarizes the main drivers and dynamics of this process and identifies some managerial recommendations as well as specific leads for further research.

STRATEGY PROCESS METHODOLOGY

Strategy process research involves a longitudinal investigation of a network of choices (strategic decision making) and implementation processes (strategic change) enacted by managers (Pettigrew 1992; Ferlie and McNulty 1997). This approach has long been proposed as a key for a better understanding of the dynamics underlying the internationalization process (e.g. Melin 1992; Andersen 1993). However, real process studies of internationalization remain scarce up until now. For this study, we zoom in on international market withdrawal, which is considered as an 'international episode' or 'a dense cluster of activities which aims at a rapid change of the international fingerprint' (Kutschker, Bäurle and Schmid 1997, p. 105), in the context of the internationalization process of a firm.

The empirical focus is limited to an in-company analysis of antecedents, (sub-)processes – both decision making and implementation – and consequences situated within an inner (e.g. the corporate strategy of the firm) and outer (e.g. local market dynamics) context of the decision to withdraw. The basic unit of analysis is the withdrawal process from an international product/market combination by a strategic business unit.

While the exploratory nature of this study requires theoretical sampling (Yin 1994), it turned out to be difficult to identify and select cases. First, no existing database was found that could help us compose a sampling frame. Moreover, companies are not eager to reveal that they have recently withdrawn from a foreign market. As a consequence, we relied upon a convenience sample of 12 multinationals – all important pan-European or global players in various business-to-business industries – to compose a shortlist of 30 foreign product/market combinations that had been withdrawn by these multinationals within the last five years. Second, we applied three proxy criteria to select extreme or polar cases from this shortlist: (1) market entry strategy (active versus reactive), (2) the maximal profitability of the venture (low/middle/high), and (3) our subjective evaluation of the company's position on the EPRG continuum at the time of withdrawal (Perlmutter 1969). Through maximal variation on each of these dimensions, we aimed at polarity among the cases and, eventually, at a study with maximal internal validity (Yin 1994). This exercise resulted in ten cases from four companies. After a first interview, two cases of these cases were not selected, respectively due to the unavailability of some key respondents, and a misfit with our definition of international market withdrawal. Ultimately, eight cases were selected (Table 3.1).

Data were collected mainly through in-depth interviews. We personally interviewed between two and five respondents per case once or twice. Respondents were selected on the basis of their role as pro- or antagonist in this particular episode. Typical respondents were general managers, international marketing managers, and area managers. Interviews lasted between one and a half and two and a half hours and topic lists were used to structure the interviews. After each interview, the transcript was sent to the interviewee for revision. By telephone, the respondent was asked to comment on this transcript and to clarify the points that could lead to misinterpretation. Additional data source triangulation was limited for two reasons. First, strict confidentiality required by all business units did not allow us to contact relevant external respondents. Second, secondary data were not available because such documents did not exist (anymore) or because the companies were not eager to release them. In general, the negative connotation of a withdrawal made it extremely difficult to identify

Table 3.1 *Eight cases of international market withdrawal*

Company	Kappa	Eta	Lambda	Sigma
Business Activity	Trading of second-hand trucks and parts	Photographic and imaging industry	Telecommunication systems and equipment	Industrial engineering, processing and contracting
Stage in the EPRG-Model	Ethnocentric → Regiocentric	Geocentric ↔ Ethnocentric → Regiocentric	Geocentric	Ethnocentric → Regiocentric
Annual Group Turnover (1999)	US$131 million (1997)	US$4.3 billion	US$22.3 billion	US$2.4 billion
International/Total Sales Ratio	90%	85%	83%	65%

Case	Spain	Belgium	Japan	Germany	Turkey	Russia	Brunei	UK
Strategic Importance of this Market	Medium → High	High → Low	High → Moderate	High	Medium	High	Low	High → Low
Profitability of this Venture	High → Losses	Medium → Losses	Losses	High	Medium → Low	High → Losses	High → Medium	High → Losses
Number of Years in the Market	1980–1990 10 years	1977–1996 19 years	1973–1998 25 years	?–1998 >20 years	1983–1995 12 years	1983–1998 15 years	1985–1995 10 years	>1970–1999 >30 years

appropriate cases and to persuade managers to cooperate in a disclosing atmosphere. Eventually 41 interviewees were held and convergence of the data across the cases gave us a strong feeling of validity (Kvale 1996). The lack of convergence between some inferred patterns could be explained by existing theory.

Inferential Pattern Coding (IPC) was adopted as the main analytic tool (Miles and Huberman 1994; Yin 1994). Equivalent to cluster and factor analytic devices in multivariate analysis, IPC (1) reduces large amounts of qualitative data into smaller numbers of analytic units or incidents, (2) helps to elaborate maps (charts or matrices) for understanding incidents and (causal) interactions between abstracted events, and (3) enables cross-case analysis by identifying common themes and time-ordered displays (Miles and Huberman 1994). For the implementation of IPC, we largely followed the analytic process as described in Miles and Huberman (1994, pp. 90–237), which consists of three analytical steps: (1) pattern coding, (2) drawing of within-case sequential incident networks, and (3) drawing of a causal network across cases. IPC was performed using QSR NUD*IST 4.0 (Sage Publications Software 1997), a Windows-based software tool for computer-aided qualitative data analysis. This tool has been indicated as an appropriate device for pattern matching methodology on which IPC is based (Richards and Richards 1998). Although driven by elaborate case data, this study is not purely inductive. Throughout the analysis, the findings and interim conclusions were regularly challenged and compared with relevant studies in organizational behavior, strategic management and political science.

UNRAVELING INTERNATIONAL MARKET WITHDRAWAL

This section describes critical incidents in the process of international market withdrawal as they were observed in and across the cases. These critical incidents are identified as the 'accelerators' in the inferred pattern, which, as a whole, comprises the strategy process of international market withdrawal. As such, these critical incidents cannot be considered in isolation. However, *ex post* and for the sake of comprehensibility, the entire pattern was divided into six phases, chronologically organized around the six most important 'accelerators'. From these findings, initial assumptions are made about the drivers, conditions and direction of the decision-making process. Later in the process, specific propositions are formulated. Both the assumptions and the propositions are critically assessed and related to theories and studies in the extant literature.

During the analysis, two cases emerged as atypical: Eta-Germany and Sigma-Brunei. For explainable reasons, these two cases behave differently in some or many of the phases. Although Eta-Germany fits in with our definition, it soon became clear that this case was just part of a major product range contraction. Case Sigma-Brunei shares many characteristics with the other cases, except for one. This venture was set up as a project venture. From the start, management knew that sooner or later it had to be broken up. This built-in deadline – and the lack of deadlines in the other cases – provides us with significant findings for comparison and discussion. Although limited space prevents us from explicitly discussing these two cases here, they offered interesting points of reference for comparing fundamentally different strategy change processes (Yin 1994).

Phase 1: Accumulating Commitment

At a certain moment in their history and before the withdrawal was decided upon, all ventures were of strategic importance to the business unit and held an important place in their respective international market portfolios. In some of the cases, organizational commitment increased gradually over the years: additional personnel were hired, more financial resources were invested, the venture obtained a higher priority position for future investments, etc. In other cases, commitment increased more dramatically due to particular events or decisions. Quoting some respondents illustrates this increasing commitment:

> First, the cowboys came out and screened the market and its opportunities in a very flexible and fast way. When additional investments were required to grab the market, it became important to get [the venture] under control. (Area Manager, Lambda-Russia)

> Over the years, our engineering activity in the UK grew steadily and large investments were made in design software. (Former Group President, Sigma-UK)

In all cases, this strategic position results in increased institutionalization of the venture and its accompanying strategy in the business unit's international market portfolio. Local marketing and organizational structures are brought in line with the international marketing strategy and control instruments are installed. Although not a causal factor of withdrawal in itself, institutionalization turns out to be a highly relevant constraint to the withdrawal decision-making later on in the process. Institutionalization is a homeostatic process, i.e. a self-supporting process that forces an organization to increase internal stability and the reliability of their decision-making. As such, the strategic logic, which had been adopted initially, has become the dominant logic. Confirming and further embedding this dominant logic is the prime goal of a homeostatic process (Huff, Huff and Thomas 1992; Haveman 1993).

This assumption of institutionalization is also relevant to distinguish the phenomenon of this study from what Welch and Wiedersheim-Paul (1980) label 'export failure' or 'missed export start'. These authors suggest that withdrawal is most likely to occur only during the earliest stages of internationalization. They argue that a lack of market knowledge and resources are constraining factors only in the first stages (Johanson and Vahlne 1990). As a consequence, it can be expected that internal intangible exit barriers are much lower in the case of a 'missed export start' compared to the withdrawal process under investigation here.

Phase 2: Increasing Stress

Under stable environmental conditions, institutionalization enhances performance through efficiency (Nelson and Winter 1982). In none of the eight cases, though, did performance materialize as expected. This performance gap was the prime, and in most cases the first, indicator of an increasing misfit between the strategic orientation of the business unit in this venture and unexpected market dynamics.

The effect of this misfit, i.e., the discrepancy between the level of aspiration and the perceived level of achievement is labeled stress (Huff, Huff and Thomas 1992; Ocasio 1995). Stress induces agents to search for causes and solutions to reduce the stress level (Huff and Clark 1978). In the observed ventures, however, management could not easily identify what caused performance to decrease. In all cases, causal ambiguity was high (Reed and DeFilippi 1990). Due to this ambiguity, individuals – in, and outside the executive business unit management team – begin to develop their personal explanations of the causes of this poor performance. Initially, a lot of different interpretations emerge.

Soon, however, these interpretations converge to form two fundamentally different perspectives. In the first perspective, unsatisfactory performance is alleged to be the result of poor implementation of the current marketing strategy. As a consequence, resolving the problem seems feasible within the scope of the current strategic approach and 'try harder' is the proposed key to success. As such, adherents of this perspective experience endogenous stress (Dutton and Duncan 1987; Barr, Stimpert and Huff 1992). Stress is labeled endogenous when failure is perceived to be due to a misfit between the strategy and its implementation. The following quote illustrates this perspective:

> They perceived the fundamental instability of the market as a temporally higher
> degree of difficulty and not as critical. . . . At that time, the business divisions'
> dictum was to try harder and certainly not to give up their autonomy. (Lambda-
> Russia, Area Director)

In the second emerging perspective, unsatisfactory performance is alleged to be the result of the increasing inappropriateness of the current strategic status quo itself. As a consequence, the proposed solution to the incurred problems lies outside the operational scope of this particular venture's current marketing strategy. In contrast to the 'try harder' solution, the advocates of this perspective do not perceive enough maneuverability within the present strategic approach. To reduce stress, the strategic status quo has to be altered. As such, the protagonists of the second perspective experience exogenous stress (Dutton and Duncan 1987; Barr, Stimpert and Huff 1992). Stress is labeled exogenous when failure is perceived to be due to a misfit between the venture's marketing strategy and the changing business environment. The following quote is illustrative:

> We had gone too far. The market was there but we had approached it in the
> wrong way. (Kappa-Spain, Marketing and Sales Manager)

Whereas most interviewees reported both endogenous and exogenous stress, in-depth analysis clearly illustrates that every agent acted upon the logic of one predominant type of stress. Moreover, personal predispositions remain fairly stable throughout the decision-making process. It was observed further that managers with inward-oriented tasks and high hierarchical power in the venture express endogenous stress. Managers that are more remote from the venture's decision center and perform more boundary-spanning activities express exogenous stress. Therefore, the following propositions are set:

P_{1a}: The higher the hierarchical power and the more inward-oriented the task of an agent within a failing venture, the more s/he experiences and acts upon endogenous stress.

P_{1b}: The more remote the agent is from the decision center and the more boundary-spanning the task of this agent within a failing venture, the more s/he experiences and acts upon exogenous stress.

The consequence of these propositions is that agents with high hierarchical power and with an inward-oriented function will stick to the current local marketing strategy in trying to redress the venture. Agents more remote from the decision center with boundary-spanning functions are expected to reject the current local marketing strategy and are expected to go for a new strategic approach.

Ample support is found for these findings. Johnson (1988) argues that scattered visions on problems tend to converge to form a limited set of conflicting perspectives. Others, such as Dutton and Duncan (1987), Barr, Stimpert and Huff (1992), and Tushman and Romanelli (1985) develop the notions of endogenous and exogenous stress. If people's frame of reference fits in with the dominant logic of the organization, stress is expected to be endogenous. As such, environmental signals are interpreted as consonant with the individual mental models as well as with the dominant logic. When an agent predominantly experiences exogenous stress, the individual mental models on this issue are dissonant with, and overrule the dominant logic of the organization (Johnson 1988). Evidently, attention of managers is likely to be allocated to information that is easily interpreted within and that supports the current frame of reference of the individual (Kuwada 1998). This individual frame of reference focuses attention on data that are compatible with the framework and restricts attention to all others (Ocasio 1995). Environmental signals may be consonant or dissonant with the agent's current frame of reference (Johnson 1988). Events that refute the present frame of reference may be disregarded or interpreted within the scope of that frame.

Phase 3: Conflicting Reactions to Increasing Stress

Stress induces reaction to reduce it. The business units initially react in a tactical way, thereby trying to improve the implementation of the current strategic approach – the 'trying harder' solution – as is illustrated by this quote:

> In 1992, I went over every week. The Belgian subsidiary incurred heavy losses. However, bringing in management capacity reversed the situation within a year. . . . When we decided to release it again, losses increased instantly. This indicated that management capacity was too low. . . . After we had dismissed the Dutch manager, we did not want to engage a new man. The sales staff would not have accepted someone new. They were convinced of the fact that they could handle the problems and reverse the situation themselves. Accordingly, we decided to install [the sales staff as] a two-headed management team. . . . Again, a year was lost. In 1994, we decided to discharge one of the managers and we appointed the more reliable of the two as managing director of the Belgian subsidiary. At the same time, however, we decided to close the place down. . . . The newly appointed director argued that this was an unfair decision; he had not had the chance to prove himself. . . . So we decided to continue for one more year. (Kappa-Belgium, Sales and Marketing Manager)

This observation of inertial, tactical and reactive behavior is made comparably across all cases. Indeed, executive business unit managers themselves are the authors of the current marketing strategy of this particular international venture. They will stick to this strategy and follow standard routines within the scope of it to redress the failing venture. Building upon this observation and proposition 1a, we propose:

> P_{2a}: To redress a failing venture, a business unit's executive management adopts tactical routine measures that remain within the scope of the venture's current marketing strategy.

Studies on organizational failure support this observation. For instance, Hambrick and D'Aveni (1988), and Barker and Duhaime (1997) reported on failing firms that initially responded to decline with increased tactical efforts to improve the implementation of the existing strategies. Indeed, the institutionalization of the venture has provided its executive management with some degree of maneuverability and an accompanying range of pre-established tactical measures. Building upon endogenous stress, executive management disregards information that may challenge the current strategic logic and further strengthens institutionalization through the implementation of these tactical measures. Combining propositions 1a and 2a implies that decreasing performance induces tactical, reactive and inertial organizational behavior, which strengthens the current strategic status quo. This conclusion is in line with threat-rigidity and organizational inertia theory (Amburgey, Kelly and Barnett 1993; Ocasio 1995).

However, soon after the first tactical measures had been implemented, challengers emerged around the experience of exogenous stress. Initially, these challengers informally rejected the current tactical measures as a valuable cure for the failing venture. Typically, challengers are middle-level players in marketing, sales, area, and project management. Their opinion feeds on continuing poor performance, remaining causal ambiguity and, in particular, on their relatively high degree of knowledge autonomy. In line with the literature, the cases confirm that the challengers' knowledge autonomy is relatively high because: (1) they are new to the organization and have no prior commitment to the current logic (Kappa-Spain; Tushman, Newman and Romanelli 1986), (2) they are involved in boundary-spanning activities (Lambda-Turkey and Lambda-Russia; Hutt, Reingen and Ronchetto 1988), and/or (3) they are operating in the foreign subsidiary itself. As such, these challengers experience (divisional) independence and have access to additional market-specific information (Kappa-Belgium, Eta-Japan and Sigma-UK; Ghertman 1988; and Hitt, Keats and DeMarie 1998).

In some cases, the challengers go beyond informal rejection of the tacti-

Table 3.2   Two types of reaction of the challenging coalition

Type of Reaction	Explanation	Cases
1. Passive rejection	A challenging coalition of middle managers rejects the current tactical measures. However, no alternative solution is proposed	Kappa-Belgium Sigma-UK
2. Pro-active rejection	A challenging coalition rejects the current tactical measures. Moreover, it initiates the development of and experimentation with a strategic alternative	Eta-Japan Lambda-Russia Kappa-Spain Lambda-Turkey

cal measures; in some of the other cases they do not. As such, two types of reaction are observed: passive and pro-active rejection (Table 3.2).

Although the tactical measures are informally rejected in Type1-cases, no challenger is able to launch and defend an alternative strategic proposal. In Type2-cases, to the contrary, challengers propose and develop an alternative strategic option. From the comparative analysis of both types, it is argued that the difference between passive rejection and pro-active rejection accrues from the level and relevance of market and business knowledge of the challengers. A quote may illustrate this:

> The real centers of power are in Paris, Stuttgart and Antwerp. However, this venture did not receive the strategic drive we would have expected. . . . I had the luck to be there when it all happened. I had hands on when the crisis emerged and saw how our competitors reacted. . . . In this case, I may conclude that this decision was taken locally and 'sold' to top management. (Lambda-Turkey, Area Director MSOD)

Building upon previous propositions and these observations, we state the following propositions:

P_{2b}: Tactical routine measures in reaction to decreasing performance induce rejection of these measures and of the current strategic logic altogether.

P_{2c}: Rejection of tactical routine measures in reaction to decreasing performance induces the creation of alternative strategic options if (1) sufficient, and (2) relevant market and business knowledge is (3) autonomously available in the venture's organization.

Support for this proposition is found in Doz and Prahalad (1987) and Burgelman (1996), who argue that lower managers may become aware of the need for strategic redirection. However, they may lack access, influence, data, and, as a consequence, receptive ears to develop and push alternative ideas. We argue that this is the case in the 'passive rejection' type. Alternatively, in the 'pro-active rejection' type, the challengers have acquired relevant knowledge, which provides them with an alternative logic for the development of a non-routine solution (Dutton and Duncan 1987; and Hutt, Reingen and Ronchetto 1988). Related to the literature on organizational learning, it is argued that the hierarchical power of the executive management induces exploitative learning within the frame of the dominant logic, whereas the knowledge power of the challengers induces exploratory learning by middle-level challengers (March 1991).

Phase 4: Power Play towards the Stress Threshold

Despite an ongoing 'try harder' approach and many tactical measures, performance continues to decrease. Nevertheless, executive management does not give up its commitment towards the current logic and the accompanying cures, to the contrary:

> The objective remained a foreign subsidiary which was able to walk on its own. It is not acceptable that we [executive management] have to be involved in managing it on a day-to-day basis. However, as soon as we had left, profitability dropped again. And this went on for many months. (Kappa-Belgium, Executive Management)

In Type1-cases ('passive rejection'), current tactical cures continue to be questioned by some middle-level managers. However, rejection fades out, as it does not take root in the organization due to a lack of a strategic alternative, a prerequisite for organizational support. As a consequence, executive management of Type1-cases continues with increasingly ineffective tactical cures until the venture reaches rock bottom.

In Type2-cases ('pro-active rejection'), increasing stress and poor performance strengthen the creative efforts of knowledgeable and independent challengers. Indeed, in all of the observed Type2-cases, challengers develop and experiment with a new strategic logic that, in all cases, goes beyond fighting the problems of the failing venture. Indeed, they start their exercise by (re)setting priorities in the international market portfolio of the business unit. Priority criteria are (re)defined, strategic goals on the short and long term are (re)set and the current international market portfolio is benchmarked against these new priorities, taking into account barriers of maneuverability within the portfolio. In all cases of this study, withdrawal of this particular venture is a logical consequence of strategic reorientation – though, evidently, not a necessary ingredient of every strategic alternative for a failing foreign venture outside our sample. In sum, the challengers' strategic alternative is formulated at the level of the entire foreign market portfolio. It has the portfolio and not the failing venture as its main focus.

Furthermore, the challengers seek and find informal support at higher echelons of the organization, i.e. beyond the executive management of this business unit. Doing so, they try to back up their increasing knowledge power with hierarchical power. As soon as the hierarchical power of the challengers increases to a certain level, authority over the venture switches from the executive management to the challengers. In some cases this transition occurs smoothly. In others, it is more dramatic, including lay-offs and a formal repositioning of executive managers. Quotes from the Lambda cases illustrate the relationship between challengers, the executive management and higher echelons in this phase:

> This . . . brought about strong reactions, especially from the business directors. They accused me of being a defeatist. . . . When this vision got accepted at HQ level, I had the business director against me. They simply did not want to accept the situation. (Lambda-Russia, Area Director MSOD)

> Another key factor is my good relationship with the director of International Operations. He is mature enough to cope with bad news. He does not panic. The thrust that existed between subsidiary and headquarters acted as a differentiator. (Lambda-Turkey, Area Director MSOD)

The extant literature underpins this dramatic evolution. Escalating commitment instructed by current executive management fits within threat-rigidity theory (e.g. Staw, Sandelands and Dutton 1981; Ocasio 1995), which argues that continuing adversity increasingly leads to a restraint of information processing, constriction of control, and increased rigidity in organizational behavior. In contrast to the rigid behavior of the executive management, the challengers are increasingly committed to the creation and adoption of a strategic alternative. Due to the ongoing search for information beyond the dominant logic and the increasing commitment to higher-order exploratory learning, causal ambiguity decreases and exogenous stress increases dramatically (Johnson 1988; and Huff, Huff and Thomas 1994). The 'real' troubling facts become clear to an increasing number of members of and beyond the business unit (Aharoni 1966). Combining the reactive threat-rigidity behavior of executive management with pro-active failure-induced learning of the challenging coalition, we claim that, as commitment to the conflicting learning paths continues to increase, both endogenous and exogenous stress increase until a threshold is reached (Schwenk 1989; Ocasio 1995).

Whereas no hierarchical power shift occurs in Type1-cases, in Type2-cases the power base shifts away from executive management towards the challengers. Indeed, over different phases of the withdrawal process, we observed an increasingly important underlying political process between the proponents of two strategic logics, which Huff, Huff and Thomas (1992) label as a dialectic between accumulating exogenous stress and accumulating inertia within the framework of the dominant logic. However, at a certain moment both endogenous and exogenous stress are at their maximum and the venture reaches rock bottom. Barr, Stimpert and Huff (1992, p. 19) define this threshold as the point where 'the level of [exogenous] stress (the level of pressure to change) exceeds the level of inertia (the level of pressure to maintain)'. The Type2-cases suggest that the impact of reaching a threshold may be extreme, depending on the preceding process. The consequences of reaching the threshold are discussed in the following section.

Phase 5: A Fait Accompli in Type2-cases

Phase 5 is operationally defined as the episode that starts at the stress threshold, i.e. where both endogenous and exogenous stress are maximal and the venture reaches rock bottom, and is ended with the formal decision to withdraw. Although in most Type2-cases (e.g. Lambda-Turkey and Lambda-Russia) this phase took less than a couple of hours, in others – mostly Type1-cases – the time gap between maximum stress and the formal decision to withdraw was considerable (e.g. in Sigma-UK up to 15 years). Since the difference between Type1- and Type2-cases culminates in this phase, we discuss them under separate headings.

In Type2-cases ('pro-active rejection'), the challengers have now gained hierarchical power over the problematic venture and in most cases even over the entire international market portfolio of this business unit. The first initiative concerning this venture is to isolate and de-institutionalize it from the rest of the international market portfolio. In all cases, the new leaders at least assess whether the venture is sufficiently isolated before the withdrawal can be implemented. Two quotes illustrate this:

> Moreover, you could say we had to stay in Japan to cover other countries in the region. However, this is not correct. Japan is really isolated. (Eta-Japan, Regional Export Manager)

> You know, Brunei was a small market, which operated independently from other operations. All engineering was performed locally. (Sigma-Brunei, Project Engineer Manager)

Second, the venture's resources are reallocated to a new strategic goal: a new product/market combination (Eta-Japan), a new entry strategy (Kappa-Spain), a new strategic thrust (Lambda-Turkey), or a new organizational set-up for growth (Lambda-Russia). As this reallocation builds upon earlier experimentation by the old challengers, the formal decision lags behind reality:

> I think that decisions of this kind are taken in the field. . . . All major decisions are taken in this way. . . . From a certain moment on, it is 'sold' to the top. However, if you have someone who strongly defends the idea, they will accept in all cases. (Lambda-Turkey, Area Director MSOD)

> The implementation is a fait accompli. . . . In fact, we do not even bring a detailed strategy to [the top management] but a vision. (Lambda-Russia, Area Director MSOD)

As such, the withdrawal is more a consequence or 'fait accompli' than a decision on its own. Moreover, interviewees of Type2-cases affirm that top management would not have accepted any of these withdrawals if they had not been the logical consequence of a larger-scale strategic reorientation, which accommodates a strategic alternative for this venture. Therefore, it is proposed that:

P_{3a}: In disregard of a failing venture's history and performance, withdrawal of a venture is not a real option if the venture cannot be isolated from the rest of portfolio and if no accepted strategic alternative is available for the freed resources.

The literature emphasizes the importance of decoupling ventures (Douglas and Craig 1995), though suggests that de-institutionalization may not be problematic if: (1) a strategic alternative for the freed resources is available, (2) the venture is isolated from the current strategic context of the venture, and (3) causal ambiguity is low (Simonson and Staw 1992; Ross and Staw 1993; Drummond 1995). Second, in many organizational change models the decision to adopt a new strategic direction is separated (in time) from the decision to leave the old strategic logic (e.g. Tushman and Romanelli 1985). Indeed, Narayanan and Fahey (1982), and Hutt, Reingen and Ronchetto (1988) argue that commitment to a strategic alternative begins to evolve during the early stages of decision making rather than after the formal decision to reallocate is made. If the challenging vision is in conflict with the status quo (Type2-cases), challengers do not wait for formal approval before implementing their project (Howell and Higgins 1990). As a consequence, the formal decision merely brings the official strategy in line with the real activities and current practices are formally routinized (Burgelman 1996). A new round of institutionalization starts here.

Phase 5: A Vacuum in Type 1-cases

When the stress threshold is reached in Type1-cases, executive management reaches the point at which it understands that none of the tactical measures has been effective. As a consequence, organizational commitment to the ventures decreases dramatically and the ventures soon become isolated from the rest of the international market portfolio:

> It is my experience that top management's interference decreases as things really begin to get worse. The message is: please continue trying hard, but don't bother us anymore. . . . The time top management devoted to these two ventures can be expressed in minutes, not in hours. (Lambda-Russia, Area Director MSOD)

However, since no strategic alternative for the venture's resources is available, the decision to withdraw is not taken and/or approved of by top management. After all, the tactical measures that had been taken had increased the institutionalization of the venture and had resulted in a context – 'we just have invested such an amount of money to redress this venture' (executive management Lambda-UK) – in which market withdrawal could not be a viable alternative. Both in Kappa-Belgium and in Lambda-UK, management's interest in the venture decreased rapidly. However, instead of withdrawing the venture, we observed that commitment began to escalate at the operational level of the venture, i.e., at the level of local non-challenging middle and lower managers. The overall driver changes from 'try harder' to 'save our souls'. The following quote illustrate this:

> During that period, we worked in a highly uncontrolled way and we hardly communicated with headquarters. There was no explicit strategy about how to redress the situation. If we communicated, it was about operational facts. So we made a plan ourselves. However, thinking about it now, we may have made major errors at the time. (Kappa-Belgium, Sales Executive)

In fact, a vacuum is created when executive management starts to detach itself from the venture without withdrawing it. In this vacuum, strategic control decreases instantly. The cases suggest that this vacuum may continue to exist for a long time – in Sigma-UK for more than 15 years. Ultimately, an externally caused dramatic event such as a major accident or the bankruptcy of a customer is necessary to wake up executive management once more and makes them to decide to exit after all, using this incident as an excuse.

P_{3b}: When a failing venture needs to be withdrawn, though the conditions of P_{3a} are not fulfilled, the venture comes into a state of strategic drift.

This observed process of increasing detachment towards strategic drift is comparable to what Ross and Staw (1993) and Burgelman (1996) describe as 'organizational de-commitment'. As economic adversity, causal ambiguity and a stream of negative information continue to increase the organization turns its head towards more promising challenges, leaving the venture to its fate. Aharoni (1966), Johnson (1988), and Drummond (1994, 1995) support our finding that a venture comes into a vacuum when no alternative real option is available at the stress threshold. Within this vacuum, local commitment begins to escalate and the venture enters a state of strategic drift. Inertial behavior and creeping rationality emanating from the dominant logic, turns into escalating commitment and strategic drift when the venture is isolated and no organizational control remains over the activities in the venture (Bowen 1987; Ross and Staw 1993). Finally, the literature suggests that an external triggering event, which has disproportionate and symbolic influence, is required to break out of this vacuum. In fact, it does not directly cause withdrawal. It only provides the last straw for top management and an excuse for business unit management to decide on the withdrawal (Gersick 1991; Huff, Huff and Thomas 1992, 1994).

In sum, extreme stress – endogenous in Type1 and exogenous in Type2 – about an increasingly de-institutionalized venture results in extreme strategic instability. However, this strategic instability is of a fundamentally different nature in Type1-cases compared to Type2-cases. In the former, venture performance reaches rock bottom and endogenous stress as well as causal ambiguity did not decrease despite increasing efforts to redress the situation. To the contrary, in the latter, a challenging logic gains momentum in the organization, causal ambiguity decreases, and a strategic alternative gains hierarchical power. Therefore, we formally distinguish between Type1- and Type2-withdrawal, which we respectively call tactical and strategic withdrawal. Both phenomena are more specifically defined in the following section.

Phase 6: Beyond the Withdrawal

In case of a tactical withdrawal (Kappa-Belgium, Sigma-UK, and Eta-Japan to a lesser extent), exploitative learning results in the unsuccessful adoption of all available routine and tactical measures. Ultimately, the organization detaches itself from the venture, not knowing what to do about the situation, and releasing strategic control. As a consequence, a painful de-institutionalization occurs through an uncontrolled process of local escalation of commitment. A tactical withdrawal is an extreme measure, which is decided upon in order to cope with strategic drift without understanding the real reason for the failure.

In case of a strategic withdrawal (Lambda-Turkey, Lambda-Russia, and Eta-Japan to a lesser extent), exploratory learning results in a strategic alternative that replaces the old dominant logic. Moreover, this strategic alternative creates a strategic context that is needed for the withdrawal (see proposition P_{3a}). In contrast to a tactical withdrawal, causal ambiguity and stress decrease dramatically as soon as the venture is withdrawn and the strategic alternative is adopted. A strategic withdrawal is decided upon as an evident measure within the framework of strategic reorientation, which is required to cope with environmental dynamics.

The cases illustrate that the stress threshold marks the beginning of an episode of instability that continues beyond the formal decision to withdraw. In the case of strategic withdrawal, this new logic allows for strategic flexibility and higher-order learning beyond the scope of the original failing venture. The cases illustrate that a strategic withdrawal of one particular venture is a germ for additional strategic reorientation at the level of the international market portfolio, or even at the level of the internationalization of the firms. In the words of an interviewee:

> We have used this crisis as a leverage to push our strategic vision. (Lambda-Russia, Area Director MSOD)

In sum, we propose:

P_{4a}: Strategic withdrawal of a failing international venture is the germ of strategic reorientation in the entire international market portfolio.

Support for this 'germ' idea is found in the literature. Gersick (1991) and Burgelman (1996) describe dramatic corporate strategic reorientations, which had been initiated by a strategic reorientation at a lower level. Aharoni (1966), Burgelman (1996) and Kuwada (1998) argue that firms who have strategically exited from a business are likely to have a better understanding of the links between their distinctive competences and the basis of competition in the industry or market. In the case of tactical withdrawal, the ventures are stigmatized as a failure, and causal ambiguity remains high. Due to organizational de-commitment hardly any learning effect was observed after a tactical withdrawal. In fact, tactical withdrawal is a reaction to strategic drift, not to the real underlying problems of the failing venture.

Four years after Kappa-Belgium had been withdrawn, an analysis of the present international market portfolio of Kappa suggests that this withdrawal had hardly influenced the overall international marketing strategy of the firm; to the contrary. At least three other subsidiaries in Eastern Europe were found that do not fit into the current global marketing perspective of the firm and, as a consequence, may need to be revised or withdrawn. Hence:

P$_{4b}$: Tactical withdrawal of a failing venture prevents learning and strategic change within and beyond this venture.

CONCLUSION

This comparative case study on the dynamics of international market withdrawal results in a six-phased process model, which is summarized in Figure 3.1. The model captures the entire withdrawal episode that starts with the perception of decreasing performance of an institutionalized venture and extends up to the consequences of this withdrawal on the business unit's international market portfolio. Critical underlying generative mechanisms are threat-rigidity and failure-induced learning, which, in their turn, are driven respectively by endogenous and exogenous stress. Equally important are political forces that interfere. While more traditional models (e.g. the Uppsala Model) of internationalization are driven by a fairly narrow conception of learning (Forsgren 2002), this study illustrates how different types of learning (exploratory versus exploitative) jointly generate progression in the internationalization process. A further extension of this dual learning perspective is promising to extend our understanding of the dynamics in the internationalization process of the firm.

Nevertheless, this study remains an exploratory and intermediate step towards the explanation of international market withdrawal and the integration of this phenomenon in internationalization process theory. Several limitations are acknowledged. Although the utmost was done to strive for a sound theoretical sample, more (polar) cases should be investigated and more effort should be made in controlling industry, corporate and market parameters. More conceptual work is necessary to explain how these two conflicting drivers (exploratory versus exploitative learning) can co-exist and how a dialectical process is able to organize their co-existence. In this respect, important added value is expected from the infusing of organizational and strategic chance concepts and models into the international management field (cf. Melin 1992). Finally, important work is still to be done in translating the central constructs and drivers of this model into measurable interrelated variables that are necessary for empirical testing.

Some important managerial lessons can be drawn. First, it is striking that none of the observed business units had contingency plans that included

	Commitment	Stress	Reactions			Fait Accompli		Withdrawal
Enactment **Executive management** *Actions*	Investing in the venture and developing a strategic logic	Increasing endogenous stress Analysis of causes	Increasing endogenous stress Tactical measures Increasing commitment	Increasing endogenous stress Tactical measures Escalation of commitment		TACTICAL WITHDRAWAL Stress is high Withdrawal as a reaction to strategic grift		TACTICAL WITHDRAWAL Withdrawal=Failure No effects on the international market portfolio
Driver	**Institutionalization**	**Threat-rigidity behavior**	**Threat-rigidity behavior**	**Threat-rigidity behavior and hierarchical power**		**Organizational de-commitment**		**None**
				CONFRONTATION				
Enactment **Challenging Middle Managers** *Actions*	Investing in the venture and implementing a strategic logic	Increasing exogenous stress Analysis of causes	Increasing exogenous stress 1. Passive rejection ⟶ 2. Pro-active rejection ➤	Increasing exogenous stress Fading out Strategic alternative	**Stress threshold**	STRATEGIC WITHDRAWAL Stress→0 – Isolation of the venture – Reallocation of resources	**Withdrawal**	STRATEGIC WITHDRAWAL Withdrawal=Opportunity Learning effects on the international market portfolio
Driver	**Institutionalization**	**Failure-induced learning**	**Failure-induced learning**	**Failure-induced learning and knowledge power**		**New strategic logic**		**Institutionalization**

Figure 3.1 A process model of international market withdrawal

withdrawal as a real option when certain deadlines were not met. In fact, no financial or time deadlines were set in any of the original strategic plans. Maneuverability within the original strategic plans was not based upon explicit tactical recipes but on unwritten, though deeply rooted, reaction styles. Furthermore, it is interesting to notice the importance of political dynamics. Although power play is a well-known characteristic of managerial decision making, too often managers and academics alike forget about the impact of it on important decisions. Understanding the intricacy of power plays is a critical factor in controlling decision-making processes. Finally, exploration and knowledge created at the boundary-spanning middle level of the organization plays a crucial and positive role in the progression of the internationalization process. Top management should understand the leverage this knowledge can create and safeguard it through stimulating bottom-up communication and lower level experimentation. It is our belief that an organization's necessary 'strategic flexibility' has its roots in this bottom-up generative mechanism.

REFERENCES

Aharoni, Yair (1966), *The Foreign Investment Decision Process*, Boston, MA: Harvard University Press.

Amburgey, Terry L., D. Kelly and W.P. Barnett (1993), 'Resetting the Clock: The Dynamics of Organizational Change and Failure', *Administrative Science Quarterly*, **38**, 51–73.

Andersen, Otto (1993), 'On the Internationalisation Process of Firms: A Critical Analysis', *Journal of International Business Studies*, **24** (2), 209–31.

Barker III, Vincent L. and I.M. Duhaime (1997), 'Strategic Change in the Turnaround Process: Theory and Empirical Evidence', *Strategic Management Journal*, **18**, 13–38.

Barr, Pamela S., J.L. Stimpert and A.S. Huff (1992), 'Cognitive Change, Strategic Action, and Organizational Renewal', *Strategic Management Journal*, **13**, 15–36.

Benito, G.R.G. (1997), 'Divestment of Foreign Production Operations', *Applied Economics*, **29**, 1365–77.

Birkinshaw, Julian and W. Ritchie (1993), 'Balancing the Global Portfolio', *Business Quarterly*, (Summer), 40–49.

Boddewyn, Jean J. (1983), 'Foreign Direct Divestment Theory: Is It the Reverse of FDI Theory?', *Weltwirtschaftliches Archiv*, **119** (2), 345–55.

Bowen, Michael G. (1987). 'The Escalation Phenomenon Reconsidered: Decision Dilemmas or Decision Errors?', *Academy of Management Review*, **12** (1), 52–66.

Burgelman, Robert A. (1996), 'A Process Model of Strategic Business Exit: Implications for an Evolutionary Perspective on Strategy', *Strategic Management Journal*, **17**, 193–214.

Calof, J.L. and P.W. Beamish (1995), 'Adapting to Foreign Markets: Explaining Internationalization', *International Business Review*, **4** (2), 115–31.

Crick, Dave (2002), 'The Decision to Discontinue Exporting: SMEs in Two U.K. Trade Sectors', *Journal of Small Business Management*, **40** (1), 66–77.

Douglas, Susan P. and C.S. Craig (1995), *Global Marketing Strategy*, New York: McGraw-Hill.

Douglas, Susan P. and C.S. Craig (1996), 'Executive Insights: Global Portfolio Planning and Market Interconnectedness', *Journal of International Marketing*, **4** (1), 93–110.

Doz, Yves L. and C.K. Prahalad (1987), 'A Process Model of Strategic Redirection in Large Complex Firms: The Case of Multinational Corporations', in Andrew M. Pettigrew (ed.), *The Management of Strategic Change*, Oxford: Basil Blackwell, pp. 63–83.

Drummond, Helga (1994), 'Escalation in Organizational Decision Making: A Case of Recruiting an Incompetent Employee', *Journal of Behavioral Decision Making*, **7**, 43–55.

Drummond, Helga (1995), 'De-escalation in Decision Making: A Case of a Disastrous Partnership', *Journal of Management Studies*, **32** (3), 265–81.

Duhaime, Irene M. and C.R. Schwenk (1985), 'Conjectures on Cognitive Simplification in Acquisition and Divestment Decision Making', *Academy of Management Review*, **10** (2), 287–95.

Dutton, Jane E. and R.B. Duncan (1987), 'The Creation of Momentum for Change Through the Process of Strategic Issue Diagnosis', *Strategic Management Journal*, **8**, 279–95.

Ferlie, Ewan and T. McNulty (1997), 'Going to Market: Changing Patterns in the Organization and Character of Process Research', *Scandinavian Journal of Management*, **13** (4), 367–87.

Fletcher, Richard (2001), 'A Holistic Approach to Internationalization', *International Business Review*, **10**, 25–49.

Forsgren, Mats (2002), 'The Concept of Learning in the Uppsala Internationalization Process Model: A Critical Review', *International Business Review*, **11**, 257–77.

Gersick, Connie J.G. (1991), 'Revolutionary Change Theories: A Multilevel Exploration of the Punctuated Equilibrium Paradigm', *Academy of Management Review*, **16** (1), 10–36.

Ghertman, Michel (1988), 'Foreign Subsidiary and Parents' Roles During Strategic Investment and Divestment Decisions', *Journal of International Business Studies*, **19** (1) (Spring), 47–67.

Hambrick, Donald C. and R.A. D'Aveni (1988), 'Large Corporate Failures as Downward Spirals', *Administrative Science Quarterly*, **33**, 1–23.

Harrigan, Kathryn R. (1985) 'Exit Barriers and Vertical Integration', *Academy of Management Journal*, **28** (3), 686–97.

Haveman, Heather A. (1993), 'Organizational Size and Change: Diversification in the Savings and Loan Industry after Deregulation', *Administrative Science Quarterly*, **38**, 20–50.

Hitt, Michael A., B.W. Keats and S.N. DeMarie (1998), 'Navigating in the New Competitive Landscape: Building Strategic Flexibility and Competitive Advantage in the 21st Century', *Academy of Management Executive*, **12** (4), 22–42.

Howell, Jane M. and C.A. Higgins (1990), 'Champions of Change: Identifying, Understanding, and Supporting Champions of Technological Innovations', *Organizational Dynamics*, **19**, 40–55.

Huff, Anne S., J.O. Huff and H. Thomas (1994), 'The Dynamics of Strategic Change', in Herman Daems and H. Thomas (eds), *Strategic Groups, Strategic Moves and Performance*, Oxford, UK: Elsevier Science, pp. 31–62.

Huff, James O. and W.A.V. Clark (1978), 'Cumulative Stress and Cumulative

Inertia: A Behavioral Model of the Decision to Move', *Environment and Planning A*, **10**, 1101–19.

Huff, James O., A.S. Huff and H. Thomas (1992), 'Strategic Renewal and the Interaction of Cumulative Stress and Inertia', *Strategic Management Journal*, **13**, 55–75.

Hutt, Michael D., P.H. Reingen and J.R. Ronchetto, Jr (1988), 'Tracing Emergent Processes in Marketing Strategy Formation', *Journal of Marketing*, **52** (January), 4–19.

Johanson, Jan and J.-E. Vahlne (1990), 'The Mechanism of Internationalization', *International Marketing Review*, **7** (4), 11–24.

Johanson, Jan-Erik and F. Wiedersheim-Paul (1975), 'The Internationalization Process of the Firm – Four Swedish Case Studies', *Journal of Management Studies*, (October), 305–22.

Johnson, Gerry (1988), 'Rethinking Incrementalism', *Strategic Management Journal*, **9**, 75–91.

Kutschker, Michael, I. Bäurle and S. Schmid (1997), 'International Evolution, International Episodes, and International Epochs – Implications for Managing Internationalization', *Management International Review*, **37** (2) (Special Issue), 101–24.

Kuwada, Kotaro (1998), 'Strategic Learning: The Continuous Side of Discontinuous Strategic Change', *Organization Science*, **9** (6), 719–36.

Kvale, Steinar (1996), *InterViews: An introduction to Qualitative Research Interviewing*. Thousand Oaks, CA: Sage Publications.

Lamb, Peter, and P. Liesch (2002), 'The Internationalization Process of the Smaller Firm: Re-Framing the Relationships between Market Commitment, Knowledge and Involvement', *Management International Review*, **42** (1), 7–27.

March, James G. (1991), 'Exploration and Exploitation in Organizational Learning', *Organization Science*, **2** (1), 71–87.

Melin, Leif (1992), 'Internationalization as a Strategy Process', *Strategic Management Journal*, **13**, 99–118.

Miles, Matthew B. and A.M. Huberman (1994), *Qualitative Data Analysis*, 2nd edn, Thousand Oaks, CA: Sage Publications.

Narayanan, V.K. and L. Fahey (1982), 'The Micro-Politics of Strategy Formulation', *Academy of Management Review*, **7** (1), 25–34.

Nelson, Richard R. and S.G. Winter (1982), *An Evolutionary Theory of Economic Change*, Cambridge, MA: The Belknap Press of Harvard University Press.

Ocasio, William (1995), 'The Enactment of Economic Adversity: A Reconciliation of Theories of Failure-Induced Change and Threat-Rigidity', *Research in Organizational Behavior*, **17**, 287–331.

Perlmutter, Howard V. (1969), 'The Tortuous Evolution of the Multinational Corporation', *Columbia Journal of World Business*, **9** (January–February), 9–18.

Pettigrew, Andrew M. (1992), 'The Character and Significance of Strategy Process Research', *Strategic Management Journal*, **13**, 5–16.

Reed, Richard and R.J. DeFillipi (1990), 'Causal Ambiguity, Barriers to Imitation, and Sustainable Competitive Advantage', *Academy of Management Review*, **15** (1), 88–102.

Richards, Thomas J. and L. Richards (1998), 'Using Computers in Qualitative Research', in Norman K. Denzin and Y.S. Lincoln (eds), *Collecting and Interpreting Qualitative Materials*, Thousand Oaks, CA: Sage Publications, pp. 211–45.

Ross, Jerry and B.M. Staw (1993), 'Organizational Escalation and Exit: Lessons from the Shoreham Nuclear Power Plant', *Academy of Management Journal*, **36** (4), 701–32.

Sage Publications (1997), *QSR NUD°IST* Rev. 4. Thousand Oaks, CA: Sage Publications.

Schwenk, Charles R. (1989), 'Linking Cognitive, Organizational and Political Factors in Explaining Strategic Change', *Journal of Management Studies*, **26** (2), 177–87.

Simonson, Itamar and B.M. Staw (1992), 'Deescalation Strategies: A Comparison of Techniques for Reducing Commitment to Losing Courses of Action', *Journal of Applied Psychology*, **77** (4), 419–26.

Staw, Barry M., L.E. Sandelands and J.E. Dutton (1981), 'Threat-Rigidity Effects in Organizational Behavior: A Multilevel Analysis', *Administrative Science Quarterly*, **26**, 501–24.

Tushman, Michael L. and E. Romanelli (1985), 'Organizational Evolution: A Metamorphosis Model of Convergence and Reorientation', *Research in Organizational Behavior*, **7**, 171–222.

Tushman, Michael L., W.H. Newman and E. Romanelli (1986), 'Convergence and Upheaval: Managing the Unsteady Pace of Organizational Evolution', *California Management Review*, **29** (1), 29–44.

Welch, Lawrence S. and R. Luostarinen (1988), 'Internationalization: Evolution of a Concept', *Journal of General Management*, **14** (2), 34–55.

Welch, Lawrence S. and F. Wiedersheim-Paul (1980), 'Initial Exports – A Marketing Failure?', *Journal of Management Studies*, (October), 333–44.

Yin, Robert K. (1994), *Case Study Research Design and Methods*, 2nd edn, Thousand Oaks, CA: Sage Publications.

4. Regionalization of multinationals: implications for research in international marketing

M. Krishna Erramilli

INTRODUCTION

A growing number of researchers are noting that multinationals are adopting a regional orientation in developing and implementing their strategies (e.g. Heenan and Perlmutter 1979; Morrison et al. 1991; Sullivan 1992; Siddiqi 2000; Rugman 2001). The region (e.g. EU, NAFTA) is becoming the focal point for identifying opportunities and exploiting them through region-specific approaches. Many strategic and operational decisions are increasingly being made at the regional level, influenced by regional considerations. Few researchers in international marketing (IM), however, have yet taken this trend into consideration. Consequently, most of them continue to make assumptions that may have become outdated.

The purpose of this chapter is broadly to describe the trend in multinational companies toward regionalization and to explore its implications for research in international marketing. To this end, the chapter reviews the relevant literature, explains its implications, describes empirical evidence from a recent study on regional headquarters of MNCs, and, finally, makes some recommendations for IM researchers. In developing this chapter, we primarily focus on research related to the choice of entry modes, although the resulting insights could be easily generalized to other IM decisions. The focus is natural given that we are most familiar with this research stream, and is justified since entry-mode choice is a very heavily researched issue in international marketing. The scope of the analysis is restricted to multinational companies (MNCs), since regionalization trends appear to be most commonly observed in these organizations. However, the findings are probably equally relevant, if not more, to small and medium-sized enterprises (SMEs) that have gone international.

REGIONALIZATION OF MNCS

In his much-cited article, Perlmutter (1969) described three major orientations of MNCs: ethnocentrism (home-country orientation), polycentrism
(host-country orientation) and geocentrism (global orientation). He also
described how these orientations shape the MNC's philosophy, decision-
making process, strategy and structure. Later, Heenan and Perlmutter
(1979) added a fourth orientation to this list, which they termed 'regiocen-
trism'. This is a tendency that predisposes MNCs to develop strategies and
structures focused on exploitation of opportunities on a regional scale.
Over the past two decades since then, a number of other scholars have
observed and studied the emergence of regionalization trends at the macro
national level (e.g. Johnson 1991; Emmerij 1992) and within MNCs (e.g.
Daniels 1986; Sullivan 1992; Siddiqi 2000). Given the objectives of this
chapter, the studies dealing with regionalization within MNCs will now be
elaborated further.

Based on research involving 115 medium and large MNCs and 103 affil-
iated subsidiaries in the US, Canada, France, Germany and Japan,
Morrison et al. (1991) observed a strong preference for regionalization over
globalization among multinational corporations. They note: 'It is within
the region that top managers determine investment locations, product mix,
competitive positioning, and performance appraisals. Managers are given
the opportunity to solve regional challenges regionally . . . regional strategies are increasingly providing the primary determinant of competitive
advantage' (p. 24).

Recently, Rugman (2001) made even stronger assertions on the trend
toward regionalization. He observed that the world's 500 largest MNCs,
based in the United States, the EU and Japan and accounting for more than
80 per cent of the world's stock of FDI and over half of world trade, are
not really global. Instead, they operated on a triad-regional basis. He goes
on to assert: 'The vast majority of MNC manufacturing and service activity is (and always been) organized regionally, not globally'. Some scholars
see the development of regionalization as an effective alternative to globalization, as a response by MNCs to the failure of globalization. For
example, Morrison et al. (1991) argue that globalization efforts by MNCs
during the 1980s failed because industry standards across the world remain
diverse, customers continue to demand locally adapted products, being an
insider player remains very important, global organizations are difficult to
manage and globalization circumvents subsidiary competencies. They
argue that regionalization represents a superior alternative because
regional operations (a) are as scale efficient as global ones, (b) can better
tailor products to local markets, (c) are relatively easier to manage, (d) give

companies the insider advantage, and (e) allow companies to leverage sub-sidiary competencies.

The emergence of regionalization strategy is also seen as a response to external geopolitical pressures, such as the formation of regional trade blocs like the EU, NAFTA and ASEAN (Lehrer and Asakawa 1999). The forma-tion of regional trade blocs increases within-region homogeneity and between-region heterogeneity, which combine together to make regional strategies more effective. For example, Lassere (1996) observed that many European multinationals established regional headquarters and developed a regional orientation in the Asia-Pacific area as the region became increas-ingly more integrated economically. In the same vein, Schutte (1997) explains why a regional Asia-Pacific strategy makes sense for many European multi-nationals. First, he explains that the growth dynamics in Asia and the rest of the world are different. Market conditions also tend to be more ambiguous and volatile in this region. Therefore, strategies successful in Europe may not be very successful in Asia. Second, he observes that the region is becoming more integrated, with intra-Asia trade and investment activities. He also notes that the business community itself, the overseas Chinese and the Japanese MNCs in particular, are driving the integration. He concludes that 'the increasing integration of Asia also enables MNCs to rationalize produc-tion activities in order to exploit cost advantages across countries, and to develop common marketing concepts adjusted to specific Asian needs and communications through increasingly regional media' (p. 440).

Lehrer and Asakawa (1999) emphasize that 'in interest of flexibility the region holds promise as an appropriate organizational compromise between global integration (efficient, but not locally flexible) and local diffe-rentiation (flexible, but not globally efficient)'. In other words, they see regionalization as a compromise approach that gives organizations the best of both worlds: the efficiency of globalization and the flexibility of local-ization. In a study of US MNCs in Europe, Daniels (1987) found a strong regional approach to marketing strategies. He discovered that regional operations bridged national and global marketing strategies, much like Lehrer and Asakawa (1999) did. He also notes other advantages of region-alization: pooling of resources, synergy among operations, standardiza-tion, and control of strategic product thrust.

The regional headquarters (RHQ) is seen as the key organizational struc-ture that helps develop, implement and coordinate regional strategies in multinational companies. The RHQ is a special subsidiary that is charged with the responsibility of integrating and coordinating the MNC's activ-ities within a certain geographic region. Based on detailed investigations of 30 Western and Japanese MNCs, Schutte (1997) found that RHQs play an important role in shaping the regional perspective in MNCs, and are instrumental in integrating the region through their support and functional activities. In studies of American multinationals in Europe, Daniels (1986, 1987) and Sullivan (1992) also re-affirm the central role of the RHQ in developing and implementing regional strategies.

Lassere (1996) defines and describes the role of RHQs broadly along two dimensions: entrepreneurial and integrative. The entrepreneurial role encompasses all tasks undertaken to identify opportunities and stimulate the company's growth in the region. This includes scouting, strategic stimulation, and signaling commitment to the region. On the other hand, integrative roles include enhancing the company's efficiency and effectiveness through coordination of regional operations, and the pooling of resources across the region.

To summarize, there appears to be an emerging conviction that a very large number of multinational companies have a regional orientation in assessing opportunities and threats and that they develop and implement strategies on a regional basis, and that the key organizational mechanism by which the multinational develops and implements regional strategies is through the regional headquarters.

REGIONALIZATION AND RESEARCH ASSUMPTIONS

Traditional international marketing researchers have implicitly or explicitly assumed that MNCs have a decision-making model as shown in Figure 4.1. All strategic decisions, such as those concerning market entry, are made at the global headquarters (GHQ) level and country managers implement them. The assumption is that there is no intermediary between the GHQ and the subsidiaries, that the country operations are strictly independent of each other, and that there is no sharing of resources or capabilities between countries.

Figure 4.2 depicts the decision-making model in a typical regionalized MNC. Although there could be many variants of this model, it captures the essential features of a regionalized MNC. Many strategic and operational decisions affecting the country operations could be made by the RHQ (or made by individuals and subsidiaries charged with relevant regional responsibilities). In many cases, the country operations could have a direct reporting relationship with the RHQ. The RHQ's role is often to coordinate country operations and encourage their integration through standardization of strategies and operating policies, and through the sharing of resources. In this model, the country may not have an independent, standalone status.

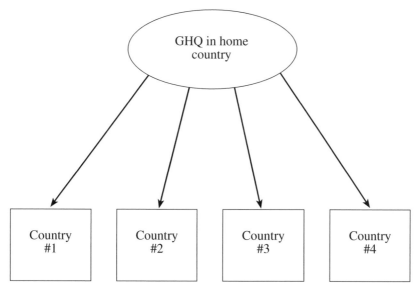

Figure 4.1   Decision making model assumed by entry mode researchers

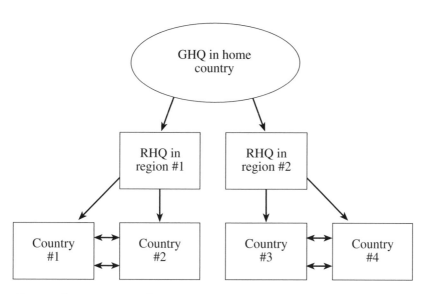

Figure 4.2   Decision making model in typical regionalized MNC

86				*Introduction*

The manner in which regionalization in MNCs affects three traditional assumptions made explicitly or implicitly by IM researchers is discussed in greater detail below. Later, some empirical evidence is presented to support some of these notions.

The Supremacy of the Global Headquarters (GHQ)

Most IM researchers unquestioningly accept the supremacy of the GHQ, typically located in the MNC's home country, in making strategic and, even, operational decisions. For example, a review of the entry mode literature reveals that there is an implicit or explicit assumption that all of the strategic decisions concerning market selection and market entry are made at the global headquarters of the multinational company. This is the reason researchers tend to survey or interview senior managers in the GHQ in their studies. But the trends toward regionalization imply that many strategic and operational decisions studied by researchers may be undertaken at the RHQ, not the GHQ. The GHQ may be involved in the establishment of region-wide priorities and resource allocation decisions, and may also reserve the right to approve all major decisions, but the actual decisions may be made by the RHQ or executives engaged in regional responsibilities. The GHQ may no longer be supreme in this respect. If this is the case, one must raise the following questions. Are GHQ-based managers directly and

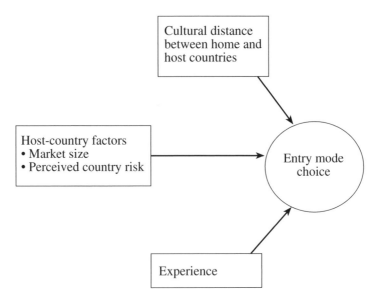

Figure 4.3   Effects need to be re-examined

fully involved in decisions concerning entry strategy into specific country markets? Do they fully understand the reality at the ground level in the region and countries? Are they aware of all the location-specific influences on these decisions? Negative answers to these questions will naturally raise concerns about the validity of data collected at the GHQ.

The Supremacy of the Host Country

Decisions made by multinationals in one host country are assumed to be independent of their decisions made in another country. Researchers tend to view host countries as being independent of each other. This explains why empirical studies typically examine influence of country-specific factors such as GDP, country risk and culture. Rarely do they consider the interdependence among a set of host countries. But regional integration means that decisions affecting countries are no longer taken independently on a stand-alone basis (Schutte 1997; Lassere 1996). If the RHQ is involved in the decisions, there is a tendency to look at the opportunities and threats on a regional scale, and to exploit host-country interdependencies. Companies will distribute their functional activities around the region and integrate them to achieve efficiencies. Entry decisions and sourcing decisions are assumed to be mutually exclusive. But regionalized companies may not differentiate between the two. The company may establish operations in a certain country in the region to serve not only the customers in that country but also the customers in the region. So researchers have to be cognizant of the fact that many of the decisions studied may be influenced by regional factors, rather than country-specific variables.

The Supremacy of the Subsidiary

Each subsidiary is assumed to be independently self-sufficient in its resources and capabilities, save for those transferred from the parent company, i.e. from the GHQ. Rarely do international marketing researchers assume the possibility that a given subsidiary may be receiving resources and capabilities from subsidiaries in the region, and contributing resources and capabilities to them. In regionalized companies, there may be extensive sharing of resources and capabilities across countries in the region (Lassere 1996).

EMPIRICAL EVIDENCE

To better understand the role played by RHQs, the author and his associates recently undertook a survey of MNC RHQs based in Singapore.

Singapore and Hong Kong are the most important locations for the HQs in the Asia Pacific. These RHQs belong to US, European and Japanese multinationals.

A total of 190 RHQs participated in the study. Table 4.1 describes the relative importance of roles played by the RHQ. These roles roughly correspond to the ones described by Lassere (1996). As can be seen, the primary reason for establishing an RHQ is to more effectively respond to local customer needs. The 'localization' motive comes through quite strongly. For many companies, the RHQ also plays a strong entrepreneurial role: scouting opportunities, stimulating growth and signaling commitment to the region. For others, the integrative role is more important: coordinating operations and resource sharing.

Table 4.2 describes the extent to which companies enjoy autonomy from the GHQ, and the extent to which they influence country operations in the region. The RHQs in the sample seem to enjoy considerable autonomy and influence for both strategic and operational decisions. Also, there is evidence of a fairly high degree of integration with a majority of the companies agreeing that they tend to follow standard operating policies and procedures in the region and that there is considerable sharing of resources and capabilities between country operations in the region.

Table 4.3 further highlights the interdependence of countries in the region. The data show the percentage of companies serving a particular country market exporting to it from another country in the region. For example, about 11 per cent of all companies serving Australia are exporting to it from their operations located in another country within the region. However, more than 54 per cent of the companies serving Cambodia follow this strategy. The data show a remarkable pattern. The importance of such regional export-mode grows as the host country becomes smaller and less developed. It appears that MNCs in the sample are using at least some of the subsidiaries in the region to serve not only the local country market but also smaller regional markets.

These findings provide further evidence that a great deal of decision making in multinationals is occurring at the regional level, that country operations within a region are not independent of each other and that there is considerable integration within the region.

RE-EXAMINING SOME EFFECTS

The above discussion raises questions about the validity of the traditional assumptions made by international marketing researchers. If these assumptions do not hold, then is it not necessary to revisit the findings

Table 4.1 Role of RHQs when established

Role of RHQ	When the RHQ was established, how *important* was this role?			
	Mean importance (1 = Not important; 4 = Critically important)	Saying somewhat important (%)	Saying highly important (%)	Saying critically important (%)
To respond to customer needs in the region more effectively	3.44	6.3	39.7	51.9
To stimulate the growth of existing and new regional markets for your company's products and services	3.32	10.1	45.7	43.6
To coordinate regional operations more effectively	3.31	7.9	41.9	46.6
To gather market intelligence and scout for new business opportunities	3.14	14.8	52.9	31.2
To signal the commitment of your company to the region	2.93	18.5	48.1	25.9
To share resources and best practices across countries in the region	2.80	17.6	52.7	19.1

Note:
n = 190.
(1 = Not important, 2 = Somewhat important, 3 = Highly important, 4 = Critically important).

Source: M. Krishna Erramilli, Benjamin Tan and Benjamin Kartono (2001), 'Regional Headquarters of MNCs Based in Singapore', Unpublished Study.

Table 4.2 Autonomy and influence of RHQs

Statement	Mean	Agree or strongly agree with statement (%)
1. The RHQ enjoys substantial autonomy from the global headquarters (GHQ) to make all major *strategic* decisions pertaining to the region (at least within the scope of its mandate)	3.49	61.6
2. The RHQ enjoys substantial autonomy from the GHQ to make all major *tactical or operational* decisions pertaining to the region (at least within the scope of its mandate)	4.02	86.8
3. The RHQ exerts substantial influence on the countries in the region on all major *strategic* decisions made at the country level	4.01	80.6
4. The RHQ exerts substantial influence on the countries in the region on all major *tactical or operational* decisions made at the country level	3.89	75.3
5. We follow a fairly standard set of operating procedures for all our operations in the region	3.74	75.3
6. There is a great deal of sharing of information and resources among our operations across the countries in the region	3.95	81.7

Note:
$n = 190$.
(1 = Strongly disagree, 2 = Disagree, 3 = Neither agree nor disagree, 4 = Agree, 5 = Strongly agree).

Source: M. Krishna Erramilli, Benjamin Tan and Benjamin Kartono (2001), 'Regional Headquarters of MNCs Based in Singapore', Unpublished Study.

Table 4.3   *Companies serving Asia-Pacific countries through exports from the region*

Country	Companies serving this country saying they export to it from another country in the region (%)
Australia	11.2
China	12.8
South Korea	13.6
Japan	15.7
Hong Kong	16.0
Taiwan	17.5
Malaysia	18.0
North Korea	18.2
New Zealand	19.3
India	19.4
Thailand	21.2
Indonesia	27.0
Philippines	27.1
Vietnam	34.6
Pakistan	37.7
Brunei	43.6
Bangladesh	43.9
Sri Lanka	44.6
Laos	47.1
Myanmar	49.2
Cambodia	54.1

Note: $n = 190$.

Source: M. Krishna Erramilli, Benjamin Tan, and Benjamin Kartono (2001), 'Regional Headquarters of MNCs Based in Singapore', Unpublished Study.

generated by research based on these assumptions? In the entry-mode literature, the following effects have traditionally been considered to have significant impact on modal choice. However, now they may need to be examined through a new lens.

Cultural Distance between Home and Host Countries

Traditional entry-mode literature holds that firms minimize the high information costs associated with operating in culturally unfamiliar countries by seeking collaborative entry modes (Gatignon and Anderson 1988; Agarwal 1994). When the cultural distance between home and host countries is high, typically measured using Hofstede's cultural indices (see, for example, Kogut and Singh 1988; Erramilli and Rao 1993), entrants are expected to choose shared-control modes, like joint ventures. Will this hold when the MNC is regionalized? First of all, the decisions for entry-mode choice may be made at the RHQ level. Decision makers at the RHQ level are likely to be closer to the markets and, therefore, possess far greater information on local country markets than the ones in the GHQ. As such, the information costs associated with entering and operating in these countries are not likely to be high. The cultural distance between the home and host countries, as captured in these measures, is unlikely to accurately represent these information costs. Intriguingly, many of the recent studies have reported uncertain cultural distance effects (Brouthers and Brouthers 2001).

Host-country Characteristics

Many studies have highlighted the role of country risk on modal choice (Gatignon and Anderson 1988; Agarwal and Ramaswami 1992). Country risk is usually interpreted in terms of uncertainty and instability in the country of entry. High country risk could lead to a reduction in the firm's resource commitments to that market, resulting in the use of lower-control, low-resource modes (Root 1994; Gatignon and Anderson 1988). But perceptions of country risk are exacerbated by lack of market familiarity. The more a decision maker knows about a certain market, the more he/she is confident in assessing the true level of risks. When a company is contemplating entry into Indonesia, the decision maker in the GHQ, located say in New York, is likely to perceive a great deal more uncertainty than the one in the RHQ located in neighboring Singapore. Therefore, when decision making is delegated to RHQs, the impact of country risk on resource commitments in the host market might not be as strong as it might be if the decisions were undertaken at the GHQ.

Market size of the host country is another commonly used variable in entry-mode studies. This is typically measured using GDP or per capita GDP, in addition to perceptual measures. The larger the size of the host country, the greater is the likelihood of firms establishing high-control, high-investment modes (Root 1994). However, in regionalized multinationals, the entry into a particular country may not necessarily be to serve that market alone. Often, firms think about regional needs as well. Frequently subsidiaries not only serve the local market, they also act as a sourcing point for the company's regional operations. For example, a major chemical manufacturer set up a manufacturing subsidiary in Singapore to serve the entire Asia-Pacific market. Given this situation, resource commitments may not necessarily correlate strongly with the local market size. This discussion suggests that country-specific influences may be weaker than expected in regionalized MNCs.

Experience Effects

Country-specific experience is seen as an important determinant. This experience generates country-specific knowledge, which in turn reduces information costs and uncertainty of dealing with the host market. Higher experience results in companies being more aggressive in their resource commitment decisions. But country-specific experience may have less impact when such market knowledge can be generated through transfer of expertise from similar countries in the region. For example, many Western firms entering China are able to jumpstart their operations by transferring key people and capabilities from their operations in Hong Kong, Taiwan or Singapore. Thus, even certain experience effects may be weaker in regionally oriented companies.

RESEARCH IN A REGIONALIZED WORLD: RECOMMENDATIONS

Researchers studying regionalized multinationals need to carefully understand where the decision-making locus is in the companies they are studying. For many international marketing decisions, the executives in the RHQ could be a more appropriate audience than executives in the GHQ, partly because they may be directly involved in making those decisions and partly because they are closer to the ground and are able to relate to the decision-making dynamics even if they did not make those decisions. Daniels (1986, 1987) and Sullivan (1992) study many international marketing and management issues using samples of European regional offices of American MNCs.

If decision makers in the region appear to be the ones making decisions then one must question approaches that estimate the firm's familiarity with the host-country culture using measures like cultural distance between home and host countries. Even the cultural distance between the country where the RHQ is located and the host country may not be an accurate measure. RHQ managers are charged with the responsibility of understanding local markets. Consequently, they are not likely to perceive the type of uncertainty envisaged in the traditional decision-making models. If it is necessary to measure cultural familiarity, self-reported perceptual measures provided by the key decision makers in the RHQ may be more effective than the cultural distance measures based on indices like Hoftsede's.

Researchers studying marketing mix standardization decisions could focus on regional standardization and adaptation, rather than global. This is actually essential in regionalized MNCs where marketing functions tend to be centralized regionally. The regional marketing executive is probably a much better candidate to interview than a global one. The regional executives tend to understand the local conditions, regional conditions and global conditions a lot more effectively than local or global managers within a company. Sullivan (1992) writes: 'The view from the RHQ is theoretically ideal because its mission is to manage the tension between headquarters' call for global efficiency and local subsidiaries' push for national effectiveness' (p. 238).

Researchers have traditionally employed theoretical frameworks that emphasize the influence of the firm's ownership advantages, resources and capabilities on international marketing decisions, particularly on entry-mode choice (Agarwal and Ramaswami 1992; Madhok 1997; Erramilli et al. 2002). Often, the focus of these studies has been to analyze the firm-specific endowments of the parent firm and their transfer to local country-based operations. The emergence of regionalized multinationals has meant that important capabilities are being developed in regional headquarters or regionally oriented subsidiaries and are being actively shared and transferred within the region. Besides, the mandates of the RHQ may include the facilitation of country-to-country transfer of capabilities. Therefore, researchers can no longer assume that subsidiaries in new countries start from ground zero. Studies should aim to measure the capability transfer from other subsidiaries as well.

Finally, researchers need to be cautious when making assumptions about the host-country operations. In entry-mode investigations, one should not automatically assume that the subsidiary has been set up to serve the local market alone, and that it does not have a regional sourcing responsibility. If one is studying subsidiaries in a regionalized MNC, it may be insightful to first understand its role: country versus regional. The more important the subsidiary's regional role is, the weaker the country-specific influences tend to be in determining the modal choice. In subsidiaries established to fulfill regional responsibilities, the size of the region is probably a better predictor of resource commitments than size of an individual country market. Similarly, country risk may be less important than the risk pertaining to an entire region.

CONCLUSION

Mounting evidence suggests that multinationals are adopting a regiocentric approach to developing and implementing international marketing strategy. In regionalized MNCs, many strategic decisions are undertaken at the regional level by regional managers who are thoroughly grounded in regional reality. This trend has necessitated the re-examination of traditional assumptions made by international marketing researchers. It has also necessitated a re-examination of well-established research findings through a fresh regional lens. It is critical for international marketing scholars to be sensitive to the regionalization of international marketing strategy within multinationals and adapt their studies appropriately. As multinationals continue to evolve, this represents another daunting, yet interesting, challenge to international marketing researchers.

REFERENCES

Agarwal, Sanjeev (1994), 'Socio-Cultural Distance and the Choice of Joint Ventures: A Contingency Perspective', *Journal of International Marketing*, **2** (2), 63–80.
Agarwal, Sanjeev and Sridhar N. Ramaswami (1992), 'Choice of Foreign Market Entry Mode: Impact of Ownership, Location, and Internalization Factors', *Journal of International Business Studies*, **23** (First Quarter), 1–27.
Anderson, Erin and Hubert Gatignon (1986), 'Modes of Foreign Entry: A Transaction Cost Analysis and Propositions', *Journal of International Business Studies*, **17** (Fall), 1–26.
Brouthers, Keith D. and Lance Eliot Brouthers (2001), 'Explaining the National Cultural Distance Paradox', *Journal of International Business Studies*, **32** (1), 177–89.
Daniels, J.D. (1986), 'Approaches to European Regional Management by Large U.S. Multinational Firms', *Management International Review*, **26** (2), 27–42.
Daniels, J.D. (1987), 'Bridging National and Global Marketing Strategies Through Regional Operations', *International Marketing Review*, **4** (3), 29–45.
Emmerij, Louis (1992), 'Globalization, Regionalization and World Trade', *Columbia Journal of World Business*, Summer, 6–13.
Erramilli, M. Krishna and C.P. Rao (1993), 'Service Firms' International Entry Mode-Choice: A Modified Transaction-Cost Analysis Approach', *Journal of Marketing*, **57** (July), 19–38.
Erramilli, M. Krishna, Sanjeev Agarwal and Chekitan Dev (2002), 'Explaining Choice Between Non-Equity Entry Modes: An Organizational Capability Perspective', *Journal of International Business Studies*, **33** (2), 223–42.
Gatignon, Hubert and Erin Anderson (1988), 'The Multinational Corporations' Degree of Control Over Foreign Subsidiaries: An Empirical Test of a Transaction Cost Explanation', *Journal of Law, Economics and Organization*, **4** (2), 305–36.
Heenan, D.A. and Howard V. Perlmutter (1979), *Multinational Organizational Development: A Social Architecture Perspective*, Reading, MA: Addison-Wesley.
Johnson, H. (1991), *Dispelling The Myth Of Globalization: The Case For Regionalization*, New York: Praeger.
Kogut, Bruce and H. Singh (1988), 'The Effect of National Culture on the Choice

of Entry Mode', *Journal of International Business Studies*, **19** (3), 411–32.

Lassere, Philippe (1996), 'Regional Headquarters: The Spearhead for Asia Pacific Markets', *Long Range Planning*, **29** (1), 30–37.

Lehrer, Mark and Kazuhiro Asakawa (1999), 'Unbundling European Operations: Regional Management and Corporate Flexibility in American and Japanese MNCs', *Journal of World Business*, **34** (3), 267–86.

Madhok, Anoop (1997), 'Cost, Value and Foreign Market Entry Mode: The Transaction and the Firm', *Strategic Management Journal*, **18**, 39–61.

Morrison, Allen J., David A. Ricks and Kendall Roth (1991), 'Globalization Versus Regionalization: Which Way for the Multinational', *Organizational Dynamics*, **19** (3), 17–29.

Perlmutter, Howard V. (1969), 'Tortuous Evolution of the Multinational Corporation', *Columbia Journal of World Business*, **4** (1), 9–18.

Root, Franklin R. (1994), *Entry Strategies for International Markets*, New York: Lexington Books.

Rugman, Alan (2001), *The End of Globalization: Why Global Strategy is a Myth and How to Profit from the Realities of Regional Markets*, New York: AMACOM.

Schutte, Helmut (1997), 'Strategy and Organization: Challenges for European MNCs in Asia', *European Management Journal*, **15** (4), 436–45.

Siddiqi, Shahid (2000), 'Customizing Core Competencies: The Regional Challenge', *International Journal of Commerce and Management*, **10** (1), 91–104.

Sullivan, Daniel (1992), 'Organization in American MNCs: The Perspective of the European Regional Headquarters', *Management International Review*, **32** (3), 237–50.

PART II

Entry strategy

5. Managerial preferences for strategic alliance attributes: some global contrasts

David B. Montgomery and Allen M. Weiss

INTRODUCTION

In recent years there has been a dramatic increase in the number of strategic alliances between organizations. These alliances represent new forms of cooperative relationships between firms in different industries and countries. The growth in alliance activity has been fueled, in part, by technological advances, deregulation, globalization, and other similar changes that dominate the present business environment (SRI 1986). As a consequence, the competitive landscape for many industries is rapidly changing as firms reposition themselves with the alliance mechanism.

The relevance of strategic alliances to marketers is demonstrated in a survey of executive views on the relative importance of 16 aspects of global marketing issues in the 1990s (Kosnik 1991). Kosnik reports that building alliances is the fifth most important issue from the perspective of US and European managers.[1] Although these data suggest a perception of importance of alliances in the 1990s by US executives, other data suggest that there is substantial concern about them. Tyebjee (1989) reports a late 1980s study that found that one-third of US CEOs believed that strategic alliances are dangerous in contrast to only four per cent of Japanese CEOs who were surveyed. In addition, three quarters of the Japanese CEOs regarded strategic alliances as an effective means of doing business whereas only 17 per cent of the US CEOs were like-minded. These surveys suggest that strategic alliances are both an area of concern and ambivalence and that executives from different countries and cultures see them quite differently.

In an attempt to better understand how different firms may view strategic alliances, there has been a great deal of writing on the subject (e.g. Harrigan 1985, 1986). Some of this work suggests broad theoretical approaches to explaining the strategic alliance phenomenon (e.g. Borys and

Jemison 1989). However, much of the literature is highly descriptive in nature, providing mostly 'war stories' and new buzz words. In this research, we empirically investigate the nature of strategic alliances by way of the following four questions: (1) Which characteristics (i.e. attributes) are most important to managers when making strategic alliances decisions? (2) Are there any differences between US managers and non-US managers in terms of what attributes are most important to them? (3) Are there any differences between firms with different strategic orientations in terms of what attributes are most important to them? (4) Are there groups of managers who share similar alliance preferences and who differ from other groups of managers in terms of these preferences (i.e. can preference segments of managers be identified)?

By focusing on managerial preferences for strategic alliance characteristics we contribute to the current literature in several ways. First, several conventional conjectures exist about how managers view strategic alliances and our data suggest to what extent these views are actually held. Second, by documenting preferences held by managers, we also provide an empirical foundation for theoretical explanations of any systematic differences that may exist. Furthermore, to the degree that extant normative theory posits how managers should 'weight' various dimensions of these alliances when making decisions, our data provide some preliminary evidence of the extent of correspondence or deviation from these normative prescriptions. Finally, our data reveal managerial implications for locating and negotiating with alliance partners.

BACKGROUND

Our perspective begins with the assumption that a firm intends to enter into a strategic alliance and asks: how do managers make tradeoffs among the various characteristics of these agreements and what attributes have priority? There are several characteristics of strategic alliances over which managers may have *preferences* and various authors have suggested, both descriptively and normatively, the most important. Indeed, the presumed importance of these characteristics reflects some of the conventional wisdom about the strategic alliance phenomenon. Since there is little consensus in the prior literature as to what are the most important attributes, we focused our attention on the dimensions discussed below. This choice was corroborated by extensive discussions with several executives experienced in making strategic alliance decisions.

Complementary Resources

To begin, most writers characterize strategic alliances as a means for a firm to acquire complementary resources. Broadly speaking, in terms of strategic alliances, resources can take many forms, including marketing and distribution, research and development, operations, and/or finance. Moreover, there can be inter (e.g. an exchange of capital for marketing/distribution) and intra (e.g. exchanges of marketing/distribution in one country for marketing/distribution in another country) functional exchanges of complementary resources. Exchanging complementary resources provides many potential benefits to the firm including access to market information, synergies due to resource pooling, lowered costs of production, and other strategic advantages (Harrigan 1986; Nielsen 1987). Indeed, a strict economic logic for strategic alliances would posit that they exist for purposes of exploiting the complementarities of the partners' resources. Accordingly, we might expect that the acquisition of complementary resources is a key dimension of managerial preferences towards strategic alliances.

Home Area of Partner

The emergence of global partnerships is another theme that pervades the popular literature on strategic alliances (e.g. Ohmae 1989; Kobayashi 1988; Tyebjee 1988). Reflecting the importance of this topic, entire issues of various journals (e.g. *Columbia Journal of World Business* 1987) have been devoted to the issue of international corporate linkages. Ohmae (1989) states that globalization 'mandates alliances'. But to what extent, if any, do practicing managers actually place a value on linking up with a global partner, and do they have distinct preferences for the geographic location of such a partner? Conversely, is there executive preference for partners from the responding manager's own region?[2] That is, do Americans prefer Americans, Europeans prefer Europeans, etc? In particular, there appears to be a sense that while there are examples of successful alliances between American and Japanese firms, there may be some growing hesitancy of American managers to ally themselves with Japanese firms, perhaps because this allows American technological leadership to flow into the hands of Japanese firms. Same region preference might result from lower perceived risk (better the devil you know), easier communication due to common language and culture, or ease of coordination resulting from proximity in both geography and time zone. Thus, we might anticipate that the home area of the partner is an important dimension in the strategic alliance decision.

Entry strategy

Time Frame of the Relationship

Next, by their very nature strategic alliances represent longer-term relationships than the 'discrete exchanges', which characterize classical interfirm
structures. But the concept of time is quite general and firms may differ substantially on what constitutes a long time horizon. This may have profound
consequences for the nature of the alliance since goal congruence can be
manifest in terms of similarity of desired outcomes or attitudes towards the
business (e.g. *when* profits should be realized or *how long* investment in a joint
research project should be made before product launch, etc.). As such, the
time frame of the relationship represents one domain of compatibility. We
would therefore expect this to be an important dimension of the strategic
alliance decision. This is a particular concern for global partners in that firms
from different countries are more prone to have vastly different corporate
cultures and thus a different perspective on the importance of long-term relationships. For example, a common wisdom among industry observers is that
the culture of American firms may be quite incompatible with firms in other
countries in terms of their expectations about the length of the relationship;
that is, it is suspected that American managers use a relatively shorter time
frame when considering these relationships.

Partner Competitiveness

Recently, the notion of strategic allinces between competitors has attracted
attention, fueled by the observation that several alliances are beginning to
take place in businesses and regions where both partners compete (e.g.
General Motors and Toyota compete on the US market and yet share the
NUMMI facility in Fremont, California) (Doz, Hamel and Prahalad 1986).
Typically, these are instances of collaboration between large technology-
intensive competing firms. Such agreements between competitors have been
touted as characteristic of 'new strategic partnerships' that allow firms to
co-opt a competitor or block potential competitors in a market (Contractor
and Lorange 1988). However, since strategic alliances imply a sharing of
know-how and skills, respondents would seem likely to be concerned about
the extent to which the firm is competitive with a potential partner. For
example, alliances between competitors often fail because firms cannot persuade their employees to cooperate with the competition (SRI 1986; Tyebjee
1989). Do managers involved with the strategic alliance decision maintain
such a perspective on working with the 'enemy'? Perhaps they are more
inclined to work with competitors if they come from a different geographic
region. Whatever, the degree of partner competitiveness may be a key attribute in the alliance decision.

Equity Stake

A firm's equity stake typically indicates the residual claimant status of alliance profits. In some cases, the equity stake also indicates a partner's degree of control of the alliance activities (procedures, decision making, etc.). Some industry observers (e.g. SRI 1986) assert that the degree of equity participation is decreasing in importance to firms. This may be the case; however, the authors know of no systematic empirical evidence to support this claim.

In summary, strategic alliances can be characterized by several attributes, some of which have been discussed at length in the prior literature (e.g. what resources the partner will give me that I don't have already) and some which are gaining in presumed importance (e.g. the home area of the partner). What we don't know is how managers prioritize these attributes and whether there are any systematic differences that can be attributable to characteristics of the manager or his/her firm (e.g. geographic location, strategic focus). In the next section, we present a method that is capable of providing some insights on these issues.

METHOD

The methodology we used to calibrate executive preferences for selected aspects of strategic alliances is conjoint analysis. The method is designed to decompose a multiattributed situation into constituent attributes. Each attribute may take on one of several levels. The method presents a respondent with a series of rank order choices and then seeks to construct a set of part worth utilities (a utility score for each level of each included attribute) which will best reproduce the respondent's actual rank order choices. These part worth utilities may then be used to assess the relative importance of these attributes to a respondent and to predict how a respondent might choose among a set of alternative combinations of levels of these attributes. Thus, it is a particularly powerful methodology for investigating the relative importance (i.e. preference) of various attributes of strategic alliances as perceived by decision makers. In marketing, conjoint analysis has been widely used for such purposes as understanding the importance of various aspects of products and services to customers, formation of preference segments (i.e. customer segments based upon commonality in preferences), and predicting the choice share which might be obtained by design options or competitive and strategic alternatives.[3] The ability of conjoint utilities to predict market choice, although not perfect, has been found to be statistically significant and substantial. For further discussion of applications, methodology, and validity of conjoint analysis, see Montgomery (1985) and Green and Srinivasan (1990).

Research Instrument

The first phase of our research involved developing and personally pre-testing a preliminary version of our research instrument to a large sample of executives knowledgeable about strategic alliances. Based on this, a revised research instrument was developed. In this final version, we asked each respondent to choose as their focus a business unit which will most likely be involved in a strategic alliance in the future. All further questions were to be answered in the context of this specific business unit. The perspective was to be relative to a prospective future strategic alliance rather than one in which the firm currently participates. Based on our pre-test it was determined that knowledge of the idiosyncrasies of a current alliance was deemed likely to make response to the research instrument more difficult, and hence the prospective orientation.

The strategic alliance attributes and levels which were chosen for this study, based on the discussion in the previous section and our pre-test, are presented in Table 5.1. The first two reflect attributes defining what a respondent prefers to receive from and give to an alliance. The levels are: (a) marketing/distribution, (b) R&D/technology, (c) manufacturing/operations, and (d) capital. These 'receive and give' attributes should provide some insight into the complementarity issue at the level of interfunctional complementarity (e.g. between marketing and technology). To be certain, firms may also desire intrafunctional complementarity such as when firms provide reciprocal market access to different regions of the globe or when firms contribute complementary technologies to an alliance. We should get insight into this form of complementarity also. In order to see if potential partners from different global regions might be preferred to those from another, the third attribute included was the home area of the potential partner (i.e. partners based in non-triad areas as well as the three triad areas of North America, Europe, and Japan). To calibrate the degree to which respondents are concerned about the extent to which the firm is competitive with a potential partner, a partner competitiveness attribute was incorporated. The levels of this attribute relate to the degree of competitive overlap between the firm and a potential partner. Since there has been much discussion of a US executive focus on the short term at the expense of the long term, the anticipated time frame of the alliance was included in order to examine the extent to which executives differed in their preferences for participation in the alliance was included.

Respondents were asked to provide their rank order preferences for com-

Table 5.1   Attributes and levels

---

1. Partner's main contribution
   The partner's main contribution to the alliance is:
   a. Marketing/Distribution
   b. Research & Development/Technology
   c. Manufacturing/Operations
   d. Capital

2. My firm's main contribution
   My firm's main contribution to the alliance is:
   a. Marketing/Distribution
   b. Research & Development/Technology
   c. Manufacturing/Operations
   d. Capital

3. Home area of partner
   The partner is headquartered in:
   a. USA/Canada
   b. Europe
   c. Japan
   d. Other

4. Partner competitiveness with my firm
   The amount of overlap between my firm's product lines and markets in this business and those of the partner is:
   a. High (significant degree of overlap, as between direct competitors)
   b. Moderate (moderate degree of overlap, as between firms in related industries)
   c. Low (little overlap, as between firms in unrelated industries)

5. Time frame
   The partners will be bound by the relationship for:
   a. Less than 4 years
   b. 4 to 7 years
   c. More than 7 years

6. My firm's equity
   The amount of equity my firm holds in the strategic alliance is:
   a. None (my firm holds no equity in the alliance)
   b. Minority (my firm holds a minority stake in the alliance)
   c. Equal (my firm holds an equal stake in the alliance with our partner)
   d. Majority (my firm holds a majority stake in the alliance)

---

binations of levels of strategic alliance attributes taken two a time.[4] With six attributes, a total of 15, two at a time tradeoff tables is possible. In order to reduce respondent fatigue and enhance cooperation, a subset of nine tables was presented to each respondent. The attribute tables were chosen such that for any two attributes which are not directly ranked in a tradeoff table (e.g. attributes 1 and 3), they shared three common attributes to which they both were directly compared (e.g. attributes 1 and 3 were both directly compared to attributes 2, 4, and 6). This redundant overlap procedure allows reduction in the total respondent task while providing substantial latitude for the respondent to express his/her preferences.

In addition to the tradeoff tables respondents were also asked several questions relating to themselves, the business unit chosen for the conjoint task, and their experience with the questionnaire. These will be addressed in subsequent discussion.

Respondents

The sample consisted of 184 senior executives who participated in a series of executive education programs conducted at a major university. The average age was just under 44 and on average respondents reported personal involvement in 4.5 alliances. Respondents were asked to use one to seven scales (e.g. 1 = none, 7 = a great deal) to rate their personal experience working with strategic alliances (average = 3.6), how knowledgeable they are about alliances at their firm (average = 4.6), and how involved they are with alliances at their firm (average = 4.7). Thus, this executive group seems fairly experienced and knowledgeable about strategic alliances.

Their firms were substantial (mean = US$6.4 billion, median = US$1.0 billion) and had been very active in strategic alliances having participated in an average of just over 14 strategic alliances. Fifty-four per cent serve consumers, 75 per cent serve industry, 75 per cent market products, 66 per cent offer services, and 55 per cent are involved in a high-technology industry (note that the percentages add to more than 100 per cent since firms may be involved in more than one of these categories).

The questionnaire was administrated in printed form early in an executive program. The respondents were promised prior to the end of the program an analysis of their results in comparison to their peer group and a copy of subsequent analysis. Respondents reported that the questionnaire required an average of 30 minutes to complete.

The respondents thus were senior executives of substantial companies which on average have extensive involvement in strategic alliances. The respondents themselves report substantial personal experience, knowledge, and involvement in strategic alliances.

AGGREGATE ALLIANCE PREFERENCES

Aggregate Sample Results

From each executive's tradeoff rankings, LINMAP IV (Srinivasan and Shocker 1981) was utilized to compute a part worth utility for each level of each alliance attribute. Relative attribute importance weights were then derived from the raw part worth utilities. For each respondent, the raw importance weight for each attribute was taken as the difference between the highest and lowest part worth utility for that attribute. For example, if for a given respondent the highest utility for 'partner competitiveness' was 6.37 and the lowest was -8.99 for 'low competitiveness' and 'high competitiveness', respectively, then the raw importance weight of the attribute 'partner competitiveness' for that respondent would be $6.37 - (-8.99) = 15.36$. For each respondent, the importance weights are normalized to sum to 1.00 by dividing the respondent's raw importance weight for each attribute by the sum of that respondent's importance weights. These normalized attribute importance weights are then averaged across all respondents and the results reported in Table 5.2 along with the standard error of the mean importance weight and the standard deviation of the importance weight across all respondents.

If each of the six attributes were equally important to the respondents, then they would each have an importance weight equal to the mean importance weight across all attributes ($1/6 = 0.167$). Two of the importance weights, 'home area of the partner' and 'my firm's equity' have importance weights significantly above the mean at the 0.01 level of significance. One attribute, 'time frame', had an importance weight significantly below the

Table 5.2   Attribute importance aggregate sample

Attribute	Mean	Std. Error of Mean	Std. Dev. Across Rs
Home Area of Partner	0.29*	0.03	(0.35)
My Firm's Equity	0.25*	0.02	(0.33)
My Firm's Contribution	0.16	0.02	(0.26)
Partner's Main Contribution	0.14	0.02	(0.23)
Partner's Competitiveness	0.14	0.02	(0.27)
Time Frame	0.03**	0.01	(0.09)

Notes: *Significantly above average attribute importance, $p < 0.01$; **Significantly below average attribute importance, $p < 0.01$.

Table 5.3   Aggregate part worths

	Mean	Std. Dev.
1. Partner's main contribution		
a. Marketing/Distribution	4.05	(19.98)
b. Research & Development/Technology	3.48	(16.92)
c. Manufacturing/Operations	0.44	(14.96)
d. Capital	−7.97	(22.21)
2. My firm's main contribution		
a. Marketing/Distribution	5.88	(18.72)
b. Research & Development/Technology	1.94	(19.55)
c. Manufacturing/Operations	2.34	(17.12)
d. Capital	−10.17	(23.86)
3. Home area of partner		
a. USA/Canada	7.22	(27.57)
b. Europe	5.25	(22.60)
c. Japan	−1.24	(22.42)
d. Other	−11.23	(31.06)
4. Partner competitiveness with my firm		
a. High (significant degree of overlap)	−8.99	(21.94)
b. Moderate (moderate degree of overlap)	2.62	(11.72)
c. Low (little overlap)	6.37	(17.65)
5. Time frame		
a. Less than 4 years	−0.33	(10.06)
b. 4 to 7 years	1.10	(6.61)
c. More than 7 years	−0.77	(8.62)
6. My firm's equity		
a. None	−12.26	(34.14)
b. Minority	2.06	(16.89)
c. Equal	5.81	(17.99)
d. Majority	4.39	(22.71)

mean at the 0.01 level.[5] Each of the attribute importances and the corresponding part worth utilities for the attribute levels will be discussed below with the latter part worth utilities presented in Table 5.3.

'Home area of partner' was found to be the most important attribute. USA/Canada was the most preferred partner, followed closely by European headquartered partners. Japan was less preferred than USA/Canada and Europe, but it was much closer in preference to the USA/Canada and Europe than it was to partners outside the triad areas. Fifty-four per cent of the total utility of the 'home area of partner' is garnered just by being located within the triad.[6] Thus it appears that the triad of North America, Europe, and Japan are the preferred areas in which to seek an alliance.

A close second in importance, and also significantly above the equal weighting mean, was the 'my firm's equity' attribute. The aggregate part worths in Table 5.3 show that 'no equity' is by far the least preferred position. Among the equity positions equal equity is somewhat more preferred than a majority position which in turn is understandably somewhat more preferred than a minority position. The slight preference for equal over majority equity position may reflect a preference for equal incentive for partnership contributions on behalf of both partners versus the perception of control that majority equity might confer.

The third most important attribute was 'my firm's contribution'. The part worth utilities indicate a substantial preference to contribute marketing/distribution. There was a lesser desire to contribute manufacturing/operations and R&D/technology. By far the least preferred was the contribution of capital. Given the results for 'equity' and 'my contribution' it would appear that for the most part the respondents want an equity position, but want to obtain that equity by contributing something other than money to the alliance.

Close in importance was 'partner's main contribution'. Here the part worths suggest that the respondents preferred marketing/distribution and R&D/technology from their partners. There was less desire for partners to provide manufacturing/operations and by far the least preference for partner supplied capital. Perhaps the low preference for partner contributed capital in relation to other functional partner contributions reflects concern with the impact partner supplied capital might have on the more important 'equity' attribute or a concern with obtaining other strategic functional resources or both. Note that inspection of the part worth utilities for capital show that capital supplied by the partner is preferable to firm supplied capital.

Of virtual co-equal importance with the contributions of my firm and the partner is the level of competitiveness the potential partner has with the respondent's firm. Not surprisingly the preference is for little overlap with high competitive overlap the least preferred. However, note that over three-quarters of the utility range is generated between the high and the moderate degree of overlap part worths.

Thus it appears that the respondents have much less trouble considering a partner with moderate competitive overlap than they do with a high level. While the part worth results are in the ranking one would expect, the conjoint analysis has allowed a *more specific calibration* of the levels of this attribute.

Finally, the only attribute which was significantly less than the equal weighting mean was 'time frame'. The results suggest that it is substantially less important in forming preference for strategic alliances than are the other five attributes. There was a preference for four to seven years followed by less than four years and over seven years, hence the time frame scale is not monotonic in executive preferences. Interestingly, in later discussion it will be seen that non-US respondents differ from their US counterparts in their preferences for the anticipated time frame of strategic alliances.

Complementarity in Alliance Preferences

A major area in which complementarity becomes an issue is that of inter- and intrafunctional preferences. In this study the functional business areas examined are marketing/distribution, R&D/technology, manufacturing/operations, and capital. Complementarities in terms of forming an alliance in order to shore up an area of perceived relative weakness might occur both between and within these broad functional areas. For example, a US firm might need access to a foreign market such as Japan and might offer its technology as quid pro quo for a Japanese partner's assistance in gaining Japan market access. To be sure, such exchanges have often had long-term negative consequences for the US firm. Alternatively, alliance partners might exchange complementary resources within a given functional area as the result of a strategic alliance.

If one examines the issue of complementarity at the level of managerial preferences for strategic alliances, as reflected in the part worth utilities for each of the functional areas in both the firm and partner contribution attributes, there is little supporting evidence for either consistent inter- or intrafunctional complementarity. The correlations of the part worth utilities for firm contribution and partner contribution for each of the four functional areas are presented in Table 5.4. Only one correlation is greater than 0.10 in magnitude and significant at any reasonable level and that is the correlation between firm and partner contribution of R&D/technology ($r = 0.20$ @ $p = 0.01$ level). Thus there is some indication that executives who prefer to give R&D/technology also tend to prefer to receive the same from an alliance partner, and vice versa.

Other than this intra functional technology preference, there are no other indications of inter- or intrafunctional complementarity in preferences for functional area involvement in a strategic alliance.

Table 5.4   Partner firm contribution part worth correlations

Partner contribution Part worths	Firm contribution Part worths			
	Mktg/Distn.	R&D/Tech.	Mfgr/Opers.	Capital
Mktg/Distn.	−0.04	−0.1	0.02	0.03
R&D/Tech.	0.02	0.20***	−0.12	−0.09
Mfgr/Opers.	0.06	−0.08	0.04	−0.02
Capital	−0.02	−0.09	0.05	0.05

Note: ***Significant at 0.01 level.

Preference Segments

The attribute importance weights and part worth utilities were found to have substantial variation across respondents as indicated by the standard deviations reported in Tables 5.2 and 5.3. This variation across executives suggests that it might be fruitful to seek to identify groups of executives having similar strategic alliance preferences and to examine how different groups of executives might differ in their preferences. In this section consideration will be given first to a priori segments (i.e. segments based upon data from outside the conjoint analysis) and subsequently to preference clusters based upon clustering together executives having similar part worth utilities.

A Priori Segments

From the ancillary data collected when the conjoint instrument was administered, it is possible to examine certain a priori segments to ascertain whether these groups differ from one another in either importance weights or parts worths. Two such splits are considered in this section: US respondents versus those from elsewhere in the world and those emphasizing global market expansion versus those who place lesser emphasis on global markets.

US vs Non-US Results

In the respondent pool there were 125 executives from the USA and 57 from outside the USA. The non-US executives were from a wide variety of areas: Europe (25), Asia (12 including 5 Japanese), Australia (7), South Africa (6),

South America (3), Canada (2), and other (2). The US firms had more alliances, the chosen business unit had been involved in more alliances, and the US respondents had been involved in more alliances.[7] However, there were no significant differences in attribute importance weights between these two groups. But there were some interesting and statistically significant differences in the part worths of two of the attributes: 'home area of partner' and 'time frame'. These are reported in Table 5.5.

The non-US group has significantly greater preference for European-based partners and significantly less preference for Japanese-based partners than do their US counterparts, both differences significant at the 0.04 level.[8] The contrast between the US and non-US groups in their European and Japanese preferences is stark. For the non-US sample the difference in their preference for Europeans and Japanese comprised 100 per cent of the range of utilities and thereby establishes the importance weight. In contrast, for the US executives, the difference in their utility for Europeans over Japanese is only five per cent of the importance weight of 'home area of partner'. And yet the two groups do not differ significantly on their overall importance weight for this attribute. The US group has greater preference for US partners, but at the marginal 0.09 level of significance. For the non-US group, a preference for a US partner is about halfway between their preference for European versus Japanese partners.

Although the two groups do not differ in the importance of 'time frame', the US respondents have significantly greater preference for less than 4 years and significantly less preference for the longer time frame of over 7 years. In fact, the two groups are opposites. The least preferred time position for US respondents was over 7 years, while less than four years was the least preferred for non-US respondents. Note that the most preferred time frame for both groups was the midrange 4–7 years. These results are consistent with the observation that US business has a short-term bias. From these conjoint results, it appears to be imbedded in their preferences. An interesting theoretical perspective on why such a short-run bias might apply in the USA is the information asymmetry argument put forth by Jacobson and Aaker (1991).[9] In any case, the conjoint results document and calibrate a US tendency toward the short run.

Further evidence on the contrasts between the US and non-US respondents may be seen in their response to questions concerning just how many years would constitue short-, intermediate-, and long-term time frames for the business they chose as their referent in responding to the conjoint task. US respondents gave shorter periods for all three time frame levels. For the long term, non-US respondents gave an average response of 9.59 years while US executives averaged 7.17 years, a difference significant at the 0.01 level. For the intermediate term, non-US respondents averaged 4.28 years while

Table 5.5 A priori segmentation

	Non-US vs US part worths			Global market expansion strategy (Median split)		
Attribute/level	Non-US (n=57)	(Sig.)	US (n=125)	Low (n=91)	(Sig.)	High (n=91)
Partner's Main Contrib.						
Mktg./Dist.	2.97		4.20	2.29		6.30
R&D/Tech.	3.92		3.20	2.57		4.34
Mfgr./Opers.	1.72		−0.01	1.36		−0.63
Capital	−8.61		−7.40	−6.22		−10.01
My Firm's Main Contrib.						
Mktg./Dist.	7.88		4.90	2.99	(0.04)	8.87
R&D/Tech.	−1.56		3.25	1.50		2.42
Mfgr./Opers.	4.85		1.17	2.07		2.69
Capital	−11.17		−9.32	−6.56	(0.04)	−13.99
Home Area of Partner						
USA/Canada	2.23	(0.09)	9.73	13.91	(0.00)	0.38
Europe	10.52	(0.04)	2.80	−0.09	(0.00)	10.44
Japan	−6.70	(0.04)	1.63	−4.10	(0.10)	1.35
Other	−6.05		−14.15	−9.71		−12.17
Partner Competitiveness						
High	−7.08		−9.93	−8.27		−9.92
Moderate	2.87		2.55	2.06		3.24
Low	4.21		7.38	6.22		6.69

Table 5.5 (continued)

| Attribute/level | Non-US vs US part worths | | | Global market expansion strategy | | |
| | | | | | (Median split) | |
	Non-US (n = 57)	(Sig.)	US (n = 125)	Low (n = 91)	(Sig.)	High (n = 91)
Time Frame						
Less than 4 years	−2.49	(0.04)	0.67	0.28		−0.96
4 to 7 years	1.42		0.96	0.51		1.70
More than 7 years	1.07	(0.07)	−1.64	−0.79		−0.75
My Firm's Equity						
None	−16.24		−10.61	−12.60		−11.48
Minority	1.55		2.33	1.42		2.85
Equal	6.44		5.61	6.76		4.59
Majority	8.25		2.68	4.41		4.04

114

the USA averaged 3.67 years, a difference significant at the 0.06 level. While the short-term time frame answers were not significantly different, the mean US answers once again were for a shorter period. Hence it appears that not only do US executives have greater preference for shorter time frames and lesser preference for longer time frames, their definitions of short term, intermediate, and long term are all less than for non-US respondents.

USA vs. Europe vs. ROW

In Table 5.6, the non-US portion of the executive sample is further divided into Europeans and the rest of the world (ROW). The data do not support a finer disaggregation. As it is, the small sample size for Europe and ROW means that the standard errors of the means for these groups will tend to be large, thereby reducing the power of the statistical tests to detect differences. Nevertheless, this breakdown of the sample may suggest insights into differences between executive preferences from these three regions. This is particularly likely to reveal situations where the Europeans fall on the opposite side of the US executives from the ROW executives.

Perhaps the most interesting results in Table 5.6 relate to 'home area of partner', the most important aggregate attribute in Table 5.2. The new segmentation shows that the regional self-preference for alliance partners is by no means a unique US phenomenon. The highest part worth utility for the USA is the USA, for Europe is Europe, and for ROW is Other.[10] The European self-preference is significantly higher than the US or ROW preference for Europe ($p<0.05$). Likewise for the ROW self-preference. The same directional result holds for the USA but the criterion level of $p=0.05$ is not attained. Europe is the No. 2 choice of both US and the ROW executives. This attraction of European partners no doubt reflects non-European expectations of business opportunities in the unified Europe of 1992 and the recent unshackling of Eastern Europe. Europe reciprocates the US No. 2 preference for Europe by having their second highest preference for US firms. This most likely reflects the long standing commercial and cultural ties between Europe and the USA. The regional executives also exhibit preference differences for the Japanese as potential partners ($p=0.054$). The US executives are the most favorably disposed toward the Japanese followed by the Europeans. The ROW executives were particularly negative toward prospective partners from the 'other' area. Such regional preferences for geographically located partners should enter into management thinking when considering the search for alliance partners. Also trade negotiations may need to reflect an understanding of the extent of self-preferences as well.

The only significant differences in importance weights occurred for 'partner's main contribution'. This was a significantly more important

Table 5.6   A priori segmentation

Attribute/level	USA ($n = 125$)	EUROPE ($n = 25$)	ROW ($n = 32$)
Partner's Main Contrib.			
Mktg./Dist.	4.20a	8.06a	−1.00a
R&D/Tech.	3.20a	9.67a	−0.58a
Mfgr./Opers.	−0.01a	0.77a	2.56a
Capital	−7.40ab	−18.51b	−0.87a
My Firm's Main Contrib.			
Mktg./Dist.	4.90a	9.61a	6.52a
R&D/Tech.	3.25a	4.42ab	−6.23b
Mfgr./Opers.	1.17a	4.05a	5.47a
Capital	−9.32a	−18.09a	−5.76a
Home Area of Partner			
US/Canada	9.73a	5.00a	0.06a
Europe	2.80a	19.18b	3.76a
Japan	1.63a	−4.85a	−8.14a
Other	−14.15a	−19.34a	4.33b
Partner Competitiveness			
High	−9.93a	−7.88a	−6.46a
Moderate	2.55a	2.26a	3.35a
Low	7.38a	5.61a	3.12a
Time Frame			
Less than 4 years	0.67a	−1.75a	−3.06a
4 to 7 years	0.96a	2.16a	0.85a
More than 7 years	−1.64a	−0.40a	2.21a
My Firm's Equity			
None	−10.61a	−17.83a	−15.00a
Minority	2.33a	0.99a	1.98a
Equal	5.61a	6.25a	6.58a
Majority	2.68a	10.58a	6.42a

Note: Means sharing the same letter are not different at the 0.05 level of significance. The significance of the differences between the USA, European, and the rest of the world (ROW) respondents for Japan as a partner home area was significant at the 0.054 level and for a time frame of over 7 years was significant at the more modest 0.08 level.

attribute for the Europeans than for the ROW. The nub of this difference is in the average part worth utilities for capital, as seen in Table 5.6. The ROW is much more favorably disposed to partner supplied capital, whereas the Europeans are not ($p < 0.05$). Since the Europeans also do not want to supply capital,[11] it would seem that this result suggests concerns over reciprocal exchange of long-term strategic resources when developing a partnership, rather than the mere contribution of capital. It is interesting that the USA prefers to acquire markets closely followed by technology whereas the Europeans prefer to obtain technology followed closely by markets. Somewhat surprisingly, given the notion that manufacturing has been vigorously exported to non-triad areas, the receipt of partner manufacturing is of major importance to the ROW but only secondary importance to the USA and Europe.

While all areas prefer to provide markets to an alliance, the USA and Europe also have strong preference for supplying technology. The USA has substantially greater preference for providing technology to an alliance than the ROW ($p < 0.05$). This no doubt reflects the difficulty the ROW has with providing technology to the technologically advanced triad regions. Not surprisingly, given their likely labor cost advantages, the ROW has a high preference for supplying manufacturing to an alliance. Finally, with respect to the 'time frame' attribute, the USA again has the least preference for a longer-term partnership while the ROW has the highest utility for the longer level ($p = 0.08$).

Strategic Orientation – Global Market Expansion

For the chosen business unit, each respondent was asked to indicate the relative importance of potential strategic themes for the business by allocating 100 points among the following categories: global market expansion, domestic market expansion, product technology development, process technology development, and an open, self-designated category.[12] A median split on the weight accorded to global expansion as a strategic theme divided the respondents into high and low global expansion groups. The results are presented in Table 5.5. With the exception of a marginally significant difference ($p = 0.09$) in the importance of partner contribution, the high versus low global expansion groups did not differ in the attribute importances.

There were some significant differences in the part worths for 'my firm's main contribution' and 'home area of partner'. Those high on global expansion had significantly ($p = 0.04$) greater preference for providing marketing/distribution and significantly less preference for providing capital. The high global expanders had significantly greater preference for Europe and less preference for the USA/Canada ($p = 0.00$). High global expanders were also more favorably predisposed toward a Japanese partner, but only at the marginal 0.10 level of significance. While the favorite for high global expanders was Europe, for the low group, the USA/Canada was much preferred.

Table 5.7   HO global expansion interaction with home area of the partner (mean part worths)

	Global Strategy and HQ Location of Company			
Home Area of Partner	**non-US Low Global** ($n=27$)	**non-US High Global** ($n=30$)	**US Low Global** ($n=63$)	**US High Global** ($n=60$)
Importance part worths	0.26a	0.34a	0.31a	0.24a
USA/Canada	2.41a	2.06a	19.33b	− 0.47a
Europe	5.13ab	15.38a	− 2.60b	8.14a
Japan	− 4.63ab	− 8.56a	− 3.15ab	6.33b
Other	− 2.90a	− 8.88a	− 13.57a	− 13.99a

Note: Means sharing the same letter in a row are not significantly different ($p<0.05$).

The latter result could be due to the large proportion of US respondents in the executive sample. It is interesting to examine both the global expansion and the US/non-US results together. The results appear in Table 5.7 which shows that indeed, US respondents with low global expansion themes are much more favorably predisposed toward a US partner than any other group.[13] They are also much less favorable toward European partners than are the high global groups, whether US or non-US. Interestingly, US high global respondents are much more favorable toward a Japanese partner than are the non-US high global respondents. In fact, high global US respondents are nearly as favorable toward the Japanese as they are toward the Europeans.

Preference Clusters

An alternative method to identify preference segments is to cluster the executive respondents based upon their similarity in their part worth utilities from the conjoint analysis. The SPSSX K-means clustering algorithm was used to cluster the 184 executive respondents based upon their part worth utilities for the levels of the six attributes. The results are reported in Table 5.8. The results for each of the six clusters are discussed below.[14]

Table 5.8 *Mean importance weights and part worths by part worth clusters*

	Cluster No.					
	1	2	3	4	5	6
Attribute/level	(n=28) (15%)	(n=44) (24%)	(n=19) (10%)	(n=48) (26%)	(n=20) (11%)	(n=25) (14%)
Partner's Main Contrib.	**0.11a**	**0.09a**	**0.03a**	**0.30b**	**0.03a**	**0.11a**
Mktg./Dist.	2.48a	-3.61a	1.22a	16.15b	1.26a	0.42a
R&D/Tech.	6.56a	3.30a	1.04a	4.72a	0.45a	2.25a
Mfgr./Opers.	1.98a	-0.71a	0.07a	0.43a	0.49a	0.98a
Capital	-11.02ab	1.02a	-2.33a	-21.31b	-2.20a	-3.67a
My Firm's Main Contrib.	**0.05a**	**0.05a**	**0.05ab**	**0.17b**	**0.06ab**	**0.64c**
Mktg./Dist.	4.76a	2.54a	4.75a	-0.52a	2.58a	28.80b
R&D/Tech.	1.49a	0.66a	1.03a	2.75a	2.62a	3.32a
Mfgr./Opers.	-0.80a	-1.44a	-3.11a	-2.25a	1.92a	25.83b
Capital	-5.54a	-1.76a	-2.67a	0.02a	-7.12a	-57.94b
Home Area of Partner	**0.08a**	**0.12a**	**0.82b**	**0.21a**	**0.80b**	**0.14a**
USA/Canada	-5.58ac	10.47bc	11.72c	-6.74a	52.88d	2.66abc
Europe	8.15a	1.27a	29.41b	-0.69a	5.34a	2.01a
Japan	0.39a	-0.12a	23.06b	-0.12a	-41.11c	6.26a
Other	-2.96ab	-11.62a	-64.16c	7.56b	-17.10a	-10.91a

Table 5.8 (continued)

Attribute/level	Cluster No.					
	1 (n=28) (15%)	2 (n=44) (24%)	3 (n=19) (10%)	4 (n=48) (26%)	5 (n=20) (11%)	6 (n=25) (14%)
Partner Competitiveness	**0.67b**	**0.03a**	**0.04a**	**0.06a**	**0.03a**	**0.03a**
High	-52.97b	-0.43a	-3.84a	-0.41a	-2.52a	-0.38a
Moderate	10.98b	0.82a	1.88ab	0.66a	2.76ab	0.62a
Low	41.98b	-0.39a	1.96a	-0.25a	-0.24a	-0.24a
Time Frame	**0.02a**	**0.03a**	**0.01a**	**0.06a**	**0.03a**	**0.02a**
Less than 4 years	0.19a	0.37a	0.18a	-1.91a	1.97a	-1.31a
4 to 7 years	1.01a	0.85a	0.27a	2.78a	0.39a	-0.40a
More than 7 years	-1.19a	-1.21a	-0.45a	-0.86a	-2.36a	1.72a
My Firm's Equity	**0.07a**	**0.67b**	**0.06a**	**0.01a**	**0.05a**	**0.06a**
None	-6.01a	-61.55c	5.42ab	11.80b	-0.73ab	-1.37ab
Minority	0.25a	5.41a	0.41a	1.45a	1.65a	0.92a
Equal	2.17ab	27.14c	-2.55ab	-6.20a	1.67ab	5.08b
Majority	3.59a	28.99b	-3.29a	-7.05a	-2.60a	-4.63a

Notes: Means sharing the same letter in a row are not significantly different ($p < 0.05$). Mean cluster importance weights are reported on the same line as the attribute name in bold. Mean cluster part worths are reported on the corresponding line with the attribute level.

Cluster 1: Competitiveness (15 per cent of sample; 71 per cent are US respondents)

The executives in this preference segment, which comprised 15 per cent of the respondents, are particularly sensitive to the issue of partner competitiveness.[15] They are many times more positively disposed toward alliances which have low competitiveness and are correspondingly much more negatively disposed toward highly competitive alliance partners than are the other five segments (all at the 0.05 level of significance). This segment is also the most favorably predisposed toward moderate competitiveness. The dominating importance of the competitiveness issue to this preference segment is reflected in the fact that two-thirds of the total importance weight of the six alliance attributes is accounted for by the competitiveness attribute. Seventy-one per cent of this cluster are US executives.

Cluster 2: Equity (24 per cent of sample; 66 per cent are US respondents)

This was the second largest cluster (24 per cent) and its alliance preferences are dominated by a concern for the equity dimension, with two-thirds of the total attribute importances being accounted for by this one attribute. Somewhat surprisingly, this equity-dominated segment has the second lowest proportion of US executives among the six segments. One might have expected that US executives might have greater equity concern given the perception of a strong entrepreneurial penchant among US executives. Members of this preference segment have the highest part worths of any cluster for both majority and equal equity alliances. In addition, they slightly prefer majority ownership over an equal partnership. This cluster also has substantially and significantly the least part worth utility for no equity. Although this cluster has the highest preference for minority equity of any of the preference segments, it does not differ significantly from the other five segments on this attribute.

Cluster 3: Europe and Japan Partner Preference (10 per cent of sample; 74 per cent are US respondents)

This is the smallest of the six preference segments and is dominated by the importance of the home area of a prospective partner, with over 80 per cent of the total attribute importance weights accounted for by this one attribute. Executives in this cluster are substantially and significantly more favorable toward European and Japanese partners than are the other five clusters. In addition, they are much more negative toward partners from areas other than the triad than are the other preference segments. The US proportion is highest in this segment.

Cluster 4: Partner Contribution and Home Area (26 per cent of sample; 72 per cent are US respondents)

This is the largest cluster (26 per cent) and reflects a significantly greater concern than for other clusters with the contribution to be made by a prospective partner. The relative importance of partner contribution is a more modest 30 per cent than the dominating attributes found for the first three clusters. This cluster has significantly greater preference for receiving marketing/distribution from a partner and significantly lesser preference for receiving capital from the partner.[16] This cluster also has the highest preference among the preference clusters for partners from outside the triad, and in fact prefers them to any of the triad areas. Thus, although non-triad partners are not preferred by most executives, for the substantial minority represented in Cluster 4, non-triad partnerships are, in fact, preferred. The members of this cluster also have the least preference for US and European partners.

Cluster 5: US Home/Not Japan (11 per cent of sample; 70 per cent are US respondents)

This is the second cluster in which a partner's home area is a dominant issue in alliance preference and the third in which it plays a major role. This cluster represents the second smallest of the preference segments (11 per cent) and has 80 per cent of the total importance of the six attributes being associated with the home area attribute. Although this cluster has an attribute importance weight for home area very similar to Cluster 3, it differs markedly from that segment in the details of its preferences. Cluster 5 has by far the largest preference for a US-based partner of all the six clusters and the most negative preference for a Japanese partner. It is also significantly different from Cluster 3 in that it has a lower preference for Europe, and a less negative preference for Other area.[17]

Cluster 6: My Firm's Contribution (14 per cent of sample; 58 per cent are US respondents)

The sixth cluster has 64 per cent of the attribute importance focused upon the attribute relating to what the respondent's firm will contribute to a prospective alliance. This cluster has the highest preference of any cluster for contributing marketing and manufacturing to an alliance. It also has by far the least preference for contributing capital.[18] Interstingly, this cluster has the smallest proportion of US executives among the six clusters.

As indicated in the discussion above, the clusters differ from one another, both statistically and substantively, in terms of their strategic alliance preferences. This preference heterogeneity could lead to substantially different alliance decisions and future research should take cognizance of these individual differences in alliance preferences in studying the incidence of strategic alliances and their outcome.[19]

Several aspects relating to the respondent and his/her firm were examined to see if they would be differentially associated with one or more clusters. The clusters were examined in terms of firm size (US sales), the proportion of cluster firms providing services or products, the proportion involved in industrial and consumer businesses, the proportion involved in high technology, the respondent's age, respondent knowledge about the firm's strategic alliances, the respondent's involvement in the decisions about strategic alliances, the respondent's self-rated knowledge of strategic alliances, the objectives of the strategic alliance, the strategic focus of the business undertaking the alliance, and the respondent's definition of short, medium and long time frame. In all, the six clusters were subject to pairwise comparison on some 27 aspects outlined above. Of the 405 comparisons, only five were found to be significant, in contrast to the 20 which would be expected given the type 1 error of 0.05. Thus, although Table 5.8 and the above discussion indicates that the preference segments differ from each other both statistically and in substance, yet the above noted aspects of the firm and the respondents did not distinguish between the clusters. Perhaps other aspects could be found which would differentiate better. Conversely, it may be yet another example of the often found failure of demographic data to differentiate market segments. The message to managers is that there is substantial preference heterogeneity and efforts to ascertain preference information from individual decision makers should smooth communications and facilitate efforts to resolve conflict both internally and between prospective alliance partners.

DISCUSSION

Embedded in our results are a number of implications for managers as well as noteworthy insights for academic scholars who intend to pursue the investigation of strategic alliances with a grounding in empirical observation. Below, we discuss our results with an emphasis on the managerial implications.

Importance of Alliance Attributes

The general pattern of results reported suggests that practicing managers do indeed have distinct preferences for the attributes of strategic alliances.

Moreover, some attributes are clearly more important than others. The geographic location of the partner and the focal firm's equity position in the alliance are significantly more important than the average importance of all attributes included in our study. Regarding the geographic location of the partner, it appears that North America and Europe are indeed the preferred geographic regions in which to seek an alliance for the respondents in this sample. Further elaboration indicative of regional self-preference is discussed below.

Regarding the focal firm's equity position, we calibrated the degree to which various levels of equity position were preferred by our sample. The results suggest that equal equity is most preferred. Given the strong interdependencies of firms involved in these alliances, this result is not that surprising since equal equity results in equal partitioning of the residual profits *and losses* from the partnership. Equal equity positions may also both signal and call forth more equal and intense commitment by the alliance partners. However, as purported by the recent literature, equity positions can be obtained in ways other than providing financial resources. Our results support and calibrate this claim. The results demonstrate that managers want to obtain equity, but preferably by contributing other strategic resources such as R&D/technology or marketing/distribution rather than contributing capital. That this is also true for the 'partner's main contribution' suggests that these executives were more focused on exchanging strategic resources than merely financial resources.

Clearly, the attribute that was preferred least by our sample is the time frame for the alliance. This is a somewhat surprising result given that these alliances commit the firm, probably not lightly, to a longer-term relationship than 'discrete exchanges' which characterize classical interfirm structures. Also, since one domain of compatibility is the presumed length of the relationship (e.g. going for short-term versus long-term profits) and compatibility has been touted as a critical dimension of alliance success, this result is somewhat surprising.

While the previous three attributes were clearly distinguished from what one would expect if all six attributes were equally important, the other three attributes were of essentially average importance. These include the contribution of both the focal firm and the partner as well as the degree of partner's competitiveness. What is most surprising about these results is that the contribution attributes did not attain a higher relative importance status. This is a result we did not anticipate given that the most common theme in the extant literature is that strategic alliances are a means to acquire complementary resources, and this is consistent with strict economic logic. Moreover, observers of strategic alliances typically point to the synergies that arise from alliances which suggest that complementarity issues are a critical dimension of these agreements. Nonetheless, according to our results, practicing managers do not consider complementarity to be the *key* dimension in their preference rankings. Moreover, there seems to be little correlation between what managers prefer to get from an alliance and what they prefer to contribute. Future research might consider the implications of this observation for the nature of the exchange relationship between strategic alliance partners.

Preference Heterogeneity

Finally, although in the aggregate managers reflect a particular ordering of alliance attributes, there appears to be a significant degree of preference heterogeneity. To demonstrate this, we were able to identify six distinct clusters of managers with particular sets of preferences. For example, in one cluster (1) respondents were particularly sensitive to the extent of partner competitiveness and insensitive to their firm's main contribution to the alliance, and yet in another cluster (6), respondents were quite the opposite, being insensitive to the extent of partner competitiveness and particularly sensitive to their firm's main contribution to the alliance. This wide variation has direct implications for pooling group responses and suggests that future research should recognize these individual differences in alliance preferences when studying the incidence of strategic alliances and their outcomes.

The clustering also helps to clarify the role of the two most important attributes in the aggregate. For 'home area of partner', which was the most important attribute in the entire sample, there were two markedly different clusters for which this attribute was the dominating one, Clusters 3 and 5. Both represent about 10 per cent of the executives, have essentially equal and extremely large importance weights for this attribute, and differ significantly from each other on every level of the 'home area of partner' attribute. Cluster 5 has the greatest preference for the USA and the least preference for Japan of any of the preference clusters. In contrast, Cluster 3 has the highest preference for Europe and Japan and by far the lowest preference for 'other' areas among all the preference clusters. This example shows the value of clustering on the part worth utilities rather than the importance weights in that a clustering based upon importance weights would have lumped these markedly different groups of executives together and masked their virtually complete differences on the 'home area of partner' attribute. This methods issue is particularly germane when there are attributes which do not have a natural monotonic ordering of their levels (e.g. there is no natural monotonic ordering of the USA, Europe, Japan, and Other).

While all but one cluster exhibits an importance weight of well over 0.10 for 'home area' (the most important attribute), the clustering shows that a very different pattern holds for the second most important attribute, 'my firm's equity'. The aggregate importance of 'equity' derives mainly from its overwhelming importance to the executives in Cluster 2 who comprise nearly one-quarter of the executive sample. No other cluster has an importance weight for this attribute greater than 0.07. Thus, while 'home area of partner' is nearly universally important, 'equity' is of vital importance to a significant minority of executives, but of relatively less importance to the large majority. Naturally, managers involved in alliance negotiations will early on want to ascertain where they and their prospective partners stand on this issue.

Preference Differences Between US and Non-US Managers

Our a priori segmentation results suggest that there are distinct differences between US vs. non-US managers for both the specific geographic location of the partner and the time frame for the alliance. Specifically, US managers prefer US- and Japanese-based partners more and European-based partners less than their non-US counterparts. When the non-US sample was further subdivided into Europeans and ROW (rest of the world), a clear pattern of geographic self-preference emerged. US managers tended to prefer alliances with other US firms, Europeans tended to prefer alliances with other Europeans, and ROW managers preferred ROW partners. One can speculate that these regional self-preferences are due to a desire to avoid cross-cultural misunderstandings and communications problems or simply reflect the advantages of close proximity which makes potential partner identification easier and which makes alliance coordination (e.g. production scheduling, inventory management, R&D etc.) and communication easier, or alternatively, reflect regional chauvinism akin to nationalism.

When comparing non-US and US managers on the time dimension, we found that both sets of managers do not differ in their importance for this attribute. However, our investigation of differences between non-US and US managers revealed some interesting insights regarding the specific levels of this attribute. First, as suspected, US managers prefer shorter-term relationships than their non-US counterparts. Second, US managers define the various time frames differently, with the number of years they ascribe to short term, intermediate, and long term all less than for non-US managers. Recent theoretical work (e.g. Jacobson and Aaker 1991) has ascribed this difference to asymmetric information about business performance. We would encourage future research to provide other explanations of this important phenomenon.

Preference Differences Based on Strategic Objectives

Managers tended to differ on some dimensions based on whether their strategic objective was either high or low global expansion. In particular, high global expanders tended to favor European and Japanese partners while low global expanders tended to favor US and Canadian partners. Our results also indicate that US high global expanders are more favorable towards a Japanese partner than are non-US high global expanders. High global expanders also tended to prefer to contribute marketing/distribution more and capital less than low global expanders.

Additional Managerial Implications

Our results indicate that: (1) some alliance attributes are of relatively greater importance than others and (2) substantial heterogeneity exists among executives in their preferences. The managerial consequence of the first is an opportunity to more effectively focus their time and attention toward that subset of attributes which is of key importance to their potential partners. This will tend to simplify, to the extent possible, the complex negotiations surrounding the alliance formation process. For the six attributes in this study, 'home area of partner' and 'equity' clearly stood out as the two major attributes, while 'time frame' was found to be of tertiary consequence.

The second, substantial preference heterogeneity across executives, has consequences both internal to the firm and in its assessment of a potential partner. To the extent that different executives within a firm have markedly different priorities for alliances, internal miscommunication may hinder alliance decision and development efforts. The conjoint measurement process utilized in this study offers the opportunity to lay out quite clearly varying internal executive preferences, thereby, hopefully, establishing a framework within which any conflicts may be resolved. An interesting question is whether internal firm members at different organizational levels may have greatly divergent views, which if not resolved may lead to front-line sabotage of an alliance (Tyebjee 1989). For example, front-line designers and engineers may be much more sensitive to competitive overlap issues, which may lessen their willingness to share information with a partner. Again, a conjoint assessment might be of considerable diagnostic utility and provide a springboard for corrective action before a crisis of implementation is generated. Since most potential alliance partners are probably also subject to substantial inter-executive alliance preference heterogeneity, a firm should also seek to identify individual executive preferences within target partners. While such external assessments are more difficult to execute, sensitivity to preference variation and agreement within a potential partner should substantially assist a firm in the negotiations process. Thus the substantial preference heterogeneity indicated by our sample suggests the need for strategies and means to identify and focus on the key issues in negotiations and to identify what these are for specific potential partners.

An interesting result from this study concerns the prevalence of geographic 'self-preferences'. While observers of the alliance phenomena (e.g. Ohmae 1989) stress the importance of globalization and, in particular, US firms forming alliances with global partners (*Business Tokyo* 1991), this is not reflected in managerial preferences. Whatever the underlying reason, there appear to be important implications for trade policies which attempt to establish a 'level playing field' between firms in different geographic areas. As reflected in managerial preferences, there seems to be a hesitancy towards the idea of managers stretching their 'hands across the ocean' (Goldenberg 1988). For practicing managers who may find that their preferences agree with this finding and yet for whom the imperative of global partnerships is a reality, it is worthwhile to consider the costs that such regionally 'biased' preferences may create for the long-term health of their firms.

Our findings regarding the preferences for equity also have implications for understanding the nature of new strategic partnerships. According to some observers (e.g. SRI 1986), the importance of equity exchanges is decreasing. Our results point to a more refined conclusion. As suggested by aggregate managerial preferences, the equity dimension is clearly an important one, with equal or majority equity being most preferred. However, a closer look via the cluster analysis reveals that equity is by far the most important attribute for about a quarter of the executives (again, equal or majority equity is most preferred), while equity is indeed of far less importance for the large majority. In practice, this suggests that equity sometimes will be a crucial negotiating point and at other times it will not. It remains for the negotiators to ascertain in which condition a given firm finds itself.

Limitations and Future Research

This study is exploratory and subject to limitations that should be considered when interpreting our results. First, we limited our study to investigating the preferences for a single manager in a firm rather than all members of the group responsible for the strategic alliance decision. We fully recognize that these decisions involve potentially complex interactions among decision participants; nevertheless we reasoned that a good first step towards understanding this decision situation is to identify key participants in the process (our executives were of sufficient status in their organizations to have major roles in alliance decisions) and measure their preferences since they would likely have an important impact on subsequent firm behavior and their preferences are likely to correlate with choice (Montgomery 1985). We encourage future research to extend our analysis to the group context. A second limitation is that we present data from a convenience sample rather than a true random sample of managers. This limits our ability to generalize too broadly. We note, however, that because our sample consists of knowledgeable executives with a great deal of experience in these matters, our results have relevance to probably a large portion of managers involved with strategic alliances. Another limitation is that alliances were character-ized by only six specific dimensions that were gleaned from the managerial and academic literature that relate to preferences. Future research might well consider additional attributes, naturally retaining those found to be important in the present research. Finally, recall that our study focuses directly on managerial *preferences* rather than what observers say about alli-ances or, indeed, what managers actually do. To provide systematic evidence as to the ultimate implications of these preferences requires data on actual alliance agreements that were subsequently created. This is beyond the scope of the present research and clearly suggests another avenue for future research. Empirical research and theory development relating to the antece-dents of the various forms of preference heterogeneity found in this research would be useful. For example, what are the forces driving the observed regional self-preference? Additionally, is there hierarchical diversity in pref-erence within a given firm? Are R&D and designers and engineers more (or less) cautious regionally or in terms of competitive overlap in strategic alli-ances? How would Japanese executives compare to their US or European counterparts? Finally, there is an opportunity to develop alliance decision support systems, perhaps similar in concept to Rao, Mahajan and Varaiya's (1991) balance model for acquisition.

CONCLUSION

In an increasingly global business environment, the idea of strategic alliances has captured the imagination of strategists and fueled great effort on the part of globalizing corporations. Yet, while much anecdotal wisdom exists on what makes a good or bad alliance, there are few broad-sample studies of what managers actually think about alliances. This chapter outlined the results of an exploratory study of a diverse senior executive sample's prefer-ences for various characteristics of possible strategic alliances. Using conjoint analysis, we explored the tradeoffs managers perceive in selecting potential alliance partners. As in studies of consumer preference, this study revealed substantial preference heterogeneity across executives, with important implications for alliance negotiations both within and across firms. Further, while some common wisdom was confirmed (Americans tend to have shorter time frames than non-Americans), other wisdom was rejected (pronounced regional self-preferences for partners suggest that the advice to 'be global' has yet to take hold in management preferences). Future research of the determinants of preferences and their link to action offers much hope in the study of this important business phenomenon.

NOTES

1. Only adaptation to markets, assessment of customer need, service enhancement and creation of a marketing culture, were seen as more important than building alliances for the US and European executives. For these two groups of executives, it was seen as more important than ensuring quality. This latter result could, of course, reflect a belief that much progress had been made on the quality front during the 1980s and that the 1990s would require somewhat more attention to the development of alliances.
2. In a different but related marketing domain, there has been research that suggests there may be some home-country product preference and that this might relate to consumers' ethnocentrism. That is, the more ethnocentric consumers are more likely to have home-country product preference (Netemeyer et al. 1991; Shimp and Sharma 1987). Johansson et al. (1985), however, found that the country of origin effect might not be as significant as previously thought. In any case, the parallel domain of strategic alliance might well, for reasons suggested in the text, exhibit same region preferences similar to the earlier country of origin results.
3. Although it had its origin in psychometrics, conjoint analysis was judged one of the most significant developments in marketing methods in the post-war era (Meyers et al. 1979). For surveys documenting the widespread application of conjoint analysis in marketing, see Cattin and Wittink (1982) and Wittink and Cattin (1989). In other strategic marketing contexts such as the management of interfunctional interfaces, conjoint analysis has proved useful. See Hausman and Montgomery (1990) for use in focusing manufacturing upon the consumers and the development of order winning strategies.
4. An alternative to the ranking of attributes taken two at a time is the ranking of full profiles. Full profiles present a respondent with the task of ranking a set of attribute bundles which consist of one level of each of the attributes considered in the study. Wittink and Cattin (1989) suggest that use of the full profile method has been increasing, perhaps driven by a variety of computer enhancements which makes design and administration easier. Nevertheless, Montgomery (1985) reports that in a study utilizing eight attributes, the two at a time tradeoff analysis has consistent advantages versus the full profile method, i.e. it had a higher response rate, respondents required only two-thirds the response time, respondents indicated greater confidence in their answers, and it had higher *ex ante* predictive validity. Although these differences were not statistically significant at the 0.05 level due to limited sample size, all were in favor of the two at a time method and are consistent with that method being easier on the respondent than the full profile method.
5. All of the six mean attribute importance weights are significantly above zero at well beyond the 0.01 level. Since the importance weights are positive and are normalized to 1.0, this is not a particularly stringent test.
6. The calculation on which this is based is as follows: the raw importance weight for 'home

area of partner' is 7.22 −(−11.23)=18.45. The lowest-rated triad member is Japan with a part worth utility of −1.24. The utility gain from going from 'other' to Japan is −1.24 −(−11.23)=9.99. Hence a prospective alliance with any triad member yields a minimum of 9.99/18.45=0.54 or 54 per cent of the total importance weight.

7. These results were statistically significant at the 0.003, 0.071, and the 0.013 levels, respectively.

8. The fact that the non-US sample is 44 per cent European may have influenced this result. This seems supported by the US preference for the USA, if the Europeans have analogous self-preferences. Further, the Europeans have been much more aggressively resistive to Japanese inroads. Simon (1986) presents a survey that shows the Japanese executives believe the USA to be a much easier market to enter than European markets.

9. The Jacobson and Aaker (1991) analysis and empirical results suggest that while both US and Japanese stock prices reflect short-term performance in an important way, the Japanese place much greater emphasis on the longer term. Jacobson and Aaker argue that in the USA, executives have substantially greater knowledge of the firm's strategy and position than do shareholders. This information asymmetry between managers and shareholders is seen as creating an executive incentive toward short-term profits. In Japan, where a much lower percentage of shares is traded and where close, continuing business relationships and cross-shareholdings create an atmosphere of sharing of vision and strategy, the asymmetry in information is greatly diminished, thereby reducing the short-term bias.

10. Note that fully 81 per cent of the ROW sample is from outside the triad, that is from the 'other' category. This group does include Japanese executives.

11. For Europeans, the part worth for 'my firm contributes' capital is the lowest level for that attribute.

12. In the interest of space only the global expansions results will be considered in this chapter.

13. To some extent this result adds convergent validity to the results in that the responses to the tradeoff rankings yield part worth utilities which relate in the expected manner to logically related questions asked in an entirely different manner.

14. The number of clusters was chosen by first examining hierarchical cluster solutions. From this analysis, it was deemed most reasonable to retain a six cluster solution. The results as reported in Table 5.8 reflect the SPSSX K-means clusters for a six cluster solution. A seventh cluster included only 11 respondents and was not considered further. See Punj and Stewart (1983).

15. Cluster No. 1 has a significantly higher utility for moderate competitiveness than Clusters Nos 2, 4, and 6. It is not significantly different from Cluster Nos 3 and 5 at the 0.05 level.

16. Cluster No. 4 is not significantly different from Cluster No. 1 in the part worth utility for capital received from a prospective partner.

17. The total contrast between Cluster Nos 3 and 5 demonstrate the benefit of clustering on the part worth utilities rather than the importance weights. While the respondents in these two clusters closely resemble one another in importance weights, and would therefore be likely to be clustered together, they are dramatically different in their part worth utilities for partner home area. The clustering based upon the part worths has enabled this contrast to be cast into bold relief. Also this shows that about 25 per cent of the respondents have vital concern with equity. The rest have relatively little concern for this attribute. This adds to our insights from the aggregation analysis results.

18. In marketing and capital preferences, Cluster No. 6's firm contribution preferences parallels Cluster No. 4's partner contribution preferences.

19. In a balance model application to acquisitions, Rao et al. (1991) found that their four subjects were very heterogeneous in their preferences and that this had a marked impact upon the strategy implications of the balanced model.

REFERENCES

Berg, Sanford, V. and Phillip Friedman (1978), 'Joint Ventures in America Industry', *Mergers and Acquisitions*, (Summer), 28–41.

Borys, Bryan and David B. Jemison (1989), 'Hybrid Organizations as Strategic Alliances: Theoretical and Practical Issues in Organizational Combination', *Academy of Management Review*, **14** (2), 234–49.

Boyle, S.E. (1968), 'Estimate of the Number and Size Distribution of Domestic Joint Subsidiaries', *Antitrust Law and Economics Review*, **1**, 81–92.

Business Week (1986), 'Corporate Odd Couples', 21 July, 100–105.

Cattin, Philippe and Dick Wittink (1982), 'Commercial Use of Conjoint Analysis: A Survey', *Journal of Marketing*, **46** (Summer), 44–53.

Columbia Journal of World Business (1987), **22** (2), (Summer).

Contractor, F. and P. Lorange (1988), *Cooperative Strategies in International Business*, Lexington, MA: Lexington Books.

Doz, Yves, Gary Hamel and C.K. Prahalad (1986), 'Strategic Partnerships: Success or Surrender?', Working Paper, INSEAD, Fountainebleau.

Fuchs, Peter (1991), 'Strategic Alliances: How U.S. Start-Ups are Tapping into Japanese Capital, Markets, and Technology,' *Business Tokyo*, **4** (April), 22–27.

Goldenberg, Susan (1988), *Hands Across the Ocean: Managing Joint Ventures with a Spotlight on China and Japan*, Boston, MA: Harvard Business School Press.

Goldenberg, Victor (1976), 'Regulations and Administered Contracts', *Bell Journal of Economics*', **7** (August), 426–52.

Green, Paul and V. Srinivasan (1990), 'Conjoint Analysis in Marketing: New Developments with Implications for Research and Practice', *Journal of Marketing*, **4** (October), 3–19.

Harrigan, Kathryn R. (1985), *Strategies for Joint Ventures*, Lexington, MA: Lexington Books.

Harrigan, Kathryn R. (1986), *Managing for Joint Venture Success*, Lexington, MA: Lexington Books.

Harrigan, Kathryn R. (1988), 'Joint Ventures and Competitive Strategy,' *Strategic Management Journal*, **9**, 141–158.

Hausman, Warren H. and David B. Montgomery (1990), 'Making Manufacturing Market Driven,' Research Paper No. 1103, Graduate School of Business, Stanford university, 17 October.

Jacobson, Robert and David Aaker (1991), 'Measuring Our Way to Economic Decline', Working Paper, University of Washington, Seattle.

Johansson, Johny K., Susan P. Douglas and Ikujiro Nonaka (1985), 'Assessing the Impact of Country of Origin on Product Evaluations: A New Methodological Perspective', *Journal of Marketing Research*, **22** (4), (November), 388–96.

Kobayashi, Noritake (1988), 'Strategic Alliances with Japanese Firms', *Long Range Planning*, **21** (2), 29–34.

Kogut, Bruce (1988), 'Joint Ventures: Theoretical and Empirical Perspectives,' *Strategic Management Journal*, **9**, 319–32.

Kosnik, Thomas J. (1991), 'Global Marketing Issues in the 1990s: A Review of Recent Research', Unpublished note presented to the Stanford Senior Executive Program, 23 July.

Lyles, Margorie A. (1987), 'Common Mistakes of Joint Venture Experienced Firms', *Columbia Journal of World Business*, **22** (2), 79–85.

Meyers, John, Stephen A. Greyser and William F. Massy (1979), 'The Effectiveness of Marketing's "R&D" for Marketing Management: An Assessment', *Journal of Marketing*, **43** (January).

Montgomery, David B. (1985), 'Conjoint Calibration of the Customer/Competitor Interface in Industrial Markets', in Klaus Backhaus and David Wilson (eds), *New Developments in Industrial Marketing*, New York: Springer Verlag.

Moriarty, Rowland T. and David J. Reibstein (1986), 'Benefit Segmentation in Industrial Markets', *Journal of Business Research*, **14**, 3–26.

Netemeyer, Richard G., Srinivas Durvasula and Donald K. Lichtenstein (1991), 'A Cross National Assessment of the Reliability and Validity of the CETSCALE', *Journal of Marketing Research*, **28** (3), (August), 320–27.

Nielsen, Richard P. (1987), 'The Case for Cooperative Strategies', *Mckinsey Quarterly*, (Spring), 41–8.

Ohmae, Kenichi (1989), 'The Global Logic of Strategic Alliances', *Harvard Business Review*, **67** (2), (March–April), 143–54.

Pate, James L. (1969), 'Joint Venture Activity, 1960–1968', *Economic Review*, Federal Research Bank of Cleveland, (July), 16–23.

Pfeffer, Jeffrey (1972), 'Merger as a Response to Organizational Interdependence', *Administrative Science Quarterly*, **17**, 382–94.

Pfeffer, Jeffrey and Phillip Nowak (1976), 'Joint Ventures and Interorganizational Interdependence', *Administrative Science Quarterly*, **21** (September), 398–418.

Punj, G. and D.W. Stewart (1983), 'Cluster Analysis in Marketing Research: Review and Suggestions for Application', *Journal of Marketing Research*, **20**, 134–48.

Rao, Vithala R., Vijay Mahajan and Nikhil P. Varaiya (1991), 'A Balance Model for Evaluating Firms for Acquisitions', *Management Science*, **37** (March), 331–49.

Shimp, Terrence A. and Subhash Sharma (1987), 'Consumer Ethnocentrism: Construction and Validation of the CETSCALE', *Journal of Marketing Research*, **24** (3), (August), 280–289.

Simon, H. (1986) 'Market Entry in Japan: Barriers, Problems and Strategies', *International Journal of Research in Marketing*, **3**, 105–16.

SRI (1986), Business Intelligence Program, Report No. 730.

Srinivasan, V. and Allan D. Shocker (1981), 'LINMAP Version IV – User's Manual', Stanford University: Graduate School of Business.

Tse, David K. Kam-Hon Lee, Ilan Vertinsky and Donald A. Wehrung (1988), 'Does Culture Matter? A Cross-Cultural Study of Executives' Choice, Decisiveness and Risk Adjustment in International Marketing', *Journal of Marketing*, **52** (October), 81–95.

Tyebjee, Tyzoon T. (1988), 'A Typology of Joint Ventures: Japanese Strategies in the United States', *California Management Review*, **31** (1), (Fall), 75–86.

Tyebjee, Tyzoon T. (Producer) (1989), 'Strategic Alliances: Achieving Competitiveness Through Collaboration', Video Presentation, Leavey School of Business, Santa Clara University.

Wittink, Dick and Philippe Cattin (1989), 'Commercial Use of Conjoint Analysis: An Update', *Journal of Marketing*, **53** (July), 91–6.

6. The political economy explanation of international market entry mode choice: an exploratory study

Shaoming Zou, Charles R. Taylor and S. Tamer Cavusgil

OVERVIEW OF THE LITERATURE

Consistent with the prior literature (e.g. Erramilli 1991; Agarwal and Ramaswami 1992; Root 1994; Tallman and Shenkar 1994), we distinguish four major entry alternatives: exporting, licensing/franchising, joint venture, and wholly-owned subsidiary. Since prior literature has established that it is inappropriate to compare exporting cases to forms of foreign direct investment in the context of the theories that are tested in this study (Hennart 1989; Kim and Hwang 1992; Erramilli and Rao 1993), we will focus on how the TCA and BP theories explain the choice between licensing/franchising, joint ventures, and full ownership. Each of these alternatives is associated with implications for: (a) the level of control the firm will enjoy over the foreign market operations, (b) the level of investment required, and (c) the level of risk the firm faces in venturing into the foreign market (Hill, Hwang and Kim 1989). Previous researchers have observed that, in general, as a firm moves from licensing/franchising to joint venture to wholly-owned subsidiary, the degree of control that the firm has over operations, the required level of investment, and the level of risk increase accordingly (Erramilli 1991; Agarwal and Ramaswami 1992; Root 1994; Shane 1994). While a number of theories have been used in previous studies to explain firms' choice of entry mode from the low- to high-control modes, we will compare the two most frequently used theories in recent literature, transaction cost analysis (TCA) and bargaining power theory (BP). The following sections describe the two theories.

Transaction Cost Analysis (TCA)

Founded on economic premises, TCA suggests that the governance structure a firm chooses for a venture is driven by a desire to minimize the sum of transaction costs (Williamson 1985). Transaction costs refer to the costs of negotiating a contract, monitoring performance of the venture, and monitoring the behavior of those who enter into the contract. According to TCA, a firm will internalize functions that it is able to perform at lower transaction costs than it could obtain by contracting with suppliers and/or distributors (Erramilli and Rao 1993; Williamson 1985).

In the context of foreign market entry, TCA theory assumes a priori that an entering firm will favor a low-control mode of entry in a competitive market. However, the TCA acknowledges that in practice, market imperfections can make high-control options more attractive (Anderson and Coughlan 1987). In instances of market failure, TCA asserts that supplier incentive to engage in opportunistic behaviors is increased, and that the cost of enforcing the contract is also increased (Caves 1982). Under such circumstances, it is more advantageous for the international firm to use a high-control mode.

Bargaining Power Theory (BP)

Based on political bargaining, BP argues that the specific mode chosen for entering a foreign market depends on the relative bargaining power of the firm and the host country (Franko 1971; Stopford and Wells 1972; Tallman and Shenkar 1994). Bargaining power refers to the bargainer's ability to set the parameters of the discussion and to skew the outcome of the negotiation to the desired ownership alternative (Dwyer and Walker 1981). Bargaining power is heavily influenced by industry structure, competition, market conditions, and the firm and the host country's dependence on each other (Tallman and Shenkar 1994).

BP theory posits that a firm has a natural preference for a high-control mode of entry, since this is the most desirable arrangement in terms of the firm's long-run ability to dominate the market and its ability to protect its proprietary technology. However, the firm may be forced to settle for a lower-control mode if it has low bargaining power. A key concept in bargaining power theory is the notion of a party's stake in a venture. According to Yan and Gray (1994), a stake is the bargainer's level of dependence on a negotiating relationship and its outcome. As the stake increases, bargaining power decreases. Furthermore, the number and attractiveness of alternatives available to the parties has a strong influence on the negotiated entry arrangement. The party having more attractive alternatives will tend to be more powerful, since it can exercise its best alternative to a negotiated agreement (Anderson and Narus 1990; Fisher and Ury 1981).

The TCA and BP theories clearly offer different explanations of firms' foreign market entry mode choice. Consequently, it is important that the two theories be compared in the same study in order to understand their relative predictive power.

MAJOR FACTORS AND THEIR EFFECT ON ENTRY MODE CHOICE

TCA Factors

A review of the literature suggests that there are at least seven key factors within the TCA framework that play a role in explaining a firm's choice of entry mode. These are: (1) the uncertainty of demand for the product in the host country; (2) the attractiveness of the market of the host country; (3) the level of cultural similarity between the firm's home country and the targeted host country; (4) the specificity of the technology on which the firm's product and production processes are based; (5) the ability of the firm to receive (what it perceives as) a fair price for the technology it intends to transfer; (6) the frequency of transactions between the venture and the firm's other subsidiaries; and (7) the size of the MNC.

In this study, uncertainty of demand is defined as the extent to which future sales of a firm's products or services in a foreign market are difficult to predict (see Williamson 1975). Williamson (1975) notes that because managers' knowledge is bounded, they are often unable to predict future contingencies. As a result of bounded rationality, high external uncertainty mandates that the writing and enforcement of contracts that specify eventualities and consequent responses will be quite expensive (Anderson and Weitz 1989). Thus, it is expected that the uncertainty of demand a firm faces will lead the firm to choose a high-control entry mode.

Market attractiveness refers to the size and growth potential of the foreign market. In highly attractive markets, the potential for shirking is increased (Gomes-Casseres 1989). Since attractive markets (in terms of size and demand potential) offer increased opportunity for economies of scale if a high-control arrangement is chosen and are also associated with a higher risk of shirking, TCA suggests that firms will be more prone to opt for a high-control mode of entry in an attractive market.

Cultural similarity refers to the perceived similarity between the culture of a firm's home country and the culture of the host country being entered. Similarity between the cultures of the host country and the home country leads to lowered transaction costs and, in turn, a preference for low-control modes (Kim and Hwang 1992). Erramilli and Rao (1993), in studies of US service firms, found cultural similarity to be related to entry mode choice. However, the impact of this variable was mediated by level of experience and asset specificity. Generally, cultural similarity between the home and host countries should lead a firm to choose a low-control entry mode.

Specificity of technology is defined as the extent to which transaction-specific technologies exists (Anderson and Coughlan 1987). When specialized technology and investments are necessary for the transaction to take place, the market has limited ability to ascertain the fair value of the technology. Thus, the transaction cost may increase and a firm may favor a high-control mode to enter the host country (Erramilli and Rao 1993).

Ability to receive a fair price refers to the firm's perception of the extent to which it will be fairly compensated for its technology and/or products when they are sold in a foreign market. According to TCA, market imperfections can occur when there is an imperfect flow of information among companies (Williamson 1981). As a result, potential licensees or joint venture partners may disagree with the firm as to the value of its offering. In these instances, the firm will be better off by opting for a high-control entry mode as opposed to discounting its technology.

Frequency of transactions refers to the number of transactions needed between a firm and its foreign subsidiary, partner, or distributor in order to maintain and operate the venture. When volumes are large and the frequency of transactions is high, the firm is better off using a high-control mode to minimize the costs of frequent negotiations and monitoring associated with a low-control mode.

The size of the firm is defined as a firm's annual worldwide sales volume. The high-control modes involve high levels of resource commitment and risk. Large firms, being more able to absorb such risks, will be more likely to opt for high-control modes.

Table 6.1 summarizes the above discussion and list the TCA factors and their effect on a firm's foreign market entry mode choice.

The BP Factors

The literature on BP theory suggests that there are seven factors which have a key influence on firms' choice of entry mode. These factors are: (1) stake of the host country in attracting the investment; (2) stake of the MNC in making the investment; (3) the level of competition for investing in the host country; (4) government restrictions imposed by the host country; (5) the need for local contribution for the MNC to achieve success; (6) the resource commitment required by the MNC; and (7) the level of risk associated with the investment.

Stake of the host country is defined as the degree to which the host country perceives a compelling need to attract the investment. When the host country has an important stake in attracting the venture, the bargaining

Table 6.1   Summary of the TCA factors' effect on entry mode choice

TCA Factor	Type of Entry Mode
Uncertainty of demand	High control
Foreign market attractiveness	High control
Cultural similarity	Low control
Specificity of technology	High control
Inability to receive a fair price	High control
Frequency of transactions	High control
Firm size	High control

power of the host country will decrease, whereas the bargaining power of the firm will increase (Gomes-Casseres 1990). Thus, the host country is likely to yield to the firm's demand for entering with a high-control mode.

Stake of the firm is defined as the extent to which a firm perceives itself as having a critical need to enter the host country due to strategic considerations (see Hill, Hwang and Kim 1990). In general, BP theory predicts that in instances where a firm believes it has a significant strategic stake in the host country, the firm's relative bargaining power will be reduced and it may be forced to settle for a lower control mode of entry than it desires.

Competitive intensity is defined as the extent to which entry into the host country is contested by a firm's competitors. When the foreign market is being pursued by a number of different firms, BP theory suggests that the bargaining power of the host government is increased (Tallman and Shenkar 1994) and the firm may be forced to accept a low-control mode of entry.

As used in this study, government restrictions refers to the extent that the laws and regulations of a host country have an impact on the operations of a foreign firm. When restrictive regulations are imposed by the host country, the firm may simply not have the power to negotiate a high-control mode, and may have settle for a low-control mode.

Need for local contribution refers to the MNCs need for local capital, technology, or other resources in order to ensure the success of the venture. When the need for local contribution is high, the host country will enjoy an improved position in terms of relative bargaining power (Yan and Gray 1994). Thus the firm may have to accept a low-control mode to enter the host country.

Resource commitment is defined as the level to which the foreign market entry requires high levels of capital investment and/or a commitment to hiring a large number of local employees. High resource commitment levels increase the stake of both parties, but particularly that of the host country

Table 6.2   Summary of the BP factors' effect on entry mode choice

BP Factor	Type of Entry Mode
Stake of the host country	High control
Stake of the firm	Low control
Level of competition to enter	Low control
Government restrictions	High control
Need for local contribution	Low control
Resource commitment	High control
Country risk	Low control

since capital is a scarce resource (Gomes-Casseres 1990; Yan and Gray 1994). As a result, the firm's bargaining power is enhanced, and it is likely to be permitted to use a high-control mode of entry.

Country risk refers to the uncertainty associated with the success of the investment in the foreign market. A high level of risk in a foreign country tends to reduce the alternatives for the host country and increase the bargaining position of the firm, making it more likely that the MNC will be able to negotiate a high-control mode of entry.

Table 6.2 summarizes the above discussion and lists the BP factors and their effect on a firm's foreign market entry mode choice.

METHODOLOGY

Sampling Frame

A total of 1024 US manufacturing firms were identified using Dun and Bradstreet's American Corporate Families. The source listed the firm's annual sales, number of employees, and the name and address of the CEO. Only firms with at least 100 employees and US$20 million in annual sales were included. These criteria were considered necessary to enhance the relative homogeneity of the sample, and were consistent with the focus of the research, namely firms, which are of sufficient size to have a range of possibilities in terms of entry mode arrangements.

Questionnaire and Measures

A structured survey questionnaire was developed using a multi-stage process. Based on the prior entry modes literature, a list of items was developed which were potentially useful to measure these constructs. These items were then expanded into Likert-type statements, with responses to be measured on a five-point scale ranging from 'strongly agree' to 'strongly disagree'. Personal interviews with three US executives responsible for international market ventures were conducted to pretest the questionnaire. After incorporating feedback from the pretest, the questionnaire was finalized.

The dependent variable measure was type of entry mode chosen. The instructions on the questionnaire asked the respondents to apply the questions to a recent foreign market entry decision made by their firms. With the exception of size of the firm, which was divided into five categories based on the firm's sales level, the independent variables were measured using a five-point Likert scale.

Data Collection

Data collection involved three stages. In the first stage, a personalized cover letter, a copy of the questionnaire, and a postage-paid business reply envelope were sent to the CEO/President of each of the 1024 US firms in the sampling frame. In the second stage, an additional mailing, which included a replacement copy of the questionnaire, was sent out to those firms that had not responded in the first mailing. In the third stage, another mailing was sent to those firms that did not respond to the first two mailings.

Overall, 55 questionnaires were returned undelivered, and 51 were not usable, usually due to the firm indicating that it had not entered any foreign markets in the recent past. Of the remaining 918 questionnaires, 165 usable responses were obtained, resulting in an effective response rate of 18 per cent.

Assessment of Non-response Bias

Potential non-response bias was assessed by comparing the responding companies with non-responding companies in terms of annual sales and number of full-time employees, the only comparative data available for both responding and non-responding groups. The results of the *t*-test comparisons indicate that responding firms are not statistically different from non-responding ones, based on average annual sales and average number of employees. Thus, it can be concluded that there is no compelling evidence that suggests the presence of non-response bias.

ANALYSIS AND FINDINGS

Measurement Assessment

To assess the reliability of the factors, coefficient alphas were computed for those factors that were measured by multiple indicators. It is found that for the 10 factors that were measured by multiple items, five have coefficient alphas above 0.700 and five others between 0.600 and 0.700. For the remaining four factors, single indicators were used for measurement due to the non-latent nature of these factors. Given the exploratory nature of such measurement schemes, the reliability of the 10 multi-item factors is considered to be adequate (Nunnally 1967).

Testing the Effect of the TCA Factors

Consistent with previous studies and the categorical nature of the dependent variable, hypotheses were tested by multiple discriminant analysis (see Anderson and Coughlan 1987; and Erramilli and Rao 1993). Since the key research question in this study is whether the TCA and BP can predict firms' entry mode choice, the dependent variable is entry mode, which has three major categories: (1) licensing/franchising, (2) joint venture, and (3) wholly-owned subsidiary.

To test the TCA factors with multiple discriminant analysis, we randomly split the US sample into two: an analysis sample and a holdout sample. Using the analysis sample, two discriminant functions were fitted onto the seven TCA factors. The underlying assumptions of discriminant analysis were checked by computing univariate skewness and kurtosis, and by Box's M test. It was found that the skewness and kurtosis are small, offering no evidence of a non-normal distribution. Similarly, the Box's M test statistic suggests no evidence of inequality of variance-covariance matrices across the groups. Hence, multiple discriminant analysis is appropriate for the analysis in this study.

Two discriminant functions were computed for the analysis sample, but only one discriminant function was statistically significant. Table 6.3 shows the results of the factors' loadings on this significant discriminant function, as well as the significance of the loadings. When the discriminant function was used to classify the cases in the holdout sample, 56 per cent of the holdout sample cases were correctly classified, which is significantly higher than the random hit rate of 41.72 per cent. Table 6.4 contains the classification table for the hold out sample. These findings suggest that the TCA model predicts US firms' entry mode choice well.

To assess the effects of specific predictors, the discriminant loadings (the

Table 6.3   Discriminant analysis results on the analysis samples: TCA

Discriminating Factors	Analysis Sample	
	Wilks's Lambda	Discriminant Loading
Uncertainty of Demand	0.994	0.085
Market Attractiveness	0.929	0.273
Cultural Similarity	0.764	−0.560*
Asset Specificity	0.913	−0.299
Inability to Receive Fair Price	0.843	0.485*
Frequency of Transactions	0.813	0.539*
Firm Size	0.912	0.198

Notes: The discriminant loadings are reported for the one significant discriminant function only; the asterisk indicates significant loadings on the function.

Table 6.4   TCA classification of the holdout sample

Actual Group	No. of Cases	Predicted Group Membership		
		Lic./ Franchise	Joint Venture	Wholly-owned/ Subsidiary
Licensing/Franchising	8	3	2	3
		37.5%	25%	37.5%
Joint Venture	15	0	11	4
		0.0%	73.3%	26.7%
Wholly-owned Subsidiary	27	1	12	14
		3.7%	44.4%	51.9%

Notes: Per cent of Cases Correctly Classified: 56.00%; Random Hit Rate: 41.72%.

correlation between each independent factor and the significant discriminant function) were used, since well-known problems are associated with using discriminant weights and partial F-values. Based on the discriminant loadings, it can be seen that US firms tend to adopt a high-control mode to enter foreign markets when: they perceive that it will be difficult to receive a fair price for their technology and know-how; when the frequency of transactions is high; and when cultural similarity to the host country is low. The effects of other TCA factors are not significant. Since these significant findings are consistent with the TCA hypotheses, it can be concluded that the TCA model is supported by the data.

Testing the Effect of the BP Factors

As in the TCA case, multiple discriminant analysis was performed to test the effect of the BP factors. Using the analysis sample, two discriminant functions were fitted onto the seven BP factors. The skewness and kurtosis of the variables, and Box's M test reveal no evidence of violation of the basic assumptions of the discriminant analysis. The results of the discriminant analysis are presented in Table 6.5, and the classification table of the holdout sample is presented in Table 6.6. It was found that one discriminant function is statistically significant and accounts for 88 per cent of the variance. When the discriminant function was used to classify the cases in the holdout sample, however, the hit rate was only 35.56 per cent, which was below the proportional chance rate of 44.39 per cent. Thus, while the BP discriminant model explains a significant amount of the variance of the analysis sample, it failed to classify the holdout sample successfully. Thus, it can be concluded that the BP discriminant model does not adequately explain the firms' entry mode choices.

Overall, it can be concluded that three TCA factors are significant predictors of the US firms' foreign market entry mode choice. In contrast, the BP factors do not seem to accurately predict the holdout sample's foreign market entry mode choice.

Table 6.5 *Discriminant analysis results on the analysis samples: BP*

Discriminating Factors	Analysis Sample	
	Wilks's Lambda	Discriminant Loading
Stake of the Host Country	0.955	0.014
Stake of the MNC	0.845	0.524*
Level of Competition	0.981	0.169*
Government Restrictions	0.895	−0.416*
Need for Local Contribution	0.994	−0.061
Resource Commitment	0.913	0.377*
Country Risk	0.927	0.317

Notes: The discriminant loadings are reported for the one significant discriminant function only; the asterisk indicates significant loadings on the function.

Table 6.6   BP classification of the holdout sample

		Predicted Group Membership		
Actual Group	No. of Cases	Lic./ Franchise	Joint Venture	Wholly-owned/ Subsidiary
Licensing/Franchising	3	0	3	0
		0.0%	100.0%	0.0%
Joint Venture	19	4	4	11
		21.1%	21.1%	57.9%
Wholly-owned Subsidiary	23	5	6	12
		21.7%	26.1%	52.2%

Notes: Per cent of Cases Correctly Classified: 35.56%; Random Hit Rate: 44.39%.

DISCUSSION

Assessing the Competing Theories

The literature on foreign market entry has advanced several theories to explain a firm's choice of foreign market entry mode. The TCA and the BP are arguably the two leading theories. Yet, few studies have attempted to compare the two theories simultaneously. As a result, the relative explanatory power of the competing theories is unknown. On the empirical front, most prior studies have adopted secondary data when testing the entry mode choice theories. A limitation with such studies is that measures of some of the key theoretical constructs are either not available or have to be derived from proxy indicators. Consequently, the quality of measurement and the completeness of theory testing would suffer when primary data are not available.

In this exploratory study, we set out to overcome the limitations of previous studies by comparing the TCA's and the BP's explanatory power based on a cross-sectional primary data set. Using multiple discriminant analysis, our findings indicate that the TCA factors performed well in predicting the US firms' foreign market entry mode choices, whereas the BP factors could not provide a satisfactory explanation of the firms' entry mode choice. Hence, our findings suggest that the TCA works better than the BP in the context of US firms.

The key findings of our study have significant implications in theory development in the entry mode literature. They clearly point out the need for researchers to further define the boundaries within which the BP theory is applicable. It is possible that in an era of globalization of the world markets, most host countries perhaps have reduced the barriers for cross-border investment and are less involved in foreign firms' investment decisions. It is also possible that the trend toward freer markets across the world since the end of the Cold War has tilted the bargaining power in favor of the investing firms. In any case, future research is needed to explore these issues.

Managerially, our findings offer insight into the decision criteria adopted by the US managers in selecting a mode for entering the foreign markets. Since the TCA factors that are focused on the intra-firm efficiency worked well, it can be concluded that US managers are preoccupied by efficiency goals in selecting a mode for foreign market entry. At least to some extent, US managers behave like the economic 'rational man' in making foreign market entry decisions, as opposed to being the political 'deal maker' or 'bargainer. Based on TCA theory, this would suggest that, in the absence of market imperfections, US managers see an opportunity to reduce transaction costs and, in turn, enhance efficiency.

KEY TCA FACTORS AFFECTING THE ENTRY MODE CHOICE OF US FIRMS

In addition to the broad finding that TCA works better for the US data than the BP, the present study also identified several key factors that influence the entry mode decisions of US firms. Specifically, three TCA-based factors are significant predictors of US firms' choice of entry mode. A US firm tends to choose a high-control mode to enter a foreign market when the frequency of transactions between the planned venture and the firm's other subsidiaries is high. Presumably the firm can cut down the transaction costs of frequent negotiation and contract monitoring associated with a market transaction (a low-control mode) by adopting a high-control mode. A US firm is also likely to choose a high-control mode when it is difficult to get a fair price for the firm's technology and know-how in the foreign market. Due to information asymmetry and other market failures, potential licensees may not be able to fully appreciate the value of the firm's technology and know-how. As a result, they may be reluctant to pay a high licensing fee. Thus, the firm is better off by choosing a high-control mode to reduce the costs of lengthy negotiation needed to sway potential licensees and realize the full value of its technology and know-how. Finally, a US firm is inclined to choose a high-control mode when cultures are less similar between the host country and the USA. When entering a host country whose culture is dissimilar to the USA, a firm may find itself in a position where it disagrees with foreign business partners with regard to what needs to be done and how to accomplish a task. Instead of incurring high transaction costs associated with contract negotiation and monitoring, the firm may be better off adopting a high-control model so that transactions will take place within the internal market.

Limitations

This study's comparison of the TCA and BP is limited by the fact that only US firms were included. As a result, the generalizability of the findings to other cultures is unknown. Future research should investigate the applicability of the TCA and BP in other cultures. Another limitation of the present study is that only two competing theories are investigated. While the TCA and BP are the two dominant theories in the entry mode literature (Tallman and Shenkar 1994), there exist several other theories such as the eclectic paradigm and internalization theory. Given the need to limit the length of our questionnaire, these theories were not included in the present study. However, their relative explanatory power should be researched in the future in order to advance our knowledge of entry mode choice.

REFERENCES

Agarwal, Sanjeev and Sridhar N. Ramaswami (1992), 'Choice of Foreign Market Entry Mode: Impact of Ownership, Location, and Internalization Factors', *Journal of International Business Studies*, **23** (1), 1–27.

Anderson, Erin and Anne T. Coughlan (1987), 'International Marketing Entry and Expansion via Independent or Integrated Channels of Distribution', *Journal of Marketing*, **51** (January), 71–82.

Anderson, Erin and Barton Weitz (1989), 'Determinants of Continuity in Conventional Industrial Dyad Channels', *Marketing Science*, **8**, 310–23.

Anderson, James C. and James A. Narus (1990), 'A Model of Distributor Firm and Manufacturer Firm Working Partnerships', *Journal of Marketing*, **54** (January), 42–58.

Caves, Richard E. (1982), *Multinational Enterprise and Economic Analysis*, Cambridge: Cambridge University Press.

Dwyer, Frederick R. and Orville C. Walker (1981), 'Bargaining in an Assymetrical Power Structure', *Journal of Marketing*, **45** (Winter), 104–55.

Erramilli, M. Krishna (1991), 'The Experience Factor in Foreign Market Entry Behavior of Service Firms', *Journal of International Business Studies*, **22** (Fall), 479–501.

Erramilli, M. Krishna and C.P. Rao (1990), 'Choice of Foreign Market Entry Modes by Service Firms: Role of Market Knowledge', *Management International Review*, **30** (2), 135–50.

Erramilli, M. Krishna and C.P. Rao (1993), 'Service Firms' International Entry

Mode Choice: A Modified Transaction Cost Analysis Approach', *Journal of Marketing*, **57** (July), 19–38.

Fisher, R. and W. Ury (1981), *Getting to YES: Negotiating Agreement Without Giving In*. New York: Penguin Books.

Franko, Lawrence G. (1971), *Joint Venture Survival in Multinational Corporations*, New York: Praeger.

Gomes-Casseres, Benjamin (1989), 'Ownership Structures of Foreign Subsidiaries: Theory and Evidence', *Journal of Economic Behavior and Organization*, **11**, 1–25.

Gomes-Casseres, Benjamin (1990), 'Firm Ownership Preferences and Host Government Restrictions: An Integrated Approach', *Journal of International Business Studies*, **21** (1), 1–21.

Hennart, Jean (1989), 'Can the "New Forms of Investment" Substitute for the "Old Forms"? A Transaction Costs Perspective', *Journal of International Business Studies*, **20** (2), 211–34.

Hennart, Jean (1991), 'The Transaction Costs Theory of Equity Joint Ventures: An Empirical Study of Japanese Subsidiaries in the United States', *Management Science*, **21** (4), 483–97.

Hill, Charles W.L., Peter Hwang and W. Chan Kim (1989), 'An Eclectic Theory of the Choice of International Entry Mode', *Strategic Management Journal*, **11** (2), 117–28.

Kim, W. Chan and Peter Hwang (1992), 'Global Strategy and Multinationals' Entry Mode Choice', *Journal of International Business Studies*, **23** (1), 29–53.

Nunnally, J. (1967), *Psychometric Theory*, New York: McGraw-Hill.

Root, Franklin R. (1994), *Entry Strategies for International Markets*, Washington, DC: Lexington Books.

Shane, Scott (1994), 'The Effect of National Culture on the Choice Between Licensing and Foreign Direct Investment', *Strategic Management Journal*, **15**, 627–42.

Stopford, John M. and Louis T. Wells, Jr (1972), *Managing the Multinational Enterprise*, New York: Basic Books.

Tallman, Stephen B. and Oded Shenkar (1994), 'A Managerial Decision Model of International Cooperative Venture Formation', *Journal of International Business Studies*, **25** (1), 91–113.

Williamson, Oliver E. (1975), *Markets and Hierarchies: Analysis and Antitrust Implications*, New York: Free Press.

Williamson, Oliver E. (1981), 'The Modern Corporation: Origins, Evolution, Attributes', *Journal of Economic Literature*, **19** (December), 1537–68.

Williamson, Oliver E. (1985), *The Economic Institutions of Capitalism*, New York: Free Press.

Williamson, Oliver E. (1986), *Economic Organization: Firms, Markets, and Policy Control*, New York: New York University Press.

Yan, Aimin and Barbara Gray (1994), 'Bargaining Power, Management, Control, and Performance in United States–China Joint Ventures: A Comparative Case Study', *Academy of Management Journal*, **37** (6), 1478–517.

7. Foreign market entry modes: a sequentially embedded decision approach

F. Esra Gençtürk

INTRODUCTION

Mode of entry into a foreign market has consistently been singled out as a frontier issue in international business research with significant consequences for firms and policy makers (Davidson 1982; Erramilli and Rao 1993; Hill et al. 1990; Root 1987; Wind and Perlmutter 1977). For firms, entry mode choice is an important strategic decision with far-reaching consequences for competitive advantage and performance. Furthermore, since each mode of foreign market entry involves different resource deployment patterns, levels of control, and risk/return tradeoff, firms' choice of a particular mode in serving a given host market is difficult to change without considerable loss of time and money (Root 1987). At the macro regulatory level, entry mode of foreign firms is critical as it determines the degree of foreign involvement in host economies, level of foreign control of local operations, and their level of impact on the local economy.

Not surprisingly, there has been considerable research into the patterns, determinants, and consequences of foreign market entry modes. Some researchers have focused on the ownership and control issues implied by various entry modes (e.g. Agarwal and Ramaswami 1992; Anderson and Gatignon 1986; Contractor 1990; Davidson and McFetridge 1984, 1985; Erramilli 1991; Gomes-Casseres 1989; Hennart 1982, 1991; Hennart and Park 1993; Hennart and Reddy 1997). Others have examined the effect of cultural distance and host-country characteristics on the mode of entry (e.g. Cho and Radmanabhan 1995; Davidson and McFetridge 1984, 1985; Gatignon and Anderson 1988; Kogut and Singh 1988; Kwon and Konopa 1992). Research attention has also been directed, albeit to a lesser degree, to the performance implications of various modes of foreign market entry (e.g. Anand and Delios 1997; Brouthers et al. 1999; Busija et al. 1997; Li 1995; Simmonds 1990; Woodcock et al. 1994).

While this rich research tradition has resulted in a remarkable body of knowledge, providing insights into the drivers and consequences of entry mode decision, there is still a lack of conceptual integration and consistent empirical corroboration (Macharzina and Engelhard 1991). There is also confusion in terminology as well as concerns over limitations and appropriateness of frameworks used (Benito and Welch 1993; Duffy 1996; Hennart 1989; McNaughton 1999; O'Farrell et al. 1995). Moreover, by looking at foreign mode of entry choice itself as a singular discrete decision, the multifaceted and sequential nature of the phenomenon has mostly been overlooked (Kogut 1983).

In order for the research on foreign market entry choice to progress both in theory development and in attempts to synthesize disparate research findings, there is a need to understand the context within which entry mode decision is made, and above all to recognize explicitly the complex nature of this decision. Hence, precise understanding of the foreign market entry mode decision and its subsequent explanation requires identification of the components that constitute this decision. Consequently, this chapter builds upon the premise that foreign market entry decision is a complex phenomenon that is inherently ambiguous until it is separated into its component parts. The broad concerns in this chapter are with our accumulated knowledge about foreign market entry choice and the nature of this complex decision. The focus is not on specific hypotheses or empirical results but rather on the insights disparate theoretical approaches bring to foreign market entry mode decision. To this end, we build on the extant research on foreign market entry mode and identify four distinct decisions that constitute the entry mode choice in their totality. These decisions are conceptualized as representing distinct yet sequentially related considerations taking place at different levels within the firm that is expanding its geographical reach beyond the borders of its home market.

In the section below, foreign market entry choice is described with a specific emphasis on the decision itself, as well as modal choices and the attributes associated with each choice. Next, an overview of different research streams is provided with an emphasis on their theoretical underpinnings. Following a brief identification of major issues associated with extant foreign market entry choice research, an analytical model, which delineates four sequentially embedded primary decisions that constitute the foreign market entry choice, is proposed and described. The chapter concludes with a summary of its contributions and suggestions for future research.

FOREIGN MARKET ENTRY: DECISION, MODES AND ATTRIBUTES

Foreign market entry has long been one of the international business field's foremost concerns as it entails nontrivial investments with significant opportunity and switching costs. In seeking to serve and penetrate foreign markets, firms may choose from various entry modes. Typical modes of foreign market entry include exporting (indirect or direct), licensing, joint ventures, wholly owned subsidiaries (acquisitions or green-field investments). At a higher level of aggregation these market entry modes can be reclassified into two groups as nonequity and equity modes (e.g. Pan and Tse 2000). In nonequity modes such as licensing or direct and indirect exporting, the foreign firm serves the host market through arm's-length contractual agreements. In equity modes, the firm has a legal physical presence in a foreign country based on ownership interest in the form of a joint venture or a wholly owned branch or subsidiary.

The different modes of entry have been further associated with and described in terms of various behavioral dimensions or salient attributes. These attributes are: risk/return, resource commitment, and control. Based on normative decision theory, a firm is expected to choose the entry mode that offers the highest risk-adjusted return on investment. Furthermore, behavioral evidence indicates that a firm's choices may also be determined by resource availability and need for control. Resource availability refers to the financial and managerial capacity of a firm for serving a particular foreign market. Control refers to a firm's need to influence systems, methods, and decisions in that foreign market (Anderson and Gatignon 1986). It is generally assumed that higher operational control results from having a greater ownership in the foreign venture. However, risks are also likely to be higher due to the assumption of responsibility of decision making and higher commitment of resources.

Entry mode choices are, therefore, often assumed to entail a compromise among the four attributes of risk, return, resource commitment, and control. The exporting mode is conceptualized as a low resource and consequently low risk/return alternative, which provides the firm with little local control. The wholly owned subsidiary, on the other extreme, is viewed as a high resource commitment mode and consequently high risk/return alternative that also provides the firm with a high level of host-market control.

While the prevailing view considers a business' equity ownership position and its resource commitment to and control over foreign operations to be closely and systematically related, the need to distinguish among ownership, control, and resource deployment considerations has been acknowledged by several researchers (e.g. Anderson and Gatignon 1986; Gençtürk et al. 1995; Gençtürk and Aulakh 1995; Erramilli and Rao 1993; Sohn 1994). In fact, the importance of control in managing host-country activities as a distinct consideration separate from the equity ownership position is reflected in several studies. For example, Carstairs and Welch (1982) provide empirical evidence suggesting that the control exercised can vary not only across different modes of entry but also within a given mode as indicated by differences in responsibilities assumed and carried out in foreign markets. In a more recent study, Aulakh and Gençtürk (2000) argue and find empirical support for the use of various types and degrees of control in intra- as well as interorganizational exchanges. Similarly, recent trends in cross-national nonequity alliances attest to the fact that control can be exercised over foreign activities without incurring the high risk, resource commitments, and the resulting switching costs associated with equity participation. Hence, firms can use means other than equity ownership for exercising control over activities performed in the host market.

THEORETICAL FOUNDATIONS

While most areas of research in international business have been criticized for being atheoretical or superficially using borrowed frameworks without due modification, foreign market entry mode research has moved well beyond anecdotal and idiosyncratic descriptions and evolved into well-established, systematic, and grounded research streams with a rich and diverse theoretical base. There is a significant and growing volume of literature that has been devoted to providing an explanation for observed market entry mode differences in serving foreign markets.

Some of the earlier theorizing on foreign market entry behavior of firms has focused on country-specific or locational advantages to explain benefits associated with locating certain activities in particular countries. Locational advantages refer to special benefits accruing to firms because of geographic and physical location of their operations. These benefits have been found to arise from structural market imperfections such as government regulations (Rugman et al. 1985) and/or the potential to economize on production costs due to the host country's factor endowments as well as to benefit from local opportunities (Rugman 1990), including characteristics of local demand, competition, and supporting industries (Porter 1990). In fact, a fundamental tenet of the classical international trade theory is comparative advantage whereby relative cross-country differences in productivity in carrying out economic activities make it desirable for firms and nations to specialize in and export the products/services that capitalize on the country's abundant factors of production and/or reflect its superior capabilities.

In addition to comparative advantage-based explanations of firms' involvement in exporting, the host country's trade policy, such as high tariffs or rigid quotas, is viewed as one of the most important locational variables that has deterred exporting and encouraged foreign production (Caves 1971). Similarly, perceived political instability of the host country has been found to influence a firm's entry mode decision (Anderson and Gatignon 1986; Goodnow and Hanz 1972; Goodnow 1985). In nations where political instability is perceived to be high, it is unlikely that a high resource commitment entry mode such as a wholly owned subsidiary will be undertaken. In general, firms interested in expanding their operations beyond the boundaries of the home country are expected to use a selective strategy and favor entry into markets possessing location advantages such as large size, high growth rate, political stability, similarity to home country, as well as favorable economic, competitive and regulatory environment.

Another important contribution to our understanding of firms' foreign market entry mode choice comes from the behavior theory of the firm (Cyert and March 1963), which adds a dynamic component. In behaviorally oriented explanations of mode choice, foreign market entry is modeled as an adaptive process of internationalization following a path-dependent trajectory where the pattern of international involvement by a firm is a function of its past international experience (Johanson and Vahlne 1977). According to this perspective, business operations in foreign markets are inherently risky because of the different political, cultural, and market systems that the firm must adapt to. The main source of this uncertainty is the foreign firm's lack of local market knowledge regarding the new country context. Firms operating internationally respond to the uncertainty and hence the liability of their foreignness (Zaheer 1995) with a sequential market entry and penetration strategy. Process views of international expansion such as the Scandinavian School (e.g. Johanson and Vahlne 1977) and the product cycle approach (Vernon 1976, 1979) relate foreign market entry decision to a firm's international experience. They contend that the firm's experiential knowledge initially derived from the domestic market is of limited value in culturally distant markets, as measured by differences in language, values, political systems, etc. (Davidson 1983; Kogut and Singh 1988). Therefore, the cultural distance between the home and host markets affects market selection as well as choice of entry mode. Firms move to distant countries only after having established a presence in more proximate countries. In this slow process of sequential internationalization, the firm learns the habits, preferences, and market structure of the target countries. This experiential knowledge is a critical resource since it is country specific and it cannot be easily transferred between firms or business units.

In addition to sequential internationalization from culturally similar to dissimilar countries, firms are also expected to increase their commitment in a given host market sequentially by entering a foreign market with a low resource commitment mode such as exporting. As the firm acquires more knowledge and experience in that host market, it is expected to assume a higher level of resource commitment with higher levels of risk, control and profit return. The gradual incremental foreign market involvement advocated in this behavioral perspective forms the conceptual basis for modeling entry modes as a continuum of increasing levels of resource commitment, risk exposure, control, and profit potential from exports to wholly owned subsidiaries.

A similar behaviorally oriented explanation considers foreign market entry mode not only as a learning sequence but also as an adoption of innovation process. In other words, the internationalization decision is considered as an innovation for the firm with various models proposed in the extant literature based on Rogers's (1962) stages of adoption process. Accordingly, these models distinguish a number of stages, arranged as a sequential, fixed development of the internationalization process. The most notable of the innovation-related stages model of market entry decision are those proposed by Andersen (1993), Bilkey and Tesar (1977), Czinkota (1982), and Cavusgil (1980, 1982). While proposed models differ with respect to the number of stages considered and the description of the proposed stages, the underlying theoretical premise remains the same, where the emphasis in these models is on classifying the development into stages rather than on explaining how firms move from one stage to another.

In a more recent extension of the behavioral explanations of mode of entry, Chang (1995) showed that MNCs often enter foreign markets in a sequential fashion, beginning with lines of business where they have the strongest competitive advantage over local firms, and over time adding lines of business that offer little or no competitive advantage. The competitive advantage present in early entries allows the firm to overcome any liabilities of foreignness. Over time, as the firm gains experience managing in the host country, learning about local practices and building relations with local suppliers, and recruiting local employees, the liabilities of foreignness may diminish or disappear, allowing it to enter into additional lines of business where its competitive advantage over local firms is lower. That is, whereas an initial entry into a foreign market may be motivated by a desire to exploit the firm's existing competitive advantages, the later ones might seek more to tap host-country advantages.

Subsequent research rooted again in behavioral theory of the firm as well as resource-based theory of the firm has paid increased attention to the notion of firms competing primarily on the basis of capabilities (Prahalad and Hamel 1990; Cantwell 1991). While earlier attempts have focused on home-country-based capabilities that can be exploited in foreign markets (Hymer 1960; Caves 1971), more recent research supported by strategic linkage theory (Chen and Chen 1998; Nohria and Garcia-Pont 1991) and network approach (Johanson and Mattsson 1987) interprets foreign market entry decision as an attempt to access external resources in order to offset the weaknesses of the foreign investor. In other words, foreign market entry decision is viewed not as exploitation of advantages a firm possesses but as a quest for strategic advantages/resources that it lacks along with the corresponding notion of collaboration formation for the purpose of developing a firm's capabilities (Kogut 1988; Hamel 1991). The source of organizational capabilities (OC) can be the firm itself, the industry in which it operates and/or the home as well as the host countries which it serves (Porter 1990). Accordingly, in OC perspective, mode of entry decision is guided by the need to manage a firm's capabilities (Kogut and Zander 1992, 1993) in terms of developing and deploying firm-specific advantages.

A different yet equally established research stream on entry mode draws predominantly from the internalization perspective (Buckley and Casson 1976; Rugman 1980), which is closely related to transaction cost (TC) theory (Williamson 1975). Unlike the behavioral explanations which views entry mode decision as a sequential progression, internalization and TC perspectives assume that all entry choices are considered simultaneously at the same point in time. Hence, foreign market entry mode decision is treated as a static, discrete choice concerned with the minimization of transaction costs and the conditions underlying market failure. In the context of entry mode choice, market failure can be related to both natural market imperfections (e.g. public good nature of knowledge) and government-imposed market imperfections. Both internalization and TC explanations also focus on the characteristics of a transaction in order to decide on the most efficient governance mode. In the internalization perspective, foreign firms need to possess superior assets/skills to earn economic rents that are high enough to counter the disadvantage of not possessing local market knowledge and the associated cost of serving unfamiliar and distant markets. The firm is, therefore, the possessor of some rent-yielding firm-specific advantage (e.g. differentiated products, advanced R&D) and enters foreign markets in order to exploit this advantage in the most efficient manner. When the host market for this firm-specific advantage is characterized by imperfections, creating complications in its pricing and transfer, cost of transacting with an independent entry increases and internalizing the transaction becomes the more efficient mode. The decision to internalize implies that it is beneficial for the firm to exploit the advantage itself through its own subsidiary rather than selling it to independent firms with arm's-length contractual agreements such as licensing. Accordingly, the internalization and TC approaches are primarily oriented towards the selection of entry mode that minimizes transaction costs associated with the host-country exploitation of a unique advantage possessed by the foreign firm.

Given the diversity of theoretical explanations offered to account for variations in firms' foreign market entry choice, there have been periodic attempts at developing a synthesis between different theories and explanatory models (Dunning 1979, 1980, 1988; Hill et al. 1990; Huang 1996; Tallman 1991). Among these, Dunning's (1979) eclectic model identifies ownership advantages, location advantages, and internalization advantages as relevant factors for entry mode decision. Ownership advantages refer to firm-specific assets and skills such as firm size, multinational experience, or ability to develop and market a differentiated product. Location advantages refer to the attractiveness of a foreign market whereas internalization advantages refer to the benefit of retaining assets and skills within the firm when an external market is unable to impose pricing or behavioral constraints. Hill et al. (1990) provide another integrative framework where strategic variables along with transaction and environmental variables are considered as the broad groups of variables that influence entry mode choice. In the Hill et al. (1990) framework, strategic variables are hypothesized to influence entry mode choice mainly through control needs of the firm, environmental variables do so through their impact on resource commitment, and transaction variables exert their influence on choice of entry mode through their impact on risk exposure. In a similar vein, Tallman (1991) proposes a resource-based strategic management (SM) model of MNE market entry, which combines resource position, market strategy, and firm structure with economic efficiency considerations. More recently, Huang (1996) tested a model that included 10 variables grouped into transaction-specific, environmental, firm-specific, and organizational factors. Consistent with the results of similar empirical attempts, significant locational advantages and transaction-related costs were found to have a significant effect on entry mode choice.

In general, attempts to combine different theoretical perspectives into an eclectic explanation have received general acceptance but limited empirical support. More importantly, these attempts do not provide a truly integrative or unified perspective (Tallman 1991) since most represent a juxtaposition and simultaneous consideration of several explanatory variables suggested in various perspectives and not a formalized synthesis of the theoretical explanations provided by the different perspectives themselves.

From this standpoint, eclectic models have yet to constitute a material theory that would allow empirically substantiated conclusions to be drawn (Macharzina and Engelhard 1991).

MAJOR ISSUES

Using the aforementioned theories, researchers have gathered considerable evidence regarding predictors of foreign market entry mode choice. However, concerns have been raised about the limitations of the frameworks, definitional ambiguities, the operationalization of the entry mode decision, and level of analysis (Benito and Welch 1993; Duffy 1996; Hennart 1989; Kogut 1983; Macharzina and Engelhard 1991; McNaughton 1999; O'Farrell et al. 1995).

Duffy (1996) challenged the importance given to transactions costs as a determinant of entry choice, contending that costs such as tariffs, logistics, regulations and other non tariff barriers are declining worldwide, and may be lower compared to other factors. Others point to inconsistencies in how factors such as control and risk (Anderson and Gatignon 1986) are discussed in terms of entry mode choice and that prior frameworks support contradictory theoretical propositions regarding diametrically opposing entry strategies. For example, as international expansion involves a high degree of risk, transaction cost theory suggests that firms may prefer direct-entry or high-control modes. The same framework could be used to argue that some firms perceive higher uncertainty and risk levels in the internationalization process and should enter via low-control means with low resource commitments.

Furthermore, different theoretical perspectives operate at different levels of analysis and consequently have a different focus of interest. For example, while internalization and TC approaches focus on the transaction itself, organizational capabilities shift the emphasis upstream to capabilities and hence to the firm. Hence, there is a conceptual and related methodological problem of mixing variables of different levels and types of explanation without defining mediating mechanics (Macharzina and Engelhard 1991).

The appropriateness of the aforementioned theoretical frameworks for explaining the entry mode decision across the full range of choices has also been questioned. For example, Hennart (1989) argues that TCA is not an appropriate framework for comparing exporting with foreign direct investment (FDI) because the choice between exporting and FDI is based on production costs rather than on transaction costs, as it relates to production in different locations.

The concerns over the definition of entry mode choice and its operationalization have also been raised frequently in the literature. O'Farrell et al. (1995) argue that while certain modes have been excluded from analysis, high levels of aggregation of disaggregated data are also used in attempts to create a dichotomous dependent variable for the sake of expediency and methodological ease. Furthermore, entry mode choices have traditionally been characterized as a static decision-making process, assuming that establishing a presence in a particular host-market represents a singular, discrete decision. Such an approach does not recognize that for many firms entry mode choice is a sequential process consisting of distinct yet interrelated decisions. As stated by Kogut (1983), foreign direct investment decisions are not discrete, but might be best understood as part of a series of decisions that determine the volume and direction of resource flows among countries. Even in cases where foreign market entry is conceptualized as consisting of a series of decisions (e.g. Buckley and Casson 1998; Contractor 1984; Chang and Rosenzweig 2001), independent consideration of different subdecisions or the particular study's focus on a single subdecision has inevitably obscured the interdependence among the decisions which together constitute the foreign market entry mode choice. Looking at entry decision without regard to its multifaceted nature overlooks the differential importance and influence of alternative theoretical explanations. That is, theoretical explanations that account for one set of decisions may not hold for later ones or vice versa. Conversely, some explanatory factors may have a persistent importance in shaping all entry mode decisions while others vary in importance depending on the sequence.

PROPOSED ANALYTICAL FRAMEWORK

Close inspection of the foreign market entry mode decision and research reveals that the decision of interest is not a singular but a multifaceted phenomenon. In their consideration of foreign market entry mode, firms are not only concerned about which foreign markets to enter but they also need to decide on how to enter the chosen market and what structural and managerial mechanisms to use for the specific transactions performed in serving that host market. Accordingly, foreign market entry mode decision is not a singular discrete decision but consists of several different yet related decisions. For analytical purposes, the foreign market entry mode decisions can be studied at four levels of aggregation, each representing a distinct yet sequentially interrelated decision. The first is the motivation for firms to enter a foreign market; namely the entry decision itself. The second-level decision is the means by which firms choose to enter the particular product market, which is the decision regarding the location of production activities. The

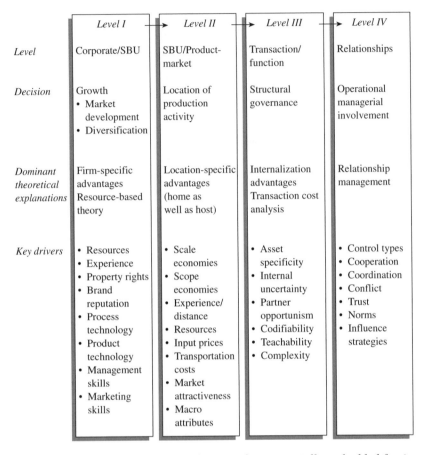

Figure 7.1   Proposed analytical framework: sequentially embedded foreign market entry mode decision

third-level decision concerns the structural presence which is the governance mode of transactions performed in the foreign market entered followed by the decision at the fourth level which concerns operational presence decisions involving management (i.e. control, coordination) of inter- or intraorganizational transactions. Each of the four decision levels are described below and summarized in Figure 7.1 along with their defining attributes.

Level I: Growth Strategy Decision

A consistent theme across different theoretical perspectives used to explain foreign market entry decision is the existence of some firm-specific assets as a prerequisite for geographical expansion of a firm's operations. Of particular importance are knowledge-based assets derived from engineering, management, and marketing expertise. These assets often have a public goods character in that they can be supplied to additional production facilities at very low cost. Because of this characteristic, these assets give rise to multiplant economies of scale (Markusen 1984; Horstmann and Markusen 1987) and hence to geographical expansion of operations.

Basically, expansion of geographic boundaries of operations and served markets represents a growth strategy of a firm. Of the different generic growth strategies, two are especially relevant for understanding firms' foreign market entry choices. One is the market development growth strategy, which represents geographic expansion of a firm's current operations, hence exploitation of existing firm-specific advantages. The other is a diversification strategy, which is represented by growth into new markets with new operations. In this case, geographical expansion into foreign markets may involve development or acquisition of firm-specific advantages that are new or at least different from those applied to current operations. Consequently, growth strategy decision would be motivated by a desire to exploit an advantage that a firm possesses in current operations, to strengthen existing advantages, or to acquire or develop a new though normally related advantage. Market entry decisions, therefore, are made under a calculus governed by considerations related to the development and deployment of a firm's capabilities.

Given the aforementioned nature of growth strategy decision, any attempt to understand and explain it should first and foremost focus on the literature on firm-specific advantages and explanatory variables suggested by associated theories of monopolistic advantages as well as the resource-based theory of the firm.

Level II: Production Location Decision

Once a firm realizes that it has or can acquire a capability that could be used to satisfy demand in a foreign country, it will then evaluate different production location options for exploiting the existing or newly developed/acquired capability. Identifying production location as a distinct albeit interdependent decision in a sequence of entry mode decisions enables consideration of where production must occur in order to maximize the returns from firm-specific advantages. The choice of a production location is based on locational advantages that maximize the value of firm-specific assets net set-up costs (Dunning 1981; Caves 1971). Rooted in trade and location theories, locational exploitation or development of organizational capabilities is influenced by characteristics of home and host markets as well as scale effects. On a strictly neoclassical view, this decision attempts to arbitrage production towards cheaper sites to attain lower costs or higher revenue.

In discerning the extent of location-specific advantages, it is useful to determine the transferability of the firm's existing capabilities/resources. Transferability may be restricted by the physical boundedness of firm-specific advantages (Rugman and Verbeke 1992) or by the inapplicability of firm-specific advantages in the host-country environment. If the motive for market development growth strategy is to exploit firm-specific advantages already possessed and the transferability of these advantages are restricted then home-country production would be favored with exporting being the resulting foreign market entry mode choice. Furthermore, economies of scale and specialization need to be large enough to warrant associated increase in international transportation and communication costs associated with export-based mode of foreign market entry.

On the other hand, if the firm-specific advantages are transferable or the motive for the growth strategy is to acquire or develop a new capability available in the host markets, then host-market-based production would be favored. The entry mode choices available in this case would be licensing/subcontracting or some type of collaborative arrangement with a local firm. As Rugman and Verbeke (1992) note, nonlocation-bound-firm specific advantages can be exploited globally, used effectively in foreign operations without substantial adaptation, and lead to benefits of scale, scope or exploitation of national differences.

It is important to note that location specificity of firm-specific advantages may not be an all or nothing phenomenon. Hence, it may be theoretically and practically more accurate to conceptualize firm-specific advantages along a continuum of location boundedness. Fundamentally, the proportion of a firm's productive activity that must take place in the home country is a function of the degree of location specificity of resources to be exploited. As Hirsch (1988) argues, a product is produced partly in isolation, independent of the consumer, and in part, simultaneously with consumption. The greater the fraction of total economic value associated with the service component (i.e. production at the time of consumption), the greater the amount of production that would occur in the host country at the site of the consumption. This would be especially true for firms whose firm-specific advantages deliver value at the downstream end of the value chain. A direct extension of this reasoning would suggest that service businesses which involve not only greater simultaneity of production and consumption but also greater economic value creation at the point of exchange would have a greater portion of their productive activity located in the host markets they serve.

Level III: Structural Presence Decision

Once the location of productive activity for the firm-specific advantage is determined, the next decision concerns the structural modality by which these firm-specific capabilities including knowledge as well as other intangible and tangible assets are to be exploited or augmented in the host country. This structural presence decision, therefore, defines the governance mode of the transactions performed in the particular host country. The appropriate unit of analysis for examining firms' structural presence decision would be the transaction where the governance modality of each transaction to be performed in the hosts country must be considered. This is where the micro-efficiency-driven explanations rooted in internalization and transaction cost analysis (TCA) would be most useful. In fact, TCA variables have consistently been found to explain a significant amount of observed variation in research specifically focusing on structural governance mode decision at the level of individual transactional activities (Agarwal and Ramaswami 1992; Anderson and Coughlan 1987; Anderson and Gatignon 1986; Erramilli and Rao 1993; Hill et al. 1990; Huang 1996; Kim and Daniels 1991; Klein et al. 1990).

Transaction cost and internalization economics offer a systematic way of analyzing the relative merits of alternative governance arrangements and a set of testable propositions relating those merits to attributes of transactions and the surrounding environment. In their basic form, TCA and internalization approaches see governance of economic exchanges as a choice between markets and a hierarchical structure, where the choice between two structural modes is governed by their relative efficiency. The principal insight from TCA- and internalization-based research is that transaction specific investments required by firms and uncertainty about allocation of outcomes make market-based performance of these transactions via arm's-length contractual agreements with external agents inefficient. Accordingly, transactions with high uncertainty to which nonfungible assets have been dedicated will be more efficiently performed when governed by the internal hierarchy of the firm than if governed by independent external agents.

Level IV: Operational Presence Decision

The fourth-level decision concerns operational presence decisions involving management (i.e., control, coordination) of inter- or intraorganizational transactions. While most of the extant mode of entry research implicitly assumes the existence of requisite administrative capabilities and control mechanisms for managing hierarchical or market-based transactions, the theoretical and practical validity of this assumption has not been tested to date and can be challenged on at least three fronts. First, it is increasingly recognized that transfer of firm-specific advantages within firms is neither easy nor without cost. For example, Zander and Kogut (1995) showed that as knowledge is less codifiable and teachable, and more complex, transferring it becomes difficult even within the boundaries of the firm. Szulanski (1996) similarly observed that causal ambiguity and the absorptive capacity of the recipient inhibits the transfer of knowledge to other parts of the organization. Inclusion of operational presence decision into the proposed analytical framework makes it clear that entry mode decision is not limited to or does not end with determination of a firm's structural presence. The firm needs to devise supporting coordination and control mechanisms as well as organizational structures that enable efficient exploitation and/or development of internalized firm-specific advantages.

Second, while Williamson (1975) originally proposed that hierarchical governance was the only means to control transaction, recent theoretical extensions include the idea that the desirable features of internal organization can also be achieved within the context of external interfirm relationships. Coughlan (1985), Jeuland and Shugan (1983), and McGuire and Staelin (1983), for example, argue that interorganizational arrangements can be managed so that they are virtually indistinguishable from internalized intraorganizational exchanges. Stinchcombe (1985) claims that unilateral provisions can be included in contracts to establish the functional equivalent of hierarchical authority. Even Williamson (1991) suggests that bilateral trading relationships can be designed to minimize potential governance problems and costs associated with arm's-length agreements with independent agents. Hence, even when host-country transactions are outsourced and performed by independent agents, the firm still faces the operational presence decision concerning the effective and efficient management of its interorganizational relationships.

Third, organizational skills in managing internalized as well as externalized transactions in a particular host market as well as throughout the global network are not constant or exogenous. Instead, these skills depend on the firm's administrative heritage and routines, thus leading to a different optimal configuration of relationships and use of coordination and control mechanisms. Firm-level routines, supporting structures as well as the regulatory and coordinative role of management, should not be ignored or implicitly assumed as being effectively applied since their unique composition can be of value and may ultimately be a source of competitive advantage.

In view of the foregoing considerations, it is argued in this study that deciding which transactions/activities to outsource and which to perform internally is a structural governance decision (Level III) that should be separate and distinct from the subsequent decision (Level IV) concerning operational management of transactions within the chosen structural governance modality. Hence, management of relationships with internal company employees as well as external independent agents emerges as an important but generally overlooked component of the broader foreign market entry decision.

CONCLUSION AND IMPLICATIONS

The rich and long tradition of research on foreign market entry mode decision constitutes considerable progress, providing invaluable insight into the drivers and consequences of entry mode choice. This research is also noteworthy, as it has benefited from a rich theoretical base rooted in different disciplines. While availability of relevant descriptive theories has been instrumental in the grounded evolution of research in this area and in revealing the complexity of the foreign market entry mode choice, there has been very little, if any, systematic investigation into the nature of this complexity and its implications. The extant research appears to have bypassed the existence of as well as the differences among the various decisions that constitute foreign market entry mode choice, treating it instead as a singular, discrete decision. Even in cases where foreign market entry choice is conceptualized as consisting of a series of decisions (e.g. Buckley and Casson 1998; Contractor 1984; Chang and Rosenzweig 2001), independent consideration of different subdecisions or the particular study's focus on a single subdecision has inevitably obscured the interdependence among the decisions which together constitute the foreign market entry mode choice. The failure to delineate the foreign market entry decision into its distinct components has limited not only the rigor with which existing explanations have been applied but also the empirical support various explanations have garnered.

The central argument of this chapter is that the relationship between foreign market entry mode choice and its determinants and consequences cannot be accurately assessed without an explicit recognition of the complex and multifaceted decision-making process that underlies this choice. Hence, in order for the extant research to progress both in theory development and in attempts to synthesize disparate research findings, there is a need to recognize and understand the inherent complexity of the foreign market entry mode decision and the diverse contexts within which this decision is made. To unravel the complexity of the foreign market entry mode choice, a systematic exposition of the dynamic and sequential decision-making calculus of firms must be undertaken. Based on this premise, this study develops and describes an analytical framework that is intended to contribute to our understanding of the sequentially embedded context within which entry mode decision is made and in surfacing its complex and multifaceted nature.

The proposed analytical framework, although subject to empirical verification, does offer guidance by highlighting factors and issues that should be considered in any attempt to understand and explain a particular component of foreign market entry decision or this decision in its totality. For instance, the framework underscores the relative importance of monopolistic firm-specific advantages and resource-based theory of the firm in considering Level I growth strategy decisions, whereas the primary focus should be on locational explanations in considering Level II decisions concerning the choice between home and host based production. Alternatively, when the unit of analysis becomes the transaction for Level III decision concerning the structural governance of operations, researchers and managers would be well advised to factor transaction cost and internalization concerns into their decision-making calculus. The final component of the foreign market entry mode choice involves decisions concerning the management of relationships with external agents as well as company employees. This is where recent research on relational exchanges with attendant interest in issues such as control, coordination, trust, and norms becomes especially relevant.

Given the differential emphasis and objectives of the decisions made at each level, it is not surprising that the relevance and relative explanatory power of the various theoretical models would vary across different decision levels and for each component of foreign market entry choice. Alternatively, certain explanatory variables can be critical at all levels for all decision components. For example, empirical findings and implications of extant mode of entry research would support the importance of perceived uncertainty as an antecedent variable exerting a significant influence on each of the four decisions delineated in the proposed framework. Yet, the source of the perceived uncertainty and the theoretical explanation provided for the hypothesized effect would be specific to the particular decision considered. More specifically, increased general as well as specific experiential knowledge about a given host market would be expected to reduce both cost and perceived risks of foreign operations. Hence, reduction in uncertainty about host-country macro operating conditions (e.g. laws, regulations) would be important in encouraging development or acquisition of new capabilities through a related diversification growth strategy at Level I. Similarly, the perception of lower contextual uncertainty would be influential at Level II concerning the location of production activity, resulting in a more favorable evaluation of host-country production. In fact, there is empirical evidence in support of a significant negative correlation between perceived macro uncertainty and host-country location of production activity (Davidson 1980; Lord and Ranft 2000). At Level III, transactional uncertainty arising internally from partner opportunism would be a critical issue influencing the structural governance decision. On the other hand, at Level IV, uncertainty associated with means–ends relationships – in evaluating the performance of internal and external agents would be critical in determining the type of control and coordination mechanism that would be used in managing these relation-ships.

The sequentially embedded decision framework proposed in this study for delineating separate yet related components of a foreign market entry mode choice is a first step necessary for progress of theory development and integration efforts on this subject matter. There are several areas for future research to refine and expand the basic framework proposed. An extremely worthwhile extension would be to generate a propositional inventory iden-tifying the expected antecedents for the decisions at each level and specify-ing the expected relationships in the form of testable hypotheses. More attention should also be focused on the congruence between theoretical explanations and operational decisions as well as the delineation of boun-daries for the applicability of different theoretical explanations.

Increased significance of nonmaterial assets as creators and/or facilita-tors of wealth should also be considered in future studies. In this context, intellectual capital has emerged as the key wealth-creating asset and has been the focus of much recent research in different disciplines. In so far as knowledge-intensive and knowledge-supporting assets have unique spatial, structural, and operational needs, it is not unreasonable to hypothesize that they will impinge on the foreign market entry decisions and related activ-ities. Equally important and even more transparent is the increased global-ization of economic activities made possible by advances in communication technologies and the emergence of electronic commerce on the Internet. Because of these technological advances and a growing number of transac-tions taking place in cyber space, the role distance plays as a physical barrier is being significantly diminished. Growing need and ease with which firms can access foreign markets, suppliers, and customers may potentially elimi-nate the need for establishing a physical presence in host markets served. One interesting question that arises in this context is whether the reduced cost and enhanced speed of communication will so reduce transaction costs that at least in some industries deintegration and contracting out will increase as a result. Hence, testing the proposed framework in diverse con-texts and under changing conditions should help gauge the strengths of the theoretical explanations and aid in empirical generalizations. It is hoped that the sequentially embedded decision framework proposed in this study will encourage conscious attention to the type of foreign market entry decision considered, generating a wave of more focused and rigorous research which provides a firmer basis for guiding firms as they expand the geographical reach of their operations.

REFERENCES

Agarwal, Sanjeev and Sridhar Ramaswami (1992), 'Choice of Foreign Entry Mode: Impact of Ownership, Location, and Internalization Factors', *Journal of International Business Studies*, **23**, 1–27.

Anand, Jaideep and Andrew Delios (1997), 'Location Specificity and the Transferability of Downstream Assets to Foreign Subsidiaries', *Journal of International Business Studies*, **28** (3), 579–603.

Andersen, Otto (1993), 'On the Internalization Process of Firms: A Critical Analysis', *Journal of International Business Studies*, **24** (2), 209–31.

Anderson, Erin and Anne T. Couglan (1987), 'International Market Entry and Expansion Via Independent or Integrated Channels of Distribution', *Journal of Marketing*, **51**, 71–82.

Anderson, Erin and Hubert Gatignon (1986), 'Modes of Foreign Entry: A Transaction Cost Analysis and Propositions', *Journal of International Business Studies*, **17** (Fall), 1–16.

Aulakh, Preet and Esra F. Gençtürk (2000), 'International Principal–Agent Relationships: Control, Governance and Performance', *Industrial Marketing Management*, **29** (6), 521–37.

Benito, G. and L. Welch (1993), 'Foreign Market Servicing: Beyond Choice of Entry Mode', *Journal of International Marketing*, **2** (2), 7–27.

Bilkey, Warren J. and George Tesar (1977), 'The Export Behavior of Smaller Wisconsin Manufacturing Firms', *Journal of International Business Studies*, **9** (Spring/Summer), 93–8.

Brouthers, Lance E., Keith D. Brouthers and Steve Werner (1999), 'Is Dunning's Eclectic Framework Descriptive or Normative?', *Journal of International Business Studies*, **30** (4), 831–44.

Buckley, Peter and Mark Casson (1976), *The Future of the Multinational Enterprise*. London, UK: Macmillan.

Buckley, Peter and Mark Casson (1998), 'Analyzing Foreign Market Entry Strategies: Extending the Internalization Approach', *Journal of International Business Studies*, **29** (3), 539–62.

Busija, Edith C., Hugh M. O'Neill and Carl P. Zeithaml (1997), 'Diversification Strategy, Entry Mode and Performance: Evidence and Choice of Constraints', *Strategic Management Journal*, **18** (4), 321–27.

Cantwell, J. (1991), 'The Theory of Technological Competence and its Application to International Production', in D. McFetridge (ed.), *Foreign Investment, Technology and Economic Growth*, Calgary: University of Calgary Press, pp. 33–67.

Carsairs, R.T. and L.S. Welch (1982), 'Licensing and the Internationalization of Smaller Companies: Some Australian Evidence', *Management International Review*, **22**, 33–44.

Caves, Richard (1971), 'International Corporations: The Industrial Economics of Foreign Investment', *Economics*, **56**, 279–93.

Cavusgil, Tamer (1980), 'On the Internationalization Process of Firms', *European Research*, **8** (November), 273–81.

Cavusgil, Tamer (1982), 'Some Observations on the Relevance of Critical Variables for Internationalization Stages', in Michael Czinkota and George Tesar (eds), *Export Management: An International Context*, New York: Praeger.

Chang, Sea-Jin (1995), 'International Expansion Strategy of Japanese Firms: Capability Building Through Sequential Entry', *Academy of Management Journal*, **38** (2), 383–407.

Chang, Sea-Jin and Philip M. Rosenzweig (2001), 'The Choice of Entry Mode in Sequential Foreign Direct Investment', *Strategic Management Journal*, **22**, 747–76.

Chen, Homin and Tain-Jy Chen (1998), 'Network Linkages and Location Choice in Foreign Direct Investment', *Journal of International Business Studies*, **29** (3), 445–68.

Cho, K.R. and R. Radmanabhan (1995), 'Acquisition Versus New Venture: The Choice of Foreign Establishment Mode by Japanese Firms', *Journal of International Management*, **1** (3), 255–85.

Contractor, Farok J. (1984), 'Choosing between Direct Investment and Licensing: Theoretical Considerations and Empirical Tests', *Journal of International Business Studies*, (Winter), 167–88.

Contractor, Farok J. (1990), 'Contractual and Cooperative Forms of International Business: Toward a Unified Theory of Modal Choice', *Management International Review*, **30**, 31–54.

Coughlan, Anne T. (1985), 'Competition and Cooperation in Marketing Channel Choice: Theory and Application', *Marketing Science*, **4** (2), 110–29.

Cyert, Richard M. and James G. March (1963), *A Behavioral Theory of the Firm*, Englewood Cliffs, NJ: Prentice-Hall.

Czinkota, Michael R. (1982), *Export Development Strategies: U.S. Promotion Policies*, New York: Praeger.

Davidson, William (1980), 'The Location of Foreign Direct Investment Activity: Country Characteristics and Experience Effect', *Journal of International Business Studies*, **11**, 9–22.

Davidson, William (1982), *Global Strategic Management*. New York: Wiley.

Davidson, William (1983), 'Market Similarity and Market Selection: Implications of International Marketing Strategy', *Journal of Business Research*, **11**, 439–56.

Davidson, William and D. McFetridge (1984), 'International Technology Transactions and the Theory of the Firm', *Journal of Industrial Economics*, **332** (3), 253–64.

Davidson, William and D. McFetridge (1985), 'Key Characteristics in the Choice of International Technology Transfer', *Journal of International Business Studies*, **16**, 5–21.

Duffy, R. (1996), 'Moving into the Global Market Place: Stages of Development', in R. Lambrix and S. Sanghvi (eds), *Global Finance 2000, A Handbook of Strategy and Organization*, New York: The Conference Board.

Dunning, John H. (1979), 'Explaining Changing Patterns of International Production: In Defense of the Eclectic Theory', *Oxford Bulletin of Economics and Statistics*, **41** (November), 269–96.

Dunning, John H. (1980), 'Toward an Eclectic Theory of International Production:

Some Empirical Tests', *Journal of International Business Studies*, **11** (Spring), 9–31.

Dunning, John H. (1981), *International Production and the Multinational Enterprise*, London: Allen & Unwin.

Dunning, John H. (1988), 'The Eclectic Paradigm of International Production: A Restatement and Some Possible Extensions', *Journal of International Business Studies*, **19** (Spring), 1–31.

Erramilli, Krishna M. (1991), 'The Experience Factor in Foreign Market Entry Behavior of Service Firms', *Journal of International Business Studies*, **22** (3), 479–501.

Erramilli, Krishna M. and C.P. Rao (1993), 'Service Firms, International Entry Mode Choice: A Modified Transaction Cost Analysis Approach', *Journal of Marketing*, **57** (July), 19–38.

Gatignon, H. and Erin Anderson (1988), 'The Multinational Corporation's Degree of Control over Foreign Subsidiaries: An Empirical Test of a Transaction Cost Explanation', *Journal of Law, Economics and Organization*, **4**, 304–36.

Gençtürk, Esra F. and Preet S. Aulakh (1995), 'The Use of Process and Output Controls in Foreign Markets', *Journal of International Business Studies*, **26** (4), 755–86.

Gençtürk, Esra F., Terry Childers and Robert Ruekert (1995), 'International Marketing Involvement: The Construct, Dimensionality and Measurement', *Journal of International Marketing*, **3** (4), 11–37.

Gomes-Casseres, Benjamin (1989), 'Ownership Structures of Foreign Subsidiaries', *Journal of Economic Behavior and Organization*, **11**, 1–25.

Goodnow, J.D. (1985), 'Development in International Mode of Entry Analysis', *International Marketing Review*, Autumn, 17–30.

Goodnow, J.D. and J.E. Hanz (1972), 'Environmental Determinants of Overseas Market Entry Strategies', *Journal of International Business Studies*, **3**, 33–50.

Hamel, Gary (1991), 'Competition for Competence and Interpartner Learning Within International Strategic Alliances', *Strategic Management Journal*, **12** (Winter Special Issue), 83–103.

Hennart, Jean-Francois (1982), *The Theory of the Multinational Enterprise*, Ann Arbor, MI: University of Michigan Press.

Hennart, Jean-Francois (1989), 'Can the "New Forms" of Investment Substitute for "Older Forms"? A Transaction Cost Perspective', *Journal of International Business Studies*, **20**, 211–34.

Hennart, Jean-Francois (1991), 'The Transaction Cost Theory of Joint Ventures: An Empirical Study of Japanese Subsidiaries in the United States', *Management Science*, **37** (4), 483–97.

Hennart, Jean-Francois and Y. Park (1993), 'Greenfield vs. Acquisition: The Strategy of Japanese Investors in the United States', *Management Science*, **39** (9), 1054–70.

Hennart, Jean-Francois and S. Reddy (1997), 'The Choice Between Mergers/ Acquisitions and Joint Ventures: The Case of Japanese Investors in the United States', *Strategic Management Journal*, **18** (1), 1–12.

Hill, Charles W., Peter Hwang and W. Chan Kim (1990), 'An Eclectic Theory of the Choice of International Entry Mode', *Strategic Management Journal*, **11** (2), 117–28.

Hirsch, Seev (1988), 'International Transactions in Services and Service-Intensive

Goods Industries', in Y. Aharoni (ed.), *Services In World Economic Growth*, Tel Aviv, Israel: Tel Aviv University.

Horstmann, Ignatius and James R. Markusen (1987), 'Licensing Versus Direct Investment: A Model of Internalization by the Multinational Enterprise', *Canadian Journal of Economics*, **10** (3), 464–81.

Huang, H. (1996), 'A Re-Examination of Entry Mode Strategies for Small Firms from NICS: Are we Eclectic Enough?', in *Competitive Advantage Through Global Networks Conference Proceedings*, pp. 351–61.

Hymer, S. (1960), *The International Operations of National Firs: A Study of Direct Foreign Investment*, PhD Thesis, Massachusetts Institute of Technology Press, Cambridge, MA, 1976.

Jeuland A. and S.M. Shugan (1983), 'Managing Channel Profits', *Marketing Science*, **2**, 239–72.

Johanson, Jan and Jan-Erik Vahlne (1977), 'The Internationalization Process of the Firm: A Model of Knowledge Development and Increasing Foreign Market Commitments', *Journal of International Business Studies*, **8**, 23–32.

Johanson, Jan and Lars-Gunnar Mattsson (1987), 'Internationalization in Industry Systems: A Network Approach', in N. Hood and Jan-Erik Vahlne (eds), *Strategies in Global Competition*, London, UK: Routledge.

Kim, J. and J.D. Daniels (1991), 'Marketing Channel Decisions of Foreign Manufacturing Subsidiaries in the US: The Case of the Metal and Machinery Industries', *Management International Review*, **31**, 123–38.

Klein, S., Gary Frasier and V. Roth (1990), 'A Transaction Cost Analysis Model of Channel Integration in International Markets', *Journal of Marketing Research*, **27**, 196–208.

Kogut, Bruce (1983), 'Foreign Direct Investment as a Sequential Process', in C.P. Kindleberger and D. Audretsch (eds), *The Multinational Corporation in the 1980s*, Cambridge, MA: MIT Press, pp. 38–56.

Kogut, Bruce (1988), 'Joint Ventures: Theoretical and Empirical Perspectives', *Strategic Management Journal*, **9** (4), 319–32.

Kogut, Bruce and Harbir Singh (1988), 'The Effect of National Culture on the Choice of Entry Mode', *Journal of Internal Business Studies*, **19** (Fall), 414–32.

Kogut, Bruce and Udo Zander (1992), 'Knowledge of the Firm, Combinative Capabilities and the Replication of Technology', *Organizational Science*, **3**, 383–97.

Kogut, Bruce and Udo Zander (1993), 'Knowledge of the Firm and the Evolutionary Theory of the Multinational Corporation', *Journal of International Business Studies*, **24** (4), 625–45.

Kwon, Y. and L. Konopa (1992), 'Impact of Host Country Market Characteristics on the Choice of Foreign Market Entry Mode', *International Marketing Review*, **10** (2), 60–76.

Li, Jiatao (1995), 'Foreign Entry and Survival: Effects of Strategic Choice on Performance in International Markets', *Strategic Management Journal*, **16** (5), 335–51.

Lord, Michael D. and Annette L. Ranft (2000), 'Organizational Learning About New International Markets: Exploring the Internal Transfer of Local Market Knowledge', *Journal of International Business Studies*, **31** (4), 573–89.

Macharzina, Klaus and Johann Engelhard (1991), 'Paradigm Shift in International Business Research: From Partist and Eclectic Approaches to the GAINS Paradigm', *Management International Review*, **31** (Special Issue), 23–43.

Markusen, James R. (1984), 'Multinationals, Multi-Plant Economies and Gains from Trade', *Journal of International Economics*, **16**, 205–26.

McGuire, T.W. and Richard Staelin (1983), 'An Industry Equilibrium Analysis of Downstream Vertical Integration', *Marketing Science*, **2**, 161–91.

McNaughton, R.B. (1999), 'Transaction Cost Analysis and the Methodology of Foreign Entry-Mode Studies', *Environment and Planning*, **31** (4), 575–96.

Nohria, Nitin and Carlso Garcia-Pont (1991), 'Global Strategic Linkages and Industry Structure', *Strategic Management Journal*, **12** (Special Issue), 105–24.

O'Farrell, P.N., L. Moffat and P.A. Wood (1995), 'Internationalization by Business Services: A Methodological Critique of Foreign-Market Entry-Mode Choice', *Environment and Planning*, **27**, 683–97.

Pan, Yigang and David K. Tse (2000), 'The Hierarchical Model of Market Entry Mode', *Journal of International Business Studies*, **31** (4), 535–54.

Porter, Michael E. (1990), *The Competitive Advantage of Nations*, New York: Free Press.

Prahalad, C.K. and Gary Hamel (1990), 'The Core Competence of the Corporation', *Harvard Business Review*, **68** (3), 79–91.

Rogers, E.M. (1962), *Diffusion of Innovations*, 3rd edn. New York: Free Press.

Root, Franklin R. (1987), *Entry Strategies for International Markets*, Lexington, MA: Lexington Books.

Rugman, Alan M. (1980), 'Internalization as a General Theory of Foreign Direct Investment: A Reappraisal of the Literature', *Weltwirtschaftliches Archiv*, **116**, 365–79.

Rugman, Alan M. (1990), *Multinationals and Canada–United States Free Trade*, Columbia, SC: University of South Carolina Press.

Rugman, Alan M., Donald J. Lecraw and Laurence D. Booth (1985), *International Business: Firm and Environment*, New York: McGraw-Hill.

Rugman, Alan M. and Alain Verbeke (1992), 'A Note on the Transnational Solution and the Transaction Cost Theory of Multinational Strategic Management', *Journal of International Business Studies*, **23** (4), 761–71.

Simmonds, P.G. (1990), 'The Combined Diversification Breadth and Mode Dimensions and the Performance of Large Diversified Firms', *Strategic Management Journal*, **11**, 399–410.

Sohn, Jung Hoon Derick (1994), 'Social Knowledge as a Control System: A Proposition and Evidence from the Japanese FDI Behavior', *Journal of International Business Studies*, **25** (2), 295–324.

Stinchcombe, A.L. (1985), 'Contracts as Hierarchical Documents', in A.L. Stinchcombe and V. Heimer (eds), *Organization Theory and Project Management*, Oslo: Norwegian University Press, pp. 121–71.

Szulanski, G. (1996), 'Exploring Internal Stickiness: Impediments to the Transfer of Best Practices Within the Firm', *Strategic Management Journal*, **17** (Winter Special Issue), 27–43.

Tallman, S.B. (1991), 'Strategic Management Models and Resource-based Strategies Among MNEs in a Host-Market', *Strategic Management Journal*, **12** (Summer Special Issue), 69–82.

Vernon, Raymond (1966), 'International Investment and International Trade in the Product Cycle', *Quarterly Journal of Economics*, **80**, 190–207.

Vernon, Raymond (1976), 'The Product Cycle Hypothesis in the New International Environment', *Oxford Bulletin of Economics and Statistics*, **41**, 255–67.

Williamson, Oliver E. (1975), *Markets and Hierarchies: Analysis and Antitrust Implications*, New York: Free Press.

Williamson, Oliver E. (1991), 'Comparative Economic Organization: The Analysis of Discrete Structural Alternatives', *Administrative Science Quarterly*, **36**, 269–96.

Wind, Yoram and H. Perlmutter (1977), 'On the Identification of the Frontier Issues in International Marketing', *Columbia Journal of World Business*, **12**, 131–9.

Woodcock, Patrick C., Paul W. Beamish and Shige Makino (1994), 'Ownership-based Entry Mode Strategies and International Performance', *Journal of International Business Studies*, **25** (2), 253–73.

Zaheer, S. (1995), 'Overcoming the Liability of Foreignness', *Academy of Management Journal*, **38** (2), 341–63.

Zander, Udo and Bruce Kogut (1995), 'Knowledge and the Speed of Transfer and Imitation of Organizational Capabilities', *Organizational Science*, **6**, 76–92.

PART III

Cross-cultural research issues

8. Measurement problems in cross-national consumer research: the state-of-the-art and future research directions

Attila Yaprak

INTRODUCTION

Comparative study of behavior across cultures has become a fascinating scholarly pursuit in the social sciences. Along this journey, researchers have come across a wide variety of problems they have had to contend with in drawing meaning from their comparisons. For example, they have had to cope with inequalities in the meanings of phenomena across cultural groups, the sometimes inappropriateness of the measurement instruments used across cultures, difficulties in generalizing findings to national or cultural populations of interest, and so forth. Importantly, they have had to learn that their research has to be able to navigate through these barriers while exploring, explaining, and interpreting cross-national similarities and differences in behavior (Craig and Douglas 2000; Mullen 1995; Steenkamp and Baumgartner 1998; Van de Vjver and Leung 1997).

Scholars of international marketing, for their part, have discovered that a better understanding of their concepts and constructs, and hence, the advancement of their field as an academic field of inquiry, required that their models and measures had to be psychometrically sound across countries and cultures (Bagozzi and Baumgartner 1994; Steenkamp and Baumgartner 1998). These scholars have had to address, for example, the question of whether the behavioral similarities and differences they were observing in their research across cultures were in fact real. If their observed findings were different than expected (statistical significance was not achieved or the reliability coefficients were low for example), they learned to question whether measurement problems had attenuated their findings; that is, whether these findings were scaling or measurement artifacts or true cultural differences (Mullen 1995). In this context, Steenkamp and Baumgartner (1998) have recently warned that while cross-national differences might be due to 'true' differences among societies on the underlying constructs, they might also be due to other sources, such as differences in scale reliability or nonequivalence of the constructs themselves. Van de Vjver and Leung (1997) have cautioned, in a similar vein, that bias may flow into cross-national studies while (a) conceptualizing the theoretical constructs relevant to the study, (b) formulating the hypotheses or the research questions, (c) designing the study, or (d) choosing and administering the research instruments and/or data analysis.

While a variety of mechanisms have been discussed in the literature to assess, and cope with, various aspects of measurement nonequivalence in cross-national research (described in Hui and Triandis 1985, for example), in recent critical reviews of the literature, scholars of the field have lamented that there is still a general lack of concern for establishing measurement equivalence (Kumar 2000; Craig and Douglas 2000; Myers et al. 2000; Singh 1995; Mullen 1995; Aulakh and Kotabe 1993; Netemeyer, Durvasula and Lichtenstein 1991; Parameswaran and Yaprak 1987). Steenkamp and Baumgartner (1998) attribute this problem to a variety of causes: (1) the many types of measure invariance that plague multicultural/multinational studies; (2) the lack of agreement on a terminology with which to refer to these types of invariance among scholars of cross-national research; (3) researchers' relative unfamiliarity with testing measurement models that incorporate variable means; (4) the methodological complexities involved in testing for, and assuring, measurement equivalence; (5) the lack of agreement among cross-national researchers about the extent to which measures have to be equivalent in order for particular cross-national comparisons to be meaningful; and (6) the absence of guidelines among the research community as to how to ascertain whether or not a measure exhibits adequate cross-national invariance.

The purpose of this chapter is to address this void in the international marketing literature. To accomplish this purpose, I review the array of measurement problems discussed in the extant literature in marketing, consumer behavior and cross-cultural studies. This review helps chart the portfolio of methodological issues researchers in a broad array of disciplines have faced, and continue to face, while conducting cross-national studies. In light of this review, I present a relatively comprehensive array of 'antidotes' researchers have used, and suggest others they might use, in coping with, and enhancing, the psychometric qualities of their findings. This inventory of problems and coping mechanisms should provide a guiding light to, and hence help foster a better understanding of, international marketing phenomena, particularly those in cross-national consumer behavior. Having taken stock of the current literature, I suggest future research avenues that emanate from this review with the hope of inspiring new studies focused on improving the quality of scientific inference in cross-national marketing studies.

THE TYPES OF MEASUREMENT PROBLEMS ENCOUNTERED IN CROSS-NATIONAL RESEARCH

Scholars of cross-national research have identified at least two groups of measurement problems. These include issues of nonequivalence and difficulties in establishing reliability and validity of measures (Parameswaran and Yaprak 1987; Mintu, Calantone and Gassenheimer 1994). Equivalency issues include ensuring construct, measure, and administration equivalencies while validity and reliability issues center on establishing the psychometric soundness of research measures. The following is a brief discussion of some of these.

The Problem Umbrella

Perhaps the most pressing concern in cross-national research is that phenomena under study are defined and operationalized in a Western (typically the United States) country, and then applied in other country settings, when in fact, the conceptual domain, measurement, and applicability of these concepts may not be (totally) transferable. Another concern stems from the fact that we typically measure perceptions in cross-cultural consumer research, and are unsure whether we are in fact measuring attitudes (cognitions) or beliefs (attribute evaluations). As we typically hope to understand cultural 'standards' that are used in attributions to make reasonably accurate generalizations about a society's behavior, measurement of perceptions, and not beliefs or values themselves, may lead to misinterpretations of phenomena. Yet another problem relates to the fact that both emotional constructs and relevant motive sets may vary across cultures, and when we conduct research we can not really isolate the impact of emotions from that of rational motives. For instance, Maslow's hierarchy may be inapplicable in another culture in concept or context or may find expression in a different hierarchy (Nevis 1983 has actually shown this for North American and Chinese societies). Further, sets of values and value change propensities may vary across cultures, possibly affecting our effort at identifying and working with sets of 'modal' salient beliefs in different cultural groups. As well, different cultures may follow different paths to ensuring correspondence among action (need to buy a car), target (a van), context (for the family) and time (soon) in expressing purchase intentions, or they may be comfortable with some incongruence, and measurement problems may taint our outcome assessments (likelihood of purchase, for example). Finally, the mental processes cultural groups use to integrate existing attitudes with personality characteristics, cognitive styles, and social contexts, and the ways they blend these to respond to research instruments can vary by culture, thereby making cross-cultural generalizations difficult.

These examples provide an umbrella of the types of general problems we face in drawing conclusions from cross-national studies. I shall now discuss, more specifically, the key methodological problems we face in these studies, and offer alternative mechanisms that might help us cope with them.

Establishing Construct Equivalence

When comparing research data from one country to another, the researcher needs to establish construct equivalence to ensure that concepts being studied are equivalent in all cultural settings. This requires establishing that the phenomena under investigation actually exist across the countries/cultures under study, that consumers interpret the stimuli, objects or behavior they observe in similar fashion, and that these concepts are expressed in similar ways in all countries/cultures of interest (Craig and Douglas 2000). Construals of concepts such as the self and others, and therefore of ethnocentrism and of values such as parochialism or cosmopolitanism are likely to vary among societies (Inglehart 1997). Beliefs, such as those in secularism or traditionalism, and social rituals such as those involved in holidays or gift exchanges might also make it difficult to establish pan-cultural conceptual equivalence (Inglehart and Baker 2000).

The second element of concern in establishing construct equivalence relates to whether the objects, concepts and behaviors under study serve the same function in all populations of interest (Craig and Douglas 2000). The typical example of nonequivalence given in the literature is bicycles, a recreation item in most of the USA, but a transportation mode in China. The significance of certain rituals, like coffee drinking, can also vary by culture; while coffee drinking may be associated with perking up in the morning in some cultures, it may evoke a social occasion function in other cultures. While shopping may be viewed as a chore in some cultures, it may have social interaction connotations in others, and so on (Craig and Douglas 2000).

The third type of construct equivalence relates to the way each population of interest categorizes each stimulus, object or behavior. What might be a fashion item, a discount distributor, or a meal drink will most likely vary across cultures as will occupational categories, socio-demographic groupings, and product categories (Craig and Douglas 2000). For example, some American eateries such as pizza chains, typically categorized as convenience restaurants in North America, may be categorized as chic, fashionable cafes in some developing countries. Demographic classifications of the United States may have to be adjusted in the modernizing societies to make them more equivalent, and so forth (Craig and Douglas 2000).

Van de Vjver and Leung (1997) discuss several common causes of *construct* nonequivalence. One of these relates to incomplete overlap of the definitions or concepts of the construct across cultures. The second is sourced in the differences in the appropriateness of the test content; that is, when skills about which subjects are being questioned do not belong to the repertoire of one of the cultural groups, for example. The final cause relates to incomplete coverage of the construct, that is, poor sampling of all relevant behaviors of interest or when less than all relevant domains of the construct are sampled in all societies of interest.

Establishing Measure Equivalence

The second type of nonequivalence in cross-national research involves measure nonequivalence. Since the measure is an operational definition of the construct, measure and construct equivalencies are closely related (Craig and Douglas 2000). The literature suggests that the following need to be considered in this context: the calibration system used in the measurement, the translation of the research instrument, and the metric equivalence of the instrument (Mullen 1995).

Establishing calibration equivalence involves achieving parity in tangible items such as monetary units and measures of weight and the like, and in intangible units such as perceptual cues. Care needs to be taken in establishing integrity in these measures since studies in cognitive and cross-cultural psychology suggest that the ability to interpret and differentiate among these and develop gradations in these schemata can vary among cultures (Craig and Douglas 2000, p. 161). For instance, Bagozzi and Baumgartner (1994) discuss a study where the perceptions associated with organ donation to a member of one's nuclear family, close relatives, ethnic strangers, and distant strangers vary significantly among black Americans, white Americans, Hong Kong Chinese and Chinese Americans.

Establishing translation equivalence is a key task in ensuring construct equivalence since this is where the construct is defined in operational terms. The objective here is to ensure that the same questionnaire items measure the same latent constructs in the populations of interest. While establishing equivalence of verbal stimuli is relatively easy, ensuring equivalence of nonverbal stimuli so that they evoke similar desired images across cultures is much more difficult (Craig and Douglas 2000). Back-translation techniques and decentering (discussed later) are typically used to ensure this type of equivalence (Hui and Triandis 1985; Craig and Douglas 2000).

The third element of measure equivalence researchers must contend with involves ensuring that subjects in different cultural/national samples are responding to the measurement scales in the same manner. Typically, two elements of equivalence are considered here. The first concerns equivalence of the scale (or scoring procedure) used to establish the measure, and the second, the equivalence of response to a given measure in different countries. Establishing scalar equivalence, that is ensuring that the score obtained in one cultural context has the same meaning in another cultural context, is important as different scales have been shown to be more effective than others in different countries (Craig and Douglas 2000). For instance, while some societies have been found to be more comfortable with 5 to 7 point scales, others have been found to prefer 10 point scales. Further, as norms of each society reinforce desirable behaviors in that culture rather than some universal mandate, culturally-bounded response set characteristics are likely to influence response scores. In addition, test batteries including nonequivalent items and researchers' bias in interpreting findings based on their own experiences exacerbate these problems (Mintu et al. 1994).

Van de Vjver and Leung (1997), Mullen (1995), Singh (1995), and Hui and Triandis (1985) show that these problems stem from a variety of causes. One of these is unfamiliarity with scaling and/or scoring formats or research methodologies that lead to inconsistent, sometimes even frivolous, scoring. Cultural differences such as those in social desirability, acquiescence, evasiveness, humility, tendency for yea- or nay-saying (extreme response styles) and to respond 'no opinion' to a question appears to be another cause. Differences in stimulus familiarity, poor item translation, inadequate item formulation (such as complex wording), items invoking additional traits, and differences in appropriateness of the item content appear to be yet other causes. Whatever the cause, these appear to add systematic error to measurements, and threaten measure reliability and validity in cross-cultural comparisons (Craig and Douglas 2000; Van de Vjver and Leung 1997).

Establishing Data Collection and Research Administration Equivalence

In addition to establishing construct and measure equivalence, it is also important to establish equivalencies in data collection and research administration procedures. Key concerns here are the comparability of the samples drawn from the different research settings and the extent to which the samples are representative of their populations of interest. Differences in sampling frames and responding sampling units may lead to unintended conclusions from the research. Reliability of the sampling procedures and the survey administration processes used in the research may vary among countries. Differences in the interview procedures employed (mail in one country, telephone in another or mall intercept technique in one country, in-class interviewing in another, etc.), differences in the physical conditions of the administration, and communication problems in the conduct of the research caused by researchers representing different cultural backgrounds and different research philosophies can all lead to administration non-equivalencies (Craig and Douglas 2000).

Establishing Reliability

While often costly and time-consuming, establishing reliability is a key ingredient in ensuring psychometric quality in cross-national studies. Despite the best intentions of researchers to design an instrument that is equally valid in all societies of interest, they often find that their instruments are not equally reliable in all cultures. The more complex measures used in the research, such as psychographic and behavioral constructs, may vary in their degrees of reliability across national samples (Davis, Douglas and Silk 1981). Country of origin of the products being studied across markets as well as demographic characteristics of the respondent (e.g. male vs. female, well educated vs. poorly educated), for example, can influence reliabilities of constructs (Parameswaran and Yaprak 1987). The stability of data may also vary in time. As these disturbances tend to attenuate the interpretations of findings, it is essential to establish reliability in cross-national research.

Other Problem Sources

In addition to these problems attached to establishing equivalence and reliability, cross-national researchers also have to attend to other sources of bias that arise in their studies. Craig and Douglas (2000) suggest at least six sources of bias in cross-cultural settings: a respondent's desire to be socially acquiescent; the desire to provide the socially acceptable response; the impact of certain underlying cultural traits unique to that society; specific respondent characteristics unique to individual respondents; the nature of the topic being studied; and the tendency not to respond to certain types of questions.

Social acquiesence bias is more common in societies, such as those in Asia, where the respondent might be concerned about disappointing or offending the researcher with his/her responses, leading to a tendency to respond to assertions in a positive manner regardless of the respondent's real position on the item in question. Where responses may be intended not only to please the researcher, but also to reflect behavior perceived to be socially acceptable by the interviewer, we might find social desirability bias, especially in the urban populations in developing societies. Where topics such as one's income or sex life are considered sensitive, the researcher will likely face topic bias. Certain types of respondents are also particularly prone to give less reliable responses compared to other respondents. Certain cultures also vary with regard to their willingness to respond to questions and in their involvement in particular topics, leading to non-responses in some societies. Finally, there may be differences in comfort with various response formats among societies that might lead the researcher to use pictorial stimuli in some while using verbal or numerical in another, exacerbating difficulties in establishing the comparability of findings (Craig and Douglas 2000; Kumar 2000).

Problems might also arise from sampling difficulties, such as incomparability of the samples or sampling frames (one sample more upscale than the other, for example), the particular sampling techniques or procedures used (convenience sampling in one society and random sampling in another, or single stage sampling in one country and multistage in another, etc.), and data collection procedures (electronic surveys in one country and personal interviews in another, etc.).

While this portfolio of problems might paint a bleak picture for researchers conducting cross-national studies, we have developed an impressive set of coping mechanisms that help desensitize the interpretations we draw from our findings. We discuss these next.

COPING MECHANISMS FOR NAVIGATING THROUGH THE PROBLEMS

Realizing that these methodological problems attenuate and/or accentuate parameter estimates and statistical tests in their studies, cross-national researchers have been searching for coping mechanisms that will help them navigate through these problems, and have succeeded in developing 'antidotes' for them. Craig and Douglas (2000) and Kumar (2000) discuss a wide variety of mechanisms researchers have discovered to attend to such problems as establishing reliability of measures across samples, overcoming sources of possible bias, and ensuring equivalence in construct development and measurement. For example, establishing consistency of responses across individuals over time and ensuring internal consistency of scales in ascertaining cross-national reliability are described thoroughly by these authors. In the paragraphs below, I discuss some of the more recent, and the more exciting, coping mechanisms found in the literature.

Mullen (1995), for example, provides a comprehensive review of the ways with which we might be able to cope with these difficulties. He suggests the use of the back translation method, visual examination of factor patterns for similarities (and differences), establishing factor structure invariance, and the use of multiple group LISREL (to test measurement models for common form and invariance of factor loadings) as methods to alleviate instrument nonequivalencies. In similar fashion, he recommends the comparison of reliabilities and the use of multiple group LISREL (to test for equality of measurement error variances) to establish consistent scoring. He also suggests the use of multiple measurement methods, exploration of response set bias with Profile analysis, examining underlying metrics by optimal scaling data, and the use of multiple group LISREL (to test for equality of measurement error variances) to ensure scalar equivalence. Finally, he suggests independent checks of conversions of measurement units to establish calibration equivalence.

Mullen (1995) also laments, however, that even these treatments may be insufficient in coping with measurement invariance in cross-national research. For instance, he points out that researchers have not yet developed a statistical test for comparing the power of reliability tests, such as Cronbach's alpha, across groups, a concern also expressed by Parameswaran and Yaprak (1987). In the same vein, Mullen argues that multiple methods assessment might be too costly and too time-consuming for the marginal benefit the researcher receives in explanatory power. Similarly, he argues that profile analysis, used to determine if the differences between the data sets are caused by systematic response bias, does not indicate, sufficiently well, whether the differences in means between (cultural/national) groups are caused by real differences in the variables or by response set bias. He argues that there is no diagnostic method available to assess cross-national differences in scalar equivalence with confidence (Mullen 1995).

In similar fashion, Singh (1995) demonstrates through structural equations modeling that inferences drawn from a three-nation study can be improved by four corrective procedures. These are: standardizing the unstandardized (or unstandardizing the standardized) coefficients (as necessitated by the objectives of the research), accounting for measurement error by adjusting unequal reliabilities among national samples, controlling the overall error rate via simultaneous analysis, and ensuring construct equivalence. He shows by replicating a previously published study, but now with these corrective measures, that the earlier work had underestimated or overestimated the magnitude and direction of various main effects and had overlooked a significant cross-national difference between Japanese and

American respondents. He demonstrates through this work that the inter-active effects of measurement issues can be pervasive, complex, and unpredictable unless corrective measures such as the ones he employs are applied on data before making sound inferences about findings.

In a similar vein, Steenkamp and Baumgartner (1998) propose a procedure for assessing and coping with measurement invariance in cross-national consumer research. Their work, which involves a multiple-sample confirmatory factor analysis (which is similar to multiple-group LISREL), helps clarify the conditions under which meaningful comparisons of construct conceptualizations, construct means, and relationships between constructs might be possible. They propose, specifically, that researchers investigate factor covariance invariance, factor variance invariance, and error variance invariance in the analysis of the data before drawing conclusions from research. They empirically illustrate how this method might enhance the cross-national psychometric qualities of CETSCALE, a scale used to measure the ethnocentrism construct, through data collected in Belgium, Great Britain and Greece. Their proposed procedure also shows us how we might be able to improve upon some of the nonequivalence problems in cross-national studies.

Myers et al. (2000) propose the extension of the use of the multiple group structural equation modeling (SEM) technique in measurement equivalence analysis by demonstrating the use of formal tests that help identify some specific sources of nonequivalence. By applying multiple group SEM on three constructs, attitude toward an ad, attitude toward a brand, and buyer intentions used in a previously published cross-national study, they suggest a procedure that goes beyond Mullen's (1995), Singh's (1995), and Steenkamp and Baumgartner's (1998) methods. The first step involves testing for configural invariance to assess whether the same simple structure of factor loadings is obtained in all country samples. The second step examines factor covariance invariance to establish overall measurement structure consistency across groups. In the third step, metric invariance is tested to ensure equality of scale intervals for all groups. In the fourth step, consistency of factor structures across countries and whether latent constructs are composed differently with respect to the measured variables are tested through examination of factor correlations and factor loadings. The final step examines the invariance of the measurement error variances by constraining these to be equal across groups. Myers et al. (2000) show that this method can help us determine sources of differences in the way constructs are composed and interpreted in different cultures, and aid in judging which items, if any, in a construct are sources of concern and whether the concerns are national culture or research instrument based.

They, too, lament, however, that even though their procedure, one of several extensions to the use of multiple group SEM proposed in the literature, is a step forward in diagnosing measure nonequivalencies in cross-national research, neither their method nor others are really capable of solving measurement problems in this arena. This is sourced, they argue, at least in part, in the limitations to the SEM technique (also discussed by Mullen 1995). For instance, large sample size requirements often limit the use of this technique or its derivatives. Also, the technique simply helps us confirm findings rather than offer a remedy to cross-national measurement nonequivalence (utmost care in the data-gathering process before analysis remains about the only preventive measure here). Finally, the application of this technique might be counter to a theory-driven research agenda, that is, the true value of the methodology might be in avoiding findings that may be skewed by measurement nonequivalence across national/cultural groups rather than providing real remedies to method problems in cross-national research (Myers et al. 2000).

Craig and Douglas (2000) discuss a number of other methods that might help researchers cope with some of these problems. These include, for example, developing and comparing decentered scales, analyzing data at different levels of aggregation, applying multiple multivariable techniques in data analysis, triangulation, and ipsatization.

According to Craig and Douglas (2000), developing decentered scales involves participation by collaborators in all countries where the research is to be conducted in the development of culture-specific (emic) dimensions of the constructs under study, and a weaning process through which the final, relatively culture-free (etic) scale is developed. This process might also involve pilot surveys of consumers in each country, and the use of a multi-cultural panel of judges who help determine, from a combined item pool, which dimensions of a construct are common to all (or most) societies and which are not. Triangulation involves the use of multiple, and diverse, methods to examine the same construct or phenomenon through different lenses to inspire greater confidence in the results of the research. For example, a phenomenon studied through qualitative as well as a number of quantitative methods is likely to command greater confidence than one studied through one set of these techniques. Convergence of results after different methodologies and research approaches have been used will lead to greater confidence in the findings when compared to single approach studies, and so forth. Ipsatization involves forcing respondents to make choices among competing alternative responses to overcome such problems as central tendency or extreme response bias (that is, choosing the cautious middle or the bold extreme options on each item), social desirability bias (that is, tendency to report what the respondent feels s/he ought to say, not what is really true), and unstandardized responses (that is, respondents adopting their own idiosyncratic response patterns typically encountered in the use of normative scales). The idea here is that with ipsative scales, respondents are faced with a common scale and choices are made between items matched in terms of the types of bias discussed (Craig and Douglas 2000).

In sum, this overview of the methodological problems typically encountered in cross-national research and the suggested remedies to counter them exemplify the wide range of discussions that are underway in the literature about how we might improve the psychometric qualities of the findings from our cross-national studies.

CONCLUSIONS AND AVENUES FOR FUTURE RESEARCH

It should be clear from this review of the methodological problems commonly faced in cross-national research and the mechanisms we have developed so far to cope with them that we have come a long way, indeed, in bringing rigor and meaning to our cross-cultural comparisons. For example, in the 25-year period since Green and White's critical review (1976), we have learned to develop conceptually more equivalent constructs, use psychometrically sounder measures, and apply more rigorous methodologies in our research. We have learned to test for, and establish, the reliability and validity of our measures and have become much more sensitive to working with multi-nationally, rather than uni-nationally, developed and validated measures. We have started applying multiple-item, rather than few-item scales and have learned to involve our research partners in many, if not all, phases of our research. Psychometric properties of many of our constructs, especially of those such as country image that have been popular in consumer research, have been placed under rigorous scrutiny, and have become 'tighter' concepts as a result (Craig and Douglas 2000; Mullen 1995; Parameswaran and Yaprak 1987).

It should also be clear, however, that our long journey into discovery is only beginning; that we need to learn much more along this sojourn. As our discipline and its practice become increasingly global and we operate in increasingly more complex and heterogeneous environments, we will have to become even more careful about conducting our research with greater integrity and drawing sounder interpretations from our findings. Craig and Douglas (2000) discuss the following as examples of the immediate challenges we will face in that quest. (For discussions of similar challenges, also see Mullen 1995 and Van de Vjver and Leung 1997.)

First, we will need to become much more proactive about including a broader range of socio-cultural contexts, and participants from them, in designing our research. We will have to pay greater attention to identifying, and working with, culture-specific constructs and learn to assess, much more deeply, the cultural embeddedness and situational dependency of constructs. This will involve not only determining how best to construe a concept in different cultural settings and a more rigorous examination of the equivalency of our constructs, but also desensitizing the dominance of our governing culture or research philosophy through decentering procedures to guard against forced-framing of research questions in cultures where they might be inappropriate or irrelevant. It may also involve the use of, and greater reliance on, unstructured approaches for further probing the cultural embeddedness of our concepts and constructs. Examining our constructs and the interrelationships among them in a broader range of cultural settings is likely to improve our understanding of the nature and extent of influence of these constructs on behavior, their universality or cultural embeddedness, and how these might vary in different sociological contexts. We will need to begin viewing cross-cultural segments, rather than country markets, as our units of analysis and learn to better isolate confounding influences from our main effect variables (Craig and Douglas 2000).

Second, we will need to bring a longitudinal, longer-term dimension to our research, especially that conducted in the rapidly transforming emerging economies. Rapid economic change, and the political and sociological transformations paralleling it in the developing countries is leading to emerging market segments and consumer behavior patterns in these societies, and tracking these with integrity over time is becoming increasingly critical. Here too, we need to be able to distinguish between the impacts of the structural (economic) changes from those associated with consumer value transformations and isolate away the effects of spurious, confounding variables (Craig and Douglas 2000).

Third, we will need to get better at establishing the equivalence of our constructs through more rigorous and better calibrated measures. We will need to devote greater attention to examining whether our instrument in fact measures what it purports to measure or whether measuring the construct in a given culture is, in fact meaningful. To overcome this problem, we will have to learn to conduct pretests more frequently, administer our instruments to wider groups of subjects, and develop (and test) new formulations and adaptations of our constructs. Further, wherever feasible, we will need to use a diverse portfolio of methods to ensure cross-method consistency in responses. Also, we will need to employ more demanding analytical techniques in our analysis, such as the SEM procedures described above, to incorporate multiple levels of analysis (i.e., at the country, individual, within-country segment, or socio-cultural group levels) to the interpretation and comparison of our findings. This will help determine whether observed patterns of measurement or constructs are invariant across countries or individual sampling units (Craig and Douglas 2000).

As scholars of international marketing, we have made considerable progress in identifying and coping with many of the methodological problems that plague our cross-national/cultural research efforts. This chapter also showed, however, that much remains to be done in our continuous improvement quest. It showed specifically that we need to pay greater attention to rigor in conceptualization, design, and application of our research tools; ensure construct and other equivalencies much more carefully; ensure the relevance of our theories in the socio-cultural contexts in which we conduct our research; and develop and use more rigorous analyses in drawing conclusions from our findings. We hope this chapter provides a roadmap that will take us to new destinations along this promising and fascinating journey.

REFERENCES

Aulakh, Preet and M. Kotabe (1993), 'An Assessment of Theoretical and Methodological Developments in International Marketing', *Journal of International Marketing*, **1** (2) 5–28.

Bagozzi, Richard P. and H. Baumgartner (1994), 'The Evaluation of Structural Equation Models and Hypothesis Testing', in Richard Bagozzi (ed.), *Principles of Marketing Research*, Cambridge, MA: Blackwell, pp. 386–422.

Craig, Samuel C. and S.P. Douglas (2000), *International Marketing Research*, 2nd edn, New York: John Wiley & Sons.

Davis, H.L., S.P. Douglas and A.J. Silk (1981), 'Measure Unreliability: A Hidden Threat to Cross-National Marketing Research', *Journal of Marketing*, **45** (1) 98–109.

Green, R.T. and P. White (1981), 'Methodological Considerations in Cross-National Research', *Journal of International Business Studies*, **7** (Fall), 81–97.

Hui, Harry C. and H.C. Triandis (1985), 'Measurement in Cross-Cultural Psychology: A Review and Comparison of Strategies', *Journal of Cross-Cultural Psychology*, **16** (June), 131–52.

Inglehart, Ronald (1997), *Modernization and Postmodernization: Cultural, Economic, and Political Change in 43 Societies*, Princeton: Princeton University Press.

Inglehart, Ronald and W. Baker (2000), 'Modernization, Cultural Change and the Persistence of Traditional Values', *American Sociological Review*, **65** (1), 19–51.

Kumar, V.K. (2000), *International Marketing Research*, New York: Prentice Hall.

Mintu, Alma, R. Calantone and J. Gassenheimer (1994), 'Towards Improving Cross-Cultural Research: Extending Churchill's Research Paradigm', *Journal of International Consumer Marketing*, **7** (2), 5–23.

Mullen, Michael R. (1995), 'Diagnosing Measurement Equivalence in Cross-National Research', *Journal of International Business Studies*, **26** (3) 573–96.

Myers, Matthew B., R. Calantone, T.J. Page and C.R. Taylor (2000), 'An Application of Multiple-Group Causal Models in Assessing Cross-Cultural Measurement Equivalence', *Journal of International Marketing*, **8** (4), 108–21.

Netemeyer, Richard G., S. Durvasula and D. Lichtenstein (1991), 'A Cross-National Assessment of the Reliability and Validity of the CETSCALE', *Journal of Marketing Research*, **28** (3), 320–27.

Nevis, Edwin C. (1983), 'Cultural Assumptions and Productivity', *Sloan Management Review*, (Spring), 11–29.

Parameswaran, Ravi and A. Yaprak (1987), 'A Cross-National Comparison of Consumer Research Measures', *Journal of International Business Studies*, **18** (2), 61–73.

Singh, Jagdip (1995), 'Measurement Issues in Cross-National Research', *Journal of International Business Studies*, **26** (3), 597–619.

Steenkamp, Jan Benedict and H. Baumgartner (1998), 'Assessing Measurement Invariance in Cross-National Research', *Journal of Consumer Research*, **25** (June), 78–90.

Van de Vjver, Vons and K. Leung (1997), *Methods and Data Analysis for Cross-Cultural Research*, London: Sage.

9. Experimental economic approaches to international marketing research[1]

Nancy R. Buchan

INTRODUCTION

> One possible way of figuring out economic laws . . . is by controlled experiments.
> . . . Economists [unfortunately] . . . cannot perform the controlled experiments
> of chemists or biologists because they cannot easily control other important
> factors. Like astronomers or meteorologists, they generally must be content
> largely to observe. (From the economics text of Samuelson and Nordhaus, 1985,
> p. 8, edited out in later editions)

Unlike traditional economists, who were hesitant to accept experimentation as a valid methodology, marketers have long understood its value.[1] As
is evidenced by the recent proliferation of experimental economic work,
economists now also recognize that 'it is indeed possible to generate economic data under controlled conditions, and that by doing so economists
are better able to understand existing theories and develop new ones' (Hey
1991, p. 2). The goal of this chapter is to discuss the unique value experimental economics offers researchers in marketing, and the potential this
methodology provides in understanding and developing international marketing theories.

Many marketing phenomena are addressed by economic theory: an
antique buyer's decision to take a dealer's offer rather than leave it, a
premium wine-maker holding its high prices constant in a competitive
market, an e-commerce auction company learning which features to add to
its web site through trial and error, competing firms deciding on timing of
market entry, or channel partners deciding to invest in innovation to
increase joint profit and how that profit will be distributed.

Not surprisingly, many of these issues have been studied directly or indirectly by experimental economists and behavioral game theorists. These
examples illustrate the following topics, respectively: ultimatum games
(antique buyers and sellers), signaling (wine pricing), learning (e-commerce),
mixed strategy equilibria (competitors), and coordination games, trust
games or gift giving (channel relationships).

Given that all the marketing phenomena just mentioned increasingly occur in the global arena with multinational players, experimental economic methodology provides an additional theory-based tool for international marketers to deepen our understanding of global marketing transactions and relationships. The remainder of this chapter is an introduction to experimental economics and a discussion of the value it has in advancing international marketing research. Specifically, the following sections define economics experiments and how they are conducted. Next, three categories of economics experiments are introduced with a discussion of the avenues for inquiry each provides for international marketing researchers. Finally, the potential and limitations of the methodology are offered.

A BRIEF REVIEW OF EXPERIMENTAL ECONOMICS

In the *Handbook of Experimental Economics* Alvin Roth identifies three streams of experimental economic research beginning in the 1930s as having initiated more formal streams of experimental investigation that continue today (1995).[2] These experiments all rely on the predictions of expected utility theory (EUT) and its concern with precisely specified 'rules of the game' to provide focus to experiments.

The first stream of experiments concerns those designed to test theories of individual choice. The most famous of these is the 'Allais paradox.' Allais asked subjects to make two hypothetical choices. The first choice was between alternatives A and B defined as:

A: Certainty of receiving 100 million (francs)

and

B: Probability 0.10 of receiving 500 million
Probability 0.89 of receiving 100 million
Probability 0.01 of receiving zero

and the second choice was between alternatives C and D defined as

C: Probability 0.11 of earning 100 million (francs)
Probability 0.89 of earning zero

and

D: Probability 0.10 of receiving 500 million
Probability 0.90 of receiving zero

An expected utility maximizer who prefers A to B, should also prefer C to D. Allais demonstrated that most people prefer A to B, but then D to C. In the first situation people are unwilling to give up the certainty of winning 100 million francs for the risk (however small) of receiving nothing. In the second situation, the difference in the probabilities is so small, people are often willing to try for the much larger amount.

The choices people make in the Allais paradox are consistent with a more general theory introduced 25 years later by Kahneman and Tversky (1979). Prospect theory, like EUT, has spawned a whole generation of experimental research on individual behaviors – focusing on how people interpret probabilities (e.g. exhibiting a tendency to overweight very small probabilities and underweight large ones), and how we value losses and gains (e.g. feeling more pain from a loss than pleasure from an equal amount of gain).

The second stream of research concerns tests of game-theoretic hypotheses. In 1950, Dresher and Flood conducted an experiment that continues to have far-reaching influence – in economics, business, psychology, sociology, biology, and political science. Their game, the prisoner's dilemma, provided a test of Nash's prediction (1950) of how rational players would behave in a situation in which one's outcome was vulnerable to the play of another. A 100-fold repetition of the matrix below was conducted between a fixed pair of subjects who communicated only their choices of row (A or B) or column (1 or 2). The first number in each cell is the earnings of the row player and the second number is the earnings of the column player.

	(1)	(2)
(A)	$-1,2$	$1/2,1$
(B)	$0,1/2$	$1,-1$

Subjects were awarded earnings (in pennies) over the 100 repetitions of the game. The unique Nash equilibrium is for players to choose (2,1), the second row and the first column, in each of the 100 plays (yielding US$0.00 earnings for the row player, and 50 cents for the column player over the hundred rounds). For the row player, (B) is better than (A) no matter what the column player chooses ($0 > -1$, $1 > 1/2$). For the column player, (1) is better than (2), no matter what the row player does ($2 > 1$, $1/2 > -1$). However, this outcome is inefficient. If players would instead play (1,2) in every period, their earnings over the 100 rounds would be 50 cents for the row player, and US$1.00 for the column player. Thus, equilibrium play is less profitable than cooperative play. The Dresher and Flood results have been replicated time and again; people tend to choose strategies that leave them with payoffs far from equilibrium, but also that fall short of complete cooperation.

The prisoner's dilemma has motivated hundreds of experiments testing how the level of cooperation responds to various kinds of manipulation. One key finding of relevance to researchers studying channels relationships is that even in repeated games in which cooperation usually unravels, cooperation may occur at the end due to players' motivations to build reputations as the type of player who will cooperate when faced with cooperation (Kreps et al. 1982).

These early game theoretic experiments illustrated important issues in experimental design and theory testing. Experimenters came to understand factors that affect behavior; for example, playing the game repeatedly or only once, possessing knowledge of one's own and the partner's payoffs or inclinations, providing incentives proportional to payoffs in the games, and designing payoffs such that one becomes more prominent than another (Roth 1995). Regarding this last point, Schelling demonstrated that in many situations the problem facing economic agents is one of coordination, and thus, by focusing on outcomes that might be 'prominent' some of the costs of coordination failure may be avoided. As Roth notes, Schelling's findings are a lesson to experimenters to be acutely aware of the details of how the experiment is being conducted and the influence they might have on behavior, even if those details do not directly concern the theory being tested (1995).

The third stream of research in experimental economics concerns the organization and functioning of markets. In 1948, Chamberlin designed an experimental market with known supply and demand curves. Chamberlin devised a method of inducing the aggregate supply and demand curves of a market by providing each buyer or seller with a reservation price for each unit they demand or supply. This method of induced valuation continues to be widely used to study various forms of market organization, and has been described as 'the crux move in the development of experimental economics' (Camerer forthcoming).

Building on this work, Smith embarked on a fruitful series of experiments intending to produce environments in which competitive equilibrium would be observed (1962). His double auction market is such an environment; results show convergence of auction prices toward competitive equilibrium within a few rounds. Importantly, in a later experiment Smith reproduced his results (involving hypothetical payments) with results involving real monetary payments. Research on double auction markets continues today – having evolved from demonstrating that competitive equilibrium can occur, to greater investigation of the causes and conditions under which it does occur.

These three streams of early experimental economic work precipitated a steady growth of the field in the 1960s and 1970s and explosive growth in the 1980s and 1990s, bringing experimentation into the 'mainstream' of traditional economics (Roth 1995).[3] Importantly, this work set a foundation for the research that followed it. First, this early research elevated the concern for testing general theories in specific, controlled environments. Second, it began the evolution in methodological protocols – providing guidelines regarding how to conduct economic experiments, and what factors need be controlled to yield the clearest interpretation of how the results address theory.

CONDUCTING ECONOMIC EXPERIMENTS

The discussion in the previous section was an introduction to experimental economics – meant to provide a rough understanding of its history and the issues investigated. This section will present a brief 'how to' guide to conducting economic experiments internationally. In the next section three 'uses' of experimental economics will be presented accompanied by a discussion of how international marketers also might employ this methodology.

Experimental Design

For experimental economists, the beauty of their method lies in the simplicity of their (experimental) games. Camerer (forthcoming) states, 'Simple games are particularly useful because only one or two basic principles are needed to make a prediction. If the prediction is wrong, we know which principles are at fault, and the results usually suggest an alternative principle which predicts more accurately' (p. 7).

Because economic theory rarely specifies how adding realistic details will affect behavior in a given situation, these details are left out of the experimental design. Essentially, what experimental subjects face is a very bare-bones context, where behaviors (such as cooperation, trust, or fairness) are measured by a common metric, and differences in these behaviors are starkly revealed through statistical analysis and control.

As an example of such a game, a standard experimental approach used to demonstrate the role of fairness in bargaining is the ultimatum game. This game allows us to quantifiably measure the extent to which bargaining behavior deviates from the purely self-interested (subgame) perfect equilibrium; this deviation is attributed to concerns for fairness (Thaler 1988).[4] By comparing deviations from the equilibrium across subject pools, for example, we can determine the extent to which concerns for fairness enter into bargaining behaviors across contexts, cultures, or countries.

In an ultimatum game the 'buyer' is given an amount, say, US$10, and is told to divide it in any way she chooses with the 'seller'. At the same time, the seller is told to list the minimum amount he would accept from the buyer. If the buyer's offer equals or exceeds the seller's minimum demand, the offer is accepted, and the two players divide the money as proposed by the buyer. If the buyer's offer is less than the seller's demand, the offer is rejected, and neither player receives anything. Since any amount of money is better than no money, the self-interested utility-maximizing buyer should offer (and the seller should demand) the smallest amount over zero; this amount ε, is the equilibrium.[5]

The temptation to add contextual details to such a game scenario is strong, especially when conducting cross-cultural research. However, balancing this temptation is the need to preserve consistency in meaning of the scenario across cultures, and preserving the clarity our results provide regarding theories of off-equilibrium behavior. For example, while the concept of salary negotiations might provide a rich and relevant context, that context would have different meanings among say, Japanese and American subjects. Any differences in behavior that result would likely be confounded by differences in contextual salience across the subject pools.

Instructions

Each economics experiment should have a clear instructional script, which enables precise replication; this is crucial when running an experiment across subject pools that vary in language. These instructions ensure that subjects know what decision they will be making, how they will make it, how and where they should record it, and the possible outcomes (Croson forthcoming).

A common convention is that the instructions include a quiz with hypothetical examples of decisions. Providing this quiz not only ensures that subjects understand the game they are about to play, but also provides the researcher with confidence that the results are not influenced by subject misunderstanding.

Additionally, instructions should be read aloud in the experimental room in view of all subjects, thereby operationalizing 'common knowledge' (all subjects know that all other subjects have received the same information) usually assumed in economic theory. Of course, some experiments are designed to test asymmetric information conditions. Here, all subjects should be explicitly told that some participants are informed, and some are not.

Anonymity

If subjects know the identity of the person with whom they interact, this knowledge is likely to influence their behavior. Furthermore, these social effects of knowledge of the partner's identity are exacerbated in cultures where 'face saving' behaviors – or the need or desire to behave in socially acceptable ways – are prominent (throughout most of East Asia, for example) (Bond and Hwang 1995). To reduce the likelihood of such demand effects (pleasing others in the experiment or pleasing the experimenter) many researchers take the precaution of running experiments with double-blind procedures; subjects are anonymous to other subjects, and subjects are anonymous to the experimenter.

Incentives

It is rare today to see an experiment published in an economics journal that does not use monetary, non-hypothetical payments. Yet, the evidence remains mixed as to whether payment, and how much, significantly influences behavior in economic games – and the debate involving the relative efficacy (and cost) of using performance-based incentives in experiments remains lively. Thaler (1987) reviews many studies in which the differences between real and hypothetical payments did not yield important differences in results. He states, 'Asking purely hypothetical questions is inexpensive, fast, and convenient. This means that many more experiments can be run with much larger samples than is possible in a monetary-incentives methodology' (p. 120).

Despite this, the strong tradition and preference for performance-based incentives continues in economics, likely prompted by deeper philosophical concerns as stated by Croson (forthcoming), 'In economics, the validity of the experiment rests on the link between behavior and payoffs. If subjects are deceived about that link, the validity of their decisions is called into doubt' (p. 31).

Cross-country Controls

The international character of our research warrants that we control specific variables that could influence results for country or culture. Within economics, these controls were first addressed by Roth et al. (1991) in their multi-country comparison of bargaining behavior.

Controlling for Subject Pool Equivalency

Ensuring that subjects are as similar as possible is a daunting task. For example, the demographics of a 'typical' college junior in each country are likely to be influenced by gender (one experiment I ran had a 90 per cent male subject pool in Korea versus a 50 per cent male pool in the USA), age (in many countries students complete military service before beginning college), intelligence or wealth (in many developing countries only a minute percentage of people attend college, versus 40–50 per cent in the USA), or courses taken in college (many countries do not have business schools as in the USA, leaving one to decide if an economics major, for example, is equivalent to a marketing major). However, the researcher must try to promote maximum equivalency by, for example, selecting students from similarly tiered universities in each country. If the researcher believes that these other demographic factors, such as gender or income, may influence behavior, these variables should be added to the analysis as covariates.

Controlling for Currency Effects

Purchasing power parity can be controlled for by choosing denominations such that the monetary incentives relative to subject income and living standards are approximately equal. Camerer (forthcoming) provides three suggestions: (1) converting a baseline sum into local currency, (2) controlling for stakes in terms of labor supply by equalizing number of hours of work required to earn the stake amount, and (3) in less developed cultures, constructing a cost-of-living index by measuring local prices of commonly used items.

Controlling for Language Effects

Controlling for any nuances in language is crucial lest these nuances influence consistency in meaning of instructions across countries. The standard method is to have all experimental materials translated and back-translated using separate external translators.

Controlling for Experimenter Effects

As mentioned previously, the identity and the behavior of the experimenter may influence subjects' behavior. The worst option for an experimenter is to have separate experimenters in each country – thus confounding whether any significant results are due to real culture differences or to differences in the manner in which the experimenter behaved or was perceived in each country. A better option is to have each experimenter conduct experiments in different cultures – thereby allowing estimation of an experimenter main effect. When running multi-country experiments, I have done the following. First, I was present when each experiment was being run to ensure equivalency of procedures (room layout, presentation of instructions, etc.). Second, an extremely thorough protocol was designed (and translated and back-translated) based upon the procedure used in the USA and used to train experimenters in each country. The protocol included information such as the positioning of the experimenter in the room, and the method to be used in answering subject questions. Third, I trained all experimenters and conducted a pilot session with them.

THREE CATEGORIES OF ECONOMIC EXPERIMENTS

Addressing the question of what is the purpose of economic experiments, Roth suggested a categorization based on how the experiments are motivated and their audience (1995). Although most experiments contain elements of more than one category, roughly, the uses of experimentation divide into three. First are experiments that 'Speak to Theorists' – that are designed to address economic theory. Second are experiments that 'Search for Facts' – that are designed to study the effects of variables (the anomalies) about which theory has little to say. Third are experiments that 'Whisper in the Ears of Princes' – that are designed to inform public policy.

These categories are helpful in that they point out areas where international marketers too can address theory and speak to specific audiences – theorists in our field, economists, and policy makers. Given that relatively little work has been conducted internationally in experimental economics, and almost no work has appeared in international marketing using the methodology, these three categories provide ample opportunity for consumer researchers interested in individual decision making, channels and strategy researchers interested in game theory, and public policy researchers interested in market structure, to study and increase our understanding of important economic phenomena. In this section I present some international work from economics and other fields that has been conducted within each of these categories, and discuss potential areas research for marketers.

Experiments Addressing Theory

One body of theory-addressing research that has attracted attention from international researchers concerns risk aversion. Camerer (1995) describes that, contrary to formal economic models of thirty years ago, today's models assume that decision makers make choices under risk and uncertainty, over time. However, as the models grow more complex, decision makers are assumed to have more rationality – making it more likely that the models will be violated. It is in this way that individual decision-making research can speak to economic theory – providing the how and why of rationality violations.

A fascinating stream of such research initiated by Weber and Hsee (1998, 1999) uses different methods of risk-taking assessment (e.g. pairwise choices between gambles and sure amounts or willingness-to-pay for risky options) to compare behaviors internationally. They show that respondents from China are less risk-averse in risky financial decisions than their counterparts in the United States. To account for these robust results, Weber and Hsee propose the 'cushion hypothesis' (1999): 'members of socially collectivist cultures, such as the Chinese culture, can afford to take greater financial risks because their social networks insure them against catastrophic outcomes. The social network serves as a "cushion" which could protect the person if she took risks and fell "ill"' (p. 14).

The cushion hypothesis yields a number of predictions, tested by Weber and Hsee. They demonstrate first, that the size and quality of a respondent's social network serves as a mediating factor between nationality and risk preference. (Not surprisingly, Chinese have much larger and stronger social networks than Americans.) Second, that Chinese are significantly more risk-seeking than Americans in financial domains, but not in other domains such as academic or medical decisions. In these other domains, they suggest, it would be more difficult for a social network to provide a remedy should something go wrong (Hsee and Weber 1999).

In addition to the work by Weber and Hsee, there have also been rich streams of research investigating cultural influence on probability judgments (e.g. Yates 1989) and on culture and risk perception (e.g. Bontempo et al. 1997), which also shed light on economic decision-making internationally.

Avenues for International Marketing Research

This research demonstrates the value and contribution that a careful and motivated international researcher can make to our understanding of economic behavior. All of this research informs the how and why of 'irrational' decision making. Yet, importantly, it also expands boundaries in that it looks at factors, such as risk aversion, which may have been assumed to be hard-wired to the human race (based mainly on studies conducted in the West), and demonstrates that there are significant differences in these processes across cultures. Therein lies the opportunity for international marketing researchers.

The area of behavioral decision research has become prominent in marketing in the last decade, phenomena such as mental accounting, intertemporal choice, framing effects, the endowment effect, and risk aversion, to name a few, are common currency in the language of consumer researchers. Yet, there are few, if any, published studies that have examined these phenomena on a cross-cultural basis. As shown by the work of Weber and Hsee, making such an examination, and providing a deeper explanation for any differences (or similarities) in cross-cultural effects greatly enhances our understanding of such phenomena, and of how they operate across cultures. This allows us to think more specifically about the implications of these cultural differences for how consumers buy, sellers sell, and agents in firms interact on a global basis.

EXPERIMENTS ADDRESSING ANOMALIES

A second category of economic experiment demonstrates the influence of factors – anomalies – not captured by theoretical models. 'An experimental result qualifies as an anomaly if it is difficult to "rationalize" or if implausible assumptions are necessary to explain it within the (self-interested, rational) paradigm' (Camerer and Thaler 1995, p. 209). The anomalies I concentrate on in this section focus on norms.

In 1991, Roth et al. compared behavior in a two-person bargaining situation (the ultimatum game) with behavior in a multiple person market environment in Japan, Israel, the Slovak Republic and the United States. Each game was repeated for ten rounds with different anonymous partners in each round. In the bargaining and market environments, the unique (subgame) perfect equilibrium was that one player would receive all the wealth (or almost all when payoffs were discrete). The authors demonstrated that outcomes in the market environment converged very quickly to equilibrium everywhere, with no relevant payoff differences across countries. Outcomes from the bargaining environment however remained different from the equilibrium across all rounds, and substantial differences in offers and rejection rates were revealed across countries (with the differences increasing as the rounds progressed). Specifically, offers in the USA and Slovenia (mean = 45 per cent of the pie) tended to be more generous than those in Japan and Israel (10 per cent lower). Despite the lower offers, rejection rates in Japan and Israel were no higher than rates in the other two countries. Roth et al. conclude, 'the subject–pool differences observed in this experiment are related to different expectations about what constitutes an acceptable offer, rather than different propensities to trespass on a shared notion of what constitutes an acceptable offer' (1991, p. 1092). To suggest why behavior converged to equilibrium in the market game but did not in the ultimatum game, they state 'The observed bargaining behavior is dominated by concerns about fairness which are context dependent and do not arise in the market environment' (Roth et al. 1991, p. 1093).

This question of what is fair, what contextual factors influence fairness, and the relationship between fair beliefs and actual behavior, prompted a study by Buchan et al. looking again at a repeated ultimatum game in Japan and the USA (2002). Our experiment differed from the Roth et al. (1991) experiment in key ways. First, we manipulated the balance of power between the players in the experiment. Second, in addition to observing behavior, we asked subjects what they believed was the fair offer or demand. Third, we ran the ultimatum game using a different method from Roth et al. We conducted the experiment using the 'strategy method'; buyers and sellers submit their offers and demands, the two are matched and if the demand is equal to or less than the offer, the division is made as proposed by the buyer. Roth et al. ran their ultimatum experiment using the 'game method'; the buyer's offer is presented to the seller, and the seller accepts or rejects it.

We suggested that collectivists would behave differently in the strategy method ultimatum game than would individually oriented subjects. Specifically, we proposed that subjects from Japan, a relatively more collectivist culture, would prefer divisions that were closer to an even split of the pie, than would the more individualist American subjects. This hypothesis was supported, with offers and demands about 12 per cent higher in Japan than in the USA. We also suggested that power would have a more differential influence in Japan than in the USA. In the USA, people relate to power as a means to an end in a negotiation; Japanese people tend to view power as much more relational. Sociologist Doi (1971) explains that in Japan, societal norms dictate that the more powerful party is responsible, in part, for the well-being of the less powerful. Thus, we hypothesized that whereas offers by a more powerful partner in the USA would decrease (relative to the condition where power was equal between the partners), offers by a more powerful partner in Japan would actually increase. Interestingly, this hypothesis was not supported in Japan by actual behavior data, but was supported by data showing what subjects believed to be the fair behavior. These results highlight the relationship between behavior and fairness beliefs in the ultimatum game. In regression analyses, fairness beliefs accounted for only 16 per cent of the variance in offers or demands, suggesting that while fairness is a component motivating behavior in the game, clearly other motivations, such as strategy, are salient as well.

One noteworthy result is our failure to replicate Roth et al.'s results; although American offers and demands were not significantly different across the two experiments, in our experiment Japanese offers were more generous, and the rejection rate was higher in Japan than in the USA. This difference is interesting in that its roots may lie in the differing experimental methods used, thus highlighting the value of using various methods to tap into different cultural tendencies. Prior research on cross-cultural negotiation styles demonstrates that the divergence between intended action and action taken is larger among Japanese negotiators than among American negotiators (Ohbuchi and Takahashi 1994). This implies that in the Roth et al. game method, Japanese sellers may have accepted lower offers as they were presented them (not wanting to say 'no'), although if given a chance beforehand, their stated minimum acceptable offer may have been higher.

The results of these two studies suggest cultural and methodological explanations for the differences in 'fair' behavior observed in Japan and the USA. From an anthropologist's view, however, these two cultures are actually very similar. A much more dramatic anthropologist-led bargaining study examined behavior in 12 small-scale cultures (including Peru's Machiguenga farmers, Paraguay's Ache headhunters, and Indonesia's Lamerlara whalers). This study reveals startling differences in behavior across cultures and addresses the influence of market development on off-equilibrium behavior (Henrich et al. 2001). For example, Machiguengas, a culture which is extremely isolated socially and economically, offered much less in the ultimatum game than has been observed in any other subject pool – with a mode at 15 per cent, and only one rejected offer. At the other extreme, the Ache headhunters and Lamelara whalers, cultures where potlatch is common, exhibited more generosity than seen with any other subject pool – offering more than half on average.

In regression analyses two variables account for the variance in offers across the 12 cultures ($R^2 = 0.68$). Cultures with more cooperative activity (e.g. collective hunting of whales) and market integration (an index combining the existence of a national language, a labor market for cash wages, and farming of crops for cash) have sharing norms closer to equal splits.

This research very quickly caught the attention of economists. After all, it was Adam Smith who observed that markets are effective because of the baker's pursuit of self-interest rather than his generosity. This research suggests something different: that a great deal of real world, 'encultured' market experience tempers rather than amplifies the pursuit of self-interest.

Avenues for International Marketing Research

The increased interest among economists in behaviors prompted by norms such as fairness has been concurrent with the increased recognition in marketing of the importance of shared norms within the channel relationship. The existence of these norms, if shared, provides a means of communication and control (Weitz and Jap 1995; Heide and John 1992), and has been shown to increase the performance of both the channel and individual channel members (Lusch and Brown 1996). Given this converging interest in norms, experimental economics may offer a different and interesting new lease to the study of the influence of norms on international trading agreements and behavior. The Roth et al. (1991) and Buchan et al. (2001a) studies demonstrate the possibilities of measuring the strength of a norm such as fairness across cultures, and of manipulating contextual factors, such as power, that may influence fair beliefs or behavior.

The norm of trust, also, has gained much attention among researchers in economics and marketing, prompted by the important work of Williamson in demonstrating the role of trust as a lubricant in market transactions (1981). Using experimental economic games, Buchan et al. (forthcoming), have demonstrated experimentally the strong (and differing) influence across cultures of group boundaries in determining who is trusted and how much, while Buchan et al. (2001b) show that cultures are similar in their trusting response to different types of non-strategic communication. Buchan et al. (2001a) examined trust in a prisoner's dilemma setting and found the trusting behavior of Japanese participants, specifically, to increase in the presence of monitoring or sanctioning mechanisms in the game. Finally, Croson and Buchan (1999) crossed gender with country in their analysis and demonstrate that while men and women trust equally, women tend to be more reciprocal (which encourages future trust and cooperation.) As with the work on fairness, this research on trust demonstrates the potential economic experiments provide for examining the influence and possible interaction of cultural and contextual factors on norms and strategic behaviors that have important ramifications on international marketing research and practice.

Given that international experimental economic research is in its infancy, there are many topics yet to be explored. As just two examples, one might apply Hall's work on high and low context cultures (1959) to the implementation of contracts and the role of trust in a strategic setting, or one might examine whether the differing attitudes and acceptance of collusion displayed across cultures by Hampden-Turner and Trompenaars (1993) influences the demonstration of fair behavior in international markets.

The anthropological research by Henrich et al. (2001) is also provocative for marketers in that it alerts us to the need to better understand the role of market development in influencing (possibly dynamic) norms and subsequent economic behavior.

Experiments That Testbed Policies

When new policies are being considered, an experiment can be run to testbed the policy, investigate and hopefully illuminate any unintended consequences, and to suggest parameters that policy makers might consider in their final implementation (Croson forthcoming).

The greatest triumph of this line of inquiry is evidenced in the application of game theory to the auctions of airwaves to telecommunications companies. In several different countries, regulatory agencies decided to put airwave spectrum up for auction. Ideally, the auctions would raise government revenue, and ensure that a public resource is awarded to the firms who are most able to create value from it. In most countries, the auctions were designed in collaboration with game theorists whose testbedding helped detect any unanticipated weaknesses in proposed designs (Camerer, forthcoming).

Avenues for International Marketing Research

Interestingly, two articles have appeared in marketing journals in the past five years urging greater game theoretic exploration of the method by which products are sold, and how efficiency might be increased (McAfee and McMillan 1996; Bazerman 2001). The advent of global electronic markets (in B2B, B2C, and C2C) provides an exciting forum for international researchers to better understand the implications of various market structures for buyers and sellers (e.g. differences in behavior in auction markets). Additionally, marketing researchers could make a valuable contribution to understanding and prompting efficient market development internationally. In discussing various testbed experiments involving markets for computer resources, gas, and electrical power grids, Friedman and Sunder state, 'Given the accelerating pace of transformation in the formerly centrally planned economies and given continuing deregulation in Western countries, the scope for institutional engineering of this sort is large and increasing' (1994, p. 9).

THE LIMITATIONS AND POTENTIAL OF ECONOMIC EXPERIMENTS

In this final section I will address the most commonly mentioned limitations of this methodology (as discussed by Croson forthcoming), but also reiterate its potential for advancing our knowledge of marketing phenomena.

One common objection of this methodology has to do with the nature of the subject pool; specifically questioning whether the behavior of college undergraduates represents what real business people would do. A first defense is that students are people too, and in fact, represent the professionals of tomorrow. A more scientific defense lies in the fact that multiple experiments have been conducted using student and professional demonstrating no significant differences in behavior. For example, Dyer et al. (1989) found no significant differences in bidding behavior of experienced business executives in construction compared to that of students and Bontempo et al. (1997) also found no differences in risk aversion among students versus security analysts.

A second objection deals with the size of the monetary payoffs; specifically, that stakes commonly used in experiments are too small to induce optimal behavior. Interestingly, a number of international experiments (at least two dozen in fact) address this argument. Experiments have been conducted in developing countries where purchasing power is so low that modest sums (by developed-country standards), amount to several weeks' or months of pay. For example, Cameron (1999) conducted the ultimatum game in Indonesia, manipulating a 40-fold change in stakes from 5000 to 200 000 rupiah – allowing some subjects to leave with the equivalent of three months expenditures. A robust conclusion of these experiments is that results under higher stakes conditions are generally very close to those with lower stakes.

A final objection to this methodology usually involves external validity; what can these simple games tell us about transactions in the real world? The strategic situation can be scaled down to their barest elements – players, information, actions, outcomes – in order to best teach readers what to look for, what behaviors to expect, and how they might behave in response. In essence that is the value of this methodology as well; it allows us to map social situations onto simple games in order to best understand the implications of behavior (Camerer forthcoming). However, once we have that initial understanding, we have every reason to build upon it to better model and understand the more complex situation we actually face. As Camerer states, 'Doubts about generalizability are a demand for more elaborate experiments, not a dismissal of the experimental method . . . More ambitious experiments with teams of players, complex environment, communication, overlapping generations, would enhance generalizability and should be the wave of the future' (forthcoming, p. 4).

The methodology of experimental economics presents international marketing researchers with a challenge. We are particularly well-equipped to understand the variables in the international environment that need be controlled when running basic games; additionally, we have developed a deep understanding of the nature of global marketing transactions. Using this new tool of controlled economic experiments, we can now build upon basic games, adding layers of contextual realism. The value of this method is that as we add on each layer of context – developing eventually into a systematic stream of research – we will be able to clearly discern its influence on individual-level behaviors, strategic interactions, and transactions in a given market structure. In this way we will lend the clearest interpretation of how our results speak to theory in economics and in marketing.

NOTES

1. Among the earliest examples of experimental work is Haire's shopping list study published in the *Journal of Marketing* in 1950.
2. Roth actually credits Bernoulli's work on the St Petersburg paradox in 1738 as being the *first* economic experiment. Bernoulli asked people to name the price at which they would buy a chance in a lottery with an infinite expected value. In showing that most people would pay only a modest sum, Bernoulli suggested that the value of an addition to a person's wealth decreases the more wealthy they become. The resulting concave utility curve explains the reluctance of people to buy into this lottery; the extra utility of high earnings from unlikely outcomes is no longer high enough to compensate for its low probability. This desire to avoid taking risks – even the reluctance to gamble on even bets – is called risk aversion.
3. Maurice Allais won the 1998 Nobel Prize in Economics.
4. Whether these concerns are motivated by a real desire to 'be fair' or by the desire to simply 'appear fair' is a subject of debate and is addressed in Buchan et al. 2002.
5. There are two methods of running the ultimatum game – the strategy method just described, and the game method. These differences will be elaborated upon here, in the section concerning 'Experiments Addressing Anomalies'.

REFERENCES

Bazerman, Max (2001), 'Consumer Research for Consumers', *Journal of Consumer Research*, **27**, 499–504.

Bernoulli, Daniel (1738), 'Specimen Theoriae Novae de Mensura Sortis', *Commentarii Academiae Scientiarum Imperialis Petropolitanae*, **5**, 175–92.

Bond, Michael and Kwang-kuo Hwang (1995), 'The Social Psychology of Chinese People', in Michael Harris Bond (ed.), *The Psychology of Chinese People*, Hong Kong: Oxford University Press.

Bontempo, R.N., W.P. Bottom and Elke Weber (1997), 'Cross-cultural Differences in Risk Perception: A Model-based Approach', *Risk Analysis*, **17**, 479–88.

Buchan, Nancy R., Peter Dickson and Diana Haytko (2001a), 'International Differences in Manufacturer–Distributor Trust', University of Wisconsin-Madison Working Paper.

Buchan, Nancy R., Eric J. Johnson and Rachel T.A. Croson (2001b), 'Trust, Reciprocity, and Altruism: An International Experiment', University of Wisconsin-Madison Working Paper.

Buchan, Nancy R., Eric J. Johnson and Rachel T.A. Croson (2002), 'Understanding What's Fair: Cross-Cultural Differences in Fairness Norms in Japan and the United States', University of Wisconsin-Madison Working Paper.

Buchan, Nancy R., Rachel T.A. Croson and Robyn M. Dawes (forthcoming), 'Swift Neighbors and Persistent Strangers: A Cross-Cultural Investigation of Trust and Reciprocity in Social Exchange', *American Journal of Sociology*.

Camerer, Colin F. (1995), *Individual Decision Making*, in John H. Kagel and Alvin E. Roth (eds), *The Handbook of Experimental Economics*, Princeton, NJ: Princeton University Press.

Camerer, Colin F. (forthcoming), *Behavioral Game Theory: Experiments on Strategic Interaction*, Princeton, NJ: Princeton University Press.

Camerer, Colin F. and Richard H. Thaler (1995), 'Anomalies: Ultimatums, Dictators and Manners', *Journal of Economic Perspectives*, **9** (2), 209–19.

Cameron, Lisa (1999), 'Raising the Stakes in the Ultimatum Game: Experimental Evidence from Indonesia', *Economic Inquiry*, **37** (1), 47–59.

Chamberlain, Edward H. (1948), *The Theory of Monopolistic Competition*, Cambridge: Harvard University Press.

Croson, Rachel T.A. (forthcoming), 'Why and How to Experiment: Methodologies from Experimental Economics', *University of Illinois Law Review*.

Croson, Rachel T.A. and Nancy R. Buchan (1999), 'Gender and Culture: International Experimental Evidence from Trust Games', *American Economic Review*, **84**, 386–91.

Doi, Takeo (1971), *The Anatomy of Dependence*, Tokyo, Japan: Kodansha Press.

Dyer, Douglas, John Kagel and Dan Levin (1989), 'A Comparison of Naïve and Experienced Bidders in Common Value Offer Auctions: A Laboratory Analysis', *Economic Journal*, **99** (394), 108–15.

Flood, Merrill M. (1952), 'Some Experimental Games', Research Memorandum RM-789, RAND Corporation, June.

Friedman, Daniel and Shyam Sunder (1994), *Experimental Methods: A Primer for Economists*, New York: Cambridge University Press.

Haire, Mason (1950), 'Projective Techniques in Marketing Research', *Journal of Marketing*, **14** (5), 649–56.

Hall, Edward (1959), 'Key Concepts: Underlying Structures of Culture', in *The Silent Language*, Garden City, NY: Doubleday Press.

Hampden-Turner, Charles and Alfons Trompenaars (1993), *The Seven Cultures of Capitalism*, New York: Doubleday.

Heide, Jan and George John (1992), 'Do Norms Matter in Marketing Relationships?', *Journal of Marketing*, **56** (2), 22–44.

Henrich, Joseph, Robert Boyd, Samuel Bowles et al. (2001), 'In Search of Homo Economicus: Behavioral Experiments in 15 Small-Scale Economies', *Economics and Social Behavior*, **91** (2), 73–8.

Hey, John D. (1991), *Experiments in Economics*, Cambridge, MA: Basil Blackwell.

Kahneman, Daniel and Amos Tversky (1979), 'Prospect Theory: An Analysis of Decision under Risk', *Econometrica*, **47**, 263–91.

Kreps, David, Paul Milgrom, John Roberts and Robert Wilson (1982), 'Reputation and Imperfect Information', *Journal of Economic Theory*, **27**, 253–79.

Lusch, Robert and James Brown (1996), 'Interdependency, Contracting and Relational Behavior in Marketing Channels', *Journal of Marketing*, **60**, 19–38.

McAfee, Preston and John McMillan (1996), 'Competition and Game Theory', *Journal of Marketing Research*, **33** (3), 263–67.

Nash, John F. (1950), 'The Bargaining Problem', *Econometrica*, **18**, 155–62.

Ohbuchi, Ken-Ichi and Yumi Takahashi (1994), 'Cultural Styles of Conflict Management in Japanese and Americans: Passivity, Covertness, and Effectiveness of Strategies', *Journal of Applied Social Psychology*, **24**, 1345–66.

Roth, Alvin (1995), 'Introduction to Experimental Economics', in John H. Kagel and Alvin Roth (eds), *The Handbook of Experimental Economics*, Princeton, NJ: Princeton University Press.

Roth, Alvin, Vesna Prasnikar, Masahiro Okuno-Fujiwara and Shmuel Zamir, (1991), 'Bargaining and Market Behavior in Jerusalem, Ljubljana, Pittsburgh, and Tokyo: An Experimental Study', *American Economic Review*, **81** (5), 1068–95.

Samuelson, Paul and William Nordhaus (1985), *Principles of Economics*, 12th edn New York: McGraw-Hill.

Smith, Vernon L. (1962), 'An Experimental Study of Competitive Market Behavior', *Journal of Political Economy*, **70**, 111–37.

Thaler, Richard H. (1987), 'The Psychology of Choice and Assumptions of Economics', in Alvin Roth (ed.), *Laboratory Experimentation in Economics: Six Points of View*, Cambridge: Cambridge University Press.

Thaler, Richard H. (1988), 'The Ultimate Game', *Journal of Economic Perspectives*, **2**, 195–206.

Weber, Elke and Christopher Hsee (1998), 'Cross-cultural Differences in Risk Perception, but Cross-cultural Similarities in Attitudes Towards Perceived Risk', *Management Science*, **44** (9), 1205–18.

Weber, Elke and Christopher Hsee (1999), 'Models and Mosaics: Investigating Cross-cultural Differences in Risk Perception and Risk Preference', *Psychonomic Bulletin and Review*, **4** , 611–17.

Weitz, Barton and Sandy Jap (1995), 'Relationship Marketing and Distribution Channels', *Journal of the Academy of Marketing Science*, **23** (4), 305–21.

Williamson, Oliver E. (1981), 'The Economics of Organization: The Transaction Cost Approach', *American Journal of Sociology*, **87**, 548–77.

Yates, J. Frank, Ying Zhu, David Ronis et al. (1989), 'Probability Judgment Accuracy: China, Japan, and the United States', *Organizational Behavior and Human Decision Processes*, **43** (2), 145–72.

10. Culture theory in international marketing: an ontological and epistemological examination

Cheryl C. Nakata

INTRODUCTION

The body of international marketing studies has steadily grown over the last 25 years. From 1976 to 1982, just 112 papers on international marketing were published, whereas from 1983 to 1986, they numbered 262, followed by 363 from 1987 to 1990 (Albaum and Peterson 1984; Aulakh and Kotabe 1993). A significant trend in this burgeoning literature is an increasing interest in culture. From 1990 to 1995, 25 per cent of international marketing articles published in the leading scholarly journals incorporated culture, and from 1995 to 2000, the percentage rose to 44 per cent (Dubois and Reeb 2000; Hult et al. 1997; Nakata and Huang 2001). The dramatic increase suggests that culture is becoming a, perhaps the, leading theory in international marketing. Culture has been used to explain and predict everything from export channel controls, use of humor in global advertising, and new product diffusion to consumer innovativeness, word-of-mouth effects among industrial firms, and marketer adaptations to immigrant consumers (Alden et al. 1993; Bello and Gilliland 1997; Money et al. 1998; Penaloza and Gilly 1999; Steenkamp et al. 1999).

Far and away the most popular culture theory in international marketing is Hofstede's value paradigm. Hofstede identified four universal values – individualism, power distance, uncertainty avoidance, and masculinity – through factor analysis of cross-cultural survey data, and then developed indices so that countries can be compared directly on their levels of these values. Indicative of dominance, Hofstede's work received more than six times the number of citations as the next most popular culture theory from 1987 to 1997. And it was the most often specified culture theory in the top-ranked academic marketing and international business journals in the last decade (Nakata and Huang 2001; Sivakumar and Nakata 2001).

While Hofstede's value framework has largely overshadowed competing culture theories, two are noteworthy: Hall's (1976) and Triandis's (1989). Using ethnographic and secondary research, Hall proposed that cultures could be categorized as high or low context based on their communications propensities. High context cultures prefer complex, embedded, implicit forms of communications, whereas low context cultures emphasize direct, transparent, explicit communications. Hall did not develop measures for context, so it remains a purely theoretical framework. Hall's work was cited 147 times from 1987 to 1997 according to the Social Sciences Citations Index (compared to Hofstede's 1101 times), and in 10 per cent of international marketing articles referencing culture in the leading academic journals from 1990 to 2000. These statistics make it the second most popular culture paradigm, though considerably lagging behind Hofstede's (Nakata and Huang 2001; Sivakumar and Nakata 2001).

Like Hofstede, Triandis (1989) offered a trait theory of culture: every society can be described by its intensity on a particular personality characteristic, namely individualism–collectivism. This is in essence the same variable as one of Hofstede's four factors, but nuanced by horizontal and vertical forms. Horizontal individualism emphasizes individuals making decisions without group considerations but with equality as the norm. Vertical individualism is likewise independent decision making, but inequality among society's members is acceptable. Horizontal and vertical collectivism pressure individuals to adhere to group norms and preferences, discouraging autonomous action; the difference is that in the horizontal form nonmembers of a group are clearly deemed as outsiders and with a measure of hostility, whereas in vertical collectivism a strong hierarchy exists within the group, most often expressed in the form of a 'headman' who leads and protects followers in exchange for authority and power. Triandis and Gelfand developed and validated an instrument to measure these constructs (1998). Triandis's theory is the third most frequently applied culture theory in international marketing, though its use is considerably behind Hofstede's (Nakata and Huang 2001).

In view of the expanding literature, rising interest in culture, and prominence of Hofstede's, Hall's and Triandis's works in particular, it is timely to examine culture theory in international marketing research. Another reason to do so is to understand the potential of culture theory to advance the field. It has noted that much of the literature has been comparative in nature, identifying similarities and differences among countries (Albaum and Peterson 1984; Boddewyn 1981). While these studies have provided insights, without an underlying conceptual glue, they present 'merely interesting but detached fragments' (Clark 1990, p. 67). On the other hand, if studies incorporate culture explicitly, thereby providing a means for explaining patterns of international marketing phenomena, disparate findings can be integrated and lead over time to a coherent body of knowledge (Clark 1990).

But what aspects of culture theory in international marketing should be examined? The argument put forth is to look at assumptions about what culture is and how to go about studying it in the global context; in other words, assess the ontological and epistemological underpinnings of the major culture frameworks in international marketing. Theories are bounded by assumptions, including implicit values of theorists and explicit restrictions around the phenomenon of interest. Assumptions form a critical, but often overlooked, aspect of theories, perhaps because of their embedded nature (Bacharach 1989; Whetten 1989). Examining assumptions is not a philosophical and therefore perfunctory exercise, but rather vital for ensuring culture theory contributes to international marketing, however limited or great those contributions ultimately are. Stripping frameworks to their core premises enables scholars to direct and if necessary redirect their research efforts to get at 'truth' – the essential scientific enterprise. Vigorous discussions on and investigations into marketing theories – their structure, content, and implicit bases – have been critical to the progression of the discipline, as indicated by the debate several years ago between positivistic and relativistic philosophies (neither term intended pejoratively) (Hunt 1983).

The purpose of this chapter is twofold: (1) to discuss the ontological and epistemological presuppositions of predominant culture paradigms, and (2) to suggest directions for the development of culture theory in international marketing. The method is reflexive consideration of culture writings from the social sciences, including sociology, anthropology, history, and political science. By no means are the writings inclusive of all thoughts and views on culture, but they are suggestive of those found in other domains that may be instructive and relevant to international marketing, a relatively young discipline. Sociology and anthropology in particular have much to offer since they have studied culture for two centuries.

DEFINITIONS

Hofstede's definition of culture as the 'collective programming of the mind' is undoubtedly the most widely known in international marketing and the broader domain of business studies. However, in order to encompass the spectrum of views on and conceptualizations of culture, including those explicated in related social sciences, Tylor's definition of culture was adopted herein: 'that complex whole which includes knowledge, belief, art, morals, law, custom, and any other capabilities and habits acquired by man as a member of society' (Tylor 1958, p. 1). This definition indicates that culture can be cognitions as indicated by Hofstede, but also habits, practices, norms, and other characteristics and aspects of group life. Tylor, the father of anthropology, initially offered this view in 1871 in his book *Primitive Culture*. It is noteworthy that more than a century after its introduction, it is still heavily cited in the scholarly literature, indicating an enduring relevance.

What the term 'theory' refers to has been the subject of considerable discussion among researchers. True consensus is not yet at hand in the behavioral sciences (DiMaggio 1995; Weick 1995). Nonetheless, the definition offered by Bacharach (1989, p. 496) and elaborated by Sutton and Staw (1995, p. 375) appears useful: 'a theory is a statement of relations among concepts within a set of boundary assumptions and constraints', 'a theory must also explain why variables or constructs come about or why they are connected'. This definition captures the essence of other formulations as well, including Hunt's well-known explication. Additionally, because it offers the benefit of succinctness, it was used to guide this study.

ASSUMPTIONS ABOUT CULTURE IN INTERNATIONAL MARKETING

Culture as Coherent and Unified

A presupposition in the international marketing literature is that culture is coherent and unified: coherent in the sense that patterns make it comprehensible; unified in that its dimensions are convergent rather than conflicting. This view is evident in Hofstede's work. His theory is coherent in that a handful of universal traits are said to represent the complex totality of culture. The attraction, some would say seduction, of the paradigm is its beguiling parsimony. Hence the French culture can be adequately described based on where it falls on a continua of four values: high in individualism and power distance, moderate in uncertainty avoidance, and low on masculinity. This profile implies a unity of culture in that subtle variability or inherent paradoxes are not reflected. Thus the French culture is not nuanced as both individualistic and collectivistic such that the two tendencies co-exist, but as individualistic given its above median score on this dimension.

Casting culture as internally consistent and externally comprehensible has been and is still a well-accepted practice in the social sciences. Classical sociological and anthropological theory is largely in this vein (Crane 1994,

pp. 3–4). Ruth Benedict, whose *Patterns of Culture* (1934) is often refer-
enced for its groundbreaking views on culture, wrote of identifiable patterns in every society. She observed that, despite the fecundity and intricacy
in forms of common life, societies make selections about which are to be
installed as ways of life. Selection necessarily results in a narrowing, a
reduction of heterogeneity in favor of homogeneity. Talcott Parsons
(Thompson et al. 1990, pp. 184–5), another major influence in anthropology, argued that culture has an inherent logic. In his *Voluntaristic Theory
of Action*, Parsons placed primacy on commonly shared values as constituting culture, noting that people generally uphold such values by submit-
ting to norms. These norms, called 'pattern variables', come in pairs such
as universalism-particularism and specificity-diffuseness. Societies differ in
their tendency to favor one side of a pair or another.

A contrasting assumption reflected in some current social science
research is that culture is indeterminant and fragmented. This belief represents a post-modernist *zeitgeist*, whereas the previous one reflects a mod-
ernist *zeitgeist*. The notion of culture as disjunctive rests partially on the
observance of variability in values, customs, and habits (Levine 1984,
p. 67). Variability is especially salient in an age of rapid change in social
structures and the dissolution of nation states. What was once, for example,
the Soviet Union is now several new countries with distinct systems and
worldviews. Even within a state, the renewal of ethnic group affiliations has
resurrected long-dormant animosities in places like Afghanistan,
Yugoslavia, and Russia (Chechnya). Civilizational identities, often relig-
iously rooted, have created such severe social fissures in some places that
they have brought governments and social systems to the brink of collapse
(Huntington 1996). Culture in these cases has clearly disintegrative effects
(Crane 1994, p. 7; Schudson 1994, p. 8).

The premise of cultural discontinuity is reflected not only in current, but
also in past, cultural works. Chief among them are writings by Weber, who
rejected arguments for a coalescing national culture because of what he
deemed to be the lack of empirical evidence. For Weber, primary paradigms
were the inter-relations among status groups, and the transformative power
of religion, best articulated in his theory of the Protestant Work Ethic.
Weber (1905) emphasized the order-altering quality of culture. Even
Durkheim, while observing societies as having a 'collective conscience',
acknowledged that there are instances when commonalities are absent or
inadequate across members of a society to regulate their lives. He termed
this condition 'anomie', essentially a state of chaos (Thompson et al. 1990,
pp. 137–41).

Culture as Immutable

Another notion underlying leading culture theories in international marketing is that culture is immutable. Embedded, for instance in Hall's theory, is the assumption of constancy. Hall describes high context cultures as using implicit communications, developing refined art forms, and having a deep regard for the past. These cultures, such as the Japanese, maintain these characteristics despite the inroads of modernization and Westernization (Hall 1976). Similarly, the high context propensities of the French can be traced from monarchical and Napoleonic times to contemporary French life, such as in a continuous emphasis on protocol and hierarchy, and particularity about and articulation of ideas (Bourdieu 1984).

The immutability of culture has empirical support. Cultural characteristics have been observed as remarkably enduring. Almost a century ago, French sociologist Alexis de Tocqueville in *Democracy in America* described the people of the land as optimistic, pragmatic, straightforward, trusting, and somewhat unrefined (Tocqueville 1945). These traits are still largely intact and descriptive of American national character despite a civil war, inter-racial conflicts, waves of immigration, and increasing social heterogeneity (Fukuyama 1997). Even when groups change geographies, they cling to certain customs and tendencies. The Chinese have engaged in entrepreneurial and educational activities fervently, regardless of living in British-ruled Hong Kong of the nineteenth century or among an Islamic majority in twentieth century Indonesia. Similarly the Germans and British have pursued technological and economic achievements whether residing in their countries of origin or upon immigration to the USA, Chile, Argentina, or Australia. As noted by one historian:

> Despite prevailing 'social science' approaches which depict people as creatures of their surrounding environment, or as victims of social institutions immediately impinging upon them, both emigrant and conquerors have carried their hard won patterns of skills and behaviors – their cultures – to the farthest regions of the planet, in the most radically different societies, and these patterns have often persisted for generations or even centuries. (Sowell 1994, pp. 1–2, 25–7)

The contrasting perspective is that cultures undergo construction, dismantlement, and reconstruction as societies continuously change their alignments of priorities, loyalties, and orientations (Bernardi 1975, pp. 75–87; Hanson 1975, pp. 13–14). This assumption allows for the interjection of time and history. Some social scientists argue that implicit in the notion of culture as static is an ahistorical, perhaps anti-historical, view that gives no place to the past, to intent, or even to accident and the commingling of circumstances (Thompson et al. 1990, p. 80). One reason to interject time and thus change into cultural theories is to help explain apparent paradoxes. Perplexing contradictions become meaningful when time – and an adequate frame – is placed around observations, as in this case about the British:

> The British were the world's leading slave traders in the 18th century – and the most implacable and relentless enemies of slave trading in the 19th and 20th centuries. These facts do not contradict one another, or cancel each other, nor is it necessary to attempt a net balance for 'the British.' Both facts are realities of history, and it is only our use of a single inter-temporal abstraction called 'the British' for a changing collection of people with changing ideas and commitments that makes the facts seem inconsistent. (Sowell 1994, p. 254)

Cultures also change because individuals continuously accept and at other times reject or modify extant beliefs, norms, and behaviors (Bernardi 1975, p. 76). Immigrants or individuals who are a generation or two removed from their parents' country of birth are a case in point. Such cultural sojourners decide moment to moment, depending on circumstance or setting, which social mores take precedence. Along this line, Swidler (1986) offered a theory in which people are active, skilled culture users rather than takers, differing in their capacities to translate values into action but by no means waiting to be pushed around by a monolithic culture. Swidler and some other contemporary sociologists have concluded that the notion of culture as permanent and omnipotent had long ago 'ceased to be compelling' (Crane 1994, p. 11; Derne 1994, p. 267).

Culture as Cognition

Hofstede defines culture as the 'collective programming of the mind', reflecting a common assumption that culture is cognitive, i.e. it is what people think. Culture in effect becomes these thoughts, or most often values, but writ large across an entire social system. Triandis is similar in his emphasis on personality traits as constituting culture. The appeal stems from both the primacy that cognition has long held in the social sciences as well as research pragmatism: culture can be measured objectively through attitude instruments. Inglehart's massive sociological values survey is an exemplar of this assumption and approach (1995).

This premise has dominated the social sciences in general, and is considered characteristic of classical sociological and social anthropological theories (Crane 1994, p. 2; Derne 1994, p. 267; Harris 1999, p. 19). It is favored not just by researchers who amass individual psychological profiles as indicators of collective mental tendencies, but also by linguists, social psychologists, and anthropologists trained in the semiotics tradition. The latter group has used ethnography and related interpretive techniques to study language, rituals, events, social arrangements, belief systems, and other symbols as carriers or embodiments of culture (Bonnel and Hunt 1999, pp. 1–34). Determining the semiotics structure in these various texts, as with using questionnaires to gauge values or attitudes, reflects a focus on people's cognitions and interpretations as indicators of culture (Gamst and Norbeck 1976, pp.18–19).

While the notion that culture is a mental good has characterized cultural studies since the late 1950s, it has also attracted considerable criticism (Bidney 1976, p. 6; Shweder 1984, p. 7). Among the most vocal critics are leading anthropologists such as Shweder and Geertz:

> At the same time the revolution was going on where people were putting things inside people's heads a counter-revolution was going the other way – criticizing the whole myth of inner reality, the whole myth of private language. The one thing anthropologists hadn't said about culture is that it is a conceptual structure. What does it mean to say that? . . . . The reason I'm against putting things in people's heads is that it reduces the tension between cultural analysis and psychological analysis. (Geertz 1973, p. 8)

What Geertz and others have found particularly problematic with the cognitive view is that it ignores the role of behaviors or actions in formulating, constituting, or expressing culture (Derne 1994, p. 267). This is not to say that cognition, especially as represented by values or attitudes, is unimportant but it does not constitute the whole of culture. Moreover, cognition is not always what leads to behaviors but the reverse is also true:

> Yet when we define culture as pure idea, and describe ideas as guiding social behavior, we are actually advocating a popular paradigmatic principle whose scientific value is scarcely self-evident. Indeed, from my cultural–materialist perspective, the emphasis on the proposition that ideas guide behavior, but not the reverse, is the mother error of contemporary anthropological theories . . . . Clearly, behaviors and ideas must be seen as elements in a feedback relationship. In the short run, ideas do guide behaviors, but in the long run behavior guides and shapes ideas. (Harris 1999, p. 20)

Some researchers have even gone further, discounting cognition and arguing that behaviors are more integral to culture. In the end it's not what people say are important to them that matters, but rather what they actually do. Thus the practice of using attitude surveys to get at culture is argued as misguided, misleading, and unproductive (Kaplan 1954; Shweder 2000):

> Attempts to measure cultural differences between groups by attitude surveys, however, miss the crucial point that culture is expressed in behavior – not lip service. The values of a culture are revealed by the choices actually made – and the sacrifices endured – in pursuing some desired goals at the expense of other

desired goals. Education and personal safety may be valued by a wide range of human beings in a great variety of cultures, but what they are prepared to do – to sacrifice – in pursuit of those goals varies enormously. (Sowell 1994, p. 10)

Contemporary social theorists are thus reformulating the notion of culture to include all social practices, not just norms, values, and beliefs. Among them, reflecting a post-structuralist orientation and garnering considerable attention across the social sciences, is Bourdieu (1977, 1984), who introduced the notion of cultural capital.

Culture as Bounded

The last assumption underlying international marketing studies is that culture is bounded, and most typically by national borders. All three of the leading culture theories – those of Hofstede, Hall, and Triandis – rest explicitly or tacitly on this assumption. Hence, Chinese collectivism goes from the northern reaches of Outer Mongolia to the southern shores of Hainan, spilling and disappearing into the East and South China Seas. The assumption is not unreasonable on two counts. First, it is generally recognized among social scientists that nations do possess a culture (Schudson 1994, p. 24). As an illustration, historians would be hard pressed to explain Germany's role and actions in World War II without discussing how the National Socialist Party appealed to the German people's sense of a common heritage and destiny to mobilize the nation toward war, and once in it sustain the cause. Second, despite regional integration and globalization, the nation state is still an extremely relevant unit of analysis. Supranational entities such as the European Union have come into existence, but their fractured nature suggests people's allegiances are more closely tied to their localities than to regional organizations. The nation state is still the most significant political and economic entity today. It is nations that sign treaties, build armies, trade goods and services, educate people, have an economy, and are admired, envied or despised. Nations possess a psychic – almost primordial – power, generating among its citizenry deeply held ties and identities (Anderson 1991):

> the nation has asserted its priority over other cultural forms, most obviously in its claim to a political embodiment. It is the nation – not religion, political principle, local community, or social class – which demands its own state. And it could not sustain this claim to priority unless national identity was experienced as more fundamental than others. (Poole 1999, pp.15–16)

Nonetheless, it is widely acknowledged that equating nations with cultures has limitations, and that nations are at best surrogates or proxies. Culture as de facto 'national culture' or 'national character' is challenged by the notion that there are other equally valid ways, besides the nation state, to circumscribe a culture (Clark 1990). Among these at the macro level are regions, border zones, continents, trading areas, and – per Huntington – civilizations; at the micro level, options are subcultures within a country, community, business organization, or family (e.g. between generations). Researchers have moreover pointed out that culture is a social force, and therefore cannot be contained by the artifice of geo-political borders (Schudson 1994, p. 21; Sowell 1994, p. 4):

> defining culture is a question of defining boundaries that are essentially political – boundaries of oppression, and of defense against oppression. The boundaries must necessarily be arbitrary in the sense that the case for drawing the boundaries at one point rather than at another is seldom logically tight. Who is an Arab? What is good music? Or even what is music? Is Confucianism a religion? It is clear that the boundaries depend on definitions, and that these definitions are not universally shared, or even consistent over time. Further of course at any given time all Arabs do not speak Arabic, all Englishmen are not individualists, some Jews and some Moslems are atheists. (Wallerstein 1997, p. 94)

Even if culture could be geographically contained, borders change. The last century witnessed radical political reconstitutions, precipitated by the fall of the Berlin Wall and proceeding to the dramatic collapse of the Soviet Union. Seemingly overnight the world's map was redrawn. Is it likely, for instance, that the Soviet culture, which had come into being and been nurtured since the Bolshevik Revolution and was itself a product of the Slavic-Eastern Orthodox culture preceding it, disappeared with the creation of Russia and the Newly Independent States?

Finally, it has long been contended that cultures mix, interact, influence, blend, squash, and compete with one another in a dynamic tension, and this occurs in both intra- and international contexts (Robertson 1997, p. 89; Sowell 1994, pp. 4–5). At the borders of any culture, there is a bleeding of sorts, as groups meet, collide, and spill into each other in conflicting or harmonizing ways. Thus cultures as truly autonomous and untouched represent a delicate, albeit useful, fiction. Social scientists have developed a rich stream of theories about the interactions of cultures and subcultures, particularly as differentiated by class and power. A long tradition centers on the theme of domination (hegemony theories). The main intellectual roots are in the works of Karl Marx (Smelser 1992, p.14), who argued that the underclass would engage in a struggle to overcome domination by the ruling class of elites and capitalists. Those who have carried on the tradition of hegemony theory, though playing down notions of economic reductionism and determinism, include Gramsci (1971), Marcuse (1964),

Habermas (1975), and Bordieu (1977). Gramsci offered his internal coloni-
alism theory, in which the center of a society is the home of the dominant
class, which promotes its worldview at the expense of others. Subordinate
groups accept this worldview as common sense, conspiring in their own
subordination by the unequal distribution of power and rewards.

Directions for the development of culture theory
The leading culture theories in international marketing, notably Hofstede's,
have certain ontological and epistemological underpinnings, namely that
culture is coherent and unified, immutable, cognitive, and bounded. These
assumptions have considerable legitimacy and acceptance in the social sciences, aligning well with classical theory. Nonetheless, for each of these
interpretations about the nature of culture, there is an antipode of thought
expressed in both contemporary and traditional writings. The notion for
instance of coherent, unified cultures contrasts with that of disjunctive,
fragmented social spheres. Observing clashing values and groups, Weber in
the past and Huntington in the present have pointed out the discordant
properties of cultures.

Based on the above, there are several directions suggested for the development of culture theory in international marketing. First, extend the range
of presuppositions and conceptual frameworks on culture. The reason is not
variety for its own sake, but rather to explore fully culture's theoretical
promise and ensure true knowledge advancement. We can look to two disciplines for models of development in particular, sociology and anthropology, which have long been investigating culture. Both fields have engaged in
intensive debate about culture – its essence, how it should be studied, and
why it matters at all. At some junctures, suppositions similar to those
current in international marketing reigned, and at other times opposing
beliefs offered a strong counterbalance. Through this process, the disciplines
have embraced a spectrum of assumptions and corresponding frameworks
on culture, enriching their theoretical landscape. It is difficult to imagine
sociology today without Durkheim on the one hand and Bourdieu on the
other. Both have been profoundly influential to a generation or more of
scholars, and not limited to sociology. International marketing, perhaps
reflecting its relative youth as an area of inquiry, has adhered more or less
to one set of assumptions and one theory. The popularity of Hofstede's paradigm may rest on conceptual strength, but it may rest as much on its apparent ease of use: it represents culture, in all its acknowledged complexity, with
four discrete parallel values (parallel because they are rarely looked at in
conjunction or interactively), and this representation is highly amenable to
study through country-level indexes. A question, though, is whether this
theoretical monopoly is best for international marketing in the long run. If

knowledge advancement is the end goal, enriching the stock of assumptions and cultures theories would be prudent.

A parallel can be found in international business. Recently Sullivan (1998a) completed an analysis of the state and ontological nature of international business research, concluding that the field had become narrower over time in terms of the complexity and range of theories studied, a view shared by other observers (e.g. Daniels 1991; Inkpen and Beamish 1994; Toyne 1997). The author raised the concern that an increasing focus on methodology was relegating theory to the backwaters. More technically competent studies were being produced but of lesser consequence. The study is suggestive that international marketing (considered by some to be a subfield of international business) is venturing down the same course unless efforts are made to avert premature constriction:

> The pitfalls of a narrow vision are dire. Scholars produce more studies, yet our cumulative findings may lead us to know more about less precisely because they obscure that these parts are of some whole. Many findings, while technically impressive and statistically significant, may stifle insight by collaring innovative perspectives. Furthermore, the tendency of some researchers to build consensus through iterative replication or trivial refinement may contribute to reports that preclude the creative processes that prompt genuine shifts in intellectual direction. . . . IB's increasingly 'impeccable micro logic is creating macro nonsense' by encouraging cognitive processes that precisely pinpoint the trees to the neglect of the forest. (Sullivan 1998b, p. 838)

A more specific direction is to generate and apply theories with differing premises than those of the current leading theories. Until now, the predominant theories in international marketing have largely framed culture as a powerful causal force that is relatively fixed and comprehensible. Culture imprints itself through various means, such as families and schools, and resides in the mental formations of people. People are passive recipients of a larger force deemed to be cultural in nature. The purpose of culture is to maintain social order in that it informs and guides individuals in how they are to see themselves, others, and the larger world around them and operate within that world. Durkheim (1976, p. 44) possibly summed this best:

> collective ways of acting or thinking have a reality outside the individuals who, at every moment of time, conform to it. These ways of thinking and acting exist in their own right. He is therefore obliged to reckon with them. It is difficult (we do not say impossible) for him to modify them in direct proportion to the extent that they share in the material and moral supremacy of society over its members. . . . These types of conduct or thought are not only external to the individual, but are, moreover, endowed with coercive power, by virtue of which they impose themselves upon him, independent of his individual will.

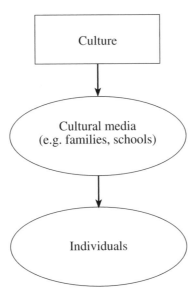

Figure 10.1   Idealist–superorganic view of culture

Consistent with this view is the search for patterns of mental frames characteristic of a given population. Hence, we see Hofstede's factor analysis to identify uncertainty avoidance (1980), Triandis and Gelfand's measurements for horizontal and vertical individualism (1998), and Inglehart's global surveys of regard for traditional versus rational forms of authority (2000). This approach and concomitant theories can be called the Idealist–Superorganic View in that culture has an all-encompassing deterministic nature and can be abstracted as universal cognitive principles as depicted in Figure 10.1.

Since theories with the Idealist–Superorganic View have already been well embraced in international marketing, theories with differing premises should be examined to invigorate the pool. These are theories in which culture is not positioned as a fixed causal force but is continuously acting on and being acted upon by the prime movers or creators of culture, namely individuals. While individuals may accept a particular aspect of a culture, they also may reformulate it for their own consumption, combine it with a dimension of another culture, or reject it altogether. Culture is a contested arena, where values, practices, habits, and products are juxtaposed, integrated, eliminated, and buttressed against one another. Individuals actively interpret, generate, reject, and even exterminate cultures or aspects of cultures in the dialectic between themselves and larger social structures.

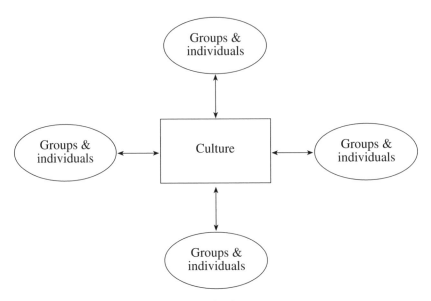

Figure 10.2   Realist–organic view of culture

Competition among subcultures in a society is one mechanism for this process. The purpose of culture is both to maintain and transform order, and the conflict between those purposes is what generates social dynamism. Important in such schemas are the themes of domination (representing the order maintaining aim of culture) and rebellion (representing the order transforming function).

All of this falls under what is called the Realist–Organic View. As the name suggests, instead of reifying culture as an external abstraction outside of people, culture is an organic entity negotiated at the mundane, concrete level of human interactions, i.e. people do things with, and in respect of each other using means that can be ascribed as cultural. Examples of theories in this vein are Carrithers's sociality theory (1992), and Bourdieu's theory of cultural capital (1984). The view is depicted in Figure 10.2. The Realist–Organic View requires examining societies at lower levels, say subcultures within a country, than the Idealist–Superorganic View. It also suggests using fine-grained research methods, including in-depth interviewing, observation, integration of extensive secondary data, and ethnography.

A third and final direction is to generate more focused discussion on theory *per se* – whether on culture or not – within international market-ing. Literature reviews are one means of doing so. Recent reviews have pointed out the evolving structure of research streams (e.g. Cavusgil 1998; Li and Cavusgil 1995) or growth of theory-based over descriptive research (e.g. Aulakh and Kotabe 1993), but there has been infrequent examination of the content of extant and evolving theories, evaluation of their contributions to knowledge building, and what these all imply for the future development of the discipline. Other reviews have been devoted to methodological concerns, and it seems we are progressing on this front, whether with respect to, say, equivalence issues or sample design (e.g. Douglas and Craig 1983; Sin et al. 1999). These efforts are still vital. However, when a research domain is characterized by epistemic predominance, knowledge development may depend as much, perhaps more, on 'competing logics vigorously contesting the merits of ideas' (Sullivan 1998a, p. 853). Clark's piece is one of the few to have commented explicitly on theory. Therefore, there is need for more literature reviews and articles aimed at evaluation, discussion, and promotion of theory. Particularly welcomed would be 'think pieces' that lay out or pioneer novel representations of international marketing concerns, which can then stimulate empirical research. Another avenue are forums devoted to theory in international marketing. These can be conferences, workshops, and seminars where researchers exchange divergent ideas on conceptual developments. This particular conference is an example of a forum where there is an emphasis on bringing new perspectives together and deliberating over them. More such opportunities would engender rich and useful discourse, furthering theoretical development and thereby the accumulation of knowledge in international marketing.

REFERENCES

Albaum, Gerald and Robert A. Peterson (1984), 'Empirical Research in International Marketing: 1976–1982', *Journal of International Business Studies*, **15**, (1), (Spring/Summer), 161–73.

Alden, Dana L., Wayne D. Hoyer and Chol Lee (1993), 'Identifying Global and Culture-Specific Dimensions of Humor in Advertising: A Multinational Analysis', *Journal of Marketing*, **57** (April), 64–75.

Anderson, Benedict (1991), *Imagined Communities: Reflections on the Origin and Spread of Nationalism*, 2nd edn, London: Verso.

Aulakh, Preet S. and Masaaki Kotabe (1993), 'An Assessment of Theoretical and Methodological Development in International Marketing', *Journal of International Marketing*, **1** (2), 5–28.

Bacharach, Samuel B. (1989), 'Organizational Theories: Some Criteria for Evaluation', *Academy of Management Review*, **14** (4), 496–515.

Bello, Daniel C. and David I. Gilliland (1997), 'The Effect of Output Controls, Process Controls, and Flexibility on Export Channel Performance', *Journal of Marketing*, **61** (January), 22–38.

Benedict, Ruth F. (1934), *Patterns of Culture*, Boston: Houghton-Mifflin.

Bernardi, Bernado (1975), 'The Concept of Culture: A New Presentation', in Bernado Bernardi (ed.), *The Concept and Dynamics of Culture*, Paris, The Hague: Mouton, pp. 75–88.

Bidney, David (1976), 'On the Concept of Culture and Some Cultural Fallacies', in Frederick C. Gamst and Edward Norbeck (eds), *Ideas of Culture: Sources and Uses*, New York: Holt, Rinehart & Winston, pp. 71–81.

Boddewyn, Jean J. (1981), 'Comparative Marketing: The First Twenty-Five Years', *Journal of International Business Studies*, **12** (1), 61–79.

Bonnel, Victoria E. and Lynn Hunt (1999), 'Introduction', in Victoria Bonnel and Lynn Hunt (eds), *Beyond the Cultural Turn: New Directions in the Study of Society and Culture*, Berkeley: University of California Press, pp. 1–34.

Bourdieu, Pierre (1977), *Outline of a Theory of Practice*, Cambridge: Cambridge University Press.

Bourdieu, Pierre (1984), *Distinction: A Social Critique of the Judgement of Taste*, translated by Richard Nice, Cambridge: Harvard University Press.

Carrithers, Michael (1992), *Why Humans Have Cultures: Explaining Anthropology and Social Diversity*, Oxford: Oxford University Press.

Cavusgil, S. Tamer (1998), 'Perspectives: Knowledge Development in International Marketing', *Journal of International Marketing*, **6** (2), 103–12.

Clark, Terry (1990), 'International Marketing and National Character: A Review and Proposal for an Integrative Theory', *Journal of Marketing*, **54** (October), 66–79.

Crane, Diane (1994), 'Introduction: The Challenge of the Sociology of Culture to Sociology as a Discipline', in Diane Crane (ed.), *The Sociology of Culture: Emerging Theoretical Perspectives*, Oxford: Blackwell.

Daniels, John D. (1991), 'Relevance in International Business Research: A Need for More Linkages', *Journal of International Business Studies*, **22** (3), 177–86.

Derne, Steve (1994), 'Cultural Conceptions of Human Motivation and Their Significance for Cultural Theory', in Diane Crane (ed.), *The Sociology of Culture: Emerging Theoretical Perspectives*, Oxford: Blackwell, pp. 267–88.

DiMaggio, Paul J. (1995), Comments on 'What Theory is Not', *Administrative Science Quarterly*, **40**, 391–7.

Douglas, Susan P. and C. Samuel Craig (1983), *International Marketing Research*, Englewood Cliffs, NJ: Prentice-Hall.

Dubois, Frank L. and David Reeb (2000), 'Ranking the International Business Journals', *Journal of International Business Studies*, **31** (4), (4th Quarter), 689–704.

Durkheim, Emile (1976), *Rules of Sociological Method*, 8th edn, 1938, reprinted, in Frederick C. Gamst and Edward Norbeck (eds), *Ideas of Culture: Sources and Uses*, New York: Holt, Rinehart & Winston, pp. 44–5.

Fukuyama, Francis (1997), *Trust: The Social Virtues and the Creation of Prosperity*, New York: Free Press.

Gamst, Frederick C. and Edward Norbeck (1976), *Introduction: Cultural Anthropology and Concepts in Culture*, in Frederick C. Gamst and Edward Norbeck (eds), *Ideas of Culture: Sources and Uses*, New York: Holt, Rinehart, & Winston.

Gannon, Martin J. (2001), *Cultural Metaphors: Readings, Research Translations, and Commentary*, Thousand Oaks, CA: Sage.

Geertz, Clifford (1973), *The Interpretation of Cultures*, New York, NY: Basic Books.

Graham, John (1988), 'Deference Given the Buyer: Variations Across Twelve Cultures', in Farok Contractor and Peter Lorange (eds), *Cooperative Strategies in International Business*, Lexington: Lexington Books, pp. 473–85.
Gramsci, Antonio (1971), *Selections from the Prison Notebooks*, New York: International Press.
Habermas, Jurgen (1975), *Legitimization Crisis*, Boston: Beacon Press.
Hall, Edward T. (1976), *Beyond Culture*, Garden City: Anchor Press/Doubleday.
Hanson, F. Allan (1975), *Meaning in Culture*, London: Routledge & Kegan Paul.
Harris, Marvin (1999), *Theories of Culture in Postmodern Times*, London: Altamira Press.
Hofstede, Geert (1980), *Culture's Consequences: International Differences in Work-Related Values*, Beverly Hills: Sage.
Hult, G. Tomas, William T. Neese and R. Edward Bashaw (1997), 'Faculty Perceptions of Marketing Journals', *Journal of Marketing Education*, 19 (Spring), 37–44.
Hunt, Shelby D. (1983), *Marketing Theory: The Philosophy of Marketing Science*, Homewood, IL: Irwin.
Huntington, Samuel P. (1996), *The Clash of Civilizations and the Remaking of the World Order*, New York: Simon & Schuster.
Inglehart, Ronald (1995), 'Changing Values, Economic Development, and Political Change', *International Social Science Journal*, 145, (September), 379–403.
Inglehart, Ronald (2000), 'Culture and Democracy', in Lawrence E. Harrison and Samuel P. Huntington (eds), *Culture Matters: How Values Shape Human Progress*, New York: Basic Books, pp. 80–97.
Inkpen, Andrew C. and Paul W. Beamish (1994), 'An Analysis of Twenty-Five Years of Research in the *Journal of International Business Studies*', *Journal of International Business Studies*, 25 (4), 703–13.
Kaplan, B. (1954), 'A Study of Rorschach Responses in Four Cultures', *Papers of the Peabody Museum of Archaeology and Ethnology*, 42 (2), Cambridge: Harvard University.
Levine, Robert A. (1984), 'Properties of Culture: An Ethnographic View', in Richard A. Shweder and Robert A. Levine (eds), *Culture Theory: Essays on Mind, Self, and Emotion*, Cambridge: Cambridge University Press, pp. 67–87.
Li, Tiger and S. Tamer Cavusgil (1995), 'A Classification and Assessment of Research Streams in International Marketing', *International Business Review*, 4 (3), 251–77.
Marcuse, H. (1964), *One-Dimensional Man*, Boston: Beacon Press.
Money, R. Bruce, Mary C. Gilly and John L. Graham (1998), 'Explorations of National Culture and Word-of-Mouth Referral Behavior in the Purchase of Industrial Services in the United States and Japan', *Journal of Marketing*, 62 (October), 76–87.
Nakata, Cheryl and Yili Huang (2001), 'Culture Theory in International Marketing: Recent Trends and Future Directions', Unpublished working paper.
Penaloza, Lisa and Mary C. Gilly (1999), 'Marketer Acculturation: The Changer and the Changed', *Journal of Marketing*, 63 (July), 84–104.
Poole, Ross (1999), *Nation and Identity*, London: Routledge.
Robertson, Roland (1997), 'Social Theory, Cultural Relativity and the Problem of Globality', in Anthony D. King (ed.), *Culture, Globalization and the World-System*, Minneapolis: University of Minnesota Press, pp. 69–90.
Schudson, Michael (1994), 'Culture and the Integration of National Societies', in

Diane Crane (ed.), *The Sociology of Culture: Emerging Theoretical Perspectives*, Oxford: Blackwell, pp. 21–44.

Shweder, Richard (1984), 'Preview: A Colloquy of Culture Theories', in Richard Shweder and Robert Levine (eds), *Culture Theory: Essays on Mind, Self, and Emotion*, New York: Press Syndicate of the University of Cambridge, pp. 1–24.

Shweder, Richard (2000), 'Moral Maps, "First World" Conceits, and the New Evangelists', in Lawrence E. Harrison and Samuel P. Huntington (eds), *Culture Matters: How Values Shape Human Progress*, New York: Basic Books, pp. 158–77.

Sin, Leo Y.M., Gordon W.H. Cheung and Ruby Lee (1999), 'Methodology in Cross-Cultural Consumer Research: A Review and Critical Assessment', *Journal of International Consumer Marketing*, **11** (4), 75–96.

Sivakumar, K. and Cheryl Nakata (2001), 'The Stampede Toward Hofstede's Framework: Avoiding the Sample Design Pit in Cross-Cultural Research', *Journal of International Business Studies*, **32** (3), (3rd Quarter), 555–74.

Smelser, Neil J. (1992), 'Culture: Coherent or Incoherent', in Richard Much and Neil J. Smelser (eds), *Theory of Culture*, Berkeley: University of California Press, pp. 3–28.

Sowell, Thomas (1994), *Race and Culture: A World View*, New York: Basic Books.

Steenkamp, Jan-Benedict, E.M. Frenkel ter Hofstede and Michel Wedel (1999), 'A Cross-National Investigation into the Individual and National Cultural Antecedents of Consumer Innovativeness', *Journal of Marketing*, **63** (April), 55–69.

Sullivan, Daniel (1998a), 'Cognitive Tendencies in International Business Research: Implications of a "Narrow Vision"', *Journal of International Business Studies*, **29** (4), (4th Quarter), 837–62.

Sullivan, Daniel (1998b), 'The Ontology of International Business: A Comment on International Business: An Emerging Vision', *Journal of International Business Studies*, **29** (4), 877–86.

Sutton, Robert I. and Barry M. Staw (1995), 'What Theory is Not', *Administrative Science Quarterly*, **40**, 371–84.

Swidler, Ann (1986), 'Culture in Action: Symbols and Strategies', *American Sociological Review*, **51**, 273–86.

Thompson, Michael, Richard Ellis and Aaron Wildavsky (1990), *Cultural Theory*, Boulder: Westview Press.

Tocqueville, Alexis de (1945), *Democracy in America*, Vols I and II, New York: Knopf.

Toyne, Brian (1997), 'International Business Inquiry: Does It Warrant a Separate Domain?', in Brian Toyne and Douglas Nigh (eds), *International Business: An Emerging Vision*, Columbia: University of South Carolina Press.

Triandis, Harry C. (1989), 'The Self and Behavior in Differing Cultural Contexts', *Psychological Review*, **96** (July), 506–52.

Triandis, Harry C. and M. Gelfand (1998), 'Converging Measurement of Horizontal and Vertical Individualism and Collectivism', *Journal of Personality and Social Psychology*, **74**, 118–28.

Tylor, Edward Burnett (1958), *The Origins of Culture*, Torchbook Edition, appearing earlier as Chapters I–X of *Primitive Culture*, 1871, Glouster: Harper & Row.

Wallerstein, Immanuel (1997), 'The National and the Universal: Can There Be Such a Thing as World Culture?', in Anthony D. King (ed.), *Culture, Globalization and the World-System*, Minneapolis: University of Minnesota Press, pp. 91–106.

Weber, Max (1905), 'Protestant Asceticism and the Spirit of Capitalism', *Gesammelte Aufsatze zur Religionssoziologie*, **16**, 163–206.

Weick, Karl E. (1995), 'What Theory is Not, Theorizing Is', *Administrative Science Quarterly*, **40**, 385–90.

Whetten, David A. (1989), 'What Constitutes a Theoretical Contribution?', *Academy of Management Review*, **14** (4), 490–95.

11. Language and culture: linguistic effects on consumer behavior in international marketing research

Shi Zhang, Bernd H. Schmitt and Hillary Haley

INTRODUCTION

In recent years, there has been a wealth of research examining the relevance of culture to consumer behavior. This chapter reviews a particular line of work within this larger body of research: work investigating the unique relevance of language. Our review finds that both structural features of language (properties of grammar) and lexical-semantic and phonological features of language (related to writing systems) are important. More specifically, current work suggests that these language features affect how consumers perceive, and also respond to, various marketing stimuli (e.g. advertisements and brand names). Our review summarizes and integrates a number of related findings, and highlights their practical significance.

International marketing research has focused more and more heavily on the topic of cross-cultural consumer behavior. And this research has observed important cross-cultural differences in the processing, evaluation, and judgment of brand and product information. Much of this work suggests that cultural differences stem from pervasive socio-cultural or cognitive factors. For example, a good deal of research demonstrates that people have broad, culture-specific cognitive dispositions, like individualism or collectivism, which can guide consumer behavior (e.g. Aaker and Williams 1998; Hofstede 1980; Triandis 1989). Other work has built upon these fundamental findings, showing that there are specific conditions under which such dispositions are especially likely to affect consumer choice (e.g. Aaker and Lee 2001; Briley, Morris and Simonson 2000; Weber and Hsee 2000).

Another line of research has turned the focus to language. This research, with roots in cognitive psychology and marketing alike, submits that a given culture's language can play a vital role in determining consumer perceptions, evaluations, and decisions (e.g. Hunt and Agnoli 1991; Luna and Peracchio 2001; Schmitt, Pan and Tavassoli 1994; Schmitt and Zhang 1998;

Tavassoli 1999, 2001; Tavassoli and Han 2001; Zhang and Schmitt 1998). In this chapter, we will take a closer look at this psycholinguistic research, and discuss how this research informs current thinking about cross-cultural marketing issues.

Specifically, we will discuss two areas of current psycholinguistic work: work on the structural features of language (properties of grammar), and work on the phonological and lexical-semantic features of language (related to writing systems). Turning our attention first to work on structural features, it should be noted that such work stems from the so-called 'Whorfian Hypothesis' (Whorf 1956), or the basic idea that language can affect cognition. In 1991, Hunt and Agnoli combined this original hypothesis with knowledge from cognitive psychology to propose that language might affect consumer categorization of both single objects and groups of objects (Hunt and Agnoli 1991). These early predictions were important, as they laid the ground for fruitful empirical work. Namely, in recent work conducted in a consumer behavior marketing context, we have found that structural aspects of a language can in fact critically affect one of the most basic aspects of consumer behavior – categorization of products (Schmitt and Zhang 1998; Zhang and Schmitt 1998).

The second area of research we will discuss concerns the phonological and lexical-semantic aspects related to different types of languages and their writing systems (Zhang and Schmitt 2001, 2002). Like grammar, phonology and semantics are fundamental building blocks to a linguistic system and should therefore have an impact on consumer behavior. In our research, we have explored phonology and semantics by looking at naming in the context of phonological and logographic writing systems. This research shows that how much consumers like a brand name (specifically, a brand name translation) can importantly depend on whether that name depicts phonological or semantic characteristics of the original name. As we will see, this research involves very practical implications for marketers and brand managers operating in a global environment.

EFFECTS OF LANGUAGE STRUCTURE ON PERCEPTION, CATEGORIZATION AND EVALUATION

How do the structural properties of language affect people's thinking and behavior? In addressing this question, we will focus on just one grammatical structure, a lexical-syntactic structure called a 'classifier' (Lucy 1992). Classifiers are present in languages like Chinese, Japanese, Korean, and Thai, as well in as the Navajo and Yucatan-Mayan languages, but they are virtually absent in Indo-European languages such as English, Spanish, French, and German (Lucy 1992). What, exactly, is a classifier? It is a structure that provides people with an 'object frame', or reference point for object categorization. As an example, the Chinese counterpart to the English phrase 'that umbrella' is 'nei ba yusan', where 'yusan' is a noun (umbrella), 'nei' is a determiner ('that'), and 'ba[3]'[1] is the classifier – in this case signifying that the object (an umbrella) can be grasped, or held in one's hand. Similarly, Chinese uses the classifier 'duo[3]' in conjunction with nouns such as flame, cloud, and spray to denote that these objects are all amorphous, or shapeless. Classifiers may indicate either the conceptual properties of an object (e.g. graspability, flexibility) or the physical properties of an object (e.g. shape, length). Importantly, however, classifiers are not 'optional' the way English adjectives are. While not every noun in the Chinese language is associated with a classifier, when a noun is associated with a classifier it is generally mandatory that the classifier be used. In other words, many nouns are associated with a specific classifier, and omission of the classifier is typically ungrammatical.

Given this understanding of classifiers, we suspected that classifiers could affect how people perceive and categorize objects. That is, we expected that speakers of Mandarin Chinese (who use one classifier system) would perceive and categorize stimuli differently from speakers of Japanese (who use another classifier system), and, most significantly, from speakers of English (who use no classifier system at all). For example, we expected that Chinese speakers would be especially likely to conceptualize and categorize umbrellas as graspable objects, while English speakers would not tend to construe umbrellas in any one particular way (i.e. they might well think of umbrellas as graspable objects, collapsible objects, or protective objects).

In a series of more than ten experiments (Schmitt and Zhang 1998; Zhang and Schmitt 1998), we presented strong support for the Whorfian hypothesis by testing a number of specific predictions. First, we predicted that native Chinese speakers would be more likely to see two separate objects as similar if those objects shared a common classifier than if they did not, while native English speakers would show no such tendency. For the purpose of this research, we randomly selected 14 of the total 35 classifiers Chinese speakers commonly use (see Chao 1968; Liu, Pan and Gu 1983), and then created a list of objects (e.g. ruler, mirror, bell) that might be associated with these classifiers (based on Chao 1968). Table 11.1 lists all of the classifiers we selected, along with many of the stimulus objects we used.

Thirty-one native Chinese speakers (who were barely familiar with English) and 30 native English speakers (who did not know Chinese) were

Table 11.1   The specific classifiers used and examples of the associated object stimuli used

Classifier		
Pinying[a]	Semantic Features[b]	Examples of Stimulus Objects Used
ba[3]	can be grasped	door key, umbrella, ruler, pliers
ding[3]	top	hat, mosquito net, tent
duo[3]	amorphous	mushroom, flame, cloud, spray
geng[1]	root or root-like thing	sausage, nail, stick, braid
ke[1]	bead-like item	tooth, star, pearl, heart
kou[3]	openings	vat, coffin
jia[4]	wooden frame-like	airplane, swing
jie[2]	a cut section	battery, railroad car
mien[4]	surface	flag, wall, mirror, drum
mu[4]	round piece	stamp, ring, political button
pian[4]	slice	meat, snowflake, tablet
shan[4]	fan-like	window, divider
tiao[2]	long, slender strip; pliable	snake, river, soap bar, fish, cable
zuo[4]	seat or seat-like things	house, bell, temple, mountain

Note:
[a] Pinying: standard transliteration used for Chinese characters.
[b] Semantic Features: the perceptual and conceptual features that each classifier conveys.

presented, in their native language, with the object stimuli. They were then asked to make pair-wise similarity ratings of the objects. As predicted, there was a significant interaction effect. Similarity ratings were contingent upon both language (Chinese versus English) and classifier (whether or not the two objects rated shared a common classifier in the Chinese language). Chinese speakers gave pairs that shared a (Chinese) classifier much higher similarity ratings than those that did not share a classifier, whereas English speakers gave almost identical ratings to both types of pairs.

These results were perfectly in accord with our predictions, and, importantly, they were replicated using different subjects and different sets of stimuli. These findings therefore strongly suggested that classifiers were influencing how Chinese speakers perceived relationships between different objects. However, these findings did not explicitly show that classifiers influence Chinese speakers' mental representations of objects.

We therefore decided to directly test the idea that classifiers affect mental representations. Since several different objects are typically associated with any one classifier, we reasoned that Chinese speakers would group, or cluster, classifier-sharing objects in their cognitive representations. How could such cognitive representations be measured? According to several memory researchers, the sequence in which people recall information can serve as an indicator of how they are grouping objects mentally. In other words, when object x triggers a person's recall for objects y and z, but not for objects a and b, it is likely that the person's mental representation of x is clustered together with y and z, but not with a and b. We reasoned that Chinese speakers would tend to mentally categorize objects in accordance with their classifiers, and we therefore predicted that they would be more likely to recall classifier-sharing objects in clusters than would English speakers.

To test this prediction, we recruited a sample of 59 Chinese speakers and 53 English speakers similar to those used in our previous studies. We provided participants with a list of words drawn from the same pool as those shown in Table 11.1, and then asked participants to remember those words. We were interested, of course, in whether or not Chinese speakers, relative to English speakers, would show classifier-related clustering. Using Pellegrino and Hubert's (1982) clustering index, this is exactly what was found.

Chinese speakers, as expected, were more likely to cluster according to (Chinese) classifier than were English speakers. It is important to recognize that this effect emerged despite the fact that on some occasions Chinese and English speakers might have naturally clustered objects in the same way (e.g. due to conceptual similarities among objects that are apparent to everyone). In other words, above and beyond the kinds of clustering that are common to both Chinese and English speakers (e.g. clustering of 'toothbrush' and 'toothpaste'), there were still significant classifier-related effects on the cognitive associations that Chinese speakers made.

So far, we have shown that classifiers affect the perceived similarity of objects and the association of objects in people's minds. But can conceptual knowledge, represented in classifiers, also guide people's expectations, evaluations and preferences? In other words, do classifiers influence consumer behavior in practically relevant ways? We suspected that the answer would be yes. We noted that in China many retail displays reflect classifier groupings; for example, Chinese department stores typically group together objects that share the classifier 'tai[3]' (used for electric and mechanical equipment), such as blow dryers, TVs, radios, washing machines, computers, electric fans, and electric cooking knives, whereas their US counterparts virtually never group such items together. If classifiers relate to things like retail displays, we suspected that they could indeed affect people's behavior in practically relevant ways.

We decided to test the effect of classifiers on expectations and preferences in a significant and very practical domain: advertising. Because people who speak languages that have classifiers apparently use classifiers when perceiving objects, we predicted that they would also show a preference for ads relevant to a product's classifier as opposed to ads not relevant to a product's classifier. We tested this prediction in a very straightforward experiment. We asked 40 native Chinese speakers to judge the advisability of using different photographs (all similar to one another in terms of layout and product display) in an advertising campaign. All participants were presented with potential campaign photos for eight different products: four products associated with the classifier 'ba[3]', denoting a graspable object (brush, cane, umbrella, and cable), and four products associated with the classifier 'tiao[2]', denoting a long, thin, and flexible object (pants, cord, rope, and cable). Half of the participants, however, were shown potential ad campaign photos that related to the classifier 'ba[3]' (photos depicting a hand grasping an object), while the other half were instead shown potential campaign photos that did not relate to 'ba[3]' (photos with no hand). We predicted that when the product in question was associated with the classifier 'ba[3]', participants would prefer the hand-present, or classifier-relevant, photos more than the hand-absent photos. When the product in question was not associated with 'ba[3]', however, we predicted that participants would evaluate hand-present and hand-absent photos as equally good. This is, in fact, precisely what we found (see Figure 11.1).

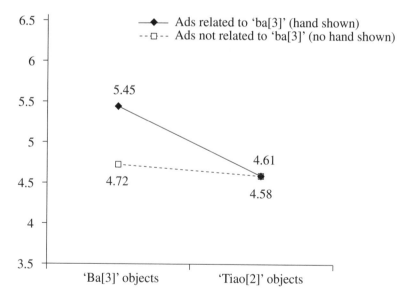

Figure 11.1   *Chinese speakers' evaluations of ads related and unrelated to the classifier 'ba[3]'; for objects having the classifier 'ba[3]' versus objects having the classifier 'tiao[2]'*

To rule out the possibility that this pattern of findings resulted from idiosyncratic characteristics of 'ba[3]' products (as opposed to 'tiao[2]' products), we asked 30 native Japanese speakers to participate in the same experiment. In the Japanese language, the same single classifier ('hon') is associated with all of the eight stimuli products. Notably, we found no significant effects with this Japanese sample (i.e. Japanese speakers liked the hand-present and hand-absent photos about the same, regardless of the product in question). Our results therefore strongly suggested that evaluations of ads are dependent upon the relevance of ad components (such as photos) to a product's classifier.

In sum, our research on classifiers has shown that grammatical differences between Chinese and English, differences that separate many other pairs of languages as well, play a powerful role in shaping consumer behavior. Classifiers affect the perceived similarity among objects, clustering in recall, and expectations and preferences. In two additional studies not described here (Schmitt and Zhang 1998), we have shown that classifiers also affect consumer inferences and choice. Thus, these grammatical structures color all aspects of consumer behavior. In the next section, focused on name translation, we will show that phonological and lexical-semantic aspects of language are just as important.

EVALUATIONS OF NAMES IN PHONOGRAPHIC AND LOGOGRAPHIC SYSTEMS

As marketers become more and more globally oriented, the question of how to best translate a brand name from one language into another has become especially important (e.g. Aaker 1991; Aaker and Joachimsthaler 2000; Javed 1993; Schmitt and Simonson 1997). While translation often appears to be a straightforward process, in many cases it is not. It should be noted that linguists have distinguished two major types of writing systems: phonographic systems, including English, where written words represent the sound components of the spoken language; and logographic systems, including Chinese, where written 'sign' symbols represent both words and concepts (Akmajian et al. 1992, p. 467). In short, in phonographic systems like English it is possible to 'sound out' an unknown written word but not possible to guess its meaning, while in logographic systems like Chinese the reverse is often true.

What challenges does this situation present to marketers who wish to translate a brand name from a phonological system into a logographic system? The major challenge is that the translation can be performed using one of three different methods (see, e.g., Nida and Tabert 1969). Major multinational companies have used all of these methods to translate English names into Chinese. In the first method, the phonetic method, the Chinese name is created simply on the basis of the sound of the original English name. The Chinese name for Nabisco, for example, sounds similar to its English counterpart. In the second method, the semantic method, the Chinese name is created simply on the basis of the meaning of the English name. The Chinese name for Microsoft, 'wei-ruan', meaning 'micro/tiny-soft', was translated in this way. Finally, in the phono-semantic method, names are created based on some combination of sound plus meaning. For example, the Chinese name for Colgate, created with the phono-semantic method, sounds similar to the original English name and also conveys semantic, or meaningful, information (signifying that the product is 'minty' and clean).

In our research, we sought to determine whether an accounting of the differences between phonological and logographic systems could lead us to a better understanding of when and why one translation method (e.g. a pho-netic translation) might be more effective than another (e.g. a semantic trans-lation). At first glance, it would appear that phonetic-semantic translations would consistently be the most effective (as they would appear to combine the benefits of both 'sound alone' and 'meaning alone' translations). In experiments investigating English–Chinese brand name translation, however, we found a more refined pattern of perception and evaluation.

Before reporting on the findings of these experiments, some context will be helpful. Many Western products have entered the Chinese marketplace in recent years, and prominent among them are products that were initially developed using the English language. These products are packaged for Chinese consumers in a variety of different ways. Typically, however, pack-aging includes the product's original English name as well as its Chinese name. Some products emphasize the English (with a bold typeface, for example), while others emphasize the Chinese. The main point is that Chinese consumers are quite familiar with 'bilingual' product packaging. Because such packaging includes both phonological (English) and logo-graphic (Chinese) representations of the brand name – the former more tied to sound and the latter more tied to meaning – we suspected that Chinese consumers would be most inclined to favor phonetic translations if the English name was emphasized but favor semantic translations if the Chinese name was emphasized (see Pan and Schmitt 1996). In other words, if the (logographic) Chinese name were the focal point of a product, then a consumer might be inclined to favor a Chinese name that conveyed the 'meaning' of the product (best approximated by a semantic method). On the other hand, if the (phonological) English name were highlighted, then a consumer might prefer a Chinese name 'sounding like', or 'matching with', the English name (best approximated by a phonetic translation). In the case of phono-semantic translations, however, we did not expect to see any differences relating to language emphasis.

We tested these predictions with a sample of 183 native Chinese speakers in Shanghai. Importantly, in terms of their proficiency in English, these participants were highly representative of the young consumer market: they were familiar with the alphabetic writing system; they could read and understand basic English; and they could easily distinguish between phonetic, semantic, and phono-semantic English–Chinese translations. Participants were told that they were to evaluate a series of six fictitious Chinese brand names (translated from original English names) that might ultimately be used for real product packaging. The stimuli included fictitious names for products such as shampoo, crackers, and contact lenses. In presenting the names to subjects, we systematically varied both the translation method used for the Chinese name (phonetic, semantic, or phono-semantic) and the language of emphasis (Chinese or English). We then collected three separate measures of name evaluation.

Consistent with our predictions, it was not the case that any one translation method was seen as the best. Instead, evaluations of differently translated names depended, as predicted, on whether there was an emphasis on the Chinese name or the English name (see Figure 11.2). Our results indicated that our participants favored phonetic translations over both other types of translations when they were presented with a product that emphasized the English name. In other words, it seems as if the English emphasis focused participants' attention on phonetic aspects, resulting in a proclivity to favor phonetically translated names. Also as expected, our participants saw phono-semantic translations as equally good, regardless of whether a product emphasized the Chinese name or the English name. But contrary to our predictions (though trends conformed to expectations), we did not find that semantic translations were evaluated significantly better in the case of Chinese emphasis rather than English emphasis, possibly because cases of 'purely' semantic translation are quite rare in the Chinese marketplace. Despite this last finding, the general pattern that emerged in this study was suggestive: Chinese speakers might be more inclined to favor one type of name translation over another depending on language-related contextual cues.

We explored this possibility further in another experiment. We recognized that priming effects have been shown to occur in the case of immediate contextual cues (such as name emphasis on product packaging), as well as in the case of cues present in people's long-term memories (see, for example, Higgins and King 1981; Sinclair, Mark and Shotland 1987; Bargh 1989; Fiske and Taylor 1991). Consistent with such findings, we proposed

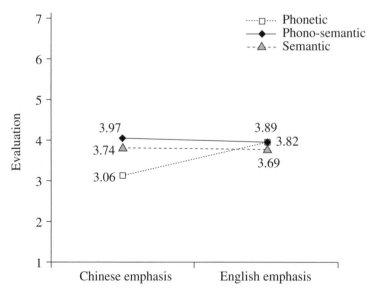

Note: 95% confidence intervals for each $\bar{X}$ are as follows: 3.97 (4.30, 3.64), 3.82 (4.28, 3.47); 3.74 (4.10, 3.38), 3.69 (4.49, 3.49); 3.06 (3.40, 2.72), 3.89 (4.31, 3.47).

Figure 11.2   *Chinese speakers' evaluations of different types of brand names as a function of language name emphasis*

that in addition to relatively immediate linguistic cues present in people's environments, long-term linguistic cues stored in people's memories could also affect preferences for different types of name translations. More specifically, we proposed the following hypothesis: when consumers are asked to evaluate fictitious names for a new product, and they know that existing successful products in the same category were created with a given translation method, then they should show a preference for fictitious names that have been created using the same method.

To test this hypothesis, we recruited 120 Shanghai consumers. Participants were told that their opinions were needed in order to help a group of managers decide which Chinese names (presented in a 'bilingual' format) to use for different products. In this experiment, we focused only on phonetic and phono-semantic name translations. We told half of our participants that prior successful products (in the same respective categories) had used the phonetic method, while we told the other half that prior successful products had used the phono-semantic method. Additionally, we presented half of our participants with products that emphasized the Chinese name, and the other half with products that emphasized the English name. Participants were then asked to evaluate a series of fictitious names, some created by phonetic translation and others created by phono-semantic translation.

The results of this study strongly supported our overall predictions. As expected, when participants were informed that prior products used phonetic translations, they in turn showed a preference for new phonetic names (see Figure 11.3a). When informed that prior products used phono-semantic translations, on the other hand, they showed a preference for the new phono-semantic names (see Figure 11.3b). These results suggested that name translation conventions in a given product category could serve as important primes, setting up cognitive expectations and preferences *vis-à-vis* new brand names. Importantly, additional analyses allowed us to rule out the notion that these effects stemmed from foreign 'image' rather than linguistic cues.

SUMMING UP

In this chapter, we have summarized two separate streams of research. First, we have discussed research on classifiers – the grammatical structures present in Chinese and other languages that require speakers to 'frame' or 'preface' objects. In such research, it was found that Chinese speakers tend to rely on classifiers when assessing similarity among products, when organizing mental representations of products, and when evaluating the different ways products might be displayed (e.g. in advertising). This research illustrated that the structural properties of language can have a significant impact on how consumers view products. Our discussion then turned to branding and naming, and the ways in which an understanding of the phonological and lexical-semantic properties of language (related to writing systems) can inform marketers' naming and branding decisions. This second stream of research showed that of the three methods available for translating English names into Chinese names, no one method is always preferable to Chinese speakers. Instead, preferences are apparently contingent upon both immediate, environment-based linguistic cues, and long-term, memory-based linguistic cues. This research therefore demonstrated the practical importance of the phonological and lexical-semantic properties of language.

Taken together, our research suggests that an understanding of different types of languages, including their grammatical structures and writing systems, can importantly inform marketers' decision making. Our research indicates, for example, that in countries that use classifiers, advertisers could benefit significantly by simply identifying the classifiers associated with their products and making an effort to incorporate those classifiers into their ad campaigns. Moreover, in a retailing environment, managers

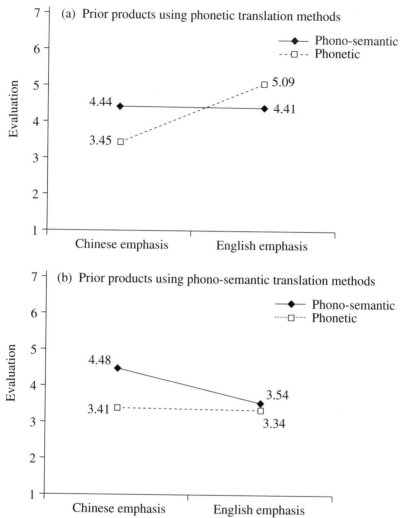

Note: (a) 95% confidence intervals for each $\bar{X}$ are as follows: 4.44 (4.73, 4.15), 4.41 (4.72, 4.10); 3.45 (3.69, 3.23), 5.09 (5.38, 4.80).
Note: (b) 95% confidence intervals for each $\bar{X}$ are as follows: 4.48 (4.78, 4.18), 3.54 (3.90, 3.18); 3.41 (3.77, 3.05), 3.34 (3.68, 3.00).

Figure 11.3   *Chinese speakers' evaluations of different types of brand names as a function of prior naming methods*

might benefit from using classifier-based product arrangements. Regarding brand names, our research suggests that when marketers make naming decisions – decisions that often entail significant amounts of time and resources – they must pay close attention to which name (the original or the translation) should be emphasized in product packaging and marketing communications.

What other language-based effects should future research examine? Research should explore the relevance of structural aspects other than classifiers to consumer cognition and behavior. For example, a product's characteristics may be lexically and semantically encoded in the form of a classifier or an adjective that depicts the function of the product. Although there are similarities in the linear occurrence of classifiers and adjectives in a noun phrase (both appear before nouns), there are also semantic and representational distinctions between the two. Namely, while adjectives describe specific instances within a class (e.g. the adjective 'flat' could be used for a specific table), classifiers instead describe classes of objects (e.g. the classifier 'zhang [1]' is used to denote that an object is part of the class 'tables' – regardless of whether it is flat). Future research might ask: how do adjectives impinge on consumer mental processing and behavior? How do consumers respond when product attributes are inconsistent with classifier attributes (e.g. a curved table)? Similarly, research might explore how structural differences in sentence construction influence consumer processing of ad messages. For example, given that languages like Chinese and Japanese employ topic structures, we might expect that these languages facilitate encoding and recall for the topics and themes of ads (e.g. the products' function). In contrast, languages that explicitly repeat or use anaphoric expressions to refer to the topics of ads (like English in the form of pronouns) might instead be expected to facilitate encoding and recall for brand names.

In terms of naming and branding, research might move beyond the general distinction among phonetic, semantic, and phono-semantic translations to examine other types of differences among translations (e.g. high versus low tones, metaphorical versus literal meanings, or idiomatic versus formal structures). Future work might also explore how visual elements, such as logos and symbols, interface with linguistic characteristics to affect cognition and behavior (e.g. see Schmitt and Simonson 1997). More generally, future research should broaden the topic of language-based cognition and choice to include additional properties of language such as word formation and sentence construction. Finally, given the increasing number of bilingual speakers in many key markets, future research would do well to examine how second-language proficiency might influence various language-based consumer effects.

As marketers become more and more international in focus, researchers are in turn spending more time investigating cross-cultural differences in consumer judgment and behavior. Within this larger stream of research, our work has examined a more specific topic: how does language shape the way consumers perceive, evaluate, and ultimately respond to different products and product features? Taken as a whole, our findings have indicated that a thorough consideration of language-based effects will be critical for future research in cross-cultural consumer and marketing research.

NOTE

1. Chinese is a tonal language, meaning that different tones signify different meanings. The numbers in parentheses are used for the four tones in Mandarin Chinese: high [1]; rising [2]; falling–rising [3]; and falling [4].

REFERENCES

Aaker, David (1991), *Managing Brand Equity*, New York: Free Press.
Aaker, David and Erich Joachimsthaler (2000), *Brand Leadership*, New York: Free Press.
Aaker, Jennifer L. and Angela Y. Lee (2001), 'I Seek Pleasures and We Avoid Pains: The Role of Self-Regulatory Goals in Information Processing and Persuasion', *Journal of Consumer Research*, **28**, 33–49.
Aaker, Jennifer L. and Patti Williams (1998), 'Empathy versus Pride: The Influence of Emotional Appeals Across Cultures', *Journal of Consumer Research*, **25**, 241–61.
Akmajian, Adrian, Richard A. Demers, Ann K. Farmer and Robert M. Harnish (1992), *Linguistics: An Introduction to Language and Communication*, Cambridge, MA: MIT Press.
Bargh, John A. (1989), 'Conditional Automaticity: Varieties of Automatic Influence in Social Perception and Cognition', in J.S. Uleman and J.A. Bargh (eds), *Unintended Thought*, New York: Guilford Press.
Briley, Donald A., Michael W. Morris and Itamar Simonson (2000), 'Reasons as Carriers of Culture: Dynamic vs. Dispositional Models of Cultural Influence on Decision Making', *Journal of Consumer Research*, **27**, 157–78.
Chao, Yuan-Ren (1968), *A Grammar of Spoken Chinese*, Berkeley, CA: University of California Press.
Fiske, Susan and Shelley Taylor (1991), *Social Cognition*. New York: McGraw-Hill.
Higgins, E. Tory and Gillian A. King (1981), 'Accessibility and Social Constructs: Information Processing Consequences of Individual and Contextual Variability', in Nancy Cantor and John F. Kihlstrom (eds), *Personality, Cognition and Social Interaction*, Hillsdale, NJ: Erlbaum.
Hofstede, Geert (1980), *Culture's Consequences: International Differences in Work-Related Values*, Beverly Hills, CA: Sage.
Hunt, Earl and Franca Agnoli (1991), 'The Whorfian Hypothesis: A Cognitive Psychology Perspective', *Psychological Review*, **98**, 377–89.
Javed, Naseem (1993), *Naming for Power*, Ontario: Linkbridge Publishing.

Liu, Yue-hua, Wenyu Pan and Hua Gu (1983), *A Guide to the Grammar of Contemporary Chinese*, Beijing, China: Press of the Institute of Foreign Languages.
Lucy, John A. (1992), *Language Diversity and Thought: A Reformulation of Whorfian Hypothesis*, Cambridge, UK: Cambridge University Press.
Luna, David and Laura A. Peracchio (2001), 'Moderators of Language Effects in Advertising to Bilinguals: A Psycholinguistic Approach', *Journal of Consumer Research*, **28**, 284–95.
Nida, Eugene A. and Charles R. Tabert (1969), *The Theory and Practice of Translation*, published for the United Bible Societies, Leiden, Netherlands: E.J. Brill.
Pan, Yigang and Bernd Schmitt (1996), 'Language and Brand Attitudes: The Impact of Script and Sound Matching in Chinese and English', *Journal of Consumer Psychology*, **5**, 263–77.
Pellegrino, James W. and Lawrence J. Hubert (1982), 'The Analysis of Organization and Structure in Free Recall', in C. Richard Puff (ed.), *Handbook of Research Methods in Human Memory and Cognition*, New York: Academic Press, pp. 129–72.
Schmitt, Bernd H., Yigang Pan and Nader T. Tavassoli (1994), 'Language and Consumer Memory: The Impact of Linguistic Differences between Chinese and English', *Journal of Consumer Research*, **21**, 419–31.
Schmitt, Bernd and Alex Simonson (1997), *Marketing Aesthetics: The Strategic Management of Brands, Identity and Image*. New York: Free Press.
Schmitt, Bernd and Shi Zhang (1998), 'Language Structure and Categorization: A Study of Classifiers in Consumer Cognition, Judgment and Choice', *Journal of Consumer Research*, **25**, 108–22.
Sinclair, Robert C., Melven M. Mark and R. Lance Shotland (1987), 'Construct Accessibility and Generalizability Across Response Categories', *Personality and Social Psychology Bulletin*, **13**, 239–252.
Tavassoli, Nader T. (1999), 'Temporal and Associative Memory in Chinese and English,' *Journal of Consumer Research*, **26**, 170–81.
Tavassoli, Nader T. (2001), 'Color Memory and Evaluations for Alphabetical and Logographic Brand Names', *Journal of Experimental Psychology: Applied*, **7**, 104–11.
Tavassoli, Nader T. and Jin K. Han (2001), 'Scripted Thought: Processing Korean Hancha and Hangul in a Multimedia Context', *Journal of Consumer Research*, **28**, 482–93.
Triandis, Harry C. (1989), 'The Self and Social Behavior in Differing Cultural Contexts', *Psychological Review*, **96**, 506–20.
Weber, Elke U. and Christopher K. Hsee (2000), 'Culture and Individual Judgment and Decision Making', *Applied Psychology: An International Review*, **49**, 32–61.
Whorf, Benjamin (1956), *Language, Thought and Reality: Selected Writings of Benjamin Lee Whorf*, edited by John B. Carroll, Cambridge, MA: MIT Press.
Zhang, Shi and Bernd Schmitt (1998), 'Language-Dependent Classification: The Role of Classifiers in Cognition, Memory and Ad Evaluation', *Journal of Experimental Psychology: Applied*, **4**, 375–85.
Zhang, Shi and Bernd H. Schmitt (2001), 'Creating Local Brands in Multilingual International Markets', *Journal of Marketing Research*, **38**, 313–25.
Zhang, Shi and Bernd H. Schmitt (forthcoming), 'Activating Sound and Meaning: The Role of Language Proficiency in Bilinguals Environments', *Journal of Consumer Research*, **30** (June).

PART IV

Marketing strategy

12. International product strategies: an integrative framework

Preet S. Aulakh

INTRODUCTION

In recent years, because of the opening of new markets around the world and the shift in competition from individual countries to a global level, firms have tried to pursue global or international marketing strategies. Product policy in international markets represents a key component of a global marketing strategy for a firm. However, given the diversity of environmental factors across countries, managing the international product policy poses unique challenges and opportunities for marketing managers. Some of the key questions facing a firm pursuing global product strategy are: how to develop new products for different foreign markets; the degree of standardization of products across markets; the timing of product introductions in various markets; and managing the international product policy to exploit the synergies across countries accruing due to the location of manufacturing facilities or sourcing of product components from different locations.

However, despite the complexity of international product policy decisions, the standardization of international marketing programs represents much of the research accumulated to date. While the marketing standardization (of which product standardization is a part) argument is not new (e.g. Bartels 1968; Buzzell 1968; Fayerweather 1969; Sorenson and Wiechmann 1975), renewed interest in the topic was generated following Levitt's (1983) article where he proposed the concept of a 'global product' and called for proactive identification of similar market segments around the world. Subsequent research rekindled a great deal of controversy over what can be standardized in global marketing and to what extent it can be done (e.g. Douglas and Wind 1987; Jain 1989; Samiee and Roth 1992; Walters 1986). The consensus that emerges from this debate is that a distinction should be made between standardization of marketing programs (i.e. marketing mix) and the managerial processes through which these programs are developed (Kotabe 1992), as performance implications of standardization are not universal (Aulakh,

245

Kotabe and Teegen 2000; Carpano and Chrisman 1995; Cavusgil and Zou 1994).

A second component of international product policy is the timing of product introduction in foreign markets. For instance, multinational firms are realizing that the key to growth and survival is the continuous development of new products that can be introduced in numerous markets (Keegan 1989). Thus a key question facing multinational firms is about decisions regarding the launching of a new product in global markets. The traditional approach to a product's timing of entry into foreign markets was based on Vernon's (1966, 1974, 1979) international product cycle thesis. According to this view, product innovations occurred in the United States because of its high per capita income which increased the demand for new products and abundant skilled labor that could innovate new products to satisfy the demand. After the home-country demand was met, the excess supply of new products was exported to countries having similar income levels to the USA. In terms of international product policy, this life cycle argument implies that products are introduced in different markets in a hierarchical fashion or follow what Ohmae (1987) calls the waterfall model.

A third component of international product policy is the location of production facilities. Since multinational firms are establishing multiple production facilities in different countries either due to government pressures or to exploit the comparative and competitive advantages of countries, they are in a position to serve different markets from these production facilities. Leroy (1976) provides a typology of multinational product strategies based on three dimensions: the location of the development of the product know-how, the location of markets in which the product is sold, and the location of the production of the product.

Evidently, research to-date on international product policy has concentrated (though unequally) on three aspects: level of product standardization, the timing of entry of new products in different markets, and the location of production facilities across countries. While researchers have provided conditions determining the level of each dimension, there has been no systematic attempt to integrate these three dimensions of international product policy. In this chapter, by drawing from various theoretical and empirical perspectives, an integrative framework of international product policy is developed along three dimensions: core component standardization, timing of market entry, and location of production facilities. It is argued in this chapter that to understand the various dimensions of international product strategies, one not only has to determine the conditions under which a particular strategy within the three dimensions will be most appropriate, but also understand how the different levels of each dimension are associated with the other dimensions of international product strategy. Furthermore, since the eventual goal of each strategy is to increase firm performance, it is proposed that the different levels of each of the three dimensions of strategy, by themselves, should not affect performance, but the fit between the antecedent conditions and the appropriate strategy should lead to higher performance.

The rest of the chapter is organized as follows. In the next section, the existing literature along the three dimensions of international product strategy is reviewed and the interrelationships between the three dimensions are outlined. Following this section, the antecedent conditions of the three strategies are identified. Then, the performance implications of each type of strategy are considered. In the final section, the implications of the proposed framework are discussed and directions for future research are provided.

LITERATURE REVIEW

In this section, the existing perspectives on the three dimensions of international product strategy are discussed: subsequently the possible interrelationships between the three dimensions are outlined.

Core Component Standardization

In one of the earliest articles on standardization, Keegan (1969) outlined five multinational product strategies depending on three conditions in foreign markets: product function or need satisfied, conditions of product use, and ability to buy the product. Keegan suggested that depending on the combination of these three variables, multinationals could use different product and communication strategies that could be an extension of their home-market strategies, adaptation to local markets, or an invention approach. In most of the subsequent research, there is no clear distinction made between standardization of the product itself and other elements of the marketing mix.

Furthermore, despite the differentiation between program and process standardization (Sorenson and Wiechmann 1975), it is not clear how the standardization within the elements of the marketing mix is accomplished and what are the determinants of these standardizations. For instance, Jain (1989) integrated the literature on program standardization and proposed that the degree of standardization will be a function of target market characteristics, the market position of the firm, the nature of the product, environmental factors in the host market, and organizational characteristics of the firm. Thus, no distinction was made between the degrees of standard-ization for the different elements of the marketing mix. Further, in terms of international product strategy, the only distinction is made between indus-trialized and consumer products, where the former are considered to be more suitable for standardization than the latter (Jain 1989; Samiee and Roth 1992).

A potential problem of product standardization research may be due to the extant literature's exclusive reliance on final product standardization, i.e. the degree to which a product used by consumers is standardized or adapted. More recently, researchers have elaborated on the concept of 'core components standardization' (e.g. Kotabe 1992; Walters and Toyne 1989) whereby universal products are developed which require only cosmetic changes to cater to differing needs across countries or market segmenta-tions (Takeuchi and Porter 1986). Furthermore, the core components stan-dardization has become more meaningful because of a growing trend in outsourcing of components by major multinational corporations to gain economies of scale and scope. Thus, by having standardized components, a firm can achieve economies of scale from the supply-side considerations, while at the same time adapt these products by offering a wide range of models according to the special needs of different country segments. Finally, as outlined by Buzzell (1968) and Douglas and Wind (1987), there are numerous constraints to global marketing standardization. For the purpose of product standardization, the two major constraints are different consumer preferences and governmental and trade restrictions. One major government constraint is local content rules that specify that products contain a specified proportion of components manufactured locally. Similarly heterogeneous consumer preferences or host government policies may force the company to change the packaging of products or the product features offered. Also global products such as Coca-Cola and personal computers, although marketed with a uniform appeal, nonetheless are sub-jected to minor adaptations in different markets. In these cases, the core product or the core components of the product may be standardized although the final product sold to the consumer may be modified to cater to idiosyncratic conditions. This lack in differentiating the final product from the core components may have led to inconsistent results in the empir-ical studies on product standardization (Walters 1986). Because of these reasons, in this chapter, the issue of product standardization is considered in terms of 'core components standardization'. Since the advantage of standardization across countries is because of lower manufacturing costs, an emphasis on core product standardization rather than final product standardization allows the realization of lower manufacturing costs without sacrificing flexibility in the other elements of the marketing mix.

Timing of Product Entry in Foreign Markets

As mentioned earlier, the timing of product entry in foreign markets has been guided by Vernon's product cycle thesis. According to this view, innovations trickle down in a slow-moving cascade from the most to the least technologically advanced countries (Kalish, Mahajan and Muller 1995). That is, after successfully launching a new product in domestic markets, multinational firms introduce it into other advanced countries and then into less developed countries. Although the international product cycle model has descriptive value, many authors have been critical of its explanatory power (Ayal 1981; Giddy 1978; Kotabe 1992). Some key deficiencies relate to the model's failure to explain the global expansion paths of non-US firms and the operational interdependence among affiliates of multinational firms. First, Jatusripitak, Fahey and Kotler (1985) found that the Japanese companies did not strictly follow the path outlined by the international product cycle model. In their global expansion path, Japanese companies followed three strategies of new product introductions:

1. Japan → Developing Countries → Developed Countries
2. Japan → Developed Countries → Developing Countries
3. Other Developed Countries → Japan → Developing Countries

This anecdotal evidence from Japanese multinationals suggests that not only are firms introducing products in foreign markets in a way that does not follow the hierarchical path suggested by Vernon (1966), but also that new product innovations originate away from the domestic market (also see Kotabe 1992). Second, the international product cycle model does not view the multinational firm as a proactive player, with simultaneous goals of establishing a global sourcing system, serving multiple global markets, and proactively driving the manufacturing and marketing experience curves (Leroy 1976; Porter 1986). Finally, while empirical evidence (e.g. Davidson and Harrigan 1977) of US-based based multinationals suggests the argument that the hierarchical path of product introductions is followed, the same study posits that in the 1970s, the lead-time between new product development and introduction into foreign markets has shrunk considerably.

Thus, along with the acceleration of new product introductions in foreign markets and the shortening of innovation lead-time, the migration of competitive advantage from the original innovator to follower firms is not just a function of changing factor costs and demand patterns, as predicted in the product life cycle model (Davidson and Harrigan 1977). Rather the innovator's slow response to emerging competitive threats around the world will cut short its competitive advantage over competition. If the innovator fails to maintain the original advantage by pursuing a global strategy aimed at dominating a set of product-market segments, the follower firms can gain the advantage at the expense of the innovator (Rapp 1973). Given that there are similar market segments at least in the Triad region, Ohmae (1987) suggests that with increased global competition, firms should follow a 'sprinkler strategy' whereby products are introduced simultaneously in all markets. In this chapter, instead of taking the dichotomous strategy of waterfall versus sprinkler models of product introductions in foreign markets, a continuous variable, lead-time between product development (or introduction in one market) and product introduction in another market, is used. The timing of entry based on a continuum is more appropriate because it is impossible to enter different markets simultaneously due to infrastructure constraints, government regulations, or firm characteristics. Thus the lead-time between product introductions in different markets may provide a more useful measure of market entry decisions.

Location of Production Facilities

As with the timing of entry, the traditional view about the location of production facilities was guided by the international product cycle model and its implications drawn from the trade theories. However, in the 1970s, there was intense research activity trying to explain the investment patterns of multinational corporations in foreign countries (see Calvet 1981 for a review of this literature). Borrowing from industrial organization literature, Hymer (1976) proposed that a multinational enterprise (MNE) should be considered as an institution for international production, rather than international exchange. Accordingly, the aim of foreign direct investment by MNEs is to create market imperfections to gain monopolistic advantage through the use of asset power accruing because of firm-specific (ownership) advantages. Subsequent research on foreign direct investments used the transaction cost framework, and its international counterpart, internalization theory, to explain foreign production by multinational corporations in terms of market imperfections with the ultimate aim of the firm being efficiency rather than profit maximization (e.g. Buckley and Casson 1976; Hennart 1982; Williamson 1975). Dunning (1988) integrated the various perspectives by proposing an eclectic paradigm of international production. Accordingly, the decision to have production facilities in a given foreign market will depend on the ownership advantages that the MNE has (i.e. firm-specific advantages) in order to compete with local competition, the internalization advantages of producing itself rather than contracting to outside parties, and the location advantages that the foreign country offers in terms of factor endowments and market potential.

In the strategy literature, the extensive geographical expansion of multinational firms has led to a growing realization of the potential competitive advantages gained in coordinating and integrating operations across national boundaries (Kogut 1985; Porter 1986). Thus a key managerial issue is to rationalize the international production process in order to determine which production units will serve which particular markets (McGrath 1992; Starr 1984). Kotabe (1992) classifies production locations into three groups: home country, market country, and third-party country. The decision about production location in a third country can be further subclassified into a developed third country (capital abundant) and a developing third country (labor abundant). Since a decision to choose the production location from any one of three groups will be a function of the ownership, internalization, and location advantages, this three-level production variable is considered in this chapter.

RELATIONSHIP BETWEEN EXTENT OF STANDARDIZATION, TIMING OF MARKET ENTRY AND LOCATION OF PRODUCTION

As discussed in the previous section, international product strategy has three components: extent of product (core component) standardization, the timing of market entry, and the location of production. While each of these strategies has been studied independently, there has been no attempt to integrate the three strategy types into a comprehensive framework of international product strategy. It is argued in this chapter that different levels of each strategy will interact with other strategy types.

A major issue in developing a strategy to support a globally standardized product is closely related to how components for that product will be sourced (Kotabe 1992). Leroy (1976) found that firms are likely to shift production facilities to the market country when the product needs to be adapted to the socio-cultural environment of the host market. Thus, the degree of core component standardization is likely to be low when firms are using multiple production facilities in the target market countries. On the other hand, if MNEs are sourcing their products from a third country, the location advantages of that particular country are the major motive for use of these production facilities. Since this third-country production facility is providing products for other markets, there is a greater likelihood of these products (components) being standardized. Thus, the degree of core component standardization will interact with the location of production. If the

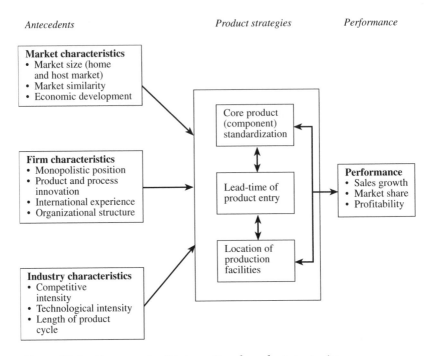

Figure 12.1   Framework of international product strategies

core component is standardized for global markets, the diffusion of the products into multiple markets will require less time. Therefore, it can be anticipated that the degree of core component standardization will be negatively related to the lead-time between product introductions in different markets. Also, if the product is developed in the home market but production facilities are located in the market or third country, the lead-time will be greater than if the product development process and the production facilities are located in the market country. (See Figure 12.1.)

DETERMINANTS OF THE THREE PRODUCT STRATEGIES

In this section, the various determinants that will affect the levels of the three strategies are identified. These determinants can be grouped into three types: market characteristics (home- and host-country markets), firm characteristics (structural and behavioral), and industry characteristics.

Market Characteristics

The first determinant that will impact the three product strategies is the potential size of the markets (both home and host). Jatusripitak, Fahey and Kotler (1985) found that Japanese product expansion strategies followed wherever a potential market existed. Thus, the Japanese firms targeted the USA for product introductions even before introducing them in the Japanese market for high-technology products in the 1970s. Even the implications of the international product cycle thesis imply that product innovations originate when there is a demand for such products. It is therefore suggested that product innovations will occur when the market size for the product is large enough to cover the costs incurred in product development and introduction. However, if there are multiple markets that have similar demand patterns, a firm has to choose the timing of market entry for each of these markets. When the size of the different markets is large, and because of the presence of inter-market segments across countries (Hill and Still 1984), firms should follow sprinkler strategies. Thus the size of the foreign markets will be negatively related to the lead-time between product development and product introductions. Furthermore, if the size of the different markets is large, a firm may be willing to start production in the different target markets so as to avoid the transportation costs between different markets (Leroy 1976). For smaller markets, not only is the lead-time of product introductions greater, but in these markets, firms may be less willing to adapt the core components to local market conditions. On the other hand, if the host market is large enough, there is greater likelihood that the core components will be adapted. In addition, the location of production facilities will determine the extent of core component standardization. If all components are produced in different production locations, then the economic advantages of core component standardization are mitigated, and the firm will adapt its products to local conditions.

Besides the size of the market, the economic similarity between the host and home markets will determine how and when a product is introduced in a host market. Rostow (1990) suggests that the level of economic development of a country determines the demand patterns for particular products as well as the absorptive capacity of technologies used in the production process. Thus, the similarity in the stage of economic development between the host and home markets will affect the product usage conditions, product functions, and the ability to buy the products (Keegan 1968) and therefore will be positively related to core component standardization (Jain 1989). In addition, if the two markets are similar in economic development, there is a greater likelihood that a firm is willing to transfer the technology to the host market and start production facilities. Finally, the lead-time in product introductions between the two markets will be lower if the markets are economically similar.

In foreign markets, firms often encounter different physical, political, and legal environments (Douglas and Wind 1987). These differences hinder the realization of global production rationalization by MNEs. For instance, local content rules in foreign markets affect the global sourcing strategies of firms because firms can no longer achieve economies of scale by sourcing components from the lowest cost production facilities. Also, differences in physical environments (infrastructure, distribution channels, etc.) and legal issues (e.g. product standards, trademark laws) will necessitate a change in product strategies to meet host-country conditions. Thus, the greater the differences in physical, political, and legal environments in the host market from the home market, the lower will be the product standardization, and the greater the lead-time in product introductions. Finally, a firm will be willing to start production in the host market if the size of the market is large, the host government requires investment in the host market, and there are potential learning effects by being physically present in the market through manufacturing facilities.

Firm Characteristics

Two types of firm characteristics will affect the levels of the three product strategies. First, structural characteristics such as the monopolistic position of the firm, the extent of process innovations, and the centralization of decision making will influence the level of each strategy. If an MNE firm enjoys a monopolistic position in its home (or 'key') market and/or the decision making is centralized in the home-country headquarters, the less pressure there is for the firm to enter foreign markets, thus increasing the lead-time in product introductions (Kalish, Mahajan and Muller 1995; Mascarenhas 1992). On the other hand, as suggested by Hymer (1976), a monopolist may want to extend its market power in other foreign countries by starting production facilities in the host market. Further, first-mover advantages in foreign markets may extend the monopolistic advantages from a single country to a global level (see Kerin, Varadarajan and Peterson 1992 for a review of first-mover advantages). This would imply that the lead-time between product introduction may be shorter if a firm wants to enter foreign markets to enhance market power and erect barriers to entry for the follower firms. From the preceding arguments, it would imply that the lead-time will be greater when a firm is entering a foreign market through exporting, but will be lower when firms decide to extend their first-mover advantages into foreign markets. Another factor that may effect the strategy type is the degree of process innovations of the MNE. Kotabe (1992) compared European and Japanese multinationals and found that process innovating firms tended to standardize the manufacturing processes, which, in turn meant greater core product standardization. In addition, process innovating firms developed products in-house instead of contracting to third parties, and firms developed products in-house instead of contracting to third parties, and thus a greater amount of concentration of production facilities in a few locations.

Second, the behavioral dimensions of the MNE will impact the strategy type. Jain (1989) suggests that effective global strategy is accomplished through tight linkages of the subsidiaries with the headquarters. When managers of the subsidiaries share common goals with the overall corporate objectives, the implementation of a global strategy is easier. For instance, a well-intended global standardization decision by Parker Pen Company went awry because of its local subsidiaries' resistance to a sudden product policy change introduced in 1982 (Kotabe 1992). Therefore, it can be anticipated that if the key managers in different countries share common corporate goals, there will be greater core component standardization in order to achieve economies of scale, the lead-time between product introductions in different markets will be lower, and there will be greater production rationalization since different production facilities will specialize in certain components and serve global or regional rather than national markets. The international experience of a firm will also impact the degree of standardization. Firms with greater international experience usually follow a polycentric instead of an ethnocentric approach. Firms experienced in foreign markets will, therefore, be more sensitive to local conditions and more willing to adapt their products. On the other hand, firms with international experience are able to identify inter-market segments that can be served through standardized products and also decrease the lead-time in product introductions. Finally, it has been suggested that the international experience of firms is negatively related to internal uncertainty in the host markets (Hennart 1982), and thus firms are more willing to invest in production facilities in different markets. Thus it can be expected that international experience will be positively related to production facilities in numerous markets to exploit location-specific advantages of different countries.

Industry Characteristics

Firms facing global competition in their product markets are more likely to use a waterfall strategy of product introductions so as not to allow their competitors to gain market share and thus achieve greater economies of scale (Kalish, Mahajan and Muller 1995). Therefore, competition in an industry will be negatively related to lead-time of product introductions. Closely related to this argument is the fact that since competitive pressures in the industry warrant quick entry into global markets, firms have time constraints to adapt their products to local conditions. Industry competition will, therefore, be positively related to core product standardization. In addition, the rate of technological change in the industry will be positively related to core component standardization and negatively related to lead-time (Samiee and Roth 1992) since firms will want a quick recovery of their fixed costs before the technology reaches obsolescence. Finally, the life cycle of the product will affect the strategy type. If a product has a long life cycle, there will be less pressure to standardize. In fact, for certain products, firms can enhance the life cycle by following a waterfall strategy using adapted technologies in different markets. For example, Suzuki of Japan gained a 50 per cent market share of the Indian car market by introducing lagged technology that produced cars that were appropriate in the Indian market.

PERFORMANCE IMPLICATIONS OF DIFFERENT PRODUCT STRATEGIES

In the final analysis, the decision to use particular levels of each of the strategy dimension should be based on economic payoff, which includes financial performance, market share, competitive advantage, and other factors. Concern for financial performance, specially in the context of marketing standardization, has been expressed by a number of researchers (e.g. Buzzell 1968; Keegan 1969; Jain 1989). While the reasons for standardization of marketing activities in foreign countries have been expressed in terms of performance implications, the actual measurement of firm performance because of different strategies has been given little attention. It was only in a recent article by Samiee and Roth (1992) that the performance implications of global marketing standardization were studied. The authors concluded that although the different environmental contexts determined the degree of standardization, firms pursuing a global standardized strategy did not perform better than firms who did not standardize.

This lack of performance implications of global standardization in the aforementioned study may be caused by two factors. First, Samiee and Roth's (1992) method of measuring the standardization construct reflected the need for standardization (or standardizability) in the product category instead of the actual standardization done in foreign marketing programs. In this case, therefore, though the managers may realize the benefits, organizational or other constraints may delay the actual implementation of standardization. A second, and related reason, is that inter-market segments may exist for a large number of products across different countries. However, to effectively access those inter-market segments as well as achieve the benefits of a standardization strategy, facilitating factors related to the environment, firm resources, as well as global reporting structures have to be in place. Thus, the relationship between degree of standardization and performance is seen from the perspective of a congruence approach where an unconditional association between the two variables is hypothesized.

It is argued in this chapter that the level of strategy along the three dimensions: core component standardization, timing of market entry, and location of production, by itself should not affect performance. Instead, since various market, firm, and industry characteristics determine the level of each strategy, and since there are interactions between the different strategy types, the performance outcomes of a particular strategy would be contingent upon the determinants of each strategy level. Thus, in order to study the performance implications, researchers should use a contingency approach whereby a conditional association of the determinants of strategy and the appropriate strategy type is seen to affect performance. Since, standardization and adaptation, sprinkler and waterfall market entry strategies, and countries where production facilities are located, are all appropriate strategies under different conditions, it is only when a firm deviates from the ideal strategy given the antecedent conditions, that it would experience lower performance.

CONCLUSIONS AND DIRECTIONS FOR FUTURE RESEARCH

The main purpose of this chapter was to clarify the different aspects of international product strategy and to integrate the various perspectives into a conceptual framework. By drawing from various theoretical and empirical studies, the determinants of core product standardization, timing of market entry, and location of production facilities were related to strategy types. Since, in the previous research, the three strategy types were studied independently of each other, only determinants for each strategy were considered. In this chapter, it is argued that the firms are simultaneously trying to make decisions on the type of strategy along the three dimensions. Consequently, there will be significant interactions among the three dimensions.

In terms of future research directions, it is suggested that researchers should concentrate on both the substantive and methodological problems associated with international product strategies. On the substantive side, more precise hypotheses showing the interrelationships of the various constructs are required for the framework provided in this chapter to be empirically tested. While broad directions of the relationships have been alluded to, it is suggested that future research should concentrate on studying the effects of interactions between different determinants of strategy. From the methodological perspective, some of the constructs outlined have either not been or have been inadequately measured. Furthermore, to understand the performance implications of the different product strategies, a contingency framework of coalignment needs to be developed. Although contingency models have been popular in the management literature, there remain theoretical and methodological concerns related to the use of these models, especially when multiple contingencies are involved. Since the framework provided in this chapter involves multiple independent and dependent variables that have performance implications for a number of factors, the existing contingency models may be inadequate to understand the various aspects of international product strategies.

REFERENCES

Aulakh, Preet S., Masaaki Kotabe and Hildy Teegen (2000), 'Export Strategies and Performance of Firms from Emerging Economies: Evidence from Brazil, Chile and Mexico', *Academy of Management Journal*, **43** (3), 342–61.
Ayal, Igal (1981), 'International Product Life Cycle: A Reassessment and Product Policy Implications', *Journal of Marketing*, **45** (Fall), 91–6.
Bartels, Robert (1968), 'Are Domestic and International Marketing Dissimilar?', *Journal of Marketing*, **34** (October), 84–94.
Buckley, Peter J. and Mark C. Casson (1976), *The Future of the Multinational Enterprise*, London: Macmillan.
Buzzell, Robert D. (1968), 'Can You Standardize Multinational Marketing?', *Harvard Business Review*, **46** (November–December), 102–13.
Calvet, A.L. (1981), 'A Synthesis of Foreign Direct Investment Theories and Theories of the Multinational Firms', *Journal of International Business Studies*, **12** (Spring/Summer), 43–59.
Carapellotti, Lawrence R. and Saeed Samiee (1984), 'The Use of Portfolio Models for Production Rationalization in Multinational Firms', *International Marketing Review*, (Spring/Summer), 5–13.
Carpano, Claudio and J.J. Chrisman (1995), 'Performance Implications of International Product Strategies and the Integration of Marketing Activities', *Journal of International Marketing*, **3** (1), 9–27.
Cavusgil, S. Tamer and Shaoming Zou (1994), 'Marketing Strategy–Performance Relationship: An Investigation of the Empirical Link in Export Market Ventures', *Journal of Marketing*, **58** (1), 1–21.
Davidson, William H. and Richard Harrigan (1977), 'Key Decisions in International Marketing: Introducing New Product Abroad', *Columbia Journal*

of World Business, (Winter), 15–23.

Douglas, Susan P. and Yoram Wind (1987), 'The Myth of Globalization', *Columbia Journal of World Business*, **22** (Winter), 19–29.

Dunning, John H. (1988), 'The Eclectic Paradigm of International Production: A Restatement and Some Possible Extensions', *Journal of International Business Studies*, **19** (Spring), 1–31.

Fayerweather, John (1969), *International Business Management: A Conceptual Framework*, New York: McGraw-Hill Book Company.

Giddy, Ian H. (1978), 'The Demise of the International Product Cycle Model in International Business Theory', *Columbia Journal of World Business*, **13** (Spring), 90–97.

Hennart, J-F. (1982), *Theory of Multinational Enterprise*, Ann Arbor: University of Michigan Press.

Hill, John S. and Richard R. Still (1984), 'Effects of Urbanization on Multinational Product Planning: Markets in Lesser-Developed Countries', *Columbia Journal of World Business*, **19** (2), 62–7.

Hymer, Stephen (1976), *The International Operations of National Firms: A Study of Direct Investment*, Boston: MIT Press.

Jain, Subhash C. (1989). 'Standardization of International Marketing Strategy: Some Research Hypotheses', *Journal of Marketing*, **53** (January), 70–79.

Jatusripitak, Somkid, Liam Fahey and Philip Kotler (1985), 'Strategic Global Marketing', *Columbia Journal of World Business*, **19** (Spring), 47–53.

Kalish, Shlomo, Vijay Mahajan and Eitan Muller (1995), 'Waterfall and Sprinkler New-Product Strategies in Competitive Global Markets', *International Journal of Research in Marketing*, **12** (July), 105–19.

Kashani, Kamran (1989), 'Beware the Pitfalls of Global Marketing', *Harvard Business Review*, **67** (September/October), 91–8.

Keegan, Warren J. (1968), 'Multinational Product Planning: Strategic Alternatives', *Journal of Marketing*, **33** (January), 58–62.

Keegan, Warren J. (1989), *Global Marketing Management*, Englewood Cliffs, NJ: Prentice-Hall.

Kerin, Roger A., P. Rajan Varadarajan and Robert A. Peterson (1992), 'First-Mover Advantage: A Synthesis, Conceptual Framework, and Research Propositions', *Journal of Marketing*, **56** (4), 33–52.

Kogut, Bruce (1985), 'Designing Global Strategies: Comparative and Competitive Value-Added Chains', *Sloan Management Review*, **26** (Summer), 15–28.

Kotabe, Masaaki (1992), *Global Sourcing Strategy: R&D, Manufacturing, and Marketing Interfaces*, New York: Quorum Books.

Leroy, Georges (1976), *Multinational Product Strategy: A Typology for Analysis of Worldwide Product Innovation and Diffusion*, New York: Praeger.

Levitt, Theodore (1983), 'The Globalization of Markets', *Harvard Business Review*, **61** (May–June), 92–102.

Mascarenhas, Briance (1992), 'Research Notes and Communications: First-Mover Effects in Multiple Dynamic Markets', *Strategic Management Journal*, **13**, 237–43.

McGrath, Michael E. (1992), 'Manufacturing's New Economies of Scale', *Harvard Business Review*, (May–June), 94–102.

Ohmae, Kenichi (1987), 'The Triad World View', *Journal of Business Strategy*, **7** (Spring), 8–19.

Onkvisit, Sak and John J. Shaw (1983), 'An Examination of the International

Product Life Cycle and Its Application within Marketing', *Columbia Journal of World Business*, **18** (3), 73–9.

Porter, Michael E. (1986), *Competition in Global Industries*, Boston: Harvard Business School Press.

Rapp, William V. (1973), 'Strategy Formulation and International Competition', *Columbia Journal of World Business*, **8** (Summer), 98–112.

Rostow, W.W. (1990), *The Stages of Economic Growth: A Non-Communist Manifesto*, Cambridge: Cambridge University Press.

Ryans, Adrian B. (1988), 'Strategic Market Entry Factors and Market Share Achievement in Japan', *Journal of International Business Studies*, (Fall), 389–409.

Samiee, Saeed and Kendall Roth (1992), 'The Influence of Global Marketing Standardization on Performance', *Journal of Marketing*, **56** (April), 1–17.

Sorenson, Ralph Z. and Ulrich E. Wiechmann (1975), 'How Multinationals View Marketing Standardization?', *Harvard Business Review*, **53** (May–June), 38–56.

Starr, Martin K. (1984), 'Global Production and Operations Strategy', *Columbia Journal of World Business*, **19** (4), 17–23.

Still, Richard R. and John S. Hill (1985), 'Multinational Product Planning: A Meta-Market Analysis', *International Marketing Review*, (Spring), 54–64.

Takeuchi, Hirotaka and Michael E. Porter (1986), 'Three Roles of International Marketing in Global Strategy', in Michael E. Porter (ed.), *Competition in Global Industries*, Boston: Harvard Business School Press, pp. 111–46.

Vernon, Raymond (1966), 'International Investment and International Trade in the Product Cycle', *Quarterly Journal of Economics*, **80** (May), 190–207.

Vernon, Raymond (1974), 'The Location of Economic Activity,' in John H. Dunning (ed.), *Economic Analysis and the Multinational Enterprise*, London: George Allen & Unwin, pp. 89–114.

Vernon, Raymond (1979), 'The Product Cycle Hypothesis in a New International Environment', *Oxford Bulletin of Economics and Statistics*, **41** (November), 255–67.

Walters, Peter (1986), 'International Marketing Policy: A Discussion of the Standardization Construct and Its Relevance for Corporate Policy', *Journal of International Business Studies*, **17** (Summer), 55–70.

Walters, Peter G.P. and Brian Toyne (1989), 'Product Modification and Standardization in International Markets: Strategic Options and Facilitating Policies', *Columbia Journal of World Business*, **24** (4), 37–44.

Whitelock, Jeryl M. (1987), 'Global Marketing and the Case of International Product Standardization', *European Journal of Marketing*, **21** (9), 32–43.

Williamson, Oliver E. (1975), *Markets and Hierarchies: Analysis and Antitrust Implications*, New York: Free Press.

Wills, James, A. Coskun Samli and Laurence Jacobs (1991), 'Developing Global Products and Marketing Strategies: A Construct and Research Agenda', *Journal of the Academy of Marketing Science*, **19** (1), 1–10.

Yip, George S. (1991), 'Do American Businesses Use Global Strategy?', *Marketing Science Institute*, Report No. 91.

13. Dynamics of international brand architecture: overview and directions for future research

Susan P. Douglas and C. Samuel Craig

INTRODUCTION

Branding is a key element of a firm's marketing strategy. Strong brands help establish the firm's identity in the marketplace, and develop a solid customer franchise (Aaker 1996; Kapferer 1997; Keller 1998). Owning the number one or two brand in the product category provides manufacturers with a weapon to counter growing retailer power (Barwise and Robertson 1992). A strong brand name can also provide the basis for brand extensions, which further strengthen the firm's position in the marketplace as well as potentially enhancing the brand's value (Aaker and Keller 1990). As firms move into international markets, branding plays an important role in their marketing strategy. In particular, a judicious branding strategy provides a means to enhance the firm's visibility and integrate strategy across national markets (see Khermouch, Holmes and Ihlwan 2001).

In markets outside the USA the concept of building strong brands in order to establish market position is relatively recent (Court et al. 1997). Markets are often fragmented, characterized by small-scale distribution, and lack the potential or size to warrant the use of heavy mass media advertising needed to develop strong brands (Barwise and Robertson 1992). In addition, firms have typically expanded the geographic scope of operations on a piecemeal basis by acquiring companies in other countries or entering into alliances across national boundaries. As a result they often acquire national brands or ones with limited visibility. Consequently, companies operating internationally need to identify opportunities for strengthening their position through improved coordination and harmonization of brands across countries and building a cohesive and effective architecture for their brands.

An international brand architecture provides a structure and a rationale for branding decisions at different levels of the organization and for different geographic locations. In essence, this architecture provides the principles that guide the effective use of brands so as to develop a strong positional advantage in international markets. It should establish which brands should be emphasized at what level in the organization, i.e. corporate, product business and product, how brands are used and extended across product lines and country, and how far branding is harmonized and coordinated across national borders. Without a well-conceived international brand architecture, the firm will be at a competitive disadvantage, suffering from inconsistencies in brand identity across national markets, lack of a strong corporate or product identity in international markets, and the inability to maximize the value of brands across national boundaries.

The present chapter develops a framework for understanding the design and composition of a firm's international brand architecture. Current perspectives on international branding and brand architecture are first examined. A conceptual framework identifying the elements of international brand architecture is developed based on the findings of a field survey of the international branding strategies of a number of large consumer goods companies in Europe. Each of its components and the typical patterns of brand architecture found in these companies are then discussed in more detail. Finally, some directions for future research, designed to provide improved understanding of this important area of research, are suggested.

PERSPECTIVES ON INTERNATIONAL BRANDING

Most discussion and research on branding, whether in domestic or international markets, focuses on the equity or value associated with a brand name and the factors which create or are the underlying source of value (Aaker 1996; Kapferer 1997; Keller 1998). Considerable attention has, for example, been devoted to examining how the value embodied in a brand and its equity can be extended to other products without resulting in dilution of value (Aaker and Keller 1990). This interest has been stimulated in part by the increasing market power and value associated with a strong brand and in part by the prohibitive costs of launching a successful new brand. In international markets, interest has been centered around global branding – defining the meaning of a global brand, discussing the advantages and pitfalls, and the conditions under which building a global brand is most likely to be successful (Roth 1995a,b; Quelch 1999).

While this focus is appropriate for a relatively few high-profile brands such as Nike or Coca-Cola, it ignores the complexity of the issues faced by the vast majority of multinational firms who own a variety of national, regional and international brands, at different levels in the organization, spanning a broad range of diverse country markets. Typically, these brands differ in their strength, associations, target market and the range of products covered, both within and across markets. Equally the use of brands at different organizational levels may vary from company to company. Some firms such as Sony, IBM or Phillips emphasize branding at the corporate level. Others such as Beiersdorf mostly have brands at the product business level, such as Nivea and Juvena, while yet others such as P&G, have primarily product level brands.

In determining whether to emphasize branding at the corporate level as opposed to the product-level or whether to adopt a hybrid structure, the firm needs to consider the role of corporate image as well as the diversity of its product businesses. Corporate brands provide strong identity for the firm's products in the marketplace, but do not enable differentiation of specific product businesses or product lines. Equally, negative publicity relating to a specific product or the firm's policies will affect all products and product businesses. Product-level brands facilitate differentiation from competing products, but may be less cost efficient and result in loss of potential synergies. The number of brands at each level of the organization and the range of product lines across which a brand is used, must also be considered. Parsimony in the number of brands helps to achieve cost efficiencies but may weaken brand strength if used across highly diverse product lines. Multiplicity of brands facilitates responsiveness to specific customer or segment needs and clear product differentiation, but may be cost inefficient and hamper building of a strong position in the marketplace.

As the firm expands in international markets, issues relating to brand architecture become even more complex. In addition to determining the number of levels in the hierarchy, another dimension, namely the degree of brand coordination or standardization across countries, needs to be assessed. Of key importance is whether to use the same brand name in different countries, leveraging brand strength across boundaries, or whether to focus on local brands responding to local customer preferences. Using the same brand name in different countries has the advantage of enhancing visibility and reach, but may have negative connotations in some markets or result in lack of adaptation to local market conditions and the competitive environment.

Often the nature and cohesiveness of a firm's international brand architecture depends on how it has expanded internationally, and how its international operations are organized. Some firms, such as P&G, have expanded through leveraging strong domestic brands in international markets. Consequently, as they seek to expand further, they have to consider whether to develop brands geared to specific regional or national preferences. Others such as Nestlé and Unilever have traditionally adopted country-centered strategies, building or acquiring a mix of national and international brands. Such companies have to decide whether to move towards greater harmonization of brands and integration of their brand architecture across countries, and if so, how to do so. Furthermore, if the company expands through acquisition or strategic alliances, the question of whether and how brand architectures of different firms are merged, arises. In particular, how far and in what way branding structures are integrated or harmonized across countries has to be determined.

INTERNATIONAL BRAND ARCHITECTURE

A field study of consumer goods company executives based in Europe (Douglas, Craig and Nijssen 2001) was conducted to gain some insights into their international brand architecture, and how these were evolving. Of particular interest were the dominant patterns of international brand architecture and how these varied across firms. The factors that underlay the formation of these patterns were also studied as well as how these were evolving in the light of the changing international environment. Also of interest, was whether or not the firm had an explicit international brand architecture, or policies for harmonizing national branding structures and for managing international brands.

The study consisted of semi-structured interviews conducted with 24 senior executives. These executives were either at the product division level in major consumer goods companies, or in advertising agencies, market research companies, and consulting companies who were responsible for international brands and branding strategies. All were based in Europe, either with European companies, or the European divisions of major US companies. This information was supplemented by secondary data – such as company reports, journal and newspaper articles on other companies, etc.

The interviews typically lasted between one and a half to two hours and followed an interview protocol relating to the firm's branding strategy in international markets. This covered issues relating to the firm's brand architecture and how this had evolved, as well as the relative importance placed on corporate- as opposed to product-level brands. The underlying rationale, as well as whether the firm had an explicit policy with regard to international brand architecture and the management of brands in international markets were also discussed, as well as issues relating to the international coordination of national branding structures and policy.

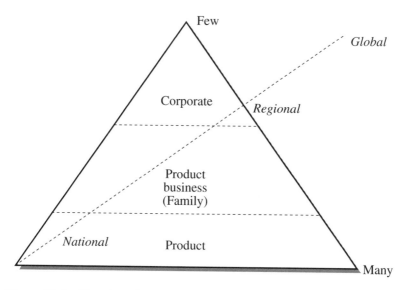

Figure 13.1   Firm brand architecture

A Framework for Examining International Brand Architecture

Overall, the results of the study suggest that a firm's international brand architecture can be categorized based on three key dimensions: the level of the brand within the organization; the geographic scope of the brand (i.e. the number of countries in which the brand is marketed); and the product scope (i.e. number of products on which the brand was used). These three dimensions provide the basis for defining their role in the firm's international marketing strategy as shown in Figure 13.1.

Organizational level
The primary dimension for classifying brands is their level in the organization. This ranges from the corporate level, the product business or group level to the product or product variant level.

Corporate level   Corporate brands rely on the use of the corporate name or logo to establish brand identity in the marketplace. For Phillips, Benetton, Shell, Apple and Nike, the corporate logo is an important element in creating a visual identity for the firm (Schmitt and Simenson 1997). Use of corporate branding typically occurs among firms organized by product lines or divisions, often with a highly centralized structure.

Product business level   Typically, firms with a number of diverse product businesses tend to emphasize brands at the product business level. For example, Unilever uses names such as Walls and Algida for its ice-cream business, and uses the Calvin Klein brand in personal products. Similarly, Philip Morris has multiple cigarette brands and uses the Kraft brand for its cheese products, Nabisco for its biscuits, and Miller for its beer.

Product level   This is most common where marketing and advertising strategy are developed and managed separately for each product line, as, for example, by brand managers. For example, P&G uses the Pampers brand for diapers in North America, Latin America, Europe, Middle East, Africa and Asia, and owns brands such as Camay in personal hygiene and Pert Plus and Pantene in shampoos.

Geographic scope
The second dimension is that of the number and breadth of markets in which the brand was used. This is clearly related to the level of branding insofar as corporate brands were invariably used in all markets in which the company sold its products. However, at the product business level and more frequently the product level, the same brand is not necessarily used in all geographic markets in which the product business operated. The geographic scope of the brand could therefore range from global, regional or several-country markets to a single-country market, or even a region within a country.

Global   Corporate brands are invariably global in scope unless the company only operates in a limited number of geographic markets or regions of the world, as for example, Kao. At the product business or product group level some brands are global, especially where the company is organized by product division. For example, the Nivea brand is used worldwide by Beiersdorf for its skin products. Equally, Mars uses the Pedigree brand name for its dog food products worldwide. At the product level, brands are also sometimes global in scope. P&G typically uses the same product brands worldwide, for example, Pantene, Head and Shoulders, Pert Plus and Pampers. Equally, Unilever owns international brands such as Bertolli olive oil and Lipton tea, and has obtained through the acquisition of Best Foods, Hellmann's, Knorr dehydrated soups, and condiments, etc.

Regional   In some cases, product division or product group brands are regional or used in some markets or regions but not in others. For example, Unilever uses the Walls brand for its ice-cream business in the UK and all new markets it enters, such as China, except those where a local ice-cream business with an established brand such as Ola or Algida has been acquired. Similarly, Nestlé has a number of regional brands at the product division or group level, such as the Stouffer brand name used on frozen foods in the USA, and the Contadina brand of tomato and spaghetti sauce products (Parsons 1996). Product-level brands are also sometimes regional in scope, as for example, Euro-brands, or brands used on products in Eastern Europe. In the detergent industry, brands are often regional in scope. For example, P&G has brands such as Ariel and Vizir in Europe, and Tide and Cheer in the USA.

National Equally some brands are national in scope. These are typically at the product level, except in the case of extremely large national markets, such as the USA or China, where companies may have product businesses that operate independently or only have operations in that market (for example, Unilever's Stouffer frozen entrées and dinners is only used in the USA).

In some instances these brands relate to niche products that are sold in single- or at most two-country markets, such as Nestlé's Marmite brand of vegetable extract, which is marketed only in the UK and in Australia under the Vegemite brand. In other cases, the same or very similar products may be sold in different countries under different brand names, as, for example, Unilever's low fat margarine is sold under the name Flora in the UK and Germany, and Promise in the USA.

Product scope
The third component is related to the number of product lines on which a brand is used, or conversely the diversity of brands within a given product line. Beiersdorf uses the Nivea brand name for its major product lines including skin care, lip care, hair care, body wash, deodorant and hand care products. The Futuro brand is used for health support products such as hosiery and arm supports. The Juvena and La Prairie brands are used for advanced skin care and cosmetic products. P&G uses a range of brands within most of its product lines. For example, P&G has 23 different brands of powder detergents including Ariel, Cheer, Fairy, Tide and Vizir. In addition, P&G has 12 liquid detergents. All but three of these are also powder detergent brands. P&G also has six brands of bar detergents and two of the brands, Ariel and Tide, are used for powder and liquid detergent.

The range of products on which a brand is used is both a function of the level of the brand within the organization, and the diversity of the firm's product offering. At the corporate level, the number of product lines on which the brand is used will depend on the number of product businesses of the firm and the diversity of their product lines. For example, the Disney brand is used on movies, books, toys, clothing, theme parks, etc. Similarly, the Phillips brand is used on all the firm's product businesses, on products ranging from TVs and audio-equipment to light bulbs.

Equally at the product business or group level the range of products which a brand covers is likely to be a function of the breadth of the product lines in the business or product group. In some cases, however, a firm may have different brands for different product lines that are targeted or positioned toward different customers, as for example, private label, or premium vs. mass-market segments, or different age groups. For example, Benetton has the Sisley clothing brand targeted to young fashion-conscious consumers, as well as the Benetton brand.

TYPOLOGY OF BRANDING STRUCTURES

Consistent with the typology proposed by Olins (1989) and the findings of a single-country study by Laforêt and Saunders (1994), this study revealed three major patterns of brand architecture: corporate-dominant, product-dominant and hybrid or mixed structures (see Figure 13.2). There is, however, considerable variation even within a given type of structure depending to a large extent on the firm's administrative heritage and international expansion strategy as well as the degree of commonality among product lines or product businesses. In addition, these structures are continually evolving in response to the changing configuration of markets or as a result of the firm's expansion strategy in international markets.

Corporate-dominant architecture tends to be most common among firms with a relatively limited range of products or product divisions, or with a clearly defined target market, e.g. Shell, Kellogg's, Nike, Benetton, etc. Product-dominant architecture, on the other hand, is typically found among firms such as Akzo Nobel with multiple national or local brands, or firms such as P&G or Mars that had expanded internationally by leveraging 'power' brands. The most common are hybrid or mixed structures, consisting of a mix of global corporate, regional and national product-level brands, or corporate endorsement of product brands or different structures for different product divisions.

Both corporate- and product-dominant structures are evolving towards hybrid structures. Firms with corporate-dominant structures are adding brands at other levels, for example, the house or product level, to differentiate between different product divisions. Product-dominant structures, on the other hand, especially where these emphasized multiple local (national) brands are moving toward greater integration or coordination

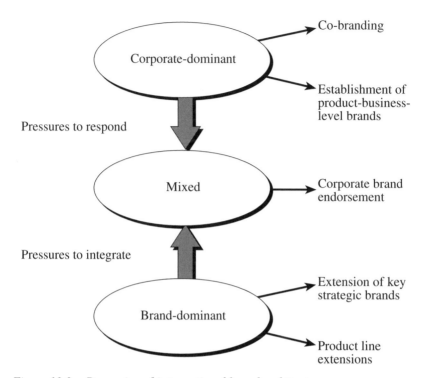

Figure 13.2   Dynamics of international brand architecture

across markets through corporate endorsement of local products. These companies also vary in the extent to which they have a clearly articulated international brand architecture to guide this evolution. Some, for example, lay out the different levels at which brands were to be used, the interrelation between brands at different levels, and the geographic scope of each brand and the product lines on which a brand was to be used, while others have few or no guidelines concerning international branding. (For an example of Nestlé's international brand architecture, see Parsons, 1996.)

Corporate-dominant Branding

A few of the companies studied have a very simple brand structure based on the corporate name, as for example, Shell, Phillips, etc. In general, these are business-to-business organizations with a heavy emphasis on corporate branding, or a relatively narrow and coherent product line. Other cases include consumer goods companies focused on a global target segment such as Nike or Benetton (Court et al. 1997). Their prime objective is to establish a strong global identity for the brand rather than respond to local market conditions. A recent survey showed that the top ten brands worldwide were all corporate brands (Khermouch, Holmes and Ihlwan, 2001). In some instances, the corporate logo and visual identification (Apple and Nike) play a major role in identifying the brand and defining brand image worldwide.

Product-dominant Branding

Other companies, for example, P&G and Reckitt Benckiser, use a product-dominant strategy. This strategy is common among US firms who had expanded internationally by leveraging 'power' brands, as, for example, P&G with brands such as Camay and Pampers. Firms with domestic product-dominant structures that have expanded by acquiring national companies often acquire a substantial number of national and local product brands, in addition to their own global and regional product brands. For example, Reckitt Benckiser has international product brands such as Dettol, Woolite, and Harpic, as well as national product brands such as Dettox surface cleanser sold only in the UK.

A few international companies, though this seemed to be rare, have structures consisting almost exclusively of national product brands. Often these are well-established traditional brand names known for their quality and reliability. For example, Akzo Nobel owns brands such as Diamond Salt in the USA and Sikkens's paint brand in Europe. Products are tailored to local preferences and product innovation is relatively low. Since customer preferences are highly localized with few links across national boundaries, management sees few potential synergies from harmonizing brands across borders.

Hybrid Branding Strategies

A number of companies have hybrid brand structures with a combination of corporate and product brands. Coca-Cola, for example uses the Coca-Cola name on its cola brand worldwide, with product variants such as Cherry Coke, Coke Lite, Diet Coke or caffeine-free Coke, in some, but not all countries. In addition, Coca-Cola has a number of local or regional soft drink brands, such as Lilt in various fruit flavors in the UK, TabXtra, a sugar-free cola drink in Scandinavia, and Cappy, a fruit drink in Eastern Europe and Turkey (Echikson and Foust 2000).

In other cases, companies use the corporate name for some product businesses, but not on others. Mars, for example, uses the Mars name on its ice-cream, soft drink and confectionery lines, but used the Pedigree house brand for pet food. This is intended to create separate and distinct images for the confectionery and pet food businesses. Similarly, Danone uses the Dannon/Danone name on yogurt worldwide, on bottled water in the USA and on cookies in China and Malaysia. Danone also owns the Lu and Jacob brands which are used on biscuits in Europe, Asia, the USA, India, and Brazil, as well as other bottled water brands such as Evian, sold worldwide, Volvic and Badoit only sold in France, as well as Kronenbourg and Kanterbrau beers, and Vivagel and Marie frozen foods in Europe.

Other companies have different brand architectures in different product divisions. For example, Unilever has predominantly global brands in its personal products division. The yellow fats division consists mostly of local brands with some harmonization in positioning or brand name across countries. Other foods are global product brands, while the ice-cream division had a combination of local and global product brands such as Magnum, Cornetto and Solero. These are endorsed by country or regional house brands such as Walls and Algida, and all share a common logo worldwide.

THE EVOLUTION OF INTERNATIONAL BRAND ARCHITECTURE

A firm's brand architecture is continually evolving. As it enters new countries or markets, acquired brands are integrated into the architecture, new brand extensions or product lines are added, and positioning may be modified or radically changed. With rising media, promotional costs and the trend towards globalization, brand architecture is increasingly subject to pressures at both the corporate and product levels to become more cost effective and better integrated across country markets. As a result, increasingly complex brand structures are beginning to emerge, characterized by corporate endorsement of product brands in order to consolidate branding structure, and by extension of strong brands across countries and product businesses so as to achieve cost economies.

Corporate Endorsement

International expansion and consumers' need for reassurance about product quality and reliability is resulting in a shift toward corporate endorsement of product brands. This helps to forge a global corporate identity for the firm as it gathers its products under a global umbrella, thus generating potential cost savings through promotion of the global corporate brand, rather than multiple independent product brands (Melewar and

Saunders 1999). At the same time, endorsement by the corporate brand provides reassurance for the customer of a reliable corporate image and enhances visibility.

Corporate endorsement of product-level brands is also increasingly used as a mechanism to integrate brand structure across country markets, providing a unifying element across product offerings. For example, Cadbury uses the Cadbury name on all its confectionery products, in conjunction with product brands such as Dairy Milk, Whispers, etc. Equally, a house brand is sometimes used on a product business worldwide. For example, Akzo Nobel places the Sikkens name on all its paint products. The relative size of the corporate or house name and the brand name varies from one company to another. In some cases, e.g. Cadbury or Nestlé, the corporate brand has equal prominence to the product name. In other cases, it is smaller and used primarily as an endorsement rather than an identifier.

In some cases, the prominence and role of the corporate brand or logo varies from country to country. For example, Douwe Egbert uses the Friesen lady logo on its coffee in all countries, but the size of the lady and also the positioning statement vary from country to country. In Spain, for example, the positioning emphasizes the richness of the coffee and the master brewer. In the UK it emphasizes its continental taste, and in Holland the association with family and comfort are featured.

Brand Extension

At the same time, rising media costs, coupled with the importance of building high visibility and the need to obtain cost economies, create pressures to extend strong brands across product lines and country borders. Increasingly, new products and variants are launched under existing brand names to take advantage of their strength and consumer awareness. Mars, for example, has launched an ice-cream line as well as a soft drink under the Mars brand name. Cadbury's Milk Tray brand has been extended to desserts, leveraging the brand's association with creaminess.

Strong international brands often have high visibility and are prime candidates for brand extensions, especially for entry into new and emerging markets such as Eastern Europe or China. In some cases, a well-known brand name is used on a product line which is marketed under another brand name elsewhere. For example, Danone uses the Danone name to market biscuits in China and Malaysia in order to leverage customer familiarity with the name. Similarly, Nestlé's Maggi brand, used on sauces and seasonings, has high recognition in Eastern Europe and so was extended to frozen foods prior to divesture of this division in 1999.

DIRECTIONS FOR FUTURE RESEARCH

Building a clear and coherent brand architecture is a critical component of the firm's international market strategy. A well-articulated brand architecture provides guidance for managers and helps ensure that the value of the firm's brands is maximized across markets. Key to the establishment of an effective brand architecture is the identification of how brands are used at different levels of the organization and the interrelationship between these different levels (Douglas, Craig and Nijssen 2001). The geographic scope of each brand and the range of product categories on which a brand will be used also have to be determined. Building this architecture provides a framework to coordinate and harmonize branding strategy across countries and develop a strong and consistent identity for the firm's products in the global marketplace.

Relatively few firms appear to have established such an explicit architecture or developed the principles to guide its construction and management (for a counterexample, see Parsons 1996). Rather, a firm's brand structure tends to evolve on an ad hoc and piecemeal basis, as new brands are acquired or new products developed. The firm's brand structure is thus continually changing as the firm grows, and must be monitored to ensure that this structure maintains a balance and is both internally coherent and consistent across countries and product markets.

The lack of attention among academics to examining brand architecture and understanding the principles guiding the building of an effective brand architecture in an international market setting underscores the importance of further research. First, a better grasp of patterns of international brand architecture and the key components is needed in order to identify relevant issues. Here, an important first step is to identify the role of firm-specific drivers, which account for differences between firms. Furthermore, brand architecture is continually evolving as the firm grows and expands in international markets. Consequently, research into the evolution of these patterns, and trends toward corporate brand endorsement and extension of strategic brands into other product markets and countries should be undertaken. Finally, research is needed on effective mechanisms and procedures for managing brand architecture and assigning custody for strategic brands.

Understanding Patterns of Brand Architecture

In the first place, further research is needed to identify and understand patterns of brand architecture. In this chapter, three components of brand architecture have been identified: the level in the organization, the geographic scope of the brand, and the range of products on which it is used. These components need to be verified on a broader sample of firms. Additional elements or complexities may need to be considered. For example, the same product may be sold under different brand names in different countries. Conversely, the same brand name may be used on different product categories in different countries.

An inventory of all brands in a broad sample of firms from different industries, or of different sizes, including diversified, multi-product businesses as well as businesses with a narrow product range, should be conducted in order to verify the generality of the proposed framework. For example, the geographic scope of each brand could be measured based on the number of countries in which it is present, and the product scope, based on the number of distinct product lines on which it is used. The patterns observed for each firm can then be charted and a taxonomy developed based on differences in the patterns, for example, the number of brands at each organizational level, their geographic and product market scope.

Patterns need to be compared across industries, i.e. diversified vs. single product businesses, and by firms of different national origins, i.e. US, European and Japanese firms. This would help determine the extent to which product market structure or firm structure condition the emergence of different architectures as opposed to the macroeconomic environment, national organizational or other contextual factors.

Another critical issue is to determine whether certain architectures are more effective in maximizing the value of brand assets across country markets than others. While complex, research should focus on defining outcome and performance measures linked to different brand architecture and assessing the extent to which different patterns are more effective and under what conditions. While it may be difficult to isolate the impact of brand architecture from other elements of the firm's marketing strategy, a comparison of average performance levels of firms with a similar pattern to those with different patterns will help to provide some initial insights. Performance can be assessed based on a variety of indicators, including long-term measures such as firm visibility, customer brand recognition and awareness, as well as market share, sales growth and cost efficiency at the corporate, product business and product levels. Key principles in redesigning brand architecture to respond to evolving market conditions should also be studied. International markets are changing rapidly and a brand architecture that was appropriate under one set of conditions may no longer be so. This research will begin to reveal how brand strategy and organization affect firm performance. More importantly, it will suggest how brand architecture should be changed to enhance performance.

Examining Firm-specific Drivers of Brand Architecture

Another important issue is to examine firm-specific drivers of international brand architecture. A firm's brand architecture at any given point in time is in large measure a consequence of past management decisions and its response to competitive realities in the marketplace (Douglas, Craig and Nijssen 2001). These in turn reflect the firm's goals and expansion strategy in international markets as well as its organizational structure and corporate philosophy with regard to branding. Investigation of firm-specific factors can thus provide insights into how patterns of brand architecture are formed and evolve.

The firm's organizational structure and administrative heritage often play an important role in fashioning its international brand strategy (Bartlett and Ghoshal 1989). Firms with a decentralized or country-by-country organizational structure where country managers have substantial autonomy typically have a plethora of national brands, whereas those with a centralized structure are likely to have fewer brands launched by local managers targeted to specific local needs. Consequently, firms with a centralized structure or those organized by global product divisions are likely to have more parsimonious streamlined brand architecture. This can be investigated by comparing the number of brands at each level in firms with centralized and decentralized organizational structures.

The firm's international market expansion strategy also impacts patterns of brand architecture and how they evolve (Douglas and Craig 1996). Firms that have expanded by leveraging domestic corporate- or product-level brands are likely to have fewer brands and a more coherent architecture than firms that have expanded by acquiring other firms and hence have to absorb these brands into their structure, resulting in a multiplicity of brands at any given level. Equally, firms that have expanded through strategic alliances may have more complex, dual structures.

The significance attached to corporate identity is another factor influencing brand architecture. Firms such as Sony and Apple that focus on developing a strong corporate identity in international markets are, for example, more likely to focus and emphasize corporate-level brands. In Japan, considerable importance is attached to trust in a company and its reliability. Consequently, corporate- rather than product-level branding is emphasized. However, companies of other national origins such as Siemens, GE, Phillips or Exxon, also emphasize corporate identity. As a result, the underlying rationale and driving force for corporate-level branding merits further investigation.

Examining the Dynamics of International Brand Architecture

Since a firm's architecture is continually evolving, it is important to trace this pattern over time and to identify triggers to changes. This aids in understanding the role and significance of branding in the firm's international strategy and provides insights into the way the firm has attempted to maximize the value of its brand assets at different stages of international market expansion.

In this context, as an increasing number of firms are endorsing local product brands with corporate-level brands to develop international visibility, an important issue is to examine whether and how far this strategy adds value. This can be examined from multiple standpoints. It can be examined in terms of the consumer's standpoint i.e. whether the addition of the corporate brand adds to customer value or enhances the brand's visibility, increases customer recall or enhances customer loyalty and strengthens feelings of trust. Equally, the extent to which corporate endorsement of brands provides greater leverage with retailers, facilitating negotiation of improved shelf placement for the brand, a high number and greater depth of facings might also be investigated.

Similarly, the value of strategic brand extensions might be studied. As firms increasingly designate key brands as 'strategic' international brands, which form the basis for brand or product line extensions in international markets, the impact of these extensions on brand image or brand value needs to be further examined. Extension of a key brand to markedly different product lines or categories often results in dilution. Consequently, the tradeoff between dilution and lower media cost or enhanced image when extending brands to different product categories, or to products with substantially different target segments or channels of distribution, might be investigated.

Equally, the importance of brand positioning consistency across country and product markets needs to be examined. Inconsistent brand positioning across countries can result in ambiguous images and confusion among customers and distributors where there is substantial movement across borders and exposure to images and products from other countries (DeMooij 1997). Again, the impact on brand, image, strength and visibility merits further investigation.

Examining the Management of International Brand Architecture

In addition to further understanding patterns of international brand architecture and their evolution, another important issue relates to the management of international brand architecture. The crucial role of key strategic brands in international markets makes it imperative to assign custody of each brand to an individual or unit within the organization and to establish mechanisms to coordinate and harmonize brand positioning across markets as well as to sanction brand extensions (Aaker and Joachimsthaler 1999).

Widely different approaches can be adopted for managing brands ranging from loosely negotiated solutions between different units within the firm, to the appointment of a brand champion with responsibility for monitoring the brand and authorizing brand extensions. The effectiveness of alternative approaches and the interplay with the firm's organizational structure, the strength of local country managers and the importance of the brand in a given market as well as its history need to be further examined. Better understanding of custody procedures adopted by different firms and in different product markets, as well as barriers to their implementation, will help to shed light on these issues.

The use of various mechanisms to ensure consistency of brand positioning across countries, such as brand manuals, standardized positioning and use of corporate logos and identifiers also needs to be further studied (Schmitt and Simenson 1997). While a wide variety of different procedures and mechanisms are used, relatively little is known about their efficacy, or under what conditions they are most likely to be effective.

CONCLUSION

The central role of branding in establishing the firm's identity and building its position in the global marketplace among customers, retailers and other market participants, makes it increasingly imperative for firms to establish a clear-cut international branding strategy. A key element of success is the framing of a harmonious and consistent brand architecture across countries and product lines, defining the number of levels and brands at each level. Of particular importance is the relative emphasis placed on corporate brands as opposed to product-level brands and the degree of integration across markets. The findings of this exploratory study suggest that there is no one optimal pattern of brand architecture. Each firm has its own unique structure, depending on its prior branding history, mode of expansion, and corporate culture. Further research on these issues is critical, so firms are able to build a strong and coherent identity in international markets and sustain their positional advantage in international markets in the long run.

REFERENCES

Aaker, David (1996), *Building Strong Brands*, New York: Free Press.
Aaker, David and Erich Joachimsthaler (1999), 'The Lure of Global Branding', *Harvard Business Review*, **77** (November/December), 137–44.
Aaker, David and Kevin Keller (1990), 'Consumer Evaluations of Brand Extensions', *Journal of Marketing*, **54** (1), 27–33.
Bartlett, Christopher A. and Sumantra Ghoshal (1989), *Managing Across Borders*, Boston, MA: Harvard Business School Press.
Barwise, Patrick and Thomas Robertson (1992), 'Brand Portfolios', *European Management Journal*, **10** (3), 277–85.
Court, David C., Anthony Freeling, Mark C. Lerter and Andrew J. Parsons (1997), 'If Nike Can "Just Do It" Why Can't We?', *McKinsey Quarterly*, **3**, 25–34.
DeMooij, Marieke (1997), *Global Marketing and Advertising, Understanding Cultural Paradoxes*, Thousand Oaks, CA: Sage.
Douglas, Susan P. and C. Samuel Craig (1996), 'Global Portfolio Planning and Market Interconnectedness', *Journal of International Marketing*, **4** (1), 93–110.
Douglas, Susan P., C. Samuel Craig and Edwin J. Nijssen (2001), 'Integrating Branding Strategy Across Markets: Building International Brand Architecture', *Journal of International Marketing*, **9** (2), 97–114.
Echikson, William and Dean Foust (2000), 'For Coke, Local Is It', *Business Week*, (July 3), 122.
Kapferer, Jean-Noel (1997), *Strategic Brand Management*, 2nd edn, London: Kogan Page.
Keller, Kevin (1998), *Strategic Brand Management*, Englewood Cliffs, NH: Prentice-Hall.
Khermouch, Gerry, Stanley Holmes and Moon Ihlwan (2001), 'The Best Global Brands', *Business Week*, (August 6), 50–57.
Laforêt, Sylvie and John Saunders (1994), 'Managing Brand Portfolios: How the Leaders Do It', *Journal of Advertising Research*, (September/October), 64–76.
Melewar, T.C. and John Saunders (1999), 'International Corporate Visual Identity: Standardization and Localization', *Journal of International Business Studies*, **30** (3), 583–98.
Olins, W. (1989), *Corporate Identity*, London: Thames & Hudson.
Parsons, Andrew (1996), 'Nestlé: The Visions of Local Managers', *McKinsey Quarterly*, **2**, 5–29.
Quelch, John (1999), 'Global Brands: Taking Stock', *Business Strategy Review*, **10** (1), 1–14.
Roth, Marvin S. (1995a), 'Effects of Global Market Conditions on Brand Image Customization and Brand Performance', *Journal of Advertising*, **24** (4), 55–72.
Roth, Marvin S. (1995b), 'The Effects of Culture and Socioeconomics on the Performance of Global Brand Image Strategies', *Journal of Marketing Research*, **32** (May), 163–75.
Schmitt, Bernd H. and Alex Simenson (1997), *Marketing Aesthetics: The Strategic Management of Brands, Identity and Image*, New York: Free Press.

14. Global brands: does familiarity breed contempt?

Johny K. Johansson and Ilkka A. Ronkainen

INTRODUCTION

The recent recognition of strong brand names as a key competitive asset
has led to increased emphasis on the management of a firm's top brands.
Today strategic marketing management involves leveraging brand portfolios so as to maximize brand strength and financial brand equity.
Consequently, given the importance of market expansion in the measurement of brand equity, it is not surprising to see that the emphasis on branding has in turn led to an increased stress on creating global brands. Brand
management, now also a top management preoccupation, involves strong
brand promotions, brand extensions and expansion into new markets,
often overseas.

Resource constraints in the typical firm suggest that managers concentrate their effort behind a few top brands, and focus on product categories
where the firm can claim a leadership position. Thus, an international
expansion strategy typically involves creating high levels of awareness and
a positive image in several markets for a selected few 'global' brands. Global
brands should be found everywhere, and everyone should know of their
existence.

However, since brand equity tends to rise with the 'distinction' or
'esteem' of a brand, an all-out effort to make the brand familiar may not
always be the best strategy. As a brand becomes a familiar presence in a
market, it may lose its aura of distinction and be perceived more as a commonplace good in the eyes of the customer. For example, it is possible that
as people in previously untapped markets become aware and gradually
more familiar with a brand, the brand may also lose some of its sense of
mystery and unattainability. After the initial surge of consumer interest and
trial, the Moscow McDonald's has settled into a predictable and not very
special eatery. When Coors beer was finally made available outside of the
Western states, its cachet pretty soon disappeared. It is not clear, therefore,
that both objectives of higher familiarity and higher esteem can be achieved

simultaneously. Does higher brand familiarity lead to higher or lower esteem? This is the question this study attempts to answer.

In what follows, the way brand equity is typically measured will be presented first. Then the linkage between brand 'familiarity' and the 'global' brand attribute will be explored. The following section presents several alternative predictions concerning the relationship between 'Familiarity' and 'Esteem'. The data against which these alternatives will be tested are then introduced, followed by the results for the 1990 data. These results are analyzed and employed to predict changes for the 1999 data. The analysis of the 1999 data is then presented, including a test of whether being a global brand makes a difference for esteem. The chapter ends with a brief summary and conclusions section.

MEASURING BRAND EQUITY

There are several ways of conceptualizing and measuring brand equity, but they all tend to share certain basic characteristics (Aaker 1996, Ch. 10; Keller 1998, Ch. 10). To get at the financial value of a brand, the typical approach is to analyze the historical brand profit record, and then subtract the level that would have been reached for a comparable generic product. The remaining profits are considered due to the brand itself. The potential future earnings are then forecast based on the assessment of present and future brand strength, and the resulting profit stream is capitalized using a discounted net present value analysis.

The present and future brand strength is typically a multidimensional construct. There have to be some indicators of brand awareness and of brand image (Keller 1998, p. 381). The awareness measures should include not only recall and recognition of the brand name at the individual level, but some measure of how extensive the awareness is, including foreign markets. The image measures need to involve specific perceptions of the unique character of the brand but also its meaning and the favorability of the perceptions. Most publicly available brand equity indices are based on a number of these and related types of indicators. The Interbrand Powerbrand measure of brand equity, for example, uses seven factors weighed together to arrive at an index of brand strength, as shown in Table 14.1.

The maximum scores available for each of the factors show also the relative weight of each factor. For our purposes it is interesting to note that 'Geographic spread' together with 'Leadership' represent the most important factors. Given these weights, it is not surprising to find that companies try very hard to be one of the top brands in each product category

Table 14.1   Seven factors weighted to arrive at an index of brand strength

Factor	Maximum score
Leadership	25
Stability	15
Market	10
Geographic spread	25
Trend	10
Support	10
Protection	5
Total	100

('Leadership') and also attempt to 'globalize' their brands, expanding into more and more markets ('Geographic spread').

When single brand equity scores are based on survey data from consumers, the aggregation is not only across the selected factors. There is also a need to aggregate across individual respondents, and, in the case of data from several countries, across markets. The most typical approach is to average across individuals and the markets selected. This necessarily tends to hide individual differences, and one needs to be careful when interpreting the data. For example, in our case we will be using data on brand 'Familiarity' and brand 'Esteem'. These scores, for a given country market, are computed as the arithmetic mean across the survey respondents in that country. That is, a brand with a score of, say, 4 on a 7-point item of 'Familiarity', might have all respondents around 4, or, alternatively, could have a bipolar distribution with some respondents very low on familiarity and others high. In the first case the brand is relatively well known to everybody, while in the second case the brand is more of a niche brand, very well known to some but not at all to others. In either case the single number is the same. A similar effect can occur if the aggregation is done across countries, as in the Interbrand case, and holds also for the 'Esteem' scores.

This ambiguity affects any analytical results for such data, including the results presented later in this study. In particular, one cannot hope to identify whether the hypothesis that higher familiarity breeds contempt, if supported, reflects an individual's reaction to a boring familiarity or a sense of the brand not being exclusive enough. This is because high familiarity scores coupled with low esteem scores can come from either extreme cases of a few individual scores (the boredom case) or relatively high familiarity and low esteem scores from the majority of the sample (the lack of exclusivity case).

LINKING 'FAMILIARITY' TO 'GLOBAL'

Strictly speaking this study is about brand 'familiarity', not 'global' branding. As will be seen, it couches the theoretical and empirical discussion in terms of level of brand knowledge and familiarity, regardless of whether the brand is global or not. Nevertheless, the impetus for the study is the declared benefit of 'brands' going 'global' by becoming well known in many countries and regions. That is, expansion into a new market of a brand involves necessarily the promotion of the brand to make the potential customers 'aware' of its existence and availability. Typically, the more global the brand, the more people in different countries are aware of and familiar with the brand. As we saw above, this is reflected also in brand equity measures. When knowledge of, or familiarity with, a brand rises, so does brand equity. Thus, one way of building equity in a brand is to make more consumers aware of it, extending it into new markets. 'Global' brands are likely to score higher on 'familiarity' across countries.

Of course, a firm can also raise the amount of knowledge that any one individual possesses, a kind of 'local penetration' strategy. Such promotional efforts are likely to include additional attitudinal factors rather than simple 'awareness' or 'knowledge'. Thus, the firm has to allocate brand-building moneys between new markets (market development) and existing customers (a penetration strategy). Which way the balance is struck depends on many factors, including what measures are used to assess brand equity. For a given level of penetration, however, brand equity will rise with expansion into new markets, not only foreign but also new segments 'at home'.

We do not assume that in any one country a global brand has higher familiarity than a local brand, not even if the global brand is domestic. 'Domestic global' brands are those brands which are globally available (such as Coca-Cola) and which also comes from the respondent's home country (so, for an American, Coca-Cola is a domestic brand). Such a brand might not show higher familiarity than a local domestic brand. For example, RCA, a quintessential 'American' brand with limited presence overseas, might show higher familiarity scores in the USA than, say, Gillette, a perennial 'global' brand with headquarters in Boston (this was actually the case in the 1990 data used below). Accordingly, although such cases might be rare, there is not a simple one-to-one relationship between 'global' reach and brand 'familiarity'.

In this study we focus on relating 'Familiarity' to 'Esteem', trying to tease out the relationship across brands for different countries and across time. We do introduce a split between 'global' and 'local' brands into the analysis, but for the reasons explained, we don't equate 'High Familiarity' with 'Highly Global'.

FAMILIARITY VERSUS ESTEEM

There are at least three alternative explanations why higher brand familiarity would be associated with higher esteem. The simplest explanation might be that well-known brands tend to have higher status. This line of reasoning derives partly from Veblen's famous conspicuous consumption theory. There is plenty of anecdotal evidence to support the idea that well-known luxury brands in particular engender desire and envy, two elements of the conspicuous consumption notion. Furthermore, for some segments where peer group influence is strong (say, teenagers), the cachet of a well-known brand name is likely to go beyond the luxury category (into apparel and shoes, for example).

A second argument in support of a positive relationship derives from research on the role of familiarity in country of origin studies. Here it has been shown that familiarity with a country's products helps reduce the country of origin biases that are typically observed. Thus, even though information about a country's economic and social conditions is used to infer the likely quality of its products, increased familiarity help place the quality judgments on a more product-specific footing. Even when the overall evaluation of a country's capability is less than positive, increased familiarity reduces the degree to which the negative valuation is an obstacle to considering a brand (Johansson et al. 1994). Familiarity seems to create a 'comfort zone' for individual judgment.

A third reason why higher familiarity would lead to higher esteem can be deduced from an efficient market hypothesis. As advanced for, say, advertising spending, the hypothesis suggests that an inferior brand would do best by staying out of the limelight. By contrast, then, the very fact that a brand is heavily advertised is sufficient as a signal of high quality. Similarly, one could argue that high levels of familiarity, however generated, should be associated with a presumption of high quality and esteem. As individuals we might never forget the lemon brands we acquired, but on the whole we would hopefully be better acquainted with more desirable brands.

But there are also reasons why one might expect higher familiarity to be associated with no increase of or even lower esteem. Two possible reasons will be given here.

First, once familiarity is high, there is no longer a need to infer quality from sheer awareness. That is, as opposed to the efficient market hypothesis, one might predict that quality is judged on the basis of direct experience with the brand. Although this post-experience re-evaluation might or might not be lower, one would not a priori expect a positive quality rating. Thus, the correlation between 'familiarity' and 'esteem' would approach zero. Furthermore, drawing on the evidence that customer dissatisfaction generates more emotion than simple satisfaction, one might venture the hypothesis that familiarity is very high when the brand is of very low quality, pushing the correlation into the negative range (see, for example, Zeithaml and Bitner 2000, pp. 36–40).

A simpler explanation for a negative relationship is the possibility that high familiarity brands incur a cost of 'common-ness' among consumers. Although largely a common-sense notion in the 'familiarity breeds contempt' tradition, it is not difficult to derive a similar prediction from the typical branding discussions. For example, when a luxury brand loses its exclusivity because of lower-end product-line extensions, one would expect 'Esteem' also to come down. When 'almost everyone' drives a Mercedes, the Veblen effect is reduced. Brand equity might still be rising because of increased 'Relevance', but a higher 'Familiarity' rating might be accompanied by lower 'Esteem' scores.

It is very likely that there is also a product-specific effect involved in the relationship between familiarity and esteem, even if the database is too small to investigate it here. In the case of convenience goods, one would expect the relationship to be positive, familiarity positively related to the ease of choosing in the store and trusting the brand. By contrast, luxury goods might show the opposite pattern, with scarcity necessary for high esteem but also leading to low familiarity.

THE LANDOR BRAND DATA

The data used to check these alternative predictions empirically were drawn from the data base collected by Landor Inc., a Young & Rubicam affiliate specializing in brand research. Drawing on large representative surveys of consumers in different countries, the Landor Brand Asset Valuator (BAV) model is built around four main constructs: Differentiation, Relevance, Esteem and Knowledge.

The differentiation construct identifies how distinctive a brand is in the marketplace. A high differentiation score suggests that the brand has unique competitive advantages while a low score makes it difficult to pursue anything but a low cost strategy. The relevance construct indicates whether a brand has personal relevance for the respondent. Is it meaningful to the respondent and personally appropriate? A brand which is highly relevant to a number of people suggests that the size of the potential target market is large.

Esteem measures whether the brand is held in high regard and considered the best in its class. This measure is closely related to perceived quality and the extent to which the brand is growing in popularity. Knowledge is a measure of the degree to which individuals know what a brand represents and stands for. A brand that scores high on knowledge tends to be very familiar to respondents. This multi-item measure of knowledge is not identical to the single-item familiarity measure often used in surveys ('On a scale from 1 through 7, how familiar are you with this brand?'), but captures a sense of intimacy which represents a deeper meaning of familiarity (Aaker 1996, p. 307). In the analysis presented here, the knowledge scores are used as the 'Familiarity' measures.

The first two constructs 'Differentiation' and 'Relevance' together make up what Landor calls Brand Strength. A brand's strength is calculated as the arithmetic mean of the differentiation and the relevance scores. 'Knowledge' and 'Esteem' together make up what Landor calls Brand Stature, measured as the average of a brand's 'Knowledge' and 'Esteem' scores.

In the data collection, multiple indicators are used for the constructs. The brand names are identified in the questionnaires, and Landor claims that virtually all the major brands in a country are listed. By rotating brand names across questionnaires it is possible to cover a large number of brands without fatiguing the respondent (Owen 1993).

The Landor cross-country surveys were done in 1990 and again in 1999 (a Japanese survey was run in 1997). The representative surveys are exhaustive, large sample studies covering several countries and hundreds of brands. Although the studies are proprietary and the company is reluctant to give out many details, some information is available. For example, the 1990 survey covered 2000 brands in the USA alone with a sample size of 5000 respondents. In the same year 13 other countries were covered, with the number of brands ranging from 400 (Poland) to 1600 (UK). Eight Western European countries were covered with 500 respondents each, while Japan had 1000 respondents. The 1999 data had even wider coverage.

From the 1990 survey, the data available for this study consisted of the 'Familiarity' and 'Esteem' scores for the top brands in each of eight different countries. The top brands were identified based on their average score on the two measures (the Brand Stature measure). The countries included were France, Germany, Italy, Japan, Spain, Sweden, UK and the USA. The top 50 brands were available for the USA and Japan, the top 25 brands for the remaining countries.

The 1999 data available (1997 for Japan) covered the same countries, but were extended to include the top 50 brands for all eight countries. However, the company refused to reveal the actual scores on 'Familiarity' and 'Esteem', instead supplying the rankings of the top brands on both measures. Furthermore, the top brands for the 1999 data were selected on the basis of 'Relevance', also different from the 1990 data. Thus, the data are not strictly comparable, although our judgment is that the differences are not serious since the study does not follow individual brands over time. In addition, of course, the alternative hypotheses presented above do not deal with over-time changes.

THE 1990 RESULTS

Given that the 'Familiarity' and 'Esteem' scores in the 1990 data were computed from multiple indicators, it seems reasonable to use standard Pearson correlation measures to measure the bivariate relationship between 'Familiarity' and 'Esteem'. The results for the eight countries are given in Table 14.2.

Table 14.2 The 1990 data

USA	− 0.126 (0.384)	n.s. ($n = 50$)
UK	− 0.074 (0.725)	n.s. ($n = 25$)
France	− 0.004 (0.984)	n.s. ($n = 25$)
Spain	− 0.301 (0.143)	n.s. ($n = 25$)
Sweden	− 0.117 (0.578)	n.s. ($n = 25$)
Italy	− 0.364 (0.074)	sig.? ($n = 25$)
Japan	− 0.424 (0.002)*	sig. ($n = 50$)
Germany	0.508 (0.010)*	sig. ($n = 25$)

Note: Correlation coefficients between 'Familiarity' and 'Esteem' (sig. levels, sample size in parenthesis; * = sig. at 0.05 level; n.s. = not significant).

The results are somewhat perplexing. The lack of a significant relationship in the first five countries suggests that when seen across a variety of brands as done here, the empirical evidence suggests that on average 'Familiarity' and 'Esteem' are simply not correlated. On the other hand, in Italy possibly, and in Japan unequivocally, the relationship is negative, supporting the 'familiarity breeds contempt' hypothesis. Then comes Germany with an equally forceful positive relationship, suggesting that Germans at least hold familiar brands in higher regard.

EXPLAINING THE 1990 RESULTS

Trying to resolve the paradox, we went back to the data to look at exactly what the top brands in different countries were. One piece of information which we already had been aware of was that to a surprising extent (to us) the top brands in each country were domestic (although many still global). For example, in the case of the United States, the first non-domestic brand was Sony in 37th place. In Germany 24 of 25 top brands were domestic, Lego from Denmark appearing in 18th place. Japan had five non-domestic brands among its top 25. Only the results for the other European countries were as we had expected, with domestic and foreign brands more evenly mixed.

One possible explanation for the significantly negative results in Japan (and to a lesser extent in Italy) would be the cultural explanation that domestic brands were rated lower on 'Esteem' than foreign brands. This would align with the notion that in Japan 'foreignness' provides a cachet, a remnant of the historical isolation and remoteness of the country. This was tested by running the correlation between a dummy variable indicating 'Domestic' brand. This correlation was significantly negative at -0.231 (sig. level 0.107), suggesting that the esteem of domestic brands was systematically lower than for foreign brands, and offering support for this cultural-based hypothesis. A similar analysis of the Italian data by contrast yielded a correlation coefficient of 0.128 (sig. level 0.542), which, although insignificantly different from zero, at least was in the other direction, not supporting any pro-foreignness on the part of the Italians.

A similar culture-based hypothesis that the positive relationship in Germany is due to a pro-domestic sentiment on the part of the Germans could perhaps be advanced. However, with the lack of foreign brands in the database, this hypothesis could not be tested.

EXPECTATIONS FOR THE 1999 DATA

Given the results for the 1990 data, what could one expect from a replication on the 1999 data? Here it is useful first to entertain the basic hypothesis that as globalization proceeds, with trade barriers lower and equalization between countries' marketplaces, a 'liberalization' hypothesis would suggest that the more artificial market effects would disappear. One such artificial effect is the 'pent-up' demand in newly opened markets – the McDonald's in Moscow effect alluded to in the beginning of the chapter. Relatedly, consumers in these new markets should become more experienced and sophisticated, less awed by distant and 'foreign' products and brands. There should be a slackening off of any provincialism, and an increase in the efficiency of the market. A strong brand would need to earn its cachet honestly, so to speak. Over time, the more familiar brands would also be the ones with the highest esteem, as people bought the best they could.

Thus, for the 1999 data, it seemed possible that the basic pattern might be construed to generate a more positive relationship between 'Familiarity' and 'Esteem'. As globalization progressed in the 1990s, open markets and free trade created a more competitive marketplace in many countries. If so, the efficient market hypothesis and its stress on visibility as a signal of quality could be used to suggest that higher 'Familiarity' should lead to higher 'Esteem'.

At the same time, however, the actual experience with the new brands might prove less than rewarding, the economic wherewithal to partake of the new affluence might not be readily forthcoming, and the resulting frustration could lead to the kind of anti-globalization attitude already witnessed in some parts of the world. Then there could be increasing avoidance of global brands despite higher esteem, and a turn towards a domestic local brand regardless of perceived quality. In terms of familiarity and esteem, the result would be to turn the relationship negative, the more familiar local brands rated lower on esteem but garnering the sales.

In the end, the relationship might stay the same, with low or no correlation between 'Familiarity' and 'Esteem', and possibly eliminating the significant correlations for Japan and German. That is, as globalization progressed through the 1990s, the cachet of 'foreignness' would evaporate in the Japanese market (although there might still be specific country of origin effects). There would be no significant influence from the split between foreign and domestic, possibly also neutralizing any German pro-domestic sentiment. Since data for 50 brands were available for each country in the 1999 database, these expectations could be tested out.

THE 1999 RESULTS

Because the 1999 data consisted of rankings rather than multiple scale scores, the proper analysis involves non-parametric statistics. The Spearman rank correlations between 'Familiarity' and 'Esteem' are given in Table 14.3.

Even though the figures are not strictly comparable, as can be seen in Table 14.3, the results are quite different from 1990. With the exceptions of France and Spain, where the correlations are still insignificantly different from zero, all correlations are now significantly positive. Even Italy and Japan, previously negative, now show a pattern where higher 'Familiarity' is associated with higher 'Esteem'. Since the results are in line with the globalization and efficient market hypothesis, one might venture the interpretation that globalization has helped make the markets more 'rational' in the economists' sense. By contrast, France seems relatively untouched by the

Table 14.3   The 1999 data

USA	0.483 (0.000)*	sig. ($n = 50$)
UK	0.515 (0.000)*	sig. ($n = 50$)
France	− 0.003 (0.983)	n.s. ($n = 50$)
Spain	0.127 (0.379)	n.s. ($n = 50$)
Sweden	0.496 (0.000)*	sig. ($n = 50$)
Italy	0.392 (0.005)*	sig. ($n = 50$)
Japan 1997	0.432 (0.002)*	sig. ($n = 50$)
Germany	0.486 (0.000)*	sig. ($n = 50$)

Note: Spearman rank correlations between 'Familiarity' and 'Esteem' (sig. levels, sample size in parenthesis; * = sig. at 0.05 level; n.s. = not significant).

globalization forces, a not uninteresting result considering its stubborn insistence on cultural purity.

With a larger sample of 50 top brands in each country, the 1999 data also makes it possible to do the 'Domestic' versus 'Foreign' brand split by country. Creating the dummy variable, its correlation with 'Familiarity' was significantly positive in every country. That is, in every country consumers were overall more familiar with domestic brands than with foreign brands. Running the same correlation between 'Domestic' and 'Esteem', the extent of pro-domestic (or pro-foreign) bias was checked. With one exception, these correlations were uniformly insignificant, even in the case of Japan where a pro-foreign sentiment had existed in 1990. The exception was Germany, where the correlation between 'Domestic' and 'Esteem' ran at 0.386, with a significance level of 0.006. In 1999 the Germans held domestic brands in higher esteem than foreign brands.

Since a domestic brand may or may not be a global brand, the brands in the 1999 database were then coded 'Global' or 'Local' (more precisely 'Non-global') by judgment. Although a judgmental procedure is by definition imperfect, the majority of the brands clearly fall into one or the other category, and anyway, by changing the coding in questionable cases and doing a sensitivity analysis of the results it is possible to derive quite credible results. Given the relatively small samples sizes in the present study, the results should still be seen as quite tentative.

The first analysis was to simply check whether 'Global' brands scored higher or lower on familiarity and esteem than 'Local' brands. The results are given in Table 14.4.

When interpreting the results, note that the 'null hypothesis' average rank for the set of 50 brands will be 25.5 for both 'Familiarity' and 'Esteem'. As can be seen in Table 14.4, global brands scored significantly higher in

Table 14.4   The 1999 data

	Familiarity			Esteem			(%) Global brand
	Global	Local	(sig.)	Global	Local	(sig.)	
USA	19.6	28.5	(0.040)*	24.5	26.0	(0.724)	34
UK	29.1	22.7	(0.129)	24.2	26.5	(0.576)	44
France	28.0	23.7	(0.307)	22.4	27.7	(0.208)	42
Spain	27.0	24.4	(0.537)	22.8	27.6	(0.253)	44
Sweden	25.6	25.5	(0.984)	24.4	26.2	(0.668)	40
Italy	26.6	24.5	(0.619)	20.3	29.7	(0.021)*	48
Japan 1997	27.2	24.6	(0.550)	19.6	28.8	(0.031)*	36
Germany	27.1	24.1	(0.475)	25.4	25.3	(0.983)	44

Note: Average ranks of 'Familiarity' and 'Esteem' for global brands (significance of difference with 'Local' in parenthesis; * = sig. at the 0.05 level).

'Familiarity' than local brands only in the United States (lower scores indicate a higher rank). In terms of 'Esteem', there is significantly higher esteem for global brands only in Italy and Japan. There is no evidence of any negative effects from the 'Global' attribute at all.

Next the correlations between 'Familiarity' and 'Esteem' were re-run for 'Global' brands only. If there were some negative effects from globality, these correlations would differ from those in Table 14.3. They would possibly show a negative correlation, indicating that higher familiarity with global brands was associated with lower esteem. Or, even if there were no negative relationships, the positive correlations in Table 14.3 would be lower. The resulting correlations are given in Table 14.5.

With one exception, the results are very similar to the correlations in Table 14.3. The relationship between familiarity and esteem is clearly positive also when only global brands are analyzed. Given the smaller sample sizes, it is even surprising how robust the positive relationship seems to be. Note also that because of the relative lack of significant differences in Table 14.4, looking only at 'Global' brands does not mean that only one tail of each distribution is included, a typical problem when analyzing sub-samples.

The one glaring exception is Japan. Here a previously very strong positive relationship (correlation of 0.432 in Table 14.3) has been reduced to a mere 0.154. Checking the standard error of the estimate in Table 14.3 yields a figure of 0.130, suggesting that the drop in the correlation coefficient is statistically significant at the 0.05 level. Doing a sensitivity analysis by re-coding five more brands into the 'Global' category (including Bandai and

Table 14.5   The 1999 data, 'Global' brands only

USA	0.447 (0.072)	sig.? ($n=17$)
UK	0.600 (0.003)*	sig. ($n=22$)
France	0.212 (0.356)	n.s. ($n=21$)
Spain	0.127 (0.379)	n.s. ($n=50$)
Sweden	0.467 (0.038)*	sig. ($n=20$)
Italy	0.623 (0.001)*	sig. ($n=24$)
Japan 1997	0.154 (0.542)	n.s. ($n=18$)
Germany	0.381 (0.080)	sig.? ($n=22$)

Note: Spearman rank correlations between 'Familiarity' and 'Esteem' (sig. levels, sample size in parenthesis; * = sig. at the 0.05 level; n.s. = not significant).

Table 14.6   The 1999 data estimated regression coefficients

	Coefficients		Adjusted R-square
	Familiarity	Global	
USA	0.51 (0.000)*	2.97 (0.466)	0.21 ($n=50$)
UK	0.56 (0.000)*	− 5.89 (0.111)	0.28 ($n=50$)
France	0.02 (0.868)	− 5.40 (0.209)	0.01 ($n=50$)
Spain	0.14 (0.322)	− 5.16 (0.220)	0.01 ($n=50$)
Sweden	0.50 (0.000)*	− 1.88 (0.617)	0.22 ($n=50$)
Italy	0.42 (0.002)*	− 10.22 (0.006)*	0.25 ($n=50$)
Japan 1997	0.46 (0.000)*	− 10.40 (0.007)*	0.28 ($n=50$)
Germany	0.49 (0.000)*	− 1.37 (0.711)	0.21 ($n=50$)

Note: 'Esteem' regressed on 'Familiarity' and 'Global' (significance levels, sample size in parenthesis; * = sig. at the 0.05 level).

Kirin) increased the correlation coefficient to 0.279, with a significance level of 0.197. With the small sample size limiting the degrees of freedom, the indication still is that the more global brands have a weaker 'Familiarity' to 'Esteem' relationship in Japan.

It is likely that these results are due to the significant effect of globality on the esteem rankings for Japan shown in Table 14.4 above. Testing this out can be done by running a regression of 'Esteem' on both 'Familiarity' and 'Global'. For completeness, this was done for all the countries. The results are presented in Table 14.6.

As can be seen, the relationship between 'Familiarity' and 'Esteem' stays very much the same as in the bivariate analysis in Table 14.3. The difference here is that the effect from the 'Global' variable adds a cachet to the esteem for Japan and for Italy (remember that the negative sign pushing the 'Esteem' score down implies that the ranking actually rises). Thus, in line with the results for Table 14.4, for those two countries a global brand seems to fetch a cachet. The negative signs for the other countries, although insignificant, are in line with this result. Only the United States estimate differs, but the global coefficient is statistically insignificant.

SUMMARY AND CONCLUSIONS

According to these empirical results from 1999 across a wide variety of brands in eight different countries, a high level of brand 'Familiarity' seems to be associated with higher levels of 'Esteem'. Possibly due to the progress of globalization – including the promotional efforts of firms 'going global' – this pattern has largely emerged over the 1990s. In the less global markets of 1990, intimate familiarity with a brand was no guarantee that the brand was perceived to be superior. Brands with high familiarity in a country, many local brands only, were apparently not necessarily very highly regarded.

With a larger data set available, the 1999 patterns were analyzed further. Overall, people seem more familiar with domestic brands, but except for Germany there was no indication of lowered esteem for foreign brands. 'Familiarity' with global brands was no different from non-global brands except in the United States where familiarity with global brands was higher. As for 'Esteem', there seems to be no particular preference for either global or local, except in the case of Japan and Italy where global brands were ranked higher in esteem. Analyzing global brands separately, the results suggest that the relationship between familiarity and esteem stays unchanged, the correlations lower only for Japan. Testing this relationship further, it was found that once the effect from familiarity to esteem has been accounted for, the net effect from globality is largely positive, significantly so in the case of Japan and Italy.

The results support the argument that in free and open markets the most visible brands will emerge as winners. Promotional funds spent to create brand awareness and knowledge also help to create esteem. And 'going global' apparently helps esteem as well. But, if the efficient market hypothesis is correct, visibility is not enough. The brand also has to be able to stand closer scrutiny that comes with the limelight. In this sense the results also support globalization, because in free and open markets the best products and brands will win.

REFERENCES

Aaker, David A. (1996), *Building Strong Brands*, New York: Free Press.

Aaker, David A. and Erich Joachimsthaler (2000), *Brand Leadership*, New York: The Free Press.

Alden, Dana L., Jan-Benedict E.M. Steenkamp and Rajeev Batra (1999), 'Brand Positioning Through Advertising in Asia, North America and Europe: The Role of Global Consumer Culture', *Journal of Marketing*, **63** (January), 75–87.

Batra, Rajeev (2001), *Consumer Evaluation of Global Brands*, Presentation at the Conference on Global Branding, Georgetown University, 4–6 May.

DeMooij, Marieke (1998), *Global Marketing and Advertising: Understanding Cultural Paradoxes*. Thousand Oaks, CA: Sage Publications.

Douglas, Susan P., C. Samuel Craig and Edwin J. Nijssen (2001), 'Integrating Branding Strategy Across Markets: Building International Brand Architecture', *Journal of International Marketing*, **9**, (2), 97–114.

Johansson, Johny K., Ilkka A. Ronkainen and Michael R. Czinkota (1994), 'Negative Country-of-Origin Effects: The Case of the New Russia', *Journal of International Business Studies*, **XXV** (1), 157–76.

Kapferer, Jean-Noel (1997), *Strategic Brand Management*, 2nd edn, London: Kogan-Page.

Keller, Kevin Lane (1998), *Strategic Brand Management*, Upper Saddle River, NJ: Prentice-Hall.

Klein, Naomi (2000), *No Logo*, London: Flamingo.

Owen, Stewart (1993), 'The Landor ImagePower Survey: A Global Assessment of Brand Strength', in David A. Aaker and Alexander L. Biel (eds), *Brand Equity and Advertising*. Hillsdale, NJ: Lawrence Erlbaum Associates.

Ricks, David A. (1993), *Blunders in International Business*, Cambridge, MA: Blackwell.

Roth, Martin S. (1995), 'The Effects of Culture and Socioeconomics on the Performance of Global Brand Image Strategies', *Journal of Marketing Research*, **32** (May), 163–75.

Usunier, Jean-Claude (1996), *Marketing Across Cultures*, 2nd edn, London: Prentice-Hall.

Yip, George S. (1992), *Total Global Strategy*, Englewood Cliffs, NJ: Prentice-Hall.

Zeithaml, Valarie A. and Mary Jo Bitner (2000), *Services Marketing*, 2nd edn, Burr Ridge, IL: Irwin/McGraw-Hill.

Zhang, Shi and Bernd H. Schmitt (2001), 'Creating Local Brands in Multilingual International Markets', *Journal of Marketing Research*, **38** (August), 313–25.

15. International advertising research: standardization/adaptation and the future

John K. Ryans, Jr and David A. Griffith

INTRODUCTION

Theoretical advancement necessitates strong theories and frameworks, as well as gestalt shifts in paradigmatic perspectives (Anderson 1983; Hunt 1983). Foundational to the advancement of scientific thought is an underlying theoretical grounding, e.g. systematic related statements, including law-like generalizations that are empirically testable, derived from laws or principles that serve as a basis for prediction, decision and action (Bartels 1951; Hunt 1971). In a critical evaluation of international business research, Sullivan (1998) states that there is a tendency to build consensus through iterative replication or trivial refinement that precludes genuine shifts in intellectual direction. From a theoretical standpoint, Sullivan's (1998) criticism is no more evident than in the field of international advertising research, specifically related to the study of standardization and adaptation.

For nearly eight decades, international advertising standardization has been the central focus of academics and practitioners (Agarwal 1995). Most notably, in the last 40 years, a tremendous growth in academic conjecture and research has focused on this topic (e.g. Levitt 1983; Boddewyn, Soehl and Picard 1986; Baalbaki and Malhotra 1993, 1995; Agarwal 1995; Solberg 2000; Laroche et al. 2001). While the rigor of the research employed in studying the issue has increased significantly over the period, with general frameworks being developed (e.g. Jain 1989) and more sophisticated statistical methodologies employed (e.g. Cavusgil and Zou 1994), the primary underlying elements of research in this area have remained relatively constant. These include researchers' inability to substantiate (or in many cases failure to explore) some of the key underlying assumptions regarding the value of standardization. Further, most research in the area over the last 40 years lacks empirical verification (e.g. Ryans 1969; Levitt

1983; Kernan and Domzal 1993; Harvey 1993) and, of the empirical research that has been conducted, most has been either replicative in nature, or encumbered in small theoretical advances, thus generating a status of stagnation in thought and action related to the topic.

The underlying purpose of this chapter is to critically review prior research in the area of standardization/adaptation of international advertising, thus providing a necessary assessment of the field's progress, and to provide new theoretical directions upon which the field may be able to advance. We begin by discussing the underlying impetus for the topic. Next, we outline the generally accepted components of theory. Employing a selection of seminal advertising standardization/adaptation research we critique the fundamental theories explored from a developmental perspective. And, as such provide insights into the foundational exploratory work and today's confirmatory assessments. Finally, we suggest answers to the question 'where do we go from here?'. In particular, we discuss theories that may provide opportunities to advance the field.

THE HISTORICAL FOUNDATIONS OF ADVERTISING STANDARDIZATION

Early economic theory postulated that economic development was predicated on the surplus of exports over imports (e.g. Smith 1776), under a mercantilistic trade orientation. Under this directive, a manufacturing mentality developed in which nations attempted to increase the amount of exports over imports, often via a minimization of production costs to enhance exports (cf. Vernon 1966). As trade expanded, firms found that their ability to maintain trade imbalances in their favor by focusing solely on the minimization of production costs was no longer economically feasible. The economic and competitive circumstances had changed.

From an evolutionary perspective, marketing thought, and its strategic focus, has developed from simple production and product-related strategies to more outward-oriented strategies placing greater emphasis on consumer and societal needs. Fullerton (1988) noted that a traditional evolutionary view of marketing categorizes marketing philosophy and strategy into specific eras of dominance. For example, the production era of 1870–1930 in the USA was characterized by the advent of mass production and the increase of market supply focused on minimization of costs. This provided lower-priced products not only domestically, but for export markets as well. However, as economic conditions deteriorated during the global depression, firms made a strategic marketing shift from being simple suppliers of low-cost products to product innovators, and then to advocates of their products within the market. As such, the underlying positioning of a firm during the period incurred a shifting asset base from machinery and output to human resources capable of persuading the customer that the firm's products would solve the customer's problems, i.e. a focus shift from products to customers.

Further, during this time period firms began to compete in a new world order, characterized by a greater number of suppliers attempting to obtain scarce consumer buying power. As companies began to expand globally, either via exporting or direct investment, new market strategies needed to be developed, or the existing approaches needed to be examined, to obtain overseas viability. Thus, the stage was set for fundamental decisions regarding a firm's foreign marketing strategies and particularly its advertising programs.

During this growing internationalization initiative, practitioners became widely split over the international advertising standardization issue. This was reflected by the different views in 1923 held by Goodyear's David Brown and Bausch & Lomb's Carl Propson. Whereas Brown (1923) viewed humanity as possessing common attributes, thus allowing for standardization, Propson (1923) argued that adaptation was often necessary to appeal to divergent local markets. Subsequent examples in the early years established a pattern for disagreement on this fundamental issue, with some advertising agency executives and corporate advertising executives perceiving adaptation to be key to global success (Vladimir 1950; Delaforce 1964; Lindsey 1964; Marcus 1964; Sutton 1974; Bari 1979; Theophilopoulos 1979), while others viewed standardization as more appropriate (Cornejo 1958; Elinder 1961; Fatt 1967; Deschampsneufs 1967; Patterson 1967; Barnes 1968; Ettinger 1969; Peebles 1967). From its outset, the focal debate practitioners have engaged in, although a few peripheral topics have been explored, has been the issues of cost savings (via economies of scale) and market similarity (the underlying homogeneity/heterogeneity of consumer needs).

Given the great importance of this debate to practitioners, academics began actively engaging in the study of the issue in the late 1950s (Pratt 1956, etc.) and 1960s (Miracle 1968; Buzzell 1968; Ryans 1969), with the first dissertation on the topic written in 1968 by Donnelly. From this time, research has continued to proliferate on the topic and remained unabated (e.g. Donnelly and Ryans 1969; Green, Cunningham and Cunningham 1975; James and Hill 1991; Kanso 1992; Shao, Shao and Shao 1992; Harvey 1993; Kernan and Domzal 1993; Agarwal 1995; Onkvisit and Shaw 1999; Sirisagul 2000; Solberg 2000; Chandra, Griffith and Ryans 2002). However, although a plethora of research has been conducted, and refinements made, such as the identification of antecedents to advertising standardization or adaptation, little progress has been made related to the development of a unifying theory. In fact, Onkvisit and Shaw (1999) argue that 'almost four decades have passed without providing much of the scientific and direct evidence to confirm or contradict the validity of international advertising standardization.' Thus, the critical issue that is raised is 'why has so little been learned in this area that has consumed so many academic resources?'. To explore this issue, general tenets of social science theory are used to gain greater insights into the field's underlying theory.

INTERNATIONAL ADVERTISING STANDARDIZATION/ADAPTATION: THEORETICAL CRITIQUE

The movement toward theoretical development in the field of marketing derived from the general arguments of whether marketing was an art, in which marketers and marketing scholars applied basic theoretical principles developed in other disciplines to the study of marketing, or whether it was a science, with scientists discovering generalizable laws through systematic research endeavors (Bartels 1951; Hunt 1971, 1983; Anderson 1983). While the debate continues (e.g. Anderson 1994), a basis for either approach is the necessity of a strong underlying theory (i.e., when one creates the theory or merely applies the theory). Similarly, for the field of advertising standardization/adaptation to advance, a strong theoretical foundation is required. As such, one must first delineate the components of theory and then apply those standards to the research in the field.

Theory can be viewed as systematic-related statements, including lawlike generalization that are empirically testable, derived from laws or principles that serve as a basis for prediction, decision and action (Bartels 1951; Hunt 1971; Dubin 1978; Kerlinger 1986). Fundamental to the development of strong theory is the general scientific approach to the topic, consisting of elements of problem identification, construct delineation and interaction, boundary setting, hypothesis development and empirical testing (Dubin 1978; Kerlinger 1986). These issues are central to theory development whether one works under the general framework of Dubin (1978) or Kerlinger (1986), or one of the many other theory-building scholars in the area. As such, the issues involved in standardization/adaptation of international advertising will be examined within this framework.

Focal Issue

Theoretical development begins with an obstacle to understanding (Kerlinger 1986). This forms the foundation of theory building as the goals of science are prediction and understanding (although these goals are most often addressed individually and drive differences in theory construction and research design) (Dubin 1978). Given the depth of practitioner concern since the 1920s, academic researchers began to formulate the question they wished to investigate. Central from its inception, and consistent today, the general question posed by academics has been whether 'standardized or adapted international advertising is more effective' (e.g. Miracle 1968; Buzzell 1968; Donnelly and Ryans 1969; Ryans 1969; Green et al. 1975; Onkvisit and Shaw 1987, 1999; James and Hill 1991; Kanso 1992; Shao et al. 1992; Harvey 1993; Kernan and Domzal 1993; Agarwal 1995; Solberg 2000)

Central Constructs

Adherent to this research question are the central constructs of advertising strategy (standardized or adapted) and effectiveness. As such, two key constructs pose the central tenet of the theoretical domain. To explore this issue one must define each construct, setting the boundary parameters under which the construct is defined. When one explores the seminal literature regarding advertising strategy one immediately notes that the field has not developed a rigorous, or consistent, conceptualization of advertising strategy as it relates to international advertising standardization/adaptation. When examining a selection of seminal articles in the field, divergence in conceptual domains is quickly evident. For example, Jain (1989) defined standardization as a common promotion program on a worldwide basis, whereas James and Hill (1991) examined only the message component, Cavusgil and Zou (1994) viewed the issue under the general 'degree' of adaptation, and Harvey (1993) argued that while prior researchers have conceptualized advertising standardization/adaptation as a binary debate (e.g. Kanso 1992), one needs to conceptualize the construct as multidimensional, looking at each specific element of advertising strategy, thus harkening back to the perspective taken by Donnelly and Ryans (1969). Clearly, a consensus eludes researchers in the definition and boundary of the most central of constructs. While one might consider the evolutionary perspective of first examining the general construct, and then delineating the individual elements as evidence of theoretical advancements, unfortunately progress in this area is unobservable as noted by Onkvisit and Shaw (1999).

Further, the conceptual domain of effectiveness encounters similar difficulties. In most cases, the effectiveness of a firm's international advertising standardization/adaptation efforts is measured in terms of one performance aspect or another. For instance, Jain (1989, p. 76) argued that 'standardization should be based on economic payoff, which includes financial performance, competitive advantage and other aspects.' Cavusgil and Zou (1994) conceptualized performance as the extent to which a firm's objectives, both economic and strategic, are achieved through planning and execution. Others, taking a more consumer orientation, explored the acceptability to consumers of product attributes, messages, brands, etc. (e.g. Green et al. 1975; Dawar and Parker 1994; Aaker, Benet-Martinez and Garolera 2001). Still others sidestep the issue of effectiveness by not conceptually defining it, but rather assuming it to be generally understood (e.g. Ryans 1969; Kernan and Domzal 1993). As such, the lack of general consensus on the conceptual definition and domain of effectiveness minimizes the ability for substantive advancement of the field, as comparability of results across studies becomes invalid.

Given the diversity of conceptual definitions of both advertising strategy standardization/adaptation and the lack of consistency related to the conceptualization of effectiveness, it is not surprising that inconsistencies have been found within the literature relating to this issue (see for example, Shoham 1995; Onkvisit and Shaw 1999). While the issue of conceptual domain remains in conflict, the underlying tenet of the relationship between the two constructs remains similarly unclear. Specifically, the arguments for and against standardization of international advertising strategy revolve around two key components (cost savings – via economies of scale – and enhanced value delivery through adaptation) both driven by the question of homogeneity of markets, or lack thereof.

Underlying Theoretical Foundations

The theoretical foundations of the standardization/adaptation debate center on the perception of consumer homogeneity and/or the movement toward homogeneity (Donnelly and Ryans 1969; Levitt 1983; Higgs 1984; Shoham 1995; Hu and Griffith 1997). Those researchers who view markets, or consumer wants and needs, as being homogeneous argue that the standardization of advertising is more 'effective' as it allows for the lowering of costs, via economies of scale, and thus increasing margins for a firm (Peebles, Ryans and Vernon 1978; Levitt 1983; Jain 1989). Alternatively, those who view markets as being heterogeneous, and therefore containing consumers with differing consumer wants and needs, perceive greater value delivery via adaptation (Donnelly and Ryans 1969; Higgs 1984; Harvey 1993).

Despite its centrality to the focal research issue, the extent of homogeneity of markets for advertising standardization has been given little attention within the literature. Rather than focusing attention on market homogeneity directly, researchers have instead explored a number of consumer response elements believed important to global advertising cross-culturally, such as brand loyalty, risk perception and most recently brand personality across countries (e.g. Tse, Belk and Zhou 1989; Biswas, Olsen and Carlet 1992; Mueller 1992; Yavas, Verhage and Green 1992; Kanwar 1993; Lin 1993; Griffin, Viswanath and Schwartz 1994; Harris 1994; Aaker et al. 2001). For example, Yavas et al. (1992) examined brand loyalty and risk perceptions of products across six countries, finding differences indicating the need for adaptation. Kanwar (1993) found differences in perceived risk across two countries, thus suggesting that advertising would need to be adapted. Aaker et al. (2001) found that the dimensions of brand personality, while sharing certain dimensions, differed across countries, thus suggestive of the need to adapt elements of a firm's advertising. Given the disparity of consumer response in these studies, it appears as though the empirical evidence would contradict the argument for homogeneity of markets, violating Levitt's (1983) central assumption and casting doubt on the merits of standardization (Shoham 1995).

However, let us assume for a moment that research regarding the homogeneity of markets was credible and supportive of market similarity, as we can find some studies that find in favor of specific universals (e.g. Alden, Hoyer and Lee 1993; Dawar and Parker 1994), potentially suggesting homogeneity with respect to certain elements influencing advertising fundamentals. Thus, an exploration of the cost argument must occur. For, it is argued, when homogeneity of market characteristics occur, firms can employ standardized advertising (adapting for language, etc., as necessary) in order to reap lower costs and larger margins.

Although this has been the argument since the initiation of the international advertising standardization/adaptation debate, little if any empirical research has explored this issue. As such, researchers, eight decades after the practitioner debate and four decades after the initiation of the academic debate, are still left with an underlying assumption that has not been empirically validated. While researchers may argue that the empirical validation of the argument is unnecessary as logic would indicate that standardization of advertising reduces costs by spreading advertising development costs over a greater number of markets, thus reducing its average cost per exposure, the theoretical linkage is that lower costs achieved through standardization increase 'effectiveness'. Thus, while most researchers have not argued with the lower-cost basis of the tenet, given the theoretical foundation of economies of scale (derived from the economics literature), some would question the ability to translate these cost savings into effectiveness (within an advertising contextual domain and as conceptualized by performance standards). A simple, yet strong, argument against the need to prove performance effectiveness is embedded within the conceptualization of value delivery. That is to say, if a standardized advertisement does not provide value to the market it is less likely to increase sales. If the advertisement is unable to increase sales (or achieve its desired response, which is typically to stimulate sales although other alternatives exist), the investment in the standardized advertisement inefficiently employs valuable corporate resources. Therefore, without verification of the economies of scale argument, the direct influence of advertising standardization on performance becomes suspect.

Alternatively, proponents of adaptation argue that international advertising adaptation that meets local consumer needs and wants is more effective (James and Hill 1991; Shao et al. 1992; Harvey 1993). When examining the empirical literature on this relationship it is evident that there appears to be consistency in the relationship between adaptation of advertising, or elements of promotion, with increased performance. For example, Cavusgil and Zou (1994) found a positive relationship between promotion adaptation and export performance. While empirical support exists for the relationship between adaptation and performance, the issue of effectiveness of the advertisement remains. For instance, could an adapted advertisement be effective, yet not increase performance? Of course, it could depend on its objectives. An advertisement can have many differing objectives, such as informative, etc. The direct linkage between adaptation and performance may not be comprehensive – or at the least, fully explanatory (however the relationship of adaptation to performance is clearly a central issue in terms of effectiveness).

In summary, when viewing the underlying constructs, relationships, and the underlying theoretical development over the past four decades of academic research it becomes most evident that the field has failed to develop strong theoretical foundations for its advancement. Today, almost four decades after the initialization of an academic research agenda on the topic, we are little closer to understanding this issue than we were when we began (without the scientific and direct evidence to confirm or contradict the validity of international advertising standardization (Onkvisit and Shaw 1999)). These results are clearly not for a lack of attention to the topic, or the lack of insightful and diligent scholars working in the field. Rather, it appears, and this is subject to debate, that the field of international advertising research is without a strong theoretical foundation. While we have clearly identified the research question, we, as a field, have failed to appropriately designate the conceptual domains of our constructs (and develop consensus on these conceptual domains), to develop laws of interaction among the constructs, and to verify the underlying assumptions of the theories used to support the laws of interaction (empirically testing the assumptions and the laws themselves). This is not to indicate that all was for naught. Rather, we have gained a great understanding of the complexities of the topic, exploring the fundamentals of process versus program standardization (Sorenson and Weichmann 1975; Jain 1989), implementation issues (Harvey 1993; Laroche et al. 2001; Chandra et al. 2002), as well as antecedent conditions (Donnelly and Ryans 1969; Ryans 1969; Jain 1989; Harvey 1993; Cavusgil and Zou 1994; Chandra et al. 2002), and a plethora of other concerns. However, for the field to gain credibility and advance as an academic discipline, it must now establish a strong theoretical position. Simply stated, a clear research agenda needs to be put forth to solidify the core advances, for we have not met the standard theory building criteria necessary for scientific advancement (as explicated by Hunt 1971; Dubin 1978; Kerlinger 1986).

CONDITIONS FOR THEORETICAL ADVANCEMENT

So, where do we go from here? First and foremost, the determination of the future of the field necessitates the clear enumeration of the constructs being employed. We are past the stage of using a generalized construct such as 'standardized/adapted advertising'. Clearly, the construct is multidimensional and a generalized construct such as 'standardized/adapted advertising' will provide limited insights to the understanding of this complex issue. Thus, researchers are challenged for specificity in their conceptualization and measurement of this construct in their studies. This necessitates a movement away from broad generalizations regarding this issue, in exchange for detailed analysis. Clearly, as Harvey (1993) argues, it is the 'degree' of standardization/adaptation along each dimension of advertising, such as message, media, etc., that is at issue, rather than an either/or decision. As such, it is recommended that researchers be specific in their conceptualization and analysis for theoretical advancement.

Additionally, researchers are challenged to delineate the conceptual domain of 'effectiveness' in relation to international advertising standardization. Effectiveness is at the core of the standardization/adaptation of advertising debate. However, without a clearly defined, and agreed upon definition of the construct, the field cannot advance. Here, it is argued that we no longer simply assume the relationship between value delivery and performance, but rather explore the issue of value delivery directly. Marketers have defined value in a variety of ways (e.g. Holbrook 1994; Woodruff 1997; Slater and Narver 2000). For example, Holbrook (1994, 1999) defines value broadly as 'an interactive, relativistic, preference experience'. Consistent with this conceptualization, it is suggested that researchers consider customer value to be the consumer's subjective assessment of the benefits derived from the advertisement less any sacrifice/costs (e.g. Rust and Zahorik 1993; Slater and Narver 2000; Zeithaml 1988). In this perspective, value is conceptualized to have both absolute and relativistic components. Furthermore, extending Gassenheimer, Houston and Davis's (1998) work in value to the domain of international advertising standardization/adaptation, customer perceptions of value can be conceptualized to have both economic and social aspects. Perceived economic value is defined as when the perceived economic outcomes exceed economic inputs. Similarly, social value is defined as when the social benefits of the relationship exceed social inputs. In the case of international advertising standardization/adaptation, economic value can be viewed as a consumer's information enhancement, gain in confidence, etc., regarding the usage of the product. As such, it becomes an efficiency benefit. Alternatively, social value delivery can be assessed in terms of the consumer's belief that the advertisement creates, or fails to create, stronger bonds between the firm and the consumer. Typically, the issue of value delivery has been viewed from the firm's standpoint in relation to this issue, where value is determined by performance enhancement (i.e. greater firm economic value is generated when performance is enhanced – whether via standardization or adaptation of advertising), and as such has been conceptualized unidimensionally, ignoring the consumer. This perspective is still applicable, however a broader conceptualization of value is necessary, inclusive of the consumer, for deeper insight.

Next, the underlying empirical laws of interaction between the constructs should be examined (while specifying the boundary parameters of the topic). To do so, crucial theoretical explication is necessary discerning why standardization or adaptation enhances 'effectiveness', or more importantly 'consumer or firm value'. This necessitates a more explicit conceptualization of homogenization, or lack thereof, of consumer wants, needs, etc. What theories could be lent to this study? Here, it is necessary to be more than descriptive, as most previous research is (e.g. Sirisagul 2000). For instance, Hofstede (1980, 1991) clearly enumerates differences in motivations across cultures. However, are these differences necessary to translate theme into advertising impacts, as Shoham (1995) suggests, or are these examples tied to other phenomena and as such only have peripheral effects on the issue of advertising standardization/adaptation? As Jain (1989), Harvey (1993) and Cavusgil and Zou (1994), as well as a plethora of other researchers enumerate and test antecedents to standardization/adaptation of advertising strategy, clearly homogeneity of consumer wants, needs, etc. are not the only issue driving standardization or adaptation. Are these the principle constructs of a theory that can be constructed toward understanding this topic? Do we have consensus on the conceptualizations of these antecedent constructs?

Tied to these questions is the validity of the underlying assumptions of the standardization argument. Empirical verification is necessary for the underlying theoretical assumptions within international advertising research. If one is to argue homogeneity of consumer characteristics (as well as other antecedent constructs), these should be conceptualized in terms of the firm's goals and target markets, assessed via reliable and valid measures, and tested in accordance with standard protocols. Of course, this necessitates that strong cross-cultural measurement equivalence, etc., be established. Also, if one is to argue for economies of scale, empirical verification is necessary. Only through the identification and measurement of key assumptions can we hope to make substantial progress in the field.

Finally, from a pragmatic perspective, while today's research almost simplistically employs the same methods as in the past, the two sides of the dyad have dramatically changed. Over the 40-year period, advertising form and content has changed, i.e., media (print, television, and online) and coverage (national to global). The consumer has changed, becoming more accessible to advertisers and, for many, becoming more affluent in their media selections. He or she has also become more sophisticated, with extensive and varied advertising experience. The rise of television's role day to day and its satellite usage is a factor. And, as the consumer has become more experienced, he or she is perhaps more critical, thus necessitating the observation of value delivery to determine effectiveness. The advertiser has also changed, developing and employing more sophisticated research techniques to understand the consumer and to evaluate advertisements. Further, the advertisers are better able to segment the market. The advertising agency industry has concentrated; the local advertising agency is more apt to be a branch of a global agency. This latter may result in few savings if a local agency is used. This indeed is a much different situation from that faced in the simpler world of the earlier researchers.

CONCLUSIONS

As a broad statement, for too long researchers in this area have focused on 'doing research' rather than on conceptualizing research. Platt (1964) argues that for science to advance researchers must design crucial experiments, complete with alternative hypotheses, that test the very foundation of the issue under investigation, as opposed to simply conducting more experiments. It is in this vein that the call is made for more theoretical development and testing in the area of international advertising standardization/adaptation.

This is not to suggest that the work over the last 40 years failed to provide us with unique insights, but rather to challenge researchers to develop stronger theoretical frameworks to apply, to be more rigorous in their testing of this area, and to clearly describe their theory and assumptions. There have been many relevant concerns raised about standardization/ adaptation research from the very outset. Most of the research to date has focused on the advertiser side of the advertiser–consumer dyad for determining both the way in which the message is developed (process) and the nature of the advertisement itself (program). Typically, survey research has been employed and the sample is drawn from executives in global business firms. The respondent is asked to respond to a series of either program-related or process-related questions (or both). In some instances, the respondent may be asked to comment on the promotional campaign's success along some relevant measure, e.g. consumer response to the approach employed. But often this is not done. By including measures on both sides of the dyad, greater insights may be gained.

After 40-plus years of academic research activity, and over almost 80 years of practitioner debate, the standardization/adaptation issue has remained a viable topic, as measured by academic/practitioner interest and the leading journals in the field. Surprisingly, it has done so without the development of solid theory to support it and with the methodological flaws indicated. The explanation for the firm wishing to adopt some degree of standardization is usually grounded in scale economies, i.e. the assumption that localization would come at a higher cost than standardization. One could argue that actual savings may be minimal, if, for example, localization were to offer lower cost than would say TV commercials on Star TV or CNN. Management control was suggested by Laroche et al. (2001), but this standardization process explanation was focused on effectively implementing strategy rather than achieving corporate advertising goals. Other than efficiency or economies of scale rationale, what sort of theory would seem to be appropriate for the standardization/adaptation issue? This is the challenge we raise to future researchers (and ourselves) in the international advertising field. As such, it is a call for a raising of the bar, in terms of theory development and testing, across the board for researchers in the field.

REFERENCES

Aaker, Jennifer, Veronica Benet-Martinez and Jordi Garolera (2001), 'Consumption Symbols as Carriers of Culture: A Study of Japanese and Spanish Brand Personality Constructs', *Journal of Personality & Social Psychology*, **81** (3), 492–508.
Agarwal, Madhr (1995), 'Review of a 40-year Debate in International Advertising', *International Marketing Review*, **12** (1), 26–48.

Alden, Dana L., Wayne D. Hoyer and Chol Lee (1993), 'Identifying Global and Culture-Specific Dimensions in Humor in Advertising: A Multinational Analysis', *Journal of Marketing*, **57** (2), 64–75.

Anderson, L. McTier (1994), 'Marketing Science: Where's the Beef?', *Business Horizons*, **37** (1), 8–16.

Anderson, Paul F. (1983), 'Marketing, Scientific Progress, and Scientific Method', *Journal of Marketing*, **47** (4), 19–31.

Baalbaki, Imad B. and Naresh K. Malhotra (1993), 'Marketing Management Bases for International Market Segmentation: An Alternate Look at the Standardization/Customization Debate', *International Marketing Review*, **10** (1), 19–43.

Baalbaki, Imad B. and Naresh K. Malhotra (1995), 'Standardization Versus Customization in International Marketing: An Investigation Using Bridging Conjoint Analysis', *Journal of the Academy of Marketing Science*, **23** (3), 182–94.

Bari, A.A. (1979), 'Advertising in Specific Markets: Egypt', in S.W. Dunn and E.S. Lorimor (eds), *International Advertising and Marketing*, Columbus, OH: Grid Publishing, Inc.

Barnes, M.L. (1968), 'Trending Toward Centralization', *The International Advertiser*, June–July, 15–16, 29.

Bartels, Robert (1951), 'Can Marketing Be a Science?', *Journal of Marketing*, **15** (3), 319–28.

Biswas, Abhijit, Janeen Olsen and Valerie Carlet (1992), 'A Comparison of Print Advertisements from the United States and France', *Journal of Advertising*, **21** (4), 73–81.

Boddewyn, J.J., R. Soehl and Jacques Picard (1986), 'Standardization in International Marketing, Is Ted Levitt in Fact Right?', *Business Horizons*, **29** (6), 69–75.

Brown, David L. (1923), *Export Advertising*, New York, NY: Ronald Press.

Buzzell, Robert D. (1968), 'Can We Standardize Multinational Marketing', *Harvard Business Review*, **46** (6), 102–13.

Cavusgil, S. Tamer and Shaoming Zou (1994), 'Marketing Strategy–Performance Relationship: An Investigation of the Empirical Link in Export Market Venture', *Journal of Marketing*, **58** (1), 1–21.

Chandra, Aruna, David A. Griffith and John K. Ryans, Jr (2002), 'Advertising Standardisation in India: US Multinational Experience', *International Journal of Advertising*, **21** (1), 47–66.

Cornejo, O. (1958), 'Co-ordinating your Foreign Subsidiaries', *Advertising. Industrial Marketing*, **43** (August), 46–9.

Dawar, Niraj and Philip Parker (1994), 'Marketing Universals: Consumers' use of Brand Name, Price, Physical Appearance, and Retail Reputation as Signals of Product Quality', *Journal of Marketing*, **58** (2), 81–95.

Delaforce, P. (1964), 'The Individual Markets of Europe', in S.W. Dunn (ed.), *International Handbook of Advertising*, New York, NY: McGraw-Hill.

Deschampsneufs, H. (1967), *Marketing Overseas*, New York, NY: Pergamon Press.

Donnelly, James H., Jr (1968), 'An Analysis of the Role of Cultural Forces and Other Selected Variables in Non-Domestic Media Selection for Consumer Non-Durables: An Empirical Study', Unpublished Doctoral Dissertation, University of Maryland.

Donnelly, James H. Jr and John K. Ryans, Jr (1969), 'Standardized Global Advertising: A Call Yet Unanswered', *Journal of Marketing*, **33** (2), 57–64.

Dubin, Robert (1978), *Theory Building*, New York, NY: Free Press.

Elinder, Eric (1961), 'How International Can Advertising Be?', *International Advertiser*, (December), 12–16.

Ettinger, K.E. (1969), 'How BMW Achieves International Message Coordination', *The International Advertiser*, **10** (2), 18–19.

Fatt, Arthur C. (1967), 'The Danger of "Local" International Advertising', *Journal of Marketing* **31** (3), 60–62.

Fullerton, Ronald A. (1988), 'How Modern is Modern Marketing? Marketing's Evolution and the Myth of the "Production Era"', *Journal of Marketing*, **52** (1), 108–25.

Gassenheimer, Jule B., Franklin S. Houston and Charlene J. Davis (1998), 'The Role of Economic Value, Social Value, and Perceptions of Fairness in Interorganizational Relationship Retention Decisions', *Journal of the Academy of Marketing Science*, **26** (4), 322–37.

Green, Robert, William Cunningham and Isabella Cunningham (1975), 'The Effectiveness of Global Advertising', *Journal of Advertising*, **4** (3), 25–30.

Griffin, Michael, K. Viswanath and Dona Schwartz (1994), 'Gender Advertising in the US and India: Exporting Cultural Stereotypes', *Media, Culture and Society*, **16**, 487–507.

Harris, Greg (1994), 'International Advertising Standardization: What Do The Multinationals Actually Standardize?', *Journal of International Marketing*, **2** (4), 13–30.

Harvey, Michael G. (1993), 'Point of View: A Model to Determine Standardization of the Advertising Process in International Markets', *Journal of Advertising Research*, **33** (4), 57–64.

Higgs, Ray (1984), *Not Yet a Global Village. Marketing*, **18** (11), 40–42.

Hofstede, Geert (1980), *Culture's Consequences*, Beverly Hills, CA: Sage.

Hofstede, Geert (1991), *Cultures and Organizations: Software of the Mind*, Beverly Hills, CA: Sage.

Holbrook, Morris B. (1994), 'The Nature of Customer Value', in Roland T. Rust and Richard L. Oliver (eds), *Service Quality*, Beverly Hills, CA: Sage, pp. 21–71.

Holbrook, Morris B. (1999), 'Introduction to Consumer Value', in Morris B. Holbrook (ed.), *Consumer Value: A Framework for Analysis and Research*, New York: Routledge, pp. 1–28.

Hu, Michael Y. and David A. Griffith (1997), 'Conceptualizing the Global Marketplace: Marketing Strategy Implications', *Marketing Intelligence & Planning*, **15** (3), 117–23.

Hunt, Shelby D. (1971), 'The Morphology of Theory and the General Theory of Marketing', *Journal of Marketing*, **35** (2), 65–8.

Hunt, Shelby D. (1983), 'General Theories and the Fundamental Explananda of Marketing', *Journal of Marketing*, **47** (4), 9–17.

Jain, Subhash C. (1989), 'Standardization of International Marketing Strategy: Some Hypotheses', *Journal of Marketing*, **53** (1), 70–79.

James, William L. and John S. Hill (1991), 'International Advertising Messages: To Adapt or Not to Adapt', *Journal of Advertising Research*, **31** (3), 65–71.

Kanso, Ali (1992), 'International Advertising Strategies: Global Commitment to Local Vision', *Journal of Advertising Research*, **30** (1), 10–14.

Kanwar, Rajesh (1993), 'The Influence of Perceived Risk and Advertising Copy Claims on the Consumption Behavior of Asian Indian Consumers', *Journal of International Consumer Marketing*, **5** (4), 7–28.

Kerlinger, Frederick (1986), *Foundations of Behavioral Research*, 3rd edn, New York, NY: Holt, Rinehart & Winston.

Kernan, Jerome B. and Teresa J. Domzal (1993), 'International Advertising: To Globalize, Visualize', *Journal of International Consumer Marketing*, 5 (4), 51–71.

Laroche, Michel, V.H. Kirpalani, Frank Pons and Zhou Lianxi (2001), 'A Model of Advertising Standardization in Multinational Corporations', *Journal of International Business Studies*, 32 (2), 249–66.

Lenormand, J.M. (1964), 'Is Europe Ripe for the Integration of Advertising?', *The International Advertiser*, (5), 14.

Levitt, Theodore (1983), 'The Globalization of Markets', *Harvard Business Review*, **61** (3), 92–102.

Lin, Carolyn (1993), 'Cultural Differences in Message Strategies: A Comparison Between American and Japanese Commercials', *Journal of Advertising Research*, **33** (4), 40–48.

Lindsey, N.A.M. (1964), 'How to Advertise in Specific Markets: Mexico', in S.W. Dunn (ed.), *International Handbook of Advertising*, New York, NY: McGraw-Hill.

Marcus, C. (1964), 'How to Advertise in Specific Markets: France', in S.W. Dunn (ed.), *International Handbook of Advertising*, New York, NY: McGraw-Hill.

Miracle, Gordon E. (1968), *International Advertising Principles and Strategies.* *MSU Business Topics*, (Autumn), 29–36.

Mueller, Barbara (1992), 'Standardization vs. Specification: An Examination of Westernization in Japanese Advertising', *Journal of Advertising Research*, 32 (1), 15–24.

Onkvisit, Sak and John J. Shaw (1987), 'Standardized International Advertising: A Review and Critical Evaluation of the Theoretical and Empirical Evidence', *Columbia Journal of World Business*, 22 (3), 43–55.

Onkvisit, Sak and John J. Shaw (1999), 'Standardized International Advertising: Some Research Issues and Implications', *Journal of Adverting Research*, **39** (6), 19–24.

Patterson, J. (1967), 'Co-ordinating International Advertising', *The International Advertiser*, **8** (6), 35–9.

Peebles, Dean (1967), 'Goodyear's Worldwide Advertising', *The International Advertiser*, **8** (1), 19–22.

Peebles, Dean, John K. Ryans, Jr and Ivan R. Vernon (1978), 'Coordinating International Advertising', *Journal of Marketing*, 42 (1), 28–34.

Platt, John R. (1964), 'Strong Inference', *Science*, **146**, 347–53.

Pratt, E.E. (1956), 'Building Export Sales-Advertising', *The International Advertiser*, 1 (8), 19–22.

Propson, Carl, F. (1923), 'Illustrating the Foreign Campaign', in *Export Advertising Practice*, New York, NY: Prentice-Hall.

Roostal, Ilmar (1963), 'Standardization of Advertising for Western Europe', *Journal of Marketing*, 27 (4), 15–20.

Rust, Roland T. and Anthony J. Zahorik (1993), 'Customer Satisfaction, Customer Retention, and Market Share', *Journal of Retailing*, **69** (2), 193–215.

Ryans, John K., Jr (1969), 'Is It Too Soon to Put a Tiger in Every Tank?', *Columbia Journal of World Business*, 4 (2), 69–75.

Samiee, Saeed and Kendall Roth (1992), 'The Influence of Global Marketing Standardization on Performance', *Journal of Marketing*, **56** (2), 1–17.

Shao, Alan T., Lawrence P. Shao and Dale H. Shao (1992), 'Are Global Markets with Standardized Advertising Campaigns Feasible?', *Journal of International Consumer Marketing*, **4** (3), 5–46.

Shoham, Aviv (1995), 'Global Marketing Standardization', *Journal of Global Marketing*, **9** (1/2), 91–119.

Sirisagul, Kanya (2000), 'Global Advertising Practices: A Comparative Study', *Journal of Global Marketing*, **14** (3), 77–97.

Slater, Stanley F. and John C. Narver (2000), 'Intelligence Generation and Superior Customer Value', *Journal of the Academy of Marketing Science*, **28** (1), 120–27.

Smith, Adam (1776), *An Inquiry Into the Nature and Causes of The Wealth of Nations*, Edinburgh, UK: Adam Smith, LL.D.

Solberg, Carl Arthur (2000), 'Standardization or Adaptation of the International Marketing Mix: The Role of the Local Subsidiary/Representative', *Journal of International Marketing*, **8** (1), 78–98.

Sorenson, Ralph Z. and Ulrich E. Wiechmann (1975), 'How multinationals view marketing standardization', *Harvard Business Review*, **53** (3), 38–56.

Sullivan, Daniel (1998), 'Cognitive Tendencies in International Business Research: Implications of a Narrow Vision', *Journal of International Business Studies*, **29** (4), 837–62.

Sutton, T. (1974), 'Advertising at the Cross-Roads', *Advertising Marketing and Media Weekly*, July, 30–31.

Theophilopoulos, G. (1979) 'Advertising in Specific Markets: Greece', in S.W. Dunn and E.S. Lorimor (eds), *International Advertising and Marketing*, Columbus, OH: Grid Publishing, Inc.

Tse, David, Russell W. Belk and Nan Zhou (1989), 'A Longitudinal and Cross-Cultural Analysis of Print Ads from Hong Kong, the People's Republic of China, and Taiwan', *Journal of Consumer Research*, **15** (4), 457–72.

Vernon, Raymond (1966), 'International Investment and International Trade in the Product Life Cycle', *Quarterly Journal of Economics*, **80** (2), 190–207.

Vladimir, I.A. (1950), 'Industrial and Export Advertising: Export Advertising', in R. Barton (ed.), *Advertising Handbook*, New York, NY: Prentice-Hall.

Woodruff, Robert B. (1997), 'Customer Value: The Next Source of Competitive Advantage', *Journal of the Academy of Marketing Science*, **25** (2), 139–53.

Yavas, Ugur, Bornislaw J. Verhage and Robert T. Green (1992), 'Global Consumer Segmentation versus Local Market Orientation: Empirical Findings', *Management International Review*, **32** (3), 265–72.

Zeithaml, Valarie A. (1988), 'Consumer Perceptions of Price, Quality, and Value: A Means-End Model and Synthesis of Evidence', *Journal of Marketing*, **52** (3), 2–22.

PART V

Global electronic commerce

16. Competitive strategy in a global electronic marketplace: extant strategy perspectives revisited

P. Rajan Varadarajan and Manjit S. Yadav

INTRODUCTION

During the last quarter-century, the evolution of the international business literature has benefited from theoretical and empirical advances in the fields of industrial organization economics, strategic management, and marketing strategy. Theoretical, conceptual, and empirical perspectives on topics such as generic competitive strategies, competitive advantage, market pioneering advantage, strategic alliances, strategic groups and mobility barriers, and scale, scope and experience effects, have contributed to enriching the body of international business literature. A relatively recent phenomenon that has had a major impact on international business practice is the continuously expanding global communication and computer infrastructure (i.e. the Internet). The implications for international business of the changes set in motion by this technological development are likely to be many and far-reaching. E-business, e-commerce, e-customer relationship management, e-customer service, e-procurement, e-supply chain management, e-supplier relationship management, e-alliance/partner relationship management, and e-knowledge management are just a few of the many recent additions to the lexicon of business that have been qualified with the prefix 'global'.

The current high level of interest concerning the implications of e-commerce for international business education, research, and practice is evidenced by the recent conferences and special issues devoted to the topic. For instance, a conference (held in May 2000) and a special issue of the *Journal of International Business Studies* (Winter 2001) were devoted to focusing on the impact of the Internet and e-commerce on the conduct of international business and the management of multinational enterprises. Table 16.1, which presents a summary of some broad themes and specific research questions enumerated in the call for papers for the

Table 16.1   Research in global e-commerce: some themes and specific research questions

International Strategy Issues for New E-commerce Enterprises
- To what extent are the issues facing the new e-commerce companies, often said to be 'born global', similar to those facing other global companies?
- What are the strategic questions facing these firms?
- Do international business theories derived from the eclectic model, transaction costs and internalization still apply?
- Do frameworks such as integration–responsiveness work equally well?

Managing Information and the Global Value Chain
- How will the Internet change the way in which companies manage global manufacturing and service businesses?
- Will there be more virtual integration of supply chains and service networks, or will markets replace integrated chains?
- Will there be disintermediation on a global scale, or will new infomediaries appear?
- What will determine whether companies are successful at adapting their supply and service chains to these changes?

Reaching and Serving Global Markets and Consumers
- What will be the impact of the Internet on cross-national differences in consumer behavior?
- Will there be a convergence of tastes and preferences?
- Will certain elements of the marketing mix assume greater importance?
- What will be the role of global brands?

Managing Global Organizational Processes: What will be the Impact of the Internet on:
- Formal and informal organization structures, systems and culture of multinationals?
- Decision-making processes?
- Knowledge flows?
- Cross-national processes such as R&D and new product development?
- Organizational and national cultures?

Regulation of Global E-commerce
- What are the key regulatory issues related to e-commerce that cross borders?
- How will governments and international organizations change their policies toward international trade, investment, intellectual property and financial transactions?
- What will be the nature of the interaction between governments and national governments?

Table 16.1 (*continued*)

● How will governments deal with issues of privacy, consumer protection, and taxation?

National Competitiveness in an Internet World
● How will the Internet re-shape the determinants of country competitiveness?
● Will clusters and proximity become more or less important?
● How can governments intervene to encourage development and competitiveness?
● Will the Internet lead to an even more extreme 'digital divide' among nations, or to greater opportunities for poor countries to leapfrog?

Source: Adapted from the Listserv Posting in ELMAR (1999), 'Call for Papers for the May 2000 *Journal of International Business Studies* Conference on Electronic Commerce and Global Business'.

conference on e-commerce and global business, is indicative of the breadth of opportunities for future research (ELMAR 1999, Listserv Posting). As evidenced by the following research questions enumerated in Table 16.1, among the potential avenues for future research alluded to is the need for a critical assessment of the continued relevance (and/or the need for refinement) of extant strategy theories, principles, concepts, tools, techniques, and frameworks in the context of the emerging global electronic marketplace:

● Do international business theories derived from the eclectic model, transaction costs, and internalization still apply?
● Do frameworks such as integration–responsiveness work equally well?
● Will certain elements of the marketing mix assume greater importance?

Against this backdrop, this chapter revisits extant perspectives on (1) the role of industry structural forces, (2) experience curves, (3) generic competitive strategies, and (4) market pioneering advantages in the context of competitive strategy in a global electronic marketplace. Research on the role of industry structural forces on competitive strategy dates back to the 1950s (e.g. Bain 1956). Research on experience effects, generic competitive strategies, and market pioneering advantages are representative of major streams of literature that had a significant impact on the evolution of the strategy literature during the last quarter-century.

Global electronic commerce

INDUSTRY STRUCTURAL CHARACTERISTICS AND INDUSTRY PROFITABILITY

Industry structure refers to the relatively stable economic and technical dimensions of an industry that provide the context in which competition takes place (Bain 1956). Research in industrial organizational economics, strategic management, and marketing lends support for the link between the structural characteristics of an industry, the competitive strategy pursued by businesses in the industry, and the average profitability of the industry. For instance, the structure–conduct–performance (SCP) model views industry structure as determining the behavior (conduct/strategy) of businesses in an industry, and conduct as determining industry performance (Bain 1956). Porter (1978), in his seminal article titled 'How Competitive Forces Shape Strategy', and book on competitive strategy (Porter 1980), distinguishes between five competitive forces that impact on the average profitability of an industry:

- Power of suppliers.
- Power of buyers.
- Threat of new entrants.
- Competition from substitutes.
- Intensity of competition among entrenched competitors.

In a recent article, Porter (2001) elaborates on the influence of the Internet on industry structure. For instance, he notes that the Internet has the potential to bolster the bargaining power of buyers, dampen the bargaining power of channel members, and intensify rivalry among competitors (see Tapscott (2001) for a critique of Porter's article). In an attempt to shed further insights into this issue, this section focuses on the effect of the Internet on the structural characteristics of an industry and, thus, on average industry profitability. Specifically, it focuses on how extant perspectives on the relationship between industry structural characteristics and industry profitability are likely to be impacted by the spread of the Internet.

Figure 16.1 provides an overview of the relationship between power of suppliers, power of buyers, threat of new entrants, competition from substitutes, intensity of competition among entrenched competitors, and the average profitability of the focal industry. As should be evident to the reader, Figure 16.1 constitutes a departure from the standard representation of Porter's five-forces model (Porter 1980, p. 4), that one generally encounters in textbooks and journal articles (e.g. Besanko, Dranove and Shanley 1996). Specifically, in Figure 16.1, the above five forces are more explicitly modeled as antecedents of industry profitability. A more detailed

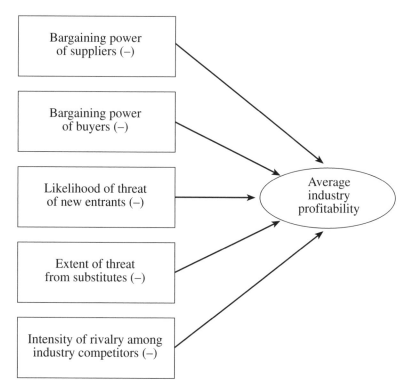

Figure 16.1   Competitive forces and industry profitability

elaboration of the dimensions underlying each of the five forces is presented in Table 16.2. Also summarized in Table 16.2 are the hypothesized relationships between specific industry structure variables underlying the five major competitive forces and industry profitability.

A consequence of the emergence of the electronic marketplace is a shift in the competitive landscape from a predominantly physical marketplace to a broader marketplace comprising both the physical and electronic marketplaces (see Varadarajan and Yadav (2002) for an extended discussion). In the next section we explore the likely impact of the Internet on industry profitability by focusing on some of the relationships enumerated in Table 16.2. While a more complete treatment of the above issue is deferred to a future work, this initial exposition explores the issue in reference to one industry structure variable underlying each of the five forces. Specifically, we focus on the following relationships delineated in Table 16.2:

Table 16.2 Competitive forces and industry profitability

Competitive Industry Forces	Impact on Industry Profitability
A. Bargaining Power of Suppliers	Impact of Supplier Forces on Industry Profitability
Supplier concentration	A supplier group that is more concentrated than the focal industry it sells to will have a negative effect on the profitability of the focal industry.
Threat of forward integration	A supplier group that poses a credible threat of forward integration in the focal industry will have a negative effect on the profitability of the focal industry.
Importance of supplier industry's inputs	A supplier group that sells a relatively important input to the focal industry will have a negative effect on the profitability of the focal industry.
Product differentiation	A supplier group whose product offerings to the focal industry are differentiated will have a negative effect on the profitability of the focal industry.
Switching costs	Inputs from a supplier group that would entail switching costs for the buyer will have a negative effect on the profitability of the focal industry.
B. Bargaining Power of Buyers	Impact of Buyer Forces on Industry Profitability
Buyer concentration and purchase volume	A buyer group that is concentrated and purchases a large volume of the total output of the focal industry will have a negative effect on the profitability of the focal industry.
Threat of backward integration	A buyer group that poses a credible threat of backward integration in the focal industry will have a negative effect on the profitability of the focal industry.
Product differentiation	A buyer group that purchases undifferentiated products from a focal industry will have a negative effect on the profitability of the focal industry.
C. Threat of New Entrants	Impact of Threat of New Entrants on Industry Profitability*
Economies of scale	Cost advantage of incumbents due to scale economies, by deterring potential new entrants, will have a positive impact on the profitability of the focal industry.

Capital requirements	Large capital requirements, by deterring potential new entrants, will have a positive impact on the profitability of the focal industry.
Switching costs	High switching costs that buyers may have to incur, by deterring potential new entrants, will have a positive impact on the profitability of the focal industry.
Access to distribution channels	Lack of access to distribution channels, by deterring potential new entrants, will have a positive impact on industry profitability.
Cost advantages independent of scale	Cost advantages independent of scale, by deterring potential new entrants, will have a positive impact on the profitability of the focal industry.
D. Threat from Substitute Products	Impact of Threat from Substitutes on Industry Profitability
Functional similarity	High functional similarity between the product offerings of the substitute industry and the focal industry will have a negative effect on the profitability of the focal industry due to higher buyer propensity to switch to substitutes.
Relative price-performance	Substitute products that provide better price-performance than the product offerings of the focal industry will have a negative effect on the profitability of the focal industry.
E. Rivalry Among Present Competitors	Impact of Rivalry Among Present Competitors on Industry Profitability
Number of competitors	Low concentration (competition between a number of firms) will have a negative effect on the profitability of the focal industry.
Industry growth rate	Low industry growth rate, by increasing market share expansion rivalry among present competitors, will have a negative effect on the profitability of the focal industry.
Diversity of competitors	Diversity among competitors (in terms of factors such as size, ownership, strategies, and origin), due to their different objectives and goals, will have a negative effect on the profitability of the focal industry.

Table 16.2 (*continued*)

Competitive Industry Forces	Impact on Industry Profitability
Fixed costs	High fixed costs by forcing competitors to frequently resort to price-cutting in an attempt to increase capacity utilization will have a negative effect on the profitability of the focal industry.
Product differentiation	Few possibilities available to firms in an industry to differentiate their product offerings from competitors' offerings will have a negative effect on the profitability of the focal industry. (The availability of a greater range of possibilities to firms in an industry to differentiate their product offerings from competitors' product offerings, by allowing multiple competitors to co-exist, will have a positive effect on the profitability of the focal industry.)
Exit barriers	High exit barriers, by deterring the exit of marginal firms, will have a negative effect on the profitability of the focal industry.

Note: * In Figure 16.1, the relationship between likelihood of threat of new entrants and industry profitability is presented as a negative relationship (i.e. greater threat of likelihood of new entrants will have a negative impact on the profitability of firms in the focal industry). However, in Table 16.2, for reasons of ease of exposition, the relationship between individual factors (e.g. economies of scale and access to distribution channels) underlying the competitive force 'threat of new entrants' and the profitability of firms in the focal industry are shown as direct positive relationships. These relationships can as well be restated as negative relationships. For example: ease of access to distribution channels to potential new entrants will have a negative impact on industry profitability.

Source: Adapted from Table 1 in: Rajan Varadarajan (1999), 'Strategy Content and Process Perspectives Revisited', *Journal of the Academy of Marketing Science*, **27** (Winter), 88–100.

- Supplier concentration, a variable underlying supplier power.
- Buyer concentration, a variable underlying buyer power.
- Access to distribution channels, a variable underlying threat of new entrants.
- Impact of the emergence of e-retailers, a potential threat from a substitute (channel) from the perspective of traditional brick-and-mortar retailers.
- Number of competitors, a variable underlying intensity of competition among entrenched competitors.

Power of Suppliers

Supplier concentration
According to Porter's (1980) five-forces model, a supplier group that is more concentrated than the focal industry it sells to will negatively impact on the profitability of the focal industry. The electronic marketplace, by serving as a meeting place for potential suppliers and buyers separated by physical distance, can be expected to impact on supplier concentration by increasing the potential pool of suppliers. The dilution of supplier concentration, in turn, can be expected to weaken the negative effect of supplier concentration on the profitability of the focal industry. Of course, a caveat that should be borne in mind is the extent to which firms feel comfortable relying on arms-length trading arrangements in buying contexts such as complex, mission critical parts and supplies (see Leamer and Storper 2001).

Relative to the physical marketplace, the electronic marketplace is more conducive to the emergence of demand aggregators in different stages of the supply chain. Here, we use the term 'upstream demand aggregators' to denote aggregator firms in the focal industry who are able to negotiate favorable prices and other terms with firms in the supplier industry on behalf of smaller buyers in the focal industry by pooling their purchases. We use the term 'downstream demand aggregators' to denote demand aggregator firms in downstream industries that are able to extract favorable prices and other terms from firms in the focal industry by pooling the purchases of smaller firms in downstream industries.

To the extent that the emergence of upstream demand aggregators results in lower prices paid by firms in the focal industry for inputs acquired from supplier industries, this will have a favorable effect on profitability of producer firms in the focal industry. In other words, the emergence of upstream demand aggregators in an industry can be expected to weaken the negative effect of supplier concentration on the profitability of the focal industry.

Power of Buyers

Buyer concentration

The five-forces model (Porter 1980) suggests that a buyer group that is concentrated and purchases a large proportion of the output of the focal industry will negatively impact on the profitability of the focal industry. As a consequence of the spread of the Internet, the pool of potential buyers for the offerings of firms in the focal industry can be expected to become larger and emanate from a more global geographic area. The likely net effect of this development will be a weakening of the negative effect of buyer concentration on the profitability of the focal industry.

However, as noted earlier, relative to the physical marketplace, the electronic marketplace is also more conducive to the emergence of both upstream and downstream demand aggregators. To the extent that the emergence of downstream demand aggregators has the effect of lowering the price paid by buyers of the offerings of the focal industry, this is likely to have a detrimental effect on profitability of producer firms in the focal industry. Hence, the emergence of downstream demand aggregators can be expected to strengthen the negative effect of buyer concentration on the profitability of the focal industry.

Threat of New Entrants

Access to distribution channels

Product categories for which channel capacity constraints are a deterrent to the entry of new competitors (e.g. retailers limiting the number of brands of bulky items they carry – such as disposable diapers – due to physical space capacity considerations) positively impacts on the profitability of the focal industry. In contrast to the physical marketplace, the amount of virtual shelf-space available in the electronic marketplace through e-retailers is unlimited and not bounded by space capacity constraints. Consequently, access to distribution channels will be less of a deterrent to the entry of new competitors. This characteristic of the electronic marketplace can be expected to weaken the positive effect of channel capacity constraints on the profitability of the focal industry.

It is important to note, however, that unlimited virtual shelf-space does not imply that physical space capacity considerations are not relevant at all (as a potential entry barrier) in the context of transactions occurring in the electronic marketplace. The incremental cost of displaying a new product on an electronic retailer's web site may be insignificant, but the fulfillment costs associated with carrying that product may not be. In fact, the emerging fulfillment infrastructure for web transaction seems to be optimized for the handling of products with a high weight/volume ratio.

Threat from Substitutes

E-retailers as an alternative channel

From the perspective of traditional retailers, the emergence of e-retailers can be construed as a threat from a potential substitute. Likewise, the increasing ability of producers to market directly to buyers also constitutes a threat from a potential substitute from the standpoint of traditional land-based retailers, e-retailers, and multi-channel retailers who maintain a presence in both the physical and the electronic marketplace. *Ceteris paribus*, an inverse relationship can be expected to exist between concentration at the intermediary level and the propensity of producers to transact directly with customers in the electronic marketplace (i.e. either resorting to total disintermediation or partial disintermediation – marketing direct to customers as well as through intermediaries). Concentration at the intermediary level implies that a relatively small number of intermediaries account for a large proportion of total industry sales to end consumers.

In the USA the air travel industry is an example of an industry characterized by low concentration at the intermediary level (numerous travel agencies, each handling a relatively small proportion of the airline industry's total sales). In such industries, the intermediaries face a greater threat from producers' attempts to develop alternative, direct channels to reach end consumers. Contrasted with the air travel industry, the small electrical home appliances industry (e.g. electric irons, toasters, and blenders) is characterized by high concentration at the intermediary level. In this industry, a few large retailers in the USA (e.g. Wal-Mart, Target, Home Depot and Lowe's) account for a large proportion of industry sales. In such industries, there is a lower likelihood of firms funneling substantial resources to transacting directly with customers in the electronic marketplace. Manufacturers' direct-to-customers initiatives in the electronic marketplace are likely to be limited to marketing of goods such as replacement parts, factory reconditioned/refurbished items, discontinued models, and services such as extended warrantees on products purchased from traditional brick-and-mortar intermediaries.

Intensity of Competition among Entrenched Competitors

Number of competitors

A product market is defined as 'the set of products judged to be substitutes within those usage situations in which similar patterns of benefits are sought by groups of customers' (Srivastava, Alpert and Shocker 1984, p. 32). By explicitly focusing on consumer perceptions, this demand-side approach to defining product markets is more insightful (from a marketing perspective) than a supply-side approach, which attempts to identify homogeneous groups of products on the basis of product attributes or manufacturing inputs and processes. One noteworthy change in recent years is that it is becoming increasingly difficult to delineate stable product-market boundaries. SIC (now NAICS)-based classifications (based on the supply-side perspective) have long served as a basis for defining 'natural markets' but have, in recent years, been losing their utility for understanding the composition and competitive dynamics of a market (Brooks 1995). Nowhere is the blurring of product-market boundaries more evident than in the arena of telecommunication and media. Three traditionally separate product markets – telephone, television, and computers – are becoming increasingly indistinguishable as firms raid each other's turf (Bane, Bradley and Collis 1998).

The blurring of product-market boundaries is not limited to the high-tech sector, although technology is usually the enabling force that enables firms to attempt a re-drawing of product-market boundaries. Sampler (1998), examining the phenomenon of product-market blurring, concludes that it is not technology *per se* but information that enables firms to re-define product-market boundaries. He argues that firms with access to the same body of information about customers have the opportunity (which firms may or may not exercise) to compete in the same product market. Thus, access to information about customers – along with other considerations – becomes an important basis for defining product-market boundaries. Increasingly, firm-to-consumer interactivity is enabling firms to significantly enhance their direct access to customers. Furthermore, firms increasingly acquire information about customers by tapping into consumer-to-consumer and firm-to-firm interactions (see Yadav and Varadarajan (2001) for a general discussion of interactivity and how it creates information generating opportunities for firms). These alternative approaches facilitate the gathering of consumer information which, following Sampler's (1998) line of reasoning, should further alter the traditional product-market boundaries. Specifically, individual firms will be emboldened to increase the number of product-markets in which they compete. As a result, the number of firms competing in any given product market is also likely to increase. Collectively, we refer to the product market changes described in this section as indications of increasing competitive overlap, which, in turn, could lead to lower industry concentration.

A large body of literature in industrial organization economics, strategic management, and marketing posits a positive relationship between industry concentration and average industry profitability. It is contended that concentrated market structures create oligopolistic coordination opportunities among competitors, resulting in lower output, higher prices, and higher rates of return (see Jacobson 1988). The emergence of the electronic marketplace significantly extends the geographic reach of firms, due to the greater ability it bestows on competing firms to promote their offerings to, communicate with, and transact with prospective buyers located farther away from their principal base of operation (i.e. from national to global). The electronic marketplace, due to its potential to bring many more companies into competition with one another, can be expected to weaken the positive effect of industry concentration on the profitability of the focal industry.

EXPERIENCE EFFECTS

In a number of industries, it has been observed that the average total cost per unit, measured in constant currency, declines by a constant percentage with every doubling of cumulative experience. Experience effects are cost reductions that are achieved by a firm as a result of proprietary learning associated with cumulative experience. Potential sources of cost reduction achieved through proprietary learning associated with cumulative experience include increased labor efficiency, work specialization and methods improvement, process improvements, and changes in the resource mix (Abell and Hammond 1978). Hence, in product categories characterized by pronounced experience effects, a firm that accumulates experience more rapidly than its competitors will be at a competitive cost advantage.

Information products refer to those products that can be stored and distributed in digital form (e.g. software, music). The production of information products is characterized by high sunk costs, modest fixed costs, and low variable costs. Sunk costs refer to costs that are incurred in developing a product (e.g. R&D expenditure and prototype development costs) that are not recoverable, should production not be undertaken or discontinued. In the limit, when the electronic marketplace is used exclusively for promotion, distribution and transaction facilitation of an information product, the variable cost associated with the production and distribution of additional units tends toward zero. A case in point would be a firm in the business of developing and marketing income tax preparation software, and primarily focusing on the electronic marketplace as a medium for product promotion, transaction facilitation and distribution (i.e. using the Internet for provision of information about the product to prospective buyers, payment for the software over the net with a credit card, and downloading of the software from the seller's server to the buyer's PC). Even in instances where other channels are used for the distribution of information products (e.g. an application software copied on a disc and marketed through land-based retail outlets), the variable costs of producing additional copies do not vary with the number of units (copies) made. Unlike physical products whose production quantity may be constrained by natural limits (capacity constraints), there are significantly fewer production-related constraints in the case of information products (Shapiro and Varian 1999; see also Arthur 1996). Relative to the high costs associated with the production of the first unit, any savings that might result from cost reductions associated with cumulative experience would be inconsequential. Hence, due to the unique cost structure of information products, competitive strategies grounded in the logic of experience curves would be inapplicable.

However, proprietary organizational learning is likely to be a potential source of significant cost reductions with respect to other cost components. For instance, the organizational learning that a producer of information products (e.g. software) may accumulate over a period of time is likely to enable the firm to achieve significant cost savings in the upgrading of its existing products as well as the development of new products. The potential to leverage organizational learning in this manner assumes increased significance in the context of a global electronic marketplace (Sawhney and Parikh 2001; Quelch and Klein 1996). The key challenge in the current environment is to create, deploy, and manage a global network architecture (Gupta and Govindarajan 2001). Comprising both physical and information resources, the network architecture must be designed to allow a firm to address problems and take advantage of business opportunities in a cost-effective and distinctive manner. According to Craig and Douglas (2000), a firm's configural advantage that results from the optimal deployment of physical and information resources in this manner is essential for succeeding in a marketplace that is becoming increasingly global as a result of the Internet.

GENERIC COMPETITIVE STRATEGIES

Porter (1980) distinguishes between two broad generic competitive strategies – cost leadership and differentiation. Cost leadership entails a business leveraging its skills and resources to achieve a defensible position of competitive cost advantage in the marketplace (i.e. being the lowest-cost producer). Differentiation entails a business leveraging its skills and resources to differentiate its product offering from its competitors' product offerings and thereby achieving a defensible position of competitive differentiation advantage in the marketplace. Cost leadership focus and differentiation focus, respectively, refer to the pursuit of a cost leadership and differentiation strategy in the context of a narrow market segment (as opposed to a broad market). Simultaneous pursuit of competitive cost advantage and differentiation advantage is viewed as not conducive to achieving superior performance. For instance, Porter (1980) cautions that a business that simultaneously pursues cost leadership and differentiation runs the risk of being stuck in the middle. The conceptual reasoning under-lying the feasibility or lack thereof of the simultaneous pursuit of compet-itive cost advantage and differentiation advantage has been the focus of extensive debate and discussion in the literature (see, e.g. Chrisman, Hofer and Boulton 1988; Murray 1988; Walker and Ruekert 1987).

A number of considerations suggest that in the evolving marketplace comprising the physical and the electronic marketplace, the simultaneous pursuit of cost leadership and differentiation is not only viable, it might also be a competitive imperative. Case in point: a source of competitive advantage enjoyed by firms such as Dell Computers that build to order (i.e., assembling a PC only after receiving a confirmed order from a customer) is their significantly lower work-in-process inventory carrying costs. In fact, conducting their business in the electronic marketplace enables these firms to achieve a significant reduction in inventory-related costs over the entire business system encompassing suppliers, the focal firm, and its customers. This is accomplished by orchestrating just-in-time delivery of parts, com-ponents and sub-assemblies by suppliers, and finished goods to customers. In effect, the pursuit of a strategy of product customization enables such firms to achieve both a competitive differentiation advantage and a com-petitive cost advantage (for additional discussion of the strategic implica-tions of product customization, see Kotha's (1995) case study of Japan's National Bicycle Company).

The simultaneous pursuit of cost and differentiation advantages in tech-nology-intensive, global markets will require fundamentally new thinking about how firms create and capture value. According to Lazer and Shaw (2000), incremental thinking is likely to yield only incremental perfor-mance-related improvements in this environment. They call for the devel-opment of new approaches and ideas that will help firms to achieve and sustain a position of competitive advantage. Price (1996) proposes a three-dimensional strategic space (comprising product, process, and consumer needs) to facilitate such thinking. In this framework, the three dimensions are related in that changes or issues pertinent to one dimension can impact other dimensions. For instance, changes in product form (e.g. analog to digital) may necessitate changes in process (technologies and production systems) to meet changed consumer needs (management of digital music collections). Price contends that the simultaneous consideration of all three dimensions while formulating strategy will help firms avoid pitfalls that often occur when they focus myopically only on one dimension at a time.

MARKET PIONEERING ADVANTAGE

A market pioneer or first-mover refers to a business being either the first to introduce a new product, employ a new process, or enter a new market. In a number of industries and product markets it has been observed that, on average, the first-mover has a higher market share than early followers, and early followers have higher market shares than later entrants. This observed pattern of relationship suggests that market pioneering can be a normative strategy conducive to superior marketplace and financial performance, and is attributed to the competitive cost and differentiation advantages associated with market pioneering (Lieberman and Montgomery 1988; Kerin, Varadarajan and Peterson 1992). A number of potential sources of market pioneering advantage have been enumerated in extant literature including the following.

Scale Preemption

The market pioneer making preemptive investments in scale in an attempt to achieve a competitive cost advantage and deterring the entry of competitors.

Spatial Preemption

The market pioneer preempting the most desirable positions in the market (locations occupied in physical space and perceptual space).

Resource Preemption

The market pioneer acquiring/contracting for factor inputs and scarce resources at more favorable terms than early followers and later entrants.

Channel Preemption

The market pioneer preempting the most important/attractive channels.

Definitional

The market pioneer either being able to set the industry standards or having a major influence in setting industry standards that later entrants are forced to adopt.

Consumer Learning and Prototypicality

The market pioneer's offerings becoming the standards in the minds of consumers with which later entrants' offerings are compared.

Consumer Use Experience and Information Asymmetry

Consumers having greater use experience and knowing more about the market pioneer's product offering than later entrants' offerings.

Consumer Risk Aversion

Users who are satisfied with the market pioneer's offerings being unwilling to take the risk of trying a later entrant's offerings.

Switching Costs

The market pioneer locking in buyers who might be unwilling to incur costs (contractual, non-contractual, and/or staggered switching costs) associated with changing suppliers.

Network Effects

Consumers favoring the market pioneer's offering due to network effects – the pioneer's offering becoming increasingly valuable to its present and potential user as the number of users of the product (i.e. the size of the network) increases.

A pertinent question in regard to pioneering advantage is whether some of the potential sources of first-mover advantage are likely to diminish in importance, and others increase in importance as the competitive landscape shifts from the physical marketplace to a hybrid marketplace encompassing both the physical and the electronic marketplace. We address this question in reference to preemptive investments in scale (of operations) as a potential source of first-mover advantage.

Preemptive Investment in Scale

Preemptive investments in manufacturing capacity can be a potential source of first-mover advantage and a credible deterrent to the entry of new competitors under conditions of the minimum efficient scale (MES) being of the same order of magnitude as the size of the market (M). As shown in Figure 16.2, when the ratio of MES/M is of the order of 1.0, a potential

Global electronic commerce

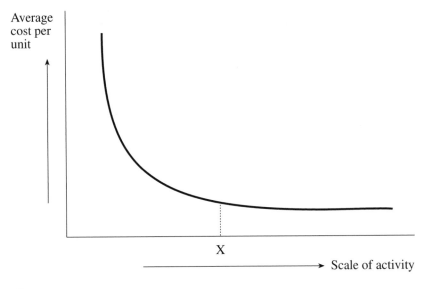

Average
cost per
unit

X

Scale of activity

Notes:
X = MES (Point asymptotic to the horizontal axis).
M = Size of market.
Y = X/M: possible values.
0.05 0.10 0.20 . . . 0.80 0.90 0.95 1.00 1.05 1.10.

*Figure 16.2   Minimum efficient scale and competitive strategy in a global
electronic marketplace*

competitor contemplating entry into the market may be deterred by the
excess capacity that its entry will lead to, and the prospect of intense price
competition that might ensue. However, under conditions of the ratio
MES/M being much smaller than 1.0, no single firm will have a scale-driven
competitive cost advantage. Under these conditions, multiple firms can
coexist in an industry. Preemptive investment in scale of operation is
unlikely either to endow the first-mover with a competitive advantage or to
deter the entry of new competitors. As noted earlier, the emergence of the
electronic marketplace significantly extends the geographic reach of firms,
due to the greater ability it bestows on competing firms to promote their
offerings to, communicate with, and transact with prospective buyers
located farther away from their principal base of operation (i.e. from
national to global). In effect, assessments of market size and market potential are likely to be based on a significantly larger and more global geographic market area. Holding 'MES' constant, a larger 'M' implies that
multiple firms can coexist in an industry and the importance of MES as a

source of first-mover advantage will diminish. Hence, relative to the physical marketplace, preemptive investment in scale of operation as a potential source of first-mover advantage can be expected to diminish in importance in the global electronic marketplace.

CONCLUSION

On one hand, a number of strategy concepts (e.g., generic competitive strategies, market pioneering advantage) subsumed within the international marketing (IM) and international business (IB) literature can be attributed to their relevance transcending products, markets, and countries. On the other hand, a number of other strategy concepts such as strategy of standardization versus adaptation are integral to IM and IB literature by virtue of their focus on the organizational and environmental conditions under which pursuit of alternative global competitive strategies may be conducive to superior performance. Our primary focus in this chapter is on strategy concepts in the genre of the former.

Responding to the Challenges and Opportunities of Global E-commerce

The widespread adoption of the Internet by firms as a tool for information dissemination, interactive communication, transaction facilitation, distribution (of digital and digitizable products), advertising and sales promotion, and other functions is indicative of its potential to have a significant impact upon the practice of international business. At the most fundamental level, the impact of e-commerce on the global marketplace manifests as firms embracing a broader and more global construal of their customers, competitors, suppliers, alliance partners and the served market. The organizational transformation that has occurred at General Electric (GE) in recent years represents an excellent blueprint of how firms can respond to the challenges and opportunities related to global e-commerce. Operating in more than 100 countries with a workforce of 300 000 people worldwide, GE is a complex, global organization.[1] It has a leading presence in more than 20 diverse 'long-cycle' businesses (e.g. power systems, medical systems, aircraft engines), 'short-cycle' businesses (e.g. plastics, appliances, broadcasting), and financial services (e.g. insurance, financing). GE focused on globalization as a major organization-wide initiative in the mid-1980s and has increased its revenues from non-domestic markets at an annual rate of 15 per cent (which is more than twice the rate at which its domestic revenues have increased over the same period of time). GE has been recognized as *Fortune's* Global Most Admired Company (1998, 1999, 2000, 2002) and the *Financial Times's* World's Most Respected Company (1998, 1999, 2000, 2001, 2002).

GE was an early adopter of e-commerce, creating its first web site in 1994 (for GE Plastics). GE's e-commerce initiatives have evolved in three phases: (1) sell-side initiatives, (2) buy-side initiatives, and (3) make-side initiatives. The sell-side initiative initially involved the development of information-only sites (starting with the web site for GE Plastics in 1994). Over the next few years, GE's efforts evolved quickly from information-only sites (the so-called brochureware) to transactional sites. GE's first transactional site (Polymerland.com) went live in 1997 and was handling about US$10000 per week in online sales at the start of 1999. By the end of 1999, online sales at Polymerland.com had jumped to more than US$6 million per week. Overall, the sell-side initiative has been very successful at GE. With almost no online sales in 1998, GE increased its online sales to US$1 billion in 1999 and US$7 billion in 2000. The buy-side initiative involved e-commerce applications designed to digitize purchasing operations and improve buyer productivity. Electronic auctions, an important component of the buy-side e-commerce initiative, accounted for US$6 billion in online purchases in 2000. GE's Global Supplier Network, which facilitates interactions and transactions with 36 000 vendors located all over the world, has emerged as the largest private electronic marketplace. Finally, GE's make-side initiative represents an effort to use digitization to reduce or eliminate manual and paper-generating processes throughout the organization. GE estimates that it can eliminate US$10 billion in costs through these digitization efforts.

Spurred by the growing strategic significance of its e-commerce initiatives, GE formally embraced digitization as its fourth organization-wide initiative in 1999 (the other three initiatives being globalization, services, and its process-improvement focus called Six Sigma). Announcing the company's decision to embrace digitization in all aspects of its business, Jack Welch, GE's former CEO and the primary force behind the company's digitization initiative, stated that it 'changed the DNA of GE forever by energizing and revitalizing every corner of the company'. The sweeping scope of this statement, we believe, applies to other organizations as well.

DIRECTIONS FOR FUTURE RESEARCH

The scope of this chapter is limited to revisiting extant perspectives on (1) the role of industry structural forces, (2) experience curves, (3) generic competitive strategies, and (4) market pioneering advantages in the context of competitive strategy in a global electronic marketplace. The implications of the emergence of the global electronic marketplace in reference to extant perspectives on a number of other strategy concepts, tools, techniques, and frameworks represents a promising avenue for further research.

In exploring these questions, there is a need for future research efforts to focus on the unique characteristics and capabilities of the emerging electronic marketplace. However, these research efforts must not overlook the role of geography as firms rethink their strategy in global markets that are increasingly connected, and impacted, by the Internet. As recent research has shown, traditional geography-related considerations remain extremely important in an environment that is increasingly becoming electronic (see, e.g. Leamer and Storper 2001; Zaheer and Zaheer 2001). The Internet seems to facilitate increased geographical dispersion of firms and increased dominance of existing geographical clusters. That is, while the ability to remotely access markets prompts firms to locate in more markets, these firms also perceive a heightened need to establish a physical presence in markets where a large number of their competitors are located. Leamer and Storper (2001) speculate that competing firms are motivated to establish a presence in the same geographical cluster to take advantage of 'knowledge spillovers' – in essence creating the ability to learn from the actions and activities of their competitors. As the non-codifiable information content of these knowledge spillovers increases (i.e. when tacit knowledge components are involved; see Polanyi 1962), a firm's ability to observe and benefit from such knowledge spillovers can be significantly curtailed. In such cases, competing firms are likely to continue gravitating toward the same geographical clusters. Research efforts are needed to better understand how firms create both physical and remote electronic access resources (see Zaheer and Manrakhan 2001) to better manage the changing competitive forces discussed here.

Kaplan and Sawhney (2000) note that a wide variety of business-to-business (B2B) initiatives that serve as meeting places for suppliers and buyers are likely to emerge as the Internet's adoption spreads across different industries. These initiatives are likely to focus both on what businesses buy (operating inputs and manufacturing inputs) and how businesses buy (systematic sourcing and spot sourcing). While the first wave of such initiatives has struggled to find acceptance, there are significant long-term productivity gains that can result from these new buying–selling arrangements (Litan and Rivlin 2001). Therefore, it is reasonable to expect that firms will continue to experiment with alternative structures and business models for these B2B marketplaces. One recent trend is towards the so-called sponsored exchanges (e.g. Covisint, with Ford, General Motors, and DaimlerChrysler as the main sponsors). One clear advantage of such exchanges is that they address the liquidity problem (i.e. attracting a critical mass of buyers and suppliers) that has plagued a number of other B2B initiatives. It remains to be seen whether the growth of such biased market-places (biased in that they presumably represent the interests of the sponsoring firms) will be able to match the ambitious projections that have been announced by the sponsoring companies.

NOTE

1. Our discussion in this section is based on the company's annual reports and related articles in the business press.

REFERENCES

Abell, Derek F. and John Hammond (1978), *Strategic Market Planning*, Englewood Cliffs, NJ: Prentice-Hall.
Arthur, Brian (1996), 'Increasing Returns and the New World of Business', *Harvard Business Review*, **74** (6), 100–109.
Bain, Joseph (1956), *Barriers to Competition*, Cambridge, MA: Harvard University Press.
Bane, P. William, Stephen P. Bradley and David J. Collis (1998), 'The Converging Worlds of Telecommunication', in Stephen P. Bradley and Richard L. Nolan (eds), *Sense and Respond: Capturing Value in the Networked Era*, Boston, MA: Harvard Business School Press, pp. 31–62.
Besanko, David, David Dranove and Mark Shanley (1996), *Economics of Strategy*, New York, NY: John Wiley & Sons.
Brooks, Geoffrey R. (1995), 'Defining Market Boundaries', *Strategic Management Journal*, **16** (Summer), 535–49.
Chrisman, James J., Charles W. Hofer and William R. Boulton (1988), 'Toward a System of Classifying Business Strategies', *Academy of Management Review*, **13**, 413–28.
Craig, C. Samuel and Susan P. Douglas (2000), 'Configural Advantage in Global Markets', *Journal of International Marketing*, **8** (1), 6–26.
ELMAR (1999), 'Call for Papers for the May 2000 Conference on Electronic Commerce and Global Business', *Journal of International Business Studies*.
Gupta, Anil K. and Vijay Govindarajan (2001), 'Converting Global Presence into Global Competitive Advantage', *Academy of Management Executive*, **15** (2), 45–58.
Jacobson, Robert (1988), 'Distinguishing Among Competing Theories of the Market Share Effect', *Journal of Marketing*, **52** (October), 62–80.
Kaplan, Steven and Mohanbir Sawhney (2000), 'E-Hubs: The New B2B Marketplaces', *Harvard Business Review*, **78** (May–June), 97–103.
Kerin, Roger A., P. Rajan Varadarajan and Robert A. Peterson (1992), 'First-Mover Advantage: A Synthesis, Conceptual Framework, and Research Propositions', *Journal of Marketing*, **56** (October), 33–52.
Kotha, Suresh (1995), 'Mass Customization: Implementing the Emerging Paradigm for Competitive Advantage', *Strategic Management Journal*, **16** (Summer), 21–42.

Lazer, William and Eric H. Shaw (2000), 'Global Marketing Management: At the Dawn of the New Millennium', *Journal of International Marketing*, **8** (1), 65–77.

Leamer, Edward E. and Michael Storper (2001), 'The Economic Geography of the Internet Age', *Journal of International Business Studies*, **32** (4), 641–65.

Lieberman, Marvin, B. and David B. Montgomery (1988), 'First-Mover Advantages', *Strategic Management Journal*, **9** (Summer), 41–58.

Litan, Robert E. and Alice M. Rivlin (2001), 'Projecting the Economic Impact of the Internet', *American Economic Review*, **91** (2), 313–17.

Murray, Allan I. (1988), 'A Contingency View of Porter's "Generic Strategies"', *Academy of Management Review*, **13** (3), 390–400.

Polanyi, M. (1962), *Personal Knowledge: Towards a Post-Critical Philosophy*, Chicago, IL: University of Chicago.

Porter, Michael E. (1978), 'How Competitive Forces Shape Strategy', *Harvard Business Review*, **57** (March–April), 43–59.

Porter, Michael E. (1980), *Competitive Strategy: Techniques for Analyzing Industries and Competitors*, New York: Free Press.

Porter, Michael E. (2001), 'Strategy and the Internet', *Harvard Business Review*, **79** (March), 63–78.

Price, Robert M. (1996), 'Technology and Strategic Advantage', *California Management Review*, **38** (3), 38–56.

Quelch, John A. and Lisa R. Klein (1996), 'The Internet and International Marketing', *Sloan Management Review*, **40** (1), 60–75.

Sampler, Jeffrey L. (1998), 'Redefining Market Structure for the Information Age', *Strategic Management Journal*, **19** (April), 343–55.

Sawhney, Mohanbir and Deval Parikh (2001), 'Where Value Lives in a Networked World', *Harvard Business Review*, **79** (1), 79–86.

Shapiro, Carl and Hal R. Varian (1999), *Information Rules: A Strategic Guide to the Network Economy*, Cambridge, MA: Harvard Business School Press.

Srivastava, Rajendra K., Mark I. Alpert and Allan D. Shocker (1984), 'A Customer-Oriented Approach for Determining Market Structures', *Journal of Marketing*, **48** (2), 32–45.

Tapscott, Don (2001), 'Rethinking Strategy in a Networked World (or Why Michael Porter Is Wrong About the Internet)', *Strategy and Business*, **24**, 1–8.

Varadarajan, Rajan (1999), 'Strategy Content and Process Perspectives Revisited', *Journal of the Academy of Marketing Science*, **27** (Winter), 88–100.

Varadarajan, Rajan and Manjit S. Yadav (2002), 'Marketing Strategy and the Internet: An Organizing Framework', *Journal of the Academy of Marketing Science*, **30** (4), 296–312.

Walker, Orville C., Jr and Robert W. Ruekert (1987), 'Marketing's Role in the Implementation of Business Strategies: A Critical Review and Conceptual Framework', *Journal of Marketing*, **51** (3), 15–33.

Yadav, Manjit S. and Rajan Varadarajan (2002),' Interactivity in the Electronic Marketplace: An Exposition of the Concept and its Implications for Consumer Research', Working Paper, Department of Marketing, Texas: A&M University.

Zaheer, Srilata and Shalini Manrakhan (2001), 'Concentration and Dispersion in Global Industries: Remote Electronic Access and the Location of Economic Activities', *Journal of International Business Studies*, **32** (4), 667–86.

Zaheer, Srilata and Akbar Zaheer (2001), 'Market Microstructures in a Global B2B Network', *Strategic Management Journal*, **22** (3), 859–73.

17. Roles and consequences of electronic commerce in global marketing

Saeed Samiee

INTRODUCTION

The Internet is one of the most significant marketing tools for the global marketplace. Estimates from various electronic commerce (e-commerce) surveys indicate that Internet users worldwide will more than double from approximately 318 million in 2000 to about 717 million in 2005 (users/1000 will also double from 53 to 111) (Pastore 1999). According to the International Data Corporation (IDC), about 60 per cent of the worldwide online audience now comes from outside the USA and is expected to generate 46 per cent of global e-commerce spending by 2003, as compared with 26 per cent in 1998 (IDC 1999). In particular, Western Europe's e-commerce sector is expected to grow at a compounded annual growth rate of 138 per cent and result in e-commerce sales of US$430 billion by 2003 as compared to just US$5.6 billion in 1998. Japan and other Asia-Pacific nations constitute the second fastest growing area.

The Internet has potentially significant ramifications and benefits for global marketing and, consequently, global e-commerce. As it continues to evolve, it is difficult to predict innovations, applications, and additional uses that will become available in the future.[1] Contemporary perspectives regarding its roles and consequences in global marketing are shaped by our current knowledge rather than infinite wisdom about the future. Thus, the Internet and the corresponding technologies being developed may have significant implications for global marketing which may render current views regarding e-commerce's roles and consequences in global marketing incomplete. With this caveat in mind, this study attempts to explore, both conceptually and pragmatically, potential roles and consequences of incorporating e-commerce in global marketing decisions.

Despite the Internet's growing international usage and unrealized potential, only a limited effort has been expended to explore the ways in which it might influence or alter global marketing planning and strategy. Accordingly, to better understand the phenomenon and identify its role and consequences, an appropriate conceptual base is necessary. The purpose of this study is to explore the issue and to make an attempt to address these gaps. Although the Internet and e-commerce denote different but complementary phenomena, contemporary e-commerce tends to be Internet dependent and marketing activities typically involve a great deal of communications that go beyond mere transactions. Thus, in this study the focus is on both the Internet and e-commerce.

This chapter is divided into six sections. First, some background information regarding the role of the Internet and e-commerce in competitive strategy is offered. Next, two complementary bases for developing a conceptual framework for global e-commerce are proposed. Third, various obstacles to the use of the Internet and e-commerce in global marketing are discussed. Fourth, perspectives regarding the Internet as a mediator of internationalization of firms and its roles for market entry and international expansion as well as development in less developed markets are explored. Finally, the role of e-commerce in global marketing strategy and concluding remarks are offered.

BACKGROUND

Although some observers view the Internet as an entirely new way of competing in domestic and global markets, experts' views on the issue are converging along the traditional means of creating economic value and, hence, competition across industries: i.e. industry structure and sustainable competitive advantage. The Internet has been a great tool that has enabled firms to reconfigure existing industries by reducing the high cost of communications, data collection, information gathering, and transaction processing (Porter 2001). However, the Internet has not fundamentally restructured industries. In other words, the rules of competition within each industry have not changed. The Internet has tacitly dampened the power structure within distribution channels by offering at least the possibility of direct links between manufacturers or suppliers and customers or the users. Indeed, by virtue of offering easier access to information, it enhances the bargaining power of the customer and widens the geographic scope of competitiors and, at least in theory, increases the number of competitors. In a global sense, however, there is a point at which it is no longer profitable to service a distant customer in the case of products that need to be shipped, installed, and/or regularly maintained. The logistical costs (e.g., packing, documentation, shipping, taxes, duties, and customs clearance) associated with ordinary consumer products also render them useless for global e-commerce. Naturally, highly differentiated, difficult to obtain products gain a competitive advantage via global e-commerce because buyers would be more likely to assume the costs associated with their purchase.

It is believed that the Internet significantly reduces search costs and, hence, leads to lower prices. However, the cost of using the Internet is by no means negligible. Consumers are routinely asked to register in order to gain access to a site, following which they need to learn how to navigate that particular site. The costs are even higher for business customers as they will need to integrate their systems to comply with the software and the rules of a group they wish to join (Porter 2001). There is also the cost and the risk associated with translation and correct interpretation of sites. It is very expensive to translate sites and no firm will make its site available in every key language. Although English is the de facto international language, customers prefer to use and function in their native language. A market targeted for global marketing, via conventional approaches or the Internet, should ideally be presented with a locally-suitable marketing plan, including communications in the local language(s).

It is also noteworthy that the use of the Internet or e-commerce offers no sustainable competitive advantage in and by itself. Firms can easily acquire the necessary hardware and software or assign third-party contractors to host their sites (Samiee 1998). Even the fancy features of a given site can be easily duplicated by other firms. It should then come as no surprise that many first-mover dotcoms were eventually beaten by their brick-and-mortar rivals who acquired or internally developed a 'web-savvy' at least as good as those of the early entrants. The CVS drugstore chain, a relative late-comer to online business, for example, set up its e-commerce site in about six months through an acquisition (*Drug Store News* 1999) and developed and implemented its Internet-based purchasing system within 60 days (Porter 2001). During the 1990s, many dotcom startups' strategy consisted of an untested, if not unrealistic, low-cost, competitive or low price strategy through which they hoped to accumulate orders over the Internet and collect payments in advance. In practice, these funds would earn interest while orders were being accumulated. When the minimum order quantities were reached, orders would be placed through pre-approved suppliers which, in turn, would ship directly or indirectly (through dotcoms) to customers. The need to build an infrastructure just like their brick-and-mortar rivals was not a serious consideration for many dotcoms because their strategies relied largely on using the existing systems. For example, Amazon's first warehouse was opened several years after it was in business. Some dotcoms drove themselves out of business by duplicating expensive and unnecessary infrastructure (e.g. Webvan and PeaPod). The cost of actually owning and operating an infrastructure, including warehouses and inventory, on top of hardware, software, and top-heavy human resource needs[2] invalidated such a strategy and placed these firms at a competitive disadvantage *vis-à-vis* their traditional competitors. In most cases the Internet has changed the front-end of these business (Porter 2001) rather than fundamentally changing the rules that govern industry structures or competitive advantage. At best only an incremental change to firms' ongoing practices has occurred. E-commerce appears to work best when it complements the existing business infrastructures of firms, as is the case for catalog operators. Lands' End maintains a successful catalog operation for several key international markets, complete with strategically-located warehouses. Its web site merely accommodates and complements its ongoing business plan rather than introducing a dramatic change or offering a new business model. Not surprisingly, it is now a successful global e-commerce firm with an infrastructure to handle global sourcing and customers. This success is a direct result of the firm's pursuit of a well-defined intermarket segment and the co-alignment of its marketing strategy to the prevailing conditions in its host markets. Theoretical support for this position is discussed in the next section.

BASIS FOR A THEORETICAL FOUNDATION

To better grasp issues and considerations that have a bearing on global e-commerce, it is necessary to establish a foundation, framework, or theory that guides the exploration. Thus far, little effort has been expended in this area in part because the focus is more often on the application of the Internet and its associated technical requirements rather than on exploring the marketing or strategic roles or changes in processes that are caused or mediated by e-commerce. Furthermore, technological platforms and related software products are dynamic by nature, which has led many to view e-commerce as a moving target and, thus, unnecessarily complicated. The lack of progress towards developing a solid conceptual footing in this area has led to a descriptive literature which is of limited help in illuminating the bigger picture.

In this study e-commerce is viewed strictly as a vehicle for exchange and, therefore, a marketing activity that, in theory, can transcend national boundaries. Exchange can be between individuals, organizations, or both. Since the marketing discipline and marketing theory are well developed, it seems reasonable to leverage off concepts upon which marketing is based.

However, an appropriate theoretical framing should also accommodate or incorporate the nature of e-commerce.

Two interrelated concepts, segmentation and strategy co-alignment, are central to marketing thought. Additionally, the five forces of competition (Porter 1980) offer important insights in assessing whether and how the structure of industries is affected by the Internet and e-commerce. First, the segmentation concept is central to the marketing plan and international marketing scholars have advocated the pursuit of intermarket segments in exploiting markets abroad (Levitt 1983; Jain 1989).[3] Using the intermarket segment concept as a basis implies that the success of e-commerce, as with the traditional marketing approach, depends on how well segments are strategically defined and reached. In other words, in the absence of solid evidence that customers around the world have actually modified their behavior as a result of the Internet, global marketing strategies should be developed in the same manner and incorporate the same components as before.

Second, there is substantial support in the strategy literature that the co-alignment of international marketing strategy (i.e. the global e-commerce plan) and the environmental context (i.e. the characteristics and macro and micro conditions of intermarket segments being targeted) have positive implications for business performance (Ginsberg and Venkatraman 1985; Venkatraman and Prescott 1990). That is, the role the Internet and e-commerce might play in a firm's global marketing program for a specific intermarket segment needs to match market conditions and customers' needs. At the present, market characteristics with regard to the penetration and use of the Internet vary significantly across markets which, in turn, hinder appropriate delineation and comprehensive coverage of intermarket segments. As shown in Table 17.1, there is a great variance in how the Internet is used in various markets. Currently, Internet users around the world tend to be younger (under 50), educated (college graduates), men who hold professional or other white-collar positions. Although such a user profile is not entirely unexpected for a high-technology product, it substantially limits segmentation and targeting in the traditional context.

Leveraging off these conceptual points, the Internet's appropriate domain in global marketing can be explored in terms of the medium's eventual penetration in various markets. Table 17.2 demonstrates that penetration rates vary significantly across different regions. Current market penetration of the Internet should not be the sole basis for developing intermarket segments. However, the lack of sufficient penetration of the Internet in many markets around the world naturally impedes significant reliance on this medium by consumer and industrial firms alike. Concurrently, the

Table 17.1   Some Internet user population and basic characteristics

Country	Population (millions)	Internet Users 2000 (millions)	Internet Penetration (%)	Male Users (%)	Other Characteristics
China	1200	8.9	0.7	85	86% college graduates
Denmark	5	n.a.	n.a.	73	63% white-collar workers or students
Finland	5	2.2	44.0	n.a.	The highest Internet penetration
Korea	45	9.4	20.8	67	68% use the Internet for information
Russia	145	5.4	3.7	62	70% professionals or students
UK	59	12.5	21.2	62	89% under 50 years old
Europe	369	98.5	26.7	31	Average age 32 years

Source: Industry statistics, worldwide internet population.
http://www.commerce.net/research/stats/wwstats.html, September 2001.

characteristics of Internet users across markets define the necessary homogeneity of intermarket segments in which the Internet somehow will play specific marketing roles.

OBSTACLES TO THE USE OF THE INTERNET IN GLOBAL MARKETING

Two sets of impediments create a formidable challenge to seamless global application of the Internet. In an earlier study, Samiee (1998) identified a series of obstacles to the use of the Internet in international marketing. These impediments are shown in Table 17.3 and consist of structural and functional barriers. Structural issues represent macro-environmental

Table 17.2 Internet users and growth by region

Region	Users (000)				Users/1000 People			
	1995	1998	2000	2005	1995	1998	2000	2005
Worldwide	39479	150887	318650	717083	6.9	25.4	52.5	110.5
North America	26217	82989	148730	229780	89.4	275.7	479.1	715.4
Western Europe	8528	34741	86577	202201	21.7	87.5	217.5	501.4
Eastern Europe	369	2983	9487	43767	1.3	10.2	32.7	151.8
Asia-Pacific	3628	24559	57607	171098	1.1	7.2	16.6	45.9
South/Central America	293	2722	10766	43529	0.6	5.5	21.1	78.6
Middle East/Africa	444	2893	7482	26708	0.5	2.9	7.2	23.6

Source: Michael Pastore (1999), 'Worldwide Internet Users to Pass 500 million Next Century', Computer Industry Almanac, CIA estimates, http://cyberatlas.internet.com/big_picture/geographics/article/0,1323,5911_200001,00.html.

Table 17.3 *Structural and functional obstacles to the deployment of the Internet in global marketing*

Structural issues	Functional issues
● Computer Literacy	● Mass Marketing vs. Segmentation
● PC Ownership	● Product vs. Service vs. Processes
● Internet Access	● Brand Equity and Knowledge
● Language	● Promotion
● Culture	● Pricing (taxes, duties, and shipping)
● Laws and Regulations	● Distribution and Logistics (customs, timely delivery, incompatible forms and supply chain systems)
● Tariff Structure and Quotas	● Information Management
● —	● Payment (methods, exchange controls)
● —	● Customer Discontent

Source: Adapted from S. Samiee (1998), 'The Internet and International Marketing: Is There a Fit?', *Journal of Interactive Marketing*, 5–21.

factors with specific reference to information technology in various markets. Such considerations as computer literacy, PC ownership, and Internet access are essential if the Internet is to play any role in marketing. Even in the highly developed nations, the penetration of the Internet is far less than 100 per cent. Finland has the highest proportion of any population (44 per cent) with access to the Internet (Table 17.1). In the USA about 40 per cent of households have access. These numbers drop sharply as the level of development of nations declines.

It is evident from the data in Tables 17.1 and 17.2 that penetration of the Internet in some countries is quite high and that substantial growth in global access to and use of the Internet is anticipated by 2005. Some developed nations, such as the USA and Finland, have historically had one of the highest Internet penetration rates. The data also indicate that some key players in international trade, such as China and Russia, have the lowest penetration and usage of the Internet and, although Internet access in their respective regions is expected to triple by 2005 (see Table 17.2), substantial use of e-commerce in these nations will take some time. However, the Internet is growing rapidly in many countries and as its overall cost falls, it will become as commonplace as the telephone in commerce and eventually play as important a role in global marketing.

Additional structural considerations include language, culture, laws and regulations, and tariffs and quotas. Language, in particular, is a daunting

Table 17.4   The languages of the Internet

Rank	Language	Number of Pages	Corrected Percentage	Estimated Number of Servers
1	English	2722	82.3	332778
2	German	147	4.0	17971
3	Japanese	101	1.6	12348
4	French	59	1.5	7213
5	Spanish	38	1.1	4646
6	Swedish	35	0.6	4279
7	Italian	31	0.8	3790
8	Portuguese	21	0.7	2567
9	Dutch	20	0.4	2445
10	Norwegian	19	0.3	2323
11	Finnish	14	0.3	1712
12	Czech	11	0.3	1345
13	Danish	9	0.3	1100
14	Russian	8	0.1	978
15	Malay	4	0.1	489
	unknown		5.6	
Total		3239	100	395984

Source: Web languages hit parade, June 1997, http://www.isoc.org:8080/palmares.en.html.

problem. Despite the availability of a variety of translation engines, the effort thus far falls far below the desired quality. In addition, web-based translation engines are available only in a limited number of languages. Reliance on the strict use of any single language or translation engine introduces unnecessary random and costly risks to marketers. As such, at the present, it is not advisable for a business to rely on a translation software to implement a global, Internet-based reach. However, even when the firm proactively avoids the temptation to internationalize in this format, it cannot stop the random surfer from using such engines to translate an entire site. In such instances, however, the risk is shifted away from the firm to the user.

English is currently both the main language of international business and *the* language of the Internet. As shown in Table 17.4, 82 per cent of web sites in the world are in English. Indeed, other key languages such as French, German, and Spanish represent a small proportion of web pages on the Internet. On the other hand, research indicates that people generally prefer to use their native tongue in personal and business matters.

This implies that, although random hits on a firm's web site are likely, a successful global e-commerce plan should be targeted for specific inter-market segments that offer greater promise and in which the firm may have a strategic advantage over its competitors. The firm then prepares specific sites for its target markets. Quelle, the German catalog operator, for example, has chosen to remain largely German whereas Lands' End has developed a specific site for each target market. Viewed in this light, it is evident that market selection, targeting, and planning in an Internet-mediated international marketing environment are not much different than in a conventional one. In other words, the e-commerce strategy adopted must be co-aligned with the environmental context within which it is implemented.

The impact of human interaction, shopping preferences, and buyer behavior (i.e. cultural differences) in Internet-mediated global marketing is also significant. If personal interaction during purchase processes is impor-tant in a given culture, then the Internet's role in marketing is likely to be limited to a support instrument for relationship management. The situation faced by Carrefour in its attempt to link its suppliers in Italy demonstrates this point. Its pilot program was designed to link its 30 Italian suppliers to their Milan buying office (Nairn 1997). Carrefour intended to use a proprie-tary software to negotiate contracts over the Internet. Carrefour's main challenge was to convince smaller suppliers to (a) invest in the appropriate hardware and software and (b) to re-engineer their business processes to conform to Carrefour's Internet-based vision. Although Carrefour com-mands significant weight as a customer and channel captain, most markets, particularly developing ones, are highly fragmented and include many small suppliers which the firm needs. As such Carrefour cannot ignore its suppliers' preferences and views. It is likely that any Internet-driven strat-egy would face such a predicament in higher context cultures. Aside from smaller firms' unwillingness to invest in the technology in these cultures, personal relationships there are often as important, if not more so, than commercial outcomes.

Another set of obstacles consists of functional or marketing strategy considerations, including segmentation versus mass marketing, the use of the Internet for transactions of products and services versus implementa-tion of marketing processes, appropriate levels of pricing distribution, promotion, information management, and potential customer discontent. A key, but implicit, issue raised in many circles is whether in an Internet-mediated environment the firm can or should attempt to delineate inter-market segments as opposed to pursuing a default-based mass-marketing approach. If access to a firm's products and prices is widely available through the Internet, then the firm can pursue a global mass-marketing approach. However, the theoretical underpinnings of monopolistic competition and market segmentation tell us that in capitalist, market economies, firms always try to be better than the competition to win more orders. In turn, this mindset leads to differentiation and, when possible, to segmentation. In any event, given the many differences across country environments, segmentation is a meaningful approach. However, segmentation through the Internet is difficult because in the absence of exclusivity through a password-protected system it tends to be accessible by everyone, that is, a reactive, default-based, bottom-up process. Traditionally, intermarket segments are proactively identified through extensive market research involving customers, based on which characteristics, preferences, behavioral patterns, and/or lifestyles are used to promote/communicate with targeted groups that match the firm's marketing strategy. In an Internet-mediated business environment, the marketer can collect a variety of personal and behavioral data (including surfing behavior) from visitors to its site (or through such suppliers as DoubleClick), in a bottom-up, reactive fashion. The downside of this approach is that the firm can never be certain of its true segment size and most likely will never reach all potential members of a targeted group. An added obstacle is the privacy regulations of many nations which prohibit collection and dissemination of personal data. These regulations, most notably in the European Union, limit the range of data that can be gathered and regulate how and when the firm might use such data.

The Internet is a suitable medium for global marketing and distribution of services that can be digitized such as audio, video, software, various information services, and marketing research. Global marketing of digitized services that do not require local maintenance are clearly ideal for the Internet. Others such as computer software, particularly proprietary ones, may need professional installation, testing, debugging, and training which may require a local presence and be less adaptable to the Internet. Business and marketing processes are clearly most suitable for the Internet. The Internet can be deployed to globally manage a number of critical marketing functions such as quality assurance measures, order processing, inventory management, accounting, and billing. Tangible products might be globally marketed and sold through e-commerce, but transportation (even from a local warehouse) is required and the transaction may involve an export license, tariffs, quotas, and other limitations, which can make the Internet less effective as a global marketing tool.

Conceptual issues pertaining to segmentation and the nature of product/service aside, 'Internet' brand equity and knowledge is the single most important functional consideration that the firm must rely on in generating business over the Internet across borders. With so many firms hoping to generate international sales over the Internet, over a billion web pages, and the many search engines that are essentially used as promotional tools (i.e. listing is prioritized through some form of payment from firms appearing on the screen), it is very difficult for an unknown firm or brand to be visible on and to generate international sales via the Internet. This implies that penetration in the international marketplace must necessarily be dependent on an international marketing strategy and a corresponding infrastructure that tend to promote the firm and its brand irrespective of the Internet.

In addition to marketing strategy issues, the Internet as the information superhighway should be viewed as a double-edged sword. On the one hand, access to a firm's site or brand information is a useful promotional tool. However, such easy access to information decreases search cost and heightens the possibility of brand switching. Ultimately, one thing that will work in favor of the marketer is that most customers do not have the inclination or the capacity to manage a large amount of information. Consumers, in particular, make their decisions on a very limited amount of information and use a sort of routine purchase decision making in many categories of products and services. Too much information may also lead to customer discontent and interfere with the firm's overall marketing strategy. Firms distribute products in various regions and stores in accordance with a plan. Not every store will receive the same models or types of merchandise. Indeed, not every retailer is willing to carry every line that a firm has to offer. In the absence of full disclosure over the Internet, a customer in Bologna may be quite content with the dozen or so models of Omega watches offered at a local store, however, the knowledge that Omega actually manufactures hundreds of models that are not available locally and are difficult to obtain through importation (i.e. foreign exchange, tariff, and regulatory issues in addition to not being able to personally see the product) has the potential of eroding his/her loyalty to the local store and possibly to the brand.

Finally, international payment for goods purchased over the Internet tends to be a problem. The use of credit cards is largely limited to developed countries. Even if available, some countries do not permit its use as a means of bypassing foreign exchange regulations. Indeed, many countries continue to impose strict exchange controls. This means that payment through official channels, even if permitted, is time consuming, expensive, and requires long lead periods. When official channels are used, then the Internet firms may be exposed to local regulatory conditions of disclosure, fair pricing, content approvals, etc. Thus, while in a local sense the Internet may bypass payment problems, on a global scale, particularly in countries where e-commerce might enhance locally available alternatives and price levels, it is rather problematic. Clearly, as the size of a given transaction grows, then the possible benefits of offers made through the Internet may exceed the cost associated with making payment arrangements.

The Internet as a Mediator of Internationalization

Since the Internet can, at least in theory, be accessed everywhere, it is commonly viewed as a global marketing medium. Furthermore, using this view as a basis, e-commerce is considered by many to be a 'born global' business that requires a global approach (Paul 1996; Telecommunications Reports 1998). Technically, anyone with a computer, appropriate software, and Internet access in the free world can access the materials posted on hundreds of millions of web pages everywhere. The exceptions are where governments seek to limit such access in general or block access to unfriendly or socially undesirable sites. As such, internationalization of the firm via the Internet is a foregone conclusion by casual observers and the anecdotal accounts of firms receiving foreign orders through their sites strengthens this belief. Many academicians and practitioners think of the Internet as key to international market entry, expansion, and potentially, globalization. The following quotes are representative of the electronic media's influence on the internationalization of the firm:

> all electronic markets are international, and understanding the role of country-specific institutional environments and the implications of omnipresent global competition among user firms is critical in developing a full appreciation of the impact of electronic markets. (Grewal, Comer and Mehta 2001, p. 30)
> Today, advances in communications technology and the growth of the Internet are radically changing existing business models and established ways of doing business in international markets. Firms can instantly 'go global', targeting a specific market segment worldwide, or reach customers by building a network of Internet sites in different languages throughout the world. So it seems there is now a need to revisit traditional approaches and formulate a new framework for doing business not only in international markets but also in cyberspace and at cyberspeed. (Douglas 2001, p. 106)

Determined as these statements sound, few have charted the course of how exactly a firm becomes international by virtue of access to the Internet or what changes in planning might fulfill the promise of global e-commerce. Less than a decade ago, there were predictions of revolutionary changes in markets and marketing.[4] Yet, the Internet has resulted in a very few discrete shopping and adoption patterns and, therefore, it is reasonable to adopt an incremental internationalization view.

Additionally, a small but growing body of literature suggests that an increasing number of firms being established are 'born global' (Oviatt and

McDougall 1991; Rennie 1993). Butler et al. (1997) predicted that many firms will be born global and 'even the smallest start-up has access to a global market for its products'. Others note that a broad range of firms from software to medical equipment are born with an eye for their golden opportunity in international markets (*San Francisco Business Times* 1997).

It is further argued that the larger, better-established firms are reorganizing themselves to become even more global and that newer technology companies are born global (Kanter 1999). New communications technologies inherently transcend national boundaries and can be deployed to rapidly create international and global alliances and networks with other firms around the world. In this sense, the possibilities may appear limitless.

These viewpoints explicitly suggest that the internationalization of firms and, indeed, the globalization of firms are at hand in the advent of the Internet and e-commerce. The Internet-based internationalization being advocated by some authors centers largely on the technology rather than the intricacies and imperative processes that internationalize the firm. The possibility of internationalizing the firm with great ease and minimum investment levels is indeed an attractive proposition to which one would enthusiastically subscribe, but one that has yet to be realized.

There is also limited evidence as to whether or not the Internet and e-commerce contribute to the internationalization of newly established firms. The internationalization of 126 dotcom firms that had gone through their initial public offering (IPO) was recently reported by Shama (2001). His findings reveal that about one-fourth had no foreign sales and another one-fourth derived less than 5 per cent of its sales from international markets. As shown in Table 17.5, however, 25 per cent of the firms in his sample had foreign sales exceeding 20 per cent, the threshold at which firms

Table 17.5   Internet firms' sales to foreign markets

International Sales As a % of Total Sales	Number of Firms	Percentage of Firms
None	31	23
Up to 5	34	25
6–10	17	13
11–20	21	15
21–30	13	10
31–50	17	13
Over 50	3	2

Source: Avraham Shama (2001), 'E-Coms and Their Marketing Strategies', *Business Horizons*, **44** (5), September–October, p. 19.

would typically become reliant and, therefore, committed to exporting. However, there is no indication in the study as to how long these firms were in operation prior to data collection. Although as dotcom firms they tend to be young, some could have been in operation for several years prior to their IPOs whereas others might be associated with larger firms in the same line of business (e.g. Barnes and Noble and BN.com) and, therefore, would have had the benefit of considerable international marketing experience. Thus, it is difficult to generalize these findings and accept them as evidence of globalization of firms at their inception through e-commerce. Furthermore, as the study does not compare dotcom firms with IPOs in brick-and-mortar operations, it is plausible that international sales generated by the latter are not significantly different from those generated by the former. Finally, no information about other characteristics of dotcom firms, for example, with respect to their international infrastructures and global marketing strategies is offered. Although studies like this seemingly defy the incremental and ecological international growth patterns by using the Internet, a variety of environmental obstacles discussed earlier inhibit growth by leaps and bounds (e.g. Samiee 1998).

INTERNATIONAL MARKET ENTRY VS. INTERNATIONAL EXPANSION

The list of obstacles shown in Table 17.3 suggests that the case for internationalization via the Internet is rather weak. However, once the firm has developed the appropriate infrastructure and is internationalized to some extent, if the Internet and e-commerce can be co-aligned with the prevailing conditions in targeted intermarket segments, then they may be deployed in a variety of ways for deeper local market penetration and expansion. The efficiencies introduced via the Internet may then release funds that can assist in exploring and entering new international markets.

Market expansion and international market entry strategies via the Internet are distinguished based on whether the firm is being proactive or reactive in its approach. An internationalization strategy with the Internet as its centerpiece is largely a reactive strategy that depends on potential customers stumbling on the firm's brand name or site. The obstacles outlined earlier generally speak against the use of the Internet as the main vehicle for internationalization. The use of the Internet as a complement to an existing international marketing infrastructure and strategy is tantamount to a proactive deployment of the technology to achieve greater efficiencies and local market penetration and expansion. It is useful to recall that capabilities and technologies that can be rapidly acquired by competitors offer no competitive advantage in the market and, in this light, the possibility of internationalizing or gaining a significant competitive advantage through the Internet is nil.

THE INTERNET AS A MEANS OF MARKET DEVELOPMENT IN LDCS

The impediments to the use of the Internet in international marketing, particularly structural limitations, make it clear that developing nations are not prime candidates for cultivation in a general, mass-market sense via e-commerce. The great majority of countries (over 165) fall into this category. However, in many of these markets, to some extent the Internet can assist in addressing the information asymmetry that permeates these societies, including communications functions. Key competitors, holding companies, educational institutions, and governments in these markets have greater business sophistication, Internet access, and the means and the inclination of accepting e-commerce and/or being reached through the Internet. Additionally, the Internet can accommodate the 'backroom operations' within MNCs operating in these markets and strategic alliance partners situated in developing markets. Cultural nuances and other considerations notwithstanding, selective use of the Internet and e-commerce is potentially possible in these markets.

It is worth nothing that LDCs have fairly complex channels of distribution structures. In the absence of a change in their economic infrastructures (Samiee 1993), the Internet will have no impact on distribution channels in these nations. Although in the fastest-growing developing nations the Internet should have an intermediate-term impact, this is limited largely to a dozen or so countries broadly referred to as 'emerging nations'. Thus, generally speaking, disintermediation is even less likely in the developing markets. As such, the main role of the Internet in these markets is that of communications and relationship maintenance rather than bypassing existing channel members.

E-COMMERCE AND GLOBAL MARKETING STRATEGY

A central decision with respect to global marketing strategy is whether to use relatively similar marketing plans across national market segments (i.e.

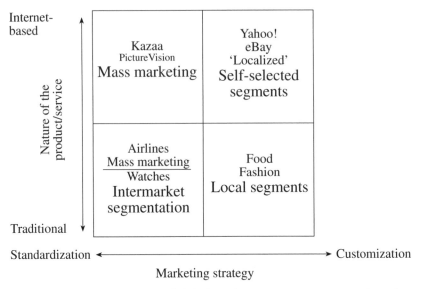

Figure 17.1   E-commerce and global marketing strategy: internet-based vs. traditional products/services

standardize across intermarket segments) or to develop a customized market strategy for each market or local segment. A question with which the firm is faced is the extent to which a given strategy should be pursued. This issue equally applies to global e-commerce.

Another factor that influences the pursuit of standardization/adaptation strategy is the extent to which the product or service being offered is Internet dependent. The Internet, as a new, innovative, interactive medium, offers the possibility of being integrated into products and services. Irrespective of other factors, when the Internet is integrated into a product, competition from conventional products is eliminated (i.e. existing off-line products and services cannot effectively compete), hence, offering a substantial competitive advantage to the firm. For example, Picture Vision.com, Yahoo!, and eBay have no true brick-and-mortar competitors. Their only competition is on the Internet.

As shown in Figure 17.1, in the case of traditional services, the Internet should be deployed as a complement to and in support of existing global marketing strategies. Thus, a firm pursuing a standardized global marketing strategy, can use the Internet for greater efficiencies and as an additional channel. Depending on the product and the firm's global strategy, either a mass-marketing (e.g. airlines) or intermarket segmentation (e.g. watches) approach via the Internet should be considered. When the firm's global market strategy calls for customization, then the firm will naturally pursue local market segments.

In the case of customized global marketing strategy, the firm seeks to identify local market segments. Given the bottom-up, self-selected nature of clientele over the Internet, market segmentation in host markets is difficult. Internet sites that face competition from brick-and-mortar rivals, in a customized global strategy environment, must identify their local segments and reach them through the Internet.

Internet-dependent services that tend to be standardized are candidates for mass marketing. First, there is little or no brick-and-mortar competition for these products. Second, by virtue of intellectual property protection afforded to some of these services, a few firms in each category seem to have emerged as key players in each sector. As such, there is little need to segment the global market or identify intermarket segments. Kazaa, for example, can use a mass-marketing approach. That is not to say that music types and preferences are the same everywhere, rather there is no need for proactive identification and cultivation of intermarket segments. The same thing is true for the purveyor of digitized photographs, PictureVision.com.[5]

Some Internet-dependent services must necessarily be customized to be of value in host markets. Internet portals such as Yahoo! compete only with other portals but need to be localized. Established in 1995, Yahoo! offers its portals in 13 languages, operates 24 global Internet network properties, has offices in 16 major cities,[6] and derives about 16 per cent of its revenues from non-US sources. Its UK portal, for example, is based there and developed for that market. Likewise, eBay is currently 'localized' in six markets through foreign direct investment, acquisitions, and joint venture agreements in a number of European and Asian markets. The key international marketing challenge of customized Internet-dependent products is that the segments to which they appeal tend to be bottom-up and self-selected.

CONCLUSIONS

The immediate conclusion derived from this study is that at best only incremental internationalization over a long period is likely through the Internet and e-commerce. This implies that in the absence of an international marketing plan at the outset, the firm will never be a serious contender in the global marketplace. This sentiment is perhaps best expressed by Chief Executive (1999):

there's also the phenomenon that a lot of new companies are being born global on the Internet. It isn't a progression from national to regional to global, they're born global and that's a whole other phenomenon. Therefore, the traditional models where industries grow up within countries, and countries negotiate how they will work together, don't really work in this new age. You need global frameworks from the beginning.

It is also posited that the roles and consequences of the Internet for global marketing are shaped by segmentation and the presence of intermarket segments, by strategy–environment co-alignment, and by forces that shape the competitive structure of markets. Furthermore, it is evident that the greatest impact of the Internet and e-commerce is in developed nations. Although only about two dozen nations are considered developed, more than 60 per cent of world trade is transacted among them. These markets lend themselves to the full deployment of the Internet and e-commerce for marketing purposes, including B2B, B2C, B2G, and P2P.[7] Limiting marketing activities to fewer nations provides an opportunity for greater familiarity and depth of knowledge regarding these markets. However, greater market potential in these markets is no secret and has attracted attention from numerous competitors. As such, these markets are among the most competitive and demand a relatively high level of quality and customer service.

There is virtually no substitute for market-sensing through some form of market presence. This means that regardless of e-commerce and Internet strategies pursued by the firm, there is a need to explore the local market, accumulate relevant knowledge for full exploitation of these markets, and monitor host markets targeted via e-commerce. Given the nature of the Internet and e-commerce, there is also an acute need for harmonization of communications, image, and firm and brand position for global consistency. As with all marketing efforts, firms should embrace global e-commerce incrementally and methodically, with a detailed strategy in hand. Global e-commerce and Internet marketing efforts should not be viewed as 'a shot in the dark'!

Finally, the different perspectives regarding e-commerce and its role in global marketing stem from the absence of well-defined terminology and concepts associated with the Internet and e-commerce. Indeed, this void has led to much confusion in interpreting the data being generated by various public and private agencies. For example, it is not entirely clear what constitutes an 'Internet firm', or how traditional Lands' End catalog orders placed though the firm's Internet site should be classified. These orders certainly do not constitute new international business or necessarily orders that were placed strictly because of the Internet. To date very few studies have addressed definition and measurement issues. The adoption of uniform definitions, along with validated measurement, will go a long way in paving the way for significant contributions to the literature that stems from a uniform platform.

NOTES

1. Using the recent accomplishment within medicine, for example, the possibilities for further applications of the Internet appear limitless. On 7 September, Madeleine Schaal, a 68-year-old French woman in Strasbourg, France, was operated on via a video monitor 3900 miles away in New York City by French surgeon Jacques Marescaux and Dr Michel Gagner (Fields-Meyer, Calandra and Lerner 2001). As such applications develop, people everywhere may eventually have access to world-class surgeons and superior medical care.
2. Although brick-and-mortar firms tend to have more employees, the average wage is lower than for cyber firms because of the latter's reliance on securing information technology expertise (hardware and software) which generally commands high salaries.
3. Intermarket segments are those that transcend national boundaries and permit firms to use identical or at least reasonably similar marketing strategies in various countries in which such segments have successfully been identified.
4. There is an abundance of e-commerce predictions that have failed to materialize. For example, Accenture has predicted that 20 per cent of grocery shopping will be non-store electronic (McGrath 1994). Maurice Saatchi has predicted that electronic retailing will replace stores in 40 years (Cope 1996). It is also expected that video-rental stores will be eliminated within 10 years (Negroponte 1995)!
5. PictureVision is an example of the type of service that substantially integrates the Internet (i.e. the product/service and the Internet are inseparable). This service allows customers to store pictures on a password-coded Internet account for a monthly fee and, for an additional fee, photo finishers scan pictures and post them to the customer's account for 30 days. Customers can (1) share photos with family and friends by sending the film identification or simply e-mailing the images to them for free, (2) download any or all images to their computers, (3) use their images in web pages, print low resolution photos, or alter them using image editing software (downloading editors is free of charge), (4) order reprints and enlargements of photos, (5) have enlargements mailed to anyone or send them to a preferred store for pickup, and (6) order gift items such as mugs, tee-shirts, and mouse pads, personalized with preferred photos. The Virginia-based PictureVision initially developed the service in conjunction with Konica. However, in 1998 Kodak acquired a 51 per cent interest in the service and acquired the rest of the firm two years later (*Discount Store News* 2000). Kodak had attempted to develop its own Internet picture service, but later decided to enter the market through this acquisition (*The Wall Street Journal* 1997).
6. As of January 2001, eBay has market presence in Buenos Aires, Copenhagen, Hong Kong, London, Madrid, Mexico City, Milan, Munich, Paris, São Paulo, Seoul, Singapore, Stockholm, Sydney, Taipei, and Toronto.
7. Business to business (B2B), business to consumer (B2C), business to government (B2G), and peer to peer (P2P).

REFERENCES

Bandyopadhyay, Soumava (2001), 'Competitive Strategies for Internet Marketers in Emerging Markets', *Competitiveness Review*, **11** (2), 16–24.
Butler, Patrick, Ted W. Hall, Alistair M. Hanna, Lenny Mendonca, Byron Auguste, James Manyika and Anupam Sahay (1997), 'A Revolution in Interaction', *The McKinsey Quarterly*, Winter, **1**, 4–21.

Chief Executive, March 15, 1999.

Cope, Nigel (1996), *Retail in the Digital Age*, London: Bowerdean.

Discount Store News (2000), Photo **39** (12), June 19, 41.

Douglas, Susan P. (2001), 'Exploring New Worlds: the Challenge of Global Marketing', *Journal of Marketing*, **65** (1), 103–7.

Drug Store News (1999), CVS Completes Soma.com Acquisition, June 28, **21** (10), 10.

Executive Speeches, August **14** (1), 1999.

Fields-Meyer, Thomas, Bob Calandra and Dietlind Lerner (2001), 'French Connection', *People*, October 8, **56** (15), 103–5.

Gisberg, Ari and N. Vankatraman (1995), 'Institutional Initiatives for Technological Change: from Issue Interpretation to Strategic Choice', *Organization Studies*, Summer, **16** (3), 425–48.

Grewal, Rajdeep, James M. Comer and Raj Mehta (2001), 'An Investigation into the Antecedents of Organizational Participation in Business-to-Business Electronic Markets', *Journal of Marketing*, July, **65** (3), 17–33.

IDC (1999), Overseas e-commerce to equal half of global spending by 2003, http://ecommerce.internet.com, August 26.

Kanter, Rosabeth Moss (1999), 'Change is Everyone's Job: Managing the Extended Enterprise in a Globally Connected World', *Organizational Dynamics*, July, **27** (1), 7.

McGrath, Betsy Grover (1994), 'Food Shopping for Couch Potatoes', *Catalog Age*, July.

Nairn, Geoff (1997), 'Trading Places: from Purchasing to Invoicing, Business are Linking up', *Financial Times*, August 27, 15.

Negroponte, Nicholas (1995), *Being Digital*, NY: Knopf.

Oviatt, Benjamin M. and Patricia P. McDougall (1991), 'Georgians Launching "Global Start-ups"', *Atlanta Business Chronicle*, November 11, **14** (24), 28.

Pastore, Michael (1999), Worldwide Internet users to pass 500 million next century. http://cyberatlas.internet.com/big_picture/geographics/article/0,1323,5911_200001,00.html.

Paul, Pallab (1996), 'Marketing on the Internet', *Journal of Consumer Marketing*, **13** (4), 27–39.

Porter, Michael E. (2001), 'Strategy and the Internet', *Harvard Business Review*, March, **29** (3), 62–78.

Quelch, John A. and Lisa R. Klein (1996), 'The Internet and International Marketing', *Sloan Management Review*, Spring, 60–75.

Rennie, W. R. (1993), 'Global Competitiveness: Born Global', *McKinsey Quarterly*, September 22, 45–52.

Samiee, Saeed (1988), 'The Internet and International Marketing: is There a Fit?, *Journal of Interactive Marketing*, **12** (4), 5–21.

Samiee, Saeed (1993), 'Retailing and Channel Considerations in Developing Countries: A Review and Research Propositions', *Journal of Business Research*, **27** (2), 103–29.

San Francisco Business Times (1997), July 25, **11** (50).

Shama, Avraham (2001), 'E-Coms and their Marketing Strategies', *Business Horizons*, September–October, **44** (5), 14–20.

Telecommunications Reports (1998), March 2, **64** (9).

The Wall Street Journal (1997), Kodak is launching service on the Internet, August 26, B-2.

Venkatraman, N. and John E. Prescott (1990), 'Environment-strategy Coalignment: an Empirical Test of its Performance Implications', *Strategic Management Journal*, January, **11** (1), 1–23.

Yip, George S. (2000), 'Global Strategy in the Internet Era', *Business Strategy Review*, December, **11** (4), 1–14.

18. Privacy protection and global marketing: balancing consumer and corporate interests

Ravi Sarathy

INTRODUCTION

Successful marketing requires obtaining information about customers. Understanding customer needs, by asking customers, surveying them, making inferences from their behavior, or observing them, are critical precursors to successful development of products and services. Customer information helps tailor products to individual needs, helps qualify prospects, increases the likelihood of enhancing customer satisfaction, and enables better retention of current customers. Growing knowledge about customer needs and satisfaction helps create better new products and services. A clothing manufacturer selling fashionable but perishable styles benefits from knowing which styles, which colors and which sizes are in demand, both at the individual level and in the aggregate. An insurer can leverage existing customers by selling additional services such as travel insurance and long-term care insurance to current term life insurance customers. Real estate agents can gain competitive advantage from knowing when a prospective customer is being transferred, their family size, their school preferences, and the amount of mortgage they pre-qualify for. The advent of location-specific information available from cell-phone users adds another opportunity, as potential customers can receive sales offers beamed to cell-phones from businesses in the vicinity of the customer, and the locations a customer visits can be factored into the algorithms that predict customer needs and behavior.

All these examples show the benefits to the well-informed marketer. The benefits and utility of information gathering about customers is magnified as marketing moves to the Internet: both because information gathering is easier, and highly individualized tailored instantaneous response is possible (Ryan 1999). Such customization facilitates bonding with the customer, offering them differentiated products and services that provide a superior value proposition. Because potential customers receive timely information about products and services which are of immediate use to them, they are more likely to respond positively, initiating purchase and otherwise responding in the manner desired by the marketer. The net effect is efficient deployment of scarce marketing funds.

Because customer information is so important, it becomes a critical firm-specific strategic asset. Database marketing is built on sources of information such as supermarket scanner data, credit card purchase histories, direct marketing firms' customer profiles and mailing lists, and Internet-based information residing in 'cookies'. Cookies are small files placed on users' computers, which identifies these individuals as they browse web sites. When an individual revisits a web site, the cookie lets the browser know who the visitor is and what their past behavior has been: which pages they visited, where they entered from, how long they stayed on the site, and whether the visitor purchased or showed other interest in the company's products or services. Such information allows the company to deliver a tailored web page or window to the visitor, containing information and advertising more likely to elicit a desired response; i.e. a purchase. A well-known example is Amazon, which maintains detailed records on its visitors and is able to greet a return visitor with an offer of a book or music CD based on what that individual had purchased in the past and what other individuals like him had purchased in the past – these being examples of collaborative filtering and presumptive marketing. An extension of this is e-mail marketing, where the individual might receive a tailored e-mail offer of products of interest to him, based on his web site browsing behavior.

The consequences of such attempted personalization can be seen in the controversy which engulfed DoubleClick, a prominent Internet advertising firm, which was one of the pioneers of 'ad servers', a technology which allows personalized ads to be sent to a visitor's computer screen as they are browsing a company's web site, based on information contained in cookies. DoubleClick attempted to enhance its personalization abilities, when it acquired a direct marketing catalog firm, Abacus Direct Corporation, a catalog direct marketer of long standing with detailed databases containing purchasing histories of millions of consumers; DoubleClick sought to combine its knowledge of each individual's web surfing behavior, with detailed individual data obtained from the direct marketing company, such as their purchasing history, age, income, and address. Individuals and public interest organizations reacted to such tactics by decrying them as an invasion of privacy and organized to stop such corporate actions. Such consumer anger and opposition destabilize the fundamental business models based on ever-increasing amounts of customer-specific information, and a resolution is necessary if both consumers and e-commerce firms are to be satisfied. Hence, the importance of considering privacy issues (see Lessig 1999; Shapiro 2000).

KEY ASPECTS OF DATA PRIVACY

There are many issues surrounding the creation and maintenance of customer-specific information. Perhaps most important is the question of ownership: who owns data about a customer? If data is gathered through a mutually agreed interaction between a customer and a company, do both parties have equal rights in the data? That is, when an individual makes a purchase from a company, does the company own data about the transaction, including customer-specific information gained from that transaction, just as much as the customer has rights to the information about himself/herself? This is an important reference point, as much of the discussion about privacy is framed around the right to privacy or the right to be left alone; at the same time, issues of ownership of intangible assets come into play. Hence, discussions about privacy must balance the interests of both customer and the firm, while understanding that it is in the best interests of the firm to obtain willing consent and collaboration from the customer in the creation and use of customer-specific databases.

The several aspects of data privacy are spelled out in Table 18.1, and discussed in detail below.

Notice

First and foremost, is the customer aware that information is being collected? The customer should know who is collecting the information – the company he is doing business with, or a third party; he should be told exactly what information is being gathered, and, how such information is being gathered: both directly through questions and surveys and indirectly through observation and inferences. Such notice arms the customer with knowledge to exercise choice and give informed consent to the data gathering.

Choice

The customer is asked for permission to allow data to be gathered, on the notice and disclosures provided. The choice can be a positive choice, with the customer specifically giving permission to allow such data gathering, or the choice can be a negative one, with the customers implicitly allowing such data gathering unless explicitly denying consent to the data gathering.

Table 18.1 Key aspects of data privacy

Notice	Who is collecting the information?
	What information is being collected?
	How is the information collected?
Choice and Consent	Are customers given a choice about data collection?
	Opt-in vs. Opt-out
Access	Will customers have access to the data about themselves?
	Is there a charge for such customer access?
	How is the access controlled?
Security and Information Protection	Is access secure?
	Who else will have access to the information?
	How is access controlled?
Disclosure	Is the information being shared with third parties?
	Will information be sold?
	Has permission been sought for such sharing or sale?
Objectives	Why is the information being collected?
	How will it be used?
Data Quality and Integrity	Is the data accurate?
	How are changes to the data controlled?
Error correction	Can customers review data about themselves?
	Are there provisions for error correction?
	Who bears the cost of such error correction?
Compliance	Is the company following customer-friendly data collection and use principles?
	Are there sanctions available to discourage and control errant behavior?

This is often referred to as opt-in vs. opt-out. Opt-in may give customers a higher standard of choice but is likely to be more costly to the firm and may result in lower volumes of customer data being gathered, hence the general preference among firms to choose opt-out; the firm may hope to benefit from inertia, as fewer customers may take the necessary additional step to opt out of data-gathering processes.

Access

Customers are likely to want to know what data has been collected on them over time, particularly when multiple data collection opportunities have been utilized over time, and when data from multiple sources has been merged; for example, third-party credit information with information provided by the customer in response to surveys and information about customer purchases with the company and with its affiliates. Customers may well feel that they have a right of access to such data since it is about themselves, and that such access should be free and available on demand. Companies however may balk at the cost of such unrestrained access and prefer to limit access to a few times a year and require advance notice. A related issue is how such access is controlled, whether it is based on password protection and if so, how unauthorized persons are prevented from accessing such information.

Security and Information Protection

The access issue noted above leads into concerns over security and protection of information in databases. Customers as well as companies should be concerned about who is authorized to access and use such data, as much sensitive information may be available in such databases, such as medical, financial and personal data. Companies need to be concerned with safeguarding such information as it is a strategic asset in addition to affecting customer well-being; hence, safeguards are necessary to prevent unauthorized access to and transfer and copying of such data, whether it is by employees or hackers or other third parties such as competitors. Information protection extends to encryption of data, storage of old information, destruction of data no longer deemed useful or obsolete, and backup and mirror images of such databases to enable quick recovery of such information in case of computer and network crashes and other disasters. As identity theft becomes more common in an e-commerce age, security of customer data will preoccupy customers intensely and create severe liabilities for corporations with lax practices in this area.

Disclosure of Sharing and Sale of Customer Information

Since customer information is scarce and has value, it is possible that companies may seek to share such information with their affiliates and subsidiaries and with third parties, often charging for such information; customers have a right to know if data collected with their permission will be shared or sold, and if so, to whom, and further, should have the right to assent to or resist such a sale or transfer. And all of the issues noted as pertinent to customer information gathered by the firm will also apply to the new recipients of such data.

Data Collection Objectives

Informed consent by customers to data collection requires that they have an understanding of the purposes of data collection, which is related to how such data will be used. The presumption is that customers will benefit from such information being available to the company, in the form of better products, superior service and greater value.

Data Quality and Integrity

The methodology used to collect information and the sources of such information will affect the quality of data collected, whether it is accurate and, in the case of inferences, whether the inferences are reasonable. Since most such information is historical in nature, a special concern is the accuracy of information over time; medical and credit histories can change, and information that was once correct may now be erroneous.

Error Correction

Error correction is in the best interests of both the customer and the firm. It is a natural consequence of the issues raised over access, security and data quality; mistakes will be made and errors will creep into the customer databases and such errors may be harmful to customers in the form of denial of service or other negative consequences. Companies therefore need to have a process in place to allow customers to point out errors and suggest corrections; errors of fact are straightforward and easy to correct while errors of interpretation and inference present more difficulties; a related problem refers to information obtained from third parties, in which case the error correction needs to be made at every point in the transfer of information all the way back to the source of the original information.

Compliance

While the issues discussed above are meant to safeguard customer interests and develop mutually satisfactory long-term relationships between customer and supplier, it is likely that not all companies will follow or implement such principles. Sanctions therefore become important: are there audit mechanisms in place to verify compliance? Will an objective third party carry out such audits? When non-compliance exists, what sanctions exist to deter such behavior? Do the sanctions have teeth, i.e. are they strong enough to promote greater voluntary compliance? Customers have an interest in seeing strong compliance processes develop as this is more likely to safeguard their interests. This is particularly so in an environment of self-regulation and the lack of legal underpinnings to strong data privacy protection.

All of these issues surrounding customer data collection and use represent an administrative burden on the company, requiring processes that will incur costs; companies may seek to save costs by attempting to diminish the control and access that customers have to such information. While the prevalent legal regime may permit such attenuation, there is the long-term possibility of damaging the customer relationship; this can be self-defeating, as the purpose of developing customer data – developing long-term relationships with the customer – is sabotaged by short-term cost-cutting behavior.

DATA PRIVACY AND INTERNATIONAL MARKETS

Data privacy becomes relevant in international markets precisely because of divergent customer expectations, and regimes governing data collection and use by corporations. In what follows, we discuss these differences, with particular reference to the divergence of data privacy regulation and expectation in the European Union (EU) and the USA, two significant markets of paramount importance to every company involved in international business.

The central difference lies between self-regulation and government regulation. Can market forces be entrusted with protecting customer privacy and balancing it with the needs of the company? Will customers willingly exchange privacy for some returns, monetary or otherwise? Or is privacy such a fundamental right that some absolute level of privacy protection must exist and govern all customer transactions?

The cultural context also affects customer and corporate attitudes towards privacy. Privacy concerns stem principally from an individualistic perspective with individuals concerned about loss of privacy, individuals concerned about safeguarding the right to be left alone, individuals concerned about privacy laws that might abridge their right of free speech and thus dissemination of information. It is conceivable that in a more collectivist culture, to use Hofstede's dichotomy, individual need for privacy may be balanced against the needs of the collectivity, whether it is the state or other organizations. Reliance on self-regulation and market forces also stems from an individualistic orientation and more collectivist-oriented cultures may prefer national regulation so as to develop a common standard governing all the members of the collectivity.

What is clear is that there is no internationally agreed-upon standard for data privacy protection. This presents a challenge for multinational corporations with customers in multiple countries, each with differing approaches to protecting customer privacy. At the customer level, companies have to figure out how to meet differing expectations of customers in each country, so as to forge successful long-term relationships and market effectively. At the governmental level, companies have to reconcile differing laws and regulations and ensure that they are in compliance with existing laws in each jurisdiction in which they operate. The complicating factor is extra-territorial application of country laws. As we shall discuss, EU laws concerning privacy protection of European customers extend beyond the EU's borders. Companies with operations in the EU must then develop one set of standards for EU customers while using different standards for customers from other countries; and such anomalous treatment can be perceived or described as discriminatory or second-best treatment rousing customer ill-will. Multinational companies have a difficult path to tread as they attempt to create company-wide policies for dealing with customer privacy issues.

US APPROACHES TO DATA PRIVACY

The USA presents the case for self-regulation at the industry level, and the case for bargains being struck by companies with their customers, with customers having the right to bargain away some levels of privacy protection in return for other goods that they value – such as products more tailored to their needs or better service or a lower price. This approach assumes that customer data is valuable and that customers can therefore 'sell' it to the company that provides them with the best value. This is an information exchange, parallel with the exchange of funds for goods and services (Culnan 1999).

The US preference for self-regulation is influenced by the conflicting demands of the First and Fourth amendments. The First Amendment guarantees free speech and limits the US government's right to regulate the flow of information, and thus limits its ability to regulate the use of information gathered by corporations. At the same time, the Fourth Amendment provides an individual freedom from unreasonable search and seizure of his home and property. Over time, this freedom has extended to and kept apace with technological developments, such as protecting an individual from unauthorized wire-tapping, on the grounds that telephone conversations are as protected as more physical assets such as a home or a car (Rosen 2001). From this stems the right to be left alone (Warren and Brandeis 1980, Tuerkheimer 1993), and thus, the question of invasion of privacy when customer information is stored in a company database. However, as suggested earlier, when there are two parties to a transaction, both parties may have rights to the information from the transaction and freedom of speech may clash with the right to be left alone.

Against this backdrop of a general predilection for self-regulation, US legislation governing privacy protection has been piecemeal and industry specific, often responding to specific problems and pressure groups focusing on an industry. This patchwork of regulation has created different standards for different industries as well as a disparity in regulations between the public and private sectors (Samuelson 1999). A variety of federal laws (see Table 18.2) govern privacy, such as the Telecommunications Act, the Cable Communications Policy Act, the Fair Credit Reporting Act and others, with an emphasis on the safeguarding of data on consumers gathered by telecom companies, cable TV companies, credit report bureaus, the health-care industry and the federal government. More recently, consumer alarm over the gathering and use of data on the Internet has led to specific industry-focused legislation such as:

- The Children's On-Line Privacy Protection Act, which requires companies operating web sites focusing on children to seek parental consent to data gathering and requires the use of comprehensive privacy policies.
- The Financial Modernization Act ('Gramm–Leach–Bilkey' Act) addresses financial institutions and places disclosure requirements and restraints on the transfer of financial information on consumers within the company and to non-affiliated third parties.
- The Electronic Signatures Act creates a framework for binding electronic signatures, thus affecting electronic contracts and privacy issues surrounding such contracts.

However, these various acts are still discrete attempts at regulating specific issues and are a reactive response to consumer concerns, quite different

Table 18.2   Federal acts designed to protect privacy on the Internet

Name of Act	Scope
Electronic Signatures in Global and National Commerce Act: E-SIGN Bill	Sets conditions for and enables legally binding electronic signature. Sen. Abraham, chief sponsor noted, 'This bill will literally supply the pavement for the e-commerce superhighway'
Gramm–Leach–Bliley Financial Modernization Act	Restrictions on disclosing nonpublic personal information about consumers to non-affiliated third parties, and disclosure of privacy policies about information sharing with affiliates and with nonaffiliated third parties
Children's Online Privacy Protection	Requires children's web site operators to post comprehensive privacy policies on their sites, notify parents about their information practices and obtain 'verifiable parental consent' before collecting information on children under age 13. The act uses flexible performance standards rather than static rules
Privacy Protection Act	Requires government officials to obtain subpoenas or voluntary cooperation when seeking evidence from individuals engaged in First Amendment activities
Internet Privacy Protection Act	Prohibits federal agencies from making individual confidential records available on the Internet
Consumer Internet Privacy Protection Act	Requires Internet providers to obtain an individual's written consent prior to the disclosure of personal information
Tax Reform Act	Protects the confidentiality of tax returns and related information
Freedom of Information Act	Regulates third-party access to government records containing personal information
Right to Financial Privacy Act	Limits government access to bank records
Fair Credit Reporting Act	Regulates the use of credit information by reporting agencies
Cable Communications Policy Act	Requires the government to obtain a court order prior to accessing cable records
Telecommunications Act	Safeguards customer information held by telecommunications carriers
Federal Records Act	Regulates the disposal of federal records

Source: Robertson and Sarathy (2002).

from the Europe-wide Data Privacy Directive which is rooted in the legal protection of privacy as a fundamental human right (George, Lynch and Marsnik 2001; Fromholz 2000).

On the issue of compliance, the USA does not have a central authority regulating customer privacy. Instead, there are multiple agencies charged with oversight of specific industries. While the Federal Trade Commission has considerable sway, it does not control the financial services industry or the airline industry, which are separately governed by the Department of Transportation and the Treasury Department. Compliance standards and the ability to enforce standards can be variably exercised, and sanctions are seen as weak and ineffective, reducing the level of actual privacy protection.

Instead, the USA has seen the rise of third-party agencies who can provide seals of compliance with high standards of privacy protection, and can perform audit functions. There is clear reliance here on market forces, replacing regulation with guarantees of trust and acceptable standards of behavior.

Another interesting direction is the use of technology to ensure greater protection for US consumers. These technology aids are most useful in an e-commerce context. They help consumers preserve privacy by allowing them to become anonymous on the Web, thus defeating the ability of cookies to identify them when they visit web sites and reduce the ability of the supplier to gather customer-specific information; while information can be gathered, customer identifiers are unavailable or disguised, circumventing the goal of building customer-specific data bases. Other examples include software from Zero Knowledge, http://www.zeroknowledge.com/privacy/default.asp, which offers personal privacy protection software; Junkbusters, which selectively blocks cookies: http://www.junkbusters.com/ht/en/ijb.html; and the Platform for Privacy Preferences, a browser-based choice, http://www.w3.org/P3P/ which allows users to set default levels of privacy protection and expectations from web sites. Another recent approach is the availability of single-use credit cards which prevents suppliers from gaining credit and purchasing data about customers beyond a specific transaction. What is interesting about these approaches is that these products for consumers assume that corporations will try to breach customer privacy and rather than seek government regulation, consumers can fight back by using technology to regain their privacy. This can even be understood as a culturally expected response, relying on individual efforts rather than governmental regulation. Further, these technology-mediated aids are viable because US consumers are more comfortable with technology and with market forces and are hence willing to use technology as an aid in defending their privacy rights.

EUROPEAN APPROACHES TO DATA PRIVACY

European approaches to privacy regulation are rooted in the notion of a fundamental right to privacy. Influenced perhaps by their history and the excesses of Nazism and the gathering of data on individuals for surveillance purposes, EU regulations create clear standards under which data on individuals may be gathered and maintained. These principles are articulated in the EU Data Privacy Directive of October 1998. While these rules have been promulgated at the level of the EU, they require enabling legislation at the national level in each of the member countries to enter into full force and complete the intended harmonization of EU Data Privacy policies (Fromholz 2000).

These rules not only govern personal data collection, but also regulate the sharing and transfer of such information; the EU regulations do not allow the transfer of personal data to countries outside the EU that do not adequately safeguard personal data privacy; the critical point is that the USA in general is not seen as having such safeguards, jeopardizing the transfer within US-based multinationals of customer data from Europe to the USA or other subsidiaries. Depending on the company and its business processes, such regulations may have the effect of a mild nuisance or result in a major interference with a company's mode of doing business.

Several principles govern the EU approach to data privacy: these are:

a. Notice.
b. Choice.
c. Regulation governing sharing of data with third parties.
d. Security systems governing access to data.
e. Protecting integrity of data.
f. Access by consumers.
g. Enforcement procedures to ensure compliance.
h. Consumer rights of redress.

These principles are discussed in Table 18.1. It is worth noting that individual countries can and are encouraged to exceed these principles in establishing their data privacy protection policies. The EU principles represent a floor that all member countries are expected to subscribe to.

IMPLICATIONS FOR INTERNATIONAL MARKETING

International marketing inevitably runs up against conflicting laws regarding individual data collection and use. Companies need to reconcile such

divergences if they are to function effectively. This involves both convergence and compromise, with a partnership of the corporation and the state
facilitating such an outcome. The US–EU Safe Harbor provisions governing data privacy protection are an example of how compromise and convergence can meet the differing interests of the various stakeholders. These
arrangements were worked out over several months as the EU and US
governments, in consultation with varied corporate interests worked out an
agreement whereby US companies could continue to do business in the EU
without the USA having to pass similar data privacy protection laws at the
national level. It provides a way for the USA's mixed approach of combining self-regulation, industry sectoral legislation and market forces, to co-
exist with the more sweeping national legislation adopted by the EU,
(George, Lynch and Marsnik 2001). Under the Safe Harbor provisions,

1. US companies voluntarily agree to adhere to EU principles of data
    privacy protection, thus complying with the EU desire to provide ade-
    quate data protection to individuals.
2. The US Department of Commerce maintains a list of US companies
    and US industry associations that have agreed to comply with the Safe
    Harbor provisions.
3. The Federal Trade Commission is charged with enforcing compliance
    including sanctions where appropriate.

Companies such as Hewlett Packard, Intel and Procter & Gamble are
among the major signatories to these Safe Harbor provisions. Not all US
corporations and US organizations are in accord with this resolution, as
complying with EU principles is seen as extra-territorial application of EU
laws; given the size of the EU and US markets, this approach is a pragmatic
resolution of a conflict that threatened to jeopardize a considerable volume
of international trade between these two trading partners. Other objections
maintain that while Safe Harbor protects US corporations, US consumer
interests have been sacrificed as they would also benefit from sweeping
national legislation similar to that passed in the EU. Finally, companies
themselves worry that Safe Harbor involves costly compliance and a better
and cheaper alternative is self-regulation, an approach that is held to be
equally effective by the companies concerned. US companies in particular
prefer leadership by the private sector to placing faith in government legislation which in their view is unnecessary, and inferior to providing incentives for self-regulation. Their preference is for minimal, clear, predictable
and cost-efficient legislation, if at all necessary.

As multinationals seek to decide whether to standardize their data
privacy practices across all markets and countries in which they operate,

they need to take into account both complying with national legislation already in existence in each of their markets, as well as attitudes towards privacy of customers and other significant business partners.

Attitudes towards data protection and privacy are influenced by several factors including the following.

Development of Economic and Marketing Systems

More developed countries are likely to have more carefully defined and well-thought-out attitudes towards customer privacy.

Political Systems, Political History

As suggested earlier, a country's experience with totalitarian regimes, war and disregard for human right is likely to shape its tolerance for invasion of piracy; Europe's greater zealousness in safeguarding individual piracy is a clear reaction to the wars and Nazi excesses of the past century; similarly, the USA's recent experience of terrorism on September 11th, 2001 has shaped a greater tolerance for reducing an individual's privacy protection in the interest of providing greater national protection against terrorists.

Legal Systems

As noted above, Europe's privacy laws are rooted in a concept of an individual's fundamental right to privacy while US laws have to reconcile the sometimes divergent pulls of the First and Fourth amendments, while also accepting piecemeal legislation aimed at specific privacy problems and specific industrial sectors, as outlined in Table 18.2.

Technological Development

Privacy concerns have increased with the spread of the Internet and e-commerce and with the diffusion of data-gathering methodologies such as supermarket scanners, GPS positioning systems and genetic screening advances; as technology continues to progress, new sources of threats to privacy will emerge and companies will constantly have to contend with balancing the opposing forces of commercially motivated privacy reduction vs. the individual and societal clamor for greater privacy protection.

Culture

Culture has an impact on notions of what is considered the domain of an individual's privacy, as well as demarcating the extent to which society's needs take precedence over an individual's need for privacy; collectivist-oriented societies are likely to expect that greater amounts of information on the individual will be made available to the state.

How then should companies behave in their approaches to managing customer privacy? The central question for a multinational is whether to adopt a standardized approach to data privacy protection or adapt policies to meet the needs and requirements of each market.

Standardization may be attractive because consumers may be hypothesized to want equal treatment across countries, and do not want to be discriminated against in comparison to their counterparts in other countries. It is also logistically difficult to implement divergent policies across markets and can lead to negative public relations.

A second consideration is the fit between privacy policies and overall marketing strategy – does the company intend to follow a strategy that is globally integrated or multi-domestic, regionally differentiated or locally responsive? If the decision is to favor local responsiveness over regional or global integration, it is likely to lead to locally differentiated privacy policies.

The nature of the industry also impacts privacy choices. Not all information is equally sensitive and customers do not care equally about safeguarding all sorts of personal information. Information that becomes quickly obsolete such as which musical groups a teenager prefers, will be less sensitive to disclosure worries as opposed to critical information about individuals, such as medical histories or credit ratings. Hence, consumers are more likely to demand uniformity of privacy treatment across industries, not across countries; for example, there is much concern being voiced about using genetic information to discriminate in accepting individuals as insurable, in providing equal access to health care and in being considered for jobs. This issue of genetic discrimination will gain increasing resonance as genetic advances continue to occur, and individuals are likely to want similar treatment of genetic information across countries. In general, individuals will seek greater protection for more sensitive information, in industries such as financial services and healthcare.

A similar divided can occur when distinguishing between information-driven vs. product-driven business; industries whose 'products' contain a high degree of digital data, and which offer value to customers principally from this digital component, are likely to face greater pressures to offer high levels of customer privacy. It is for this reason that privacy concerns are far higher in e-commerce and web-based businesses than in businesses dealing with physical products and operating in 'bricks and mortar' settings.

What this suggests is that not all customers in all industries want exactly the same level of privacy protection. Companies may find that the ideal solution lies in offering a range of privacy protection: between a floor of minimal protection and a ceiling of almost complete privacy, consumers can choose a level of privacy protection that is most satisfactory to them. Under this approach, firms can offer to buy information from consumers; payment can be direct, cash or near cash compensation, or indirect, in the form of preferred treatment, better service, early access, participation in new product development, greater prestige etc. – many of which are typical of frequent flyer programs, where airline travelers offer information about themselves such as preferred destinations, points of contact, price preferences and vacation plans all in return for access to advance reservations, priority check-in and seating, access to airport lounges, preferred discount pricing (Web-only fares) etc.

If an economics of information approach is specifically adopted in dealing with demands for customer privacy, the first step is calculating a value for customer information. If the benefits to the firm from adopting a privacy respecting strategy, i.e. the value of information and the long-term cash flows from enhanced long-term customer relationships, are greater than the price paid for the information together with the costs of implementing the privacy protection policies, then it makes sense for the company to be pro-active in formulating and implementing customer privacy-friendly proposals. While initial estimates are likely to vary widely, such estimates will gain greater precision over time, with experience and with the benefit of actual customer reaction to customer privacy policies. Over time, one would expect that companies would adopt policies in tune with the value of their customer base and specifics of needs and behavior of their customer base. Customer equity methodologies and calculations are part of this modeling approach to resolving customer privacy conflicts. However, such a cost–benefit calculus may be different in different markets, as customer value, the price to be paid for customer information and the costs of implementing specific privacy policies can all vary between markets.

In a broader sense, consumers can be educated, persuaded to trade privacy for greater satisfaction. Privacy is not a black and white proposition, and consumers may actually benefit overall from giving up some privacy. This persuasive approach is likely to result in long-term satisfactory resolution of conflicts with customers rather than blanket one size fits all policies.

As customer information becomes increasingly important as an asset, new entities will emerge whose principal business objective is to serve as international infomediaries and information brokers (Hagel and Rayport 1997).

Ethical considerations can also illuminate the decision-making process concerning customer privacy. Can an absolute ethical position towards data privacy protection be formulated, independent of countries and market differences? Companies can choose from multiple ethical stances in philosophically analyzing the customer privacy question: Utilitarian theories, theories of Rights, and theories of Justice (Robertson and Sarathy 2002). Each of these philosophical approaches can yield a different answer to the question of protecting customer privacy, depending on whether societal interests, individual interests or pragmatic considerations are paramount. Adding an ethical lens does not lead the company any closer to a clear-cut answer. It still depends on how the country and the individual view privacy, and how the company chooses to examine privacy: as a business decision having economic consequences amenable to cost–benefit analysis, or as a philosophical question not bound by market forces.

Trust also influences the privacy decision. Trust reduces the need for regulation, as trust allows consumers to feel more assured that companies will not misuse their personal information. Such trust can have a beneficial side-effect of greater loyalty and repeat purchases. Trust is intimately linked to stewardship, suggesting that companies do not own customer data, they hold it in trust for customers who expect that the data will be used in the best interests of the customers. However, the boundaries of trust can vary across cultures, who one trusts and the basis for determining trustworthy partners may themselves be culture bound (Buchan, Dickson and Haytko 2001). When customers can choose between multiple international companies, are local companies likely to be more trusted? Will trust be greater in face-to-face commerce vs. commerce at a distance – i.e. international e-commerce? And if companies can influence the degree of trust customers place in their supplier, how can an international firm gain customer trust?

One development is the rise of third party firms who furnish a seal of privacy quality and other certificates of compliance. Such firms establish standards based on customer surveys and needs, then audit firms to establish compliance levels and their seals are intended to assure customers who do not know the company well that the company is in fact protective of customer privacy. Examples of such companies in the US market are BBOOnline and eTrust. There is no business reason why such audit and certificate mechanisms cannot be extended to markets in other countries, though there may be a cultural barrier: will customers from all cultures trust third parties to develop trustworthiness indicators or will they rely on time-honored approaches to determining trustworthiness, i.e. personal interaction and experience.

Looking to the future, firms need to assess whether there will be a convergence of regulation and industry practices in the area of customer privacy protection; and will the convergence take place around regulatory approaches standardized across all markets or in a self-regulatory framework with room for market forces to allow trading of privacy for value between customers and suppliers? The answer is not clear and unlikely to be resolved soon. Lack of standardization may arrest the move to international e-commerce and personalized international marketing, while firms gradually work out a solution for their global operations. Governments are more likely to move to a convergence of data protection policies in interrelated markets (with a high degree of trade and investment). In the meantime, companies have to work out their privacy strategies piecemeal, taking into account customer needs, the industry context, cultural and political differences, regulatory imperatives and their own cost–benefit calculus. The decision is not an easy one and is likely to evolve as industries and customers change and as countries themselves move to harmonize the regulatory frameworks.

REFERENCES

Buchan, Nancy, Peter R. Dickson and Diana L. Haytko (2001), 'International Differences in Trust in Manufacturer–Distributor Relationships', University of Wisconsin Working Paper.

Culnan, Mary J. (1999), *Protecting Privacy Online: Is Self-Regulation Working?*, Georgetown: Georgetown University Press.

Economist, The (2000), '*The Internet's chastened child*', 11 November, p. 80.

EU–US Safe Harbor Agreement, http://www.usembassy.de/policy/archive/privacy. htm; http://www.export.gov/safeharbor/larussacovernote717.htm.

Fromholz, Julia M. (2000), 'The European Union Data Privacy Directive, Annual Review of Law and Technology,' *Berkeley Technology Law Journal*, **15** (1), Winter.

George, Barbara Crutchfield, Patricia Lynch and Susan J. Marsnik (2001), 'US Multinational Employers: Navigating Through the "Safe Harbor" Principles to Comply with the EU Data Privacy Directive', *American Business Law Journal*, **38** (4), Summer.

Hagel, John and Jeffery Rayport (1997), 'The Coming Battle for Customer Information', *Harvard Business Review*, January/February.

Hofstede, Geert (1991), *Cultures and Organizations: Software of the Mind*, London: McGraw-Hill.

Junkbusters: http://www.junkbusters.com/ht/en/ijb.html.

Lessig, Lawrence (1999), *Code and other Laws of Cyberspace*, New York: Basic Books.

Platform for Privacy Preferences: http://www.w3.org/P3P/.

Robertson, Chris and Ravi Sarathy (2002), 'Executive Briefing: Digital Privacy', *Business Horizons*, January/February.

Rosen, Jeffrey (2001), 'A Victory for Privacy', *The Wall Street Journal*, 18 June.

Ryan, James (1999), 'Your Online Shadow Knows', *Business 2.0*, June.

Samuel, Warren and Louis D. Brandeis (1980), 'The Right to Privacy', *Harvard Law Review*.

Samuelson, Pamela (1999), 'Data Privacy Law: A Study of United States Data Protection', *California Law Review*, **87** (3).

Shapiro, Carl (2000), 'Will E-Commerce Erode Liberty', *Harvard Business Review*, **78** (3).

Zero Knowledge Systems: http://www.zeroknowledge.com/privacy/default.asp.

PART VI

Special topics

19. Global diffusion models: back to the future

V. Kumar

INTRODUCTION

With today's market converging towards forming a dynamic and global arena for selling and buying products, sensible marketing has become the catchphrase for success. What to sell? When to sell? Where to sell? All these questions loom large over every market-based decision-making process. Even though the market is shrinking, there exist differences between any two given markets. These subtle differences can, in effect, make or break a marketing effort. A market is like a living, breathing entity with a mind of its own; each market reacting in a different way to a marketing effort. So is there a definite way, a strategy, for a firm to go about the marketing process? Is there a tried and tested way of understanding and penetrating a market? Study of multinational diffusion models is precisely the way to go about answering the previous question. This chapter is a compilation of the various studies in the field of global diffusion that tries to explain the phenomenon. This review attempts to encapsulate the past studies and the current studies in the field of multinational diffusion models and finally draws conclusions about the future of multinational diffusion models.

HISTORY

Cross-national Diffusion Research

Any diffusion model in the field of marketing today can be traced back to the Bass model, which considers the adoption of an innovation within a market or population as being influenced by two methods of communication – mass media and word of mouth. It also distinguishes the adopters into two groups, one that is influenced by mass media, known as 'innovators' and the other that is influenced by the word-of-mouth communication, known as 'imitators'. The density function according to Bass (1969) is:

$$\frac{dF}{dt} = f(t) = [p + qF(t)][1 - F(t)], \tag{19.1}$$

where, $F(t)$ denotes the cumulative function of adopters, and p and q represent the coefficients of innovation and imitation respectively.

Much of the knowledge in the field of cross-national diffusion as it stands today finds its root in three studies that were done over a period of time, all of which were developed on the Bass model. The three studies in perspective are those conducted by Gatignon, Eliashberg and Robertson (1989), Takada and Jain (1991), and Helsen, Jedidi and DeSarbo (1993) (henceforth referred to as GER, TJ and HJD, respectively). All the three studies applied diffusion model to sales data across countries to understand the nature of the diffusion process. These studies collectively act as the foundation for much of the preliminary understanding of the cross-national diffusion patterns that are useful in international marketing strategy formulation. The gist of the three studies collectively can be stated as:

1. The dissemination of an innovation is specific to the culture of the target market/country (TJ), and the differences in the rate of adoption process can be explained to a great extent by country-specific factors such as cosmopolitanism (cosmo), mobility (mobil), and women (women) in labor force (GER).
2. The later an innovation/product is introduced in a country, the faster will be the rate at which the innovation/product is adopted. There exists a time (lead–lag) effect in cross-national diffusion patterns, which results in the faster adoption rate in the lag country when compared with the lead country.
3. The country sections that can be derived on the basis of diffusion parameters (the coefficient of innovation and imitation) are unstable. These segments differ to some extent due to the nature of the product and they do not correspond with the segments/sections.

The GER study, presented a method that modeled the heterogeneity between different countries in terms of their learning to innovate and imitate. The GER study, using six consumer durable goods for 14 European countries, indicated the existence of systematic patterns of diffusion across products and countries. The TJ study found that communication in high context cultures was homophilous and therefore was more conducive to flow of information. On the other hand, in low context cultures the communication was more heterophilous and therefore was not conducive to flow of information and exchange of ideas. They also argued that the rate of adoption was likely to be faster if the innovation is introduced in the market with a time lag since it will give the potential adopter in the lag country additional time to understand the advantage of the innovation and to see if the innovation is compatible with his/her needs. TJ find support for both H1 and H2. The third study attempted to understand the advantages of country segmentation schemes depending upon multinational diffusion parameters. The constructs that represented the array of macroeconomic variables for this study were identified as mobil, cosmo, health, trade, and lifestyle. HJD used 12 countries that included the USA, Japan and 10 European countries for this study to reach both two- and three-cluster solutions. This study applied the latent structure methodology to the Bass model to determine the segments and segment-level estimates. The summary of all three studies can be seen in Table 19.1.

Though these three studies provided useful information, they also came up with contradicting results and observations. First of all, they had little in common as far as the products and countries were concerned. The TJ study came up with the finding that the diffusion process is faster in high context cultures as compared to low context cultures because the environment in high context cultures was found to be more conducive to flow of information, whereas the HJD study came up with little to support the same. Similarly, there were conflicting results between the TJ study and the HJD study with regard to the lead–lag time effect.

To help fill this gap and to study the discrepancy between the three studies, Kumar, Ganesh and Echambadi did a study in 1998 that replicated and extended the findings of the three previous studies on cross-national diffusion. The research aimed to replicate the four findings from the previous studies: the role of country-specific effects in explaining differences in diffusion parameters, the presence of the lead–lag effect, the use of cultural variables to explain systematically the diffusion patterns across countries, and the merit of country segmentation schemes based on diffusion parameters. Kumar et al. extended the previous research by integrating cross-sectional and time-lag variables into one framework and demonstrated how managers can use this single framework for forecasting the diffusion of new products in a market. For this purpose they used annual sales data from Euromonitor Publications for five product categories (VCRs, microwave ovens, cellular phones, home computers, and CD players) in the following countries: Austria, Belgium, Denmark, Finland, France, Germany, Italy, the Netherlands, Norway, Portugal, Spain, Sweden, Switzerland, and the UK. The product categories and time periods covered differ from the ones in the previous studies: some overlap exists among the countries in this study and the ones in the previous studies. One of the main objectives of this study was to replicate the three studies with

Table 19.1 Summary of the studies using the Bass diffusion model

Gatignon, Eliashberg and Robertson (1989)	Takada and Jain (1991)	Helsen, Jedidi and DeSarbo (1993)
Countries with a greater degree of cosmopolitanism (cosmo) tended to show a higher inclination to innovate and a lower inclination to imitate Supported: Yes	The rate of adoption characterized by high context culture and homophilous communication is faster (higher value for the imitation coefficient, i.e. word-of-mouth effect) than that in countries characterized by low context culture and heterophilous communication Supported: Yes	To what extent do the country segments derived from traditional analyses of macro-level data correspond to segments derived from multinational, product class-specific diffusion parameters? Supported: Only to a small extent
Mobility (mobil) is positively associated with the inclination to imitate, since it increased the opportunity for social interaction and exchange of ideas Supported: Yes	The later an innovation is introduced into a market, the faster will be the rate of adoption of the innovation. Therefore, the imitation coefficient will have a larger value for a country in which the innovation is introduced later than for a country in which the innovation is first introduced Supported: Yes	How well do variables that are typically used in macro-level country segmentation studies perform when used to profile diffusion-based country groups? Supported: Not very well
The percentage of women (women) in the labor force is negatively related to the inclination to innovate for an innovation which was time-consuming and was positively related to the inclination to imitate when the work context provided a level of hetrophilous influence Supported: Yes		How stable are the diffusion-based country segmentation schemes when estimated across different innovations Supported: Not stable

a common set of product categories and countries in an effort to reach some generalizable results that can be used in future research.

MODEL FORMULATION AND ESTIMATION PROCEDURES

Replication of GER

The econometric model from the GER study is used to estimate the diffusion model parameters and assess the influence of the characteristics of a country associated with patterns of social communication – cosmo, mobil, and women. The values for these three variables are used from the GER study. In discrete form the model proposed by GER was:

$$x(i,t) - x(i,t-1) = [p(i) + q(i)x(i,t-1) \times (1 - x(i,t-1)] + u(i,t), \quad (19.2)$$

where, $x(i,t)$ = cumulative penetration of product i at time $t[y(i,t)m(i)]$; $y(i,t)$ = cumulative sales of product in country i in time t; $p(i)$ = propensity to innovate in country i; $q(i)$ = propensity to imitate in country i; $m(i)$ = market potential; $u(i,t)$ = disturbance term.

The fluctuations of the parameters across countries are explained in the study as

$$p(i) = Z'(i)g_p + e_p(i) \qquad (19.3)$$

$$q(i) = Z'(i)g_q + e_q(i), \qquad (19.4)$$

where $Z(i)$ = vector of country i characteristics, including an element 1 (constant); g_p = vector of coefficients representing the impact of country characteristics on the propensity to innovate; g_q = vector of coefficients representing the impact of country characteristics on the propensity to imitate; $e_p(i), e_q(i)$ = disturbance terms.

Equations (19.3) and (19.4) are substituted into equation (19.2) and the GLS procedure is applied for the estimation.

Replication of TJ

Similar to TJ, the Bass diffusion model is estimated by the NLS procedure to obtain the diffusion model parameters. The country-specific effect hypothesis is tested with a 'least significant difference' t-test between countries. Time effect is tested with a regression model:

$$Y_{ijk} = \alpha + \beta X_{ijk} + u_i, \qquad (19.5)$$

where X_{ijk} and Y_{ijk} are the differences in values of imitation coefficients and introduction years for a pair of countries i and j for product k. α and β are the intercept and slope coefficients and u is the error term.

Replication of HJD

The two- and three-country segments obtained in the HJD study from macroeconomic variables are used to compare segments formed on the basis of similarity of diffusion patterns in this study. Country segments are derived for each category of product based on the similarity of the diffusion model parameters 'p' and 'q' using cluster analysis.

REPLICATION RESULTS

Replication of GER

In this study, the signs of cosmo on propensity were found to be positive and significant for four of the products, while they were not found significant for cellular phones. The signs for cosmo on propensity to imitate came up with a mixed pattern, with three negative and significant and two positive. The effect of mobil on imitation coefficient shows a mixed pattern. Out of three significant coefficients in this study, two are found to be negative. For the most part, the effect of cosmo was found as hypothesized. Out of five significant coefficients, only three were positive. However, GER did find support for an overall positive effect for mobil using a joint test. The findings of this study indicated that the effect of mobility can vary depending on the innovation itself. The results of this study show that mobility is important and positive in most of the cases, indicating support for the hypothesized positive effect. The expected negative effect for women on the innovation is seen for four of the five product categories. However, the effect of women on the coefficient of innovation did not find any support. The consistency in the signs of the coefficients for the construct variables across products in this study indicated that social communication operates similarly across innovations. Therefore, the results of this study indicated that the directional impact of the individual variables is similar to the GER study findings.

Replication of TJ

The diffusion model parameters in this study are estimated using the NLS procedure in the SAS/STAT package. The effects that were country specific were tested using the least significant difference t-test for pairwise differences in the imitation coefficients between countries. Fourteen European countries were used in the analysis. It was observed that out of the 91 pairwise differences, seven were found to be significant. Although these findings contradicted the findings from the TJ study of culture-specific effects, the results for this test were consistent with the expectations for the European countries that they may not exhibit major differences in the coefficients for imitation. These effects were also observed in the HJD study. The time effect in this study yielded a greater value. Due to availability of better infrastructure facilities and economic climate in later time periods (as compared to the previous study), the benefits of the innovations were known to consumers in a much shorter span of time. This resulted in a higher influence of time lag in the replication study. The model also estimated for each product category to see if the time effect was dependent on the type of innovation. At the aggregate level it was found that the time effect on coefficient was positive. This was similar to the result found in the TJ study. At the individual product level however, this finding held true only for four out of the five innovations.

Replication of HJD

In the replication study, it was found that countries grouped together in terms of time of introduction, and in similar time periods of introduction, geographical proximity appeared to shape the formation of clusters. Also, the cultural and economic similarity between countries seemed to influence the formation of clusters. Though these observations were based on limited evidence, this replication study offered valuable benchmarking for future studies.

No correspondence between the clustering schemes was found when the country segments solution found in this study was compared to the two-country segments solution obtained using macroeconomic factors in the HJD study. There were several reasons for this discrepancy. First, in the HJD study, clustering was based on countries from different continents, while the replication study focused on the European markets. Since cluster analysis can be sensitive to addition/deletion of countries, it was impossible to compare the HJD clustering solution based on macro-economic variables with the clustering solution from the replication study. Also since HJD did not provide the year of introduction for the innovations they studied, it was not possible to draw inferences on the patterns of clusters across product innovations. However, the replication study offered reasons as to grouping of the countries.

Although the replication study revealed some interesting facts, many questions remained unanswered regarding the diffusion process. The study was extended to include the effects of cross-sectional and time-lag variables into a single framework. Thus, the following issues were addressed: (a) to evaluate the cross-sectional time-series model for evaluating diffusion of innovations, (b) to study the ability of this model to predict the diffusion of an existing innovation in a new market, and (c) to study the performance of the model to predict the diffusion of a new product or innovation in any country. As in the replication, data on all the five consumer innovations were used for this extension study. The effect of cross-sectional and time-series variables were captured by the following formulations:

$$p(i) = Z'(i)g_p + e_p(i) \qquad\qquad (19.6)$$

$$q(i) = Z'(i)g_q + \tau_i + e_q(i) \qquad\qquad (19.7)$$

τ_i in the equation denotes the time effect or the time lag of innovation in country i relative to the lead country. All the other notations are the same as in equation (19.4). In this extension study, it was found that the effect of cosmopolitanism was positive for four cases and the influence of women on the coefficient to innovate, was negative in four cases. For propensity to imitate, cosmopolitanism was found negative in four cases and mobility and women showed a positive effect in three cases. This extension study found grounds for all the hypothesized effects. It was found that differences in the rate of diffusion of an innovation can be explained by certain country-specific and time-lag effects. This integrated model also assisted the decision makers in the decision-making process by generating forecasts of the diffusion process. The future studies meant taking up research that could model the diffusion patterns for industrial innovations. That is exactly what Ganesh and Kumar undertook in 1996, and their study is explained below. However, we would like to begin with the decision-making concerns.

INTERNATIONAL MARKET ENTRY: THE BIG LEAP

Strategy formulation for entry into international markets is a dynamic evolutionary process – one that requires meticulous planning. Among the first steps in this process are issues that pertain to initial market entry and expansion (Douglas and Craig 1992). These are some of the most important and critical decisions that a firm takes since a correct and timely entry into a target market can give the innovation the required momentum to capture the market. These decisions pertain to (a) identification and selection of potential markets as well as (b) timing and order of entry (Ayal and Zif 1979).

Up to this point, research studies on the first issue focused on analysis of macro-level country-market characteristics such as (a) attractiveness based on perceived risks, (b) growth rate, (c) foreign market size, and (d) identification of industry and the firm's product potential. Regarding the second question of the timing of market entry, research has shown that a firm entering the international market can adopt either of the following two methods of entering a new market (Kumar 2000).

Sprinkler Strategy/Approach

This strategy suggests that the firm interested in entering international markets can adopt a simultaneous approach to expansion. Under this strategy the firm enters multiple foreign markets at the same time. This is a risky method to adopt because of the high cost involved in entering multiple foreign markets.

Waterfall Strategy/Approach

This strategy suggests an approach in which the firm initially enters one or more lead markets and subsequently times the entry into other foreign countries in a sequential manner. The subsequent markets are identified depending on the performance of the product in the initial market. This strategy is more suited for internationalization. This approach is more conservative than the Sprinkler approach since researchers can study the pattern of product diffusion for a given product category and decide on the roll-out strategy. This way the company has the opportunity to cut losses in any market where its products are not accepted.

Accordingly, there are various questions that can haunt a multinational manager. First, the question can be about which strategy to adopt – the sprinkler approach or the waterfall approach (Kalish, Mahajan and Muller 1995)? Second, if a firm decides to adopt the waterfall approach, what are the initial market segments and how should it time the entry into subsequent markets? The following study attempted to address these very strategic issues facing the multinational managers by examining the cross-national diffusion of a product/technology.

Cross-national diffusion: the learning effect

Previous studies (TJ) observed that the time effect (lead–lag) caused the diffusion rate in lag countries to be faster than the rate in the country where it was first introduced. The findings suggest that lag time had a positive effect on the diffusion rate in the lag countries. However, a later study by Helsen et al. (HJD) observed a negative relationship between the time lag and the diffusion rate in lag countries. The contradictory findings suggest that time may be acting as a proxy for other schematic influences whereby the potential adopter in the lag market gets an opportunity to learn from the experiences of adopters in the lead market. This influence was called the 'learning Effect', and it was found to help lower the perceived risk associated with the new innovation among the adaptors in the lag countries and thereby caused a faster diffusion to take place in those countries.

Learning Effect

Traditionally, diffusion has been defined as the process by which the innovation is communicated through certain channels over a period of time among the members of a social system (Rogers 1983). As discussed before, this communication is mainly influenced by mass-media (external) and by word-of-mouth (internal) communication. And the diffusion theory assumes that diffusion occurs within the boundaries of a social system. The following study by Ganesh and Kumar argues that when an innovation is introduced first in one country and then is introduced in subsequent countries with a time lag, the adopters in the lag countries get an opportunity to learn from the experiences of the adopters in the lead country. This study uses the case of a retail scanner technology. It is assumed that the adopting population who are retailers in this case, in the lag countries, has the opportunity to learn from the experiences of the retailers in the lead country. The result is then used to study the influence of the diffusion process in the lead country over the diffusion process in the lag country.

The proposed learning model explicitly captured (at any given time t) the influence of the cumulative adopters in the lead market on the potential adopters in the lag country. The learning effect also implicitly captured the effect of improvements made to the technology/innovation in the lead market on the diffusion process in the lag market over the period of time. This was important because any improvements made to the technology or the marketing mix variables in the lead country influenced penetration in the lead country, which in turn, influenced the diffusion process in the lag countries.

In order to systematically capture the learning effect, a variation of the classical Bass model is used and is called the 'learning model'. This model incorporates the influence of the diffusion of one innovation on the diffusion process of another and allows for one-way interaction across a pair of products. This represents the hypothesized learning effect. The model is formulated as given below:

$$\frac{dF_1(t)}{dt} = [p + q*F_1(t) + c*F_2(t)]* [1 - F_1(t)], \qquad (19.8)$$

where: $F_1(t) = N_1(t)/m_1$ represents the cumulative penetration ratio until time t for the lag country; $F_2(t) = N_2(t)/m_2$ represents the cumulative penetration ratio until time t for the lead country; p: represents the coefficient of innovation for the lag country; q: represents the coefficient of imitation for the lag country; and c represents the learning coefficient for the lag country.

The data required for this research were individual store-level adoption data for scanners in the United States, Japan, Belgium, Germany, the UK, the Netherlands, France, Italy, Spain, and Denmark. The unit of analysis was individual retail stores in each of these 10 countries. The data for all countries were collected from the first year of introduction. The data used in this study were collected through several different sources and were cross-checked to maintain reliability.

In this case of retail scanners, spreading of information regarding the benefits of scanners in Europe and other countries based on the experience of US (lead market) retailers explained to a very large extent the faster diffusion rate in the lag markets. This process was assisted by the formation of the European Article Numbering Association (EAN), which disseminated information to its members regarding the advantages of scanning. The reports on the diffusion of scanners in the lag markets did not come across problems that came up in the lead market. This suggested that some learning had taken place and that the European retailers had learned from their US counterparts. The following was hypothesized:

H1: The diffusion process of an innovation in the lead country has a positive effect on the diffusion process in the lag country. This positive effect works to accelerate the diffusion process in the lag country.

The role that this process of learning plays in the adoption process holds true for any industrial technology where the industry that adopts the innovation has a structured arrangement to communicate. Retail scanners and similar capital-intensive technologies belong to a typical product category where the potential adopters in the lag markets constitute a small section of the market and thus play a very minimal role in the process of diffusion. Thus, here it is assumed that the diffusion of the innovation is driven mainly by the learning effect. The following was hypothesized:

H2: In the case of industrial technological innovations, the diffusion process in the lag markets is driven only by the learning that takes place between the potential adopters in the lag markets and between potential adopters in the lag market and their counterparts in the lead market.

It is seen that industrial technological innovations are, in general more complex and far-reaching. The risks related with adopting such an innovation are relatively high and need to be mitigated by integrated means of communication. In these situations, it is seen that the potential consumers in the lag markets rely very much on the experience of their counterparts in the lead market. To capture this kind of diffusion, this study puts forward the pure learning model, which is formulated as:

$$\frac{dF_1(t)}{dt} = [q^*F_1(t) + c^*F_2(t)]^*[1 - F_1(t)] \tag{19.9}$$

which is similar to the learning model in equation (19.8), but here it is without the *p* term.

The learning model and the pure learning model were used to model the diffusion process in the lag markets. The learning coefficient was estimated to examine the effects of the lead country on the lag markets. The results implied that the later the introduction of an innovation in a lag country the greater is the influence of the lead country on the diffusion process in the lag country. The estimate of the time required for scanners to peak in the lag countries was far less than that of the lead country. Where the US market took 17 years to peak, in lag countries like Germany and Belgium, it peaked in 9 years. In countries where the innovation was introduced even later showed an even faster rate of diffusion. For example, in Denmark and Sweden it peaked in 4 years. Hence, the first hypothesis was supported by the results. The results also supported the second hypothesis and it was seen that in case of an industrial technological innovation, the coefficient of innovation on the process of diffusion in the lag markets was nonexistent.

Given the importance of the learning effect in international market entry decisions, Ganesh, Kumar and Subramaniam (1997) did a study that addressed critical issues raised in past research. While previous studies suggested at most a method to capture the learning effect, these studies did not address the factors that influenced learning. This study done by the author extends the knowledge in this area by empirically capturing the learning effect and systematically explaining the factors affecting the learning effect. Also in this study diffusion of consumer durables was studied whereas the previous study by Ganesh and Kumar concentrated on industrial technological innovation.

AN EXPLORATORY INVESTIGATION OF THE LEARNING EFFECT

The main objectives of this study were to:

1. Investigate the existence of a systematic learning effect between a pair of lead and lag countries in the case of consumer durables.
2. Propose a theoretical framework that identifies the factors that influence the learning process.
3. Empirically examine the relationship between these factors and the learning effect so as to better understand the dynamics of the learning phenomenon.
4. Estimate the sales of these products in countries (not included in the estimation) to evaluate the robustness of the proposed model as a forecasting tool.

This study attempted to examine the dynamics of the interaction between social systems using the extended diffusion model. The study focused on identifying the factors that influence consumer learning and their impact on the adoption process in the lag markets. Identification and verification of these factors can assist managers in market selection and in timing and order-of-entry decisions.

Factors Influencing the Learning Process

Past research studies on international marketing and multinational diffusion suggest that several factors could potentially influence the learning process that takes place between a pair of lead and lag markets. Overall, these factors could be categorized as (a) country-specific factors, (b) the time lag between product introduction in the lead and lag markets, and (c) product-innovation-specific factors. The country-specific factors include geographical proximity, cultural similarity and economic similarity; the product-innovation-specific factors include type of innovation (continuous or discontinuous) and existence of an accepted technical standard. The study came up with the factors described in Table 19.2.

In the study, the diffusion patterns of four consumer durables – the VCR, microwave oven, home computer, and cellular phone were analyzed for 11 to 16 European countries. The countries included Belgium, Germany, the UK, the Netherlands, Italy, France, Spain, Denmark, Austria, Finland, Switzerland, Greece, Portugal, Ireland, Sweden, and Norway. The data required for modeling the diffusion process in this study were yearly sales data for each product in all the countries studied. The data were collected from the first year of intro-

Table 19.2   Factors influencing the learning process

Factor	What it means	Proposition
Geographical proximity	The flow of information is primarily dependent on the social and terrestrial barriers, which impede, divert, and channel communications	The smaller the geographical distance is between the lead and lag countries, the stronger will be the learning effect
Cultural similarity	Culturally similar countries share similar religious beliefs, language, customs, and lifestyles. Therefore, the behavior of consumers in two culturally similar countries is more likely to follow similar patterns	The more similar the lead and lag markets are culturally, the stronger will be the learning effect
Economic similarity	Identification of markets similar to the home country in terms of economic growth is expected to reduce uncertainties associated in entering foreign markets and thus assist in market-selection and mode-of-entry decisions	The more similar the lead and lag markets are economically, the stronger will be the learning effect
Time lag	Time lag provides the additional time for potential adopters in the lag market to understand the relative advantage of the product, to check whether it is compatible with their needs, to observe the usage of the product from the experiences of the adopters in the lead market	The time lag between the introduction of an innovation in the lead and lag markets is positively related to the learning effect

Table 19.2 (*continued*)

Factor	What it means	Proposition
Type of innovation	A continuous innovation is a minor innovation possessing a majority of features in common with earlier products in addition to some new features that improve performance or add some value to the product. Discontinuous innovation differs drastically from earlier forms in several relevant features or attributes	In case of continuous innovation, the learning effect will be stronger when compared with discontinuous innovations
Existence of a technical standard	Customers' resistance will be high for an innovation that does not have a standard in the industry since the perceived risk will be higher for such innovations	The existence of an industry standard for the technology enhances the learning effect; conversely, a lack of a technical standard weakens the learning effect

duction of the product in each of these countries through the time period for which the most recent data were available. Yearly sales data on each of the product categories for the different countries analyzed in this study and the data on the independent variable – economic similarity – were obtained primarily from *European Marketing Data and Statistics* (Euromonitor Publications 1984–1999). The measures for the data were as described above.

Geographical proximity was operationalized as the distance between capital cities of the lead and lag countries. There have been numerous attempts to cluster countries based on cultural factors. This study has used Hofstede's (1980) dimensions as a measure of cultural differences. Hofstede grouped countries on four dimensions: (a) power distance, (b) masculinity/feminity, (c) uncertainty avoidance, and (d) individualism. These four dimensions are postulated to constitute fundamental value orientations that underlie national differences in managerial practices, organizational patterns, and decision making. Economic similarity was operationalized as a negative index of the sum of absolute differences in the standardized

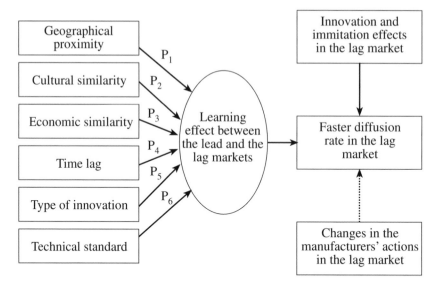

Figure 19.1   Diffusion process in a lag market

values of GDP per capita, level of urbanization, and unemployment rate between the corresponding lead and lag countries, Time lag was tested by operationalizing time lag as the difference in years of introduction of the product between the lead and lag countries. It was proposed that time lag will be positively related to the learning effect. Existence of a technical standard was operationalized as a dummy variable with a value of 1 for an innovation that lacked a technical standard while a value of 0 was assigned to the innovation that had a technical standard. (See Figure 19.1.)

Model Specification and Estimation

The classical Bass diffusion model was used to capture the diffusion process of each innovation in the individual countries. Subsequently, to capture the learning effect between the lead and lag markets, the learning model was used. The learning model (equation 19.8) is akin to the independent product model developed by Peterson and Mahajan (1978), and the learning effect is captured by the learning coefficient c. Further, it was proposed in this study that the difference in the learning effect across different lag countries could be partially explained by three sets of factors: (a) country-specific factors, (b) time lag, and (c) innovation-specific factors. The basic model was estimated using the non-linear least squares (NLS) procedure recommended by Srinivasan and Mason (1986).

RESULTS

The empirical findings suggested that five of the six factors examined in this study – cultural similarity, economic similarity, time lag, type of innovation, and existence of a technical standard – were strongly related to the learning process. The analysis revealed that geographical proximity was not significant for three of the four product categories. Hence, the findings of the study did not support the first proposition. The lack of support for the first proposition was attributed to other factors that probably play a greater role in the study.

Though the study focused on the diffusion patterns of consumer durables on an aggregate level, the findings of the study raise several interesting questions. It brought out results that provided proof of the existence of the learning effect across consumer durables. This further established the findings of the study conducted by Ganesh and Kumar (1996), which focused on the presence of the learning effect on industrial technological innovations. The study showed that investigating the factors found in the study can lead to a better understanding of the learning effect. These findings can be very beneficial when decisions regarding market entry are made. For example, a market showing a weak learning effect can be overcome by giving the market additional time for the learning to take place more effectively. The study came forward with the idea that in cases of continuous innovation, the sprinkler approach was the better option. For a discontinuous innovation, the use of the waterfall approach was more effective. The study also placed a lot of emphasis on transforming a technological innovation into a world wide standard. It also provided an opportunity for managers to get insights into future target markets, thereby helping in the decision-making process.

So far, through analyzing the sales data of a sample of new products in different countries, Takada and Jain (1991) showed that the differences in the diffusion rates in various countries could be attributed to some of the cultural differences between the countries and/or to the differences in the product introduction timing in those countries. In a different study, Gatignon et al. (1989) attributed the differences to country-specific factors such as cosmopolitanism, consumer mobility and role of women in the labor force. However, Helsen et al. (1993) could not replicate some of these results in their study. On further investigation, Kumar et al. (1998) found that the inconsistency in the past research findings was due to the specific set of countries and innovations used in those different studies. The studies mentioned above merely analyzed the diffusion processes in two countries, keeping each country in isolation, and then later compared the results on specific factors.

The interaction among the sales processes in different countries today has been modeled and studied in two methods. The first is called the lead–lag effect, which has been discussed at length in this chapter and the second method which we will be discussing, was suggested by Putsis et al. (1997), who used a 'mixing model' to empirically explore the existence of simultaneous interaction between markets. In this particular mixing model, the limiting factor was that the product should be introduced in the two countries/markets simultaneously.

$$\frac{f_1(t)}{(1 - F_1(t))} = (a_1 + c_1 \cdot (rho) \cdot F_1(t) + c_2 \cdot (1 - (rho) \cdot F_2(t))) \; mixing \; model \; (19.10)$$

'Mixing' described ways in which a population interacted. The mixing model considered the adoption of a new product in one country as affecting adoption in other countries. How the pattern of communication within and across the countries influenced the diffusion process was what this study tested. The study used the Bass model on each country tested using nonlinear least squares and then examined the correlation in the residuals across the countries. It used 10 EC countries across four product categories – VCRs (1977–1989), microwave ovens (1975–1989), CD players (1984–93), and home computers (1981–91). The study found a universally positive and often high correlation between the countries. The conclusions that the study drew from these findings were that there were significant cross-country influences that were not explained by the simple Bass model and that there were critical missing covariates that were simultaneously affecting sales in the countries.

The study defined three basic forms of mixing behavior across populations, two of which defined the ends of a continuum of possible mixing behaviors and the third defined the possibilities between the two ends. The first one was called 'pure segregation', where the probability of contact between an individual in one population and an individual from another population was zero (only contact within a population – word of mouth – was possible). The second basic form was called 'random mixing', which was on the other end of the spectrum in comparison with pure segregation. In this case, mixing occurred freely. The third basic form defined all the possibilities found between pure segmentation and random mixing and was called 'Bernoulli noise mixing' (preferred mixing). A mixing parameter (ϕ_i) was also defined in Bernoulli noise mixing, which defined a specific point on the continuum where the behavior fell ($\phi_i = 1$ for pure segmentation and $\phi_i = 0$ for random mixing). The study took the estimated diffusion parameters for individual nations of the EC from the study conducted by Mahajan and Muller (1994) and simulated sales for three countries

(Austria, Germany and Portugal). These simulations were conducted under assumptions of segregated, random, and Bernoulli mixing. Only the mixing parameter (ϕ_i) was changed during the transition from pure segmentation to random mixing. Thus, differences in sales were attributed solely to the mixing behavior.

For each of the four product categories in the study, estimations were first done allowing ϕ_i to vary and then on the same system restricting ϕ_i to be the same. For VCRs, microwave ovens, and compact disc players mixing behavior was estimated to be between segregated and random mixing with point estimates of ϕ_i for 0.551 for VCRs, 0.572 for compact disc players and 0.538 for microwave ovens. The standard error for ϕ_i was found to be very low in these instances, which suggested the better fit of Bernoulli mixing over the population of interest.

A major conclusion of this study was that if one had to understand the diffusion in one country, then it was important to not only know the diffusion parameters of that country, but also the parameters of other relevant countries. The diffusion model integrating the mixing patterns assumed that the products were introduced at the same time in all the related countries. The effect of each country on another country however was not explicitly captured by the mixing model. The simulations illustrated a number of important points. First, the timing of peak sales and the speed of the diffusion process were significantly affected by the type of mixing. Second, it was found that in general, across the entire population peak sales were higher and time to peak was shorter under random mixing versus segregation mixing. Third, the change in sales was not found proportional to change in ϕ_i. This was important to understand and interpret the estimated values of ϕ_i. The study thus put forward the idea that mixing across populations had a significant effect on the diffusion process and since the real world did not exist in a purely segregated environment, the mixing effect was a very critical factor in the diffusion process.

Thus so far, we now have two types of models that have been developed to study the interaction among the diffusion processes in two countries. Over the period of time, the initial studies captured the diffusion process using the Bass model as the base. Later, studies also found time acting as a surrogate for another phenomenon which affected the diffusion process. This phenomenon called the learning effect. This was followed by the mixing model, which studied the simultaneous effect. Though the simultaneous effect model found the significance of mixing in the diffusion process, it only acted as an initial step in understanding the factors driving the cross-country correlations. In summary, the initial studies failed to address the simultaneous effect while the mixing model failed to address the lead–lag effect. Over the period, a third effect was also observed in which the lag market affected the lead market. This effect was aptly termed the 'lag–lead effect'. In order to come up with a model that captured all these effects in a single model formulation, the following study is proposed by Kumar and Krishnan (2002). They name their model the 'flexible interaction model'.

ADDITIONAL DEVELOPMENTS

An Alternative Framework

The main objective of the following study is to propose a model that can accommodate all the three effects, namely, the lead–lag, the lag–lead and the simultaneous effects. Kumar and Krishnan (2002) proposed a model using sales data of four consumer durable innovations. In the empirical tests, evidence of the presence of all three effects is found, implying that neglect of any of the effects will undermine the ability of an international marketing manager to understand the diffusion process in multiple countries.

Proposed Model

The model is developed in two stages, first focusing on modeling the simultaneous effect and then including the lead–lag and the lag–lead effects in that model. To capture the influence of diffusion of an innovation in one country on the diffusion in the other country, diffusion of each country was modeled using the generalized Bass model (Bass, Krishnan and Jain 1994) as follows:

$$\frac{f(t)}{1 - F_i(t)} = [p_i + q_i F_i(t)]x_i(t), \ i = 1,2 \tag{19.11}$$

where, $f_i(t)/[1 - F_i(t)]$ is the hazard function of time to adoption in country i, p_i is the coefficient of innovation or external influence, $q_i F_i(t)$ is the word-of-mouth effect and $x_i(t)$ is the current marketing effort as defined in the generalized Bass model. Also $x_1(t) = 1 + \{b_{21} * [dF_2(t)/dt]\}$.

The model is now extended to include the lead–lag effect and the lag–lead effect as follows: assume that country 1 introduces an innovation at time t_1, and that countries 2 and 3 introduce the same innovation in a subsequent time period, t_2. Now, the diffusion process in countries 2 and 3 can be affected by each other (simultaneous), and by country 1 (lead–lag effect). Further, the diffusion process in country 1 can be affected by the diffusion

Table 19.3   Evaluation of forecasting performance

			CD Players ($n = 6$)
Belgium (1)	Flexible Interaction	MSE*	0.0004
		MAD*	0.0148
	No Interaction	MSE	0.0009
		MAD	0.0281
	One-way Interaction	MSE	0.0007
		MAD	0.0232
Germany (2)	Flexible Interaction	MSE	0.0003
		MAD	0.0128
	No Interaction	MSE	0.0010
		MAD	0.0302
	One-way Interaction	MSE	0.0008
		MAD	0.0262

Note: *The forecasting measures are the mean squared error (MSE) and mean absolute deviation (MAD) in each period penetration rate across the hold-out time periods.

processes in the other two countries. The framework now accommodates the lead–lag effect, the lag–lead effect and the simultaneous effect.

Apart from establishing the model, the study also evaluated forecasting performance of the model on the hold-out time periods. Table 19.3 shows a result from the forecasting evaluation on one of the product categories studied across the countries in the study. Similar forecasting evaluations were also carried out across the product categories and countries.

CONCLUSIONS

The findings of the study using the flexible interaction model are based on consumer durables and therefore, may not generalize to industrial techno-logical innovations. Also, the scope of this study was limited due to the problems associated with the reliability and availability of time-series data across multiple countries. To analyze the interaction coefficients, country-specific factors here included cultural similarity and economic similarity measures. The measures for cultural similarity were drawn from Hofstede (1980) – power distance, masculinity/feminity, uncertainty avoidance and individualism. These four dimensions were hypothesized to constitute fundamental value orientations that explain national differences in management practices, organizational pattern and decision making. Past studies

examine diffusion patterns only in European countries (predominantly
developed economies) and as such the findings cannot be generalized to
other developing and less developed economies. Future research can focus
on systematically capturing all possible effects across countries to better
understand the influence between continents and different types of innovations. Studies that investigate the factors affecting all the effects can reveal
important facts and can help in better explaining the three effects. Also, as
the countries affected increases the complexity of the effects increases, the
present study can be extended to explain the complexities. For example, if
the number of countries is large, one can segment/group the countries
based on some criteria such as Western Europe/Eastern Europe, Asia-
Pacific etc. and then apply the flexible framework suggested by Kumar and
Krishnan (2002). It is also possible to conceptualize individual or brand-
level diffusion models in the international context. This disaggregate modeling framework may offer additional insights into the adoption process of
various innovations (Krishnan, Bass, Kumar, 2000). Further, the factors
influencing the individual adoption across cultures can help managers
target countries with maximum potential for success.

REFERENCES

Ayal, Igal and Jehiel Zif (1979), 'Market Expansion Strategies in Multinational
    Marketing', *Journal of Marketing* **43** (Spring), 84–94.
Bass, M. Frank (1969), 'A New Product Growth Model for Consumer Durables',
    Management Science, **18**, January, 215–27.
Bass, M. Frank, T.V. Krishnan and Dipak Jain (1994), 'Why the Bass Model Fits
    Without Decision Variables', *Marketing Science*, **13** (3), Summer.
Douglas, Susan and C. Craig Samuel (1992), 'Advances in International
    Marketing', *International Journal of Research in Marketing*, **9**, 291–318.
Eliashberg, Jehoshua and Kris Helsen (1996), 'Modeling Lead/Lag Phenomena in
    Global Marketing: The Case of VCRs', Working Paper, University of
    Pennsylvania: The Wharton School.
Euromonitor Publications (1984–1999), *European Marketing Data and Statistics*,
    London: Euromonitor Publications Ltd.
Ganesh, Jaishankar and V. Kumar (1996), 'Capturing the Cross-National Learning
    Effect: An Analysis of an Industrial Technology Diffusion', *Journal of the
    Academy of Marketing Science*, **24** (Fall), 328–37.
Ganesh, Jaishankar, V. Kumar and V. Subramaniam (1997), 'Learning Effects in
    Multinational Diffusion of Consumer Durables: An Exploratory Investigation',
    Journal of Academy of Marketing Science, **25** (3), 214–28.
Gatinon, H., J Eliashberg and T. Robertson (1989), 'Modeling Multinational
    Diffusion Patterns: An Efficient Methodology', *Marketing Science*, **8** (Summer),
    231–47.
Gatignon, Hubert and Thomas S. Robertson (1985), 'A Prepositional Inventory for
    New Diffusion Research', *Journal of Consumer Research*, **11** (March), 849–67.

Helsen, Kristiaan, Kamel Jedidi and Wayne S. DeSarbo (1993), 'A New Approach to Country Segmentation Utilizing Multinational Diffusion Patterns', *Journal of Marketing*, **57** (October), 60–71.

Hofstede, Geert (1980), *Culture's Consequences: International Differences in Work-Related Values*, Beverly Hills, CA: Sage.

Horsky, Dan and Herbert Simon (1983), 'Advertising and the Diffusion of New Products', *Marketing Science*, **9**, 342–85.

Jain, Dipak and Ram C. Rao (1990), 'Effect of Price on the Demand for Durables: Modeling, Estimation, and Findings', *Journal of Business and Economic Statistics*, **8**, 163–70.

Kalish, Shlomo, Vijay Mahajan and Eitan Muller (1995), 'Waterfall and Sprinkler New-Product Strategies in Competitive Global Markets', *International Journal of Research in Marketing*, **12**, 105–19.

Krishnan, Trichy V., Frank M. Bass and V. Kumar (2000), 'Impact of a Late Entrant on the Diffusion of a New Product/Service', *Journal of Marketing Research*, **37** (May), 269–78.

Kumar, V. (2000), *International Marketing Research*, Upper Saddle River, NJ: Prentice-Hall.

Kumar, V. and T.V. Krishnan (2002), 'Multinational Diffusion Models: An Alternative Framework', *Marketing Science*, **21** (3), 318–30.

Kumar, V., J. Ganesh and Raj Echambadi (1998), 'Cross-National Diffusion Research: What Do We Know and How Certain Are We?', *Journal of Product Innovation Management*, **15**, 255–68.

Mahajan, Vijay and Eitan Muller (1994), 'Innovation Diffusion in a Borderless Global Market: Will the 1992 Unification of the European Community Accelerate Diffusion on New Ideas, Products and Technologies?', *Technological Forecasting and Social Change*, **45**, 221–35.

Peterson, Robert A. and Vijay Mahajan (1978), 'Multi-Product Growth Models', in Jagdish Sheth (ed.), *Research in Marketing*, Greenwich, CT: Greenwood Press.

Putsis, Jr, William P., Sridhar Balasubramaniam, Edward H. Kaplan and Subrata Sen (1997), 'Mixing Behavior in Cross-Country Diffusion', *Marketing Science*, **16** (4), 354–69.

Rogers, Everett M. (1983), *Diffusion of Innovations*, 3rd edn, New York: Free Press.

Srinivasan, V. and Charlotte H. Mason (1986), 'Nonlinear Least Squares Estimation of New Product Diffusion Models', *Marketing Science*, **5** (Spring), 169–78.

Takada, Hirokazu and Dipak Jain (1991), 'Cross-National Analysis of Diffusion of Consumer Durable Goods in Pacific Rim Countries', *Journal of Marketing*, **55** (April), 48–54.

20. Country equity and product-country images: state-of-the-art in research and implications

Nicolas Papadopoulos and Louise A. Heslop

INTRODUCTION

Country images are pervasive in society and can have a significant influence on buyers of all types. Incorporated as they are in countries' names and other formal 'trademarks' such as their flags and currencies, as well as in their music and landmarks, people and personalities, cultural and product exports, and countless other symbols, these images are an integral part of people's cognitive belief structures and often evoke strong emotions. In line with buyer behavior theory, therefore, they are by definition a potentially important driver of marketplace behavior.

This chapter is about the images of countries and other places, their effects on buyers, and their implications for a wide variety of sellers ranging from firms marketing traditional products to countries marketing them-selves to attract investment and tourism. The chapter comprises four main sections which also reflect its specific objectives. The first provides a brief background and supplies the needed context for the discussion that follows. The second outlines the methodology used to develop a near-exhaustive inventory of research in this field, which at this time numbers well over 700 publications, and the third presents the findings from the inventory. Lastly, the fourth section assesses the state of the art on the role of place images in marketing by reviewing the findings of past studies and suggesting avenues for future research.

BACKGROUND AND CONTEXT

Country- and other place-related references and symbols are omnipresent and many are noted and internalized in cognition, consciously or not, by people worldwide virtually every day. Examples range from *Italian* arias, *Persian* carpets, and the *Rio* Carnival and *New Orleans* MardiGras, to

American aid to victims of famine, *Russian* roulette, *German* engineering, a *Mexican* standoff, and *TexMex* food. Since these associations may be learned from a near-infinite variety of sources, including education, travel, exposure to the products of various countries, the news media, cultural products such as movies and books, business experiences, and, of course, word of mouth, they exist in the mental map of every person regardless of his or her particular situation.

The following brief exchange from the movie *Back to the Future III*, a comedy about time travel, between Doc, the scientist living in real-time 1955, and Marty, the young hero who has been to 1985 and back, helps to portray many of the elements that are the focus of this chapter:

> Doc: No wonder this circuit failed . . . it says 'Made in Japan'.
> Marty: What do you mean, Doc? All the best things are made in Japan.
> Doc: Unbelievable!

First, through the prism of his experiences to the mid-1950s, Doc attributes the product's (poor) performance to its provenance – while, from his vantage point of the mid-1980s, Marty has a decidedly more positive view of Japanese product performance. Second, the two time points roughly correspond to the nadir and zenith of Japan's image as a producer, and together they show that a national image can change over time as a result of a focused national strategy. Third, given their respective mindframes prior to the exchange, Doc would be highly unlikely to knowingly choose, while Marty would be highly likely to in fact seek out, a Japanese circuit – pointing to the fundamental tenet in consumer behavior theory that beliefs help to guide consumer choices. (Since he operates from a 1985 perspective and is too young to remember early Japanese products, Marty would choose the Japanese-made product even in 1955!) Fourth, whether deliberately or not the screenwriter did not write Martin's line as 'the best circuits are made in Japan', which might have been a more natural response. Marty generalizes that 'all the best things' are made in that country – that is, the country images of individual product classes may differ from one another but all are likely to be congruent with its overall image as a producer, as this may have been shaped by various factors including its most prominent products. Lastly, following the exchange Marty will likely maintain his positive view and Doc, given his response, may change his attribution of the circuit failure and be more open to products from Japan. This suggests the broad range of sources from which consumers receive origin-related product information, as noted above. This particular vignette points to product experience, advertising, and so on for Marty and to word of mouth for Doc – but also to the entertainment and scholarly media for, respectively, those who watched the movie and/or who are reading this book!

A key conclusion from the above paragraphs is that countries have images which, unlike brand or corporate images, are not directly under the marketer's control. They are developed from a myriad sources and used routinely in association with objects, events, experiences, and of course products, as people try to understand them better, categorize them, symbolize them, or process new information they receive about them (Jaffe and Nebenzahl 2001). Needless to say, some countries have stronger or more focused images than others, and different people may (and likely do) have different images of any one country – but what is important is that the images exist and may influence behavior.

Therefore, depending on whether and how they are used, country images can have a significant impact on the effectiveness of marketing strategies by virtually all sellers. The issue is of potential interest to firms aiming to penetrate foreign markets, those that need to compete at home against imports, and the governments and associations who represent them. Not surprisingly in light of their importance, product-country images (PCIs), or the place-related images with which buyers and/or sellers may associate a product, and their effects on buyers' behavior, have attracted significant research attention over the past 40 years.

This interest has increased recently as a result of the dramatic growth of foreign direct investment (FDI). The growing number of countries that use systematic marketing to attract investors from within the finite and highly competitive global capital pool has focused attention on countries as 'investment products'. This, coupled with the longstanding view of places as 'tourism products', adds the myriad government agencies, trade associations, and firms which market cities, regions, or countries to tourists and investors, to the long list of those interested in place images.

The combination of growing interest in promoting exports, defending against imports, and marketing for investment and tourism, has brought forth the notion of 'countries (or places) as brands' as a key concept in this field. In this context, 'country equity', or the net sum of a country's real or perceived strengths (assets) and weaknesses (liabilities), appears destined to become a central organizing concept that is of great and growing interest in government, business, and research. As with brand equity and image, but on a significantly broader level, strong and well-managed country equity can benefit all actors in a country, from consumers to business and governments, and of course the country at large – while a weak or poorly managed image can have the opposite effect.

As noted in the introduction, the purpose of this chapter is to discuss country images and their effects on buyers and sellers. Since the concepts of country equity and country branding are in a nascent state at best, and therefore research from this particular perspective is virtually nonexistent, the primary source for this discussion is the PCI literature which represents the bulk of research in this field. In addition, relevant references to related fields, such as social psychology and, from within marketing, consumer behavior, are used where appropriate.

METHOD

Background on Product-country Image Research

PCI research began in the 1960s and has since grown to comprise one of the most voluminous literatures within international marketing or, indeed, any disciplinary subfield. A brief overview of the evolution of this research can serve as useful background to the method used in this chapter.

The first literature review in this area, by Bilkey and Nes in 1982, used only 20 studies (including several unpublished PhD dissertations), but by 1987 Tan and Farley called this 'the most researched' issue in international buyer behavior. In 1992, Douglas and Craig referred to a 'host of studies' on this topic, while at the same time bewailing the continuing methodological weaknesses, which Bilkey and Nes (1982) had also identified, by attributing its 'popularity [more to] the ease with which data can be collected, often from "captive foreign student subjects", and less to its perceived significance'. By the time of the next thorough review, however, by Baughn and Yaprak in 1993, the situation had improved significantly and these authors were able to use 64 studies as the base for mapping out several well-defined avenues for potential future research.

By 1995, Peterson and Jolibert were calling country of origin effects 'one of the most widely studied phenomena in the international business, marketing, and consumer behavior literatures' (p. 883), placing the total number of publications at 'nearly 200' (p. 886). The 1990s also saw publication of several integrative works, including two meta-analyses (of experiments by Liefeld 1993, and of surveys by Peterson and Jolibert 1995), three PCI-specific books (Kotler, Haider and Rein 1993; Papadopoulos and Heslop 1993; Gold and Ward 1994), and three applied books on individual countries (Head 1992, Germany; Reid and Burns 1992, Canada; and Fischer and Byron 1995, Australia). Lastly, in the most recent book on this topic, in 2001, Jaffe and Nebenzahl guesstimated the number of PCI publications at 'over two hundred'.

While these estimates of the research volume on PCI are sizeable in themselves, as noted in the introduction they in fact understate reality by a wide margin, considering that our comprehensive inventory of this research includes over 700 publications. The approach used in making a more complete assessment is briefly outlined in the next two sub-sections.

Background on Surveys of Research and Literature Reviews

A review of major journals indicated that literature reviews have increased significantly in recent years in terms of the variety of approaches they use, their analytical depth, and their overall number. Twenty-six such studies were identified and used to provide guidance for developing the inventory of PCI research presented in this chapter and to decide the types of analysis to be used. Of these, 18 were 'literature reviews' or 'surveys of research' in individual fields and eight focused on research productivity.

Given their objectives, traditional literature reviews provide a valuable service by dealing with the chosen topic in depth, often discussing in detail both the specific content of individual contributions and the state of research in the field's component parts. On the other hand, such studies tend to be selective in the sources they use, since, more often than not, these are limited by the authors' knowledge of the various sub-fields, their judgment as to which sources are important enough to consult, and the extent of their effort in developing their base inventory of research for review. As a result, even the superior thematic reviews by recognized scholars, such as Bilkey (1978), Boddewyn (1981), Reid (1983), Li and Cavusgil (1991), Douglas and Craig (1992), and Leonidou and Katsikeas (1996), are not comprehensive in their coverage (nor do they intend to be or portray themselves as such).

Surveys of research, on the other hand, typically focus more on a quantitative analysis of research contributions and less, if at all, on depth regarding the substance of the issue they deal with. The number of sources used varies greatly depending on the study's objectives. Studies that focus on analyzing contributions by a single journal (e.g. Thomas, Shenkar, and Clarke 1994, on the *Journal of International Business Studies*) are limited to it by definition. Among the broader studies, those by Adler and Bartholomew (1992) and Katsikeas, Leonidou and Morgan (2000), for example, were based respectively on 73 and 33 journals. Of the surveys of research we consulted, none used publication venues other than journals.

Lastly, studies on research productivity also tend to be limited in terms of the number of sources they use (e.g. Booth and Heath (1990) and Morrison and Inkpen (1991) used 17 and nine 'key' journals, respectively), and do not normally deal with the content of the thematic area, focusing instead on an analysis of contributions by author and/or university affiliation and/or publication venue. Their typical approach is to assign contribution weights to the authors of articles (1.0, 0.5, 0.33, etc. to each author depending on how many (co-) authors were involved).

Clearly, each of the three approaches has its own advantages: literature reviews offer significant depth and insight; surveys of research offer less depth but wider coverage, exposing readers to a broader scope of the research that is being carried out in the chosen field; and comparative contribution analyses identify the main participants in the area, thus providing valuable information to a variety of potential users (e.g. PhD candidates considering which university to attend or join, researchers considering which journal to submit their work to, scholars wanting to identify other principal researchers in their field, and individual researchers and/or their institutions for career decisions such as moves or assessments; see Booth and Heath 1990; Morrison and Inkpen 1991; Pierce and Garven 1995).

In developing this chapter we decided on a hybrid approach incorporating elements from all three of those described above. This of course means that the chapter cannot go into as much depth from any of the three perspectives as it might if it focused on just one of them. However, the inventory that is used as the base for this chapter is comprehensive, placing it in the 'survey of research' domain, but also formatted so that it enables both a contribution analysis and a more in-depth consideration of the various issues, thus making it possible to attempt a rounded state-of-the-art review on the intertwined subjects of product-country images and country and place branding and equity.

Methodology for the PCI Research Database

Our a priori assumption was that since PCI researchers publish in a broad range of venues and countries, limiting our search for relevant works to selected journals would not achieve the objective of obtaining a comprehensive database. This was partly because, no matter how thorough, such an approach cannot possibly include all relevant journals. As Douglas and Craig (1992) noted, for example, it may end up misrepresenting the level of interest in a particular field, since it 'may in part be a reflection of the journals selected for inclusion' (p. 304). We also felt it would be inappropriate to limit the search to journals. As Wayland, Urban and McDermott (1992) have rightly stated in reference to the American Marketing Association and the Association for Consumer Research, 'some proceedings require a more rigorous review process than do lower level journals' (p. 316; see also Douglas and Craig 1992, p. 297). Furthermore, a considerable portion of significant PCI work has appeared in the form of papers in conference proceedings (as well as book chapters and research reports or monographs), as evidenced by their inclusion in the meta-analyses by Liefeld (1993) and Peterson and Jolibert (1995).

Therefore, it was decided to cast a wider net in an effort to generate as broad a pool as possible of relevant publications. The process used is outlined below.

1. Base approach

An iterative approach similar to that described by Peterson and Jolibert (1995) was used, consisting of five main parts:

a. Our own lists of references of PCI publications, used in our research to 1991, were compiled into a master list and converted to Microsoft Access database format for ease of analysis.
b. The lists of references of all papers in the master list were scanned to develop the base of the inventory and identify the main journals and other venues in which PCI researchers publish.
c. Of the journals and conferences identified in (b), those that appeared to contain the bulk of relevant publications were systematically monitored from that point on to identify new publications in them. Adjustments to this list were made over time to reflect the shifting interests of authors and publication venues, the appearance of new journals or conferences that host large numbers of relevant articles, and so on.
d. New works identified through (b) and (c) were also obtained in hard copy form (except for those judged to be decidedly less significant based on our knowledge of the field), and their lists of references scanned to identify new works, with this process continuing to date.
e. Articles identified through the above process were obtained either through standard library holdings and inter-library loans, or, where not otherwise available (e.g. some papers published only locally in countries outside North America), by writing to the authors (identified through the membership lists of the major marketing and international business associations and/or through the author who originally cited the particular reference).

This enabled the development of a database that benefits not only from our own knowledge of sources but also from that of virtually all researchers that are involved in this field. In particular, since authors typically tend to cite their own work and/or that of other researchers with whom they associate or of whom they are aware, this makes it possible to identify publications that might normally be too far afield to be included in any standardized listing of 'key' venues (an example is the *Finnish Journal of Business Economics*, in which Darling and his colleagues published some of their longitudinal PCI studies; see Darling and Kraft 1996). Overall, the outcome of the process was gratifying in that it helped to identify over 700 works relevant to the theme.

2. Criteria

Four criteria were used in deciding what types of publications to search for and which to eventually include for this state-of-the-art review.

1. *Relevance to the theme.* As of this writing, the complete database includes 1160 works. Almost one-third of these, however, though potentially useful to some researchers depending on their perspective in studying place images, are part of other disciplines and therefore had not been catalogued as thoroughly as those from within marketing and international business. For example, the vast literature on national images in social psychology is important but does not approach the issues from a marketing perspective; conversely, research on tourism (which is also voluminous) often is marketing oriented but is sector specific and only some works in it are relevant to image issues. Such works were excluded, leaving the inventory focused on the domain described as studies of place images from a marketing or international business perspective. Thus, for example, an article written by a marketing researcher and dealing with PCI issues from a marketing perspective would be included, while one focusing on the political implications of national stereotypes and published in a social psychology journal would not.
2. *Venue.* Most of the included works are from the academic literature, but some applied works were included if they satisfied the relevance criterion and provided sufficient depth of coverage (i.e. short journalistic articles were excluded regardless of relevance, while a few detailed government reports and extensive articles in business magazines were included).
3. *Publication type.* The initial inventory included books, book chapters, articles in journals and conference proceedings (as well as a small number of papers that were refereed and presented at, but for various reasons not published in the proceedings of, major conferences), working papers, doctoral and master's theses, and reports and monographs not falling in any of the other categories. However, as research in this field proliferated it proved impossible to track working papers and theses as systematically as other types, and these were dropped from the core of the inventory.
4. *Time.* Researchers generally acknowledge Schooler's (1965) 'Product Bias in the Central American Common Market' as the first published PCI study. While our approach identified relevant publications prior to that time, tracking earlier studies is fraught with difficulties (e.g., we

were unable to obtain a copy of a 1903 study on the legal implications of 'Made In'– labels for imports into Canada, which was cited in one of the later articles). Since coverage of earlier dates could not be comprehensive, 1950 was decided upon as the cutoff point. At the other end of the timeframe, it is important to note that, by virtue of the research method as described, the inventory is incomplete for the last two to three years. This is because, unless they are published in the venues that we selectively monitor, very recent works have not yet begun to be cited by other authors whose lists of references we scan for this purpose, and therefore are not included.

The approach described above resulted in as comprehensive an inventory as possible, by including all relevant works in the specified domain but excluding related publications from potentially important but tangential fields that could not be catalogued as exhaustively.

3. Data screening

The final inventory was generated following a three-step process. First, all publications were entered into the database and duplicates were eliminated. While these may result, for example, from a simple mis-spell of an author's name, a main cause of double entries proved to be papers published initially in conference proceedings and subsequently as journal articles and/or book chapters. The decision on whether or not such papers were substantively identical was made by referring to the original sources, and if such were the case the 'lower-order' publication was deleted. Second, the remaining entries were cleaned up or augmented by obtaining missing information (e.g. page numbers, book publisher locations, etc.). Lastly, the entry formats were standardized to enable analysis by various types of criteria and reviewed to ensure that all retained publications matched the criteria.

The net result of the above is 766 works that form the inventory and the basis of discussion in this chapter.

INVENTORY AND TAXONOMY OF PCI RESEARCH: PRINCIPAL FINDINGS

PCI Research: Time and Venues

Table 20.1 presents the database in terms of the type of publications and their frequency by year range. As can be seen, this frequency has increased significantly over time (it should be recalled that data for 1999–2001 are not complete, and therefore the average output per year is understated, particularly for the last two to three years). Specifically, of the four major decades of research in this field, the 1960s and 1970s combined account for 6 per cent, the 1980s for 30 per cent, and the 1990s for 57 per cent of the total. The volume of this research, and its maturation in terms of quality as evidenced in the reviews and meta-analyses cited earlier, suggest a continuing interest on the part of researchers which may in fact grow further as the broader themes of country branding and country equity evolve.

Turning to publications by type, journal articles clearly account for the bulk of publications (361, or almost twice as many as earlier estimates of all publications in the field), followed by articles in proceedings (285). The frequency of these two main types of publications has increased at similar rates, with about 60 to 70 per cent having appeared since 1990. Given the previously mentioned emphasis on integrative works since the early 1990s, most books, chapters, and reports have appeared over the past ten years or so. Interestingly, and in line with the move from 'PCI' as such to the broader concept of country equity discussed above, most of the research reports focus on country branding for FDI attraction.

Tables 20.2 and 20.3 show the main journals and conference proceedings in which the published articles have appeared. These tables present a rather interesting map of publishing concentration. Fully 61 per cent of all journal articles were published in the top-15 journals, which include the major outlets in marketing, international business, and international marketing. The top four of these journals account for one-third of the total. Of the 15, 12 are published in the USA, two in Europe, and perhaps surprisingly given the country's small population, one in Canada. As interesting as the publishing concentration is, it is perhaps as interesting to note that a substantial number of articles (142, or 39 per cent of the total) appeared in 86 other journals. This confirms the validity of the method used in compiling the inventory, since few of these journals would have been captured had the traditional approach of relying on a pre-selected list been used instead. The total number of journals that have published PCI research, 101, suggests the impressive scope of coverage in, and the broad exposure of a multitude of target audiences to, this area.

Similarly to journals, but to a significantly greater extent, conference papers confirm the 80/20 rule: as shown in Table 20.3, the six major academic associations account for exactly 80 per cent (261) of the total, while 38 other conferences account for the remaining 20 per cent. The Academy of Marketing Science clearly predominates, with 21 per cent of all papers. As with the journals, most conferences are held in the USA although, again, one European and one Canadian association combined represent 22

Table 20.1   PCI research by year range and type of publication

Year range	Total	Average/year	(%)	Journal articles	Conf. papers	Conf. Pres.[2]	Chapters in books	Research reports	Books
1950–1959	2	—	0	1	—	—	—	1	—
1960–1969	12	1	2	9	1	—	—	2	—
1970–1979	33	3	4	25	6	—	2	—	—
1980–1984	54	11	7	28	14	8	2	2	—
1985–1989	174	35	23	78	72	8	4	12	—
1990–1994	247	49	32	112	94	9	24	3	5
1995–1999[1]	210	42	27	97	81	16	6	9	1
2000–2001[1]	34	17	4	11	17	—	1	4	1
Total	766			361	285	41	39	33	7
(%)			100	47	37	5	5	4	1

Notes:
1. Due to the method used in compiling the inventory, not all publications for the most recent 2–3 years are included (see above).
2. As noted, this includes papers submitted to, refereed, and presented at major conferences, but not published in their proceedings.

Table 20.2   Journals publishing PCI research

Journal	Place of pub.	Total	(%)
International Marketing Review	Europe	37	10
Journal of International Consumer Marketing	USA	34	9
Journal of International Business Studies	USA	25	7
European Journal of Marketing	Europe	24	7
Journal of Global Marketing	USA	14	4
Journal of the Academy of Marketing Science	USA	13	4
Journal of Marketing Research	USA	12	3
Journal of Business Research	USA	11	3
International Journal of Advertising	USA	9	2
Journal of International Marketing	USA	8	2
Journal of Consumer Research	USA	7	2
Journal of Marketing	USA	7	2
Journal of World Business	USA	6	2
Canadian Journal of Administrative Sciences	Canada	6	2
Industrial Marketing Management	USA	6	2
Sub-total		219	61
86 other journals		142	39
Total		361	100

per cent of the papers. The total number of conferences and/or associations involved, 44, again suggests the broad scope and exposure of the topic.

Contributors to PCI Research

The net number of authors contributing one or more publications was 789, which is rather high particularly when considering the limiting criteria used in developing the inventory. The gross number of authors was 1572, which, coupled with the number of works included, results in an average of 2.05 authors per publication and suggests that multiple authorships may be more common in this field than in others (in another inventory dealing with export research, for example, we found an average of 1.6; see Papadopoulos and Rosson 1999).

This prompted an examination of publications by number of authors, shown in Table 20.4. The table shows that two-thirds of all papers involve

Table 20.3   Conference papers on PCI research[1]

Conference/Association	Usual location[2]	Total	(%)
Academy of Marketing Science (AMS)	USA and other[2]	70	21
American Marketing Association (AMA)	USA	48	15
Administrative Sciences Association of Canada (ASAC)	Canada	41	13
Academy of International Business (AIB)	USA and other[2]	36	11
Advances in Consumer Research (ACR)	USA	36	11
European Marketing Academy (EMAC)	Europe	30	9
Sub-total		261	80
38 other conferences/associations[3]		65	20
Total		326	100

Notes:
1. Includes both published (285) and presented (41) papers.
2. Some organizations occasionally hold their principal annual conference in other countries (e.g. EMAC did so in Montréal, Canada, in 2000). Also, some hold several different conferences at various intervals (e.g. in addition to its annual conference the AMS sponsors the biannual Multicultural Marketing Conference in various countries worldwide), and some publish proceedings only from selected regional or theme-specific conferences (e.g. the AIB). This listing includes all conferences sponsored by the organizations shown.
3. Includes both annual and ad hoc conferences by various organizations.

Table 20.4   Single- vs. co-authorships in PCI research

No. of authors per publication	Publications	
	Number	(%)
1	236	31
2	316	41
3	167	22
4	32	4
5 or more	15	2
Total	766	100

Table 20.5   *Summary of contributions by authors*

Authors	Number of contributions (net no. of publications: 766)			Score		
	Range	Total No.	%	Range	Total No.	%
15	9–67	351	22	5.7–28.1	157.9	21
62	2–10	270	17	2.0–5.3	172.9	23
712	1–6	951	60	0.2–1.9	433.5	57
789		1572	100		764.3	100

two or more co-authors. In fact, further analysis indicated that 166 of all publications (22%) represent the work of four-author teams whose members have tended to work together over long periods of time. This may be partly a result of some of the difficulties in conducting research in various different countries (see Malhotra, Agarwal and Peterson 1996), which encourages the principal investigators in some studies to seek partners for carrying out the research in those countries.

Tables 20.5 and 20.6 present the contribution analysis results both in absolute terms (number of publications) and based on contribution scores developed by using weights for co-authorships as described in the methodology section. It should be noted that analyses of this type are fraught with difficulties and bound to invite criticism (e.g. scholarship measures do not account for the variable quality of journals or articles within the same journal; given that alphabetical listings are rare, by assigning equal weights to co-authors regardless of order of appearance they underestimate the lead author's contribution; the weighting system praises single authorship and underestimates the value of teamwork; etc.). Since this study includes several different publication types, such issues were even more pronounced: if there is argument as to which of two journals (let alone which of two papers in the same journal) is 'worth more', how can a book chapter or ACR conference paper be weighed versus an article in a lower-level journal? To address such issues as best as possible while enabling the full use of the information in the database, we simply (a) followed the traditional approach, with no attempt to differentiate by author sequence or publication value, and (b) developed both total scores as well as partial ones by publication type, so that readers may use the criteria they prefer in assessing the data.

In this context, Table 20.5 shows that the top-15 contributors account for over one-fifth of the works included in the inventory, with each of these authors having a contribution score of 5.7 or higher and nine or more

Table 20.6 *PCI publications by contributor**

Contributor	Country	Main publications			Journal articles			Published conf. papers			Chapters in books			Books		
		sc	No.	r	sc	No.	r	sc	No.	r	sc	No.	r	sc	No.	r
Papadopoulos	Canada	21.6	55	1	3.8	12	7	12.5	36	2	4.8	6	1	0.5	1	1
Heslop	Canada	20.2	62	2	5.5	16	4	12.9	42	1	1.3	3	7	0.5	1	1
Ahmed	Canada	11.5	26	3	7.0	16	1	4.2	9	5	0.3	1	32			
d'Astous	Canada	10.5	24	4	7.0	16	1	3.2	7	11	0.3	1	32			
Liefeld	Canada	9.3	22	5	1.3	4	52	6.1	16	3	2.0	2	3			
Jaffe	Israel	9.2	20	6	5.0	11	6	2.7	6	14	1.0	2	8	0.5	1	1
Wall	Canada	9.1	27	7	2.6	7	19	6.0	19	4	0.5	1	18			
Nebenzahl	Israel	8.0	16	8	3.2	7	13	3.3	6	9	1.0	2	8	0.5	1	1
Crawford	USA	6.8	15	9	3.0	7	14	2.3	6	16	1.5	2	6			
Chao	USA	6.7	9	10	5.3	7	5	1.3	2	34						
Kaynak	USA	6.7	13	10	2.8	5	18	3.3	7	9	0.5	1	18			
Johansson	USA	6.7	12	10	3.5	7	9	1.2	3	43	2.0	2	3			
Darling	USA	6.5	9	13	6.0	8	3	0.5	1	69						
Graby	France	5.7	9	14	0.2	1	467	2.5	5	15	3.0	3	2			
Parameswaran	USA	5.2	9	15	1.0	2	69	4.2	7	5						

Notes: Legend: sc = score, No. = number of publications, r = rank. *The table includes publications in the four sub-categories shown and excludes research reports and non-published conference presentations. The ranks are based on the full list of all 789 authors.

publications. At the other end of the spectrum, a very large number of authors (712) have scores of up to 2.0 with one to six works each. Interestingly, the 62 authors between these two groups account for fewer publications than the top 15 in absolute terms (17 per cent vs. 22 per cent), but have a higher total score (23 per cent vs. 21 per cent of the total). This is probably due to the pattern of co-authorships noted above. That is, the heavy contributors work as members of larger teams, thus publishing widely but reducing the per author score.

Lastly, Table 20.6 identifies the 15 principal researchers and outlines and ranks their contributions. As noted above, the table lists publications both overall and by type, thus enabling readers who would prefer to focus on journal articles to do so. To address potential concerns about assessing contributions by non-standard means, this table also excludes research reports and non-published presentations, which would not normally be included in such analyses (works of this type are included in other parts of the analysis since their subject matter makes them of interest to researchers in this area). It is important to stress that, of course, the table is limited to PCI studies and does not reflect the authors' overall contributions to research (many also publish actively in several other areas). Conversely, due to space limits the table does not do justice to several important contributors (e.g. C. Min Han, Gabriele Morello, Attila Yaprak), who have made numerically fewer but very significant contributions to the literature.

By showing contributions both overall and by type, the table highlights the contribution rates and/or preferences of the authors concerning various types of publication venues, as well as their co-authorship preferences, and helps to differentiate between them. For instance, the first two authors overall, who also are the co-authors of this chapter, are ranked lower on journal articles alone, while the 13th author, having published numerically fewer journal articles than some others, is ranked third in journals by score as a result of having worked with fewer co-authors.

In addition to, once again, depicting a high level of concentration even within this limited group of researchers, this table also helps to highlight an interesting observation: while, as described above, the vast majority of major venues for publishing PCI work are US based, nine of the top-15 authors are based in other countries (six in Canada, two in Israel, and one in France; in fact, of the six US authors, one did the majority of his PCI-related work while stationed in Canada). This helps to explain an earlier observation, concerning the inclusion of European and Canadian journals and conferences in the top-15 and top-six lists respectively: non-US authors appear to seek international publication venues, while also publishing heavily at home where possible.

Lastly, these data reflect the total contributions of the authors over the entire 50-year time period covered by the inventory. An analysis by year (not shown separately due to lack of space) shows that, as might be expected, some stopped working in this area at some point for various reasons, while other scholars joined-in in later years. In fact, an analysis within each of the two most recent periods shows that nine of the above 15 were also on the list in 1995–1999 while six had been replaced by new researchers, and by 2000–2001 only three were still on the top-15 list.

Themes in PCI Research

Entries in the inventory were reviewed to identify the main themes that have been addressed by the various studies, and this review was used to develop a taxonomy into which each entry could be classified based on its main focus. The results are shown in Table 20.7 and enable a broad overview of the particular themes that have attracted the attention of PCI researchers. We note that, since many studies address several sub-topics, classifying the works in discrete categories may obscure somewhat the level of interest in any one area. However, since there is little reason to believe that the range of secondary objectives would differ materially from the principal foci, this analysis likely is a fairly accurate reflection of the main research thrusts.

The studies in the database were classified into six main groups and 25 categories. The distribution of publications by main group is probably not surprising, with the exception of the relative paucity of research dealing explicitly with strategic issues (7 per cent of the total), to be discussed below. The largest number of studies (191), accounting for one-quarter of the total, focus primarily on how people in one or more countries view products from one or more origins. Such research tends to be descriptive in nature and, while common and useful in the early years when the first researchers were trying to understand the PCI phenomenon, is not as popular today. Although many of these studies (particularly the more recent ones) also make theoretical contributions related to the other themes, these tend to be secondary to their main focus.

Conversely, but as might be expected, works focusing on general theoretical issues are considerably fewer (82) and include articles on research methodology (e.g. Martin and Eroglu 1993; Lim, Darley and Summers 1997), integrative models (e.g. Nebenzahl, Jaffe and Lampert 1997), meta-analyses or literature reviews such as those noted earlier (e.g. Baughn and Yaprak 1993; Liefeld 1993; Peterson and Jolibert 1995), and related themes.

In between these two groups, 434 studies comprising the bulk of research (57 per cent) deal with various topics which could technically all be called 'issues' but have been classified, instead, into three distinct groups because of noteworthy differences in their approaches. Studies in the first of these

Table 20.7   Main research themes

Principal Focus	Theme	Contributions		
		Subtotal	Total	(%)
Countries	Views about an origin(s) (109) and/or by a sample(s) (82)	191	191	25
Issues	Ethnocentrism (59) and domestic goods vs. imports (49)	108		
	Cross-national (15) and sub-national (8) studies	23		
	Hybrid products	20		
	Longitudinal studies (10) and impact of events (6)	16	167	22
Research orientation	Misc. consumer behaviour approaches (incl. gender: 4)	75		
	Info. processing, multiple-cue studies, PCI effects	67		
	Studies using socio-psychological perspectives	13	155	20
Sectors and markets	Organizational buyers (55) and FDI/ investors (21)	76		
	Specific sectors (e.g. cars, food)	28		
	Tourism from PCI perspective (5) and services (3)	8	112	15
Conceptual, methodological, theory dev.	Methodological aspects	39		
	Integrative works and models	28		
	Literature reviews, meta-analyses, research agendas	15	82	11
Strategy	General (37), adv. (11), other mix (10), legal (1)	59	59	7
Total		766	766	100

groups deal with distinct 'Issues' that have been or are of interest to practitioners, researchers, or both. Key among these is the natural concern in many nations over the growing influx of imports (e.g. Baughn and Yaprak 1996), and its counterpoint from the exporter's perspective (domestic resistance due to patriotism or other reasons) leading to the second-largest number of studies (108) at the category level – those that deal with ethnocentrism (Sharma, Shimp and Shin 1995) and views about domestic vs. foreign products (Heslop, Papadopoulos and the IKON Research Group 2000). Other studies in this group have dealt with the cross-national

(Papadopoulos, Heslop and the IKON Research Group 2000), longitudinal (Darling and Kraft 1996), and intra-national (Heslop, Papadopoulos
and Bourk 1998) stability of national images, and with the growing interest in hybrid products resulting from globalization and multi-national production (Brodowski 1998).

The second of these groups of studies is distinguished by the particular
research orientation adopted by the researchers involved. In other words,
the 155 studies in this group address a very wide variety of questions – but
each does so from a particular theoretical or methodological perspective
that sets it apart from the research in other groupings. These studies are
subdivided into categories reflecting consumer behavior perspectives such
as the effects of familiarity and perceived risk on product-country perceptions (Alden 1993; Schaefer 1997; Lee and Ganesh 1999), multi-cue experiments researching the importance of PCI relative to other extrinsic cues
(Ahmed and d'Astous 1993), consumer information processing (Zhang
1997), and insights from social psychology (Johansson and Nebenzahl
1987; Shimp, Samiee and Madden 1993; Li, Monroe and Chan 1994).

The last of these three groups contains 112 studies that are differentiated
from the others in that they deal with particular types of markets, such as
industrial buyers (Ahmed, d'Astous and El-adraoui 1994), retail buyers
(Heslop et al. 2000), and investors (Papadopoulos et al. 1997a), or with
specific sectors, ranging from tourism (Hallberg 1996) and air travel
(Bruning 1997) to food (Biljana, Worsley and Garrett 1996) and cars (Chao
and Gupta 1995). Of these studies, several have very limited generalizability given their objectives, while others, by focusing on individual sectors or
markets and therefore being able to explore PCI issues in more detail, have
been able to make substantive theoretical contributions.

As noted at the start of this section, the relatively small number of
studies in the 'Strategy' group is perhaps surprising, given the theme's
importance. A large part of the explanation for this may be that virtually
every one of the other studies does contain a section on 'implications for
practitioners', which typically discusses the strategic considerations arising
from the study's findings. However, these sections tend to be brief, often are
treated as parenthetical to the main discussion, and of course are
specifically tied to the main subject of the particular research. What
appears to be missing is broader studies of strategic PCI-related considerations, such as those of Johansson (1993), who stressed the strategic importance of PCI, Sethi and Elango (1995), who examined country of origin in
the context of multinational firms' strategies, and Fenwick and Wright
(2000), who dealt with the impact of using a PCI cue on performance.
Notably, studies on marketing mix issues are very few in number (21), and
several of those, particularly in advertising, are dated.

In summary, the above review shows a wide range of topics being researched, but only a relative few accounting for the bulk of attention. At the category level, only five (of 25) themes include 50 or more publications. A number of potentially significant issues are represented by 25 or fewer publications, including the longitudinal stability of national images (the dearth of longitudinal studies has also been noted in other marketing fields as well; see Hubbard and Armstrong 1994 and Katsikeas, Leonidou and Morgan 2000), studies of investor behavior (which number less than half as many as those of other organizational buyers), and research into national image effects on services (although some studies classified as sector-focused do deal with services, such as airlines, tourism, and banks, the total number still is less than 20).

NATURE AND ROLE OF PLACE IMAGES: THE STATE OF THE ART

Drawing from the above analysis and review, this last section attempts to answer three interrelated questions: what research has been done in this field? What have we learned from it? And what might future studies focus on in order to further improve our understanding of the PCI phenomenon and its broader contemporary context of country branding and country equity? Although full answers to these questions would require volumes, the preceding review provides sufficient information to at least attempt summary responses in this chapter.

Implications from the Summary of Time, Venue, and Contributor Findings

The inventory analysis clearly points to two diverse conclusions. First, there is a high degree of concentration in PCI research, with a small number of journals, conferences/associations, and authors predominating and with the majority of works having been published in a very brief time span (about 10 years). At the same time, it would not be much of an exaggeration to say that, for as clearly delimited a field as this, the numbers of publications, journals, conferences, and authors involved are 'huge'. These conclusions can have both positive and negative implications.

On the positive side, the concentration of authors suggests that much of the output is produced by researchers who know the area well. At the same time, the large overall number of authors, coupled with the time evolution of the research field, suggests an ongoing influx of new researchers which helps to continuously rejuvenate the thinking of those already involved and adds fresh insights that advance understanding. The majority of publications appear in well-regarded venues, which, coupled with the large overall number of venues hosting PCI research, underscores the perceived importance of the subject by reviewers, editors, and readers. The relative recency of the research suggests current and potentially growing interest. Lastly, the increasing incidence of integrative works points to the relative maturity of the field as more is learned about its particular aspects.

On the other hand, the high concentration of authors and venues may result in over-emphasizing their particular points of view, increasing the risk that differing views may not receive the exposure they may deserve. The large number of authors who account for only a small handful of publications each may reflect a lower level of familiarity with the subject and a potential tendency to write and publish research on it ad hoc rather than systematically. Lastly, the large number of venues (particularly that of conferences, which often publish quality studies that are only exposed to a very limited audience and/or readership) makes it difficult for individual researchers to follow advances in their field.

Notwithstanding the potential negative ramifications, however, on balance the above considerations do point to a vibrant research field with a multitude of participants and a broad audience, which can only augur well for future research in this field and its contribution to related disciplines within and beyond marketing and international business.

What We Have Learned

The principal findings to date from this large body of research can be summarized into several key conclusions, upon which those involved appear to be reaching various levels of consensus.

The literature as a whole leaves no doubt that place images are an extrinsic cue used by people as a stereotype, or 'applied theory', in their marketplace behavior. This use is widespread and extends not only to consumers but also to various types of business executives including industrial and retail buyers (e.g. Nes and Ghauri 1998). The role of national images in influencing behavior may be of lesser, similar, or greater importance than those of other intrinsic or extrinsic cues, ranging from product characteristics to brand name and price, as shown in various multi-cue studies (Tse and Gorn 1993; Nebenzahl and Jaffe 1996). Further, buyers appear to organize their PCI-related thought patterns in terms of seven key constructs, including a nation's level of advancement, their feelings about its people, their desire for closer links with the country, the quality, price, and level of market presence of its products, and their overall level of satisfaction with these products (Papadopoulos, Heslop and the IKON Research Group 2000).

The legally-mandated 'Made In'– designation of a product's country of origin may be important in some cases, but a product's origin association more often than not may be shaped by various other factors (e.g. advertising or the brand name itself, as in the case of Clearly Canadian bottled water) – a conclusion underscored by the research on hybrid products, which shows that buyers may distinguish between a product's country of design, manufacture, or assembly, and/or the producer's home country (Ahmed, d'Astous and El-adraoui 1994). In fact, buyers expect a price discount for products made in places with weaker images, which, in conjunction with the findings from hybrid product research, helps to explain the strategies of producers in developed countries who stress the 'country of design' and try to conceal or obscure that of manufacture when the latter is a low labor cost haven (Nebenzahl and Jaffe 1993).

Buyers' views of a country's image will likely vary by product class (Kaynak and Cavusgil 1983), but, as noted in the introductory vignette, the stronger a country's image is, the stronger those of individual product classes from it will be (Dzever and Quester 1999). This helps to explain the widespread consumer acceptance of successive waves of Japanese exports as that country moved from trinkets in the 1950s to a wide range of advanced products and services today. In fact, the research makes it clear that buyers distinguish between major, niche, and less developed countries as producers (Nes and Bilkey 1993; Heslop and Papadopoulos 1993).

The studies show that country images may be influenced over the short or longer term by significant events (Jaffe and Nebenzahl 1993; Brunner, Flaschner and Lou 1993), but that, overall, national images are strongly held stereotypes and shift slowly, if at all in some cases (Darling and Kraft 1996). This finding is at least partially supported by the relative difficulty of 'Buy Domestic' campaigns in persuading consumers to favor locally-made products over imports, at least in terms of actual purchases rather than just in engendering patriotic feelings (Jaffe and Nebenzahl 2001).

The preceding paragraphs highlight the main findings in certain key areas where a degree of consensus among substantive numbers of researchers appears to have emerged. Needless to say, a large number of other findings, too many to enumerate here, have made significant contributions to understanding the PCI/country of origin phenomenon. Examining these contributions in detail requires one or more in-depth reviews of the relevant parts of the literature – a research need that is highlighted, among others, in the next section.

What More Do We Need to Learn?

A useful start in answering this question is to benchmark the answer against the two major reviews of the literature to date. Our review of both the summary data presented above and the individual studies in the inventory makes it reasonably safe to conclude that most of the concerns expressed in Bilkey and Nes's (1982) seminal review, which focused primarily on methodological issues, have been addressed. For example, as might have been expected given the widespread impact of that review, the passage of time, and the growing sophistication in research, the incidence of student samples (also a concern of Douglas and Craig 1992) has subsided, a fairly large number of experiments have used tangible products rather than just abstract verbal cues as stimuli (Liefeld 1993), and several studies have explored the level of congruence between global and product class-specific images (Papadopoulos et al. 1997b).

On the other hand, while several of the issues identified a decade later by Baughn and Yaprak (1993) have been explored, others have not. Among the former, as illustrated in the thematic summary above, research on such topics as ethnocentrism and consumer patriotism, consumer information processing, and attitude formation, has flourished, particularly in recent years. Conversely, longitudinal studies remain rare, research into the antecedents and influencers of national image formation remains virtually nonexistent (to use these researchers' example, what is the potential effect of 'highly publicized products . . . [such as] the Anglo-French Concord'?), and studies on the behavioral (e.g. familiarity, perceived risk) and/or demographic (e.g. education, income) correlates of national images, while several in number, are far from reaching consensus.

Given the passage of time between the last major review (Baughn and Yaprak 1993) and today, and the very large number of new studies published since 1993, there appears to be a particular research need for a new literature review in this field. In fact, the number of studies within individual subfields in PCI research suggests the need for several reviews. For example, it would be useful to carry out in-depth analyses of the 108 studies dedicated to the issue of domestic versus foreign product preferences and ethnocentrism, or the 67 papers in the 'information processing, multi-cue studies, and PCI effects' category. More generally, the value of the preceding inventory-based analysis lies, in part, in demonstrating that the number of studies in several subfields is very large indeed, and therefore worthy of separate attention.

The thematic analysis (Table 20.7) has already identified several additional areas where research coverage is weak. Prominent among these is the need to broaden the perspective of PCI research beyond the traditional notion of 'product' in the sense of tangible goods (Papadopoulos 1993), in line with the more comprehensive 'countries as brands' concept. This incorporates, among others, services, tourism, FDI, and even the need to attract a qualified workforce to particular countries or places within them (international marketing for this purpose by technology firms, who try to attract skilled workers from a limited worldwide pool based on country branding, is a case in point).

Considering the case of FDI in particular, while the literature on this topic is, of course, vast, it has generally tended to deal with 'hard' (e.g. the influence of operating costs in potential target countries) rather than 'soft' (e.g. investor perceptions and attitudes) factors (Papadopoulos and Heslop 2002). As a result, a large number of questions remain unanswered (or even un-asked). For example, FDI may flow into a country from companies which may or may not already operate in it through other service modes; how do existing operations influence executives' perceptions, how do these differ from those of managers who are unfamiliar with the country, and what strategies might a country need to use for each of these two distinct target markets? Further important questions that may be explored include, do country images differ by investor nationality? Are the national images held by investors 'global' or do they differ by sector (e.g. technology-intensive versus traditional industries)? Do investors, explicitly or implicitly, use their image of the country as a whole or that of particular regions/cities in considering alternative locations? Does the influence of place images vary by type of investment, that is, do companies that acquire others care as much about their target's location as those that engage in greenfield FDI? While preliminary answers to some of these questions have begun to appear in some studies (see the thematic review), the research is not nearly enough considering the growing importance of the topic and the increasing interest in it by governments in many countries.

The review has focused so far on topics that at least have been researched, even to a small extent – but what of topics that do not even appear in Table 20.7? Three of these deserve separate mention. First, while the entire literature on product-country (or country of origin) images purports to focus on how country images affect product perceptions, the number of studies which have in fact included country measures is extremely small (the main studies include Wang and Lamb 1983; Heslop and Papadopoulos 1993; Martin and Eroglu 1993; Li, Fu and Murray 1997; Papadopoulos, Heslop and the IKON Research Group 2000). In other words, most of the research to date has implicitly assumed that a country's image is reflected in its products, and has not tried to measure it separately and then correlate it with the product measures obtained.

A prime example is the study by Han (1989), which introduced the notions of the 'halo' and 'summary' constructs as the main explanations of the PCI phenomenon. While the concept makes intuitive sense and has been accepted as fact (and much quoted and repeated) since, the study actually offers no evidence to support it. The halo and summary hypotheses assume, respectively, that the consumer knows about the country but not its products (in which case country image affects beliefs which in turn affect brand attitude), or that he/she knows little about the country and forms its image through exposure to its products (beliefs). Interestingly, however, closer examination of the study reveals that it did not use any country measures, and therefore measured both country image and beliefs through the same variables. This essentially turns the concept into a tautology (in the halo hypothesis, for example, country image is said to predict product image – which was tested by using the latter to measure the former).

Addressing this problem requires the introduction of new country-level variables, of which some have been suggested in the studies mentioned above and several more can be gleaned from the social psychology literature. This, in turn, helps to focus attention on the second area that has yet to attract significant attention by PCI researchers: cross-disciplinary integration. As noted earlier, place images are a principal research stream in several areas, including social psychology, tourism, and political science and international behavior. As well, the role of images in marketing also constitutes a major research stream, most notably in brand image studies. Yet to the best of our knowledge none of the PCI studies has systematically and explicitly attempted to bridge the gap between this field and related others. (Lack of cross-disciplinary contact is of course endemic in research. In this case, for example, national images are a key stream in social psychology, yet few of the PCI researchers have accessed it for insight. Conversely, in the book *Place Promotion* (Gold and Ward 1994), one of the co-editors is an urban geographer, the other is a planning historian, and all of their chapter contributors are in the same or similar fields – with no one being in marketing or business.) Yet borrowing methodologies, concepts, and findings from such disciplines, and applying them to the study of PCI phenomena, would seem to hold great promise in advancing knowledge in both the former and the latter.

Last, but not least, the reader must have noticed the absence of references so far, in discussing PCI research, to the themes of country branding and country equity as such. The reason for this is rather simple: while all PCI studies are by definition part of these themes and have addressed them in one way or another, the concepts and the terms themselves are new and have not yet found their way into the mainstream research vocabulary (exceptions include several articles in the April 2002 issue of the *Journal of Brand Management*, which was expressly dedicated to the issue of 'Countries as Brands'; also see Papadopoulos and Heslop 2000 and 2001). By contrast, they are rapidly gaining acceptance among government agencies worldwide as evidenced, for example, by the *Scotland: The Brand* campaign, the Branding Secretariat in Canada's Department of Industry, France's 'image committee' (Comité Image France, CIF), and the government-sponsored research projects (Table 20.1) studying branding for various purposes in these and other countries.

As already noted, the notion of country equity includes the country as exporter, importer, and potential tourism, investment, or immigration destination, making its image a matter of vital importance to anyone living or otherwise interested in it. Furthermore, a country's image as 'imperialist', 'underdeveloped', 'aggressive', or 'neutral', or a city's image as 'clean and safe' versus 'full of crime', can have a far greater range of implications than just affecting the acceptability of the former's exports or the latter's attractiveness to foreign investors: matters ranging from a country's relative influence in international affairs or its ability to attract foreign aid, to a city's ability to attract national government infrastructure funds, are dependent on their real or perceived equity.

Therefore, the issue is much more than one of vocabulary: the emergence of the country equity concept essentially represents a call for integration of several research streams that focus on the various manifestations where the image of a country (or place) may have an effect.

CONCLUSIONS

This chapter provides a quantitative and qualitative overview of research on the role of place images in the marketing and international business context based on a comprehensive inventory of the relevant publications. A general conclusion from the preceding analysis is that, in spite of the relative newness of the field, research in it is substantial, involves large numbers of scholars, and has made significant strides toward a fuller understanding of the 'country of origin' phenomenon. The previous section makes a number of suggestions for research directions that may help to address some long-standing issues but also move forward to several exciting new ones. Of these, the overarching themes of country branding and country equity will likely be the most important in the longer term.

In line with our call for greater integration of the various research substreams under the notion of country equity, an obvious suggestion would be to learn from the sibling concept of brand equity, which, while also relatively new, was developed earlier and offers several useful insights. Aaker (1991) defines brand equity (p.15) as 'a set of brand assets and liabilities linked to a brand, its name and symbol, that add to or subtract from the value provided by a product or service to a firm and/or to that firm's customers'. With suitable adjustments for context, country equity may therefore be defined as 'a set of country assets and liabilities linked to a country, its name and symbols, that add to or subtract from the value provided by the country's outputs to its various internal and external publics'.

Aaker (1991) further groups a brand's assets and liabilities into five categories (p.16): '(1) Brand loyalty, (2) Name awareness, (3) Perceived quality, (4) Brand associations in addition to perceived quality, [and] (5) Other proprietary brand assets – patents, trademarks, channel relationships, etc.'. Transferring these to the country context, the vast majority of the literature reviewed in this chapter (a) has clearly focused on the middle three of these categories, and (b) has a way to go to be able to claim that it has addressed all relevant questions within the same three categories. Therefore, the task of future country equity research would appear to be, first, to continue investigating those questions where research has already begun, and, second, to begin investigating those where it has not, including the core concept of country equity itself.

REFERENCES

Aaker, David A. (1991), *Managing Brand Equity*, New York: Free Press.

Adler, Nancy J. and Susan Bartholomew (1992), 'Academic and Professional Communities of Discourse: Generating Knowledge on Transnational Human Resource Management', *Journal of International Business Studies*, 23 (3), 551–69.

Ahmed, Sadrudin A. and Alain d'Astous (1993), 'Cross-National Evaluation of Made-in Concept Using Multiple Cues', *European Journal of Marketing*, 27 (7), 39–52.

Ahmed, Sadrudin A., Alain d'Astous and M. El-adraoui (1994), 'Country-Of-Origin Effects On Purchasing Managers' Product Perceptions', *Industrial Marketing Management*, 23 (4), 323–32.

Alden, Dana L. (1993), 'Product Trial and Country-of-Origin: An Analysis of Perceived Risk Effects', *Journal of International Consumer Marketing*, 6 (1), 7–26.

Baughn, Christopher C. and Attila Yaprak (1993), 'Mapping Country-of-Origin Research: Recent Developments and Emerging Avenues', in N. Papadopoulos and L. Heslop (eds), *Product-Country Images: Impact and Role in International Marketing*, Binghamton, NY: Haworth Press, pp. 89–116.

Baughn, Christopher C. and Attila Yaprak (1996), 'Economic Nationalism: Conceptual and Empirical Development', *Journal of Political Psychology*, 17 (4), 759–77.

Biljana, Juric, Tony Worsley and Tony Garrett (1996), 'Country of Origin Related Food Product Images', in J. Beracs, A. Bauer, and J. Simon (eds), *Marketing for an Expanded Europe, Proceedings of the European Marketing Academy* Budapest, Hungary, May, pp. 635–51.

Bilkey, Warren J. (1978), 'An Attempted Integration of the Literature on the Export Behavior of Firms', *Journal of International Business Studies*, (Spring/Summer), 33–46.

Bilkey, Warren J. and Erik B. Nes (1982), 'Country-of-Origin Effects on Product Evaluations', *Journal of International Business Studies*, 8 (Spring/Summer), 89–99.

Boddewyn, Jean J. (1981), 'Comparative Marketing: The First Twenty-five Years', *Journal of International Business Studies*, (Spring/Summer), 61–79.

Booth, Lawrence and Fred Heath (1990), 'Finance Research at Canadian Management and Administration Faculties', *Canadian Journal of Administrative Sciences*, **7** (4), 43–9.

Brodowski, Glen (1998), 'The Effects of Country of Design and Country of Assembly on Evaluative Beliefs About Automobiles and Attitudes Toward Buying them', *Journal of International Consumer Marketing*, **10** (3), 85–113.

Bruning, Edward R. (1997), 'Country of Origin, National Loyalty and Product Choice: The Case of International Air Travel', *International Marketing Review*, **14** (1), 59–73.

Brunner, James F., Alan B. Flaschner and Xiaogang Lou (1993), 'Images and Events: China Before and After Tiananmen Square', in N. Papadopoulos and L. Heslop (eds), *Product-Country Images: Impact and Role in International Marketing*, New York: International Business Press, pp. 379–400.

Chao, Paul and Pola Gupta (1995), 'Information Search and Efficiency of Consumer Choices of New Cars: Country-of-Origin Effects', *International Marketing Review*, **12** (6), 47–59.

Darling, John R. and Frederic B. Kraft (1996), 'Changes in Finnish Consumer Attitudes Toward the Products and Associated Marketing Practices of Various Selected Countries, 1975 to 1995', *Finnish Journal of Business Economics*, **44** (3), 227–42.

Douglas, Susan P. and C. Samuel Craig (1992), 'Advances in International Marketing', *International Journal of Research in Marketing*, **9** (4), 291–318.

Dzever, Sam and Pascale Quester (1999), 'Country-of-Origin Effects on Purchasing Agents' Product Perceptions: An Australian Perspective', *Industrial Marketing Management*, **28**, 165–75.

Fenwick, Graham and Cameron Wright (2000), 'Effect of a Buy-National Campaign on Member Firm Performance', *Journal of Business Research*, **47**, 135–45.

Fischer, Wolfgang Chr and Peter Byron (1995), *Buy Australian Made*, North Queensland, Australia: James Cook University.

Gold, John R. and Stephen V. Ward (eds) (1994), *Place Promotion: The Use of Publicity and Marketing to Sell Towns and Regions*, Chichester: John Wiley & Sons.

Hallberg, Annika (1996), 'Country-of-Origin Effects of Tourism: Foreign Travel and Product-Country Images', Nordisk Turisme i en Global sammenhæng, Udvalgte Papers fra det 4. *Nordiske Forskersymposium*, Copenhagen, October, pp. 149–65.

Han, Min C. (1989), 'Country image: Halo or Summary Construct?' *Journal of Marketing Research*, **XXVI** (May), 222–229.

Head, David (1992), *'Made in Germany': The Corporate Identity of a Nation* London, UK: Hodder & Stoughton.

Heslop, Louise A. and Nicolas Papadopoulos (1993), 'But Who Knows Where or When': Reflections on the Images of Countries and Their Products', in N. Papadopoulos and L.A. Heslop (eds), *Product-Country Images: Impact and Role in International Marketing*, Binghamton, NY: Haworth Press, pp. 39–77.

Heslop, Louise A., Nicolas Papadopoulos and Margie Bourk (1998), 'An Inter-Regional and Inter-Cultural Perspective on Subcultural Differences in Product Evaluations', *Canadian Journal of Administrative Sciences*, **15** (2).

Heslop, L.A., N. Papadopoulos and the IKON Research Group (2000), 'Evidence of Home Country Bias in Evaluations of Products: A 15-Country Study', in *Proceedings of the European Marketing Academy*, Rotterdam, Netherlands, May.

Heslop, Louise A., Nicolas Papadopoulos, Melissa Dowdles, Marjorie Wall, John Liefeld and Deborah Compeau (forthcoming 2005), 'Who Controls the Purse Strings: A Study of Consumers' and Retail Buyers' Reactions in a NAFTA Environment', *Journal of Business Research*.

Hubbard, Raymond and J. Scott Armstrong (1994), 'Replications and Extensions in Marketing: Rarely Published But Quite Contrary', *International Journal of Research in Marketing*, **11**, 233–48.

Jaffe, Eugene D. and Israel D. Nebenzahl (1993), 'Global Promotion of Country Image: Do the Olympics Count?', in N. Papadopoulos and L. Heslop (eds), *Product-Country Images: Impact and Role in International Marketing*, New York: International Business Press, pp. 433–52.

Jaffe, Eugene D. and Israel D. Nebenzahl (2001), *National Image and Competitive Advantage*, Copenhagen, Denmark: Copenhagen Business School Press.

Johansson, Johny K. (1993), 'Missing a Strategic Opportunity: Managers' Denial of Country-of-Origin Effects', in N. Papadopoulos and L. Heslop (eds), *Product-Country Images: Impact and Role in International Marketing*, Binghamton, NY: Haworth Press, pp. 77–86.

Johansson, Johny K. and Israel D. Nebenzahl (1987), 'Country-of-Origin, Social Norms and Behavioral Intentions', *Advances in International Marketing*, **2** (June), 65–79.

Katsikeas, Constantine S., Leonidas C. Leonidou and Neil A. Morgan (2000), 'Firm-Level Export Performance Assessment: Review, Evaluation, and Development', *Journal of the Academy of Marketing Science*, **28** (4), 493–511.

Kaynak, Erdener and S. Tamer Cavusgil (1983), 'Consumer Attitudes Towards Products of Foreign Origin: Do They Vary Across Product Classes?', *International Journal of Advertising*, **2** (April/June), 147–57.

Kotler, Philip, Donald H. Haider and Irving Rein (1993), *Marketing Places: Attracting Investment, Industry, and Tourism to Cities, States, and Nations*, New York, NY: Free Press.

Lee, Dongdae and Gopala Ganesh (1999), 'Effects of Partitioned Country Image in the Context of Brand Image and Familiarity', *International Marketing Review*, **16** (1), 18–39.

Leonidou, Leonidas C. and Constantine S. Katsikeas (1996), 'The Export Development Process: An Integrative Review of Empirical Models', *Journal of International Business Studies*, **27** (3), 517–51.

Li, Tiger and S. Tamer Cavusgil (1991), 'International Marketing: A Classification of Research Streams and Assessment of Their Development Since 1982', *Summer Educators Conference Proceedings*, Chicago, IL: American Marketing Association, pp. 592–607.

Li, Wai-Kwan, Kent B. Monroe and D.K.S. Chan (1994), 'The Effects of Country-of-Origin, Brand, and Price Information – A Cognitive-Affective Model of Buying Intentions', in *Advances in Consumer Research*, Association for Consumer Research, pp. 449–57.

Li, Zhan G., Shenzhao Fu and L. William Murray (1997), 'Country and Product Images: The Perceptions of Consumers in the People's Republic of China', *Journal of International Consumer Marketing*, **10** (1–2), 115–38.

Liefeld, John P. (1993), 'Consumer Use of Country-of-Origin Information in

Product Evaluations: Evidence from Experiments', in N. Papadopoulos and L. Heslop (eds), *Product-Country Images: Impact and Role in International Marketing*, Binghamton, NY: Haworth Press, pp. 117–56.

Lim, Jeen-Su, William K. Darley and John Summers (1997), 'An Assessment of Demand Artefacts in Country-of-Origin Studies Using Three Alternative Approaches', *International Marketing Review*, **14** (4), 201–217.

Malhotra, Naresh K., James Agarwal and Mark Peterson (1996), 'Methodological Issues in Cross-cultural Marketing Research: A State-of-the-Art Review', *International Marketing Review*, **13** (5), 7–43.

Martin, Ingrid M. and Sevgin Eroglu (1993), 'Measuring a Multi-Dimensional Construct: Country Image', *Journal of Business Research*, **28** (3), 191–210.

Morrison, Alen J. and Andrew C. Inkpen (1991), 'An Analysis of Significant Contributions to the International Business Literature', *Journal of International Business Studies*, **22** (1), 143–153.

Nebenzahl, Israel D. and Eugene D. Jaffe (1993), 'Estimating Demand Functions from the Country-of-Origin Effect', in N. Papadopoulos and L. Heslop (eds), *Product-Country Images: Impact and Role in International Marketing*, Binghamton, NY: Haworth Press, pp. 159–78.

Nebenzahl, Israel D. and Eugene D. Jaffe (1996), 'Measuring the Joint Effect of Brand and Country Image in Consumer Evaluation of Global Products', *International Marketing Review*, **13** (4), 5–22.

Nebenzahl, Israel D., Eugene D. Jaffe and Shlomo Lampert (1997), 'Towards a Theory of Country Image Effect on Product Evaluation', *Management International Review*, **37** (1), 27–49.

Nes, Erik B. and Warren J. Bilkey (1993), 'A Multi-Cue Test of Country-of-Origin Theory', in N. Papadopoulos and L.A. Heslop (eds), *Product-Country Images: Impact and Role in International Marketing*, Binghampton, NY: International Business Press, pp. 179–95.

Nes, Erik B. and Pervez N. Ghauri (1998), 'Country of Origin Effects on Industrial Products Coming from Eastern Europe', *Journal of East-West Business*, **4** (1–2), 129–40.

Papadopoulos, Nicolas (1993), 'What Product and Country Images Are and Are Not', in N. Papadopoulos and L.A. Heslop (eds), *Product-Country Images: Role and Implications for International Marketing*, Binghampton, NY: Haworth Press, pp. 1–38.

Papadopoulos, Nicolas and Louise A. Heslop (eds), (1993), *Product-Country Images: Role and Implications for International Marketing*, Binghampton, NY: Haworth Press.

Papadopoulos, N. and L.A. Heslop (2000), 'Countries as Brands: Canadian Products Abroad', *Ivey Business Journal*, (November/December), 30–36.

Papadopoulos, Nicolas and Louise A. Heslop (2001), *A Review, Analysis, and Consolidation of Research on the Business Image of Canada Among Investors and Others Abroad*, Ottawa, ON: Branding Secretariat, Investment Partnerships Canada, Industry Canada.

Papadopoulos, N. and L.A. Heslop (2002), 'Country Equity and Country Branding: Problems and Prospects', *Journal of Brand Management*, **9** (4–5), 294–314.

Papadopoulos, N. and Philip J. Rosson (1999), 'Inventory and Analysis of Canadian Research and Scholarship in Exporting and International Marketing', *Canadian Journal of Administrative Sciences*, **16** (2), 77–94.

Papadopoulos, Nicolas, Louise A. Heslop and the IKON Research Group (2000), 'A Cross-National and Longitudinal Study of Product-Country Images with a Focus on the U.S. and Japan', *Marketing Science Institute*, Report 1–106.

Papadopoulos, Nicolas, Vijay M. Jog, Louise A. Heslop and Ritoo D'Souza (1997a), 'The Investment Climate in Canada: Foreign Investor Experiences and Perceptions', in S. Preece and P. Woodcock (eds), *International Business*, **18**, St. John's, Nfld: Administrative Sciences Association of Canada, (June), 37–47.

Papadopoulos, Nicolas, Louise A. Heslop, Leslie Szamosi, Richard Ettenson and Gillian Sullivan-Mort (1997b), ' "Czech Made" or Check Mate? An Assessment of the Competitiveness of East European Products', in V. Wong and V. Shaw (eds), *Marketing: Progress, Prospects, Perspectives, Proceedings of the European Marketing Academy*, Coventry, UK, May, pp. 993–1012.

Peterson, Robert A. and Alain J.P. Jolibert (1995), 'A Meta-Analysis of Country-of-Origin Effects', *Journal of International Business Studies*, **26** (4), 883–900.

Pierce, Barbara and Garnet Garven (1995), 'Publishing International Business Research: A Survey of Leading Journals', *Journal of International Business Studies*, **26** (1), 69–89.

Reid, Angus E. and Margaret M. Burns (1992), *Canada and the World: An International Perspective on Canada and Canadians*, Toronto, Canada: Angus Reid Group.

Reid, Stanley (1983), 'Export Research in a Crisis', in M.R. Czinkota (ed.), *Export Promotion: The Public and Private Sector Interaction*, New York, NY: Praeger, pp. 129–53.

Schaefer, A. (1997) 'Consumer Knowledge and Country of Origin Effects', *European Journal of Marketing*, **37**, 56–72.

Schooler, Robert D. (1965), 'Product Bias in the Central American Common Market', *Journal of Marketing Research*, **II** (November), 394–7.

Sethi, S. Prakash and B. Elango (1995), 'Does "Country of Origin" Make a Difference in MNC Strategy Formulation and Implementation? An Exploratory Framework', Paper presented to the Academy of International Business, Seoul, S. Korea, November.

Sharma, Subhash, Terrence A. Shimp and Jeongshin Shin (1995), 'Consumer Ethnocentrism: A Test of Antecedents and Moderators', *Journal of the Academy of Marketing Science*, **23** (1), 26–37.

Shimp, Terrence A., Saeed Samiee and Thomas J. Madden (1993), 'Countries and Their Products: A Cognitive Structure Perspective', *Journal of the Academy of Marketing Science*, **21** (4), 323–30.

Tan, Chin T. and John U. Farley (1987), 'The Impact of Cultural Patterns on Cognition and Intention in Singapore', *Journal of Consumer Research*, **13** (March), 540–44.

Thomas, Anisya S., Oded Shenkar and Linda Clarke (1994), 'The Globalization of Our Mental Maps: Evaluating the Geographic Scope of JIBS Coverage', *Journal of International Business Studies*, **25** (4), 675–86.

Tse, David K. and Gerald J. Gorn (1993), 'An Experiment on the Salience of Country-of-Origin in the Era of Global Brands', *Journal of International Marketing*, **1** (1), 57–76.

Wang, C.K. and C. Lamb (1983), 'The Impact of Selected Environmental Forces Upon Consumers' Willingness to Buy Foreign Products', *Journal of the Academy of Marketing Science*, **11**, 71–83.

Wayland, Jane P., David J. Urban and Dennis R. McDermott (1992), 'The Role of

Proceedings in the Evaluation of Faculty Research Standards in AACSB-Accredited Marketing Departments', in Summer Educators Proceedings, *American Marketing Association*, **3**, 313–17.

Zhang, Yong (1997), 'Country-of-Origin Effect: The Moderating Function of Individual Difference in Information Processing', *International Marketing Review*, **14**, 266–87.

21. Introduction to a global scorecard: industry practice and international implications

Camille P. Schuster

INTRODUCTION

In an historic move, the companies from the grocery and packaged goods industries (manufacturers, retailers, brokers, wholesalers, and industry associations) met during the early 1990s to examine the threats to their industry. As a result of the discussions Kurt Salmon and Associates conducted a study to evaluate the current state of the industry. The results indicated that an integrated supply chain be created to enhance the timely, accurate, paperless flow of information while creating a smooth, continuous flow of product matched to consumption (see Figure 21.1). Savings to the industry of US$30 billion would result if the industry operated in a more efficient manner while keeping the consumer clearly in mind.[1] To follow up on these findings, the companies and associations formed the Efficient Consumer Response (ECR) organization.

A number of committees were created to analyze business activities in a particular area, conduct pilot tests and report on the results. About 40+ books documenting best practices in specific areas, such as activity-based costing, category management, effective replenishment, and effective assortment, have been published and made available to the industry so any company planning to concentrate improvement efforts in a particular area has access to the information on best practices.

One of the fundamental business behaviors resulting from this new approach to doing business is the development of greater collaboration among companies. The only way for companies to have access to timely and accurate flows of information enabling smooth continuous flow of product matched to consumption is with the use of technology to facilitate information transfer and collaboration to facilitate joint activities and decision making.

Collaboration involves both business partners examining the consumer

VISION – The ECR System

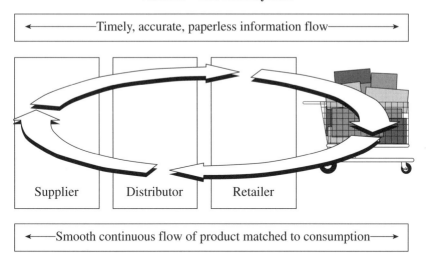

Figure 21.1   *Integrated supply chain*

demand for products, introducing the best new practices, creating promotions that are directly related to satisfying consumer needs rather than promotion deals that artificially fill the supply chain. Collaboration involves the exchange of information between business partners to create systems based upon replenishing consumer purchases rather than filling the supply chain based upon artificial forecasts. Collaboration involves the decision of competitors and a given retailer to manage categories of products to supply the right products to the right consumers at the right time at a reasonable price.

As companies began this collaborative process, questions about identifying the most critical tasks for success and measuring progress emerged. Individual companies began work on creating tools for assessing and benchmarking business activities involved in this continuous supply and demand consumer-centric supply chain. Different versions of instruments were evaluated and merged in a scorecard that could be used across companies to assess a company's current state of supply chain and demand activities and utilization of enabler and integrator tools. Eventually a European and an Asian version were developed. Global companies doing business in all three areas found the task of completing and trying to compare results from different versions of a scorecard to be time consuming and frustrating. The Global Commerce Initiative created a committee to develop a global scorecard.

This chapter focuses on the implementation of a global scorecard to facilitate collaboration. Implementation of collaborative business practices created the opportunity for companies to move beyond the traditional, adversarial approach to business transactions to a joint decision-making process in which the focus is on the consumer. Four major topics will be discussed: Collaboration as New Work, Industry Practices, Creation of a Global Scorecard, and Organizational and International Implications.

COLLABORATION AS NEW WORK[2]

Employees in the companies involved in the pilot studies and subsequent implementation efforts understood how to do their traditional activities of buying, selling, shipping, receiving accounts, or creating invoices really well. They had been trained, had lots of practice, and received good evaluations for their competence. Now they were being told that their jobs were going to change and that they would be expected to learn new behaviors. Change is always threatening.

Traditionally, employees engaged in short-term, tactical activities related to purchasing products on a deal at the lowest possible price. Employees are now being expected to purchase products that create the best assortment and fit the objectives of the category management strategy for the company. This new work is threatening because it has not been done before, because initially employees may not understand the reward structure, because sharing information is not something everyone is comfortable with yet, and because making decisions strategically rather than tactically requires a new mindset. To make the challenge even more formidable, employees have to balance their old work and this new work as the companies make the transition to this new collaborative, integrative business model.

INDUSTRY PRACTICES

The decision to collaborate with suppliers or wholesalers or brokers or retailers in an effort to create a more efficient supply chain, to create value for the consumer, and reduce costs is difficult to refute based upon the suggested US$30 billion of savings and the results of the pilot studies. However, companies have traditionally operated in a competitive environment. When there has been no trust in this adversarial business environment, how do you create trust and how do you choose the companies with whom you will collaborate?

One recommendation from companies having implemented collaborative activities is to be selfish about making initial choices: find a company that has the skills and expertise to help you improve in an area that is important to you, find a company that is large enough to have an impact on other vendors or at least a variety of departments within your company, or find a company that has a diverse product offering because different products move through different systems requiring different solutions. One analogy often offered by industry experts is that the choice of a company for collaboration is very similar to the choice of a dancing partner at a junior high dance. Choose a company with whom you feel comfortable, work with that company to learn the basic steps of the process, and then branch out to other companies filling your dance card. The process proceeds at a slow pace – one product category in one division working with one partner – and, when success results, branches out to other categories, other divisions, and other partners. Choose the initial partner carefully – someone with whom there is a level of trust and someone with expertise in an area that is of interest and importance to your company. As the new work succeeds, the transition will take on more momentum.

Companies engaging in collaboration activities for the first time find there is a great deal of misunderstanding, a lack of trust, inconsistent priorities, and a lack of accountability. Basically there are three reasons for creating an alliance: common opportunity, what can be gained together, and what can be gained individually. Unless both parties understand the opportunity and clearly see that they have something to gain, there is likely to be a great deal of misunderstanding about what is being done in general. Since each company has its own culture, mission, objectives, and jargon, business activities may not be designated the same way or performed the same way, which also can result in a great deal of misunderstanding. If the partners have never trusted one another before, why should they start now? Moving beyond self-serving goals is not easy. The companies that have created successful collaborative relationships have been able to make the transition by focusing on the consumer. The manufacturer wins if more consumers purchase its products in this retail establishment; the retailer wins if more consumers patronize this store or if consumers purchase more of this manufacturer's items in this store. Both parties and the consumers need to win. Then the shareholders will win as well. The collaborative venture results in a win–win–win–win situation.

Coordinating priorities is a new task. Each company has its own objectives and now the joint team also develops its own objectives. Ensuring consistency among these objectives is a new challenge. Deciding what success looks like for these new collaborative tasks is not easy. Since it has never been done before, how do the parties know it has been done responsibly, how do they know they selected the best tasks, and how do they know if their progress is outstanding or mediocre? Have the right opportunities been identified for my company? Have the right opportunities for the greatest impact been identified with my trading partners? While wrestling with these questions, companies began to develop a scorecard for assessing the current state of joint activities and measuring progress.

CREATION OF A GLOBAL SCORECARD

The motivation for creating a scorecard is to have an assessment tool. Assessment tools have been most highly developed in the area of education and have many purposes: set standards, focus on goals, monitor quality, reward/sanction practices, direct resources, formulate policies, determine effects, monitor progress, determine accountability, and perform evaluations.[3] These are the same issues facing the companies that began employing collaborative activities.

The initial scorecard was developed through an ECR Operating Committee Project and Scorecard Work Group (Booz-Allen and Hamilton, Fleming, General Mills, Kroger, Procter & Gamble, Supervalu, and Carey, Ahrens & Raynsford).[4] Kroger and Procter & Gamble conducted a beta test. The key findings were that scorecarding was useful, easy to use, produced meaningful results, and that gaps and opportunities did, in fact, exist. Members of the ECR group in the USA began using the scorecard.

The ECR movement was expanding to Europe, Asia, and Latin America. The need for a scorecard surfaced in these markets as well. As a result, an Asian and a European scorecard were developed. Multinational companies now had three different scorecards to use, making comparisons among scorecard results, even within their own company, difficult. In 2000, the ECR committee in the USA disbanded and most companies became involved in the Global Commerce Initiative (CGI). One of CGI's major initiatives was the creation of a global scorecard and a committee was created to undertake that task.

Viewing the supply chain from a holistic perspective with the objective of keeping consumers clearly in mind resulted in the identification of four key elements for the global scorecard: demand management, supply management, enablers, and integrators. By defining each of these four elements, creating key performance indicators (KPIs) for each element, and identifying attribute level descriptors for each KPI resulted in a global scorecard that could be used as an assessment tool around the world.[5] The four elements and their KPIs can be seen in Figure 21.2.

One KPI will be used as an illustration in this chapter: optimize assortment. One of the goals of creating value for the consumer in the integrated supply

Demand Management	**Enablers**
Demand strategy and capabilities	Common data and communication
Optimize assortments	standards
Optimize promotions	Cost/profit and value
Optimize new product introductions	measurement
Consumer value creation	
	Integrators
Supply Management	Collaborative planning
Supply strategy and capabilities	E-business, business-to-business
Responsive replenishment	
Integrated demand-driven supply	
Operational excellence	

Note: (A) designates the Advanced Global Scorecard.

Figure 21.2   Global scorecard

chain is to match movement of product with consumption; this is part of demand management. Optimizing assortment is a key performance indicator for matching product with consumption and there are three considerations when implementing this indicator: assortment planning, assortment execution, and assortment evaluation (see Figure 21.3). Each of these considerations is assessed on a scale of 0–4 with 0 being no capability of joint activity and 4 being an accurate, integrated joint process with direct benefits.

To use the scorecard, each trading partner has an internal team score itself. The team represents the company functions involved in the collaboration, such as accounts receivable and payable, shipping and receiving, buying and selling, finance, or information systems. By analyzing the internal scores, the team can identify the company's strengths and weaknesses on the four elements or individual KPIs or on specific considerations. By comparing strengths and weaknesses with company objectives, the team can develop priorities for action to either improve their areas of strength or to improve areas of weakness – whatever actions are most consistent with the company mission and objectives for providing value to the consumers.

The company team also scores their trading partner and conducts the same strength and weakness analysis for their trading partner. The team can then compare the trading partner's strengths to their own company's weak-

Key component: Demand management

Key performance indicator: Optimize assortment

Considerations: Assortment planning

                            Assortment execution

                            Assortment evaluation

0	1	2	3	4
No integrated capability	Being tested	In use with quality issues	Accurate and integrated	Accurate, with benefits

Figure 21.3   Global scorecard example

nesses or vice versa to determine areas of opportunity. Then both teams meet to discuss scores, priorities, and possible areas for collaboration.

In this collaborative discussion, success depends upon developing and enforcing some ground rules. First, the members of the team need to understand that the evaluations reflect the companies' individual and/or joint business activities and *not* the individual behaviors of members of the team. Second, the discussion needs to constantly revolve around those areas of opportunity and implementation that will provide consumer value. Success for these meetings depends upon support by top management, participation by a facilitator who is familiar with this process of collaboration, and abilities of the members to adopt new behaviors.

Companies also have the option of entering their data into the global scorecard database. Two major advantages are that (1) both companies can access the information on the Internet with password identification to facilitate entry of scores and/or modification of the scorecard used by their joint team and (2) company data can be benchmarked. The web site is maintained by IBM Consulting, formerly PriceWaterhouseCoopers. The data can be entered into either the non-verified or verified database. Any organizational representative may request and be given a password to use the non-verified database, enter data, and use the scorecard. However, the integrity of that data is not assured, which can be a problem for benchmarking. Companies wanting to have their scorecard data become part of the verified database must permit PriceWaterhouseCoopers representatives to examine the data for accuracy – not content, but whether the scorecard is completed correctly. For example, since the scoring ranges from 0–4, any scores of 5 are mistakes and the data would not be included in the verified database until corrections were made. For example, the scores are whole numbers, any decimals are mistakes and the data would not be added to the verified database until corrections were made. As a result of this process, the integrity of data in the verified database is ensured and these data become valuable for benchmarking.

Continuing to use the optimize assortment KPI as an example, four benchmarking figures have been prepared (Figures 21.4, 21.5, 21.6, 21.7). Figure 21.4 displays average figures across all 84 entries in the verified database as of 10 October 2001. The average and high scores for planning,

All countries verified	Average	High
Assortment planning	2.2	3.5
Assortment execution	2.1	4.0
Assortment evaluation	1.7	3.0

Figure 21.4   Benchmarking

Assortment planning		
All countries verified	2.2	3.5
Europe verified	2.4	3.5
Asia* verified	2.1	3.0
All countries super- and hypermarkets manufacturer	2.3	3.5
Europe super- and hypermarkets manufacturer	2.5	3.5
Asia* super- and hypermarkets manufacturer	2.3	3.0

Note: *Excluding Middle East.

Figure 21.5   Benchmarking – assortment planning

Assortment execution		
All countries verified	2.1	4.0
Europe verified	2.1	3.5
Asia* verified	1.9	3.0
All countries super- and hypermarkets manufacturer	2.3	3.5
Europe super- and hypermarkets manufacturer	2.1	3.5
Asia* super- and hypermarkets manufacturer	2.2	3.0

Figure 21.6   Benchmarking – assortment execution

Assortment evaluation		
All countries verified	1.7	3.0
Europe verified	1.8	2.5
Asia* verified	1.6	3.0
All countries super- and hypermarkets manufacturer	1.9	3.0
Europe super- and hypermarkets manufacturer	1.8	2.5
Asia* super- and hypermarkets manufacturer	1.8	3.0

Figure 21.7   Benchmarking – assortment evaluation

execution, and evaluation allow a company to compare its own score with the average in each category to find out where it stands in relation to the average for all companies completing the scorecard. In addition, a company can also compare its score with the highest score in the category to determine where it stands in relation to the 'best in class'. Companies can also compare their scores with the average and high scores for a particular region of the world, such as Europe or Asia (see Figure 21.5). In addition, a company could compare itself with particular industries and/or an element of the supply chain, such as manufacturers supplying super- and hypermarkets in general or in Europe or Asia. This information allows a company to benchmark itself in terms of its own industry, its own or other regions in the world, and against other manufacturers to determine where it stands in relation to the average and 'best in class'. This can be done for each of the three considerations: assortment planning (Figure 21.5), assortment execution (Figure 21.6), and assortment evaluation (Figure

21.7). The 'best in class' scores as well as averages are not the same in all three areas – even using the same groupings of Asia or Europe and manufacturers supplying super- and hypermarkets.

Companies can use the data to benchmark themselves on a worldwide basis, regional basis or country basis, within a particular industry, and with particular types of companies within the supply chain. As such, the global scorecard can be an important assessment tool for determining progress, comparing one company's progress with other companies, and for current information on the state of the industry.

ORGANIZATIONAL AND INTERNATIONAL IMPLICATIONS

Organizational implications

Feedback from industry experts and an analysis of case studies sponsored by the Global Scorecard Committee revealed several organizational implications regarding scorecard usage.

First, companies engaging in a scorecard activity develop a better understanding of their partner organization. Rather than reacting to constraints proposed by the trading partner as roadblocks designed to prevent progress, participants understand why the other organization has to live within certain constraints.

Second, the conversation between trading partners takes place at a strategic level rather than a tactical level. For instance, instead of discussing a particular deal to encourage a purchase, the discussion revolves around what promotion vehicles might be more effective in getting specific consumers to purchase a particular product.

Third, because the language is well-defined and shared by all members of the joint team, there is less misunderstanding. Because the considerations describe very specific business behaviors, the teams find it is possible to produce clear, common goals.

Fourth, when all members of the team have clear goals using terms that all understand and when all members of the team agree upon those goals, alignment of behavior follows. Each team member knows his or her responsibility, how specific activities fit into the overall plan, and the work is well coordinated.

Fifth, assessment of specific behavior enables the team to measure progress and benchmark their activity within the industry, across industries, and within a specific geographic area.

In the case study sponsored by the Global Scorecard Committee, joint teams were composed of companies from different countries. Not all of the comments were positive.

First, team members in some countries had difficulty understanding the concepts because business behavior and terminology vary across countries.

Second, some team members found that some concepts did not apply to their situation.

Third, not all team members understood the process of collaboration so found the scorecard activity to be confusing. In general, a lack of training appeared to be a problem.

Fourth, since some concepts were confusing and since some members did not think all the concepts applied, a suggestion was made to use the scorecard as a guideline to be generally, but not strictly, followed. A major problem with this recommendation is that if each team uses the scorecard in a different way, then the advantage of benchmarking is lost.

The organizational advantages of the scorecard appear to result when there is a clear understanding of both the terms used in the scorecard and the process of a collaboration. Training is essential. Having a facilitator, who is knowledgeable about the process of using a scorecard, present during the discussions is also essential for success. Those joint teams who found the scorecard to be a valuable tool commented that it was very helpful to have a knowledgeable facilitator present who could help them through the process when the team had difficulties. Therefore, *if* team members are trained and *if* a knowledgeable facilitator works with the team, the scorecard had major positive benefits for an organization: strategic discussions, identifications of opportunities, and mutual understanding of projects.

International Implications

The major implication for international business is in the creation of a common language related to the process of doing business. Some of the international team members suggested that they did not understand some of the concepts or that the concepts may not apply in their country. These issues have significant ramifications. Maybe there are some business processes that are not universal and may not apply across countries. That is an empirical question yet to be answered. Maybe the training process needs to focus on ensuring that everyone understands the terms, concepts, and their definitions. Once everyone understands the same terms, concepts, and definitions then the empirical question of whether they apply across countries can be addressed.

Unresolved questions relate to the uniform applicability of concepts in all cultures, the ability to which the benchmark results can be used to develop business strategies, and the relationship between scorecard results and business performance. At this point the global scorecard is still in the development process, companies are being encouraged to add their data to the verified database so that benchmarking activities can generate a greater level of detail, and the relationship between benchmark data and performance is not readily available. Much of this information is proprietary or shared with business partners and has not been made public. As the global scorecard database is more populated and benchmarking data is more broadly available, additional information addressing the performance and business strategy issues will be explored.

Once everyone understands the terms, concepts, and their definitions, as well as the rationale for engaging in those behaviors, the business practices identified in the global scorecard may become universal, thereby moving the business world one step closer to the concept of a global village. The accounting profession is working to develop a global set of standards so that numbers can be more easily compared across countries. One of the major international implications of the global scorecard may be that it is creating a set of marketing definitions that are accepted worldwide. Not only will companies be able to benchmark their scores against other companies, industries, and geographies, but also will begin doing business using similar marketing processes and practices worldwide. Observing whether the usage of the global scorecard increases over time can be one indicator of whether more companies around the world are using this set of terms and definitions to assess their activities. Businesses may be developing standard definitions for marketing activities that will be applied worldwide.

NOTES

1. Kurt Salmon and Associates (1993), *Enhancing the Efficiency*, Washington, DC: Food Marketing Institute.
2. Mike Maurer (1997 and 2001), Executive MBA Presentation in the Williams College of Business at Xavier University and Presentation at Winter AMA Educators' Conference.
3. R.J. Dietel, J.L. Herman and R.A. Knuth (1991), 'What Does Research Say About Assessment?', North Central Regional Educational Laboratory, www.ncrel.org/sdrs/areas/stw_esys/4assess.htm.
4. Ryan Mathew (1996), 'Trying to Score', *Progressive Grocer*, **75** (10), October, 59–62.
5. Definitions and the complete scorecard can be found at the following website: www.globalscorecard.net.

22. The development and use of a global marketing and sales scorecard

Robert L. Engle

INTRODUCTION

It has been suggested that assessing the company's current financial position through the use of metrics such as financial ratios is a major step in the strategic planning process. These financial ratios tend to be the major analyses tools being used by many company management teams in their attempt to evaluate and control the current and future health of their organizations (Brigham and Gapenski 1997). However, Kaplan and Norton's (1992) research of 12 companies highlighted their efforts to develop a set of metrics to measure performance that went beyond the standard financial measures. They opened their *Harvard Business Review* article with 'What you measure is what you get' (p. 71), recognizing that organizations will focus on those objectives on which they are being measured. They built a case not only for business metrics covering key financial measures that report the results of actions already taken, but also using 'operational' measures that are the critical drivers of future financial performance. This more comprehensive approach of using financial and operational measures has been labeled the 'business scorecard'.

THE BUSINESS SCORECARD

Kaplan and Norton (1992) suggested that a balanced scorecard covers four areas including: a financial perspective (How does the company look to its shareholders?); a customer perspective (How do customers see the company?); an internal business perspective (What must the company excel at?); and an innovation and learning perspective (How can the company continue to improve and create value?). These last three perspectives – customer, internal business, and innovation and learning – are the areas included in their concept of 'operational' measures. If done correctly, they argue, vision and strategy and not control are the center of the balanced scorecard. In fact, research has confirmed that financial measures alone have little correlation with the future market value of a company and that operational measures such as customer relationships and brand strength are more closely linked to value creation and share price (Roberts and Styles 2001).

Subsequent articles by Kaplan and Norton (1993, 1996a) reinforced the importance of building the scorecard from the vision and strategy of the organization and actually using the scorecard to better refine the vision and strategies. They suggested putting things in measurable terms often giving employees a much clearer picture of the sometimes-vague strategy and vision communications. They believe this is especially true when these measures are specific to the business and business growth stage, and not of a pure generic nature (1996b).

Many other researchers have furthered Kaplan and Norton's work (Epstein and Manzoni 1997; Atkinson and Holden 2000; Goulian and Mersereau 2000; Avery 2000; Roberts and Styles 2001) with some suggesting that the scorecard concept should not only be used at the overall business level, but could and should be taken deeper into the organization and used at the department level. These same researchers have agreed that non-financial metrics are an essential part of a balanced scorecard.

MARKETING AND SALES METRICS

Obviously, one of the key departments that every company should consider as a primary candidate for the scorecard concept is marketing. McCollough (2000) takes a strong position in support of marketing specific metrics by saying that 'Marketing is on the precipice of much-needed change' (p. 64), and that marketers must change senior executives' perception that marketing is an expense – to a perception of one where marketing is an enhancement of a company's overall profitability. McCollough believes that marketing metrics is the way to change senior management's perception.

Based on the results of a 30-month study by the London School of Business, Ambler (2001) argues that companies are successful due to the increase in the value of their brands and that brand equity is the upstream reservoir of cash flow. He believes that marketing metrics are the key to providing the insights necessary to assess whether or not the brand asset has truly grown which will lead to longer-term profitability. He suggests that even while the pressure is on for marketers to be more accountable, the marketers themselves have mixed feelings. While the marketers are welcoming the recognition, many are uneasy with what they perceive as more controls on what they can and cannot do if, for example, their creative approaches are not perceived to improve a given metric in the short or long term. As suggested by previous researchers, Ambler found that marketing metrics fell into categories depending on the nature of the business and are calculated differently in various business sectors. Even though he believes that firms should choose their metrics according to strategy, he admits the pressure of business practitioners to provide a short generic list of market metrics. Thus Ambler reports, with the admitted risk of being ineffective due to its generic and potentially non-strategically focused nature, the top ten brand equity metrics in the UK as:

- Awareness.
- Market share (volume or value).
- Relative price (market share value/volume).
- Number of complaints (level of dissatisfaction).
- Consumer satisfaction.
- Distribution/availability.
- Total number of customers.
- Perceived quality/esteem.
- Loyalty/retention.
- Relative perceived quality.

In another study, Clark (2000) reviewed the history of research in marketing performance measurement and suggested four categories of measures that should be addressed. These include (with sample measures):

- Health of brand or company reputation (awareness; strength of image; favorability of image; and uniqueness of image).
- Sales and profitability analysis (unit sales; and value sales).
- Health of customer base (size, growth, profitability; relative customer satisfaction; retention rate; frequency, recency, amount and type of purchases; and penetration of target market).
- Quality of marketing inputs (strategic activities specific to firm; employee surveys regarding marketing orientation; and percentage of sales from new products).

In 1987, the United States established the Malcolm Baldridge National Quality Improvement Award that has become the operational definition Total Quality Management (TQM). A relatively recent change in the Malcolm Baldridge National Quality Improvement Award criteria is also giving increased emphasis to marketing metrics (Thomas 1997). The award is now also based on customer and marketing knowledge, customer satisfaction and relationship enhancement, and analysis and review of company performance. Thus companies must now address such things as: how customer groups and/or market segments are chosen; how key product and service features and their relative importance to customers are determined; how the company's approach to listening and learning from customers and markets is evaluated; how the company improves customer contact requirements; and customer satisfaction and financial and market-results. The status of the prestigious Baldridge awards and the inclusion of these marketing-related criteria representing over 30 per cent of the total possible points obtainable are clearly adding to the emphasis and importance of marketing-related metrics (US Department of Commerce).

There are a number of other researchers who have added to the list of possible metrics that could be contained in a marketing and sales scorecard (Thomas 1997; Denby-Jones 1998; Haigh 2000). A composite of the various marketing and sales metrics suggestions and examples found in this literature review would include such things as:

- Brand awareness/leadership.
- Target market share – volume or value.
- Relative market price.
- Number of complaints – level of dissatisfaction.
- Consumer satisfaction.
- Customer profitability.
- On-time delivery – customer defined.
- Distribution/availability.
- Total number of customers.
- Perceived quality/esteem/image/uniqueness.
- Loyalty/retention.
- Frequency/recency/amount and type of customer purchases.
- New business.
- Number of firsts into the market.
- Relative perceived quality.
- Value sales/growth.
- Unit sales/growth.
- Sales backlog.
- Percent of sales from new products.
- Employee marketing orientation.
- Employee satisfaction.
- Correlation between customer and employee satisfaction.
- Pre-tax profitability/product.
- Profit forecast reliability/product.
- Project profitability.

- Marketing margin growth.
- Strategic plans geared to market/strategic quality.
- Correlation between corporate position and core marketing competencies.
- Employee empowerment.
- Employee suggestions.
- Marketing organization structure efficiency.
- Speed of response to market environment/organizational learning.
- Appropriate channels to meet market needs.
- Strength of channel relationship.
- Management hours spent with customers.
- Sustainability of competitive advantage.
- Brand Value Added™ (Haigh 2000) and relationship to economic value added.
- New product introduction vs. competition.
- Product life-cycle management.

Clearly, this brief review identifies many more than the average of 12–20 business scorecard metrics seen in company examples of this literature review. As Kaplan and Norton (1996b) point out, all scorecards may use certain generic measures such as profitability, market share, customer satisfaction, and perhaps employee skills. However, they emphasize that the real drivers of performance are those that tend to be unique for a particular company or business unit and suggest that up to a total of two dozen measures is not too many. A global marketing and sales specific scorecard might logically follow the same guidelines.

The above list suggests a wide array of potential generic content options to reinforce strategy and vision, as well as identify potential marketing and sales problems. Many of the above metrics may be seen as 'generic' in nature and may in some form be valid within companies of all industries given their particular vision and strategy. In addition to possible selections from this list of marketing and sales metrics, the recent literature suggests the importance of adding metrics that would address key marketing strategies.

A GLOBAL MARKETING AND SALES SCORECARD

While there is no shortage of suggested generic marketing and sales metrics to use in a possible scorecard approach, a literature review could find no information regarding the needs, experiences and approaches to developing global marketing and sales scorecards. One could assume the concept of developing a scorecard at the global business level would be similar to overall country business level and particular departmental approaches, but questions clearly remain. 'Is there a perceived need for a global marketing and sales specific scorecard? Should the data contained within be aggregated and/or local? To what degree should the chosen metrics be standardized between countries? How should the scorecard be developed and implemented? What should be measured and how should these measures be evaluated?'

To begin exploring these questions, a major global ethical pharmaceutical company was examined with regard to their development and implementation of global marketing and sales metrics. This multi-billion dollar company operates in approximately 70 countries and is well known for its global presence.

As with most other businesses there are a relative few countries that represent most of the global industry sales and current global industry potential for their products. The USA alone represents nearly 50 per cent of the world's sales (in value) in all pharmaceutical products and if one adds the UK, France, Germany, Japan, Italy, Spain, and Canada, then according to the market research company, IMS, you have approximately 85 per cent of the world's current potential in pharmaceutical sales. It is common within the pharmaceutical industry to refer to these countries as the 'eight main countries'.

The Worldwide Pharmaceutical Management Committee of this company set the goal of significantly improving the business marketing and sales effectiveness in these eight main countries. A sub-committee was set up to oversee this important project. A group of senior marketing and sales managers representing the 'eight main countries' and two European representatives from smaller countries were chosen to be members of the task force whose job it would be to address this project.

The first step of this task force was to complete a 'needs analysis' in each country as well as a literature review of current industry best practices and work with a consulting firm who completed a benchmarking study on key industry marketing and sales practices in a number of the main countries. One of the first important outputs of this project was a list of critical marketing and sales success factors for the marketing and sales organizations of major pharmaceutical companies. Of the critical success factors identified, seven were believed to be the most critical for this organization, i.e. having the greatest opportunity for improvement and input. One of these seven was the development and successful implementation of a global marketing and sales metrics scorecard.

The company's Worldwide Management Committee clearly agreed there was a need for a marketing and sales metrics scorecard and that these metrics should ideally be the same for all eight main countries. They believed that these main countries were essential due to their percentage of the current and potential business. They also indicated that this will allow the business and marketing management teams in each of the eight countries to focus on the issues identified as most critical for both global and local business and aid in the discussion and formulation of future global strategic actions, as well as help to focus the country managers in their sharing of best practices between countries. In addition, they believed that these metrics would also serve to reinforce the vision and appropriate strategies throughout all main countries. The management committee clearly communicated throughout the global organization their support for the development and use of a global marketing and sales scorecard.

The assigned task force began by addressing the question of 'what do we measure and against what do we evaluate these metrics?'. There was clear agreement that the metrics needed to tie to the identified critical success factors, vision, and strategies of company. The Worldwide Management Committee wanted the ability to look at specific products and performance, by countries, regions, and the world, and measure the impact of various global initiatives. They also wanted to be able to aggregate all products into product groups and total business across these parameters. It was also agreed to address both financial and operational metrics.

The international task force consisting of senior marketing and marketing research personnel from the main countries began the process of identifying what specific financial and operational related metrics needed to be used. These team members worked closely with the country managers and their marketing teams. There was no shortage of suggestions from various team members and country managers – each had something they felt strongly about, which would highlight a particular strength of their country. These suggestions were not always compatible with those suggested by other countries, or necessarily related to key strategies or vision. For example, one country wanted sales by a classification of customer group in which they were strong, but this customer category did not exist in other countries.

As could be anticipated, there were a number of challenges for this global team. Everybody wanted a different set of metrics, often arguing for those metrics that would be best for their country and arguing against those metrics that may not be as flattering. Perhaps the most significant problem reported, though, was the difference in data availability and compatibility, especially at the individual customer level. While the end-user of prescription pharmaceutical products is the patient, the real customer is, in most countries, the individual physician. Due to the sensitive nature of healthcare information, and the fact that with the exception of Japan, most prescription products are not distributed directly to the physician for sales to the patient, information on what products the individual physician is using can be difficult, or even impossible, to obtain in many countries. Related to this problem was the fact that some countries had much more secondary market research data available, or secondary data of a different type, than other countries. Financial reporting processes that impact product marketing margins also varied between some countries. Another problem was the difference between individual country marketing strategies, as this company tended to allow a great deal of freedom for individual countries, or regions, to develop country-level marketing strategies.

This latter problem of country marketing strategy difference was addressed by setting up a global marketing group whose responsibility included the coordination of appropriate global marketing strategies, such as branding and positioning, across countries. The other problems were addressed by deciding to develop this global metric scorecard in multiple phases over a period of two to three years. In this fashion, the company could begin by addressing some of the more 'generic' metrics that were immediately possible while developing the methodology and tools to address other metrics that were felt to be important. In some cases laws and/or regulations are changing in several countries that will allow better data availability in the near future.

The multiple phase approach would also allow the company to get some experience with the information systems that were being developed for these metrics and to evaluate the importance and use of this first set of metrics. This evaluation would allow for some to be deleted or altered before adding more, as it was recognized that too many metrics would dilute the visibility and perhaps value for all of them. The phased approach would also prove to marketing and sales management that senior management would not be using them for control purposes, perhaps making it easier to put more 'sensitive' metrics in later phases.

It also was agreed that individual countries would, in addition to the global metrics scorecard, have a local scorecard addressing future phases of the scorecard or items unique to a given country. A project to better coordinate financial reporting across the main countries was also begun and, finally, there were many meetings and communications between task force members to narrow down the original possible list of metrics.

The new global marketing group who generally obtain the data from the marketing research departments of the individual countries manages the global marketing and sales metrics scorecard. Phase 1 of this company's global marketing and sales scorecard included such things as:

- Net sales.
- Market share (sales value).

- Total prescriptions.
- Prescription share.
- Detailing (sales calls and number of products/call).
- Detailing share of voice.
- New prescriptions.
- Number of prescribers.
- Sales per representative.
- Sales per sales call.
- New prescriptions per sales call.
- Customer targeting, including reach and frequency.

Each metric is clearly defined and suggestions made as to how calculations should be done if there is no reliable primary or secondary data available. Each metric is by product and/or in aggregate across products, as appropriate, and measured by comparing the metric to a goal established by the local business manager and marketing team. In the case of the larger main countries, an industry benchmark for available metrics was also used for comparison. With regard to overall business marketing metrics for each country such as net sales and market share, the Worldwide Management Committee set the goals along with the local business manager. A 'traffic light' approach is used where the metric is seen on the computer screen in the color green if the metric is greater or equal to 100 per cent of goal; it is in yellow if above 90 per cent but less than 100 per cent; and it is seen in red if below 90 per cent of the stated goal. The format of the information system's screen allows for easy comparison across countries or regions.

Meanwhile, each of the individual eight main countries has developed their own marketing and sales metrics scorecard. These local scorecards not only include the Phase 1 global metrics, but are often focused on the metrics to be included in Phase 2 or Phase 3 of the global marketing and sales scorecard. The following is an early version of some of the things US local marketing and sales metrics scorecard included in addition to the global metrics:

- Gross sales in value compared to budgets.
- Marketing margins (profitability without R&D, allocations, etc.).
- Advertising and promotion spend compared to budget.
- Detailing share of voice (3-month moving average; and current month).
- Managed care and institutional product availability.
- Personnel turnover (field and HQ).
- Physician reach and frequency by decile (sales potential).
- Sales representative minutes per detail (contact minutes).

- New prescriptions per detail (company; top 20 companies; selected market).

These also represent some of the things being considered by the company for possible inclusion in Phase 2 of the global metrics marketing and sales scorecard. Since major product launches will take place for this company in the near future, the company indicated that it is probable that a product launch effectiveness metric such as stocking or availability by channel will be added. Some of the other metrics in active discussion for future phases include a customer satisfaction measure, number of marketing/sales pilot tests, management time spent with customers, company and brand image, and brand awareness.

THE FUTURE

When looking a little further out, there appears to be a number of technological and channel changes that may allow for different and perhaps more precise global marketing and sales metrics to be added to the scorecard. Two such possibilities are customer relationship management systems (CRM) and e-business.

Later phases of this company's scorecard will probably include aspects of marketing and sales that CRM will allow. CRM is a technology solution that enables a company to manage multiple points of contact that exist with a customer throughout its organization, creating a comprehensive view of the customer. With such a system the company will not only be better able to follow all contacts they have with a given customer, and as a result put them in a better position to manage their customer's needs and more efficiently communicate with them, but it will allow the company to more accurately evaluate exactly how much time, money, and other resources they are investing in each customer. CRM will make such metrics as return on investment by the customer a realistic possibility. While the use of CRM on a global scale is not without potential challenges such as different data processes, customer data formats, and definitions, CRM's promise is to allow new approaches to customer segmentation, measurement, and activity, as well as supply new measures of such things as customer satisfaction (Crosby and Johnson 2002).

One of the areas from which CRM will potentially be able to gather information is e-business activity. CRM has the capacity to tell the company, in some detail, about each customer's involvement with their web-based applications. This will give rise to a whole new sub-set of marketing and sales metrics known as e-metrics. As companies become more involved and experienced with e-business they are looking at such information as:

- Number and identity of non-customer or new customer site visits.
- Number of visits over time by customer/customer group.
- Top referring sites.
- Ad visits.
- Order patterns by customer/customer groups.
- Customer participation in e-events.
- Customer's key areas of interests or concerns.

These are but a few of possible business and marketing and sales metrics. Especially for those companies in which the internet or extranet is a key marketing channel, such metrics can be of strategic importance and should be considered for a business and/or global marketing and sales scorecard.

Overall, the management of the pharmaceutical company examined here sees a real need for global marketing and sales metrics and is moving forward to quickly move up the learning curve in how to best accomplish this goal. Senior management's commitment to, and active support of, the scorecard's development and use, is seen by the organization as key to its success.

Global marketing and sales scorecards are a potentially important tool for most companies regardless of industry, and while future research will clarify which metrics are most appropriate at the global level, either generically or for a given strategy, it is logical to assume many of the same marketing and sales metrics identified to date at the local country levels will serve well as a place for companies to begin discussion.

REFERENCES

Ambler, Tim (2001), 'What Does Successful Marketing Look Like?', *Marketing Management*, **10** (1), 12–18.
Atkinson, Philip and Malcolm Holden (2000), 'Unlocking the Secret Behind the Balanced Business Scorecard', *Management Services*, **44** (5), 6–10.
Avery, Susan (2000), 'Measuring Performance Takes on New Importance', *Purchasing*, **129** (3), 123–8.
Brigham, Eugene F. and Louis C. Gapenski (1997), *Financial Management: Theory and Practice*, 8th edn, Fort Worth, TX: Dryden press.
Clark, Bruce H. (2000), 'A Summary of Thinking on Measuring the Value of Marketing', *Journal of Targeting, Measurement and Analysis for Marketing*, **9** (4), 357–69.
Crosby, Lawrence A. and Sheree L. Johnson (2002), 'The Globalization of Relationship Marketing', *Marketing Management*, 1 March.

Denby-Jones, Sarah (1998), 'Marketing Measures for Performance', *Journal of Targeting Measurement And Analysis For Marketing*, **7** (2), 155–63.

Epstein, Marc J. and Jean-Francois Manzoni (1997), 'The Balanced Scorecard and Tableau De Bord: Translating Strategy into Action', *Management Accounting*, **79** (2), 23–36.

Goulian, Caroline and Alexander Mersereau (2000), 'Performance Measurement', *Ivey Business Journal*, **65** (1), 48–59.

Haigh, David (2000), 'Best Practice in Measuring the Impact of Marketing on Brand Equity and Corporate Profitability', *Journal of Targeting, Measurement and Analysis for Marketing*, **9** (1), 9–19.

Kaplan, Robert S. and David P. Norton (1992), 'The Balanced Scorecard – Measures That Drive Performance', *Harvard Business Review*, **70** (1), 71–9.

Kaplan, Robert S. and David P. Norton (1993), 'Putting The Balanced Scorecard to Work', *Harvard Business Review*, **71** (5), 134–47.

Kaplan, Robert S. and David P. Norton (1996a), 'Using The Balanced Scorecard as a Strategic Management System', *Harvard Business Review*, **74** (1), 75–85.

Kaplan, Robert S. and David P. Norton (1996b), 'Linking the Balanced Scorecard to Strategy', *California Management Review*, **39** (1), 53–80.

McCollough, Wayne R. (2000), 'Use Them or Lose Everything', *Marketing Management*, **9** (1), 64–6.

Roberts, John H. and Chris Styles (2001), 'Australia's Competitive Advantage: Gaining the Marketing Edge', *Australia Journal of Management*, **26** (8), 105–20.

Thomas, Michael J. (1997), 'Measuring Marketing Performance', *Journal of Targeting, Measurement and Analysis for Marketing*, **6** (3), 233–46.

23. Country of origin effect: synthesis and future direction

Narasimhan Srinivasan and Subhash C. Jain

INTRODUCTION

The country of origin (COO) effect has been examined in the literature for at least 35 years. Hundreds of journal articles and numerous doctoral dissertations have been written on the subject. Yet we have not developed a solid theory of the COO effect. Is it because researchers have pursued their work without following a common framework and assumptions? Ultimately, academic pursuits should lead to a usable framework and generalizations, and also develop guidelines attractive to practitioners. What have we learnt thus far in the area of country of origin? What direction should future research take?

For quality research, empirical examination requires a theoretical base. In inductive research, past empirical investigations is the foundation that leads to new theory building. We seek to synthesize past research and set directions for future work. A conceptual framework for gaining insights into the COO effect is proposed. Generalizations are presented, and an attempt is made to establish a research agenda on the COO effect.

As Bass and Wind (1995) note, empirical generalization is 'a pattern or regularity that repeats over different circumstances' but one that 'need not be universal over all circumstances'. Approaches include literature reviews, content analysis and meta-analysis. This study looks at the literature in major journals, books and published meta-analysis. It draws out a meaningful framework. In Bass's (1995) viewpoint, 'there is general agreement that science is a process in which data and theory interact to produce higher level explanations'. To make progress, we need to take stock periodically and set up the base levels on which we build in the future. Such a step is attempted here for understanding the COO effect.

New studies continue to be published on the topic periodically, sometimes with conflicting results. Most studies are based on data with students serving as respondents. As Peterson and Jolibert (1995) rightly note in their meta-analysis, COO effects are only somewhat generalizable, and the phenomenon is still not well understood. With increasing globalization, COO cannot remain a simple construct. It can be further decomposed as country of design, country of parts manufacture, country of assembly, and country of branding. Hence, this is an opportune time to take stock of this important construct based on decades of research in this area.

Briefly, the missing gap in most previous research is an organized theoretical framework leading to an evaluation of products of foreign origin. In this era of globalization, such a framework is of critical importance. In making production location decisions, firms would like to avoid an adverse impact on the image, positioning and acceptance of products among their customers in developed countries. At the same time, as developing countries' markets become important, the products sold there should be sourced from nations which are perceived as the 'right' countries for the product from the consumers' viewpoint.

LITERATURE REVIEW

Consumers use both intrinsic and extrinsic cues in product evaluations. Intrinsic cues are product attributes intrinsic to the product that cannot be changed without changing the physical characteristics of the product. Extrinsic cues, by contrast, refer to the product's non-physical characteristics. In the case of cars, for example, size of engine, performance durability, and quality would be intrinsic cues; price and country label would be extrinsic cues. Country of origin is a complex construct, having both intrinsic and extrinsic properties. Although it can be debated, country of manufacture can be considered intrinsic in some circumstances (e.g. chocolates made in Switzerland), whereas country of branding could be considered an extrinsic cue (e.g. Procter & Gamble's branding of detergents in Europe).

Before globalization started on its rapid growth (post-1980), many products were manufactured and sold in the same country. This identification of the country with a product was easy for the consumer. Today, however, it is common to find products that are manufactured in one country, branded in another and sold in a third country. Actually, it is even more complex: Products can be assembled in a country different from that of manufacture, use ingredients or parts from many more countries, be designed in yet another country, be developed by a company headquartered in still a different country and branded differently in the countries of sale. The emergence of new markets, intense worldwide competition and rapid growth in global sourcing has led to a world of hybrid or multinational products, making the COO effect more critical and complex. What is the state of the art now?

Most earlier works on the COO effect have been single-cue studies that attempted to measure the effect in isolation from other cues that may influence consumer choices. An early study in this category was reported by Schooler (1965). Several other single-cue studies followed: Schooler and Wildt (1968); Schooler (1971); Tonberg (1972); Lillis and Narayanan (1974); Baumgarner and Jolibert (1978); Hampton (1977); Bilkey and Nes (1982); Papadopoulos et al. (1987), and others. Practically speaking, all these studies support the important effect of COO on product evaluations, although the effect size varied significantly with a number of study characteristics. Generally, these studies established that a bias exists in consumers from developed countries favoring (a) their home-country products, and (b) products from other developed countries over products from developing countries. It is easy to realize that the COO effect could have been exaggerated in those studies where it was the only cue for evaluation.

The second stream of research comprises studies that include cues, other than COO, in testing the sensitivity of the COO effect. These studies included both intrinsic and extrinsic cues. Intrinsic cues refer to attributes that are built into the product and, therefore, cannot be changed or experimentally manipulated without changing the physical characteristics of the product, such as quality, design and performance. Extrinsic cues are attributes such as color, packaging, and brand name (Olsen and Jacoby 1972). Notable works in this group include Ettenson, Wagner and Gaeth (1988); Hong and Wyer (1989, 1990); Johansson (1989); Johansson, Douglas and Nonaka (1985); Liefeld (1993); Thorelli, Lim and Ye (1989); Erickson, Johansson and Chao (1984); Chao (1989); and d'Astous and Ahmed (1992). These studies represent an attempt to examine the cognitive processes triggered when COO is presented with information on other product attributes. The major finding of the multi-cue studies has been the statistical significance of the COO effect even when other cues (for example, price, brand name) are available.

Studies in the third category deal with hybrid products, i.e. products that were assembled in a country using parts from several other countries. In this case, consumer ethnocentrism and country stereotyping behavior have been found to be significant. In addition to its role as a quality cue, COO in these studies has symbolic and emotional meaning to consumers. Representative research in this area includes Chao (1993); Ettenson and Gaeth (1991); Johansson (1989); Kochunny et al. (1993); Haubl (1996); Li and Monroe (1992); Batra et al. (2000); Botschen and Hemettsberger (1998); Han (1989), Han and Terpstra (1988); Johansson and Nebenzahl (1987); Haubl and Elrod (1999); Insch and McBride (1996); Johansson (1997); Papadopoulos et al. (1997); Saghafi and Puig (1997); Nebenzahl and Jaffe (1997), and others. It is found that even after controlling for consumer ethnocentrism and stereotyping behavior in the case of hybrid products, the COO effect is still mostly present.

There are three dimensions of the COO effect that have been identified: cognitive, affective and normative processing (Verlegh and Steenkamp 1999). Studies in the first category use country of origin as the cue for product quality; for example, reliability and durability, signifying cognitive mechanism. The second set of studies consider country of origin as an affective mechanism that links the product to symbolic and emotional benefits, including social status. The third category represents a normative process that relates country of origin to personal norms such as buying domestic products is the right thing to do, since it supports the domestic economy. Overall, it can be concluded that country of origin is a significant consideration in product evaluation. The significance will vary depending on the country of manufacturing and branding, consumer's background based on demographics, ethnocentricity, and stereotype notions about the product from the manufacturing and branding countries.

COUNTRY OF ORIGIN FRAMEWORK

Country of origin essentially refers to the perceived nationality/nationalities of a product. Considering a simple case, in the current state of globalization, this could mean the country where the product has been manufactured and/or the country associated with the branding. Both these aspects are important in delineating the COO effect. The following key concepts underlie the rationale for the framework shown in Figure 23.1:

- A product's country of manufacture impacts judgment about its value.
- The branding country of a product effects the manufacturing country associated with a product, either positively or negatively, depending on the specific countries involved and the time period/specificity when/where the research is conducted.
- Based on the manufacturing country and the branding country of the product as well as other extrinsic and intrinsic cues, a customer assesses the value of the product.
- This value assessment is further modified by the demographic and behavior characteristics of the customer.
- Finally, the COO effect is the outcome of the interaction of the consumer, product and situation.

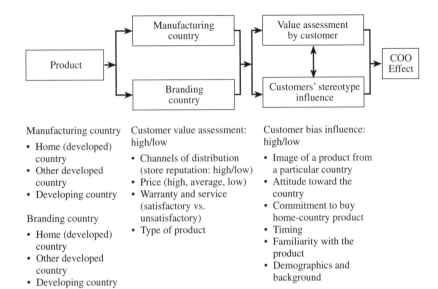

Manufacturing country
- Home (developed) country
- Other developed country
- Developing country

Branding country
- Home (developed) country
- Other developed country
- Developing country

Customer value assessment: high/low
- Channels of distribution (store reputation: high/low)
- Price (high, average, low)
- Warranty and service (satisfactory vs. unsatisfactory)
- Type of product

Customer bias influence: high/low
- Image of a product from a particular country
- Attitude toward the country
- Commitment to buy home-country product
- Timing
- Familiarity with the product
- Demographics and background

Figure 23.1   A framework for understanding the country of origin effect

COUNTRY-OF-ORIGIN SYNTHESIS

Manufacturing Country

A product may be manufactured in the home country where it was first developed and branded, or in another developed country (with high per capita and GNP), or in a developing country. For example, a Toyota car may be assembled in Japan, the USA, or Mexico. It is expected that consumers' response to products manufactured in these three countries will vary across nations.

Chao (1998) found that product quality was rated higher when the product was assembled in the USA rather than in Mexico. Similarly, product quality scored higher when parts were identified as being from the USA rather than Mexico. In another study, TVs assembled in Mexico were perceived to be lower in quality than those assembled in Taiwan. However, between Taiwan and Thailand there were no significant differences (Chao 1992). Han and Terpstra (1988) noted that the sourcing country stimulus is powerful in product evaluation. A study by Ahmed and d'Astous (1995) confirmed that products manufactured in Mexico were rated lower than those in developed countries. They found that a Toyota car made in Japan got higher ratings in Canada than a Toyota made in Canada. Similarly a

Toyota made in Belgium received lower ratings than the one made in Japan. These findings corroborate Iacocca's (1990) contention that the Japanese-made Mitsubishi brand outsold Chrysler's Colt made in Japan three to one in the USA.

Virtually, all studies have found the manufacturing location of a product to be a significant variable impacting consumer evaluation and choice. Some studies note, however, that the COO effect is not predominant, relative to other cues (d'Astous and Ahmed 1992). Consumers make judgments about product quality from product-country images, which contain beliefs about a country's products, but also about the general characteristics, like its economy, workforce and culture (Verlegh and Steenkamp 1999). Thus the following generalizations can be made:

G1a: Customers in developed countries evaluate products manufactured in their own country higher than in another country.

G1b: Customers in developed countries rate products manufactured in a developed country higher than those from a developing country.

Branding Country

The origin of a brand may be the home country, which is also a developed country (for example, a Kodak digital camera manufactured in the USA), another developed country (for example, a Sony digital camera manufactured in the USA), or a developing country (for example, a Chinese brand of digital camera manufactured in the USA). Relating manufacturing country alternatives to branding alternatives generate nine manufacturing branding options as shown in Figure 23.2.

Based on research with respondents in Germany and France, Haubl (1996) found that both brand name and the country of origin (i.e. manufacturing) have a significant impact on consumers' attitudes towards new automobiles. Conscious efforts by consumers to evaluate products involve a wide range of attributes and the country of origin is a significant determinant. But brand name came out to be a stronger criterion (Chawla, Smith and Derakshan 1995), particularly in the case of younger consumers.

Elliot and Cameron (1994) based on their research with Australian respondents found that the IBM-PC built in the USA rated as being of highest quality, the IBM-PC made in Australia ranked second, while the Singapore-made label ranked last. A Ford Laser car assembled in Japan scored highest on quality, while the one made in UK ranked second, and the Australian made came last. In the case of Florshein Brogues shoes, the ones made in the USA were rated as the best, while those made in Brazil

Branding country

		Home country	Developed country	Developing country
	Home country			
Manufacturing country	Developed country			
	Developing country			

Figure 23.2   Manufacturing branching options

and Australia scored alike. Dunlop steel tires made in Australia scored higher in terms of quality than those made in the UK. Bosch dishwashers made in Germany were rated best, with those made in Australia scoring second and the Korean-made ranking third.

Hulland (1999) showed a strong branding country effect. He noted that while the COO effects are extremely robust, brand name plays a strong and incremental role in influencing a subject's evaluations. If the brand name of the product is well recognized and respected, the country of origin impact may be lessened. Consumers may decide to buy the product on the brand's reputation without worrying about the place of manufacture (Ahmed and d'Astous 1993). Chao (1998) noted that consumers might often be unaware of or may often be indifferent about the actual place of manufacture, and rely on brand origin.

Johansson and Nebenzhal (1986) report that Japanese and American automobiles made at developing country plant locations may require large price concessions if they are to be sold in North America. This shows it is not just the brand name that consumers consider in their purchasing decision, but country of manufacture as well. D'Astous and Ahmed (1992) found brand name to be a more important cue than country of origin information for automobiles. According to Ahmed and d'Astous (1995), firms with production facilities in a less prestigious country of origin should stress the brand name in order to counter negative bias. Han and Terpstra (1988) concur with the importance of brand name to overcome the competitive advantage of foreign products. Hulland, Todino and Lecraw (1996) conclude that branding reduced the country of manufacture effect.

Based on the above discussion, the following generalizations are advanced:

G2a: A well-known brand name product manufactured in a developing country would be rated lower than if it were to be manufactured in a developed country.

G2b: A well-known brand name reduces, but does not eliminate completely, the significance of country of manufacture cue.

Value Assessment by Consumer

Given the country of manufacture and brand name of the product, consumers assess the value of the product, based on a composite of the following:

a.   Channels of distribution, e.g. reputation of the retail outlet through which the product is distributed, and implicit and explicit assurances provided by the channel outlet.

b.   Price, e.g. price break for the product manufactured in a developing country, to compensate for the perceived loss of utility (mostly attributable to the increase in perceived risk) due to the country of manufacture.

c.   Warranty and services accompanying the product purchase, e.g. a Sony television whether manufactured in a developing country or a developed country may carry the same warranty and service policy.

d.   Type of product, e.g. in the case of high involvement products, country of origin may play a more significant role than in low involvement products. In other words, where the purchasing risk is high, a consumer will be more concerned about COO than otherwise. All durable products, for example, fall in this category.

Combining the above four factors, consumers explicitly or implicitly attach a value to the product, which may be high or low. In such assessments, the COO cue comprises an important but not the sole factor. For instance, Chao (1989) noted that distributing the product through a reputed store could moderate the COO effect. He observed 'sturdy construction claim credibility is higher for a Korean-made Gold Star Stereo set if the product is distributed through Hudson's than if the product is not indicated as being carried by Hudson's. The COO effect can be circumvented through a careful selection of retail distribution'. Thus, it can be concluded that a prestigious store distribution is an effective way to generate a higher quality perception of products manufactured in developing countries. Hence, the following generalization:

> G3a: The effect of the country of origin cue diminishes where the product is distributed through a reputed/prestigious channel.

According to Cordell (1991), price concession does not eliminate the effect of country of origin. Elliot and Cameron (1994) stated that imported products need to be of markedly superior quality or attractively priced relative to their locally made counterpart if consumers are to give them first purchase preference. Hulland, Todino and Lecraw (1996) demonstrated a significant impact of price in mitigating the COO effect. Chao (1993), however, did not find that a low price necessarily connotes a lower perceived quality of an imported product. Ahmed and d'Astous (1993) also noted that the effect of price on perceptions of purchase value is not that important.

However, a number of other studies concluded that a price break could successfully make up for the poorer perceived image of products manufactured in developing countries (Johansson and Nebenzahl 1986; Chao 1989). Cline (1979) noted that manufactured imports from less developed countries (LDCs) tend to be lower priced than comparable products made in the USA or imported from industrialized countries. Hence, any cue effect of price on the perceived quality of products would tend to inter-correlate with their country of origin. This would have a reinforcing effect on negative biases regarding products sourced in LDCs.

The importance of the pricing variable leads to the following generalization:

> G3b: As the price of a product manufactured in a developing country declines, the importance of its country of origin diminishes.

However, the price discount should be substantial but not excessive – somewhere between 10 to 20 per cent seems appropriate, according to the literature.

Han and Terpstra (1988) found serviceability to be an important factor that encourages consumers to buy locally made products. Similarly, Ahmed, d'Astous and Adraoui (1994) noted that quality assurance programs can overcome the COO effect, and hence the following generalization:

G3c: Offering credible assurances of quality, i.e. after-sales service, warranty and return guarantee can overcome the COO effect for products from less developed countries.

Cordell (1991) found that consumers are more wary of products from developing countries when the financial risk is higher. Hugstad and Durr (1986) noted that sensitivity to country of origin varied by product category, but are highest for durable goods. Similar conclusions were drawn by Han and Terpstra (1988). They concluded that COO effects are product-dimension specific, i.e. certain dimensions of product evaluation would be impacted and that the contribution to the overall evaluation would then depend on the importance of the affected dimension. A similar conclusion was reached by Chao and Gupta (1995) in their study of new car choices. They found that 'country of origin effects are not only product specific but also vehicle, category specific'. They noted that consumers' perceptions, whether they be perceived risk, quality or value for the money, are important in the decision to choose a car. Consumers engage in information search to make efficient choices and country of origin is one of the variables that consumers consider in their search process.

The above discussion suggests the following generalizations:

G3d: Consumers' willingness to buy products manufactured in developing countries declines as the financial risk attached to such a purchase rises.

G3e: Country of origin, brand name, price, and quality assurance are more important for high-involvement products, relative to low-involvement products.

Customers' Stereotype Influence

Consumers have stereotype images of products from different countries. Consumers have stereotypes of countries as well. For example, countries like China, India, Mexico, Brazil, and other developing countries are considered less technologically advanced and sophisticated, and, therefore, all products originating from these nations are perceived to be of low quality. By the same token, broadly speaking, products originating from developed countries are considered wholesome. Over and above that, certain countries have established a unique reputation for specific products. For example, France is known for perfumes, Switzerland for chocolates, Japan for cars, cameras, and consumer electronics. This built-in stereotype among consumers plays a role in the evaluation of products originating from different countries.

Furthermore, people have their inherent attitudes toward different countries. For example, even if a country is known for developing quality products, an unfavorable attitude toward a country may lead the buyer to favor a product originating from another nation, if this negative bias is strong enough. Consumer ethnocentrism also affects product choices (Bailey and de Pineres 1997; Granzin and Painter 2000). Many US consumers prefer US-made cars to Japanese-made vehicles, although they are conscious of the quality differences, presumably to help the US economy.

Consumers' stereotypes of nations, their attitudes toward different nations, and their ethnocentricity can be related to their demographics, socio-economic backgrounds, and familiarity with the underlying product, and the timing factor in buying the product.

Consumers do, indeed, have a preconceived, stereotypical view of products identified as being made in certain foreign countries (Schooler and Wildt 1968; White and Cundiff 1978). It can also be asserted that there is generally a direct relationship between product quality evaluation and the perceived degree of economic development of the country of origin (Gaedeke 1973; White and Cundiff 1978; Wang and Lamb 1983; Morello 1984; Toyne and Walters 1989; Cordell 1985).

Hulland, Todino and Lecraw (1996), discovered that imported products from more industrialized countries were found to command price premiums over the same product, produced by the same company in less developed countries. Countries with a poor image require price concessions or other incentives to sell their products in developed countries (Ahmed and d'Astous 1993). Hong and Wyer (1989) noted that country of origin information about the product stimulates consumers to think more extensively about other information. In this process their own biases and attitudes become significant in evaluating the product. A number of studies have shown that country stereotypes do exist and impact product evaluations (Lin and Sternquist 1992; Richey, Rose and Dominguez 1999).

Haubl (1996) showed that ethnocentric tendencies were a stronger predictor of buying behavior than demographic variables. In another study, it was noted that the purchase of domestic products is negatively related to consumers' perceived costs of helping, and positively related to internalized responsibility of helping, i.e. a feeling of sharing a common fate with the workers, and ethnocentric orientation and patriotism (Granzin and Olsen 1998). In the same way, highly ethnocentric consumers are less likely to process new information that impacts their home-country-related beliefs in an objective manner (Gurhan-Canli and Maheswaran 2000). Brodowsky (1998) found that high ethnocentric consumers favored cars both designed and assembled in the USA.

Hence the following generalization:

G4a: Ethnocentric consumers are likely to prefer local products to foreign ones.

G4b: Consumers' stereotype image of countries and the products from these countries will affect their evaluation of products.

G4c: Consumers' familiarity and prior experience with imported products will impact their evaluation of these products.

Country of Origin Effect

It is clear from the above discussion that the COO cue does play a role in product evaluation. However, the relevance of the COO effect cannot be determined in isolation from other cues. Further, different ingredients of marketing mix as the type of product, channels, price and promotion impact COO perspectives of the product. Additionally, demographic background of the consumers, as well as their attitudes and ethnocentric tendencies, prior knowledge or experience with the product influence the COO effect. Further, the timing effect for stimulus presentation is also relevant. For example, when country of origin and intrinsic attribute information was provided simultaneously, consumers perceived country of origin as simply another product attribute. However, when presented a day before, country of origin had a greater influence on product evaluations (Hong and Wyer 1990). It has been determined that country of origin cue is more frequently used by people with higher product familiarity (Heimbach, Johansson and MacLachlan 1989). However, Akaah and Yaprak (1993) noted that neither product familiarity nor respondent nationality had significant moderating influence on country of origin effects. So, the results using familiarity have been mixed. Ettenson (1993) found that the country of origin impact varied by country. For example, Russian, Polish and Hungarian consumers attached varying importance to the country of origin. In a study conducted in the USA and Canada, younger people cared less about the country of origin of their purchases than middle-aged or older people (Hester and Yuen 1987; Chawla, Smith and Derakshan 1995). Hong and Toner (1989) did not find any gender differences in the use of country of origin information in product evaluation. To sum up, there is a need to examine the COO effect in different countries with different products under different experimental conditions.

CONCLUSIONS AND FUTURE RESEARCH

Despite decades of research in this important area of country of origin, we do not operate on a theoretical framework that has consensus. Impact of the country of origin of a product on its acceptance is an important issue. With the globalization of the economy and numerous multilateral trade agreements, more and more goods will cross borders. Therefore, companies have a stake in knowing what factors will affect the acceptance of their products in different countries. Based on the literature, a theoretical framework has been put forth in this chapter. Synthesizing previous work, several generalizations have been drawn, to lay the foundation for further progress in this important area. Directions for future research, to enhance the state of the art, are outlined below:

1. While most COO studies have been conducted in the US using student samples, it is important to investigate the COO effect in other developed countries, large emerging countries (such as China, India, Brazil and Indonesia), as well as in the Eastern European countries. Studies should be conducted using real consumers rather than the typical student samples, for increasing external validity. Demographic differences between consumers should be included to determine any patterns.

2. Research should be pursued using different kinds of products (e.g. durable goods, nondurable goods) and particularly services, where the local component may be high. The level of involvement of the product/service also needs to be measured.

3. It will be interesting to examine what product has a positive association with which country. For example, Swiss watches and chocolates are held in high esteem. Germany stands out in the case of automobiles and Japan has a reputation for manufacturing consumer electronics, cameras and cars. How about the UK, the USA, Mexico and other countries? Are there any products from these nations that are considered good quality/prestigious from these nations? Is it possible to overcome the stereotype image of a country? How might this be feasible for managers? What are the determinants of attitude changes over time?

4. Are lower prices and good customer service substitutes for lower quality? If yes, what should be the range of price discounts to enable consumers to prefer low-quality products? Is there a cut-off point beyond which lowering price does not do much for the marketer? In other words, if the price is unreasonably low, consumers may be completely turned off since this could signal an unacceptable quality.

5. What role does the distribution channel play in overcoming low-quality perception of products from developing countries? What alternative strategies might marketers employ in encouraging consumers to buy products from 'unfavorable' countries? How does the Web-based operation influence the distribution effect?

6. Research is needed to examine the role of service and warranty to posi-

tion products from developing countries to be more acceptable in developed nations. Consider Korea's automobile marketing in the USA. Anecdotally, the 100 000 mile warranty has gone a long way to boost car sales in the USA.

7. Another important question is the quality perception of goods from a country over time. How does this change occur? For example, 10 years ago, textile goods from developing countries were generally considered low in quality. Today, however, even in the best department stores, and among the famous designer items, one can find clothing from a variety of developing countries. It seems consumers are not opposed to buying expensive clothing made in China or another developing country. What factors are responsible for such changes? Managers can then plan for future strategies profitably.

8. Efforts should be made to build databases for longitudinal studies over time. It is crucial to conduct comparative studies, say, how do US autos become accepted in Poland or Germany or Russia?

9. Sometimes, it appears that country of origin of a product may not be as significant a factor in product evaluations as it has been made out to be. Is the COO effect applicable to all consumers? Are there consumers who do not care for the country of origin of the product they are considering for purchase? Can they be profiled?

10. Is there a relationship between per capita GNP of a nation and the image of its products overseas? In other words, will it be reasonable to say that products from countries with per capita GNP below US$1000 will be considered to be low quality?

11. What dimensions of COO are relevant under a given context? A recent meta-analysis (Verlegh and Steenkamp 1999) has identified those dimensions of the COO effect: cognitive, affective, and normative. Studies in the first category use country of origin as the cue for product quality; for example, reliability and durability signifying cognitive mechanism. The second set of studies considers country of origin as an affective mechanism that links the product to symbolic and emotional benefit including social status. The third category represents a normative process that relates country of origin to personal norms such as 'buying domestic products is the right thing to do', since it supports the domestic economy. Most of the past studies on COO have been concerned with cognitive dimension. Therefore, more research is needed on the symbolic and emotional aspects of country of origin.

REFERENCES

Ahmed, Sadrudin A. and Alain D'Astous (1993), 'Cross-National Evaluation of Made-in Concept Using Multiple Uses', *European Journal of Marketing*, **27** (7), 39–52.

Ahmed, Sadrudin A. and Alain D'Astous (1995), 'Comparison of Country-of-Origin Effects on Household and Organizational Buyer's Product Perceptions', *European Journal of Marketing*, **25** (3), 36–51.

Ahmed, Sadrudin A., Alain d'Astous and Mostafa Adraoui (1994), 'Country of Origin Effects on Purchasing Managers Product Perceptions', *Industrial Marketing Management*, **23** (4), 323–32.

Akaah, Ishmael P. and Attila Yaprak (1993), 'Assessing the Influence of Country of Origin on Product Evaluations: An Application of Conjoint Methodology', *Journal of International Consumer Marketing*, **5** (2), 39–53.

Anderson, W.T. and W.H. Cunningham (1972), 'Growing Foreign Product Promotion', *Journal of Advertising Research*, **12** (February), 29–34.

Bailey, William and Sheila A.G. de Pineres (1997), 'Country of Origin Attitudes in Mexico: The Malinchismo Effect', *Journal of International Consumer Marketing*, **9** (3), 25–41.

Bass, Frank M. (1995), 'Empirical Generalizations and Marketing Science: A Personal View', *Marketing Science*, **14** (3), G6–G19.

Bass, Frank M. and Jerry Wind (1995), 'Empirical Generalizations in Marketing', *Marketing Science*, **14** (3), G1–G5.

Batra, R., V. Ramaswamy, D.L. Alden, J.B. Steenkamp and S. Ramchander (2000), 'Effects of Brand Local/Non-Local Origin on Consumer Attitudes in Developing Countries', *Journal of Consumer Psychology*, **9** (2), 83–95.

Baumgarner, Gary and J.P. Alain Jolibert (1978), 'The Perception of Foreign Products in France', in H.K. Hunt (ed.), *Advances in Consumer Research*, **5**, 603–5.

Baunists, J.P. and J.A. Saunders (1978). 'U.K. Consumers' Attitudes Towards Imports: The Measurement of National Stereotype Image', *European Journal of Marketing*, **12** (6), 562–70.

Bilkey, Warren J. and Erick Nes (1982), 'Country-of-Origin Effects on Product Evaluations', *Journal of International Business Studies*, (Spring/Summer), 89–99.

Botschen, G. and A. Hemettsberger (1998), 'Diagnosing Means–End Structures to Determine the Degree of Potential Marketing Program Standardization', *Journal of Business Research*, **42** (2), 151–9.

Brodowshy, Glen H. (1998), 'The Effects of Country of Design and Country of Assembly on Evaluative Beliefs About Automobiles and Attitudes Toward Buying Them: A Comparison Between Low and High Ethnocentric Consumers', *Journal of International Consumer Marketing*, **10** (3), 85–113.

Chao, Paul (1989), 'The Impact of Country Affiliation on the Credibility of Product Attribute Claims', *Journal of Advertising Research*, (April/May), 35–41.

Chao, P. (1992), 'Partitioning Country of Origin Effects: Consumer Evaluations of a Hybrid Product', *Journal of International Business Studies*, **24** (2), 291–306.

Chao, Paul (1998), 'Impact of Country-of-Origin Dimensions on Product Quality and Design Quality Perceptions', *Journal of Business Research*, **42** (1), 1–6.

Chao, Paul and Pola B. Gupta (1995), 'Information Search and Efficiency of Consumer Choices of New Cars', *International Marketing Review*, **12** (6), 47–59.

Chawla, Sudhir K., Mary F. Smith and Foad Derakshan (1995), 'A Field Investigation of Country-of-Origin Effects on Consumer Product Evaluations', *International Journal of Management*, **12** (4), 529–37.

Cline, William R. (1979), 'Imports and Consumer Prices: A Survey Analysis', *American Retail Federation and the National Merchants Association*, Washington, DC.

Cordell, V. (1985), 'Product Sourcing from LDC's: The Impact of Competitive Context and Price on Consumer Choice', Working Paper, George Mason University.

Cordell, Victor V. (1991), 'Competitive Context and Price as Moderations of Country of Origin Preferences', *Journal of the Academy of Marketing Science*, **19** (2), 123–8.

D'Astous, Alain and Sadrudin A. Ahmed (1992), 'Multi-Cue Evaluation of Made-In Concept: A Conjoint Analysis Study in Belgium, 1992', *Journal of Euromarketing*, **2** (1), 9–29.

Elliot, Gregory R. and Ross C. Cameron (1994), 'Consumer Perception of Product Quality and the Country-of-Origin Effect', *Journal of International Marketing*, **2** (2), 49–62.

Erickson, Jerry M., Johny K. Johansson and Paul Chao (1984), 'Image Variables in Multi-Attribute Product Evaluation: Country-of-Origin Effects', *Journal of Consumer Research*, **11** (September), 694–9.

Ettenson, Richard (1993), 'Brand Name and Country of Origin Effects in the Emerging Market Economies of Russia, Poland and Hungry', *International Marketing Review*, **10** (5), 14–36.

Ettenson, R. and G. Graeth (1991), 'Consumer Perceptions of Hybrid (bi-national) Products', *Journal of Consumer Marketing*, **8** (4), 13–18.

Ettenson, Richard, Janet Wagner and Gary Gaeth (1998), 'Evaluating the Effect of Country of Origin and the "Made in U.S.A." Campaign: A Conjoint Approach', *Journal of Retailing*, **64** (Spring), 85–100.

Gaedeke, R. (1973), 'Consumer Attitudes Toward Products Made-in-Developing Countries', *Journal of Retailing*, **49** (Summer), 13–24.

Granzin, Kent L. and Jancen E. Olsen (1998), 'Americans' Choice of Domestic over Foreign Products: A Matter of Helping Behavior', *Journal of Business Research*, **43** (1), 39–54.

Granzin, Kent L. and John J. Painter (2000), 'Non-Demographic Versus Demographic Determinants of "Buy Domestic" Activities in Two Nations', *Journal of Global Marketing*, **13** (4), 73–92.

Gurhan-Canli and Durairaj Maheswaran (2000), 'Determinants of Country-of-Origin Evaluations', *Journal of Consumer Research*, **27** (June), 96–108.

Gyer, G.R. and J.K. Kalita (1997), 'The Impact of Country of Origin and Country of Manufacture Cues on Consumer Perceptions of Quality and Value', *Journal of Global Marketing*, **11** (1), 7–28.

Hampton, Gerald M. (1977), 'Perceived Risk in Buying Products Made Abroad by American Firms', *Baylor Research Studies*, **113** (August), 53–64.

Han, C.M. (1989), 'Country Image: Halo or Summary Construct?', *Journal of Marketing Research*, **26** (May), 222–9.

Han, C.M. and V. Terpstra (1988), 'Country-of-Origin Effects for Uni-National Bi-National Products', *Journal of International Business Studies*, **19** (Summer), 235–255.

Haubl, Gerald (1996), 'A Cross-National Investigation of the Effects of Country of

Origin and Brand Name on the Evaluation of a New Car', *International Marketing Review*, **13** (5), 76–97.

Haubl, Gerald and Terry Elrod (1999), 'The Impact of Congruity Between Brand Name and Country of Production on Consumers' Product Quality Judgements', *International Journal of Research in Marketing*, **4**.

Heimbach, Arthur E., Johny K. Johansson and Douglas L. MacLachlan (1989), 'Product Familiarity, Information Processing and Country of Origin Cues', *Advances in Consumer Research*, **16**, 466–7.

Hester, Susan B. and Mary Yuen (1987), 'The Influence of Country of Origin on Consumer Attitude and Buying Behavior in the United States and Canada', *Advances in Consumer Research*, **14**, 538–42.

Hong, Sung-Tai and Julie F. Toner (1989), 'Are there Gender Differences in the Use of Country-of-Origin Information in the Evaluation of Products?', *Advances in Consumer Research*, **16**, 468–72.

Hong, Sung-Tai and Robert S. Wyer, Jr (1989), 'Effects of Country-of-Origin and Product-Attribute Information on Product Evaluation: An Information Processing Perspective', *Journal of Consumer Research*, **16** (September), 175–87.

Hong, Sung Tai and Robert S. Wyer, Jr (1990), 'Determinants of Evaluation: Effects of the Time of a Product's Country of Origin and Information About its Specific Attributes', *Journal of Consumer Research*, **17** (December), 277–88.

Hugstad, P. and M. Durr (1986), 'A Study of Country of Manufacturer Impact on Consumer Perceptions', in *Developments in Marketing Science*, Academy of Marketing Science conference, Miami, Florida.

Hulland, John S. (1999), 'The Effects of Country-of-Brand and Brand Name on Product Evaluation and Consideration: A Cross-Country Comparison', *Journal of International Consumer Marketing*, **11** (1), 23–40.

Hulland, John, Honorio Todino and Donald Lecraw (1996), 'Country-of-Origin Effects on Sellers' Price Premiums in Competitive Philippine Markets', *Journal of International Marketing*, **4** (1), 57–79.

Hurdle, Joel (1992), 'A Note on the Predictive Validity of the CETSCALE', *Journal of the Academy of Marketing Science*, **20** (3), 261–4.

Iacocca, L. (1990), *American Interest*, a TV interview by public broadcasting service, 25 January.

Insch, Gary S. and J. Brad McBride (1996), 'Decomposing the Country-of-Origin Construct. An Empirical Test of Country of Design, Country of Parts, and Country of Assembly', Paper presented at the Academy of International Business Annual Meeting, Banff, Canada.

Johansson, Johny K. (1989), 'Determinants and Effects on the Use of "Made In" Labels', *International Marketing Review*, **6** (1), 47–58.

Johansson, Johny K. (1997), 'Why Country-of-Origin Effects are Stronger Than Ever', Paper Presented at the European Association for Consumer Research Conference, Stockholm, Sweden.

Johansson, Johny K. and Israel D. Nebenzahl (1987), 'Multinational Production Effect on Brand Value', *Journal of International Business Studies*, **17** (3), 101–26.

Johansson, Johny K., Susan P. Douglas and Ikujiro Nonaka (1985), 'Assessing the Impact of Country of Origin on Product Evaluations: A New Methodological Perspective', *Journal of Marketing Research*, **22** (November), 388–96.

Kochunny, C.M., E. Babukus, R. Berl and W. Marks (1993), 'Schematic Representation of Country Image: Its Effects on Product Evaluations', *Journal of International Consumer Marketing*, **5** (1), 5–25.

Li, W.K. and K.B. Monroe (1992), 'The Role of Country-of-Origin Information: An In-Depth Interview Approach', *Proceedings of the 1992 AMA Summer Educators' Conference*, Chicago, IL, pp. 272–80.

Liefeld, John (1993), 'Consumer Use of Country-of-Origin Information in Product Evaluations: Evidence from Experiments', in N. Papadopoulos and L. Heslop (eds), *Product-Country Images: Impact and Role in International Marketing*, New York: International Business Press, pp. 117–56.

Lillis, Charles and Chem Narayanan (1974), 'Analysis of "Made In" Product Images: An Exploratory Study', *Journal of International Business Studies*, **5** (1), 119–27.

Lin, L.W. and B. Sternquist (1992), 'Taiwanese Consumers' Perceptions of Product Information Cues: Country of Origin and Stage Prestige', *European Journal of Marketing*, **28** (1), 5–18.

Morello, B. (1984), 'The "Made In" Issue: A Comparative Research on the Image of Domestic and Foreign Products', *European Research*, (July), 95–100.

Nagashima, Akira (1970), 'A Comparison of Japanese and U.S. Attitudes Toward Foreign Products', *Journal of Marketing*, **34** (January), 68–74.

Nebenzahl, Israel D. and Eugene D. Jaffe (1996), 'The Dynamics of Country-of-Origin Effect: The Case of South Korea', Paper Presented at the EIBA Conference, Stockholm, Sweden.

Olsen, J.C. and J. Jacoby (1972), 'Cue Utilization in the Quality Perception Process', in *Proceedings of the Third Annual Conference*, Ann Arbor, MI: Association for Consumer Research, pp. 167–79.

Papadopoulos, Nicolas, Louise Heslop, Francoise Garby and George Avlonitis (1987), *Does 'Country of Origin' Matter? Some Findings from A Cross-Cultural Study of Consumer Views About Foreign Products Report* (87). Cambridge, MA: Marketing Science Institute, pp. 87–104.

Papadopoulos, Nicolas, Louise A. Heslop, Leslie Szanosi and Richard Ettenson (1997), '"Czech Mate or Check Mate?" An Assessment of the Competitiveness of East European Products', in *Proceedings*, 26th EMAC Conference, Warwick Business School, pp. 993–1012.

Peterson, Robert A. and Alain J.P. Jolibert (1995), 'A Meta-Analysis of Country-of-Origin Effects', *Journal of International Business Studies*, (Fourth Quarter), 883–900.

Richey, Brenda E., Patricia B. Rose and Luis Dominguez (1999), 'Perceived Value of Mexican vs. U.S. Products in Mexico, Venezuela and the United States: Implications for Mexican Firms', *Journal of Global Marketing*, **13** (2), 49–65.

Saghafi, Massoud and Rosa Puig (1997), 'Evaluation of Foreign Products of American International Industrial Buyers', in *Proceedings*, 26th EMAC Conference, Warwick Business School, pp. 1101–15.

Samiee, Saeed (1994), 'Customer Evaluation of Products in the Global Market', *Journal of International Business Studies*, (Third Quarter), 579–604.

Schooler, R.D. (1965), 'Product Bias in the Central American Common Market', *Journal of Marketing Research*, **2** (November), 394–7.

Schooler, R.D. (1971), 'Bias Phenomena Attendant to the Marketing of Foreign Goods in the U.S.', *Journal of International Business Studies*, **2** (1), 71–80.

Schooler, R.D. and A.R. Wildt (1968), 'Elasticity of Product Bias', *Journal of Marketing Research*, **6** (February), 78–81.

Thorelli, Hans B., Lim Jeen-Su and Ye Jongsuk (1989), 'Relative Importance of

Country of Origin in the Era of Global Brands', *International Marketing Review*, **6** (1), 35–46.

Tonberg, Richard C. (1972), 'An Empirical Study of Relationships Between Dogmatism and Consumer Attitudes Towards Foreign Products', PhD dissertation, Pennsylvania State University.

Toyne, B. and P. Walters (1989), *Global Marketing Management: A Strategic Perspective*, Boston: Alyn & Bacon.

Verlegh, Peeter and Jan-Benedict Steenkamp (1999), 'A Review and Meta-Analysis of Country-of-Origin Research', *Journal of Economic Psychology*, **20**, 521–46.

Wang, C. and C. Lamb (1983), 'The Impact of Selected Environmental Forces Upon Consumers' Willingness to Buy Foreign Products', *Journal of the Academy of Marketing Science*, **11** (2), 71–84.

White, P.D. and E.W. Cundiff (1978), 'Assessing the Quality of Industrial Product', *Journal of Marketing*, **15** (July), 80–85.

Index